An Introduction to Medical Statistics

An Introduction to Medical Statistics

FOURTH EDITION

Martin Bland

Professor of Health Statistics
Department of Health Sciences
University of York

OXFORD

UNIVERSITY PRESS

OXFORD
UNIVERSITY PRESS

Great Clarendon Street, Oxford, OX2 6DP,
United Kingdom

Oxford University Press is a department of the University of Oxford.
It furthers the University's objective of excellence in research, scholarship,
and education by publishing worldwide. Oxford is a registered trade mark of
Oxford University Press in the UK and in certain other countries

First Edition published in 1987
Second Edition published in 1995
Third Edition published in 2000
Fourth Edition published in 2015

Impression: 1

Published in the United States of America by Oxford University Press
198 Madison Avenue, New York, NY 10016, United States of America

British Library Cataloguing in Publication Data
Data available

Library of Congress Control Number: 2014959481

ISBN 978–0–19–958992–0

Printed in Italy by
L.E.G.O. S.p.A.

To Emily and Nicholas Bland

Preface to the Fourth Edition

This book is for medical students, doctors, medical researchers, nurses, members of professions allied to medicine, and all others concerned with medical data. When I wrote the first edition of *An Introduction to Medical Statistics*, I based the contents on the statistical methods which appeared frequently in the *Lancet* and the *British Medical Journal*. I continued to do this with each succeeding edition. Each time, the range and complexity of the methods used increased. There are two reasons for this. One is that the size and complexity of medical research studies has increased greatly and, I think, the quality has increased greatly, too. The other reason is that developments in computing have enabled statisticians to develop and bring into use new, computer-intensive methods of analysis and these have been applied in medical research.

In this fourth edition, I have added new chapters on meta-analysis and on handling missing data by multiple imputation, methods now seen routinely in major journals. I have also added a chapter explaining the Bayesian approach to data, including Markov Chain Monte Carlo methods of analysis. I have added a new chapter collecting together and expanding the material on time to event or survival data. I have also added new sections on allocation by minimization, bootstrap methods, Poisson and negative binomial regression, kappa statistics for agreement between observers, and the creation of composite scales using principal components and factor analysis, all things you will see in medical journals.

Apart from changes in the practice of statistics in medicine in general, I hope that I have changed a bit, too. Since writing the third edition, I have moved to a different university, where I now spend a lot more time on clinical trials. I have also spent 6 years on the Clinical Evaluation and Trials Board of the Health Technology Assessment programme, reading and criticising hundreds of grant applications. I hope that I have learned something along the way and I have revised the text accordingly.

I have included some new examples, though many of the old ones remain, being too good to replace, I thought. I have changed most of the exercises, to remove all calculations. I never touch a calculator now, so why should my readers? Instead, I have concentrated on understanding and interpreting analyses. I have dropped the stars for sections with material which was beyond the undergraduate course. I no longer teach medical or nursing students and I do not have my finger on that pulse. All the graphs have been redrawn using Stata12, except for one pie chart, done using Excel.

This is a book about data, not statistical theory. The fundamental concepts of study design, data collection, and data analysis are explained by illustration and example. Only enough mathematics and formulae are given to make clear what is going on. For those who wish to go a little further in their understanding, some of the more mathematical background to the techniques described is given as appendices to the chapters rather than in the main text.

The book is firmly grounded in medical data, particularly in medical research, and the interpretation of the results of calculations in their medical context is emphasized. Except for a few obviously invented numbers used to illustrate the mechanics of calculations, all the data in the examples and exercises are real, from my own research and statistical consultation or from the medical literature.

There are two kinds of exercise in this book. Each chapter has a set of multiple choice questions of the 'true or false' type, 122 in all. Multiple choice questions can cover a large amount of material in a short time, so are a useful tool for revision. As MCQs are widely used in postgraduate examinations, these exercises should also be useful to those preparing for memberships. All the MCQs have solutions, with reference to an appropriate part of the text or a detailed explanation for most of the answers. Each chapter also has a long exercise, also with suggested answers, mostly on the interpretation of data in published studies.

I wish to thank many people who have contributed to the writing of this book. First, there are the many medical students, doctors, research workers, nurses, physiotherapists, and radiographers whom it has been my pleasure to teach, and from whom I have learned so much. Second, the book contains many examples drawn from research carried out with other statisticians, epidemiologists, and social scientists, particularly Douglas Altman, Ross Anderson, Mike Banks, Barbara Butland, Beulah Bewley, Nicky Cullum, Jo Dumville, Walter Holland, and David Torgerson. These studies could not have been done without the assistance of Patsy Bailey, Bob Harris, Rebecca McNair, Janet Peacock, Swatee Patel, and Virginia Pollard. Third, the clinicians and scientists with whom I have collaborated or who have come to me for statistical advice not only taught me about medical data but many of them have left me with data which are used here, including Naib Al-Saady, Thomas Bewley, Frances Boa, Nigel Brown, Jan Davies, Caroline Flint, Nick Hall, Tessi Hanid, Michael Hutt, Riahd Jasrawi, Ian Johnston, Moses Kapembwa, Pam Luthra, Hugh Mather, Daram Maugdal, Douglas Maxwell, Georgina Morris, Charles Mutoka, Tim Northfield, Andreas Papadopoulos, Mohammed Raja, Paul Richardson, and Alberto Smith. I am particularly indebted to John Morgan, as Chapter 21 is partly based on his work.

I thank Douglas Altman, Daniel Heitjan, David Jones, Klim McPherson, Janet Peacock, Stuart Pocock, and Robin Prescott for their helpful comments on earlier drafts and Dan Heitjan for finding mistakes in this one. I am very grateful to Julian Higgins and Simon Crouch for their comments on my new chapters on meta-analysis and Bayesian methods, respectively. I am grateful to John Blase for help with converting my only Excel graphic. I have corrected a number of errors from earlier editions, and I am grateful to colleagues who have pointed them out to me. Most of all I thank Pauline Bland for her unfailing confidence and encouragement.

Since the last edition of this book, my children, Nick and Em, have grown up and have both become health researchers. It is to them I dedicate this fourth edition.

M.B.
York, April 2015

Contents

Detailed Contents

1 Introduction

1.1 Statistics and medicine

Evidence-based practice is the watchword in every profession concerned with the treatment and prevention of disease and the promotion of health and well-being. This requires both the gathering of evidence and its critical interpretation. The former is bringing more people into the practice of research, and the latter is requiring of all health professionals the ability to evaluate the research carried out. Much of this evidence is in the form of numerical data. The essential skill required for the collection, analysis, and evaluation of numerical data is Statistics. Thus Statistics, the science of assembling and interpreting numerical data, is the core science of evidence-based practice.

In the past 40 years, medical research has become deeply involved with the techniques of statistical inference. The work published in medical journals is full of statistical jargon and the results of statistical calculations. This acceptance of statistics, though gratifying to the medical statistician, may even have gone too far. More than once I have told a colleague that he did not need me to prove that his difference existed, as anyone could see it, only to be told in turn that without the magic of the P value he could not have his paper published.

Statistics has not always been so popular with the medical profession. Statistical methods were first used in medical research in the 19th century by workers such as Pierre-Charles-Alexandre Louis, William Farr, Florence Nightingale, and John Snow. Snow's studies of the modes of communication of cholera, for example, made use of epidemiological techniques upon which we have still made little improvement. Despite the work of these pioneers, however, statistical methods did not become widely used in clinical medicine until the middle of the 20th century. It was then that the methods of randomized experimentation and statistical analysis based on sampling theory, which had been developed by Fisher and others, were introduced into medical research, notably by Bradford Hill. It rapidly became apparent that research in medicine raised many new problems in both design and analysis, and much work has been done since towards solving these by clinicians, statisticians, and epidemiologists.

Although considerable progress has been made in such fields as the design of clinical trials, there remains much to be done in developing research methodology in medicine. It seems likely that this will always be so, for every research project is something new, something which has never been done before. Under these circumstances we make mistakes. No piece of research can be perfect and there will always be something which, with hindsight, we would have changed. Furthermore, it is often from the flaws in a study that we can learn most about research methods. For this reason, the work of several researchers is described in this book to illustrate the problems into which their designs or analyses led them. I do not wish to imply that these people were any more prone to error than the rest of the human race, or that their work was not a valuable and serious undertaking. Rather I want to learn from their experience of attempting something extremely difficult, trying to extend our knowledge, so that researchers and consumers of research may avoid these particular pitfalls in the future.

1.2 Statistics and mathematics

Many people are discouraged from the study of Statistics by a fear of being overwhelmed by mathematics. It is true that many professional statisticians are also mathematicians, but not all are, and there are many very able appliers of statistics to their own fields. It is possible, though perhaps not very useful, to study statistics simply as a part of mathematics, with no concern for its application at all. Statistics may also be discussed without appearing to use any mathematics at all (e.g. Huff 1954).

The aspects of statistics described in this book can be understood and applied with the use of simple algebra. Only the algebra which is essential for explaining the most important concepts is given in the main text. This means that several of the theoretical results used are stated without a discussion of their mathematical basis. This is done when the derivation of the result would not aid much in understanding the application. For many readers the reasoning behind these results is not of great interest. For the reader who does not wish to take these results on trust, several chapters have appendices in which simple mathematical proofs are given. These appendices are designed to help increase the understanding of the more mathematically inclined reader and to be omitted by those who find that the mathematics serves only to confuse.

1.3 Statistics and computing

Practical statistics has always involved large amounts of calculation. When the methods of statistical inference were being developed in the first half of the 20th century, calculations were done using pencil, paper, tables, slide rules, and, with luck, a very expensive mechanical adding machine. Older books on statistics spend much time on the details of carrying out calculations and any reference to a 'computer' means a person who computes, not an electronic device. The development of the digital computer has brought changes to statistics as to many other fields. Calculations can be done quickly, easily, and, we hope, accurately with a range of machines from pocket calculators with built-in statistical functions to powerful computers analysing data on many thousands of subjects. Many statistical methods would not be contemplated without computers, and the development of new methods goes hand in hand with the development of software to carry them out. The theory of multilevel modelling (Goldstein 1995) and the programs MLn and MLWin are a good example. Most of the calculations in this book were done using a computer and the graphs were produced with one.

There is therefore no need to consider the problems of manual calculation in detail. The important thing is to know why particular calculations should be done and what the results of these calculations actually mean. Indeed, the danger in the computer age is not so much that people carry out complex calculations wrongly, but that they apply very complicated statistical methods without knowing why or what the computer output means. More than once I have been approached by a researcher, bearing a two inch thick computer printout and asking what it all means. Sadly, too often, it means that another tree has died in vain.

The widespread availability of computers means that more calculations are being done, and being published, than ever before, and the chance of inappropriate statistical methods being applied may actually have increased. This misuse arises partly because people regard their data analysis problems as computing problems, not statistical ones, and seek advice from computer experts rather than statisticians. They often get good advice on how to do it, but rather poor advice about what to do, why to do it, and how to interpret the results afterwards. It is therefore more important than ever that the consumers of research understand something about the uses and limitations of statistical techniques.

1.4 Assumptions and approximations

Many statistical calculations give answers which are approximate rather than exact. For example, if we carry out a clinical trial and obtain a difference in outcome between two treatment groups, this applies only to the people in the trial. It is people not in the trial, those who are yet to come and to be eligible for the trial treatments, for whom we want to know the difference. Our trial can only give an approximate estimate of what that might be. As we shall see, statistical methods enable us to get an idea of how precise our estimate could be, but this, too, is only approximate. It depends on some assumptions about how the data behave. We have to assume that our data fit some kind of idealized mathematical model. The great statistician George Box said that 'essentially, all models are wrong, but some are useful'. We might add that, in medical statistics, all answers are approximate, but some approximations are useful.

The important thing will be to have an idea of how good our approximations are. We shall spend quite a lot of time investigating the assumptions underlying our statistical methods, to see how plausible they are for our data.

1.5 The scope of this book

This book is intended as an introduction to some of the statistical ideas important to medicine. It does not tell you all you need to know to do medical research. Once you have understood the concepts discussed here, it is much easier to learn about the techniques of study design and statistical analysis required to answer any particular question. There are several excellent standard works which describe the solutions to problems in the analysis of data (Armitage *et al.* 2002; Altman 1991) and also more specialized books to which reference will be made where required. It is also worth noting that, just like Medicine, Statistics does not stand still. Statisticians and other researchers are continually trying to develop new methods, often exploiting advances in computing, to give better answers to questions than those we have now. The basic principles explained in this book should apply to all of them.

What I hope the book will do is to give enough understanding of the statistical ideas commonly used in medicine to enable the health professional to read the medical literature competently and critically. It covers enough material (and more) for an undergraduate course in Statistics for students of medicine, nursing, physiotherapy, etc. At the time of writing, as far as can be established, it covers the material required to answer statistical questions set in the examinations of most of the Royal Colleges.

When working through a textbook, it is useful to be able to check your understanding of the material covered. Like most such books, this one has exercises at the end of each chapter, but to ease the tedium many of these are of the multiple choice type. There is also a long exercise, usually involving interpretation of results rather than calculations, for each chapter. The exercises can be completed quite quickly and the reader is advised to try them. Solutions are given at the end of the book, in full for the long exercises and as brief notes with references to the relevant sections in the text for MCQs. Readers who would like more numerical exercises are recommended to see Osborn (1979). For a wealth of exercises in the understanding and interpretation of statistics in medical research, drawn from the published literature and popular media, you should try the companion volume to this one, *Statistical Questions in Evidence-based Medicine* (Bland and Peacock 2000).

If you would like to try some of the analyses described, you can download some of the datasets from my website (martinbland.co.uk).

Finally, a question many students of medicine ask as they struggle with statistics: is it worth it? As Altman (1982) has argued, bad statistics leads to bad research and bad research is unethical. Not only may it give misleading results, which can result in good therapies being abandoned and bad ones adopted, but it means that patients may have been exposed to potentially harmful new treatments for no good reason. Medicine is a rapidly changing field. In 10 years' time, many of the therapies currently prescribed and many of our ideas about the causes and prevention of disease will be obsolete. They will be replaced by new therapies and new theories, supported by research studies and data of the kind described in this book, and probably presenting many of the same problems in interpretation. The practitioner will be expected to decide for her- or himself what to prescribe or advise based on these studies. So a knowledge of medical statistics is one of the most useful things any doctor, nurse, dentist, or physiotherapist could acquire during her or his training.

2 The design of experiments

2.1 Comparing treatments

There are two broad types of study in medical research: observational and experimental. In observational studies, aspects of an existing situation are observed, as in a survey or a clinical case report. We then try to interpret our data to give an explanation of how the observed state of affairs has come about. In experimental studies, we do something, such as giving a drug, so that we can observe the result of our action. This chapter is concerned with the way statistical thinking is involved in the design of experiments. In particular, it deals with comparative experiments where we wish to study the difference between the effects of two or more treatments. These experiments may be carried out in the laboratory *in vitro* or on animals or human volunteers, in the hospital or community on human patients, or, for trials of preventive interventions, on currently healthy people. We call trials of treatments on human subjects **clinical trials**. The general principles of experimental design are the same, although there are special precautions which must be taken when experimenting with human subjects. The experiments whose results most concern clinicians are clinical trials, so the discussion will deal mainly with them.

Suppose we want to know whether a new treatment is more effective than the present standard treatment. We could approach this in a number of ways.

First, we could compare the results of the new treatment on new patients with records of previous results using the old treatment. This is seldom convincing because there may be many differences between the patients who received the old treatment and the patients who will receive the new. As time passes, the general population from which patients are drawn may become healthier, standards of ancillary treatment and nursing care may improve, or the social mix in the catchment area of the hospital may change. The nature of the

disease itself may change. All these factors may produce changes in the patients' apparent response to treatment. For example, Christie (1979) showed this by studying the survival of stroke patients in 1978, after the introduction of a C-T head scanner, with that of patients treated in 1974, before the introduction of the scanner. He took the records of a group of patients treated in 1978, who received a C-T scan, and matched each of them with a patient treated in 1974 of the same age, diagnosis, and level of consciousness on admission. As the first column of Table 2.1 shows, patients in 1978 clearly tended to have better survival than similar patients in 1974. The scanned 1978 patient did better than the unscanned 1974 patient in 31% of pairs, whereas the unscanned 1974 patient did better than the scanned 1978 patient in only 7% of pairs. However, he also compared the survival of patients in 1978 who did not receive a C-T scan with matched patients in 1974. These patients also showed a marked improvement in survival from 1974 to 1978 (Table 2.1). The 1978 patient did better in 38% of pairs and the 1974 patients in only 19% of pairs. There was a general improvement in outcome over a fairly short period of time. If we did not have the data on the unscanned

Table 2.1 Analysis of the difference in survival for matched pairs of stroke patients (data from Christie 1979)

	C-T scan in 1978	No C-T scan in 1978
Pairs with 1978 better than 1974	9 (31%)	34 (38%)
Pairs with same outcome	18 (62%)	38 (43%)
Pairs with 1978 worse than 1974	2 (7%)	17 (19%)

patients from 1978, we might be tempted to interpret these data as evidence for the effectiveness of the C-T scanner. Historical controls like this are seldom very convincing, and usually favour the new treatment. We need to compare the old and new treatments concurrently.

Second, we could obtain concurrent groups by comparing our own patients, given the new treatment, with patients given the standard treatment in another hospital or clinic, or by another clinician in our own institution. Again, there may be differences between the patient groups due to catchment, diagnostic accuracy, preference by patients for a particular clinician, or you might just be a better therapist. We cannot separate these differences from the treatment effect.

Third, we could ask people to volunteer for the new treatment and give the standard treatment to those who do not volunteer. The difficulty here is that people who volunteer and people who do not volunteer are likely to be different in many ways, apart from the treatments we give them. Volunteers might be more likely to follow medical advice, for example. We will consider an example of the effects of volunteer bias in Section 2.5.

Fourth, we can allocate patients to the new treatment or the standard treatment and observe the outcome. The way in which patients are allocated to treatments can influence the results enormously, as the following example (Hill 1962) shows. Between 1927 and 1944, a series of trials of BCG vaccine were carried out in New York (Levine and Sackett 1946). Children from families where there was a case of tuberculosis were allocated to a vaccination group and given BCG vaccine, or to a control group who were not vaccinated. Between 1927 and 1932, physicians vaccinated half the children, the choice of which children to vaccinate being left to them. There was a clear advantage in survival for the BCG group (Table 2.2). However, there was also a clear tendency for the physician to vaccinate the children of more cooperative parents, and to leave those of less cooperative parents as controls. From 1933, allocation to treatment or control was done centrally, alternate children being assigned to control and vaccine. The difference in degree of cooperation between the parents of the two groups of children largely disappeared, and so did the difference in mortality. Note that these were a special group of children, from families where there was tuberculosis. In large trials using children drawn from the general population, BCG was shown to be effective in greatly reducing deaths from tuberculosis (Hart and Sutherland 1977).

Different methods of allocation to treatment can produce different results. This is because the method of allocation may not produce groups of subjects which are comparable, similar in every respect except the treatment. We need a method of allocation to treatments in which the characteristics of subjects will not affect their chance of being put into any particular group. This can be done using random allocation.

2.2 Random allocation

If we want to decide which of two people receive an advantage, in such a way that each has an equal chance

Table 2.2 Results of studies of BCG vaccine in New York City (data from Hill 1962)

Period of trial	No. of children	No. of deaths from TB	Death rate	Average no. of visits to clinic during 1st year of follow-up	Proportion of parents giving good cooperation as judged by visiting nurses
1927–32 Selection made by physician:					
BCG group	445	3	0.67%	3.6	43%
Control group	545	18	3.30%	1.7	24%
1933–44 Alternate selection carried out centrally:					
BCG group	566	8	1.41%	2.8	40%
Control group	528	8	1.52%	2.4	34%

Table 2.3 1 040 random digits

Row	1–4	5–8	9–12	13–16	17–20	21–24	25–28	29–32	33–36	37–40	41–44	45–48	49–52	53–56	57–60	61–64	65–68	69–72	73–76	77–80
1	36 45	88 31	28 73	59 43	46 32	00 32	67 15	32 49	54 55	75 17	90 51	40 66	18 46	95 54	65 89	16 80	95 33	15 88	18 60	56 46
2	98 41	90 22	48 37	80 31	91 39	33 80	40 82	38 26	20 39	71 82	55 25	71 27	14 68	64 04	99 24	82 30	73 43	92 68	18 99	47 54
3	02 99	10 75	77 21	88 55	79 97	70 32	59 87	75 35	18 34	62 53	79 85	55 66	63 84	08 63	04 00	18 34	53 94	58 01	55 05	90 99
4	33 53	95 28	06 81	34 95	13 93	37 16	95 06	15 91	89 99	37 16	74 75	13 13	22 16	37 76	15 57	42 38	96 23	90 24	58 26	71 46
5	06 66	30 43	00 66	32 60	36 60	46 05	17 31	66 80	91 01	62 35	92 83	31 60	87 30	76 83	17 85	31 48	13 23	17 32	68 14	84 96
6	61 21	31 49	98 29	77 70	72 11	35 23	69 47	14 27	14 74	52 35	27 82	01 01	74 41	38 77	53 68	53 26	55 16	35 66	31 87	82 09
7	61 05	50 10	94 85	86 32	10 72	95 67	88 21	72 09	48 73	03 97	11 57	85 67	94 91	49 48	35 49	39 41	80 17	54 45	23 66	82 60
8	15 16	08 90	92 86	13 32	26 01	20 02	72 45	94 74	97 19	99 46	22 09	29 66	15 44	76 74	94 92	48 13	75 85	81 28	95 41	36 30
9	69 13	53 55	35 87	43 23	83 32	79 40	92 20	83 76	82 61	24 20	08 29	79 37	00 33	35 34	86 55	10 91	18 86	43 50	67 79	33 58
10	37 29	99 85	55 63	32 66	71 98	85 20	31 93	63 91	77 21	99 62	65 11	14 04	88 86	28 92	04 03	42 99	87 08	20 55	30 53	82 24
11	66 22	81 58	30 80	21 10	15 53	26 90	33 77	51 19	17 49	27 14	37 21	77 13	69 31	20 22	67 13	46 29	75 32	69 79	39 23	32 43
12	51 43	09 72	68 38	05 77	14 62	89 07	37 89	25 30	92 09	06 92	31 59	37 83	92 55	15 31	21 24	03 93	35 97	84 61	96 85	45 51
13	79 05	43 69	52 93	00 77	44 82	91 65	11 71	25 37	89 13	63 87	04 30	69 08	33 81	34 92	69 86	35 37	51 81	47 95	13 55	48 33

Column

of receiving it, we can use a simple, widely accepted method. We toss a coin. This is used to decide the way football matches begin, for example, and all appear to agree that it is fair. So if we want to decide which of two subjects should receive a vaccine, we can toss a coin. Heads and the first subject receives the vaccine, tails and the second receives it. If we do this for each pair of subjects, we build up two groups which have been assembled without any characteristics of the subjects themselves being involved in the allocation. The only differences between the groups will be those due to chance. As we shall see later (Chapters 8 and 9), statistical methods enable us to measure the likely effects of chance. Any difference between the groups which is larger than this should be due to the treatment, since there will be no other differences between the groups. This method of dividing subjects into groups is called **random allocation** or **randomization**.

Several methods of randomizing have been in use for centuries, including coins, dice, cards, lots, and spinning wheels. Some of the theory of probability which we shall use later to compare randomized groups, was first developed as an aid to gambling. For large randomizations we use a different, non-physical randomizing method: random numbers generated by a mathematical process. Table 2.3 provides an example, a table of 1 040 random digits. These are more properly called **pseudo-random numbers**, as they are generated by a mathematical process. They are available in printed tables (Kendall and Babington Smith 1971) or can be produced by computer and calculators. Random allocation is now usually done by generating the numbers fresh each time, but the table will be used to illustrate the principle. We can use tables of random numbers in several ways to achieve random allocation. For example, let us randomly allocate 20 subjects to two groups, which I shall label A and B. We choose a random starting point in the table, using one of the physical methods described previously. (I used decimal dice. These are 20-sided dice, numbered 0 to 9 twice, which fit our number system more conveniently than the traditional cube. Two such dice give a random number between 1 and 100, counting '0,0' as 100.) The random starting point was row 7, column 79, and the first twenty digits were 6, 0, 1, 5, 1, 6, 0, 8, 9, 0, 9, 2, 2, 8, 6, 1, 3, 3, 2, 2, and 6. We now allocate subjects corresponding to

odd digits to group A and those corresponding to even digits to B. The first digit, 6, is even, so the first subject goes into group B. The second digit, 0, is also even, so the second subject goes into group B, the third, 1, is odd giving group A, and so on. We get the allocation shown in Table 2.4. We could allocate into three groups by assigning to A if the digit is 1, 2, or 3, to B if 4, 5, or 6, and to C if 7, 8, or 9, ignoring 0. We could allocate in a 2:1 ratio by putting 1 to 6 in A, 7 to 9 in B, and ignoring zeros. There are many possibilities.

The system described above gave us unequal numbers in the two groups, 8 in A and 12 in B. We sometimes want the groups to be of equal size. One way to do this would be to proceed as above until either A or B has 10 subjects in it, all the remaining subjects going into the other groups. This is satisfactory in that each subject has an equal chance of being allocated to A or B, but it has a disadvantage. There is a tendency for the last few subjects all to have the same treatment. This characteristic sometimes worries researchers, who feel that the randomization is not quite right. In statistical terms, the possible allocations are not equally likely. If we use this method for the random allocation described above, the 10th subject in group B would be reached at subject 18 and the last two subjects would both be in group A. We can ensure that all randomizations are equally likely by using the table of random numbers in a different way.

Table 2.4 Allocation of 20 subjects to two groups

subject	digit	group	subject	digit	group
1	6	B	11	9	A
2	0	B	12	2	B
3	1	A	13	8	B
4	5	A	14	6	B
5	1	A	15	1	A
6	6	B	16	3	A
7	0	B	17	3	A
8	8	B	18	2	B
9	9	A	19	2	B
10	0	B	20	6	B

For example, we can use the table to draw a random sample of 10 subjects from 20, as described in Section 3.4. These would form group A, and the remaining 10 group B. Another way is to put our subjects into small equal-sized groups, called **blocks**, and within each block to allocate equal numbers to A and B. This gives approximately equal numbers on the two treatments and will do so whenever the trial stops. We can also have blocks which vary in size, the size of block being chosen randomly.

The use of random numbers and the generation of the random numbers themselves are simple mathematical operations well suited to the computers which are now readily available to researchers. It is very easy to program a computer to carry out random allocation, and once a program is available it can be used over and over again for further experiments. There are several programs available, both free and commercial, which will do random allocations of different types. There is a directory on my website, martinbland.co.uk.

The trial carried out by the Medical Research Council (MRC 1948) to test the efficacy of streptomycin for the treatment of pulmonary tuberculosis is generally considered to have been the first randomized experiment in medicine. There are other contenders for this crown, but this is generally regarded as the trial that inspired others to follow in their footsteps. In this study, the target population was patients with acute progressive bilateral pulmonary tuberculosis, aged 15–30 years. All cases were bacteriologically proved and were considered unsuitable for other treatments then available. The trial took place in three centres and allocation was by a series of random numbers, drawn up for each sex at each centre. The streptomycin group contained 55 patients and the control group 52 cases. The condition of the patients on admission is shown in Table 2.5. The frequency distributions of temperature and sedimentation rate were similar for the two groups; if anything the treated (S) group were slightly worse. However, this difference is no greater than could have arisen by chance, which, of course, is how it arose. The two groups are certain to be slightly different in some characteristics, especially with a fairly small sample, and we can take account of this in the analysis using multifactorial methods (Chapter 15).

After six months, 93% of the S group survived, compared with 73% of the control group. There was a clear

Table 2.5 Condition of patients on admission to trial of streptomycin (data from MRC 1948)

		Group	
		S	C
General condition	Good	8	8
	Fair	17	20
	Poor	30	24
Max. evening temperature in first week (°F)	98–98.9	4	4
	99–99.9	13	12
	100–100.9	15	17
	101+	24	19
Sedimentation rate	0–10	0	0
	11–20	3	2
	21–50	16	20
	51+	36	29

advantage to the streptomycin group. The relationship of survival to initial condition is shown in Table 2.6. Survival was more likely for patients with lower temperatures, but the difference in survival between the S and C groups is clearly present within each temperature category where deaths occurred.

Randomized trials are not restricted to two treatments. We can compare several treatments. A drug trial might include the new drug, a rival drug, and no drug at all. We can carry out experiments to compare several factors at once. For example, we might wish to study the effect of a drug at different doses in the presence or absence of a second drug, with the subject standing or supine. This is usually designed as a factorial experiment, where every possible combination of treatments is used. These designs are unusual in clinical research but are sometimes used in laboratory work. They are described in more advanced texts (e.g. Armitage *et al.* 2002). For more on randomized trials in general, see Pocock (1983) and Johnson and Johnson (1977).

Randomized experimentation may be criticised because we are withholding a potentially beneficial treatment from patients. Any biologically active treatment is potentially harmful, however, and we are surely not justified in giving potentially harmful treatments to patients before the benefits have been demonstrated conclusively. Without properly conducted controlled

Table 2.6 Survival at six months in the MRC streptomycin trial, stratified by initial condition (data from MRC 1948)

Maximum evening temperature during first observation week	Outcome	Group	
		Streptomycin group	Control group
98–98.9°F	Alive	3	4
	Dead	0	0
99–99.9°F	Alive	13	11
	Dead	0	1
100–100.9°F	Alive	15	12
	Dead	0	5
101°F and above	Alive	20	11
	Dead	4	8

clinical trials to support it, each administration of a treatment to a patient becomes an uncontrolled experiment, whose outcome, good or bad, cannot be predicted.

2.3 Stratification

Researchers sometimes worry that the randomization process will not produce balanced groups. Just by chance, we might have all the men allocated to one group and all the women allocated to the other. This is possible, of course, but extremely unlikely. However, to be sure that it does not happen, we can **stratify** our allocation. We divide the sample to be allocated into separate, mutually exclusive groups, called **strata**. We then allocate participants to trial groups using a separate blocked allocation within each stratum. This guarantees that within each stratum we will have similar numbers of participants on each treatment. There must be enough participants in each stratum for more than one block if this is to work. This makes stratified allocation suitable only for large trials. For small trials, we can consider minimization (Section 2.14) instead.

Age and sex are often used to stratify. Each stratum is then an age group of one sex, e.g. women aged under 40 years. For stratification, we choose a variable which predicts the outcome well and is easy to observe. There is no point in stratifying by sex if the thing we are trying to influence by our treatment will not differ between the sexes. There is no point in using a stratification variable which we do not know without great effort. It means that the recruitment process takes longer and potential participants may be lost.

Some statisticians and triallists, myself included, think that stratification is often a waste of time. We need a large sample and a large sample will give similar groups anyway. We should adjust treatment estimates for participant characteristics which affect the outcome whether the groups are exactly balanced or not (Section 15.3). Stratification is usually more to make the researchers feel secure than for any practical benefit.

2.4 Methods of allocation without random numbers

In the second stage of the New York studies of BCG vaccine, the children were allocated to treatment or control alternately. Researchers often ask why this method cannot be used instead of randomization, arguing that the order in which patients arrive is random, so the groups thus formed will be comparable. First, although the patients may appear to be in a random order, there is no guarantee that this is the case. We could never be sure that the groups are comparable. Second, this method is very susceptible to mistakes, or even to cheating in the patients' perceived interest. The experimenter knows what treatment the subject will receive before the subject is admitted to the trial. This knowledge may influence the decision to admit the subject, and so lead to biased groups. For example, an experimenter might be more prepared to admit a frail patient if the patient will be on the control treatment than if the patient would be exposed to the risk of the new treatment. This objection applies to using the last digit of the hospital number for allocation.

Knowledge of what treatment the next patient will receive can certainly lead to bias. For example, Schulz *et al.* (1995) looked at 250 controlled trials. They compared trials where treatment allocation was not adequately concealed from researchers, with trials where there was adequate concealment. They found an average treatment effect 41% larger in the trials with inadequate concealment.

There are several examples reported in the literature of alterations to treatment allocations. Holten (1951) reported a trial of anticoagulant therapy for patients with coronary thrombosis. Patients who presented on even dates were to be treated and patients arriving on odd dates were to form the control group. The author reports that some of the clinicians involved found it 'difficult to remember' the criterion for allocation. Overall the treated patients did better than the controls (Table 2.7). Curiously, the controls on the even dates (wrongly allocated) did considerably better than control patients on the odd dates (correctly allocated), and even managed to do marginally better than those who received the treatment. The best outcome, treated or not, was for those who were incorrectly allocated. Allocation in this trial appears to have been rather selective.

Table 2.7 Outcome of a clinical trial using systematic allocation, with errors in allocation (data from Holten 1951)

Outcome	Even dates		Odd dates	
	Treated	**Control**	**Treated**	**Control**
Survived	125	39	10	125
Died	39 (25%)	11 (22%)	0 (0%)	81 (36%)
Total	164	50	10	206

Other methods of allocation set out to be random but can fall into this sort of difficulty. For example, we could use physical mixing to achieve randomization. This is quite difficult to do. As an experiment, take a deck of cards and order them in suits from ace of clubs to king of spades. Now shuffle them in the usual way and examine them. You will probably see many runs of several cards which remain together in order. Cards must be shuffled very thoroughly indeed before the ordering ceases to be apparent. The physical randomization method can be applied to an experiment by marking equal numbers on slips of paper with the names of the treatments, sealing them into envelopes and shuffling them. The treatment for a subject is decided by withdrawing an envelope. This method was used in another study of anticoagulant therapy by Carleton *et al.* (1960). These authors reported that in the latter stages of the trial some of the clinicians involved had attempted to read the contents of the envelopes by holding them up to the light, in order to allocate patients to their own preferred treatment.

Interfering with the randomization can actually be built into the allocation procedure, with equally disastrous results. In the Lanarkshire Milk Experiment, discussed by 'Student' (1931), 10 000 school children received three-quarters of a pint of milk per day and 10 000 children acted as controls. The children were weighed and measured at the beginning and end of the six-month experiment. The object was to see whether the milk improved the growth of children. The allocation to the 'milk' or control group was done as follows:

The teachers selected the two classes of pupils, those getting milk and those acting as controls, in two different ways. In certain cases they selected them by ballot and in others on an alphabetical system. In any particular school where there was any group to which these methods had given an undue proportion of well-fed or ill-nourished children, others were substituted to obtain a more level selection.

The result of this was that the control group had a markedly greater average height and weight at the start of the experiment than did the milk group. 'Student' interpreted this as follows:

Presumably this discrimination in height and weight was not made deliberately, but it would seem probable that the teachers, swayed by the very human feeling that the poorer children needed the milk more than the comparatively well to do, must have unconsciously made too large a substitution for the ill-nourished among the (milk group) and too few among the controls and that this unconscious selection affected secondarily, both measurements.

Whether the bias was conscious or not, it spoiled the experiment, despite being from the best possible motives.

There is one non-random method which can be used successfully in clinical trials: minimization (Section 2.14). In this method, new subjects are allocated to treatments so as to make the treatment groups as similar as possible in terms of the important prognostic factors.

2.5 Volunteer bias

People who volunteer for new treatments and those who refuse them may be very different. An illustration is provided by the field trial of Salk poliomyelitis vaccine carried out in 1954 in the USA (Meier 1977). This was carried out using two different designs simultaneously, due to a dispute about the correct method. In some districts, second grade school-children were invited to participate in the trial, and randomly allocated to receive vaccine or an inert saline injection. In other districts, all second grade children were offered vaccination and the first and third grade left unvaccinated as controls. The argument against this 'observed control' approach was that the groups may not be comparable, whereas the argument against the randomized control method was that the saline injection could provoke paralysis in infected children. The results are shown in Table 2.8. In the randomized control areas the vaccinated group clearly experienced far less polio than the control group. Since these were randomly allocated, the only difference between them should be the treatment, which is clearly preferable to saline. However, the control group also had more polio than those who had refused to participate in the trial. The difference between the control and not inoculated groups is in both treatment (saline injection) and selection; they are self-selected as volunteers and refusers. The observed control areas enable us to distinguish between these two factors. The polio rates in the vaccinated children are very similar in both parts of the study, as are the rates in the not inoculated second grade children. It is the two control groups which differ. These were selected in different ways: in the randomized control areas they were volunteers, whereas in the observed control areas they were everybody eligible, both potential volunteers and potential refusers. Now suppose that the vaccine were saline instead, and that the randomized vaccinated children had the same polio experience as those receiving saline. We would expect $200\,745 \times 57/100\,000 = 114$ cases, instead of the 33 observed. The total number of cases in the randomized areas would be $114 + 115 + 121 = 350$ and the rate per $100\,000$ would be 47. This compares very closely with the

Table 2.8 Result of the field trial of Salk poliomyelitis vaccine (data from Meier 1977)

Study group	Number in group	Paralytic polio	
		Number of cases	Rate per 100 000
Randomized control:			
Vaccinated	200 745	33	16
Control	201 229	115	57
Not inoculated	338 778	121	36
Observed control:			
Vaccinated 2nd grade	221 998	38	17
Control 1st and 3rd grade	725 173	330	46
Unvaccinated 2nd grade	123 605	43	35

rate of 46 in the observed control first and third grade group. Thus it seems that the principal difference between the saline control group of volunteers and the not inoculated group of refusers is selection, not treatment.

There is a simple explanation of this. Polio is a viral disease transmitted by the faecal–oral route. Before the development of vaccine almost everyone in the population was exposed to it at some time, usually in childhood. In the majority of cases, paralysis does not result and immunity is conferred without the child being aware of having been exposed to polio. In a small minority of cases, about one in 200, paralysis or death occurs and a diagnosis of polio is made. The older the exposed individual is, the greater the chance of paralysis developing. Hence, children who are protected from infection by high standards of hygiene are likely to be older when they are first exposed to polio than those children from homes with low standards of hygiene, and thus more likely to develop the clinical disease. There are many factors which may influence parents in their decision as to whether to volunteer or refuse their child for a vaccine trial. These may include education, personal experience, current illness, and others, but certainly include interest in health and hygiene. Thus, in this trial, the high risk children tended to be volunteered and the low risk children tended to be refused. The higher risk volunteer control children experienced 57 cases of polio per 100 000, compared with 36/100 000 among the lower risk refusers.

In most diseases, the effect of volunteer bias is opposite to this. Poor conditions are related both to refusal to participate and to high risk, whereas volunteers tend to be low risk. The effect of volunteer bias is then to produce an apparent difference in favour of the treatment. We can see that comparisons between volunteers and other groups can never be reliable indicators of treatment effects.

2.6 Intention to treat

In the observed control areas of the Salk trial (Table 2.8), quite apart from the non-random age difference, the vaccinated and control groups are not comparable. However, it is possible to make a reasonable comparison in this study by comparing all second grade children,

both vaccinated and refused, with the control group. The rate in the second grade children is 23 per 100 000, which is less than the rate of 46 in the control group, demonstrating the effectiveness of the vaccine. The 'treatment' which we are evaluating is not vaccination itself, but a policy of offering vaccination and treating those who accept. A similar problem can arise in a randomized trial, for example in evaluating the effectiveness of health check-ups (South-east London Screening Study Group 1977). Subjects were randomized to a screening group or to a control group. The screening group were invited to attend for an examination, some accepted and were screened and some refused. When comparing the results in terms of subsequent mortality, it was essential to compare the controls to the screening groups containing both screened and refusers. For example, the refusers may have included people who were already too ill to come for screening. The important point is that the random allocation procedure produces comparable groups and it is these we must compare, whatever selection may be made within them. We therefore analyse the data according to the way we intended to treat subjects, not the way in which they were actually treated. This is analysis by **intention to treat**. The alternative, analysing by treatment actually received, is called **on treatment** or **per protocol** analysis.

Analysis by intention to treat is not free of bias. As some patients may receive the other group's treatment, the difference may be smaller than it should be. We know that there is a bias and we know that it will make the treatment difference smaller, by an unknown amount. On treatment analyses, on the other hand, are biased in favour of showing a difference, whether there is one or not. Statisticians call methods which are biased against finding any effect **conservative**. If we must err, we like to do so in the conservative direction.

2.7 Cross-over designs

Sometimes it is possible to use a trial participant as her or his own control. For example, when comparing analgesics in the treatment of arthritis, participants may receive in succession a new drug and a control treatment. The response to the two treatments can then be compared for each participant. These designs have the advantage of removing variability between participants. We can carry out a trial with fewer participants than would be needed for a two group trial.

Although all subjects receive all treatments, these trials must still be randomized. In the simplest case of treatment and control, patients may be given two different regimes: control followed by treatment or treatment followed by control. These may not give the same results, e.g. there may be a long-term carry-over effect or time trend which makes treatment followed by control show less of a difference than control followed by treatment. Subjects are, therefore, assigned to a given order at random. It is possible in the analysis of cross-over studies to estimate the size of any carry-over effects which may be present.

As an example of the advantages of a cross-over trial, consider a trial of pronethalol in the treatment of angina pectoris (Pritchard *et al.* 1963). Angina pectoris is a chronic disease characterized by attacks of acute pain. Patients in this trial received either pronethalol or an inert control treatment (or placebo, see Section 2.9) in four periods of two weeks, two periods on the drug and two

on the control treatment. These periods were in random order. The outcome measure was the number of attacks of angina experienced. These were recorded by the patient in a diary. Twelve patients took part in the trial. The results are shown in Table 2.9. The advantage in favour of pronethalol is shown by 11 of the 12 patients reporting fewer attacks of pain while on pronethalol than while on the control treatment. If we had obtained the same data from two separate groups of patients instead of the same group under two conditions, it would be far from clear that pronethalol is superior because of the huge variation between subjects. Using a two group design, we would need a much larger sample of patients to demonstrate the efficacy of the treatment.

Cross-over designs can be useful for laboratory experiments on animals or human volunteers. They should only be used in clinical trials where the treatment will not affect the course of the disease and where the patient's condition would not change appreciably over the course of the trial. A cross-over trial could be used to compare different treatments for the control of arthritis or asthma, for example, but not to compare different regimes for the

Table 2.9 Results of a trial of pronethalol for the treatment of angina pectoris (data from Pritchard *et al.* 1963)

Patient number	Number of attacks while on		Difference Placebo-Pronethalol
	Placebo	Pronethalol	
1	71	29	42
2	323	348	–25
3	8	1	7
4	14	7	7
5	23	16	7
6	34	25	9
7	79	65	14
8	60	41	19
9	2	0	2
10	3	0	3
11	17	15	2
12	7	2	5

management of myocardial infarction. However, a cross-over trial cannot be used to demonstrate the long-term action of a treatment, as the nature of the design means that the treatment period must be limited. As most treatments of chronic disease must be used by the patient for a long time, a two sample trial of long duration is usually required to investigate fully the effectiveness of the treatment. Pronethalol, for example, was later found to have quite unacceptable side effects in long-term use.

For more on cross-over trials, see Senn (2002) and Jones and Kenward (1989).

2.8 Selection of subjects for clinical trials

I have discussed the allocation of subjects to treatments at some length, but we have not considered where they come from. The way in which subjects are selected for an experiment may have an effect on its outcome. In practice, we are usually limited to subjects which are easily available to us. For example, in an animal experiment we must take the latest batch from the animal house. In a clinical trial of the treatment of myocardial infarction, we must be content with patients who are brought into the hospital. In experiments on human volunteers, we sometimes have to use the researchers themselves.

As we shall see more fully in Chapter 3, this has important consequences for the interpretation of results. In trials of myocardial infarction, for example, we would not wish to conclude that, say, the survival rate with a new treatment in a trial in London would be the same as in a trial in Edinburgh. The patients may have a different history of diet, for example, and this may have a considerable effect on the state of their arteries and hence on their prognosis. Indeed, it would be very rash to suppose that we would get the same survival rate in a hospital a mile down the road. What we rely on is the comparison between randomized groups from the same population of subjects, and hope that if a treatment reduces mortality in London, it will also do so in Edinburgh. This may be a reasonable supposition, and effects which appear in one population are likely to appear in another, but it cannot be proved on statistical grounds alone. Sometimes in

extreme cases it turns out not to be true. BCG vaccine has been shown, by large, well conducted randomized trials, to be effective in reducing the incidence of tuberculosis in children in the UK. However, in India it appears to be far less effective (*Lancet* 1980). This may be because the amount of exposure to tuberculosis is so different in the two populations.

Given that we can use only the experimental subjects available to us, there are some principles which we use to guide our selection from them. As we shall see later, the lower the variability between the subjects in an experiment, the better chance we have of detecting a treatment difference if it exists. This means that uniformity is desirable in our subjects. In an animal experiment this can be achieved by using animals of the same strain raised under controlled conditions. In a clinical trial we usually restrict our attention to patients of a defined age group and severity of disease. The Salk vaccine trial (Section 2.5) only used children in one school year. In the streptomycin trial (Section 2.2) the subjects were restricted to patients with acute bilateral pulmonary tuberculosis, bacteriologically proved, aged between 15 and 30 years, and unsuitable for other current therapy. Even with this narrow definition there was considerable variation among the patients, as Tables 2.5 and 2.6 show. Tuberculosis had to be bacteriologically proved because it is important to make sure that everyone has the disease we wish to treat. Patients with a different disease are not only potentially being wrongly treated themselves, but may make trial results difficult to interpret. Restricting attention to a particular subset of patients, though useful, can lead to difficulties. For example, a treatment shown to be effective and safe in young people may not necessarily be so in the elderly. Trials have to be carried out on the sort of patients the treatment is proposed to treat.

2.9 Response bias and placebos

The knowledge that she or he is being treated may alter a patient's response to treatment. This is called the **placebo effect**. A **placebo** is a pharmacologically inactive treatment given as if it were an active treatment. This effect may take many forms, from a desire to please the doctor to measurable biochemical changes in the brain.

Mind and body are intimately connected, and unless the psychological effect is actually part of the treatment, we usually try to eliminate such factors from treatment comparisons. This is particularly important when we are dealing with subjective assessments, such as of pain or well-being. Rather surprisingly, placebos can have an effect even when the person taking them knows in advance that what they are taking has no active component. Kaptchuk *et al.* (2010) randomized people with irritable bowel syndrome to no treatment or to what they were told were 'placebo pills made of an inert substance, like sugar pills, that have been shown in clinical studies to produce significant improvement in IBS symptoms through mind-body self-healing processes'. Patients allocated to placebo reported significantly lower symptom severity and had significantly better global improvement scores after three weeks. One participant described on television her attempts to obtain further supplies of the placebo after the three weeks were over and her symptoms had returned (*Horizon* 2014).

A fascinating example of the power of the placebo effect is given by Huskisson (1974). Three active analgesics, aspirin, Codis and Distalgesic, were compared with an inert placebo. Twenty-two patients each received the four treatments in a cross-over design. The patients reported on a four point scale, from 0 = no relief to 3 = complete relief. All the treatments produced some pain relief, maximum relief being experienced after about two hours (Figure 2.1).

The three active treatments were all superior to placebo, but not by very much. The four drug treatments were given in the form of tablets identical in shape and size, but each drug was given in four different colours. This was done so that patients could distinguish the drugs received, to say which they preferred. Each patient received four different colours, one for each drug, and the colour combinations were allocated randomly. Thus some patients received red placebos, some blue, and so on. As Figure 2.2 shows, red placebos were markedly more effective than other colours, and were just as effective as the active drugs! In this study not only is the effect demonstrated of a pharmacologically inert placebo in producing reported pain relief, but also the wide variability and unpredictability of this response. We must clearly take account of this in trial design. Incidentally, we should not conclude that red placebos always work best. There is, for example, some evidence that patients being treated for anxiety prefer tablets to be in a soothing green, and depressive symptoms respond best to a lively yellow (Schapira *et al.* 1970).

In any trial involving human subjects it is desirable that the subjects should not be able to tell which treatment is which. In a study to compare two or more treatments this should be done by making the treatments as similar as possible. Where subjects are to receive no treatment, an inactive placebo should be used if possible. Sometimes when two very different active treatments are compared, a double placebo or **double dummy** can

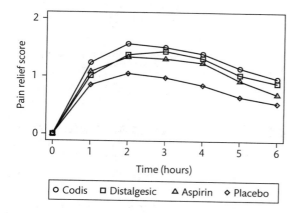

Figure 2.1 Pain relief in relation to drug or placebo (data from Huskisson 1974).

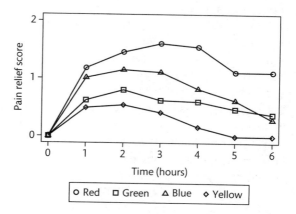

Figure 2.2 Pain relief in relation to colour of placebo (data from Huskisson 1974).

be used. For example, when comparing a drug given as a single dose with a drug taken daily for seven days, subjects on the single dose drug may receive a daily placebo and those on the daily dose a single placebo at the start.

Placebos are not always possible or ethical. In the MRC trial of streptomycin, where the treatment involved several injections a day for several months, it was not regarded as ethical to do the same with an inert saline solution and no placebo was given. Others, however, have done far more aggressive things as placebos. Moseley *et al.* (2002), for example, report that 'A total of 180 patients with osteoarthritis of the knee were randomly assigned to receive arthroscopic debridement, arthroscopic lavage, or placebo surgery. Patients in the placebo group received skin incisions and underwent a simulated debridement without insertion of the arthroscope. Patients and assessors of outcome were blinded to the treatment group assignment'. In the Salk vaccine trial, the inert saline injections were placebos. It could be argued that paralytic polio is not likely to respond to psychological influences, but how could we be really sure of this? The certain knowledge that a child had been vaccinated may have altered the risk of exposure to infection as parents allowed the child to go swimming, for example. Finally, the use of a placebo may also reduce the risk of assessment bias, as we shall see in Section 2.10.

2.10 Assessment bias and double blind studies

The response of subjects is not the only thing affected by knowledge of the treatment. The assessment by the researcher of the response to treatment may also be influenced by the knowledge of the treatment.

Some outcome measures do not allow for much bias on the part of the assessor. For example, if the outcome is survival or death, there is little possibility that unconscious bias may affect the observation. However, if we are interested in an overall clinical impression of the patient's progress, or in changes in an X-ray picture, the measurement may be influenced by our desire (or otherwise) that the treatment should succeed. It is not enough to be aware of this danger and allow for it, as we may have the similar problem of 'bending over backwards to be

fair'. Even an apparently objective measure such as blood pressure can be influenced by the expectations of the experimenter, and special measuring equipment has been devised to avoid this (Rose *et al.* 1964).

We can avoid the possibility of such bias by using **blind assessment**, that is, the assessor does not know which treatment the subject is receiving. If a clinical trial cannot be conducted in such a way that the clinician in charge does not know the treatment, blind assessment can still be carried out by an external assessor. When the subject does not know the treatment and blind assessment is used, the trial is said to be **double blind**. (Researchers on eye disease hate the terms 'blind' and 'double blind', preferring '**masked**' and '**double masked**' instead.)

Placebos may be just as useful in avoiding assessment bias as for response bias. The subject is unable to tip the assessor off as to treatment, and there is likely to be less material evidence to indicate to an assessor what it is. In the anticoagulant study by Carleton *et al.* (1960) described in Section 2.4, the treatment was supplied through an intravenous drip. Control patients had a dummy drip set up, with a tube taped to the arm but no needle inserted, primarily to avoid assessment bias. In the Salk trial, the injections were coded and the code for a case was only broken after the decision had been made as to whether the child had polio and, if so, of what severity.

In the streptomycin trial, one of the outcome measures was radiological change. X-ray plates were numbered and then assessed by two radiologists and a clinician, none of whom knew to which patient and treatment the plate belonged. The assessments were done independently, and they only discussed a plate if they had not all come to the same conclusion. Only when a final decision had been made was the link between plate and patient revealed. The results are shown in Table 2.10. The clear advantage of streptomycin is shown in the considerable improvement of over half the S group, compared with only 8% of the controls.

We should not necessarily assume that the use of a placebo guarantees that a study is double blind. In some of the trials of the controversial influenza medication Tamiflu, the active and placebo pills were different colours (Jefferson *et al.* 2014; Goldacre 2014). As we

Table 2.10 Assessment of radiological appearance at six months as compared with appearance on admission (data from MRC 1948)

Radiological assessment	S Group		C Group	
Considerable improvement	28	51%	4	8%
Moderate or slight improvement	10	18%	13	25%
No material change	2	4%	3	6%
Moderate or slight deterioration	5	9%	12	23%
Considerable deterioration	6	11%	6	11%
Deaths	4	7%	14	27%
Total	55	100%	52	100%

saw in Section 2.9, the colour of a placebo may have considerable influence on its apparent effects.

2.11 Laboratory experiments

So far we have looked at clinical trials, but exactly the same principles apply to laboratory research on animals. It may well be that in this area the principles of randomization are not so well understood and even more critical attention is needed from the reader of research reports. One reason for this may be that great effort has been put into producing genetically similar animals, raised in conditions as close to uniform as is practicable. The researcher using such animals as subjects may feel that the resulting animals show so little biological variability that any natural differences between them will be dwarfed by the treatment effects. This is not necessarily so, as the following examples illustrate.

A colleague was looking at the effect of tumour growth on macrophage counts in rats. The only significant difference was between the initial values in tumour induced and non-induced rats, that is, before the tumour-inducing treatment was given. There was a simple explanation for this surprising result. The original

design had been to give the tumour-inducing treatment to each of a group of rats. Some would develop tumours and others would not, and then the macrophage counts would be compared between the two groups thus defined. In the event, all the rats developed tumours. In an attempt to salvage the experiment my colleague obtained a second batch of animals, which he did not treat, to act as controls. The difference between the treated and untreated animals was thus due to differences in parentage or environment, not to treatment.

That problem arose by changing the design during the course of the experiment. Problems can also arise from ignoring randomization in the design of a comparative experiment. Another colleague wanted to know whether a treatment would affect weight gain in mice. Mice were taken from a cage one by one and the treatment given, until half the animals had been treated. The treated animals were put into smaller cages, five to a cage, which were placed together in a constant environment chamber. The control mice were in cages also placed together in the constant environment chamber. When the data were analysed, it was discovered that the mean initial weight was greater in the treated animals than in the control group. In a weight gain experiment this could be quite important! Perhaps larger animals were easier to pick up, and so were selected first. What that experimenter should have done was to place the mice in the boxes, give each box a place in the constant environment chamber, then allocate the boxes to treatment or control at random. We would then have two groups which were comparable, both in initial values and in any environmental differences which may exist in the constant environment chamber.

2.12 Experimental units and cluster randomized trials

In the weight gain experiment described in Section 2.11, each box of mice contained five animals. These animals were not independent of one another, but interacted. In a box the other four animals formed part of the environment of the fifth, and so might influence its growth. The box of five mice is called an **experimental unit**. An experimental unit is the smallest group of subjects in an experiment whose response cannot be affected by other subjects and which could be allocated to different treatments. We need to know the amount of natural variation which exists between experimental units before we can decide whether the treatment effect is distinguishable from this natural variation. In the weight gain experiment (Section 2.11), the mean weight gain in each box should be calculated and used as a single measurement, then the mean difference estimated using the two sample t method (Section 10.3). In human studies, the same thing happens when groups of patients, such as all those in a hospital ward or a general practice, are randomized as a group. This might happen in a trial of health promotion, for example, where special clinics are advertised and set up in GP surgeries. It would be impractical to exclude some patients from the clinic and impossible to prevent patients from the practice interacting with and influencing one another. All the practice patients must be treated as a single unit. Trials where experimental units contain more than one participant are called **cluster randomized**.

For an example of a cluster randomized trial, Richards *et al.* (2013) carried out a trial of the management of depression in primary care by adding a specialist mental health worker to the practice team, an approach called collaborative care. We had found (Richards *et al.* 2008) that if we allocated individuals attending the same primary care practice to collaborative care or to treatment as usual, there appeared to be a big contamination effect. The outcomes for patients in the same practice were more similar than we would expect. So for our main trial we allocated primary care practices to treatment groups. All the patients identified as having depression by the doctors in the Collaborative Care practices were offered collaborative care and all were invited to be in the trial. All the patients identified as having depression by the doctors in the Treatment As Usual practices received the usual treatment provided by the practice and they, too, were invited to be participants in the trial. All the patients identified with depression in the same practice formed a **cluster**.

Cluster randomized trials have become more frequent in medical research (Bland 2004). They present difficulties both in the running and in the analysis which do not arise with individually randomized trials. There may be differences in recruitment within clusters, for example, where intervention clusters are more eager to recruit participants than are control cluster. Torgerson and Torgerson (2008), chapter 9, discuss some of the practical problems. Because of these problems, cluster randomized designs should be avoided unless they are necessary. We might need to use one if the treatment can only be given to a group, such as a new hygiene regime on a hospital ward or an educational intervention in a school. For example, Cheyne *et al.* (2008) tested a new algorithm for the diagnosis of active labour in women having their first baby. This can be difficult and women are often put onto a labour ward too early. This was thought to result in unnecessary interventions when the apparent labour stopped. All the midwives in a labour unit had to be taught the algorithm and it would then be impossible for them to forget it for some deliveries and not for others. Whole delivery units had to be randomized. Some of the problems in running this trial are described by Hundley *et al.* (2010). There might be contamination between people in the same cluster, as in the Collaborative Care trial.

There are statistical problems, too. Sample size calculations are different (Section 18.8) and the clustering must be included in the analysis (Section 10.13). Statistical problems are discussed by Donner and Klar (2000) and Eldridge and Kerry (2012).

The question of the experimental unit arises when the treatment is applied to the provider of care rather than to the patient directly. For example, White *et al.* (1989) compared three randomly allocated groups of GPs, the first given an intensive programme of small group education to improve their treatment of asthma, the second a lesser intervention, and the third no intervention at all. For each GP, a sample of her or his asthmatic patients was selected. These patients received questionnaires about their symptoms, the research hypothesis being that the intensive programme would result in fewer symptoms among their patients. The experimental unit was the GP, not the patient. The asthma patients treated by an individual GP were used to monitor the effect of the intervention on that GP. The proportion of patients who reported symptoms was used as a measure of the GP's effectiveness and the mean of these proportions was compared between the groups using one-way analysis of variance (Section 10.9). The patients of the GP formed a cluster.

The most extreme case arises when there is only one experimental unit per treatment. For example, consider a health education experiment involving two schools. In one school a special health education programme was mounted, aimed at discouraging children from smoking. Both before and afterwards, the children in each school completed questionnaires about cigarette smoking. In this example the school is the experimental unit. There is no reason to suppose that two schools should have the same proportion of smokers among their pupils, or that two schools which do have equal proportions of smokers will remain so. The experiment would be much more convincing if we had several schools and randomly allocated them to receive the health education programme or to be controls. We would then look for a consistent difference between the treated and control schools, using the proportion of smokers in the school as the variable.

2.13 **Consent in clinical trials**

I started my research career in agriculture. Our experimental subjects, being barley plants, had no rights. We sprayed them with whatever chemicals we chose and burnt them after harvest and weighing. We cannot treat human subjects in the same way. We must respect the rights of our research subjects and their welfare must be our primary concern. This has not always been the case, most notoriously in the Nazi death camps (Leaning 1996). The Declaration of Helsinki (*BMJ* 1996a), which lays down the principles which govern research on human subjects, grew out of the trials in Nuremburg of the perpetrators of these atrocities (*BMJ* 1996b).

If there is a treatment, we should not leave patients untreated if this in any way affects their well-being. The world was rightly outraged by the Tuskegee Study, where men with syphilis were left untreated to see what the long-term effects of the disease might be (Brawley 1998; Ramsay 1998). This is an extreme example but it is not the only one. Women with dysplasia found at cervical cytology have been left untreated to see whether cancer developed (Mudur 1997). Patients are still being asked to enter pharmaceutical trials where they may get a placebo, even though an effective treatment is available, allegedly because regulators insist on it. In 2014, Facebook came under great criticism for experiments in which the news feed of subscribers was biased either to give to positive news or to give negative news, to see whether this affected posts users subsequently produced (Kramer *et al.* 2014). Subscribers were not aware of the experiment.

People should not be treated without their consent. This general principle is not confined to research. Patients should also be asked whether they wish to take part in a research project and whether they agree to be randomized. They should know to what they are consenting, and usually recruits to clinical trials are given information sheets which explain to them randomization, the alternative treatments, and the possible risks and benefits. Only then can they give informed or valid consent. For children who are old enough to understand, both child and parent should be informed and give their consent, otherwise parents must consent (Doyal 1997). People get very upset and angry if they think that they have been experimented on without their knowledge and consent, or if they feel that they have been tricked into it without being fully informed. A group of women with cervical cancer were given an experimental radiation treatment, which resulted in severe damage, without proper information (Anon 1997). They formed a group which they called RAGE, which speaks for itself.

Patients are sometimes recruited into trials when they are very distressed and very vulnerable. If possible they should have time to think about the trial and discuss it with their family. Patients in trials are often not at all clear about what is going on and have incorrect ideas about what is happening (Snowdon *et al.* 1997). They may be unable to recall giving their consent, and deny having given it. They should always be asked to sign consent forms and should be given a separate patient information sheet and a copy of the form to keep.

A difficulty arises with the **randomized consent** design (Zelen 1979, 1992). In this, we have a new, active treatment and either no control treatment or usual care. We randomize subjects to active or control. We then offer the new treatment to the active group, who may refuse, and the control group gets usual care. The active group is asked to consent to the new treatment and all subjects are asked to consent to any measurement required. They might be told that they are in a research study, but not that they have been randomized. Thus only patients in the active group can refuse the trial, though all can refuse measurement. Analysis is then by intention to treat (Section 2.6). For example, Dennis *et al.* (1997) wanted to evaluate a stroke family care worker. They randomized patients without their knowledge, then asked them to consent to follow-up consisting of interviews by a researcher. The care worker visited those patients and their families who had been randomized to her. McLean (1997) argued that if patients could not be informed about the randomization without jeopardizing the trial, the research should not be done. Dennis (1997) argued that to ask for consent to randomization might bias the results, because patients who did not receive the care worker might be resentful and be harmed by this. My own view is that we should not allow one ethical consideration, informed consent, to outweigh all others and this design can be acceptable (Bland 1997).

There is a special problem in cluster randomized trials (Section 2.12). Participants cannot consent to randomization, but only to treatment. In a trial where general practices are allocated to offer health checks or not to offer them, for example, patients can consent to the health checks only if they are in a health check practice, though all would have to consent to an end of trial assessment.

Research on human subjects should always be approved by an independent ethics committee, whose role is to represent the interests of the research subject. Where such a system is not in place, terrible things can happen. In the USA, research can be carried out without ethical approval if the subjects are private patients in a private hospital without any public funding, and no new drug or device is used. Under these circumstances, plastic surgeons carried out a trial comparing two methods of performing face-lifts, one on each side of the face, without patients' consent (Bulletin of Medical Ethics 1998).

2.14 Minimization

Stratification (Section 2.3) ensures that we have randomized groups which are similar for specified variables, but

it works only for large samples. **Minimization** is an alternative approach suggested by Taves (1974). This sets out to allocate non-randomly so as to balance the groups on selected variables.

I shall explain via an example (Bland 2014). A television company, Outline Productions, wanted to do some randomized control trials of novel remedies, for a series called *Health Freaks*, first broadcast in the UK on Channel 4, 21st October, 2013. One remedy for psoriasis was using oatmeal in a bath. The plan was to allocate about 20 volunteers either to oatmeal or a control treatment using a regular bath. There was the usual concern that random allocation would result in imbalance on some important variable. I promised to avoid this by minimization. They wanted the groups to be balanced for age, gender, and severity of psoriasis. I decided to classify age as <30 years or 30+. Severity was graded as mild, moderate, or severe.

I received a list of participants and their characteristics as shown in Table 2.11. The minimization algorithm which I used allocated the first participant, #13, at random, to Control. We then consider the participant #6. For each of the variables, we count the number with the same characteristic as the new participant and sum these over all variables, for each group. For Oatmeal, which has no-one allocated, this is $0 + 0 + 0 = 0$. For Control it is also $0 + 0 + 0 = 0$, because the participant #6 is in a different age category, has different gender, and different severity, from the first. The totals are the same, the imbalance will be the same whichever group we put #6 into, so #6 was allocated randomly, to Control. We then consider #1. The sum for Oatmeal is $0 + 0 + 0 = 0$. For Control it is $1 + 1 + 1 = 3$, because #6 is in the same age category and the same gender category and #13 is in the same severity category. The total for Oatmeal is less than for Control, the imbalance will be greater if we put #1 into Control than if we put #1 into Oatmeal, so we allocate to Oatmeal. We then consider #3. The sum for Oatmeal is $1 + 1 + 0 = 2$. For Control it is $1 + 1 + 1 = 3$. We allocate to Oatmeal. We continue like this until all have been allocated.

Age group and severity were quite well balanced, younger:older ratio for Oatmeal being 5:4 and for Control 3:4 and mild:moderate:severe being 1:4:4 for Oatmeal and 1:3:3 for Control. Gender was less well

Table 2.11 Characteristics of volunteers for the oatmeal bath trial, with subsequent allocated group

Participant	Age group	Gender	Psoriasis severity	Allocated group
13	Younger	Male	Moderate	Control
6	Older	Female	Mild	Control
1	Older	Female	Moderate	Oatmeal
3	Older	Female	Mild	Oatmeal
5	Younger	Male	Severe	Oatmeal
7	Younger	Female	Severe	Control
11	Younger	Male	Moderate	Oatmeal
10	Younger	Female	Severe	Control
2	Older	Female	Severe	Oatmeal
14	Younger	Male	Severe	Control
16	Older	Female	Moderate	Control
15	Older	Female	Moderate	Control
8	Younger	Female	Severe	Oatmeal
9	Younger	Female	Moderate	Control
12	Older	Male	Moderate	Oatmeal
4	Older	Male	Severe	Control

balanced, F:M ratio for Oatmeal being 6:3 and for Control 4:3. Exact balance is not possible in a sample of 13 people. Some of the participants withdrew before the trial and a further list of participants arrived which I allocated in the same way, having removed the dropouts.

An obvious objection to this procedure is that it is quite deterministic and predictable. The second person allocated is very likely to get the opposite allocation to the first for example. I randomized the order of the list of participants to make it more random, but this can be done only if we have a list at the start. In most trials participants are recruited one by one and this is not possible. Some minimization algorithms introduce a random element by finding the group preferred to reduce imbalance and then allocating the participant to that group with a random element, e.g. 3:1 in favour of the indicated group, 1:3 in favour of the other group.

Minimization is often used in cluster randomized trials (Section 2.12), because the number of clusters is usually quite small. For example, in the Collaborative Care trial (Section 2.12), 51 primary care practices were allocated separately by minimization in four different geographic locations, using practice list size, number of doctors at the practice, and index of multiple deprivation for the practice area as minimization variables. We did not start with a list of practices but recruited them in ones and twos. The Collaborative Care arm had 24 practices, average list size 6 615 patients, average number of doctors (whole time equivalents) 3.8, and average index of multiple deprivation rank 9 210. For the 27 practices in the Treatment as Usual arm, the figures were 7 152, 4.0, and 8 449 respectively, so the balance was quite good.

Because of the predictability, some drug regulators do not accept minimized trials. I understand their feelings, but it is really a method for small trials, not regulatory trials, and for them it can be useful, particularly for anxious researchers.

2.15 Multiple choice questions: Clinical trials

(Each branch is either true or false.)

2.1 When testing a new medical treatment, suitable control groups include patients who:
  (a) are treated by a different doctor at the same time;
  (b) are treated in a different hospital;
  (c) are not willing to receive the new treatment;
  (d) were treated by the same doctor in the past;
  (e) are not suitable for the new treatment.

2.2 In an experiment to compare two treatments, participants are allocated using random numbers so that:
  (a) the sample may be referred to a known population;
  (b) when deciding to admit a participant to the trial, we do not know which treatment that participant would receive;
  (c) the participants will get the treatment best suited to them;
  (d) the two groups will be similar, apart from treatment;
  (e) treatments may be assigned according to the characteristics of the participant.

2.3 In a double blind clinical trial:
  (a) the participants do not know which treatment they receive;
  (b) each participant receives a placebo;
  (c) the participants do not know that they are in a trial;
  (d) each participant receives both treatments;
  (e) the clinician making the assessment does not know which treatment the participant receives.

2.4 In a trial of a new vaccine, children were assigned at random to a 'vaccine' or a 'control' group. The 'vaccine' group were offered vaccination, which two-thirds accepted. The control group were offered nothing:
  (a) the group which should be compared with the controls is all children who accepted vaccination;
  (b) those refusing vaccination should be included in the control group;
  (c) the trial is double blind;
  (d) those refusing vaccination should be excluded;
  (e) the trial is useless because not all the treated group were vaccinated.

2.5 Cross-over designs for clinical trials:
  (a) may be used to compare several treatments;
  (b) involve no randomization;
  (c) require fewer participants than do designs comparing independent groups;
  (d) are useful for comparing treatments intended to alleviate chronic symptoms;
  (e) use the participants as their own controls.

2.6 Placebos are useful in clinical trials:
  (a) when two apparently similar active treatments are to be compared;
  (b) to guarantee comparability in non-randomized trials;
  (c) because the fact of being treated may itself produce a response;
  (d) because they may help to conceal the subject's treatment from assessors;
  (e) when an active treatment is to be compared with no treatment.

2.16 Exercise: The 'Know Your Midwife' trial

The Know Your Midwife (KYM) scheme was a method of delivering maternity care for low-risk women. A team of midwives ran a clinic, and the same midwife would give all antenatal care for a mother, deliver the baby, and give postnatal care. The KYM scheme was compared with standard antenatal care in a randomized trial (Flint and Poulengeris 1986). It was thought that the scheme would be very attractive to women and that if they knew it was available, they might be reluctant to be randomized to standard care. Eligible women were randomized without their knowledge to KYM or to the control group, who received the standard antenatal care provided by St George's Hospital. Women randomized to KYM were sent a letter explaining the KYM scheme and inviting them to attend. Some women declined and attended the standard clinic instead. The mode of delivery for the women is shown in Table 2.12. Normal obstetric data were recorded on all women, and the women were asked to complete questionnaires

Table 2.12 Method of delivery in the KYM study (data from Flint and Poulengeris 1986)

Method of delivery	Accepted KYM		Refused KYM		Control women	
	%	n	%	n	%	n
Normal	80.7	352	69.8	30	74.8	354
Instrumental	12.4	54	14.0	6	17.8	84
Caesarean	6.9	30	16.3	7	7.4	35

(which they could refuse) as part of a study of antenatal care, though they were not told about the trial.

2.1 The women knew what type of care they were receiving. What effect might this have on the outcome?

2.2 What comparison should be made to test whether KYM has any effect on method of delivery?

2.3 Do you think it was ethical to randomize women without their knowledge?

3 Sampling and observational studies

3.1 Observational studies

In this chapter we shall be concerned with observational studies. Instead of changing something and observing the result, as in an experiment or clinical trial, we observe the existing situation and try to understand what is happening. Most medical studies are observational, including research into human biology in healthy people, the natural history of disease, the causes and distribution of disease, the quality of measurement, and the process of medical care.

One of the most important and difficult tasks in medicine is to determine the causes of disease, so that we may devise methods of prevention. We are working in an area where experiments are often neither possible nor ethical. For example, to determine that cigarette smoking caused cancer, we could imagine a study in which children were randomly allocated to a '20 cigarettes a day for 50 years' group and a 'never smoke in your life' group. All we would have to do then would be to wait for the death certificates. However, we could not persuade our subjects to stick to the treatment, and deliberately setting out to cause cancer is hardly ethical. We must therefore observe the disease process as best we can, by watching people in the wild rather than under laboratory conditions.

We can never come to an unequivocal conclusion about causation in observational studies. The disease effect and possible cause do not exist in isolation but in a complex interplay of many intervening factors. We must do our best to assure ourselves that the relationship we observe is not the result of some other factor acting on both 'cause' and 'effect'. For example, it was once thought that the African fever tree, the yellow-barked acacia, caused malaria, because those unwise enough to camp under them were likely to develop the disease. This tree grows by water where mosquitos breed, and provides an ideal day-time resting place for these insects, whose bite transmits the plasmodium parasite that produces the disease. The water and the mosquitos were the important factors, not the tree. Indeed, the name 'malaria' comes from a similar incomplete observation. It means 'bad air' and comes from the belief that the disease was caused by the air in low-lying, marshy places, where the mosquitos bred. Epidemiological study designs must try to deal with the complex interrelationships between different factors to deduce the true mechanism of disease causation. We also use a number of different approaches to the study of these problems, to see whether all produce the same answer.

There are many problems in interpreting observational studies, and the medical consumer of such research must be aware of them. We have no better way to tackle many questions and so we must make the best of them and look for consistent relationships that stand up to the most severe examination. We can also look for confirmation of our findings indirectly, from animal models and from dose–response relationships in the human population. However, we must accept that perfect proof is impossible and it is unreasonable to demand it. Sometimes, as with smoking and health, we must act on the balance of the evidence.

We shall start by considering how to get descriptive information about populations in which we are interested. We shall go on to the problem of using such information to study disease processes and the possible causes of disease.

3.2 Censuses

One simple question we can ask about any group of interest is how many members it has. For example, we need to know how many people live in a country and how many of them are in various age and sex categories, in order to monitor the changing pattern of disease and to plan medical services. We can obtain this information by a **census**. In a census, the whole of a defined population is counted. In the UK as in many developed countries, a population census is held every 10 years (although this great institution may not continue). This is done by dividing the entire country into small areas called enumeration districts, usually containing between 100 and 200 households. It is the responsibility of an enumerator to identify every household in the district and to ensure that a census form is completed, listing all members of the household and providing a few simple pieces of information. Even though completion of the census form is compelled by law, and enormous effort goes into ensuring that every household is included, there are undoubtedly some which are missed. The final data, though extremely useful, are not totally reliable.

The medical profession takes part in a massive, continuing census of deaths, by providing death certificates for each death that occurs, including not only the name of the deceased and cause of death, but also details of age, sex, place of residence, and occupation. Census methods are not restricted to national populations. They can be used for more specific administrative purposes too. For example, we might want to know how many patients are in a particular hospital at a particular time, how many of them are in different diagnostic groups, in different age/sex groups, and so on. We can then use this information together with estimates of the death and discharge rates to estimate how many beds these patients will occupy at various times in the future (Bewley *et al.* 1975; 1981).

3.3 Sampling

A census of a single hospital can only give us reliable information about that hospital. We cannot easily generalize our results to hospitals in general. If we want to obtain information about the hospitals of the UK, two courses are open to us: we can study every hospital, or we can take a representative sample of hospitals and use that to draw conclusions about hospitals as a whole.

Most statistical work is concerned with using samples to draw conclusions about some larger population. In the clinical trials described in Chapter 2, the patients act as a sample from a larger population consisting of all similar patients. We do the trial to find out what would happen to this larger group were we to give them a new treatment.

The word 'population' is used in common speech to mean 'all the people living in an area', commonly of a country. In statistics, we define the term more widely. A **population** is any collection of individuals in which we may be interested, where these individuals may be anything, and the number of individuals may be finite or infinite. Thus, if we are interested in some characteristics of the British people, the population is 'all people in Britain'. If we are interested in the current treatment of diabetes the population is 'all people with diabetes'. If we are interested in the blood pressure of a particular patient, the population is 'all possible measurements of blood pressure in that patient'. If we are interested in the toss of two coins, the population is 'all possible tosses of two coins'. The first two examples are finite populations and could, in theory if not in practice, be completely examined; the second two are infinite populations and could not. We could only ever look at a **sample**, which we will define as being a group of individuals taken from a larger population and used to find out something about that population.

How should we choose a sample from a population? The problem of getting a representative sample is similar to that of getting comparable groups of patients, as discussed in Section 2.1. We want our sample to be representative, in some sense, of the population. We want it to have all the characteristics in terms of the proportions of individuals with particular qualities as has the whole population. In a sample from a human population, for example, we want the sample to have about the same proportions of men and women as in the population, the same proportions in different age groups, in occupational groups, with different diseases, and so on. In addition, if we use a sample to estimate the proportion of people with a disease, we want to know how reliable this estimate is, how far from the proportion in the whole population the estimate is likely to be.

It is not sufficient to choose the most convenient group. For example, if we wished to predict the results of an election, we would not take as our sample people waiting in bus queues. These may be easy to interview, at least until the bus comes, but the sample would be heavily biased towards those who cannot afford cars and thus towards lower income groups. In the same way, if we wanted a sample of medical students we would not take the front two rows of the lecture theatre. They may be unrepresentative in having an unusually high thirst for knowledge, or poor eyesight.

How can we choose a sample that does not have a built-in bias? We might divide our population into groups, depending on how we think various characteristics will affect the result. To ask about an election, for example, we might group the population according to age, sex, and social class. We then choose a number of people in each group by knocking on doors until the quota is made up, and interview them. Then, knowing the distributions of these categories in the population (from census data, etc.), we can get a far better picture of the views of the population. This is called **quota sampling**. In the same way, we could try to choose a sample of rats by choosing given numbers of each weight, age, sex, etc. There are difficulties with this approach. First, it is rarely possible to think of all the relevant classifications. Second, it is still difficult to avoid bias within the classifications, by picking interviewees who look friendly, or rats that are easy to catch. Third, we can only get an idea of the reliability of findings by repeatedly doing the same type of survey, and of the representativeness of the sample by knowing the true population values (which we can actually do in the case of elections), or by comparing the results with a sample that does not have these drawbacks. Quota sampling can be quite effective when similar surveys are made repeatedly, as in opinion polls or market research. It is less useful for medical problems, where we are continually asking new questions. We need a method where bias is avoided and where we can estimate the reliability of the sample from the sample itself. As in Section 2.2, we use a random method: random sampling.

3.4 Random sampling

The problem of obtaining a sample that is representative of a larger population is similar to that of allocating patients into two comparable groups. We want a way of choosing members of the sample that does not depend on their own characteristics. The only way to be sure of this is to select them at random, so that whether or not each member of the population is chosen for the sample is purely a matter of chance.

For example, to take a random sample of five students from a class of 80, we could write all the names on pieces of paper, mix them thoroughly in a hat or other suitable container, and draw out five. All students have the same chance of being chosen, and so we have a random sample. All samples of five students are equally likely, too, because each student is chosen quite independently of the others. This method is called **simple random sampling**.

As we have seen in Section 2.2, physical methods of randomizing are often not suitable for statistical work. We usually use tables of random digits, such as Table 2.3, or random numbers generated by a computer program. We could use Table 2.3 to draw our sample of five from 80 students in several ways. For example, we could list the students, numbered from 1 to 80. This list from which the sample is to be drawn is called the **sampling frame**. We choose a starting point in the random number table (Table 2.3), say row 10, column 45. This gives us the following pairs of digits:

14 04 88 86 28 92 04 03 42 99 87 08. We could use these pairs of digits directly as subject numbers. We choose subjects numbered 14 and 4. There is no subject 88 or 86, so the next chosen is number 28. There is no 92, so the next is 4. We already have this subject in the sample, so we carry on to the next pair of digits, 03. The final member of the sample is number 42. Our sample of five students is thus numbers 3, 4, 14, 28, and 42.

There appears to be some pattern in this sample. Two numbers are adjacent (3 and 4) and three are divisible by 14 (14, 28, and 42). Random numbers often appear to us to have pattern, perhaps because the human mind is always looking for it. On the other hand, if we try to make the sample 'more random' by replacing either 3 or 4 by a subject near the end of the list, we are imposing a pattern of uniformity on the sample and destroying its randomness. All groups of five are equally likely and may happen, even 1, 2, 3, 4, 5.

This method of using the table is fine for drawing a small sample, but it can be tedious for drawing large samples, because of the need to check for duplicates. There are many other ways of doing it. For example, we can drop the requirement for a sample of fixed size, and only require that each member of the population will have a fixed probability of being in the sample. We could draw a 5/80 = 1/16 sample of our class by using the digits in groups to give a decimal number, say,

.1404   .8886   .2892   .0403   .4299   .8708.

We then choose the first member of the population if 0.1404 is less than 1/16. It is not, so we do not include this member, nor the second, corresponding to 0.8886, nor the third, corresponding to 0.2892. The fourth corresponds to 0.0403, which is less than 1/16 (0.0625) and so the fourth member is chosen as a member of the sample, and so on. This method is only suitable for fairly large samples, as the size of the sample obtained can be variable in small sampling problems. In the example there is a higher than 1 in 10 chance of finishing with a sample of two or fewer.

As with random allocation (Section 2.2), random sampling is an operation ideally suited to computers. There are many programs available to do this. Some computer programs for managing primary care practices actually have the capacity to take a random sample for any defined group of patients built in.

Random sampling ensures that the only ways in which the sample differs from the population will be a result of chance. It has a further advantage, because the sample is random, we can apply the methods of probability theory to the data obtained. As we shall see in Chapter 8, this enables us to estimate how far from the population value the sample value is likely to be.

The problem with random sampling is that we need a list of the population from which the sample is to be drawn. Lists of populations may be hard to find, or they may be very cumbersome. For example, to sample the adult population in the UK, we could use the electoral roll. A simple random sample drawn from across the country might be difficult to study, for example, if we had to interview them. In practice we would first take a random sample of electoral wards, and then a random sample of electors within these wards. This is, for obvious reasons, a **multi-stage random sample**. This approach contains the element of randomness, and so samples will be representative of the populations from which they are drawn. However, not all samples have an equal chance of being chosen, so it is not the same as simple random sampling. An electoral roll sample might also be biased, too, because not everybody is included in the electoral roll.

We can also carry out sampling without a list of the population itself, provided we have a list of some larger units that contain all the members of the population. For example, we can obtain a random sample of schoolchildren in an area by starting with a list of schools, which is quite easy to come by. We then draw a simple random sample of schools and all the children within our chosen schools form the sample of children. This is called a **cluster sample**, because we take a sample of clusters of individuals. Another example would be sampling from any age/sex group in the general population by taking a sample of addresses and then taking everyone at the chosen addresses who matched our criteria.

Sometimes it is desirable to divide the population into different strata (Section 2.3), for example into age and sex groups, and take random samples within these. This is rather like quota sampling, except that within the strata we choose at random. If the different strata have different values of the quantity we are measuring, this **stratified random sampling** can increase our precision considerably. There are many complicated sampling schemes for use in different situations. For example, in a study of cigarette smoking and respiratory disease in Derbyshire schoolchildren, we drew a random sample of schools, stratified by school type (single sex/mixed, selective/non-selective, etc.). Some schools which took children to age 13 then fed into the same 14+ school were combined into one sampling unit. Our sample of children was all children in the chosen schools who were in their first secondary school year (Banks *et al.* 1978). We thus had a stratified random cluster sample. These sampling methods affect the estimate obtained. Stratification improves the precision, cluster sampling worsens it. The sampling scheme should be taken into account in the analysis (Cochran 1977; Kish 1994). Often it is ignored, as was done by Banks *et al.* (1978) (that is, by me), but it should not be and results may be reported as being more precise than they really are.

In Section 2.3 I looked at the difficulties that can arise using methods of allocation which appear random but do not use random numbers. In sampling, two such methods are often suggested by researchers. One is to take every tenth subject from the list, or whatever fraction is required. The other is to use the last digit of some reference number, such as the hospital number, and take as the sample subjects where this is, say, 3 or 4. These sampling methods are **systematic** or **quasi-random**. It is not usually obvious why they should not give 'random' samples, and it may be that in many cases they would be just as good as random sampling. They are certainly easier. To use them, we must be very sure that there is no pattern to the list which could produce an unrepresentative group. If it is possible, random sampling seems safer.

Volunteer bias can be as serious a problem in sampling studies as it is in trials (Section 2.4). If we can only obtain data from a subset of our random sample, then this subset will not be a random sample of the population. Its members will be self-selected. It is often very difficult to get data from every member of a sample. The proportion for whom data is obtained is called the **response rate** and in a sample survey of the general population is likely to be between 70% and 80%. The possibility that those lost from the sample are different in some way must be considered. For example, they may tend to be ill, which can be a serious problem in disease prevalence studies. In the school study of Banks *et al.* (1978), the response rate was 80%, most of those lost being absent from school on the day. Now, some of these absentees were ill and some were truants. Our sample may thus lead us to underestimate the prevalence of respiratory symptoms, by omitting sufferers with current acute disease, and the prevalence of cigarette smoking by omitting those who have gone for a quick smoke behind the bike sheds.

One of the most famous sampling disasters, the *Literary Digest* poll of 1936, illustrates these dangers (Bryson 1976). This was a poll of voting intentions in the 1936 US presidential election, fought by Roosevelt and Landon. The sample was a complex one. In some cities every registered voter was included, in others one in two, and for the whole of Chicago one in three. Ten million sample ballots were mailed to prospective voters, but only 2.3 million, less than a quarter, were returned. Still, two million is a lot of Americans, and these predicted a 60% vote to Landon. In fact, Roosevelt won with 62% of the vote. The response was so poor that the sample was most unlikely to be representative of the population, no matter how carefully the original sample was drawn. Two million Americans can be wrong! It is not the mere size of the sample, but its representativeness which is important. Provided the sample is truly representative, 2 000 voters is all you need to estimate voting intentions to within 2%, which is enough for election prediction if they tell the truth and don't change their minds (see Section 18.10).

3.5 Sampling in clinical and epidemiological studies

Having extolled the virtues of random sampling and cast doubt on all other sampling methods, I must admit that most medical data are not obtained in this way. This is partly because the practical difficulties are immense. To obtain a reasonable sample of the population of the UK, anyone can get a list of electoral wards, take a random sample of them, buy copies of the electoral rolls for the chosen wards, and then take a random sample of names from it. But suppose you want to obtain a sample of patients with carcinoma of the bronchus. You could get a list of hospitals easily enough and get a random sample of them, but then things would become difficult. The names of patients will only be released by the consultant in charge should she or he so wish, and you will need her or his permission before approaching them. Any study of human patients requires ethical approval, and you will need this from the ethics committee of each of your chosen hospitals. Getting the cooperation of so many people is a task to daunt the hardiest, and obtaining ethical approval alone can take more than a year. In the UK, we now have a system of multi-centre research ethics committees, but as local approval must also be obtained the delays may still be immense.

The result of this is that clinical studies are done on the patients to hand. I have touched on this problem in the context of clinical trials (Section 2.8) and the same applies to other types of clinical study. In a clinical trial we are concerned with the comparison of two treatments and we hope that the superior treatment in Stockport will also be the superior treatment in Southampton. If we are studying clinical measurement, we can hope that a measurement method which is repeatable in Middlesbrough will be repeatable in Maidenhead, and that two different methods giving similar results in one place will give similar results in another. Studies that are not comparative give more cause for concern. The natural history of a disease described in one place may differ in unpredictable ways from that in another, because of differences in the environment and the genetic makeup of the local population. Reference ranges for quantities of clinical interest, the limits within which values from most healthy people will lie (Section 20.7), may well differ from place to place.

Studies based on local groups of patients are not without value. This is particularly so when we are concerned with comparisons between groups, as in a clinical trial, or relationships between different variables. However, we must always bear the limitations of the sampling method in mind when interpreting the results of such studies.

In general, most medical research has to be carried out using samples drawn from populations which are much more restricted than those about which we wish to draw conclusions. We may have to use patients in one hospital instead of all patients, or the population of a small area rather than that of the whole country or planet. We may have to rely on volunteers for studies of normal subjects, given most people's dislike of having needles pushed into them and disinclination to spend hours hooked up to batteries of instruments. Groups of normal subjects contain medical students, nurses, and laboratory staff far more often than would be expected by chance. In animal research the problem is even worse, for not only does one batch of one strain of mice have to represent the whole species, it often has to represent members of a different order, namely humans.

Findings from such studies can apply only to the population from which the sample was drawn. Any conclusion which we come to about wider populations, such as all patients with the disease in question, depends on evidence which is not statistical and often unspecified, namely our general experience of natural variability and experience of similar studies. This may let us down, and results established in one population may not apply to another. We have seen this in the use of the BCG vaccine in India (Section 2.8). It is very important wherever possible that studies should be repeated by other workers on other populations, so that we can sample the larger population at least to some extent.

In two types of study, case reports and case series, the subjects come before the research, as the research is suggested by their existence. There is no sampling. They are used to raise questions rather than to answer them.

A case report is a description of a single patient whose case displays interesting features. This is used to generate ideas and raise questions, rather than to answer them. This clearly cannot be planned in advance; it arises from the case. For example, Velzeboer et al. (1997) reported the case of an 11-month-old Pakistani girl, who was admitted to hospital because of drowsiness, malaise, and anorexia. She had stopped crawling or standing up and scratched her skin continuously. All investigations were negative. Her 6-year-old sister was then brought in with similar symptoms. (Note that there are two patients here, but they are part of the same case.) The doctors guessed that exposure to mercury might be to blame. When asked, the mother reported that 2 weeks before the younger child's symptoms started, mercury from a broken thermometer had been dropped on the carpet in the children's room. Mercury concentration in a urine sample taken on admission was 12.6 micrograms/l (slightly above the accepted upper normal value of 10 micrograms/l). Exposure was confirmed by a high mercury concentration in her hair. After 3 months treatment the symptoms had disappeared totally and urinary mercury had fallen below the detection limit of 1 micrograms/l. This case called into question the normal values for mercury in children.

A case series is similar to a case report, except that a number of similar cases have been observed. For example, Shaker et al. (1997) described 15 patients examined for hypocalcaemia or skeletal disease, in whom the diagnosis of coeliac disease was subsequently made.

In 11 of the patients, gastrointestinal symptoms were absent or mild. They concluded that bone loss may be a sign of coeliac disease and this diagnosis should be considered. The design does not allow them to draw any conclusions about how often this might happen. To do that they would have to collect data systematically, using a cohort design (Section 3.7) for example.

3.6 Cross-sectional studies

One possible approach to the sampling problem is the **cross-sectional study**. We take some sample or whole narrowly defined population and observe them at one point in time. We get poor estimates of means and proportions in any more general population, but we can look at relationships within the sample. For example, in an epidemiological study, Banks *et al.* (1978) gave questionnaires to all first year secondary school boys in a random sample of schools in Derbyshire (Section 3.4). Among boys who had never smoked, 3% reported a cough first thing in the morning, compared with 19% of boys who said that they smoked one or more cigarettes per week. The sample was representative of boys of this age in Derbyshire who answer questionnaires, but we want our conclusions to apply at least to the UK, if not the developed world or the whole planet. We argue that although the prevalence of symptoms and the strength of the relationship may vary between populations, the existence of the relationship is unlikely to occur only in the population studied. We cannot conclude that smoking causes respiratory symptoms. Smoking and respiratory symptoms may not be directly related, but may both be related to some other factor. A factor related to both possible cause and possible effect is called **confounding**. For example, children whose parents smoke may be more likely to develop respiratory symptoms, because of passive inhalation of their parent's smoke, and also be more influenced to try smoking themselves. We can test this by looking separately at the relationship between the child's smoking and symptoms for those whose parents are not smokers, and for those whose parents are smokers. As Figure 3.1 shows, this relationship in fact persisted and there was no reason to suppose that a third causal factor was at work.

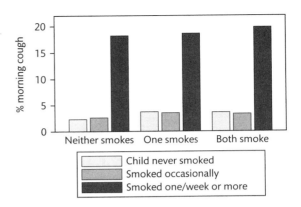

Figure 3.1 Prevalence of self-reported cough first thing in the morning in Derbyshire schoolboys, by their own and their parents' cigarette smoking (data from Banks *et al.* 1978).

Most diseases are not suited to this simple cross-sectional approach, because they are rare events. For example, lung cancer accounts for 9% of male deaths in the UK, and so is a very important disease. However the proportion of people who are known to have the disease at any given time, the **prevalence**, is quite low. Most deaths from lung cancer take place after the age of 45, so we will consider a sample of men aged 45 and over. The average remaining life span of these men, in which they could be diagnosed with lung cancer, will be about 30 years. The average time from diagnosis to death is about a year, so of those who will contract lung cancer only 1/30 will have been diagnosed when the sample is drawn. Only 9% of the sample will develop lung cancer anyway, so the proportion with the disease at any time is 1/30 × 9% = 0.3% or 3 per thousand. We would need a very large sample indeed to get a worthwhile number of lung cancer cases.

Cross-sectional designs are used in clinical studies also. For example, Rodin *et al.* (1998) studied polycystic ovary disease (PCO) in a random sample of Asian women from the lists of local general practices and from a local translating service. We found that 52% of the sample had PCO, very high compared with that found in other UK samples. However, this would not provide a good estimate for Asian women in general, because there may be many differences between this sample, such as their regions of origin, and Asian women living elsewhere. We also found that PCO women had higher fasting glucose levels than non-PCO women. As this is a comparison within the sample, it seems plausible to conclude that among Asian women, PCO tends to be associated with raised glucose. We cannot say whether PCO raises glucose or whether raised glucose increases the risk of PCO, because they are measured at the same time.

3.7 Cohort studies

One way of getting round the problem of the small proportion of people with the disease of interest is the **cohort study**. We take a group of people, the **cohort**, and observe whether they have the suspected causal factor. We then follow them over time and observe whether they develop the disease. This is a **prospective** design, as we start with the possible cause and see whether this leads to the disease in the future. It is also **longitudinal**, meaning that subjects are studied at more than one time. A cohort study usually takes a long time, as we must wait for the future event to occur. It involves keeping track of large numbers of people, sometimes for many years, and often very large numbers must be included in the sample to ensure sufficient numbers will develop the disease to enable comparisons to be made between those with and without the factor.

A noted cohort study of mortality in relation to cigarette smoking was carried out by Doll and Hill (1956). They sent a questionnaire to all members of the medical profession in the UK, who were asked to give their name, address, age, and details of current and past smoking habits. The deaths among this group were recorded. Only 60% of doctors co-operated, so in fact the cohort does not represent all doctors. The results for the first 53 months are shown in Table 3.1.

The cohort represents doctors willing to return questionnaires, not people as a whole. We cannot use the death rates as estimates for the whole population, or even for all doctors. What we can say is that, in this group, smokers were far more likely than non-smokers to die from lung cancer. It would be surprising if this relationship were only true for doctors, but we cannot definitely say that this would be the case for the whole population, because of the way the sample has been chosen.

We also have the problem of other intervening variables. Doctors were not allocated to be smokers or non-smokers as in a clinical trial; they chose for themselves. The decision to begin smoking may be related to many things (social factors, personality factors, genetic factors), which may also be related to lung cancer. We must consider these alternative explanations very carefully before coming to any conclusion about the

Table 3.1 Standardized death rates per year per 1 000 men aged 35 or more in relation to most recent amount smoked, 53 months follow-up (data from Doll and Hill 1956)

| Cause of death | Death rate among | | | | |
| | Non-smokers | Smokers | Men smoking a daily average weight of tobacco of | | |
			1–14g	15–24g	25g+
Lung cancer	0.07	0.90	0.47	0.86	1.66
Other cancer	2.04	2.02	2.01	1.56	2.63
Other respiratory	0.81	1.13	1.00	1.11	1.41
Coronary thrombosis	4.22	4.87	4.64	4.60	5.99
Other causes	6.11	6.89	6.82	6.38	7.19
All causes	13.25	15.78	14.92	14.49	18.84

causes of cancer. In this study there were no data to test such hypotheses.

The same technique is used, usually on a smaller scale, in clinical studies. For example, Casey *et al.* (1996) studied 55 patients with severe rheumatoid arthritis affecting the spine and the use of all four limbs. These patients were operated on in an attempt to improve their condition and their subsequent progress was monitored. We found that only 25% had a favourable outcome. We could not conclude from this that surgery would be worthwhile in 25% of such patients generally. Our patients might have been particularly ill or unusually fit, our surgeons might be the best or they might be (relatively speaking) ham-fisted butchers. However, we compared these results with other studies published in the medical literature, which were similar. These studies together gave a much better sample of such patients than any study alone could do (see Chapter 17, Meta-analysis). We looked at which characteristics of the patients predicted a good or bad outcome and found that the area of cross-section of the spinal cord was the important predictor. We were much more confident of this finding, because it arose from studying relationships between variables within the sample. It seems quite plausible from this study alone that patients whose spinal cords have already atrophied are unlikely to benefit from surgery.

Cohort studies can become more and more valuable as follow-up continues. For example, Richard Doll was able to continue to follow his cohort of doctors for 50 years (Doll *et al.* 2004). He reported the estimated mortality rate over 50 years to be 19.38 per 1 000 men per year for lifelong non-smokers, whereas for those smoking 25 cigarettes a day or more it was 45.34 per 1 000 per year, more than twice as much. I'm glad I stopped smoking when I was 22.

3.8 Case–control studies

Another solution to the problem of the small number of people with the disease of interest is the **case–control study**. In this we start with a group of people with the disease, the cases. We compare them to a second group without the disease, the controls. In an epidemiological study, we then find the exposure of each subject to the

possible causative factor and see whether this differs between the two groups. Before their cohort study, Doll and Hill (1950) carried out a case–control study into the aetiology of lung cancer. Twenty London hospitals notified all patients admitted with carcinoma of the lung, the cases. An interviewer visited the hospital to interview the case, and, at the same time, selected a patient with diagnosis other than cancer, of the same sex and within the same 5-year age group as the case, in the same hospital at the same time, as a control. When more than one suitable patient was available, the patient chosen was the first in the ward list considered by the ward sister to be fit for interview. Table 3.2 shows the relationship between smoking and lung cancer for these patients. A smoker was anyone who had smoked as much as 1 cigarette a day for as much as 1 year. It appears that cases were more likely than controls to smoke cigarettes. Doll and Hill concluded that smoking is an important factor in the production of carcinoma of the lung.

The case–control study is an attractive method of investigation, because of its relative speed and cheapness compared with other approaches. However, there are difficulties in the selection of cases, the selection of controls, and obtaining the data. Because of these, case–control studies sometimes produce contradictory and conflicting results.

The first problem is the selection of cases. This usually receives little consideration beyond a definition of the type of disease and a statement about the confirmation of the diagnosis. This is understandable, as there is usually little else that the investigators can do about it. They start with the available set of patients. However, these

Table 3.2 Numbers of smokers and non-smokers among lung cancer patients and age- and sex-matched controls with diseases other than cancer (data from Doll and Hill 1950)

	Non-smokers	Smokers	Total
Males:			
Lung cancer patients	2 (0.3%)	647 (99.7%)	649
Control patients	27 (4.2%)	622 (95.8%)	649
Females:			
Lung cancer patients	19 (31.7%)	41 (68.3%)	60
Control patients	32 (53.3%)	28 (46.7%)	60

patients do not exist in isolation. They are the result of some process which has led to them being diagnosed as having the disease and thus being available for study. For example, suppose we suspect that oral contraceptives might cause cancer of the breast. We have a group of patients diagnosed as having cancer of the breast. We must ask ourselves whether any of these were detected at a medical examination which took place because the woman was seeing a doctor to receive a prescription. If this were so, the risk factor (pill) would be associated with the detection of the disease rather than its cause. This is called **ascertainment bias**.

Far more difficulty is caused by the selection of controls. We want a group of people who do not have the disease in question, but who are otherwise comparable with our cases. We must first decide the population from which they are to be drawn. There are two main sources of controls: the general population and patients with other diseases. The latter may be preferred because of its accessibility. Now these two populations are clearly not the same. For example, Doll and Hill (1950) gave the current smoking habits of 1014 men and women with diseases other than cancer, 14% of whom were currently non-smokers. They commented that there was no difference between smoking in the disease groups comprising respiratory disease, cardiovascular disease, gastrointestinal disease, and others. However, in the general population the percentage of current non-smokers was 18% for men and 59% for women (Todd 1972). The smoking rate in the patient group as a whole was high. Since their report, of course, smoking has been associated with diseases in each group. Smokers get more disease and are more likely to be in hospital than non-smokers of the same age.

Intuitively, the comparison we want to make is between people with the disease and healthy people, not people with a lot of other diseases. We want to find out how to prevent disease, not how to choose one disease or another! However, it is much easier to use hospital patients as controls. There may then be a bias because the factor of interest may be associated with other diseases. Suppose we want to investigate the relationship between a disease and cigarette smoking using hospital controls. Should we exclude patients with lung cancer from the control group? If we include them, our controls may have more smokers than the general population, but if we exclude them we may have fewer. This problem is usually resolved by choosing specific patient groups, such as fracture cases, whose illness is thought to be unrelated to the factor being investigated. In case–control studies using cancer registries, controls are sometimes people with other forms of cancer. Sometimes more than one control group is used.

Having defined the population, we must choose the sample. There are many factors that affect exposure to risk factors, such as age and sex. The most straightforward way is to take a large random sample of the control population, ascertain all the relevant characteristics, and then adjust for differences during the analysis, using methods described in Chapter 15. The alternative is to try to match a control to each case, so that for each case there is a control of the same age, sex, etc. Having done this, then we can compare our cases and controls knowing that the effects of these intervening variables are automatically adjusted for. If we wish to exclude a case we must exclude its control, too, or the groups will no longer be comparable. We can have more than one control per case, but the analysis becomes complicated.

Matching on some variables does not ensure comparability on all. Indeed, if it did there would be no study. Doll and Hill matched on age, sex, and hospital. They recorded area of residence and found that 25% of their cases were from outside London, compared with 14% of controls. If we want to see whether this influences the smoking and lung cancer relationship, we must make a statistical adjustment anyway. What should we match for? The more we match for, the fewer intervening variables there are to worry about. On the other hand, it becomes more and more difficult to find matches. Even matching on age and sex, Doll and Hill could not always find a control in the same hospital, and had to look elsewhere. Matching for more than age and sex can be very difficult.

Having decided on the matching variables, we then find in the control population all the possible matches. If there are more matches than we need, we should choose the number required at random. Other methods, such as that used by Doll and Hill who allowed the ward sister to choose, have obvious problems of potential bias.

If no suitable control can be found, we can do two things. We can widen the matching criteria, say age to within 10 years rather than 5, or we can exclude the case.

There are difficulties in interpreting the results of case–control studies. One is that the case–control design is often **retrospective**, that is, we are starting with the present disease state, e.g. lung cancer, and relating it to the past, e.g. history of smoking. We may have to rely on the unreliable memories of our subjects. This may lead both to random errors among cases and controls and systematic **recall bias**, where one group, usually the cases, recalls events better than the other. For example, the mother of a child with a disability may be more likely than the mother of a child with typical development to remember events in pregnancy which may have caused damage. There is a problem of assessment bias in such studies, just as in clinical trials (Section 2.10). Interviewers will very often know whether the interviewee is a case or control and this may well affect the way questions are asked. These and other considerations make case–control studies extremely difficult to interpret. The evidence from such studies can be useful, but data from other types of investigation must be considered, too, before any firm conclusions are drawn.

The case–control design is used clinically to investigate the natural history of disease by comparing patients with healthy subjects or patients with another disease. For example, Kiely et al. (1995) were interested in lymphatic function in inflammatory arthritis. Arthritis patients (the cases) were compared with healthy volunteers (the controls). Lymphatic flow was measured in the arms of these subjects and the groups compared. It was found that lymphatic drainage was less in the cases than in the control group, but this was only so for arms which were swollen (oedematous).

3.9 Questionnaire bias in observational studies

In observational studies, many data may have to be supplied by the subjects themselves. The way in which a question is asked may influence the reply. Sometimes the bias in a question is obvious. Compare these:

(a) Do you think people should be free to provide the best medical care possible for themselves and their families, free of interference from a state bureaucracy?

(b) Should the wealthy be able to buy a place at the head of the queue for medical care, pushing aside those with greater need, or should medical care be shared solely on the basis of need for it?

Version (a) expects the answer yes, version (b) expects the answer no. We would hope not to be misled by such blatant manipulation, but the effects of question wording can be much more subtle than this. Hedges (1978) reports several examples of the effects of varying the wording of questions. He asked two groups of about 800 subjects one of the following:

(a) Do you feel you take enough care of your health, or not?

(b) Do you feel you take enough care of your health, or do you think you could take more care of your health?

In reply to question (a), 82% said that they took enough care, whereas only 68% said this in reply to question (b). Even more dramatic was the difference between this pair:

(a) Do you think a person of your age can do anything to prevent ill-health in the future, or not?

(b) Do you think a person of your age can do anything to prevent ill-health in the future, or is it largely a matter of chance?

Not only was there a difference in the percentage who replied that they could do something, but as Table 3.3 shows this answer was related to age for version (a) but not for version (b). Here version (b) is ambiguous, as it is quite possible to think that health is largely a matter of chance but that there is still something one can do about it. Only if it is totally a matter of chance is there nothing one can do.

Table 3.3 Replies to two similar questions about ill-health, by age (data from Hedges 1978)

	Age (years)			
	16–34	35–54	55+	Total
Can do something (a)	75%	64%	56%	65%
Can do something (b)	45%	49%	50%	49%

Sometimes the respondents may interpret the question in a different way from the questioner. For example, when asked whether they usually coughed first thing in the morning, 3.7% of the Derbyshire schoolchildren replied that they did. When their parents were asked about the child's symptoms, 2.4% replied positively, not a dramatic difference. Yet when asked about cough at other times in the day or at night, 24.8% of children said yes, compared with only 4.5% of their parents (Bland *et al.* 1979). These symptoms all showed relationships to the child's smoking and other potentially causal variables, and also to one another. We are forced to admit that we are measuring something, but that we are not sure what!

Another possibility is that respondents may not understand the question at all, especially when it includes medical terms. In an earlier study of cigarette smoking by children, we found that 85% of a sample agreed that smoking caused cancer, but that 41% agreed that smoking was not harmful (Bewley *et al.* 1974). There are at least two possible explanations for this: being asked to agree with the negative statement 'smoking is not harmful' may have confused the children, or they may not see cancer as harmful. We have evidence for both of these possibilities. In a repeat study in Kent we asked a further sample of children whether they agreed that smoking caused cancer and that 'smoking is bad for your health' (Bewley and Bland 1976). In this study 90% agreed that smoking causes cancer and 91% agreed that smoking is bad for your health. In another study (Bland *et al.* 1975), we asked children what was meant by the term 'lung cancer'. Only 13% seemed to us to understand and 32% clearly did not, often saying 'I don't know'. They nearly all knew that lung cancer was caused by smoking, however.

The setting in which a question is asked may also influence replies. Opinion pollsters International Communications and Market Research conducted a poll in which half the subjects were questioned by interviewers about their voting preference and half were given a secret ballot (McKie 1992). By each method 33% chose 'Labour', but 28% chose 'Conservative' at interview and 7% would not say, whereas 35% chose 'Conservative' by secret ballot and only 1% would not say. Hence the secret method produced most votes for the Conservatives, as at the then recent general election, and the open interview most for Labour. For another example, Sibbald *et al.* (1994) compared two random samples of GPs. One sample were approached by post and then by telephone if they did not reply after two reminders, and the other were contacted directly by telephone. Of the predominantly postal sample, 19% reported that they provided counselling themselves, compared with 36% of the telephone sample, and 14% reported that their health visitor provided counselling compared with 30% of the telephone group. Thus the method of asking the question influenced the answer. One must be very cautious when interpreting questionnaire replies.

Often the easiest and best method, if not the only method, of obtaining data about people is to ask them. When we do it, we must be very careful to ensure that questions are straightforward, unambiguous, and in language the respondents will understand. If we do not do this, then disaster is likely to follow.

3.10 Ecological studies

Ecology is the study of living things in relation to their environment. In epidemiology, an **ecological study** is one where the disease is studied in relation to characteristics of the communities in which people live. For example, we might take the death rates from heart disease in several countries and see whether this is related to the national annual consumption of animal fat per head of population.

Esmail *et al.* (1997) carried out an ecological study of factors related to deaths from volatile substance abuse (VSA, also called solvent abuse, inhalant abuse, or glue

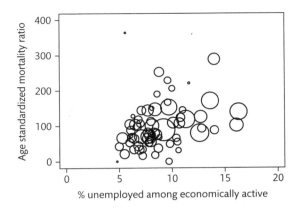

Figure 3.2 Volatile substance abuse mortality and unemployment in the counties of Great Britain (data from Esmail *et al.* 1997). (The area of the circle is proportional to the population of the county, so reflects the importance of the observation.)

sniffing). The observational units were the administrative counties of Great Britain. The deaths were obtained from a national register of deaths held at St George's and the age and sex distribution in each county from national census data. These were used to calculate an index of mortality adjusted for age, the standardized mortality ratio (Section 21.3). Indicators of social deprivation were also obtained from census data. Figure 3.2 shows the relationship between VSA mortality and unemployment in the counties. Clearly, there is a relationship. The mortality is higher in counties where unemployment is high.

Relationships found in ecological studies are indirect. We must not conclude that there is a relationship at the level of the person. This is the **ecological fallacy**. For example, we cannot conclude from Figure 3.2 that unemployed people are at a greater risk of dying from VSA than the employed. The peak age for VSA death was among school-children, who are not included in the unemployment figures. It was not the unemployed people who were dying. Unemployment is just one indicator of social deprivation, and VSA deaths are associated with many of them.

Ecological studies can be useful to generate hypotheses. For example, the observation that hypertension is common in countries where there is a high intake of dietary salt might lead us to investigate the salt consumption

and blood pressure of individual people, and a relationship there might in turn lead to dietary interventions. These leads often turn out to be false, however, and the ecological study alone is never enough.

3.11 Multiple choice questions: Observational studies

(Each branch is either true or false.)

3.1 In statistical terms, a population:
  (a) consists only of people;
  (b) may be finite;
  (c) may be infinite;
  (d) can be any set of things in which we are interested;
  (e) may consist of things which do not actually exist.

3.2 A 1-day census of in-patients in a psychiatric hospital could:
  (a) give good information about the patients in that hospital at that time;
  (b) give reliable estimates of seasonal factors in admissions;
  (c) enable us to draw conclusions about the psychiatric hospitals of Britain;
  (d) enable us to estimate the distribution of different diagnoses in mental illness in the local area;
  (e) tell us how many patients there were in the hospital.

3.3 In simple random sampling:
  (a) each member of the population has an equal chance of being chosen;
  (b) adjacent members of the population must not be chosen;
  (c) likely errors cannot be estimated;
  (d) each possible sample of the given size has an equal chance of being chosen;
  (e) the decision to include a subject in the sample depends only on the subject's own characteristics.

3.4 Advantages of random sampling include:
  (a) it can be applied to any population;
  (b) likely errors can be estimated;
  (c) it is not biased;
  (d) it is easy to do;
  (e) the sample can be referred to a known population.

3.5 In a case–control study to investigate whether eczema in children is related to cigarette smoking by their parents:

(a) parents would be asked about their smoking habits at the child's birth and the child observed for subsequent development of eczema;

(b) children of a group of parents who smoke would be compared with children of a group of parents who are non-smokers;

(c) parents would be asked to stop smoking to see whether their children's eczema was reduced;

(d) the smoking habits of the parents of a group of children with eczema would be compared with the smoking habits of the parents of a group of children without eczema;

(e) parents would be randomly allocated to smoking or non-smoking groups.

3.6 To examine the relationship between alcohol consumption and cancer of the oesophagus, feasible studies include:

(a) questionnaire survey of a random sample from the electoral roll;

(b) comparison of history of alcohol consumption between a group of oesophageal cancer patients and a group of healthy controls, matched for age and sex;

(c) comparison of current oesophageal cancer rates in a group of alcoholics and a group of teetotallers;

(d) comparison by questionnaire of history of alcohol consumption between a group of oesophageal cancer patients and a random sample from the electoral roll in the surrounding district;

(e) comparison of death rates from cancer of the oesophagus in a large sample of subjects whose alcohol consumption has been determined in the past.

3.7 In a study of hospital patients, 20 hospitals were chosen at random from a list of all hospitals. Within each hospital, 10% of patients were chosen at random:

(a) the sample of patients is a random sample;

(b) all hospitals had an equal chance of being chosen;

(c) all hospital patients had an equal chance of being chosen at the outset;

(d) the sample could be used to make inferences about all hospital patients at that time;

(e) all possible samples of patients had an equal chance of being chosen.

3.12 Exercise: *Campylobacter jejuni* infection

Campylobacter jejuni is a bacterium causing gastro-intestinal illness, spread by the faecal–oral route. It infects many species, and human infection has been recorded from handling pet dogs and cats, handling and eating chicken and other meats, and via milk and water supplies. Treatment is by antibiotics.

In May, 1990, there was a fourfold rise in the isolation rate of *C. jejuni* in the Ogwr District, Mid-Glamorgan. The mother of a young boy admitted to hospital with febrile convulsions resulting from *C. jejuni* infection reported that her milk bottles had been attacked by birds during the week before her son's illness, a phenomenon which had been associated with campylobacter infection in another area. This observation, with the rise in *C. jejuni*, prompted a case–control study (Southern *et al.* 1990).

A 'case' was defined as a person with laboratory confirmed *C. jejuni* infection with onset between 1 May and 1 June 1990, resident in an area with Bridgend at its centre. Cases were excluded if they had spent one or more nights away from this area in the week before onset, if they could have acquired the infection elsewhere, or were members of a household in which there had been a case of diarrhoea in the preceding 4 weeks.

The controls were selected from the register of the general practice of the case, or in a few instances from practices serving the same area. Two controls were selected for each case, matched for sex, age (within 5 years), and area of residence.

Cases and controls were interviewed by means of a standard questionnaire at home or by telephone. Cases were asked about their exposure to various factors in the week before the onset of illness. Controls were asked the same questions about the corresponding week for their matched cases. If a control or member of his or her family had had diarrhoea lasting more than 3 days in the week before or during the illness of the respective case, or had spent any nights during that week away from home, another control was found. Evidence of bird attack included the pecking or tearing off of milk bottle tops. A history of bird attack was defined as a previous attack at that house.

Table 3.4 Doorstep delivery of milk bottles and exposure to bird attack (data from Southern *et al.* 1990)

	No. (%) exposed	
	Cases	**Controls**
Doorstep milk delivery	29 (91%)	47 (73%)
Previous milk bottle attack by birds	26 (81%)	25 (39%)
Milk bottle attack in week before illness	26 (81%)	5 (8%)
Protective measures taken	6 (19%)	14 (22%)
Handling attacked milk bottle in week before illness	17 (53%)	5 (8%)
Drinking milk from attacked bottle in week before illness	25 (80%)	5 (8%)

Table 3.5 Frequency of bird attacks on milk bottles (data from Southern *et al.* 1990)

Number of days of week when attacks took place	Cases	Controls
0	3	42
1–3	11	3
4–5	5	1
6–7	10	1

Fifty-five people with campylobacter infection resident in the area were reported during the study period. Of these, 19 were excluded and four could not be interviewed, leaving 32 cases and 64 matched controls. There was no difference in milk consumption between cases and controls, but more cases than controls reported doorstep delivery of bottled milk, previous milk bottle attack by birds, milk bottle attack by birds in the index week, and handling or drinking milk from an attacked bottle (Table 3.4). Cases reported bird attacks more frequently than controls (Table 3.5). Controls were more likely to have protected their milk bottles from attack or to have discarded milk from attacked bottles. Almost all subjects whose milk bottles had been attacked mentioned that magpies and jackdaws were common in their area, though only three had actually witnessed attacks and none reported bird droppings near bottles.

None of the other factors investigated (handling raw chicken; eating chicken bought raw; eating chicken, beef, or ham bought cooked; eating out; attending barbecue; cat or dog in the house; contact with other cats or dogs; and contact with farm animals) were significantly more common in controls than cases. Bottle attacks seemed to have ceased when the study was carried out, and no milk could be obtained for analysis.

3.1 What problems were there in the selection of cases?

3.2 What problems were there in the selection of controls?

3.3 Are there any problems with data collection?

3.4 From the information provided, do you think there is convincing evidence that bird attacks on milk bottles cause campylobacter infection?

3.5 What further studies might be carried out?

4 Summarizing data

4.1 Types of data

In Chapters 2 and 3 we looked at ways in which data are collected. In this chapter we shall see how data can be summarized to help to reveal information they contain. We do this by calculating numbers from the data which extract the important material. These numbers are called **statistics**. A statistic is anything calculated from the data alone.

It is often useful to distinguish between three types of data: qualitative, discrete quantitative, and continuous quantitative. **Qualitative** data arise when individuals may fall into separate classes. These classes may have no numerical relationship with one another at all, e.g. sex: male, female; types of dwelling: house, maisonette, flat, lodgings; eye colour: brown, grey, blue, green, etc. **Quantitative** data are numerical, arising from counts or measurements. If the measurements can have only certain specific values, like the number of people in a household, or number of teeth which have been filled, those data are said to be **discrete**. Discrete variables usually have integer or whole number values. If the values of the measurements can take any number in a range, such as height or weight, the data are said to be **continuous**. In practice there is overlap between these categories. Most continuous data are limited by the accuracy with which measurements can be made. Human height, for example, is difficult to measure more accurately than to the nearest millimetre and is more usually measured to the nearest centimetre. So only a finite set of possible measurements is actually available, although the quantity 'height' can take an infinite number of possible values, and the measured height is really discrete. However, the methods described below for continuous data will be seen to be those appropriate for its analysis.

We shall refer to qualities or quantities such as sex, height, age, etc., as **variables**, because they vary from one member of a sample or population to another. A qualitative variable is also termed a **categorical variable**, **nominal variable**, or an **attribute**. We shall use these terms interchangeably.

4.2 Frequency distributions

When data are purely qualitative, the simplest way to deal with them is to count the number of cases in each category. For example, in the analysis of the census of a psychiatric hospital population (Section 3.2), one of the variables of interest was the patient's principal diagnosis (Bewley *et al.* 1975). To summarize these data, we count the number of patients having each diagnosis. The results are shown in Table 4.1. The count of individuals having a particular quality is called the **frequency** of that quality. For example, the frequency of schizophrenia is 474. The proportion of individuals having the quality is called the

Table 4.1 Principal diagnosis of patients in Tooting Bec Hospital (data from Bewley *et al.* 1975)

Diagnosis	Number of patients
Schizophrenia	474
Affective disorders	277
Organic brain syndrome	405
Subnormality	58
Alcoholism	57
Other and not known	196
Total	1 467

relative frequency or **proportional frequency**. The relative frequency of schizophrenia is 474/1467 = 0.32 or 32%. The set of frequencies of all the possible categories is called the **frequency distribution** of the variable.

In this census we assessed whether patients were 'unlikely to be discharged', 'possibly to be discharged', or 'likely to be discharged'. The frequencies of these categories are shown in Table 4.2. Likelihood of discharge is a qualitative variable, like diagnosis, but the categories are ordered. This enables us to use another set of summary statistics, the cumulative frequencies. The **cumulative frequency** for a value of a variable is the number of individuals with values less than or equal to that value. Thus, if we order likelihood of discharge from 'unlikely', through 'possibly' to 'likely', the cumulative frequencies are 871, 1 210 (= 871 + 339), and 1 467. The **relative cumulative frequency** for a value is the proportion of individuals in the sample with values less

than or equal to that value. For the example they are 0.59 (= 871/1 467), 0.82, and 1.00. Thus we can see that the proportion of patients for whom discharge was not thought likely was 0.82 or 82%.

As we have noted, likelihood of discharge is a qualitative variable, with ordered categories. Sometimes this ordering is taken into account in analysis, sometimes not. Although the categories are ordered these are not quantitative data. There is no sense in which the difference between 'likely' and 'possibly' is the same as the difference between 'possibly' and 'unlikely'.

Table 4.3 shows the frequency distribution of a quantitative variable, parity. This shows the number of previous pregnancies for a sample of women booking for delivery at St George's Hospital. Only certain values are possible, as the number of pregnancies must be an integer, so this variable is discrete. The frequency of each separate value is given.

Table 4.2 Likelihood of discharge of patients in Tooting Bec Hospital (data from Bewley *et al.* 1975)

Discharge:	Frequency	Relative frequency	Cumulative frequency	Relative cumulative frequency
Unlikely	871	0.59	871	0.59
Possible	339	0.23	1 210	0.82
Likely	257	0.18	1 467	1.00
Total	1 467	1.00	1 467	1.00

Table 4.3 Parity of 125 women attending antenatal clinics at St George's Hospital (data supplied by Rebecca McNair, personal communication)

Parity	Frequency	Relative frequency (per cent)	Cumulative frequency	Relative cumulative frequency (per cent)
0	59	47.2	59	47.2
1	44	35.2	103	82.4
2	14	11.2	117	93.6
3	3	2.4	120	96.0
4	4	3.2	124	99.2
5	1	0.8	125	100.0
Total	125	100.0	125	100.0

Table 4.4 FEV1 (litres) of 57 male medical students (data from Physiology practical class, St George's Hospital Medical School)

2.85	3.19	3.50	3.69	3.90	4.14	4.32	4.50	4.80	5.20
2.85	3.20	3.54	3.70	3.96	4.16	4.44	4.56	4.80	5.30
2.98	3.30	3.54	3.70	4.05	4.20	4.47	4.68	4.90	5.43
3.04	3.39	3.57	3.75	4.08	4.20	4.47	4.70	5.00	
3.10	3.42	3.60	3.78	4.10	4.30	4.47	4.71	5.10	
3.10	3.48	3.60	3.83	4.14	4.30	4.50	4.78	5.10	

Table 4.4 shows a continuous variable, forced expiratory volume in one second (FEV1) in a sample of male medical students. As most of the values occur only once, to get a useful frequency distribution we need to divide the FEV1 scale into class intervals, e.g. from 3.0 to 3.5, from 3.5 to 4.0, and so on, and count the number of individuals with FEV1s in each class interval. The class intervals should not overlap, so we must decide which interval contains the boundary point to avoid it being counted twice. It is usual to put the lower boundary of an interval into that interval and the higher boundary into the next interval. Thus the interval starting at 3.0 and ending at 3.5 contains 3.0 but not 3.5. We can write this as '3.0 − ' or '3.0 − 3.5⁻' or '3.0 − 3.499'. Including the lower boundary in the class interval has this advantage: most distributions of measurements have a zero point below which we cannot go, whereas few have an exact upper limit. If we were to include the upper boundary in the interval instead of the lower, we would have two possible ways of dealing with zero. It could be left as an isolated point, not in an interval. Alternatively, it could be included in the lowest interval, which would then not be exactly comparable with the others as it would include both boundaries while all the other intervals only included the upper.

If we take a starting point of 2.5 and an interval of 0.5, we get the frequency distribution shown in Table 4.5. Note that this is not unique. If we take a starting point of 2.4 and an interval of 0.2, we get a different set of frequencies.

The frequency distribution can be calculated easily and accurately using a computer. Manual calculation is not so easy and must be done carefully and systematically.

Table 4.5 Frequency distribution of FEV1 in 57 male medical students (data from Physiology practical class, St George's Hospital Medical School)

FEV1	Frequency	Relative frequency (per cent)
2.0 −	0	0.0
2.5 −	3	5.3
3.0 −	9	15.8
3.5 −	14	24.6
4.0 −	15	26.3
4.5 −	10	17.5
5.0 −	6	10.5
5.5 −	0	0.0
Total	57	100.0

One way recommended by many older texts (e.g. Hill 1977) is to set up a tally system, as in Table 4.6. We go through the data and for each individual make a tally mark by the appropriate interval. We then count up the number in each interval. In practice this is very difficult to do accurately, and it needs to be checked and double-checked. Hill (1977) recommends writing each number on a card and dealing the cards into piles corresponding to the intervals. It is then easy to check that each pile contains only those cases in that interval and count them. This is undoubtedly superior to the tally system. Another method is to order the observations from lowest to highest before marking the interval

Table 4.6 Tally system for finding the frequency distribution of FEV1 (data from Physiology practical class, St George's Hospital Medical School)

FEV1		Frequency
2.0 –		0
2.5 –	///	3
3.0 –	///// ////	9
3.5 –	///// ///// ////	14
4.0 –	///// ///// /////	15
4.5 –	///// /////	10
5.0 –	///// /	6
5.5 –		0
Total		57

boundaries and counting, or to use the stem and leaf plot described below. Personally, I always use a computer.

4.3 Histograms and other frequency graphs

Graphical methods are very useful for examining frequency distributions. Figure 4.1 shows a graph of the cumulative frequency distribution for the FEV1 data. This is

called a **step function**, because the frequency increases in abrupt steps. We can smooth this by joining successive points where the cumulative frequency changes by straight lines, to give a **cumulative frequency polygon**. Figure 4.2 shows this for the cumulative relative frequency distribution of FEV1.

The most common way of depicting a frequency distribution is by a **histogram**. This is a diagram where the class intervals are on an axis and rectangles with heights or areas proportional to the frequencies erected on them. Figure 4.3 shows the histogram for the FEV1 distribution in Table 4.5. The vertical scale shows frequency, the number of observations in each interval.

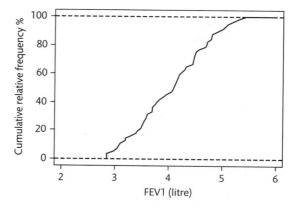

Figure 4.2 Cumulative frequency polygon of FEV1 (data from Physiology practical class, St George's Hospital Medical School).

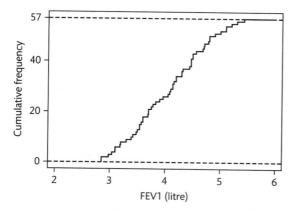

Figure 4.1 Cumulative frequency distribution of FEV1 in a sample of male medical students (data from Physiology practical class, St George's Hospital Medical School).

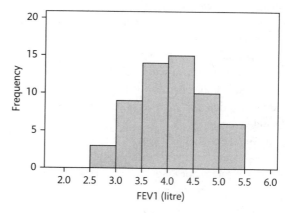

Figure 4.3 Histogram of FEV1: frequency scale (data from Physiology practical class, St George's Hospital Medical School).

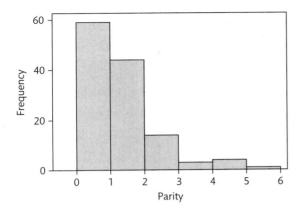

Figure 4.4 Histogram of parity (Table 4.3) using integer cut-off points for the intervals (data supplied by Rebecca McNair, personal communication).

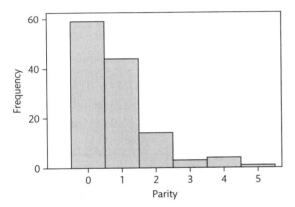

Figure 4.5 Histogram of parity (Table 4.3) using fractional cut-off points for the intervals (data supplied by Rebecca McNair, personal communication).

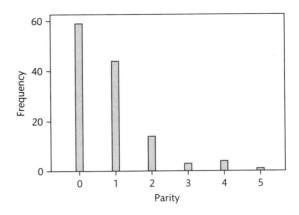

Figure 4.6 Histogram of parity (Table 4.3) using fractional cut-off points and narrow intervals (data supplied by Rebecca McNair, personal communication).

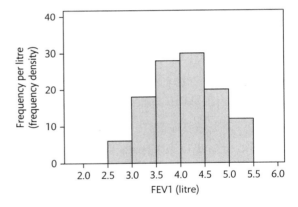

Figure 4.7 Histogram of FEV1: frequency per unit FEV1 or frequency density scale (data from Physiology practical class, St George's Hospital Medical School).

Sometimes we want to show the distribution of a discrete variable (e.g. Table 4.3) as a histogram. If our intervals are $0 - 1^-$, $1 - 2^-$, etc., the actual observations will all be at one end of the interval (Figure 4.4). Making the starting point of the interval a fraction rather than an integer gives a slightly better picture (Figure 4.5). This can also be helpful for continuous data when there is a lot of digit preference (Section 20.1). For example, where most observations are recorded as integers or as something point five, starting the interval at something .75 can give a more accurate picture. We can also emphasize the discrete nature of the variable by using a narrow interval (Figure 4.6). We could even use simple vertical lines.

Figure 4.7 shows a histogram for the same distribution as Figure 4.3, with frequency per unit FEV1 (or frequency density) shown on the vertical axis. The distributions appear identical and we may well wonder whether it matters which method we choose. We see that it does matter when we consider a frequency distribution with unequal intervals, as in Table 4.7. If we plot the histogram using the heights of the rectangles to represent relative frequency in the interval we get the histogram in Figure 4.8, whereas if we use the relative frequency per year we get the histogram in Figure 4.9. These histograms tell different stories. Figure 4.8 suggests that the most common age for accident victims is between 15 and 44 years,

Table 4.7 Distribution of age in people suffering accidents in the home (data from Whittington 1977)

Age group	Relative frequency (per cent)	Relative frequency per year (per cent)
0–4	25.3	5.06
5–14	18.9	1.89
15–44	30.3	1.01
45–64	13.6	0.68
65+	11.7	0.33

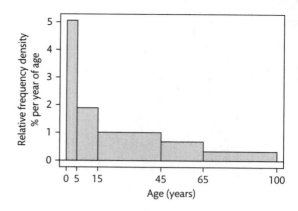

Figure 4.9 Histogram of age distribution of home accident victims using the relative frequency density scale (data from Whittington 1977).

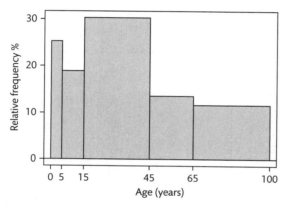

Figure 4.8 Histograms of age distribution of home accident victims using the relative frequency scale (data from Whittington 1977).

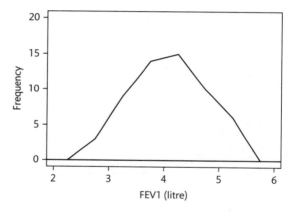

Figure 4.10 Frequency polygon of FEV1 in medical students (data from Physiology practical class, St George's Hospital Medical School).

whereas Figure 4.9 suggests it is between 0 and 4. Figure 4.9 is correct, Figure 4.8 being distorted by the unequal class intervals. It is therefore preferable in general to use the frequency per unit (frequency density) rather than per class interval when plotting a histogram with unequal class intervals. The frequency for a particular interval is then represented by the area of the rectangle on that interval. Only when the class intervals are all equal can the frequency for the class interval be represented by the height of the rectangle. The computer programmer finds equal intervals much easier, however, and histograms with unequal intervals are now uncommon. I have used equal intervals and the frequency scale in most of this book.

Rather than a histogram consisting of vertical rectangles, we can plot a **frequency polygon** instead. To do

this we join the centre points of the tops of the rectangles, then omit the rectangles (Figure 4.10). Where a cell of the histogram is empty, we join the line to the centre of the cell at the horizontal axis (Figure 4.11, males). This can be useful if we want to show two or more frequency distributions on the same graph, as in Figure 4.11. When we do this, the comparison is easier if we use relative frequency or relative frequency density rather than frequency. This makes it easier to compare distributions with different numbers of subjects.

A different version of the histogram has been developed by Tukey (1977), the **stem and leaf plot** (Figure 4.12). The rectangles are replaced by the numbers themselves. The 'stem' is the first digit or digits of

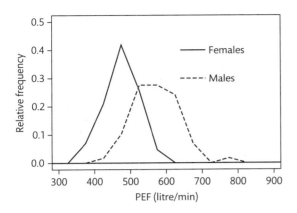

Figure 4.11 Frequency polygons of PEF in medical students (data from Physiology practical class, St George's Hospital Medical School).

```
2 | 8 8 9
3 | 0 1 1 1 2 3 3 4 4 5 5 5 5 6 6 6 7 7 7 7 8 9 9
4 | 0 0 1 1 1 1 2 2 3 3 3 4 4 4 4 5 5 5 6 7 7 7 8 8 9
5 | 0 1 1 2 3 4
```

Figure 4.12 Stem and leaf plot for the FEV1 data, rounded down to one decimal place (data from Physiology practical class, St George's Hospital Medical School).

the number and the 'leaf' the trailing digit. The first row of Figure 4.12 represents the numbers 2.8, 2.8, and 2.9, which in the data are 2.85, 2.85, and 2.98. The plot provides a good summary of data structure while at the same time we can see other characteristics such as a tendency to prefer some trailing digits to others, called digit preference (Section 20.1). It is also easy to construct and much less prone to error than the tally method of finding a frequency distribution.

4.4 Shapes of frequency distribution

Figure 4.3 shows a frequency distribution of a shape often seen in medical data. The distribution is roughly symmetrical about its central value and has frequency concentrated about one central point. The most frequent value is called the **mode** of the distribution and the interval with the greatest frequency is called the **modal**

interval or **modal class**. Figure 4.3 has one such point. It is **unimodal**. Figure 4.13 shows a very different shape. Here there are two distinct modes, one near 100 mm Hg and the other near 170 mm Hg. There is pronounced dip in the region between 120 and 160 mm Hg, where we might expect the systolic pressures of many members of the general population to be found. This distribution is **bimodal**. We must be careful to distinguish between the unevenness in the histogram which results from using a small sample to represent a large population and that resulting from genuine bimodality in the data. The trough between 120 and 160 in Figure 4.13 is very marked and might represent a genuine bimodality. In this case we

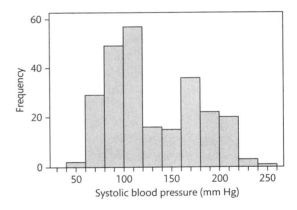

Figure 4.13 Systolic blood pressure in a sample of patients in an intensive therapy unit (data from Friedland *et al.* 1996).

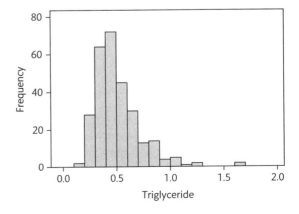

Figure 4.14 Serum triglyceride in cord blood from 282 babies (Table 4.8) (data supplied by Tessi Hanid, personal communication).

Table 4.8 Serum triglyceride measurements in cord blood from 282 babies (data supplied by Tessi Hanid, personal communication)

0.15	0.29	0.32	0.36	0.40	0.42	0.46	0.50	0.56	0.60	0.70	0.86
0.16	0.29	0.33	0.36	0.40	0.42	0.46	0.50	0.56	0.60	0.72	0.87
0.20	0.29	0.33	0.36	0.40	0.42	0.47	0.52	0.56	0.60	0.72	0.88
0.20	0.29	0.33	0.36	0.40	0.44	0.47	0.52	0.56	0.61	0.74	0.88
0.20	0.29	0.33	0.36	0.40	0.44	0.47	0.52	0.56	0.62	0.75	0.95
0.20	0.29	0.33	0.36	0.40	0.44	0.47	0.52	0.56	0.62	0.75	0.96
0.21	0.30	0.33	0.36	0.40	0.44	0.47	0.52	0.56	0.63	0.76	0.96
0.22	0.30	0.33	0.36	0.40	0.44	0.48	0.52	0.56	0.64	0.76	0.99
0.24	0.30	0.33	0.37	0.40	0.44	0.48	0.52	0.56	0.64	0.78	1.01
0.25	0.30	0.34	0.37	0.40	0.44	0.48	0.53	0.57	0.64	0.78	1.02
0.26	0.30	0.34	0.37	0.40	0.44	0.48	0.54	0.57	0.64	0.78	1.02
0.26	0.30	0.34	0.37	0.40	0.44	0.48	0.54	0.58	0.64	0.78	1.04
0.26	0.30	0.34	0.38	0.40	0.45	0.48	0.54	0.58	0.65	0.78	1.08
0.27	0.30	0.34	0.38	0.40	0.45	0.48	0.54	0.58	0.66	0.78	1.11
0.27	0.30	0.34	0.38	0.41	0.45	0.48	0.54	0.58	0.66	0.80	1.20
0.27	0.31	0.34	0.38	0.41	0.45	0.48	0.54	0.59	0.66	0.80	1.28
0.28	0.31	0.34	0.38	0.41	0.45	0.48	0.55	0.59	0.66	0.82	1.64
0.28	0.32	0.35	0.39	0.41	0.45	0.48	0.55	0.59	0.66	0.82	1.66
0.28	0.32	0.35	0.39	0.41	0.46	0.48	0.55	0.59	0.67	0.82	
0.28	0.32	0.35	0.39	0.41	0.46	0.49	0.55	0.60	0.67	0.82	
0.28	0.32	0.35	0.39	0.41	0.46	0.49	0.55	0.60	0.68	0.83	
0.28	0.32	0.35	0.39	0.42	0.46	0.49	0.55	0.60	0.70	0.84	
0.28	0.32	0.35	0.40	0.42	0.46	0.50	0.55	0.60	0.70	0.84	
0.28	0.32	0.36	0.40	0.42	0.46	0.50	0.55	0.60	0.70	0.84	

have people in intensive care, who are very sick. Some have a condition which results in dangerously high pressure, others a condition which results in dangerously low pressure. We actually have multiple populations represented with some overlap between them. However, almost all distributions encountered in medical statistics are unimodal.

Figure 4.14 differs from Figure 4.3 in a different way (Table 4.8). The distribution of serum triglyceride is **skewed**, that is, the distance from the central value to the extreme is much greater on one side than it is on the other. The parts of the histogram near the extremes are called the **tails** of the distribution. If the tails are similar in length the distribution is **symmetrical**, as in

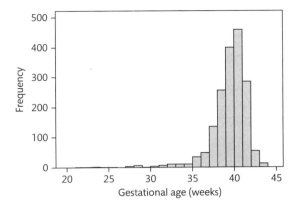

Figure 4.15 Gestational age at birth for 1 749 deliveries at St George's Hospital (data supplied by Rebecca McNair, personal communication).

Figure 4.3. If the tail on the right is longer than the tail on the left as in Figure 4.14, the distribution is **skewed to the right** or **positively skewed**. If the tail on the left is longer, the distribution is **skewed to the left** or **negatively skewed**. This is unusual, but Figure 4.15 shows an example. The negative skewness comes about because babies can be born alive at any gestational age from about 20 weeks, but soon after 40 weeks the baby will have to be born. Pregnancies will not be allowed to go on for more than 44 weeks; the birth would be induced artificially. Most distributions encountered in medical work are symmetrical or skewed to the right, for reasons we shall discuss later (Section 7.4).

4.5 Medians and quantiles

We often want to summarize a frequency distribution in a few numbers, for ease of reporting or comparison. The most direct method is to use quantiles. The **quantiles** are values which divide the distribution such that there is a given proportion of observations below the quantile. For example, the median is a quantile. The **median** is the central value of the distribution, such that half the observations are less than or equal to it and half are greater than or equal to it. We can estimate any quantiles easily from the cumulative frequency distribution or a stem and leaf plot. For the FEV1 data the median is 4.1, the 29th value in Table 4.4. If we have an even number

of points, we choose a value midway between the two central values.

In general, we estimate the q quantile, the value such that a proportion q will be below it, as follows. We have n ordered observations which divide the scale into $n + 1$ parts: below the lowest observation, above the highest, and between each adjacent pair. The proportion of the distribution which lies below the ith observation is estimated by $i/(n + 1)$. We set this equal to q and get $i = q(n + 1)$. If i is an integer, the ith observation is the required quantile estimate. If not, let j be the integer part of i, the part before the decimal point. The quantile will lie between the jth and $j + 1$th observations. We estimate it by

$$x_j + (x_{j+1} - x_j) \times (i - j)$$

For the median, for example, the 0.5 quantile, $i = q(n + 1)$ = 0.5 × (57 + 1) = 29, the 29th observation as before.

Other quantiles which are particularly useful are the **quartiles** of the distribution. The quartiles divide the distribution into four equal parts, called **fourths** or **quarters**. The second quartile is the median. For the FEV1 data the first and third quartiles are 3.54 and 4.53. For the first quartile, $i = 0.25 \times 58 = 14.5$. The quartile is between the 14th and 15th observations, which are both 3.54. For the third quartile, $i = 0.75 \times 58 = 43.5$, so the quartile lies between the 43rd and 44th observations, which are 4.50 and 4.56. The quantile is given by 4.50 + (4.56 – 4.50) × (43.5 – 43) = 4.53. We often divide the distribution at 99 **centiles** or **percentiles**. The median is thus the 50th centile. For the 20th centile of FEV1, $i = 0.2 \times 58 = 11.6$, so the quantile is between the 11th and 12th observations, 3.42 and 3.48, and can be estimated by 3.42 + (3.48 – 3.42) × (11.6 – 11) = 3.46. We can estimate these easily from Figure 4.2 by finding the position of the quantile on the vertical axis, e.g. 0.2 for the 20th centile or 0.5 for the median, drawing a horizontal line to intersect the cumulative frequency polygon, and reading the quantile off the horizontal axis. The term 'quartile' is often used incorrectly to mean the fourth or quarter of the observations which fall between two quartiles. The related words 'quintile' and 'tertile' often suffer in the same way.

Tukey (1977) used the median, quartiles, maximum and minimum as a convenient five figure summary of a distribution. He also suggested a neat graph, the **box and whisker plot**, which represents this (Figure 4.16). The box shows the distance between the quartiles, with the median marked as a line, and the 'whiskers' show the extremes. The different shapes of the FEV1 and serum triglyceride distributions are clear from the graph. For display purposes, an observation whose distance from the edge of the box (i.e. the quartile) is more than 1.5 times the length of the box (i.e. the interquartile range, Section 4.7) may be called an **outlier**. Outliers may be shown as separate points, as for the serum triglyceride measurements in Figure 4.16. The plot can be useful for showing the comparison of several groups (Figure 4.17).

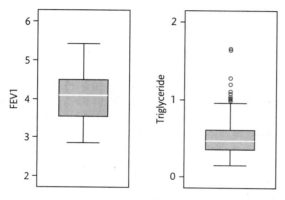

Figure 4.16 Box and whisker plots for FEV1 and for serum triglyceride (data from Physiology practical class, St George's Hospital Medical School/Tessi Hanid).

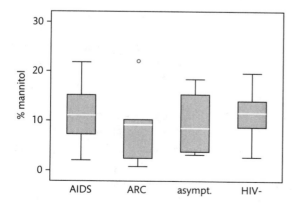

Figure 4.17 Box plots showing a roughly symmetrical variable in four groups, with an outlying point (data in Table 10.7) (data supplied by Moses Kapembwa, personal communication).

4.6 The mean

The median is not the only measure of central value for a distribution. Another is the **arithmetic mean** or **average**, usually referred to simply as the **mean**. This is found by taking the sum of the observations and dividing by their number. For example, consider the following hypothetical data:

$$2 \quad 3 \quad 9 \quad 5 \quad 4 \quad 0 \quad 6 \quad 3 \quad 4$$

The sum is 36 and there are nine observations, so the mean is 36/9 = 4.0. At this point we need to introduce some algebraic notation, widely used in statistics. We denote the observations by

$$x_1, x_2, \ldots, x_i, \ldots, x_n$$

There are n observations and the ith of these is x_i. For the example, $x_4 = 5$ and $n = 9$. The sum of all the x_i is

$$\sum_{i=1}^{n} x_i$$

The summation sign is an upper case Greek letter, sigma, the Greek S. When it is obvious that we are adding the values of x_i for all values of i, which runs from 1 to n, we may abbreviate this to $\sum x_i$ or simply to $\sum x$. The mean of the x_i is denoted by $\bar{x}$ ('x bar'), and

$$\bar{x} = \frac{1}{n} \sum x_i = \frac{\sum x_i}{n}$$

The sum of the 57 FEV1s is 231.51 and hence the mean is 231.51/57 = 4.06. This is very close to the median, 4.1, so the median is within 1% of the mean. This is not so for the triglyceride data. The median triglyceride (Table 4.8) is 0.46 but the mean is 0.51, which is higher. The median is 10% away from the mean. If the distribution is symmetrical, the sample mean and median will be about the same, but in a skewed distribution they will usually not. If the distribution is skewed to the right, as for serum triglyceride, the mean will usually be greater, if it is skewed to the left the median will usually be greater. This is because the values in the tails affect the mean but not the median.

The sample mean has much nicer mathematical properties than the median and is thus more useful for the comparison methods described later. The median is a very useful descriptive statistic, but not much used for other purposes.

4.7 Variance, range, and interquartile range

The mean and median are measures of the position of the middle of the distribution, which we call the **central tendency**. We also need a measure of the spread or variability of the distribution, called the **dispersion**.

One obvious measure is the **range**, the difference between the highest and lowest values. For the data of Table 4.4, the range is 5.43 – 2.85 = 2.58 litres. The range is often presented as the two extremes, 2.85–5.43 litres, rather than their difference. The range is a useful descriptive measure, but has two disadvantages. Firstly, it depends only on the extreme values and so can vary a lot from sample to sample. Secondly, it depends on the sample size. The larger the sample is, the further apart the extremes are likely to be. We can see this if we consider a sample of size 2. If we add a third member to the sample, the range will only remain the same if the new observation falls between the other two, otherwise the range will increase. We can get round the second of these problems by using the **interquartile range**, the difference between the first and third quartiles. For the data of Table 4.4, the interquartile range is 4.53 – 3.54 = 0.99 litres. The interquartile range, too, is often presented as the two extremes, 3.54–4.53 litres. However, the interquartile range is quite variable from sample to sample and is also mathematically intractable. Although a useful descriptive measure, it is not the one preferred for purposes of comparison.

The most frequently used measures of dispersion are the variance and standard deviation. We start by calculating the difference between each observation and the sample mean, called the **deviations from the mean** (Table 4.9). If the data are widely scattered, many of the observations x_i will be far from the mean $\bar{x}$ and so many deviations $x_i - \bar{x}$ will be large. If the data are narrowly scattered, very few observations will be far from the mean and so few deviations $x_i - \bar{x}$ will be large. We need some kind of average deviation to measure the scatter. If we add all the deviations together, we get zero, because $\sum(x_i - \bar{x}) = \sum x_i - \sum \bar{x} = \sum x_i - n\bar{x}$ and $n\bar{x} = \sum x_i$. Instead we square the deviations and then add them, as shown in Table 4.9. This removes the effect of sign;

Table 4.9 Deviations from the mean of nine observations

Observations x_i	Deviations from the mean $x_i - \bar{x}$	Squared deviations $(x_i - \bar{x})^2$
2	–2	4
3	–1	1
9	5	25
5	1	1
4	0	0
0	–4	16
6	2	4
3	–1	1
4	0	0
36	0	52

we are only measuring the size of the deviation, not the direction. This gives us $\sum(x_i - \bar{x})^2$, in the example equal to 52, called the **sum of squares about the mean**, usually abbreviated to **sum of squares**.

Clearly, the sum of squares will depend on the number of observations as well as the scatter. We want to find some kind of average squared deviation. This leads to a difficulty. Although we want an average squared deviation, we divide the sum of squares by $n-1$, not n. This is not the obvious thing to do and puzzles many students of statistical methods. The reason is that we are interested in estimating the scatter of the population, rather than the sample, and the sum of squares about the sample mean is proportional to $n - 1$ (Appendix 4A, Appendix 6B). Dividing by n would lead to small samples producing lower estimates of variability than large samples. The minimum number of observations from which the variability can be estimated is two, a single observation cannot tell us how variable the data are. If we used n as our divisor, for $n = 1$ the sum of squares would be zero, giving a variance of zero. With the correct divisor of $n - 1$, $n = 1$ gives the meaningless ratio 0/0, reflecting the impossibility of estimating variability from a single observation. The estimate of variability is called the **variance**, defined by

$$\text{variance} = \frac{1}{n-1}\sum(x_i - \bar{x})^2$$

We have already said that $\sum(x_i - \bar{x})^2$ is called the sum of squares. The quantity $n - 1$ is called the **degrees of freedom** of the variance estimate (Appendix 7A). We have:

$$\text{variance} = \frac{\text{sum of squares}}{\text{degrees of freedom}}$$

We shall usually denote the variance by s^2. In the example, the sum of squares is 52 and there are nine observations, giving 8 degrees of freedom. Hence $s^2 = 52/8 = 6.5$.

The formula $\sum(x_i - \bar{x})^2$ gives us a rather tedious calculation. There is another formula for the sum of squares, which makes the calculation easier to carry out. This is simply an algebraic manipulation of the first form and gives exactly the same answers. We thus have two formulae for variance:

$$s^2 = \frac{1}{n-1}\sum\left(x_i - \bar{x}^2\right)$$

$$s^2 = \frac{1}{n-1}\left(\sum x_i^2 - \frac{(\sum x_i)^2}{n}\right)$$

The algebra is quite simple and is given in Appendix 4B. For example, using the second formula for the nine observations, we have:

$$\sum x_i^2 = 2^2 + 3^2 + 9^2 + 5^2 + 4^2 + 0^2 + 6^2 + 3^2 + 4^2$$
$$= 4 + 9 + 81 + 25 + 16 + 0 + 36 + 9 + 16$$
$$= 196$$

$$\sum x_i = 36$$

$$s^2 = \frac{1}{n-1}\left(\sum x_i^2 - \frac{(\sum x_i)^2}{n}\right)$$

$$= \frac{1}{9-1}\left(196 - \frac{36^2}{9}\right)$$

$$= \frac{1}{8}(196 - 144)$$

$$= 52/8$$

$$= 6.5$$

as before. On a calculator this is a much easier formula than the first, as the numbers need only be put in once.

It can be inaccurate, because we may subtract one large number from another to get a small one. For this reason the first formula would be used in a computer program.

4.8 Standard deviation

The variance is calculated from the squares of the observations. This means that it is not in the same units as the observations, which limits its use as a descriptive statistic. The obvious answer to this is to take the square root, which will then have the same units as the observations and the mean. The square root of the variance is called the **standard deviation**, usually denoted by s. Thus,

$$s = \sqrt{\frac{1}{n-1}\sum(x_i - \bar{x})^2}$$

$$= \sqrt{\frac{1}{n-1}\left(\sum x_i^2 - \frac{(\sum x_i)^2}{n}\right)}$$

Returning to the FEV data, we calculate the variance and standard deviation as follows. We have $n = 57$, $\sum x_i = 231.51$, $\sum x_i^2 = 965.45$.

$$\text{Sum of squares} = \sum x_i^2 - \frac{(\sum x_i)^2}{n}$$

$$= 965.45 - \frac{231.51^2}{57}$$

$$= 965.45 - 940.296$$

$$= 25.154$$

$$s^2 = \frac{\text{sum of squares}}{n-1}$$

$$= \frac{25.154}{57-1}$$

$$= 0.449$$

The standard deviation is $s = \sqrt{s^2} = \sqrt{0.449} = 0.67$ litres.

Figures 4.18 and 4.19 show the relationship between mean, standard deviation, and frequency distribution. For FEV1, we see that the majority of observations are within one standard deviation of the mean, and nearly all within two standard deviations of the mean (Figure 4.18). There is a small part of the histogram outside the $\bar{x} - 2s$ to $\bar{x} + 2s$ interval, on either side of this symmetrical histogram. Figure 4.19 shows the same thing for the highly skewed triglyceride data. In this case, however, the outlying observations are all in one tail of the distribution. In general, we expect roughly two-thirds of observations to

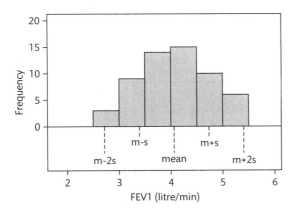

Figure 4.18 Histogram of FEV1 with mean and standard deviation (data from Physiology practical class, St George's Hospital Medical School).

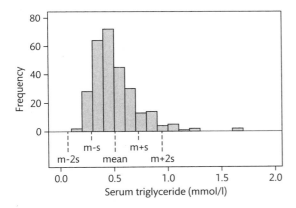

Figure 4.19 Histogram of triglyceride with mean and standard deviation (data supplied by Tessi Hanid, personal communication).

lie within one standard deviation of the mean and 95% to lie within two standard deviations of the mean, but where the outlying observations are will depend on symmetry or skewness.

4.9 Multiple choice questions: Summarizing data

(Each branch is either true or false.)

4.1 Which of the following are qualitative variables:
(a) sex;
(b) parity;
(c) diastolic blood pressure;
(d) diagnosis;
(e) height.

4.2 Which of the following are continuous variables:
(a) blood glucose;
(b) peak expiratory flow rate;
(c) age last birthday;
(d) exact age;
(e) family size.

4.3 When a distribution is skewed to the right:
(a) the median is greater than the mean;
(b) the distribution is unimodal;
(c) the tail on the left is shorter than the tail on the right;
(d) the standard deviation is less than the variance;
(e) the majority of observations are less than the mean.

4.4 The shape of a frequency distribution can be described using:
(a) a box and whisker plot;
(b) a histogram;
(c) a stem and leaf plot;
(d) mean and variance;
(e) a table of frequencies.

4.5 For the sample 3, 1, 7, 2, 2:
(a) the mean is 3;
(b) the median is 7;
(c) the mode is 2;
(d) the range is 1;
(e) the standard deviation is 6.0.

4.6 Diastolic blood pressure has a distribution which is slightly skewed to the right. If the mean and standard deviation were calculated for the diastolic pressures of a random sample of men:
(a) there would be fewer observations below the mean than above it;
(b) the standard deviation would be approximately equal to the mean;
(c) the majority of observations would be more than one standard deviation from the mean;
(d) the standard deviation would estimate the accuracy of blood pressure measurement;
(e) about 95% of observations would be expected to be within two standard deviations of the mean.

4.10 Exercise: Student measurements and a graph of study numbers

There are two sets of data in this exercise. The first, observations made during a student anatomy practical, provide practice in reading histograms and standard deviations. The second, from a publication on the numbers of participants in studies, presents a challenging graphical interpretation.

Figure 4.20 shows the distribution of the mid upper arm circumferences of 120 female biomedical sciences, medical, nursing, physiotherapy, and radiography students.

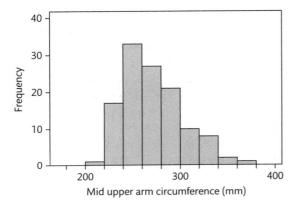

Figure 4.20 Distribution of the mid upper arm circumferences of 120 female students (data from Anatomy practical class, St George's Hospital Medical School).

4.1 What kind of variable is arm circumference?

4.2 What kind of graph is Figure 4.20?

4.3 On the graph, where are the mode, the lower tail, and the upper tail of this distribution?

4.4 From the graph, how would you describe the shape of the distribution of arm circumference and why?

4.5 From the graph, approximately what would you estimate the median and the first and third quartiles to be? Where would they appear along the horizontal axis?

4.6 From the graph, approximately what would you estimate the mean and the standard deviation to be? Where would they appear along the horizontal axis?

Table 4.10 shows eye colour, as recorded by another student, for male and female students.

Table 4.10 Recorded eye colour by sex for 183 students

Eye colour	Sex		
	Female	Male	Total
Black	6	4	10
Brown	47	32	79
Blue	27	16	43
Grey	10	1	11
Hazel	9	5	14
Green	16	4	20
Other	4	1	5
Missing	1	0	1
Total	120	63	183

4.7 What kind of variable is eye colour? What kind of variable is sex?

My friend and colleague Doug Altman sent me this interesting graph. Shiraishi *et al.* (2009) analysed studies of diagnostic tests reported in the journal *Radiology* between 1997 and 2006. They looked at all the studies of diagnostic methods which used a numerical variable with a particular cut-off value to decide the diagnosis. Such studies are analysed and presented using a ROC curve, or Receiver Operating Characteristic curve (Section 20.6). Shiraishi *et al.* looked at the total number of people, both with and without the condition under investigation, who were included in each of these studies. They gave a graph similar to Figure 4.21 for the distribution of the number of participants included.

4.8 How would you describe the shape of this distribution?

4.9 What feature of the intervals makes it difficult to draw a histogram for these data?

4.10 If we were to present this distribution as a histogram, what would the horizontal scale show?

4.11 If we were to present this distribution as a histogram, what would the vertical scale show?

4.12 Think about how this might appear as a valid histogram. How would you describe the shape of this distribution?

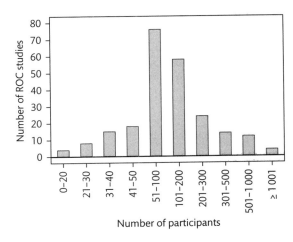

Figure 4.21 Numbers of participants for each study in a sample of 233 diagnostic studies (reproduced from Shiraishi J *et al.* Experimental design and data analysis in receiver operating characteristic studies: lessons learned from reports in *Radiology* from 1997 to 2006. *Radiology* 2009 253:(3) 822–830, with permission from the Radiological Society of North America).

Appendix 4A: The divisor for the variance

The variance is found by dividing the sum of squares about the sample mean by $n - 1$, not by n. This is because we want the scatter about the population mean, and the scatter about the sample mean is always less. The sample mean is 'closer' to the data points than is the population mean. We shall try a little sampling experiment to show this. Table 4.11 shows a set of 100 random digits which we shall take as the population to be sampled. They have mean 4.74 and the sum of squares about

the mean is 811.24. Hence the average squared difference from the mean is 8.1124. We can take samples of size two at random from this population using a pair of decimal dice, which will enable us to choose any digit numbered from 00 to 99. The first pair chosen was 5 and 6 which has mean 5.5. The sum of squares about the population mean 4.74 is $(5 - 4.74)^2 + (6 - 4.74)^2 = 1.655$. The sum of squares about the sample mean is $(5 - 5.5)^2 + (6 - 5.5)^2 = 0.5$.

The sum of squares about the population mean is greater than the sum of squares about the sample mean, and this will always be so. Table 4.12 shows this for 20 such samples of size two. The average sum of squares about the population mean is 13.6, and about the sample mean it is 5.7. Hence dividing by the sample size ($n = 2$), we have mean square differences of 6.8 about the population mean and 2.9 about the sample mean. Compare this with 8.1 for the population as a whole. We see that the sum of squares about the population mean is quite close to 8.1, while the sum of squares about the sample mean is much less. However, if we divide the sum of squares about the sample mean by $n - 1$, i.e. 1, instead of n we have 5.7, which is not much different from the 6.8 from the sum of squares about the population mean.

Table 4.13 shows the results of a similar experiment with more samples being taken. The table shows the two average variance estimates using n and $n - 1$ as the divisor of the sum of squares, for sample sizes 2, 3, 4, 5, and 10. We see that the sum of squares about the sample mean divided by n increases steadily with sample size, but if we divide it by $n - 1$ instead of n, the estimate does not change as the sample size increases. The sum of squares about the sample mean is proportional to $n - 1$.

Table 4.11 Population of 100 random digits for a sampling experiment

9	1	0	7	5	6	9	5	8	8	1	0	5	7	6	5	0	2	2	2
1	8	8	8	5	2	4	8	3	1	6	5	5	7	4	1	7	3	3	3
2	8	1	8	5	8	4	0	1	9	2	1	6	9	4	4	7	6	1	7
1	9	7	9	7	2	7	7	0	8	1	6	3	8	0	5	7	4	8	6
7	0	2	8	8	7	2	5	4	1	8	6	8	3	5	8	2	7	2	4

Table 4.12 Sampling pairs from Table 4.11

Sample		$\sum(x_i - \mu)^2$	$\sum(x_i - \bar{x})^2$	Sample		$\sum(x_i - \mu)^2$	$\sum(x_i - \bar{x})^2$
5	6	1.655	0.5	8	3	13.655	12.5
8	8	21.255	0.0	5	7	5.175	2.0
6	1	15.575	12.5	5	2	5.575	4.5
9	3	21.175	18.0	5	7	5.175	2.0
5	5	0.135	0.0	8	8	21.255	0.0
7	7	10.215	0.0	3	2	10.535	0.5
1	7	19.095	18.0	0	4	23.015	8.0
9	8	28.775	0.5	9	3	21.175	18.0
3	3	6.055	0.0	5	2	7.575	4.5
5	1	14.055	8.0	6	9	19.735	4.5
Mean						13.6432	5.7

Table 4.13 Mean sums of squares about the sample mean for sets of 100 random samples from Table 4.12

Number in sample, n	Mean variance estimates	
	$\frac{1}{n}\sum(x_i - \bar{x})^2$	$\frac{1}{n-1}\sum(x_i - \bar{x})^2$
2	4.5	9.1
3	5.4	8.1
4	5.9	7.9
5	6.2	7.7
10	7.2	8.0

Appendix 4B: Formulae for the sum of squares

The different formulae for sums of squares are derived as follows:

$$\text{sum of squares} = \sum(x_i - \bar{x})^2$$
$$= \sum(x_i^2 - 2x_i\bar{x} + \bar{x}^2)$$
$$= \sum x_i^2 - \sum 2x_i\bar{x} + \sum \bar{x}^2$$
$$= \sum x_i^2 - 2\bar{x}\sum x_i + n\bar{x}^2$$

because $\bar{x}$ has the same value for each of the n observations. Now, $\sum x_i = n\bar{x}$, so

$$\text{sum of squares} = \sum x_i^2 - 2\bar{x}n\bar{x} + n\bar{x}^2$$
$$= \sum x_i^2 - 2n\bar{x}^2 + n\bar{x}^2$$
$$= \sum x_i^2 - n\bar{x}^2$$

and putting $\bar{x} = \frac{1}{n}\sum x_i$

$$\text{sum of squares} = \sum x_i^2 - n\left(\frac{1}{n}\sum x_i\right)^2$$
$$= \sum x_i^2 - \frac{(\sum x_i)^2}{n}$$

We thus have three formulae for variance:

$$s^2 = \frac{1}{n-1}\sum(x_i - x)^2$$
$$= \frac{1}{n-1}\left(\sum x_i^2 - n\bar{x}^2\right)$$
$$= \frac{1}{n-1}\left(\sum x_i^2 - \frac{(\sum x_i)^2}{n}\right)$$

5 Presenting data

5.1 Rates and proportions

Having collected our data as described in Chapters 2 and 3 and extracted information from it using the methods of Chapter 4, we must find a way to convey this information to others. In this chapter we shall look at some of the methods of doing that. We begin with rates and proportions.

When we have data in the form of frequencies, we often need to compare the frequency with certain conditions in groups containing different totals. In Table 2.1, for example, two groups of patient pairs were compared, 29 where the later patient had a C-T scan and 89 where neither had a C-T scan. The later patient did better in 9 of the first group and 34 of the second group. To compare these frequencies we compare the proportions 9/29 and 34/89. These are 0.31 and 0.38, and we can conclude that there appears to be little difference. In Table 2.1, these were given as percentages, that is, the proportion out of 100 rather than out of 1, to avoid the decimal point. In Table 2.8, the Salk vaccine trial, the proportions contracting polio were presented as the number per 100 000 for the same reason.

A **rate** expresses the frequency of the characteristic of interest per 1 000 (or per 100 000, etc.) of the population, per unit of time. For example, in Table 3.1, the results of the study of smoking by doctors, the data were presented as the number of deaths per 1 000 doctors per year. This is not a proportion, as a further adjustment has been made to allow for the time period observed. Furthermore, the rate has been adjusted to take account of any differences in the age distributions of smokers and non-smokers (Section 21.2). Sometimes the actual denominator for a rate may be continually changing. The number of deaths from lung cancer among men in England and Wales for 1983 was 26 502. The denominator for the death rate, the number of males in England and

Wales, changed throughout 1983, as some died, some were born, some left the country, and some entered it. The death rate is calculated using a representative number, the estimated population at the end of June 1983, the middle of the year. This was 24 175 900, giving a death rate of 26 502/24 175 900, which equals 0.001 096, or 109.6 deaths per 100 000 at risk per year. A number of the rates used in medical statistics are described in Section 21.5.

The use of rates and proportions enables us to compare frequencies obtained from unequal sized groups, base populations, or time periods, but we must beware of their use when their bases or denominators are not given. Victora (1982) reported a drug advertisement sent to doctors which described the antibiotic phosphomycin as being '100% effective in chronic urinary infections'. This is very impressive. How could we fail to prescribe a drug which is 100% effective? The study on which this was based used eight patients, after excluding 'those whose urine contained phosphomycin-resistant bacteria'. If the advertisement has said the drug was effective in 100% of eight cases, we would have been less impressed. Had we known that it worked in 100% of eight cases selected because it might work in them, we would have been still less impressed. The same paper quotes an advertisement for a cold remedy, where 100% of patients showed improvement. This was out of five patients! As Victora remarked, such small samples are understandable in the study of very rare diseases, but not for the common cold.

Sometimes we can fool ourselves as well as others by omitting denominators. I once carried out a study of the distribution of the soft tissue tumour Kaposi's sarcoma in Tanzania (Bland *et al.* 1977), and while writing it up I came across a paper setting out to do the same thing (Schmid 1973). One of the factors studied was tribal group, of which there are over 100 in

Tanzania. This paper reported 'the tribal incidence in the Wabende, Wambwe and Washirazi is remarkable ... These small tribes, each with fewer than 90 000 people, constitute the group in which a tribal factor can be suspected'. This is based on the following rates of tumours per 10 000 population: national, 0.1; Wabende, 1.3; Wambwe, 0.7; Washirazi, 1.3. These are very big rates compared with the national, but the populations on which they are based are small, 8 000, 14 000, and 15 000, respectively (Egero and Henin 1973). To get a rate of 1.3/10 000 out of 8 000 Wabende people, we must have 8 000 × 1.3/10 000 = 1 case! Similarly we have 1 case among the 14 000 Wambwe and 2 among the 15 000 Washirazi. We can see that there are not enough data to draw the conclusions which the author has done. Rates and proportions are powerful tools but we must beware of them becoming detached from the original data.

5.2 Significant figures

When we calculated the death rate because of lung cancer among men in 1983, we quoted the answer as 0.001 096 or 109.6 per 100 000 per year. This is an approximation. The rate to the greatest number of figures my calculator will give is 0.001 096 215 653 and this number would probably go on indefinitely, turning into a recurring series of digits. The decimal system of representing numbers cannot in, general, represent fractions exactly. We know that 1/2 = 0.5, but 1/3 = 0.333 333 33 . . . , recurring infinitely. This does not usually worry us, because for most applications the difference between 0.333 and 1/3 is too small to matter. Only the first few non-zero digits of the number are important and we call these the **significant digits** or **significant figures**. There is usually little point in quoting statistical data to more than three significant figures. After all, it hardly matters whether the lung cancer mortality rate is 0.001 096 or 0.001 097. The value 0.001 096 is given to four significant figures. The leading zeros are not significant, the first significant digit in this number being '1'. To three significant figures we get 0.001 10, because the last digit is 6 and so the 9 which precedes it is rounded

up to 10. Note that significant figures are not the same as decimal places. The number 0.00110 is given to five decimal places, the number of digits after the decimal point. When rounding to the nearest digit, we leave the last significant digit, 9 in this case, if what follows it is less than 5, and increase by 1 if what follows is greater than 5. When we have exactly 5, I would always round up, i.e. 1.5 goes to 2. This means that 0, 1, 2, 3, 4 go down, and 5, 6, 7, 8, 9 go up, which seems unbiased. Some writers take the view that 5 should go up half the time and down half the time, as it is exactly midway between the preceding digit and that digit plus 1. Various methods are suggested for doing this but I do not recommend them myself. In any case, it is usually a mistake to round to so few significant figures that this matters.

How many significant figures we need depends on the use to which the number is to be put and on how accurate it is anyway. For example, if we have a sample of 10 sublingual temperatures measured to the nearest half degree, there is little point in quoting the mean to more than three significant figures. What we should *not* do is to round numbers to a few significant figures before we have completed our calculations. In the lung cancer mortality rate example, suppose we round the numerator and denominator to two significant figures. We have 27 000/24 000 000 = 0.001 125 and the answer is only correct to two figures. This can spread through calculations causing errors to build up. We always try to retain several more significant figures than we require for the final answer.

Consider Table 5.1. This shows mortality data in terms of the exact numbers of deaths in 1 year. The table is taken from a much larger table, which shows the numbers dying from every cause of death in the International Classification of Diseases (ICD), which gives numerical codes to many hundreds of causes of death. Table 5.1 shows deaths for broad groups of diseases called ICD chapters. This table is not a good way to present these data if we want to get an understanding of the frequency distribution of cause of death, and the differences between causes in men and women. This is even more true of the 70-page original. This is not the purpose of the table, of course. It is a source of data, a reference document from which users extract information for their own

Table 5.1 Deaths by sex and cause, England and Wales, 2012 (data from the Office for National Statistics)

ICD code and type of disease		Number of deaths	
		Males	**Females**
A00-B99	Infectious and parasitic	2 271	2 838
C00-D48	Neoplasms (cancers)	76 695	68 700
D50-D89	Blood and blood forming organs	422	521
E00-E90	Endocrine, nutritional, and metabolic diseases	3 132	3 578
F00-F99	Mental disorders	11 710	24 155
G00-G99	Diseases of the nervous system	9 499	11 674
H00-H59	Diseases of the eye and adnexa	11	9
H60-H95	Diseases of the ear and mastoid process	14	7
I00-I99	Diseases of the circulatory system	69 516	71 846
J00-J99	Diseases of the respiratory system	33 463	37 245
K00-K93	Diseases of the digestive system	11 766	12 807
L00-L99	Diseases of the skin and subcutaneous tissue	564	1 111
M00-M99	Diseases of the musculoskeletal system and connective tissue	1 397	2 933
N00-N99	Diseases of the genitourinary system	4 080	5 682
O00-O99	Pregnancy, childbirth, and the puerperium		46
P00-P96	Certain conditions originating in the perinatal period	114	91
Q00-Q99	Congenital malformations, deformations, and chromosomal abnormalities	595	554
R00-R99	Symptoms, signs, and abnormal clinical and laboratory findings, not elsewhere classified	2 800	7 923
U509, V01-Y89	External causes of morbidity and mortality (injury, etc.)	10 993	6 469
Total		240 238	259 093

purposes. Let us see how Table 5.1 can be simplified. First, we can reduce the number of significant figures. Let us be extreme and reduce the data to one significant figure (Table 5.2). This makes comparisons rather easier, but it is still not obvious which are the most important causes of death. We can improve this by re-ordering the table to put the most frequent cause, diseases of the circulatory system, first (Table 5.3). I have increased the number of significant figures for this and put the counts in thousands. We can also combine a lot of the smaller categories into an 'others' group. I did this arbitrarily, by combining all those accounting for less than 3% of the total. Now it is clear at a glance that the most important causes of death in England and Wales are neoplasms, diseases of the circulatory system, and diseases of the respiratory system, and that these dwarf all the others. Of course, mortality is not the only indicator of the importance of a disease. ICD codes M00-M99, diseases of the musculoskeletal system and connective tissues, are easily seen from Table 5.2 to be only minor causes of death,

Table 5.2 Deaths by sex and cause, England and Wales, 2012, rounded to one significant figure (data from the Office for National Statistics)

ICD code and type of disease		Number of deaths	
		Males	**Females**
A00–B99	Infectious and parasitic	2 000	3 000
C00–D48	Neoplasms (cancers)	80 000	70 000
D50–D89	Blood and blood forming organs	400	500
E00–E90	Endocrine, nutritional, and metabolic diseases	3 000	4 000
F00–F99	Mental disorders	12 000	20 000
G00–G99	Diseases of the nervous system	9 000	12 000
H00–H59	Diseases of the eye and adnexa	10	9
H60–H95	Diseases of the ear and mastoid process	10	7
I00–I99	Diseases of the circulatory system	70 000	70 000
J00–J99	Diseases of the respiratory system	30 000	40 000
K00–K93	Diseases of the digestive system	10 000	10 000
L00–L99	Diseases of the skin and subcutaneous tissue	600	1 000
M00–M99	Diseases of the musculoskeletal system and connective tissue	1 000	3 000
N00–N99	Diseases of the genitourinary system	4 000	6 000
O00–O99	Pregnancy, childbirth, and the puerperium		50
P0 P00–P96	Certain conditions originating in the perinatal period	100	90
Q00–Q99	Congenital malformations, deformations, and chromosomal abnormalities	600	600
R00–R99	Symptoms, signs, and abnormal clinical and laboratory findings, not elsewhere classified	3 000	8 000
U509, V01–Y89	External causes of morbidity and mortality (injury, etc.)	10 000	6 000
Total		200 000	300 000

but this group includes arthritis and rheumatism, most important illnesses in their effects on daily activity.

5.3 Presenting tables

Tables 5.1 to 5.3 illustrate a number of useful points about the presentation of tables. Like all the tables in this book, they are designed to stand alone from the text. There is no need to refer to material buried in some

paragraph to interpret the table. A table is intended to communicate information, so it should be easy to read and understand. A table should have a clear title, stating clearly and unambiguously what the table represents. The rows and columns must also be labelled clearly.

When proportions, rates, or percentages are used in a table together with frequencies, they must be easy to distinguish from one another. This can be done, as in Table 2.10, by adding a '%' symbol, or by including a place

Table 5.3 Deaths by sex, England and Wales, 2012, for major causes (data from the Office for National Statistics)

Type of disease	Number of deaths	
	Males	**Females**
Neoplasms (cancers)	77 000	69 000
Circulatory system	70 000	72 000
Respiratory system	33 000	37 000
Mental disorders	12 000	24 000
Digestive system	12 000	13 000
Nervous system	9 000	12 000
External causes	11 000	6 000
Others	15 000	25 000
Total	240 000	259 000

of decimals. The addition in Table 2.10 of the 'total' row and the '100%' makes it clear that the percentages are calculated from the number in the treatment group, rather than the number with that particular outcome or the total number of patients.

5.4 Pie charts

It is often convenient to present data pictorially. Information can be conveyed much more quickly by a diagram than by a table of numbers. This is particularly useful when data are being presented to an audience, as here the information must be put across in a limited time. It can also help a reader get the salient points of a table of numbers. Unfortunately, unless great care is taken, diagrams can also be very misleading and should be treated only as an addition to numbers, not a replacement.

We have already discussed methods of illustrating the frequency distribution of a quantitative variable. We will now look at an equivalent of the histogram for qualitative data, the **pie chart** or **pie diagram**. This shows the relative frequency for each category by dividing a circle into sectors, the angles of which are proportional to the relative frequency. We thus multiply each relative frequency by 360, to give the corresponding angle in degrees.

Table 5.4 shows the calculation for drawing a pie chart to represent the distribution of cause of death for females, using the data from Tables 5.1 and 5.3. (The total degrees are 358 rather than 360 because of rounding errors in the calculation of degrees.) The resulting pie chart is shown in Figure 5.1. This diagram is said to resemble a pie cut into pieces for serving, hence the name.

5.5 Bar charts

A **bar chart** or **bar diagram** shows data in the form of horizontal or vertical bars. For example, Table 5.5 shows

Table 5.4 Calculations for a pie chart of the distribution of cause of death, 2012, men (data from the Office for National Statistics)

Cause of death	Frequency	Relative frequency	Angle (degrees)
Neoplasms (cancers)	76 695	0.319 25	115
Circulatory system	69 516	0.289 36	104
Respiratory system	33 463	0.139 29	50
Mental disorders	11 710	0.048 74	18
Digestive system	11 766	0.048 98	18
Nervous system	9 499	0.039 54	14
External causes	10 993	0.045 76	16
Others	15 400	0.064 10	23
Total	294 227	1.000 00	358

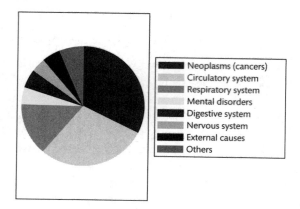

Figure 5.1 Pie chart showing the distribution of cause of death among males, England and Wales, 2012 (data from the Office for National Statistics).

Table 5.5 Deaths from cancer: standardized mortality rate per 1 000 000 per year, males, England and Wales, 2000–2012 (data from the Office for National Statistics)

Year	Mortality rate	Year	Mortality rate
2000	8 477	2007	6 996
2001	8 230	2008	6 906
2002	8 134	2009	6 628
2003	8 039	2010	6 467
2004	7 617	2011	6 236
2005	7 412	2012	6 191
2006	7 167		

the mortality caused by all cancers among men in England and Wales over a 13-year period. Figure 5.2 shows these data in the form of a bar chart, the heights of the bars being proportional to the mortality.

There are many uses for bar charts. As in Figure 5.2, they can be used to show the relationship between two variables, one being quantitative and the other either qualitative or a quantitative variable which is grouped, as is time in years. The values of the first variable are shown by the heights of bars, one bar for each category of the second variable.

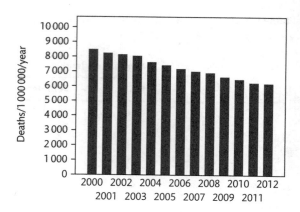

Figure 5.2 Bar chart showing the relationship between mortality caused by cancer and year, males, England and Wales, 2000–2012 (data from the Office for National Statistics).

Bar charts can be used to represent relationships between more than two variables. Figure 5.3 shows the relationship between children's reports of breathlessness and cigarette smoking by themselves and their parents. We can see quickly that the prevalence of the symptom increases both with the child's smoking and with that of their parents. In the published paper reporting these respiratory symptom data (Bland *et al.* 1978), the bar chart was not used; the data were given in the form of tables. It was thus available for other researchers to compare

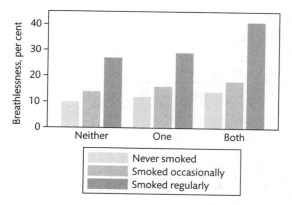

Figure 5.3 Bar chart showing the relationship between the prevalence of self-reported breathlessness among schoolchildren and two possible causative factors (data from Bland *et al.* 1978).

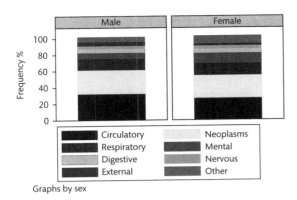

Figure 5.4 Stacked bar chart showing data for main causes of death from Table 5.1 (data from the Office for National Statistics).

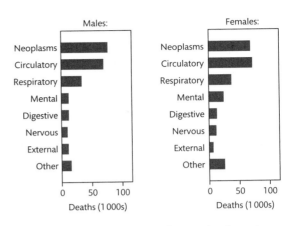

Figure 5.6 Horizontal bar charts showing data for main causes of death from Table 5.1 (data from the Office for National Statistics).

to their own or to carry out calculations on. The bar chart was used to present the results during a conference, where the most important thing was to convey an outline of the analysis quickly.

Bar charts can also be used to show frequencies. For example, Figure 5.4 shows the relative frequency distributions of the main causes of death among men and women. This is a **stacked bar chart**, so called because the bars have sub-bars stacked one above the other. Figure 5.5 shows the frequency distribution of cause of death among men and women as two separate bar charts, one above the other. There are many variations on the bar chart theme. The important thing is that the information should be conveyed quickly, clearly, and without ambiguity.

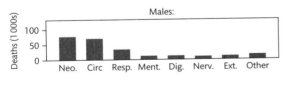

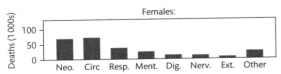

Figure 5.5 Paired bar charts showing data for main causes of death from Table 5.1 (data from the Office for National Statistics).

The bar charts in Figure 5.5 look very like histograms. The distinction between these two terms is not clear. Most statisticians would describe Figures 4.3, 4.4, and 4.6 as histograms, and Figures 5.2 and 5.3 as bar charts, but I have seen books which actually reverse this terminology and others which reserve the term 'histogram' for a frequency density graph, like Figures 4.7 and 4.9.

Sometimes it is useful to rotate bar charts like Figure 5.5, so that the bars are horizontal. Figure 5.6 shows an example. This enables us to extend the labels for the bars so that they can be read more easily. We shall see the same thing for forest plots in Chapter 17.

5.6 Scatter diagrams

The bar chart would be a rather clumsy method for showing the relationship between two continuous variables, such as vital capacity and height (Table 5.6). For this we use a **scatter diagram** or **scattergram** (Figure 5.7). This is made by marking the scales of the two variables along horizontal and vertical axes. Each pair of measurements is plotted with a cross, circle, or some other suitable symbol at the point indicated by using the measurements as coordinates.

Table 5.7 shows serum albumin measured from a group of alcoholic patients and a group of controls (Hickish *et al.* 1989). We can use a scatter diagram to

Table 5.6 Vital capacity (VC) and height for 44 female medical students (data from Physiology practical class, St George's Hospital Medical School)

Height (cm)	VC (litres)	Height (cm)	VC (litres)	Height (cm)	VC (litres)	Height (cm)	VC (litres)
155.0	2.20	161.2	3.39	166.0	3.66	170.0	3.88
155.0	2.65	162.0	2.88	166.0	3.69	171.0	3.38
155.4	3.06	162.0	2.96	166.6	3.06	171.0	3.75
158.0	2.40	162.0	3.12	167.0	3.48	171.5	2.99
160.0	2.30	163.0	2.72	167.0	3.72	172.0	2.83
160.2	2.63	163.0	2.82	167.0	3.80	172.0	4.47
161.0	2.56	163.0	3.40	167.6	3.06	174.0	4.02
161.0	2.60	164.0	2.90	167.8	3.70	174.2	4.27
161.0	2.80	165.0	3.07	168.0	2.78	176.0	3.77
161.0	2.90	166.0	3.03	168.0	3.63	177.0	3.81
161.0	3.40	166.0	3.50	169.4	2.80	180.6	4.74

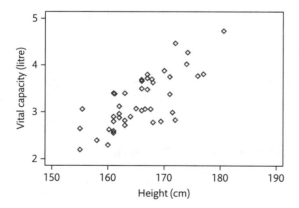

Figure 5.7 Scatter diagram showing the relationship between vital capacity and height for a group of female medical students (data from Anatomy practical class, St George's Hospital Medical School).

present these data also. The vertical axis represents albumin and we choose two arbitrary points on the horizontal axis to represent the groups.

In Table 5.7 there are many identical observations in each group, so we need to allow for this in the scatter diagram. If there is more than one observation at the

same coordinates, we can indicate this in several ways. We can use the number of observations in place of the chosen symbol, but this method is becoming obsolete. As in Figure 5.8, we can displace the points slightly in a random direction (called **jittering**). This is what Stata does and so what I have done in most of this book. Alternatively, we can use a systematic sideways shift, to

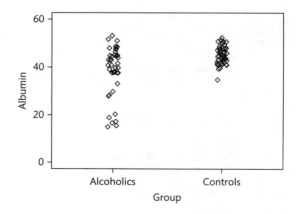

Figure 5.8 Scatter diagram showing the data of Table 5.7, with random jitter (data from Hickish *et al.* 1989).

Table 5.7 Albumin measured in alcoholics and controls (data from Hickish *et al.* 1989)

Alcoholics						Controls						
15	28	39	41	44	48	34	41	43	45	45	47	50
16	29	39	43	45	48	39	42	43	45	45	47	50
17	32	39	43	45	49	39	42	43	45	45	48	50
18	37	40	44	46	51	40	42	43	45	46	48	50
20	38	40	44	46	51	41	42	44	45	46	48	54
21	38	40	44	46	52	41	42	44	45	47	49	
28	38	41	44	47		41	42	44	45	47	49	

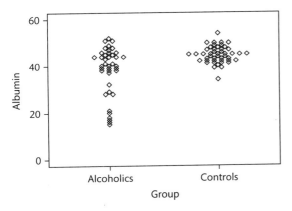

Figure 5.9 Scatter diagram showing the data of Table 5.7, with horizontal shift (data from Hickish *et al.* 1989).

form a more orderly picture as in Figure 5.9. The latter is often used when the variable on the horizontal axis is categorical rather than continuous. Such scatter diagrams are very useful for checking the assumptions of some of the analytical methods which we shall use later. A scatter diagram where one variable is a group is also called a **dot plot**. As a presentational device, they enable us to show far more information than a bar chart of the group means can do. For this reason, statisticians usually prefer them to other types of graphical display.

5.7 Line graphs and time series

The data of Table 5.5 are ordered in a way that those of Table 5.6 are not, in that they are recorded at intervals in time. Such data are called a **time series**. If we plot a scatter diagram of such data, as in Figure 5.10, it is natural to join successive points by lines to form a line graph. We do not even need to mark the points at all; all we need is the line. This would not be sensible in Figure 5.7, as the observations are independent of one another and quite unrelated, whereas in Figure 5.10 there is likely to be a relationship between adjacent points. Here the mortality rate recorded for cancer will depend on a number of things which vary over time, including possibly causal factors, such as tobacco and alcohol consumption, and clinical factors, such as better diagnostic techniques and methods of treatment.

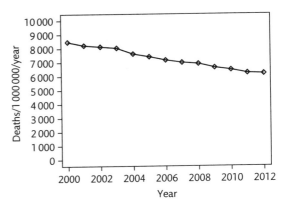

Figure 5.10 Line graph showing changes in cancer mortality over time (data from the Office for National Statistics).

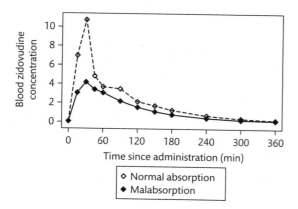

Figure 5.11 Line graph to show the response to administration of zidovudine in two groups of AIDS patients (data from Kapembwa *et al.* 1996).

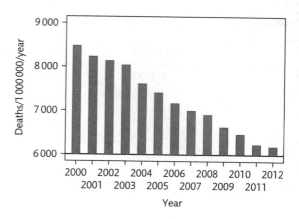

Figure 5.12 Bar chart with zero omitted on the vertical scale.

Line graphs are particularly useful when we want to show the change of more than one quantity over time. Figure 5.11 shows levels of zidovudine (AZT) in the blood of AIDS patients at several times after administration of the drug, for patients with normal fat absorption and with fat malabsorption (Section 10.7). The difference in response between the two conditions is very clear.

5.8 Misleading graphs

Figure 5.2 is clearly titled and labelled and can be read independently of the surrounding text. The principles of clarity outlined for tables apply equally here. After all, a diagram is a method of conveying information quickly and this object is defeated if the reader or audience has to spend time trying to sort out exactly what a diagram really means. Because the visual impact of diagrams can be so great, further problems arise in their use.

The first of these is the missing zero. Figure 5.12 shows a second bar chart representing the data of Table 5.5. This chart appears to show a very rapid decrease in mortality, compared to the gradual decrease shown in Figure 5.2. Yet both show the same data. Figure 5.12 omits most of the vertical scale, and instead stretches that small part of the scale where the change takes place. Even when we are aware of this, it is difficult to look at this graph and not think that it shows a large decrease in mortality. It helps

if we visualize the baseline as being somewhere near the middle of the page.

There is no zero on the horizontal axis in Figures 5.2 and 5.12, either. There are two reasons for this. There is no practical 'zero time' on the calendar; we use an arbitrary zero. Also, there is an unstated assumption that mortality rates vary with time and not the other way round.

The zero is omitted in Figure 5.7. This is almost always done in scatter diagrams, yet if we are to gauge the importance of the relationship between vital capacity and height by the relative change in vital capacity over the height range, we need the zero on the vital capacity scale. The origin is often omitted on scatter diagrams because we are usually concerned with the existence of a relationship and the distributions followed by the observations, rather than its magnitude. We estimate the latter in a different way, described in Chapter 11.

Line graphs are particularly at risk of undergoing the distortion of a missing zero. Many computer programs resist drawing bar charts like Figure 5.12, but will produce a line graph with a truncated scale as the default. Figure 5.13 shows a line graph with a truncated scale, corresponding to Figure 5.12. Just as there, the message of the graph is a dramatic decrease in mortality, which the data themselves do not really support. We can make this even more dramatic by stretching the vertical scale and compressing the horizontal scale as in Figure 5.14. The effect is now really impressive and looks much more

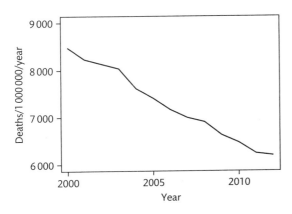

Figure 5.13 Line graph with a missing zero.

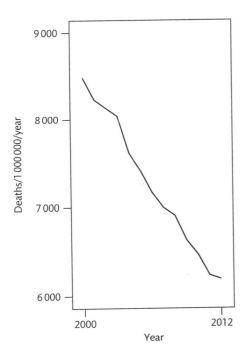

Figure 5.14 Line graph with a missing zero and with a stretched vertical and compressed horizontal scale, a 'gee whiz' graph.

likely than Figure 5.10 to attract research funds, Nobel prizes, and interviews on television. Huff (1954) aptly named such horrors 'gee whiz' graphs. They are even more dramatic if we omit the scales altogether and show only the plunging or soaring line.

This is not to say that authors who show only part of the scale are deliberately trying to mislead. There are often good arguments against graphs with vast areas of boring blank paper. In Figure 5.7, we are not interested in vital capacities near zero and can feel quite justified in excluding them. In Figures 5.13 and 5.14, we certainly are interested in zero mortality; it is surely what we are aiming for. The point is that graphs can so easily mislead the unwary reader, so let the reader beware.

The advent of powerful personal computers led to an increase in the ability to produce complicated graphics. Simple charts, such as Figure 5.1, are informative but not visually exciting. One way of decorating such graphs is to make them appear three-dimensional. Figure 5.15 shows the effect. The angles are no longer proportional to the numbers which they represent. The areas are, but because they are different shapes it is difficult to compare them. This defeats the primary object of conveying information quickly and accurately. Another approach to decorating diagrams is to turn them into pictures. In a **pictogram** the bars of the bar chart are replaced by pictures. Pictograms can be highly misleading, as the height of a picture, drawn with three-dimensional effect, is proportional to the number represented, but what we see is the volume. Such decorated graphs are like the illuminated capitals of medieval manuscripts: nice to look at but hard to read. I think they should be avoided.

Huff (1954) recounts that the president of a chapter of the American Statistical Association criticised him for accusing presenters of data of trying to deceive. The statistician argued that incompetence was the problem.

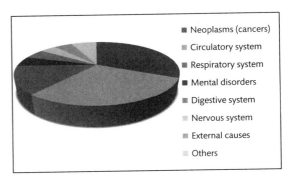

Figure 5.15 Figure 5.1 with three-dimensional effects (data from the Office for National Statistics).

Huff's reply was that diagrams frequently sensationalize by exaggeration and rarely minimize anything, that presenters of data rarely distort those data to make their case appear weaker than it is. The errors are too one-sided for us to ignore the possibility that we are being fooled. When presenting data, especially graphically, be very careful that the data are shown fairly. When on the receiving end, beware!

5.9 Using different colours

Colour can be useful in graphs. Graphs like Figure 5.1 and 5.15 are often shown using different colours for the segments of the pie, graphs like Figure 5.3 and 5.4 with different colours for the categories, and graphs like Figure 5.11 with different colours for the lines. Care is needed if this is not to become misleading for some readers. About one in 12 men, and a small number of women, cannot easily distinguish between red and green, because they have the most frequent type of colour-blindness. We should always avoid using red and green together without some other distinguishing feature, such as solid and broken lines. There are other kinds of colour blindness, too, so the best guide is never to rely on colour alone to distinguish elements in a graph. Always draw graphs which use colour so that they could be read clearly if reproduced in black and white.

5.10 Logarithmic scales

Figure 5.16 shows a line graph representing the fall in tuberculosis mortality in England and Wales over 100 years (DHSS 1976). We can see a rather unsteady curve, showing the continuing decline in the disease. Figure 5.17 shows the mortality plotted on a logarithmic (or log) scale. A **logarithmic scale** is one where two pairs of points will be the same distance apart if their ratios are equal, rather than their differences. Thus the distance between 1 and 10 is equal to that between 10 and 100, not to that between 10 and 19. (See Appendix 5A if you do not understand this.) The logarithmic line shows a clear kink in the curve about 1950, when a number of effective anti-TB measures, chemotherapy

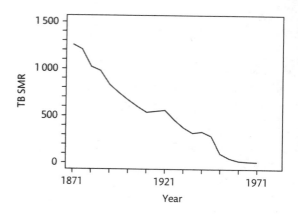

Figure 5.16 Tuberculosis mortality in England and Wales, 1871 to 1971 (data from DHSS 1976).

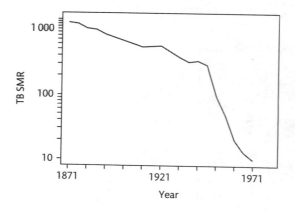

Figure 5.17 Tuberculosis mortality in England and Wales, 1871 to 1971, log scale (data from DHSS 1976).

with streptomycin, BCG vaccine, and mass screening with X-rays, were introduced. If we consider the properties of logarithms (Appendix 5A), we can see how the log scale for the tuberculosis mortality data produced such sharp changes in the curve. If the relationship is such that the mortality is falling with a constant proportion, such as 10% per year, the absolute fall each year depends on the absolute level in the preceding year:

mortality in 1960 = constant × mortality in 1959

So if we plot mortality on a log scale we get:

log(mortality in 1960) = log(constant)
+ log(mortality in 1959)

For mortality in 1961, we have

$$\log(\text{mortality in 1961}) = \log(\text{constant})$$
$$+ \log(\text{mortality in 1960})$$
$$= \log(\text{constant})$$
$$+ \log(\text{constant})$$
$$+ \log(\text{mortality in 1959})$$
$$= 2 \times \log(\text{constant})$$
$$+ \log(\text{mortality in 1959})$$

Hence we get a straight line relationship between log mortality and time t:

$$\log(\text{mortality at } t \text{ years}) = t \times \log(\text{constant})$$
$$+ \log(\text{mortality at start})$$

When the constant proportion changes, the slope of the straight line formed by plotting log(mortality) against time changes and there is a very obvious kink in the line.

Log scales are very useful analytic tools. However, a graph on a log scale can be very misleading if the reader does not allow for the nature of the scale. The log scale in Figure 5.17 shows the increased rate of reduction in mortality associated with the anti-TB measures quite plainly, but it gives the impression that these measures were important in the decline of TB. This is not so. If we look at the corresponding point on the natural scale, we can see that all these measures did was to accelerate a decline which had been going on for a long time (see Radical Statistics Health Group 1976).

Another use of logarithmic scales is to plot several variables on the same graph, even though their ranges are quite different. Figure 5.18 shows the mortality rates from all cancers, from carcinoma of the bronchus and lung, and from malignant melanoma, on a linear scale. Figure 5.19 shows the same mortality rates on a logarithmic scale. It is easier to compare the patterns over time on the logarithmic scale than on the linear. We can see that the melanoma mortality rate rose while the rates for all cancers and for lung fell.

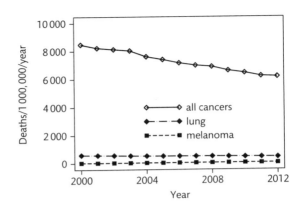

Figure 5.18 Mortality rate from all cancers, lung, and melanoma, males, England and Wales, 2000–2012, on a linear scale (data from the Office for National Statistics).

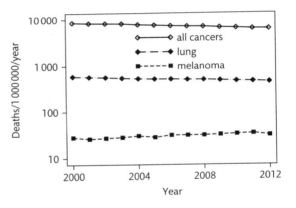

Figure 5.19 Mortality rate from all cancers, lung, and melanoma, males, England and Wales, 2000–2012, on a logarithmic scale (data from the Office for National Statistics).

5.11 Multiple choice questions: Data presentation

(Each branch is either true or false.)

5.1 'After treatment with Wondermycin, 66.67% of patients made a complete recovery'
  (a) Wondermycin is wonderful;
  (b) This statement may be misleading because the denominator is not given;
  (c) The number of significant figures used suggest a degree of precision which may not be present;

(d) Some control information is required before we can draw any conclusions about Wondermycin;

(e) There might be only a very small number of patients.

5.2 The number 1 729.543 71:

(a) to two significant figures is 1 700;

(b) to three significant figures is 1 720;

(c) to six decimal places is 1 729.54;

(d) to three decimal places is 1 729.544;

(e) to five significant figures is 1 729.5.

5.3 Figure 5.20:

(a) shows a histogram;

(b) should have the vertical axis labelled;

(c) should show the zero on the vertical axis;

(d) should show the zero on the horizontal axis;

(e) should show the units for the vertical axis.

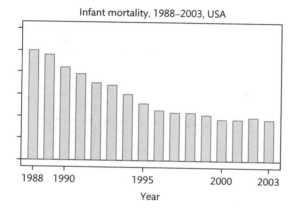

Infant mortality, 1988–2003, USA

1988   1990   1995   2000   2003
Year

Figure 5.20 A dubious graph.

5.4 Logarithmic scales used in graphs showing time trends:

(a) show changes in the trend clearly;

(b) often produce straight lines;

(c) give a clear idea of the magnitude of changes;

(d) should show the zero point from the original scale;

(e) compress intervals between large numbers compared with those between small numbers.

5.5 The following methods can be used to show the relationship between two variables:

(a) histogram;

(b) pie chart;

(c) scatter diagram;

(d) bar chart;

(e) line graph.

5.12 Exercise: Creating presentation graphs

In this exercise we shall think about how to display graphically some of the data we have studied so far.

5.1 Table 4.1 shows diagnoses of patients in a hospital census. How would you display these data as a graph?

5.2 Table 2.8 shows the paralytic polio rates for several groups of children. What would a bar chart look like for the results from the randomized control areas?

5.3 Table 3.1 shows some results from the study of mortality in British doctors. How might we show these graphically?

Appendix 5A: Logarithms

Logarithms are not simply a method of calculation dating from before the computer age, but a set of fundamental mathematical functions. Because of their special properties they are much used in statistics. We shall start with logarithms (or logs for short) to base 10, the common logarithms used in calculations. The log to base 10 of a number x is y where

$$x = 10^y$$

We write $y = \log_{10}(x)$. Thus for example $\log_{10}(10) = 1$, $\log_{10}(100) = 2$, $\log_{10}(1\,000) = 3$, $\log_{10}(10\,000) = 4$, and so on. If we multiply two numbers, the log of the product is the sum of their logs:

$$\log(xy) = \log(x) + \log(y)$$

For example,

$$100 \times 1\,000 = 10^2 \times 10^3 = 10^{2+3} = 10^5 = 100\,000$$

Or in log terms:

$$\log_{10}(100 \times 1\,000) = \log_{10}(100) + \log_{10}(1\,000)$$
$$= 2 + 3 = 5$$

Hence, $100 \times 1\,000 = 10^5 = 100\,000$. This means that any multiplicative relationship of the form

$$y = a \times b \times c \times d$$

can be made additive by a log transformation:

$$\log(y) = \log(a) + \log(b) + \log(c) + \log(d)$$

This is the process underlying the fit to the Lognormal distribution described in Section 7.4.

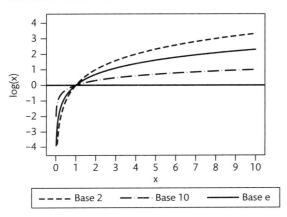

Figure 5.21 Logarithmic curves to three different bases.

There is no need to use 10 as the base for logarithms. We can use any number. The log of a number x to base b can be found from the log to base a by a simple calculation:

$$\log_b(x) = \frac{\log_a(x)}{\log_a(b)}$$

Ten is convenient for arithmetic using log tables, but for other purposes it is less so. For example, the gradient, slope, or differential of the curve $y = \log_{10}(x)$ is $\log_{10}(e)/x$, where $e = 2.718\,281\ldots$ is a constant which does not depend on the base of the logarithm. This leads to awkward constants spreading through formulae. To keep this to a minimum we use logs to the base e, called natural or Napierian logarithms after the mathematician John Napier. This is the logarithm usually produced by LOG(X) functions in computer languages.

Figure 5.21 shows the log curve for three different bases, 2, e, and 10. The curves all go through the point (1,0), i.e. $\log(1) = 0$. As x approaches 0, $\log(x)$ becomes a larger and larger negative number, tending towards minus infinity as x tends to zero. There are no logs of negative numbers. As x increases from 1, the curve becomes flatter and flatter. Though $\log(x)$ continues to increase, it does so more and more slowly. The curves all go through ($base$, 1) i.e. $\log(base) = 1$. The curve for log to the base 2 goes through (2,1), (4,2), (8,3) because $2^1 = 2$, $2^2 = 4$, $2^3 = 8$. We can see that the effect of replacing data by their logs will be to stretch out the scale at the lower end and contract it at the upper.

We often work with logarithms of data rather than the data themselves. This may have several advantages. Multiplicative relationships may become additive, curves may become straight lines and skew distributions may become symmetrical.

We transform back to the natural scale using the **antilogarithm** or **antilog**. If $y = \log_{10}(x)$, $x = 10^y$ is the antilog of y. If $z = \log_e(x)$, $x = e^z$ or $x = \exp(z)$ is the antilog of z. If your computer program doesn't transform back, most calculators have e^x and 10^x functions for this purpose.

6 Probability

6.1 Probability

We use data from a sample to draw conclusions about the population from which it is drawn. For example, in a clinical trial we might observe that a sample of patients given a new treatment respond better than patients given an old treatment. We want to know whether an improvement would be seen in the whole population of patients, and if so how big it might be. The theory of probability enables us to link samples and populations, and to draw conclusions about populations from samples. We shall start the discussion of probability with some simple randomizing devices, such as coins and dice, but the relevance to medical problems should soon become apparent.

We first ask what exactly is meant by 'probability'. In most of this book I shall take the frequency definition: the **probability** that an event will happen under given circumstances may be defined as the proportion of repetitions of those circumstances in which the event would occur in the long run. For example, if we toss a coin it comes down either heads or tails. Before we toss it, we have no way of knowing which will happen, but we do know that it will either be heads or tails. After we have tossed it, of course, we know exactly what the outcome is. If we carry on tossing our coin, we should get several heads and several tails. If we go on doing this for long enough, then we would expect to get as many heads as we do tails. So the probability of a head being thrown is half, because in the long run a head should occur on half of the throws. The number of heads which might arise in several tosses of the coin is called a **random variable**, that is, a variable which can take more than one value with given probabilities. In the same way, a thrown die can show six faces, numbered one to six, with equal probability, 1/6. We can investigate random variables such as the number of sixes in a given number of throws, the number of throws before the first six, and so on.

There is another, broader definition of probability which leads to a different approach to statistics, the Bayesian school, to which I shall return in Chapter 22.

The frequency definition of probability also applies to continuous measurement, such as human height. For example, suppose the median height in a population of women is 168 cm. Then half the women are above 168 cm in height. If we choose women at random (i.e. without the characteristics of the woman influencing the choice) then, in the long run, half the women chosen will have heights above 168 cm. The probability of a woman having height above 168 cm is one half. Similarly, if 1/10 of the women have height greater than 180 cm, a woman chosen at random will have height greater than 180 cm with probability 1/10. In the same way we can find the probability of height being above, below, or between any given values. When we measure a continuous quantity we are always limited by the method of measurement, and so when we say a woman's height is 170 cm we mean that it is between, say, 169.5 cm and 170.5 cm, depending on the accuracy with which we measure. So what we are interested in is the probability of the continuous random variable taking values between certain limits rather than particular values.

6.2 Properties of probability

The following simple properties follow from the definition of probability.

1 A probability lies between 0.0 and 1.0. When the event never happens the probability is 0.0, when it always happens the probability is 1.0.

2 **Addition rule.** Suppose two events are **mutually exclusive**, i.e. when one happens the other cannot happen. Then the probability that one or the other happens is the sum of their probabilities. For example,

a thrown die may show a one or a two, but not both. The probability that it shows a one or a two = 1/6 + 1/6 = 2/6.

3 **Multiplication rule**. Suppose two events are **independent**, i.e. knowing one has happened tells us nothing about whether the other happens. Then the probability that both happen is the product of their probabilities. For example, suppose we toss two coins. One coin does not influence the other, so the results of the two tosses are independent, and the probability of two heads occurring is 1/2 × 1/2 = 1/4. Consider two independent events A and B. The proportion of times A happens in the long run is the probability of A. As A and B are independent, of those times when A happens, a proportion, equal to the probability of B, will have B happen also. Hence the proportion of times that A and B happen together is the probability of A multiplied by the probability of B.

6.3 Probability distributions and random variables

Suppose we have a set of events which are mutually exclusive and which includes all the events that can possibly happen, which is called **exhaustive**. The sum of their probabilities is 1.0. The set of these probabilities make up a **probability distribution**. For example, if we toss a coin the two possibilities, head or tail, are mutually exclusive and these are the only events which can happen. The probability distribution is:

$$PROB(Head) = 1/2$$

$$PROB(Tail) = 1/2$$

Now, let us define a variable, which we will denote by the symbol X, such that $X = 0$ if the coin shows a tail and $X = 1$ if the coin shows a head. X is the number of heads shown on a single toss, which must be 0 or 1. We do not know before the toss what X will be, but do know the probability of it having any possible value. X is a random variable (Section 6.1) and the probability distribution is also the distribution of X. We can represent this with a diagram, as in Figure 6.1.

What happens if we toss two coins at once? We now have four possible events: a head and a head, a head and

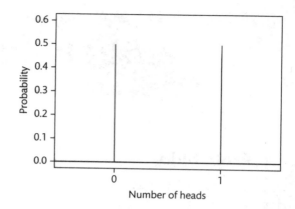

Figure 6.1 Probability distributions for the number of heads shown in the toss of one coin.

a tail, a tail and a head, a tail and a tail. Clearly, these are equally likely and each has probability 1/4. Let Y be the number of heads. Y has three possible values: 0, 1, and 2. $Y = 0$ only when we get a tail and a tail and has probability 1/4. Similarly, $Y = 2$ only when we get a head and a head, so has probability 1/4. However, $Y = 1$ either when we get a head and tail, or when we have a tail and a head, and so has probability 1/4 + 1/4 = 1/2. We can write this probability distribution as:

$$PROB(Y = 0) = 1/4$$

$$PROB(Y = 1) = 1/2$$

$$PROB(Y = 2) = 1/4$$

The probability distribution of Y is shown in Figure 6.2.

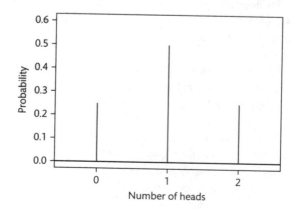

Figure 6.2 Probability distributions for the number of heads shown in tosses of two coins.

6.4 The Binomial distribution

We have considered the probability distributions of two random variables: X, the number of heads in one toss of a coin, taking values 0 and 1, and Y, the number of heads when we toss two coins, taking values 0, 1, or 2. We can increase the number of coins; Figure 6.3 shows the distribution of the number of heads obtained when 15 coins are tossed. We do not need the probability of a 'head' to be 0.5: we can count the number of sixes when dice are thrown. Figure 6.4 shows the distribution of the number of sixes obtained from 10 dice. In general, we can think of the coin or the die as trials, which can have outcomes success (head or six) or failure (tail or one to five). The distributions in Figures 6.1, 6.2, 6.3, and 6.4 are all examples of the Binomial distribution, which arises frequently in medical applications. The **Binomial distribution** is the distribution followed by the number of successes in n independent trials when the probability of any single trial being a success is p. The Binomial distribution is in fact a family of distributions, the members of which are defined by the values of n and p. The values which define which member of the distribution family we have are called the **parameters** of the distribution.

Simple randomizing devices like coins and dice are of interest in themselves, but not of obvious relevance to medicine. However, suppose we are carrying out a random sample survey to estimate the unknown prevalence, p, of a disease. As members of the sample are

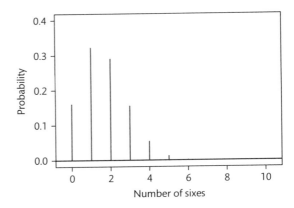

Figure 6.4 Distribution of the number of sixes shown when 10 dice are thrown, an example of the Binomial distribution.

chosen at random and independently from the population, the probability of any chosen subject having the disease is p. We thus have a series of independent trials, each with probability of success p, and the number of successes, i.e. members of the sample with the disease, will follow a Binomial distribution. As we shall see later, the properties of the Binomial distribution enable us to say how accurate is the estimate of prevalence obtained (Section 8.4).

We could calculate the probabilities for a Binomial distribution by listing all the ways in which, say, 15 coins can fall. However, there are $2^{15} = 32\,768$ combinations of 15 coins, so this is not very practical. Instead, there is a formula for the probability in terms of the number of throws and the probability of a head. This enables us to work these probabilities out for any probability of success and any number of trials. In general, we have n independent trials with the probability that a trial is a success being p. The probability of r successes is

$$\text{PROB}(r \text{ successes}) = \frac{n!}{r!(n-r)!} p^r (1-p)^{(n-r)}$$

where $n!$, called n factorial, is $n \times (n-1) \times (n-2) \times \cdots \times 2 \times 1$. This rather forbidding formula arises like this. For any particular series of r successes, each with probability p, and $n-r$ failures, each with probability $1-p$, the probability of the series happening is $p^r(1-p)^{(n-r)}$, as the trials are independent and the multiplicative rule applies. The number of ways in which r things may be chosen from

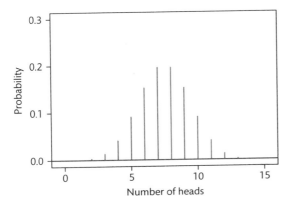

Figure 6.3 Distribution of the number of heads shown when 15 coins are tossed, an example of the Binomial distribution.

n things is *n*!/*r*!(*n* – *r*)! (Appendix 6A). Only one combination can happen at one time, so we have *n*!/*r*!(*n* – *r*)! mutually exclusive ways of having *r* successes, each with probability $p^r(1 - p)^{(n-r)}$. The probability of having *r* successes is the sum of these *n*!/*r*!(*n* – *r*)! probabilities, giving the formula above. Those who remember the binomial expansion in mathematics will see that this is one term of it, hence the name Binomial distribution.

We can apply this to the number of heads in tosses of two coins. The number of heads will be from a Binomial distribution with *p* = 0.5 and *n* = 2. Hence the probability of two heads (r = 2) is:

$$PROB(r = 2) = \frac{n!}{r!(n-r)!}p^r(1-p)^{(n-r)}$$

$$= \frac{2!}{2!0!}0.5^2 \times 0.5^0$$

$$= \frac{2}{2 \times 1} \times 0.25 \times 1$$

$$= 0.25$$

Note that 0! = 1 (Appendix 6A), and anything to the power 0 is 1. Similarly for *r* = 1 and *r* = 0:

$$PROB(r = 1) = \frac{2!}{1!1!}0.5^1 \times 0.5^1$$

$$= \frac{2}{1 \times 1} \times 0.5 \times 0.5$$

$$= 0.5$$

$$PROB(r = 0) = \frac{2!}{0!2!}0.5^0 \times 0.5^2$$

$$= \frac{2}{1 \times 2} \times 1 \times 0.25$$

$$= 0.25$$

This is what was found for two coins in Section 6.3. We can use this distribution whenever we have a series of trials with two possible outcomes. If we treat a group of patients, the number who recover is from a Binomial distribution. If we measure the blood pressure of a group of people, the number classified as hypertensive is from a Binomial distribution.

Figure 6.5 shows the Binomial distribution for *p* = 0.3 and increasing values of *n*. The distribution becomes more symmetrical as *n* increases. It is converging to the Normal distribution, described in the next chapter.

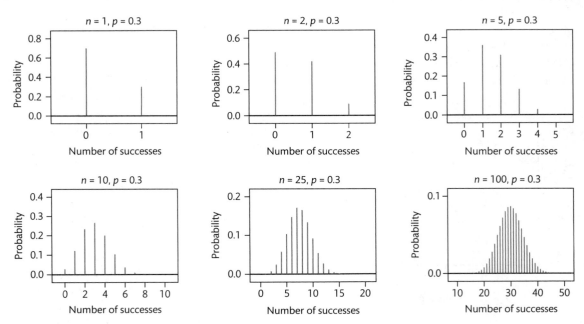

Figure 6.5 Binomial distributions with different *n*, *p* = 0.3.

6.5 Mean and variance

The number of different probabilities in a Binomial distribution can be very large and unwieldy. When n is large, we usually need to summarize these probabilities in some way. Just as a frequency distribution can be described by its mean and variance, so can a probability distribution and its associated random variable.

The **mean** is the average value of the random variable in the long run. It is also called the **expected value** or **expectation** and the expectation of a random variable X is usually denoted by $E(X)$. For example, consider the number of heads in tosses of two coins. We get 0 heads in $\frac{1}{4}$ of pairs of coins, i.e. with probability $\frac{1}{4}$. We get 1 head in $\frac{1}{2}$ of pairs of coins, and 2 heads in $\frac{1}{4}$ of pairs. The average value we should get in the long run is found by multiplying each value by the proportion of pairs in which it occurs and adding:

$$0 \times \frac{1}{4} + 1 \times \frac{1}{2} + 2 \times \frac{1}{4} = 0 + \frac{1}{2} + \frac{1}{2} = 1$$

If we kept on tossing pairs of coins, the average number of heads per pair would be 1. Thus for any random variable which takes discrete values the mean, expectation, or expected value is found by summing each possible value multiplied by its probability.

Note that the expected value of a random variable does not have to be a value that the random variable can actually take. For example, for the mean number of heads in throws of one coin we have either no heads or 1 head, each with probability half, and the expected value is $0 \times 1/2 + 1 \times 1/2 = 1/2$. The number of heads must be 0 or 1, but the expected value is half, the average which we would get in the long run.

The **variance** of a random variable is the average squared difference from the mean. For the number of heads in tosses of two coins, 0 is 1 unit from the mean and occurs for 1/4 of pairs of coins, 1 is 0 units from the mean and occurs for half of the pairs and 2 is 1 unit from the mean and occurs for 1/4 of pairs, i.e. with probability 1/4. The variance is then found by squaring these differences, multiplying by the proportion of times the difference will occur (the probability) and adding:

$$\text{Variance} = (0-1)^2 \times \frac{1}{4} + (1-1)^2 \times \frac{1}{2}$$
$$+ (2-1)^2 \times \frac{1}{4}$$
$$= (-1)^2 \times \frac{1}{4} + 0^2 \times \frac{1}{2} + 1^2 \times \frac{1}{4}$$
$$= \frac{1}{2}$$

We denote the variance of a random variable X by $VAR(X)$. In mathematical terms,

$$VAR(X) = E(X - E(X))^2 = E\left(X^2\right) - (E(X))^2$$

The square root of the variance is the standard deviation of the random variable or distribution. We often use the Greek letters μ, pronounced 'mu', and σ, 'sigma', for the mean and standard deviation of a probability distribution. The variance is then σ^2.

The mean and variance of the distribution of a continuous variable, of which more in Chapter 7, are defined in a similar way. Calculus is used to define them as integrals, but this need not concern us here. Essentially what happens is that the continuous scale is broken up into many very small intervals and the value of the variable in that very small interval is multiplied by the probability of being in it, then these are added.

6.6 Properties of means and variances

When we use the mean and variance of probability distributions in statistical calculations, it is not the details of their formulae which we need to know, but some of their simple properties. Most of the formulae used in statistical calculations are derived from these. The reasons for these properties are quite easy to see in a non-mathematical way.

If we add a constant to a random variable, the new variable so created has a mean equal to that of the original variable plus the constant. The variance and standard deviation will be unchanged. Suppose our random variable is human height. We can add a constant to the height by measuring the heights of people standing on a box. The mean height of people plus box will now be the mean height of the people plus the constant height of the box. The box will not alter the variability of the heights, however. The difference between the tallest and smallest, for example, will be unchanged. We can subtract a constant by asking the people to stand in a constant hole to be measured. This reduces the mean but leaves the variance unchanged as before.

If we multiply a random variable by a positive constant, the mean and standard deviation are multiplied by the constant, the variance is multiplied by the square of the constant. For example, if we change our units of measurements, say from inches to centimetres, we multiply each measurement by 2.54. This has the effect of multiplying the mean by the constant, 2.54, and multiplying the standard deviation by the constant as it is in the same units as the observations. However, the variance is measured in squared units, and so is multiplied by the square of the constant. Division by a constant works in the same way. If the constant is negative, the mean is multiplied by the constant and so changes sign. The variance is multiplied by the square of the constant, which is positive, so the variance remains positive. The standard deviation, which is the square root of the variance, is always positive. It is multiplied by the absolute value of the constant, i.e. the constant without the negative sign.

If we add two random variables, the mean of the sum is the sum of the means, and, *if the two variables are independent*, the variance of the sum is the sum of their variances. We can do this by measuring the height of people standing on boxes of random height. The mean height of people on boxes is the mean height of people + the mean height of the boxes. The variability of the heights is also increased. This is because some short people will find themselves on small boxes, and some tall people will find themselves on large boxes. If the two variables are not independent, something different happens. The mean of the sum remains the sum of the means, but the variance of the sum is not the sum of the variances. Suppose our people have decided to stand on the boxes, not just at a statistician's whim, but for a purpose. They wish to change a light bulb, and so must reach a required height. Now the short people must pick large boxes, whereas tall people can make do with small ones. The result is a reduction in variability to almost nothing. On the other hand, if we told the tallest people to find

the largest boxes and the shortest to find the smallest boxes, the variability would be increased. Independence is an important condition.

If we subtract one random variable from another, the mean of the difference is the difference between the means, and, if the two variables are independent, the variance of the difference is the *sum* of their variances. Suppose we measure the heights above ground level of our people standing in holes of random depth. The mean height above ground is the mean height of the people minus the mean depth of the hole. The variability is increased, because some short people stand in deep holes and some tall people stand in shallow holes. If the variables are not independent, the additivity of the variances breaks down, as it did for the sum of two variables. When the people try to hide in the holes, and so must find a hole deep enough to hold them, the variability is again reduced.

The effects of multiplying two random variables and of dividing one by another are much more complicated. Fortunately, we rarely need to do this.

We can now find the mean and variance of the Binomial distribution with parameters n and p. First consider $n = 1$. Then the probability distribution is:

value	probability
0	$1 - p$
1	p

The mean is therefore $0 \times (1-p) + 1 \times p = p$. The variance is

$$(0 - p)^2 \times (1 - p) + (1 - p)^2 \times p$$
$$= p^2(1 - p) + p(1 - p)^2$$
$$= p(1 - p)(p + 1 - p)$$
$$= p(1 - p)$$

Now, a variable from the Binomial distribution with parameters n and p is the sum of n independent variables from the Binomial distribution with parameters 1 and p. So its mean is the sum of n means all equal to p, and its variance is the sum of n variances all equal to $p(1 - p)$. Hence the Binomial distribution has mean $= np$ and variance $= np(1-p)$. For large sample problems, these are more useful than the Binomial probability formula.

The properties of means and variances of random variables enable us to find a formal solution to the problem of degrees of freedom for the sample variance discussed in Chapter 4. We want an estimate of variance whose expected value is the population variance. The expected value of $\sum (x_i - \bar{x})^2$ can be shown to be $(n - 1)\text{VAR}(x)$ (Appendix 6B) and hence we divide by $n - 1$, not n, to get our estimate of variance.

lung cancer in 1 year among people in an occupational group, such as coal miners, will be an observation from a Poisson distribution, and we can use this to make comparisons between mortality rates (Section 21.3).

Figure 6.6 shows the Poisson distribution for four different means. You will see that as the mean increases the Poisson distribution looks rather like the Binomial distribution in Figure 6.5. We shall discuss this similarity further in the next chapter.

6.7 The Poisson distribution

The Binomial distribution is one of many probability distributions which are used in statistics. It is a discrete distribution, that is, it can take only a limited set of possible values. It is the discrete distribution most frequently encountered in medical applications. One other discrete distribution is worth discussing at this point, the Poisson distribution. Although, like the Binomial, the Poisson distribution arises from a simple probability model, the mathematics involved is more complicated and will be omitted.

Suppose events happen randomly and independently in time at a constant rate. The **Poisson distribution** is the distribution followed by the number of events which happen in a fixed time interval. If events happen with rate μ events per unit time, the probability of r events happening in unit time is

$$\frac{e^{-\mu}\mu^r}{r!}$$

where $e = 2.718\ldots$, the mathematical constant. If events happen randomly and independently in space, the Poisson distribution gives the probabilities for the number of events in a unit volume or area.

There is seldom any need to use individual probabilities of this distribution, as its mean and variance suffice. The mean of the Poisson distribution for the number of events per unit time is simply the rate, μ. The variance of the Poisson distribution is also equal to μ. Thus the Poisson is a family of distributions, like the Binomial, but with only one parameter, μ. This distribution is important, because deaths from many diseases can be treated as occurring randomly and independently in the population. Thus, for example, the number of deaths from

6.8 Conditional probability

Sometimes we need to think about the probability of an event if another event has happened. For example, we might ask what is the probability that a patient has coronary artery disease if he or she has tingling pain in the left arm. This is called a **conditional probability**, the probability of the event (coronary artery disease) given a condition (tingling pain). We write this probability thus, separating the event and the condition by a vertical bar:

PROB(Coronary artery disease | Tingling pain)

Conditional probabilities are useful in statistical aids to diagnosis (Section 22.3). For a simpler example, we can go back to tosses of two coins. If we toss one coin then the other, the first toss alters the probabilities for the possible outcomes for the two coins:

PROB(Both coins heads | First coin head) = 0.5
PROB(Head and tail | First coin head) = 0.5
PROB(Both coins tails | First coin head) = 0.0

and

PROB(Both coins heads | First coin tail) = 0.0
PROB(Head and tail | First coin tail) = 0.5
PROB(Both coins tails | First coin tail) = 0.5

The multiplicative rule (Section 6.2) can be extended to deal with events which are not independent. For two events A and B:

PROB(A and B) = PROB(A | B)PROB(B)
= PROB(B | A)PROB(A)

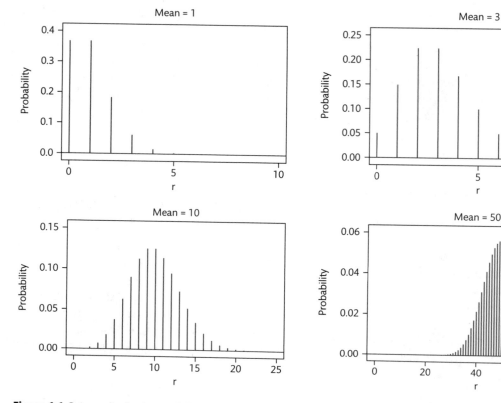

Figure 6.6 Poisson distributions with four different means.

It is important to understand that PROB(A | B) and PROB(B | A) are not the same. For example, Table 6.1 shows the relationship between two diseases, hay fever and eczema, in a large group of children. The probability that in this group a child with hay fever will have eczema also is

PROB(eczema | hay fever) = 141/1 069 = 0.13,

Table 6.1 Relationship between hay fever and eczema at age 11 in the National Child Development Study (data from the National Child Development Study)

	Hay fever		
Eczema	**Yes**	**No**	**Total**
Yes	141	420	561
No	928	13 525	14 453
Total	1 069	13 945	15 014

the proportion of children with hay fever who have eczema also. This is clearly much less than the probability that a child with eczema will have hay fever,

PROB(hay fever | eczema) = 141/561 = 0.25,

the proportion of children with eczema who have hay fever also.

This may look obvious, but confusion between conditional probabilities is common and can cause serious problems, for example in the consideration of forensic evidence. Typically, this will produce the probability that a material found a crime scene (DNA, fibres, etc.) will match the suspect as closely as it does given that the material did not come from the subject. This is

PROB(Evidence | Suspect not at crime scene).

It is not the same as

PROB(Suspect not at crime scene | Evidence),

but this is often how it is interpreted, an inversion known as the **prosecutor's fallacy**.

6.9 Multiple choice questions: Probability

(Each branch is either true or false.)

6.1 The events A and B are mutually exclusive, so:
(a) PROB(A or B) = PROB(A) + PROB(B);
(b) PROB(A and B) = 0;
(c) PROB(A and B) = PROB(A) PROB(B);
(d) PROB(A) = PROB(B);
(e) PROB(A) + PROB(B) = 1.

6.2 The probability of a woman aged 50 having condition X is 0.20 and the probability of her having condition Y is 0.05. These probabilities are independent:
(a) the probability of her having both conditions is 0.01;
(b) the probability of her having both conditions is 0.25;
(c) the probability of her having either X, or Y, or both is 0.24;
(d) if she has condition X, the probability of her having Y also is 0.01;
(e) if she has condition Y, the probability of her having X also is 0.20.

6.3 The following variables follow a Binomial distribution:
(a) number of sixes in 20 throws of a die;
(b) human weight;
(c) number of a random sample of patients who respond to a treatment;
(d) number of red cells in 1 ml of blood;
(e) proportion of hypertensives in a random sample of adult men.

6.4 Two parents each carry the same recessive gene which each transmits to their child with probability 0.5. If their child will develop clinical disease if it inherits the gene from both parents and will be a carrier if it inherits the gene from one parent only then:
(a) the probability that their next child will have clinical disease is 0.25;
(b) the probability that two successive children will both develop clinical disease is 0.25 × 0.25;

(c) the probability their next child will be a carrier without clinical disease is 0.50;
(d) the probability of a child being a carrier or having clinical disease is 0.75;
(e) if the first child does not have clinical disease, the probability that the second child will not have clinical disease is 0.75^2.

6.5 If a coin is spun twice in succession:
(a) the expected number of tails is 1.5;
(b) the probability of two tails is 0.25;
(c) the number of tails follows a Binomial distribution;
(d) the probability of at least one tail is 0.5;
(e) the distribution of the number of tails is symmetrical.

6.6 If X is a random variable, mean μ and variance σ^2:
(a) $E(X + 2) = \mu$;
(b) $VAR(X + 2) = \sigma^2$;
(c) $E(2X) = 2\mu$;
(d) $VAR(2X) = 2\sigma^2$;
(e) $VAR(X/2) = \sigma^2/4$.

6.7 If X and Y are independent random variables:
(a) $VAR(X + Y) = VAR(X) + VAR(Y)$;
(b) $E(X + Y) = E(X) + E(Y)$;
(c) $E(X - Y) = E(X) - E(Y)$;
(d) $VAR(X - Y) = VAR(X) - VAR(Y)$;
(e) $VAR(-X) = -VAR(X)$.

6.10 Exercise: Probability in court

In November 1999, a woman was convicted of the murder of her two children. They had originally been diagnosed as cot deaths, sudden infant death syndrome. There was no obvious medical reason for them to die. One of the pieces of evidence brought to court was that the probability that two children would both die from cot death was very small. It was stated, by a paediatrician, to be one in 73 million (Watkins 2000). This was calculated from the estimated proportion of similar children dying from cot death as about one in 8 540. 8 540 times 8 540 = 73 million. This was claimed to be so unlikely that we could not believe they were cot deaths and therefore they must have been murdered.

6.1 What property of probability was used here?

6.2 What assumption about cot death is being made? Do you think it is plausible?

6.3 What would be the effect of this assumption on the probability of two cot deaths?

6.4 If it were correct, what would the probability of one in 73 million tell us about the deaths of these two children?

6.5 What probability might be more useful here?

6.6 What fallacy was the paediatrician making?

Appendix 6A: Permutations and combinations

For those who never knew, or have forgotten, the theory of combinations, it goes like this. First, we look at the number of permutations, i.e. ways of arranging a set of objects. Suppose we have n objects. How many ways can we order them? The first object can be chosen n ways, i.e. any object. For each first object there are $n - 1$ possible second objects, so there are $n \times (n - 1)$ possible first and second permutations. There are now only $n - 2$ choices for the third object, $n - 3$ choices for the fourth, and so on, until there is only one choice for the last. Hence, there are $n \times (n - 1) \times (n - 2) \times \ldots \times 2 \times 1$ permutations of n objects. We call this number the **factorial** of n and write it '$n!$'.

Now we want to know how many ways there are of choosing r objects from n objects. Having made a choice of r objects, we can order those in $r!$ ways. We can also order the $n - r$ not chosen in $(n - r)!$ ways. So the objects can be ordered in $r!(n - r)!$ ways without altering the objects chosen. For example, say we choose the first two from three objects, A, B, and C. Then if these are A and B, two permutations give this choice, ABC and BAC. This is, of course, $2! \times 1! = 2$ permutations. Each combination of r things accounts for $r!(n - r)!$ of the $n!$ permutations possible, so there are

$$\frac{n!}{r!(n - r)!}$$

possible combinations. For example, consider the number of combinations of two objects out of three, say A, B, and C. The possible choices are AB, AC, and BC. There is no other possibility. Applying the formula, we have $n = 3$ and $r = 2$ so

$$\frac{n!}{r!(n - r)!} = \frac{3!}{2!(3 - 2)!} = \frac{3 \times 2 \times 1}{2 \times 1 \times 1} = 3$$

Sometimes in using this formula we come across $r = 0$ or $r = n$ leading to $0!$. This cannot be defined in the way we have chosen, but we can calculate its only possible value, $0! = 1$. Because there is only one way of choosing n objects from n, we have

$$1 = \frac{n!}{n!(n - n)!} = \frac{n!}{n! \times 0!} = \frac{1}{0!}$$

so $0! = 1$.

For one more example, in the UK National Lottery players choose six out of 49 possible numbers. The number of possible choices is

$$\frac{49!}{6! \times (49 - 6)!} = 13\,983\,816$$

hence the one in approximately 14 million chance of winning.

Appendix 6B: Expected value of a sum of squares

The properties of means and variances described in Section 6.6 can be used to answer the question raised in Section 4.7 and Appendix 4A about the divisor in the sample variance.

We ask why the variance from a sample is

$$s^2 = \frac{1}{n - 1}\sum(x_i - \bar{x})^2$$

and not

$$s_n^2 = \frac{1}{n}\sum(x_i - \bar{x})^2$$

We shall be concerned with the general properties of samples of size n, so we shall treat n as a constant and x_i and $\bar{x}$ as random variables. We shall suppose x_i has mean μ and variance σ^2.

From Appendix 4A, the expected value of the sum of squares is

$$E\left(\sum(x_i - \bar{x})^2\right) = E\left(\sum x_i^2 - \frac{1}{n}\left(\sum x_i\right)^2\right)$$

$$= E\left(\sum x_i^2\right) - \frac{1}{n}E\left(\left(\sum x_i\right)^2\right)$$

because the expected value of the difference is the difference between the expected values and n is a constant. Now, the population variance σ^2 is the average squared distance from the population mean μ, so

$$\sigma^2 = E\left((x_i - \mu)^2\right)$$

$$= E\left(x_i^2 - 2\mu x_i + \mu^2\right)$$

$$= E\left(x_i^2\right) - 2\mu E(x_i) + \mu^2$$

because μ is a constant. Because $E(x_i) = \mu$, we have

$$\sigma^2 = E\left(x_i^2\right) - 2\mu^2 + \mu^2 = E\left(x_i^2\right) - \mu^2$$

and so we find $E(x_i^2) = \sigma^2 + \mu^2$ and so $E(\sum x_i^2) = n(\sigma^2 + \mu^2)$, being the sum of n numbers all of which are $\sigma^2 + \mu^2$. We now find the value of $E\left((\sum x_i)^2\right)$. We need

$$E\left(\sum x_i\right) = \sum E(x_i) = \sum \mu = n\mu$$

$$\text{VAR}\left(\sum x_i\right) = \sum \text{VAR}(x_i) = n\sigma^2$$

Just as $E(x_i^2) = \sigma^2 + \mu^2 = \text{VAR}(x_i) + (E(x_i))^2$ so

$$E\left(\left(\sum x_i\right)^2\right) = \text{VAR}\left(\left(\sum x_i\right)\right) + \left(E\left(\sum x_i\right)\right)^2$$

$$= n\sigma^2 + (n\mu)^2$$

So

$$E\left(\sum (x_i - \bar{x})^2\right) = E\left(\sum x_i^2\right) - \frac{1}{n}E\left(\left(\sum x_i\right)^2\right)$$

$$= n(\sigma^2 + \mu^2) - \frac{1}{n}\left(n\sigma^2 + n^2\mu^2\right)$$

$$= n\sigma^2 + n\mu^2 - \sigma^2 - n\mu^2$$

$$= (n-1)\sigma^2$$

So the expected value of the sum of squares is $(n-1)\sigma^2$ and we must divide the sum of squares by $n-1$, not n, to obtain the estimate of the variance, σ^2.

We shall find the variance of the sample mean, $\bar{x}$, useful later (Section 8.2):

$$\text{VAR}(\bar{x}) = \text{VAR}\left(\frac{1}{n}\sum x_i\right) = \frac{n\sigma^2}{n^2} = \frac{\sigma^2}{n}$$

7 The Normal distribution

7.1 Probability for continuous variables

When we derived the theory of probability in the discrete case, we were able to say what the probability was of a random variable taking a particular value. As the number of possible values increases, the probability of a particular value decreases. For example, in the Binomial distribution with $p = 0.5$ and $n = 2$, the most likely value, 1, has probability 0.5. In the Binomial distribution with $p = 0.5$ and $n = 100$ the most likely value, 50, has probability 0.08. In such cases we are usually more interested in the probability of a range of values than one particular value.

For a continuous variable, such as height, the set of possible values is infinite and the probability of any particular value is zero (Section 6.1). We are interested in the probability of the random variable taking values between certain limits rather than taking particular values. If the proportion of individuals in the population whose values are between given limits is p, and we choose an individual at random, the probability of choosing an individual who lies between these limits is equal to p. This comes from our definition of probability, the choice of each individual being equally likely. The problem is finding and giving a value to this probability.

When we find the frequency distribution for a sample of observations, we count the number of values which fall within certain limits (Section 4.2). We can represent this as a histogram such as Figure 7.1 (Section 4.3). One way of presenting the histogram is as relative frequency density, the proportion of observations in the interval per unit of X (Section 4.3). Thus, when the interval size is 5, the relative frequency density is the relative frequency divided by 5 (Figure 7.1). The relative frequency in an interval is now represented by the width of the interval multiplied by the density, which gives the area of the rectangle. Thus, the relative frequency between any two points can be

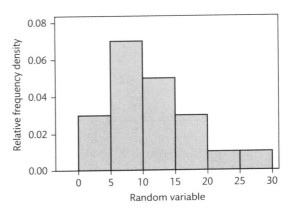

Figure 7.1 Histogram showing relative frequency density.

found from the area under the histogram between the points. For example, to estimate the relative frequency between 10 and 20 in Figure 7.1 we have the density from 10 to 15 as 0.05 and between 15 and 20 as 0.03. Hence the relative frequency is

$$0.05 \times (15 - 10) + 0.03 \times (20 - 15)$$
$$= 0.25 + 0.15$$
$$= 0.40$$

If we take a larger sample we can use smaller intervals. We get a smoother looking histogram, as in Figure 7.2, and as we take larger and larger samples, and so smaller and smaller intervals, we get a shape very close to a smooth curve (Figure 7.3). As the sample size approaches that of the population, which we can assume to be very large, this curve becomes the relative frequency density of the whole population. Thus we can find the proportion of observations between any two limits by finding the area under the curve, as indicated in Figure 7.3.

If we know the equation of this curve, we can find the area under it. (Mathematically we do this by integration, but we do not need to know how to integrate to use or to

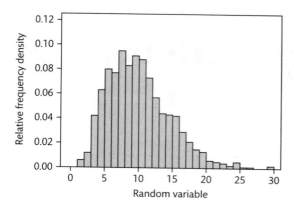

Figure 7.2 The effect on a frequency distribution of increasing sample size.

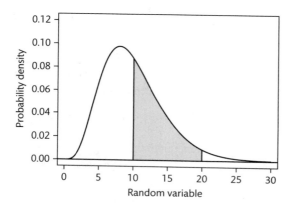

Figure 7.3 Relative frequency density or probability density function, showing the probability of an observation between 10 and 20.

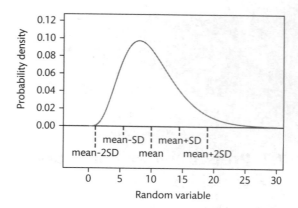

Figure 7.4 Mean, μ, standard deviation, σ, and a probability density function.

understand practical statistics—all the integrals we need have been done and tabulated, or will be performed by a computer program when we need them.) Now, if we choose an individual at random, the probability that X lies between any given limits is equal to the proportion of individuals who fall between these limits. Hence, the relative frequency distribution for the whole population gives us the probability distribution of the variable. We call this curve the **probability density function**.

Probability density functions have a number of general properties. For example, the total area under the curve must be one, as this is the total probability of all possible values of the variable. Continuous random variables have means, variances, and standard deviations defined in a similar way to those for discrete random variables

and possessing the same properties (Section 6.5). The mean will be somewhere near the middle of the curve and most of the area under the curve will be between the mean minus two standard deviations and the mean plus two standard deviations (Figure 7.4).

The precise shape of the curve is more difficult to ascertain. There are many possible probability density functions and some of these can be shown to arise from simple probability situations, as were the Binomial and Poisson distributions. However, most continuous variables with which we have to deal, such as height, blood pressure, serum cholesterol, etc., do not arise from simple probability situations. As a result, we do not know the probability distribution for these measurements on theoretical grounds. As we shall see, we can often find a standard distribution whose mathematical properties are known, which fits observed data well and which enables us to draw conclusions about them. Further, as sample size increases, the distribution of certain statistics calculated from the data, such as the mean, becomes independent of the distribution of the observations themselves, and follows one particular distribution form, the Normal distribution. We shall devote the remainder of this chapter to a study of this distribution.

7.2 The Normal distribution

The Normal distribution, also known as the Gaussian distribution, may be regarded as the fundamental probability distribution of statistics. The word 'normal' is not used here in its common meaning of 'ordinary or common', or its medical meaning of 'not diseased'. The usage relates to its older meaning of 'conforming to a rule or pattern', and as we shall see, the Normal distribution is the form to which the Binomial distribution tends as its parameter n increases. There is no implication that most variables follow a Normal distribution.

We shall start by considering the Binomial distribution as n increases. We saw in Section 6.4 that, as n increases, the shape of the distribution changes. The most extreme possible values become less likely and the distribution becomes more symmetrical. This happens whatever the value of p. The position of the distribution along the horizontal axis, and its spread, are still determined by p, but the shape is not. A smooth curve can be drawn which goes very close to these points. This is the Normal distribution curve, the curve of the continuous distribution which the Binomial distribution approaches as n increases. Any Binomial distribution may be approximated by the Normal distribution of the same mean and variance provided n is large enough. Figure 7.5 shows the Binomial distributions of Figure 6.3 with the corresponding Normal distribution curves. From $n = 10$ onwards the two distributions are very close. Generally, if both np and

$n(1-p)$ exceed 5, the approximation of the Binomial to the Normal distribution is quite good enough for most practical purposes. See Section 8.4 for an application. The Poisson distribution has the same property, as Figure 6.4 suggests.

The Binomial variable may be regarded as the sum of n independent identically distributed random variables, each being the outcome of one trial taking value 1 with probability p. In general, if we have any series of independent, identically distributed random variables, then their sum tends to a Normal distribution as the number of variables increases. This is known as the **central limit theorem**. As most sets of measurements are observations of such a series of random variables, this is a very important property. From it, we can deduce that the sum or mean of any large series of independent observations follows a Normal distribution.

For example, consider the **Uniform** or **Rectangular distribution**. This is the distribution where all values between two limits, say 0 and 1, are equally likely and no other values are possible. Observations from this arise if we take random digits from a table of random numbers such as Table 2.3. Each observation of the Uniform variable is formed by a series of such digits placed after a

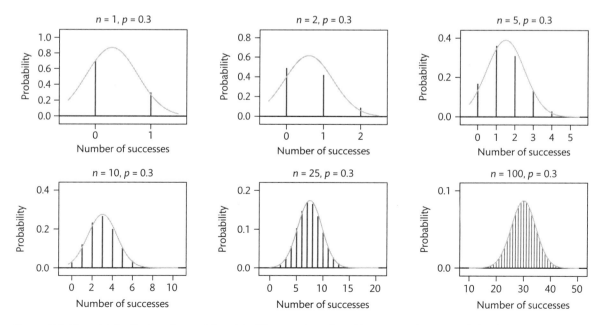

Figure 7.5 Binomial distributions for $p = 0.3$ and six different values of n, with corresponding Normal distribution curves.

decimal point. On a microcomputer, this is usually the distribution produced by the RND(X) function in the BASIC language. Figure 7.6 shows the histogram for the frequency distribution of 5 000 observations from the Uniform distribution between 0 and 1. It is quite different from the Normal distribution. Now suppose we create a new variable by taking two Uniform variables and adding them (Figure 7.6). The shape of the distribution of the sum of two Uniform variables is quite different from the shape of the Uniform distribution. The sum is unlikely to be close to either extreme, here 0 or 2, and observations are concentrated in the middle near the expected value. The reason for this is that to obtain a low sum, both the Uniform variables forming it must be low; to make a high sum both must be high. But we get a sum near the middle if the first is high and the second low, or the first is low and second high, or both first and second are moderate. The distribution of the sum of two is much closer to the

Normal than is the Uniform distribution itself. However, the abrupt cut-off at 0 and at 2 is unlike the corresponding Normal distribution. Figure 7.6 also shows the result of adding four Uniform variables and six Uniform variables. The similarity to the Normal distribution increases as the number added increases and for the sum of six the correspondence is so close that the distributions could not easily be told apart.

The approximation of the Binomial to the Normal distribution is a special case of the central limit theorem. The Poisson distribution is another. If we take a set of Poisson variables with the same rate and add them, we will get a variable which is the number of random events in a longer time interval (the sum of the intervals for the individual variables) and which is therefore a Poisson distribution with increased mean. As it is the sum of a set of independent, identically distributed random variables, it will tend towards the Normal as the mean increases.

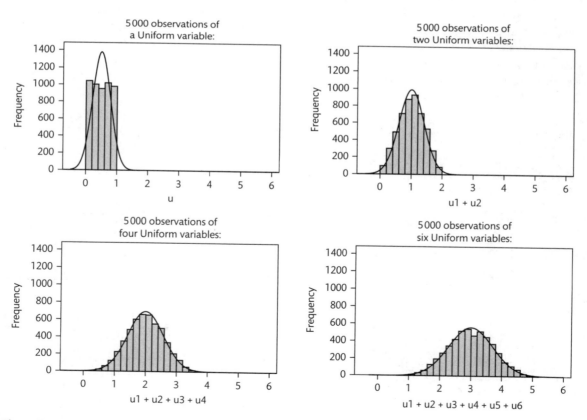

Figure 7.6 Sums of observations from a Uniform distribution.

Hence as the mean increases the Poisson distribution becomes approximately Normal. For most practical purposes this is when the mean exceeds 10. The similarity between the Poisson and the Binomial noted in Section 6.7 is a part of a more general convergence shown by many other distributions.

7.3 Properties of the Normal distribution

In its simplest form the equation of the Normal distribution curve, called the **Standard Normal distribution**, is usually denoted by $\phi(z)$, where ϕ is the Greek letter 'phi':

$$\phi(z) = \frac{1}{\sqrt{2\pi}} \exp\left(-\frac{z^2}{2}\right)$$

where π is the usual mathematical constant. The medical reader can be reassured that we do not need to use this forbidding formula in practice. The Standard Normal distribution has a mean of 0, a standard deviation of 1, and a shape as shown in Figure 7.7. The curve is symmetrical about the mean and often described as 'bell-shaped' (though I've never seen a bell like it). We can

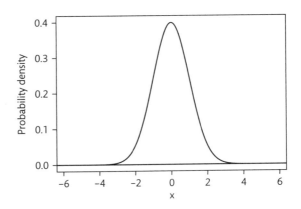

Figure 7.7 The Standard Normal distribution.

note that most of the area, i.e. the probability, is between –1 and +1, the large majority between –2 and +2, and almost all between –3 and +3.

Although the Normal distribution curve has many remarkable properties, it has one rather awkward one: it cannot be integrated. In other words, there is no simple formula for the probability of a random variable from a Normal distribution lying between given limits. The areas under the curve can be found numerically, however, and these have been calculated and tabulated. Table 7.1 shows the probability that a variable from a Standard

Table 7.1 The Normal distribution

z	Φ(z)	z	Φ(z)	z	Φ(z)	z	Φ(z)	z	Φ(z)	z	Φ(z)
–3.0	0.001	–2.0	0.023	–1.0	0.159	0.0	0.500	1.0	0.841	2.0	0.977
–2.9	0.002	–1.9	0.029	–0.9	0.184	0.1	0.540	1.1	0.864	2.1	0.982
–2.8	0.003	–1.8	0.036	–0.8	0.212	0.2	0.579	1.2	0.885	2.2	0.986
–2.7	0.003	–1.7	0.045	–0.7	0.242	0.3	0.618	1.3	0.903	2.3	0.989
–2.6	0.005	–1.6	0.055	–0.6	0.274	0.4	0.655	1.4	0.919	2.4	0.992
–2.5	0.006	–1.5	0.067	–0.5	0.309	0.5	0.691	1.5	0.933	2.5	0.994
–2.4	0.008	–1.4	0.081	–0.4	0.345	0.6	0.726	1.6	0.945	2.6	0.995
–2.3	0.011	–1.3	0.097	–0.3	0.382	0.7	0.758	1.7	0.955	2.7	0.997
–2.2	0.014	–1.2	0.115	–0.2	0.421	0.8	0.788	1.8	0.964	2.8	0.997
–2.1	0.018	–1.1	0.136	–0.1	0.460	0.9	0.816	1.9	0.971	2.9	0.998
–2.0	0.023	–1.0	0.159	0.0	0.500	1.0	0.841	2.0	0.977	3.0	0.999

Normal distribution will be less than a given value, z. For a value z, the table shows the area under the curve to the left of z, i.e. from minus infinity to z, denoted by $\Phi(z)$ (Figure 7.8). Thus $\Phi(z)$ is the probability that a value chosen at random from the Standard Normal distribution will be less than z. Φ is the Greek capital 'phi'. Note that half this table is not strictly necessary. We need only the half for positive z as $\Phi(-z) + \Phi(z) = 1$. This arises from the symmetry of the distribution. To find the probability of z lying between two values a and b, where $b > a$, we find $\Phi(b) - \Phi(a)$. To find the probability of z being greater than a we find $1 - \Phi(a)$. These formulae are all examples of the additive law of probability. Table 7.1 gives only a few values of z, and much more extensive tables are available (Lindley and Miller 1955; Pearson and Hartley 1970). Good statistical computer programs will calculate these values when they are needed.

There is another way of tabulating a distribution, using what are called percentage points. The **one sided** P **percentage point** of a distribution is the value z such that there is a probability P% of an observation from that distribution being greater than or equal to z (Figure 7.9). The **two sided** P **percentage point** is the value z such that there is a probability P% of an observation being greater than or equal to z or less than or equal to –z (Figure 7.10). Table 7.2 shows both one sided and two sided percentage points for the Normal distribution. The probability is quoted as a percentage because when we use percentage points we are usually concerned with rather small probabilities, such as 0.05 or 0.01, and use of

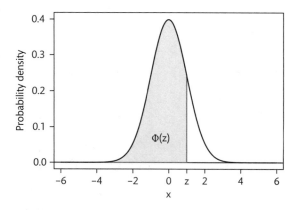

Figure 7.8 The Standard Normal distribution function.

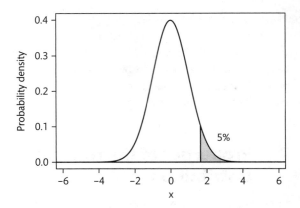

Figure 7.9 One sided percentage point (5%) of the Standard Normal distribution.

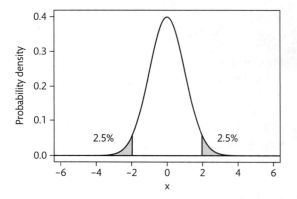

Figure 7.10 Two sided percentage points (5%) of the Standard Normal distribution.

the percentage form, making them 5% and 1%, cuts out the leading zero.

So far we have examined the Normal distribution with mean 0 and standard deviation 1. If we add a constant μ to a Standard Normal variable, we get a new variable which has mean μ (see Section 6.6). Figure 7.11 shows the Normal distribution with mean 0 and the distribution obtained by adding 1 to it together with their two sided 5% points. The curves are identical apart from a shift along the axis. On the curve with mean 0 nearly all the probability is between –3 and +3. For the curve with mean 1 it is between –2 and +4, i.e. between the mean –3 and the mean +3. The probability of being a given number of units from the mean is the same for both distributions, as is also shown by the 5% points.

Table 7.2 Percentage points of the Normal distribution

One sided		Two sided	
$P_1(z)$	z	$P_2(z)$	z
50	0.00		
25	0.67	50	0.67
10	1.28	20	1.28
5	1.64	10	1.64
2.5	1.96	5	1.96
1	2.33	2	2.33
0.5	2.58	1	2.58
0.1	3.09	0.2	3.09
0.05	3.29	0.1	3.29

The table shows the probability $P_1(z)$ of a Normal variable with mean 0 and variance 1 being greater than z, and the probability $P_2(z)$ of a Normal variable with mean 0 and variance 1 being less than $-z$ or greater than z.

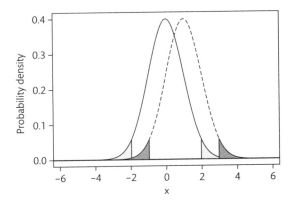

Figure 7.11 Normal distributions with different means, showing two sided 5% points.

If we take a Standard Normal variable, with standard deviation 1.0, and multiply by a constant σ we get a new variable which has standard deviation σ. Figure 7.12 shows the Normal distribution with mean 0 and standard deviation 1 and the distribution obtained by multiplying by 2. The curves do not appear identical. For the distribution with standard deviation 2, nearly all the probability is between –6 and +6, a much wider interval than the –3 and +3 for the standard distribution.

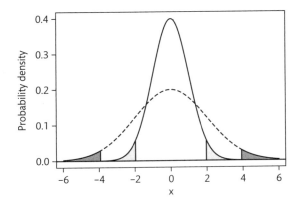

Figure 7.12 Normal distributions with different variances, showing two sided 5% points.

The values –6 and +6 are –3 and +3 standard deviations. We can see that the probability of being a given number of standard deviations from the mean is the same for both distributions. This is also seen from the 5% points, which represent the mean plus or minus 1.96 standard deviations in each case.

In fact, if we multiply a Standard Normal variable by σ and add μ, we get a Normal distribution of mean μ and standard deviation σ. Tables 7.1 and 7.2 apply to it directly, if we denote by z the number of standard deviations above the mean, rather than the numerical value of the variable. Thus, for example, the two sided 5% points of a Normal distribution with mean 10 and standard deviation 5 are found by $10 - 1.96 \times 5 = 0.2$ and $10 + 1.96 \times 5 = 19.8$, the value 1.96 being found from Table 7.2.

This property of the Normal distribution, that multiplying or adding constants still gives a Normal distribution, is not as obvious as it might seem. The Binomial does not have it, for example. Take a Binomial variable with $n = 3$, possible values 0, 1, 2, and 3, and multiply by 2. The possible values are now 0, 2, 4, and 6. The Binomial distribution with $n = 6$ has also possible values 1, 3, and 5, so the distributions are different and the one which we have derived is not a member of the Binomial family.

We have seen that adding a constant to a variable from a Normal distribution gives another variable which follows a Normal distribution. If we add two variables from Normal distributions together, even with different means and variances, the sum follows a Normal distribution. The difference between two variables from Normal distributions also follows a Normal distribution.

7.4 Variables which follow a Normal distribution

So far we have discussed the Normal distribution as it arises from sampling as the sum or limit of other distributions. However, many naturally occurring variables, such as human height, appear to follow a Normal distribution very closely. We might expect this to happen if the variable were the result of adding variation from a number of different sources. The process shown by the central limit theorem may well produce a result close to Normal. Figure 7.13 shows the distribution of height in a sample of pregnant women, and the corresponding Normal distribution curve. The fit to the Normal distribution is very good.

If the variable we measure is the result of multiplying several different sources of variation, we would not expect the result to be Normal from the properties discussed in Section 7.2, which were all based on addition of variables. However, if we take the log transformation of such a variable (Appendix 5A), we would then get a new variable which is the sum of several different sources of variation and which may well have a Normal distribution. This process often happens with quantities which are part

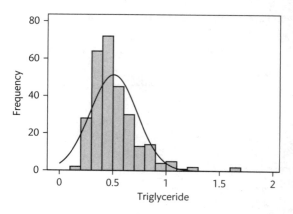

Figure 7.14 Distribution of serum triglyceride (Table 4.8) in cord blood for 282 babies, with corresponding Normal distribution curve.

of metabolic pathways, the rate at which the reaction can take place depending on the concentrations of other compounds. Many measurements of blood constituents exhibit this, for example. Figure 7.14 shows the distribution of serum triglyceride measured in cord blood for 282 babies (Table 4.8). The distribution is highly skewed and quite unlike the Normal distribution curve. However, when we take the logarithm of the triglyceride concentration, we have a remarkably good fit to the Normal distribution (Fig. 7.15). If the logarithm of a random variable follows a Normal distribution, the random variable itself follows a **Lognormal distribution**.

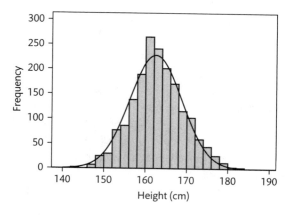

Figure 7.13 Distribution of height in a sample of 1794 pregnant women (data from Brooke *et al.* 1989).

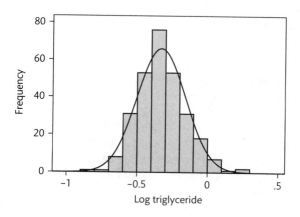

Figure 7.15 Distribution of $\log_{10}$ serum triglyceride in cord blood for 282 babies, with corresponding Normal distribution curve.

We often want to change the scale on which we analyse our data so as to get a Normal distribution. We call this process of analysing a mathematical function of the data rather than the data themselves **transformation**. The logarithm is the transformation most often used, the square root and reciprocal are others (see also Section 10.4). For a single sample, transformation enables us to use the Normal distribution to estimate centiles (Section 4.5). For example, we often want to estimate the 2.5th and 97.5th centiles, which together enclose 95% of the observations. For a Normal distribution, these can be estimated by $\bar{x} \pm 1.96s$. We can transform the data so that the distribution is Normal, calculate the centile, and then transform back to the original scale.

Consider the triglyceride data of Figure 7.14 and Table 4.8. The mean is 0.51 and the standard deviation 0.22. The mean for the $\log_{10}$ transformed data is −0.33 and the standard deviation is 0.17. What happens if we transform back by the antilog? For the mean, we get $10^{-0.33} = 0.47$. This is less than the mean for the raw data. The antilog of the mean log is not the same as the untransformed arithmetic mean. In fact, this the **geometric mean**, which is the nth root of the product of the observations. If we add the logs of the observations, we get the log of their product (Appendix 5A). If we multiply the log of a number by a second number, we get the log of the first raised to the power of the second. So if we divide the log by n, we get the log of the nth root. Thus the mean of the logs is the log of the geometric mean. On back transformation, the reciprocal transformation also yields a mean with a special name, the **harmonic mean**, the reciprocal of the mean of the reciprocals.

The geometric mean is in the original units. If triglyceride is measured in mmol/litre, the log of a single observation is the log of a measurement in mmol/litre. The sum of n logs is the log of the product of n measurements in mmol/litre and is the log of a measurement in mmol/litre to the nth. The nth root is thus again the log of a number in mmol/litre and the antilog is back in the original units, mmol/litre (see Appendix 5A).

The antilog of the standard deviation, however, is not measured in the original units. To calculate the standard deviation we take the difference between each log

observation and subtract the log geometric mean, using the usual formula $\sum(x_i - \bar{x})^2/(n - 1)$ (Section 4.8). Thus we have the difference between the log of two numbers each measured in mmol/litre, giving the log of their ratio (Appendix 5A) which is the log of a dimensionless pure number. It would be the same if the triglycerides were measured in mmol/litre or mg/100ml. We cannot transform the standard deviation back to the original scale.

If we want to use the standard deviation, it is easiest to do all calculations on the transformed scale and transform back, if necessary, at the end. For example, the 2.5th centile on the log scale is −0.33 − 1.96 × 0.17 = −0.6632 and the 97.5th centile is −0.33 + 1.96 × 0.17 = 0.0032. To get these we took the log of something in mmol/litre and added or subtracted the log of a pure number (i.e. multiplied on the natural scale), so we still have the log of something in mmol/litre. To get back to the original scale, we antilog to get 2.5th centile = 0.2188 and 97.5th centile = 1.0074 mmol/litre, which we can round to 0.22 and 1.01.

Transforming the data to a Normal distribution and then analysing on the transformed scale may look like cheating. I don't think it is. The scale on which we choose to measure things need not be linear, though this is often convenient. Other scales can be much more useful. We measure pH on a logarithmic scale, for example. Should the magnitude of an earthquake be measured in mm of amplitude (linear) or on the Richter scale (logarithmic)? Should spectacle lenses be measured in terms of focal length in cm (linear) or dioptres (reciprocal)? We often choose non-linear scales because they suit our purpose and for statistical analysis it often suits us to make the distribution Normal, by finding a scale of measurement where this is the case.

7.5 The Normal plot

Many statistical methods should be used only if the observations follow a Normal distribution (see Chapters 10 and 11). There are several ways of investigating whether observations follow a Normal distribution. With a large sample we can inspect a histogram to see whether it looks like a Normal distribution curve.

This does not work well with a small sample, and a more reliable method is the **Normal quantile plot**, usually shortened to **Normal plot**. This is a graphical method, which used to be done using ordinary graph paper and a table of the Normal distribution or with specially printed Normal probability paper, and now, much more easily, using a computer. Any good general statistical package will give Normal plots; if it doesn't then it isn't a good package. The Normal plot method can be used to investigate the Normal assumption in samples of any size, and is a very useful check when using methods such as the t distribution methods described in Chapter 10.

The Normal plot is a plot of the cumulative frequency distribution for the data against the cumulative frequency distribution for the Normal distribution. First, we order the data from lowest to highest. For each ordered observation we find the expected value of the observation if the data followed a Standard Normal distribution. There are several approximate formulae for this. I shall follow Armitage *et al.* (2002) and use for the *i*th observation z where $\Phi(z) = (i - 0.5)/n$. Some books and programs use $\Phi(z) = i/(n + 1)$ and there are other more complex formulae. It doesn't make much difference which is used. We find from a table of the Normal distribution the values of z which correspond to $\Phi(z) = 0.5/n$, $1.5/n$, etc. (Table 7.1 lacks detail for practical work, but will do for illustration.) For 5 points, for example, we have $\Phi(z) = 0.1$, 0.3, 0.5, 0.7, and 0.9, and z = −1.3, −0.5, 0, 0.5, and 1.3. These are the points of the Standard Normal distribution which correspond to the observed data. Now, if the observed data come from a Normal distribution of mean μ and variance σ^2, the observed point should equal $\sigma z + \mu$, where z is the corresponding point of the Standard Normal distribution. If we plot the Standard Normal points against the observed values, we should get something close to a straight line. We can write the equation of this line as $\sigma z + \mu = x$, where x is the observed variable and z the corresponding quantile of the Standard Normal distribution. We can rewrite this as

$$z = \frac{x}{\sigma} - \frac{\mu}{\sigma}$$

which goes through the point defined by $(\mu, 0)$ and has slope $1/\sigma$ (see Section 11.1). If the data are not from a Normal distribution we will not get a straight

Table 7.3 Vitamin D levels measured in the blood of 26 healthy men (data of Hickish *et al.* 1989)

14	20	22	25	26	27	31	32	42	46	52	54	67
17	21	24	26	26	30	31	35	43	48	54	63	83

line, but a curve of some sort. Because we plot the quantiles of the observed frequency distribution against the corresponding quantiles of the theoretical (here Normal) distribution, this is also referred to as a **quantile–quantile plot** or **q-q plot**.

Table 7.3 shows vitamin levels measured in the blood of 26 healthy men. The calculation of the Normal plot is shown in Table 7.4. Note that the $\Phi(z) = (i - 0.5)/26$ and z are symmetrical, the second half being the first half with opposite sign. The value of the Standard Normal deviate, z, can be found by interpolation in Table 7.1, by using a fuller table, or by computer. Figure 7.16 shows the histogram and the Normal plot for these data. The distribution is skew and the Normal plot shows a pronounced curve. Figure 7.16 also shows the vitamin D data after log transformation. It is quite easy to produce the Normal plot, as the corresponding Standard Normal deviate, z, is unchanged. We only need to log the observations and plot again. The Normal plot for the transformed data conforms very well to the theoretical line, suggesting that the distribution of log vitamin D level is close to the Normal.

A single bend in the Normal plot indicates skewness. A double curve indicates that both tails of the distribution are different from the Normal, usually being too long, and many curves may indicate that the distribution is bimodal (Figure 7.17). When the sample is small, of course, there will be some random fluctuations.

There are several different ways to display the Normal plot. Some programs plot the data distribution on the vertical axis and the theoretical Normal distribution on the horizontal axis, which reverses the direction of the curve. Some plot the theoretical Normal distribution with mean $\bar{x}$, the sample mean, and standard deviation s, the sample standard deviation. This is done by calculating $\bar{x} + sz$. Figure 7.18(a) shows both these features, the Normal plot drawn by the program Stata's 'qnorm' command. The straight line is the line of equality. This plot is identical to the second plot in Figure 7.16, except for the

Table 7.4 Calculation of the Normal plot for the vitamin D data (data from Hickish *et al.* 1989)

i	Vit D	Φ(z)	z	i	Vit D	Φ(z)	z
1	14	0.019	−2.07	14	31	0.519	0.05
2	17	0.058	−1.57	15	32	0.558	0.15
3	20	0.096	−1.30	16	35	0.596	0.24
4	21	0.135	−1.10	17	42	0.635	0.34
5	22	0.173	−0.94	18	43	0.673	0.45
6	24	0.212	−0.80	19	46	0.712	0.56
7	25	0.250	−0.67	20	48	0.750	0.67
8	26	0.288	−0.56	21	52	0.788	0.80
9	26	0.327	−0.45	22	54	0.827	0.94
10	26	0.365	−0.34	23	54	0.865	1.10
11	27	0.404	−0.24	24	63	0.904	1.30
12	30	0.442	−0.15	25	67	0.942	1.57
13	31	0.481	−0.05	26	83	0.981	2.07

$$\Phi(z) = (i - 0.5)/26$$

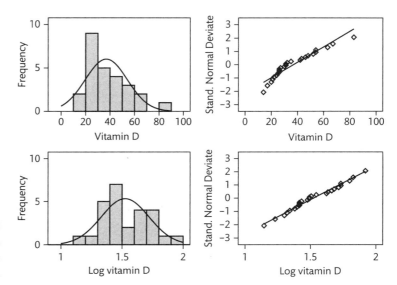

Figure 7.16 Blood vitamin D levels and log₁₀ vitamin D for 26 healthy men, with Normal plots (data from Hickish *et al.* 1989).

change of scale and switching of the axes. A slight variation is the **standardized Normal probability plot** or **p-p plot**, where we standardize the observations to zero mean and standard deviation one, $y = (x - \bar{x})/s$, and plot the cumulative Normal probabilities, $\Phi(y)$, against

$(i - 0.5)/n$ or $i/(n + 1)$ (Figure 7.18(b)), produced by the Stata command 'pnorm'). There is very little difference between Figures 7.18(a) and 7.18(b) and the quantile and probability versions of the Normal plot should be interpreted in the same way.

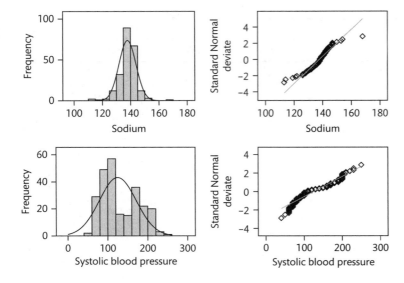

Figure 7.17 Blood sodium and systolic blood pressure measured in 250 patients in the Intensive Therapy Unit at St George's Hospital, with Normal plots (data from Friedland *et al.* 1996).

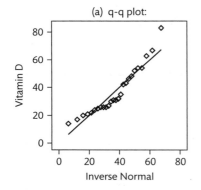

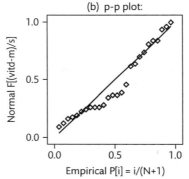

Figure 7.18 Variations on the Normal plot for the vitamin D data (data from Hickish *et al.* 1989).

7.6 Multiple choice questions: The Normal distribution

(Each branch is either true or false.)

7.1 The Normal distribution:
  (a) is also called the Gaussian distribution;
  (b) is followed by many variables;
  (c) is a family of distributions with two parameters;
  (d) is followed by all measurements made in healthy people;
  (e) is the distribution towards which the Poisson distribution tends as its mean increases.

7.2 The Standard Normal distribution:
  (a) is skew to the left;
  (b) has mean = 1.0;
  (c) has standard deviation = 0.0;
  (d) has variance = 1.0;
  (e) has the median equal to the mean.

7.3 The PEFRs of a group of 11-year-old girls follow a Normal distribution with mean 300 l/min and a standard deviation 20 l/min:
  (a) about 95% of the girls have PEFR between 260 and 340 l/min;
  (b) 50% of the girls have PEFR above 300 l/min;
  (c) the girls have healthy lungs;
  (d) about 5% of girls have PEFR below 260 l/min;
  (e) all the PEFRs must be less than 340 l/min.

7.4 The mean of a large sample:
  (a) is always greater than the median;
  (b) is calculated from the formula $\sum x_i/n$;

(c) is from an approximately Normal distribution;

(d) increases as the sample size increases;

(e) is always greater than the standard deviation.

7.5 If *X* and *Y* are independent variables which follow Standard Normal distributions, a Normal distribution is also followed by:

(a) $5X$;

(b) X^2;

(c) $X + 5$;

(d) $X - Y$;

(e) X/Y.

7.6 When a Normal plot is drawn with the Standard Normal deviate on the *y* axis:

(a) a straight line indicates that observations are from a Normal distribution;

(b) a curve with decreasing slope indicates positive skewness;

(c) an 'S' shaped curve (or ogive) indicates long tails;

(d) a vertical line will occur if all observations are equal;

(e) if there is a straight line, its slope depends on the standard deviation.

7.7 Exercise: Distribution of some measurements obtained by students

Table 7.5 shows blood glucose levels obtained from a group of medical students. Figure 7.19 shows a plot of these data.

Table 7.5 Random blood glucose levels from a group of first year medical students (mmol/litre)

2.2	3.3	3.6	3.7	3.8	4.0	4.2	4.4	4.7	4.9
2.9	3.4	3.6	3.7	3.9	4.1	4.3	4.5	4.7	5.0
3.3	3.4	3.6	3.8	4.0	4.1	4.4	4.6	4.8	5.1
3.3	3.4	3.6	3.8	4.0	4.1	4.4	4.7	4.9	6.0

7.1 What kind of graph is Figure 7.19?

7.2 From Figure 7.19, how closely do these data appear to follow a Normal distribution?

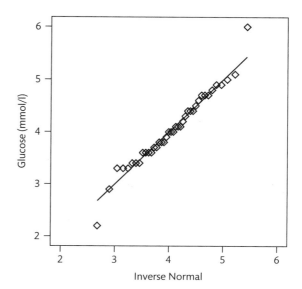

Figure 7.19 Plot of the random glucose measurements in Table 7.5.

7.3 Figure 7.20 shows a different plot of these data. What kind of graph is this? Does the interpretation differ from Figure 7.19?

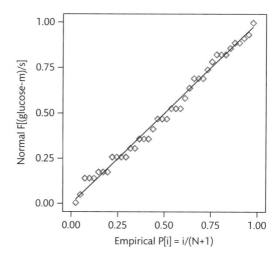

Figure 7.20 Alternative plot of the random glucose measurements in Table 7.5.

7.4 Figure 7.21 shows the self-reported heights of a convenience sample of students and their friends and family, collected as part of a course exercise. Figure 7.22 shows a

Normal plot. How would you describe the shape of this distribution?

7.5 Suggest a possible explanation for the unusual shape of the distribution shown in Figures 7.21 and 7.22.

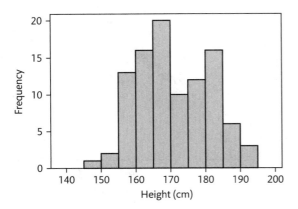

Figure 7.21 Histogram showing heights of 99 postgraduate students and their friends and family.

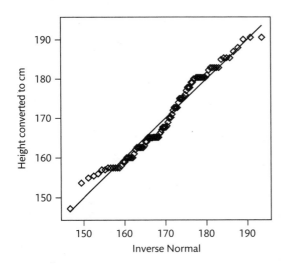

Figure 7.22 Normal plot showing heights of 99 postgraduate students and their friends and family.

7.6 Figure 7.23 shows the self-reported body mass index (BMI, weight/height squared) of female members of a convenience sample of students and their friends and family, collected as part of a course exercise. How would you describe the shape of this distribution?

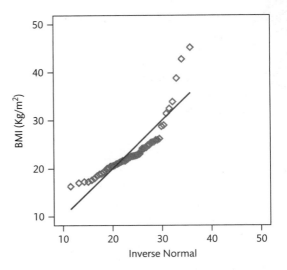

Figure 7.23 Normal plot showing body mass index (BMI) of 58 female postgraduate students and friends and family.

Appendix 7A: Chi-squared, t, and F

Less mathematically inclined readers can skip this section, but those who persevere should find that applications like chi-squared tests (Chapter 13) appear much more logical.

Many probability distributions can be derived for functions of Normal variables which arise in statistical analysis. Three of these are particularly important: the Chi-squared, t and F distributions. These have many applications, some of which we shall discuss in later chapters.

The Chi-squared distribution is defined as follows. Suppose Z is a Standard Normal variable, so having mean 0 and variance 1. Then the variable formed by Z^2 follows the Chi-squared distribution with 1 degree of freedom. If we have n such independent Standard Normal variables, $Z_1, Z_2, \ldots, Z_n$ then the variable defined by

$$\chi^2 = Z_1^2 + Z_2^2 + \cdots + Z_n^2$$

is defined to be the **Chi-squared distribution with n degrees of freedom**. χ is the Greek letter 'chi', pronounced 'ki' as in 'kite'. The distribution curves for several different numbers of degrees of freedom are shown in

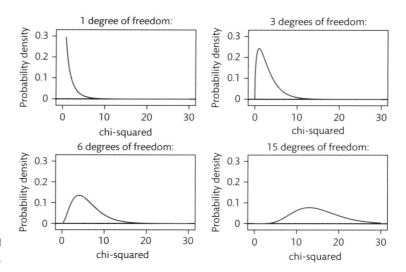

Figure 7.24 Some Chi-squared distributions.

Figure 7.24. The mathematical description of this curve is rather complicated, but we do not need to go into this.

Some properties of the Chi-squared distribution are easy to deduce. As the distribution is the sum of n independent identically distributed random variables it tends to the Normal as n increases, from the central limit theorem (Section 7.2). The convergence is slow, however, (Figure 7.24) and the square root of chi-squared converges much more quickly. The expected value of Z^2 is the variance of Z, the expected value of Z being 0, and so $E(Z^2) = 1$. The expected value of chi-squared with n degrees of freedom is thus n:

$$E(\chi^2) = E\left(\sum_{i=1}^{n} Z_i^2\right) = \sum_{i=1}^{n} E(Z_i^2) = \sum_{i=1}^{n} 1 = n$$

The variance is $VAR(\chi^2) = 2n$. The square root of χ^2 has mean approximately equal to $\sqrt{n - 0.5}$ and variance approximately 0.5.

The Chi-squared distribution has a very important property. Suppose we restrict our attention to a subset of possible outcomes for the n random variables $Z_1, Z_2, \ldots, Z_n$. The subset will be defined by those values of $Z_1, Z_2, \ldots, Z_n$ which satisfy the equation $a_1 Z_1 + a_2 Z_2 + \cdots + a_n Z_n = k$, where $a_1, a_2, \ldots, a_n$, and k are constants. (This is called a **linear constraint**.) Then under this restriction, $\chi^2 = \sum Z_i^2$ follows a Chi-squared distribution with $n - 1$ degrees of freedom. If there are m such constraints such that none of the

equations can be calculated from the others, then we have a Chi-squared distribution with $n - m$ degrees of freedom. This is the source of the name 'degrees of freedom'.

The proof of this is too complicated to give here, involving such mathematical abstractions as n dimensional spheres, but its implications are very important. First, consider the sum of squares about the population mean μ of a sample of size n from a Normal distribution, divided by σ^2. $\sum(x_i - \mu)^2/\sigma^2$ will follow a Chi-squared distribution with n degrees of freedom, as the $(x_i - \mu)/\sigma$ have mean 0 and variance 1 and they are independent. Now suppose we replace μ by an estimate calculated from the data, $\bar{x}$. The variables are no longer independent, they must satisfy the relationship $\sum(x_i - \bar{x}) = 0$ and we now have $n - 1$ degrees of freedom. Hence $\sum(x_i - \bar{x})^2/\sigma^2$ follows a Chi-squared distribution with $n - 1$ degrees of freedom. The sum of squares about the mean of any Normal sample with variance σ^2 follows the distribution of a Chi-squared variable multiplied by σ^2. It therefore has expected value $(n - 1)\sigma^2$ and we divide by $n - 1$ to give the estimate of σ^2.

Thus, provided the data are from a Normal distribution, not only does the sample mean follow a Normal distribution, but the sample variance is from a Chi-squared distribution times $\sigma^2/(n - 1)$. Because the square root of the Chi-squared distribution converges quite rapidly to the Normal, the distribution of the sample standard deviation is approximately Normal for

100 **Chapter 7** The Normal distribution

n > 20, provided the data themselves are from a Normal distribution. Another important property of the variances of Normal samples is that, if we take many random samples from the same population, the sample variance and sample mean are independent if, and only if, the data are from a Normal distribution.

Student's t distribution with n degrees of freedom is the distribution of $Z/\sqrt{\chi^2/n}$, where Z is a Standard Normal variable and χ^2 is independent of it and has n degrees of freedom. It is the distribution followed by the ratio of the mean to its standard error (Appendix 10A). The combined variance in the two sample t method (Section 10.3) is to give the single sum of squares on the bottom row of the t ratio, so it will have a Chi-squared distribution.

The F distribution with m and n degrees of freedom is the distribution of $(\chi_m^2/m)/(\chi_n^2/n)$, the ratio of two independent χ^2 variables each divided by its degrees of freedom. This distribution is used for comparing variances. If we have two independent estimates of the same variance calculated from Normal data, the variance ratio will follow the F distribution. We can use this for comparing two estimates of variance (Section 10.8), but its main uses are in comparing groups of means (Section 10.9) and in examining the effects of several factors together (Section 15.2).

8 Estimation

8.1 Sampling distributions

We saw in Chapter 3 how samples are drawn from much larger populations. Data are collected about the sample so that we can find out something about the population. We use samples to estimate quantities such as disease prevalence, mean blood pressure, mean exposure to a carcinogen, etc. We also want to know by how much these estimates might vary from sample to sample.

In Chapters 6 and 7 we saw how the theory of probability enables us to link random samples with the populations from which they are drawn. In this chapter we shall see how probability theory enables us to use samples to estimate quantities in populations, and to determine the precision of these estimates. First we shall consider what happens when we draw repeat samples from the same population. Table 8.1 shows a set of 100 random digits which we can use as the population for a sampling experiment. The distribution of the numbers in this population is shown in Figure 8.1. The population mean is 4.7 and the standard deviation is 2.9.

The sampling experiment is done using a suitable random sampling method to draw repeated samples from the population. In this case decimal dice were a convenient method. A sample of four observations was chosen: 6, 4, 6, and 1. The mean was calculated: 17/4 = 4.25. This

was repeated to draw a second sample of four numbers: 7, 8, 1, 8. Their mean is 6.00. This sampling procedure was done 20 times altogether, to give the samples and their means shown in Table 8.2.

These sample means are not all the same. They show random variation. If we were able to draw all of the 3 921 225 possible samples of size 4 and calculate their means, these means themselves would form a distribution. Our 20 sample means are a sample from this distribution. The distribution of all possible sample means is called the **sampling distribution** of the mean.

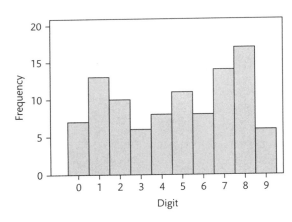

Figure 8.1 Distribution of the population of Table 8.1.

Table 8.1 Population of 100 random digits for a sampling experiment

9	1	0	7	5	6	9	5	8	8	1	0	5	7	6	5	0	2	1	2
1	8	8	8	5	2	4	8	3	1	6	5	5	7	4	1	7	3	3	3
2	8	1	8	5	8	4	0	1	9	2	1	6	9	4	4	7	6	1	7
1	9	7	9	7	2	7	7	0	8	1	6	3	8	0	5	7	4	8	6
7	0	2	8	8	7	2	5	4	1	8	6	8	3	5	8	2	7	2	4

Table 8.2 Random samples drawn in a sampling experiment

Sample	6	7	7	1	5	5	4	7	2	8
	4	8	9	8	2	5	2	4	8	1
	6	1	2	8	9	7	7	0	7	2
	1	8	7	4	5	8	6	1	7	0
Mean	4.25	6.00	6.25	5.25	5.25	6.25	4.75	3.00	6.00	2.75
Sample	7	7	2	8	3	4	5	4	4	7
	8	3	5	0	7	8	5	3	5	4
	7	8	0	7	4	7	8	1	8	6
	2	7	8	7	8	7	3	6	2	3
Mean	6.00	6.25	3.75	5.50	5.50	6.50	5.25	3.50	4.75	5.00

In general, the sampling distribution of any statistic is the distribution of the values of the statistic which would arise from all possible samples.

8.2 Standard error of a sample mean

For the moment we shall consider the sampling distribution of the mean only. As our sample of 20 means is a random sample from it, we can use this to estimate some of the parameters of the distribution. The 20 means have their own mean and standard deviation. The mean is 5.1 and the standard deviation is 1.1. Now the mean of the whole population is 4.7, which is close to the mean of the samples. But the standard deviation of the population is 2.9, which is considerably greater than that of the sample means. If we plot a histogram for the sample of means (Figure 8.2), we see that the centre of the sampling distribution and the parent population distribution are the same, but the scatter of the sampling distribution is much less.

Another sampling experiment, on a larger scale, will illustrate this further. This time our parent distribution will be the Normal distribution with mean 0 and standard deviation 1. Figure 8.3 shows the distribution of a random sample of 1000 observations from this distribution. Figure 8.3 also shows the distribution of means from 1000 random samples of size 4 from this population, the same sample size as in Figure 8.2. Figure 8.3

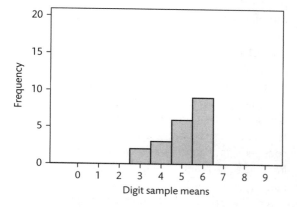

Figure 8.2 Distribution of the sample of the means of Table 8.2.

also shows the distributions of 1000 means of samples of size 9 and of size 16. In all four distributions the means are close to zero, the mean of the parent distribution. But the standard deviations are not the same. They are, in fact, approximately 1 (parent distribution); 1/2 (means of 4), 1/3 (means of 9), and 1/4 (means of 16). In fact, if the observations are independent of one another, the sampling distribution of the mean has standard deviation $\sigma/\sqrt{n}$ or $\sqrt{\sigma^2/n}$, where σ is the standard deviation of the parent distribution and n is the sample size (Appendix 8A). The mean of the sampling distribution is equal to the mean of the parent distribution. The actual, as opposed to simulated, distribution of the mean of four observations from a Normal distribution is shown in Figure 8.4.

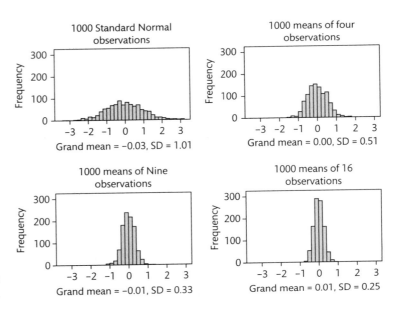

Figure 8.3 Samples of means from a Standard Normal variable.

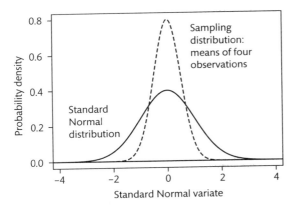

Figure 8.4 Sampling distribution of the mean of four observations from a Standard Normal distribution.

The sample mean is an estimate of the population mean. The standard deviation of its sampling distribution is called the **standard error** of the estimate. It provides a measure of how far from the true value the estimate is likely to be. In most estimation, the estimate is likely to be within one standard error of the true mean and unlikely to be more than two standard errors from it. We shall look at this more precisely in Section 8.3.

In almost all practical situations we do not know the true value of the population variance σ^2 but only its estimate s^2 (Section 4.7). We can use this to estimate the standard error by $s/\sqrt{n}$. This estimate is also referred to

as the standard error of the mean. It is usually clear from the context whether the standard error is the true value or that estimated from the data.

When the sample size n is large, the sampling distribution of the sample mean, $\bar{x}$, tends to a Normal distribution (Section 7.3). Also, we can assume that s^2 is a good estimate of σ^2. So for large n, $\bar{x}$ is, in effect, an observation from a Normal distribution with mean μ and standard deviation estimated by $s/\sqrt{n}$. So with probability 0.95 or for 95% of possible samples, $\bar{x}$ is within 1.96 standard errors of μ. With small samples we cannot assume either a Normal distribution or, more importantly, that s^2 is a good estimate of σ^2. We shall discuss this in Chapter 10.

For an example, consider the 57 FEV1 measurements of Table 4.4. We have $\bar{x} = 4.062$ litres, $s^2 = 0.449\,174$, $s = 0.67$ litres. Then the standard error of $\bar{x}$ is $\sqrt{s^2/n} = \sqrt{0.449\,174/57} = \sqrt{0.007\,880} = 0.089$. The best estimate of the mean FEV1 in the population is then 4.06 litres with standard error 0.089 litres.

The mean and standard error are often written as 4.062 ± 0.089. This is rather misleading, as the true value may be up to two standard errors from the mean with a reasonable probability. This practice is not recommended.

There is often confusion between the terms 'standard error' and 'standard deviation'. This is understandable, as the standard error is a standard deviation (of the sampling distribution) and the terms are often interchanged in this context. The convention is this: we use the term 'standard error' when we measure the precision of estimates, and the term 'standard deviation' when we are concerned with the variability of samples, populations, or distributions. If we want to say how good our estimate of the mean FEV1 measurement is, we quote the standard error of the mean. If we want to say how widely scattered the FEV1 measurements are, we quote the standard deviation, s.

8.3 Confidence intervals

The estimate of mean FEV1 is a single value and so is called a **point estimate.** There is no reason to suppose that the population mean will be exactly equal to the point estimate, the sample mean. It is likely to be close to it, however, and the amount by which it is likely to differ from the estimate can be found from the standard error. What we do is find limits which are likely to include the population mean, and say that we estimate the population mean to lie somewhere in the interval (the set of all possible values) between these limits. This is called an **interval estimate**.

For instance, if we regard the 57 FEV measurements as being a large sample we can assume that the sampling distribution of the mean is Normal, and that the standard error is a good estimate of its standard deviation (see Section 10.6 for a discussion of how large is large). We therefore expect about 95% of such means to be within 1.96 standard errors of the population mean, μ. Hence, for about 95% of all possible samples, the population mean must be greater than the sample mean minus 1.96 standard errors and less than the sample mean plus 1.96 standard errors. If we calculated $\bar{x} - 1.96se$ and $\bar{x} + 1.96se$ for all possible samples, 95% of such intervals would contain the population mean. In this case these limits are 4.062 − 1.96 × 0.089 to 4.062 + 1.96 × 0.089 which gives 3.89 to 4.24, or 3.9 to 4.2 litres, rounding to two significant figures. 3.9 and 4.2 are called the **95% confidence limits** for the estimate, and the set of values between 3.9 and 4.2 is called the **95% confidence interval**. The confidence limits are the values at the ends of the confidence interval.

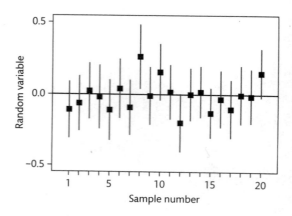

Figure 8.5 Mean and 95% confidence interval for 20 random samples of 100 observations from the Standard Normal distribution.

Strictly speaking, it is incorrect to say that there is a probability of 0.95 that the population mean lies between 3.9 and 4.2, though it is often put that way (even by me, though I try to avoid this). The population mean is a number, not a random variable, and has no probability. (This is the Frequency School view of probability, see Chapter 22 for a different, Bayesian view.) It is the probability that limits calculated from a random sample will include the population value which is 95%. Figure 8.5 shows confidence intervals for the mean for 20 random samples of 100 observations from the Standard Normal distribution. The population mean is, of course, 0.0, shown by the horizontal line. Some sample means are close to 0.0, some further away, some above, and some below. The population mean is contained by 19 of the 20 confidence intervals. In general, for 95% of confidence intervals it will be true to say that the population value lies within the interval. We just don't know which 95%. This is sometimes expressed by saying that we are 95% confident that the mean lies between these limits.

In the FEV1 example, the sampling distribution of the mean is Normal and its standard deviation is well estimated because the sample is large. This is not always true and although it is usually possible to calculate confidence intervals for an estimate, they are not all quite as simple as that for the mean estimated from a large sample. We shall look at the mean estimated from a small sample in Section 10.2.

There is no necessity for the confidence interval to have a probability of 95%. For example, we can also calculate 99% confidence limits. The upper 0.5% point of the Standard Normal distribution is 2.58 (Table 7.2), so the probability of a Standard Normal deviate being above 2.58 or below −2.58 is 1% and the probability of being within these limits is 99%. The 99% confidence limits for the mean FEV1 are therefore, 4.062 − 2.58 × 0.089 and 4.062 + 2.58 × 0.089, i.e. 3.8 and 4.3 litres. These give a wider interval than the 95% limits, as we would expect as we are more confident that the population mean will be included. The probability we choose for a confidence interval is a compromise between the desire to include the estimated population value and the desire to avoid parts of scale where there is a low probability that the mean will be found. For most purposes, 95% confidence intervals have been found to be satisfactory.

Standard error is not the only way in which we can calculate confidence intervals, although at present it is the one used for most problems. Others are described in Section 8.9, Section 8.10, and Section 8.11. There are others, which I shall omit because they are rarely used.

8.4 Standard error and confidence interval for a proportion

The standard error of a proportion estimate can be calculated in the same way. Suppose the proportion of individuals who have a particular condition in a given population is p, and we take a random sample of size n, the number observed with the condition being r. Then the estimated proportion is r/n. We have seen (Section 6.4) that r comes from a Binomial distribution with mean np and variance $np(1 - p)$. Provided n is large, this distribution is approximately Normal. So r/n, the estimated proportion, is from a Normal distribution with mean given by $np/n = p$, and variance given by

$$\text{VAR}\left(\frac{r}{n}\right) = \frac{1}{n^2}\text{VAR}(r)$$

$$= \frac{1}{n^2}np(1 - p)$$

$$= \frac{p(1 - p)}{n}$$

as n is constant, and the standard error is

$$\sqrt{\frac{p(1 - p)}{n}}$$

We can estimate this by replacing p by r/n. As for the sample mean, this standard error is only valid if the observations are independent of one another. For example, in a random sample of first year secondary schoolchildren in Derbyshire (Banks et al. 1978), 118 out of 2 837 boys said that they usually coughed first thing in the morning. This gave a prevalence estimate of 118/2 837 = 0.041 6, with standard error $\sqrt{0.041\,6 \times (1 - 0.041\,6)/2\,837}$ = 0.003 7. The sample is large so we can assume that the estimate is from a Normal distribution and that the standard error is well estimated. The 95% confidence interval for the prevalence is thus 0.041 6 − 1.96 × 0.003 7 to 0.041 6 + 1.96 × 0.003 7 = 0.034 to 0.049. Even with this fairly large sample, the estimate is not very precise. This confidence interval, using the standard error, is called the **Wald interval**.

The standard error of the proportion is only of use if the sample is large enough for the Normal approximation to apply. A rough guide to this is that np and $n(1 - p)$ should both exceed 5. This is usually the case when we are concerned with straightforward estimation. If we try to use the method for smaller samples, we may get absurd results. For example, in a study of the prevalence of HIV in ex-prisoners (Turnbull et al. 1992), of 29 women who did not inject drugs, one was HIV positive. The authors reported this to be 3.4%, with a 95% confidence interval −3.1% to 9.9%. The lower limit of −3.1%, obtained from the observed proportion minus 1.96 standard errors, is impossible. As Newcombe (1992) pointed out, the correct 95% confidence interval can be obtained from the exact probabilities of the Binomial distribution and is 0.1% to 17.8% (Section 8.9).

8.5 The difference between two means

In many studies we are more interested in the difference between two population parameters than in their absolute value. These could be means, proportions, the slopes of lines, and many other statistics. When samples are large we can assume that sample means and proportions are observations from a Normal distribution, and that the calculated standard errors are good estimates of the standard deviations of these Normal distributions. We can use this to find confidence intervals.

For example, suppose we wish to compare the means, $\bar{x}_1$ and $\bar{x}_2$, of two independent large samples, sizes n_1 and n_2. The expected difference between the sample means is equal to the difference between the population means, i.e. $E(\bar{x}_1 - \bar{x}_2) = \mu_1 - \mu_2$. What is the standard error of the difference? The variance of the difference between two independent random variables is the sum of their variances (Section 6.6). Hence, the standard error of the difference between two independent estimates is the square root of the sum of the squares of their standard errors. The standard error of a mean is $\sqrt{s^2/n}$, so the standard error of the difference between two independent means is

$$\sqrt{\frac{s_1^2}{n_1} + \frac{s_2^2}{n_2}}$$

For an example, in a study of respiratory symptoms in schoolchildren (Bland *et al.* 1974), we wanted to know whether children reported by their parents to have respiratory symptoms had worse lung function than children who were not reported to have symptoms. Ninety-two children were reported to have cough during the day or at night, and their mean PEFR was 294.8 litre/min with standard deviation 57.1 litre/min, and 1643 children were not reported to have this symptom, their mean PEFR being 313.6 litre/min with standard deviation 55.2 litre/min. We thus have two large samples, and can apply the Normal distribution. We have

$$n_1 = 92, \quad \bar{x}_1 = 294.8, \quad s_1 = 57.1,$$
$$n_2 = 1643, \quad \bar{x}_2 = 313.6, \quad s_2 = 55.2$$

The difference between the two group means is $\bar{x}_1 - \bar{x}_2 = 294.8 - 313.6 = -18.8$. The standard error of the difference is

$$\sqrt{se_1^2 + se_2^2} = \sqrt{\frac{s_1^2}{n_1} + \frac{s_2^2}{n_2}}$$
$$= \sqrt{\frac{57.1^2}{92} + \frac{55.2^2}{1643}}$$
$$= 6.11$$

We shall treat the sample as being large, so the difference between the means can be assumed to come from a Normal distribution and the estimated standard error to be a good estimate of the standard deviation of this distribution. (For small samples see Section 10.3 and Section 10.6) The 95% confidence limits for the difference are thus $-18.8 - 1.96 \times 6.11$ and $-18.8 + 1.96 \times 6.11$, i.e. -6.8 and -30.8 l/min. The confidence interval does not include zero, so we have good evidence that, in this population, children reported to have day or night cough have lower mean PEFR than others. The difference is estimated to be between 7 and 31 litre/min lower in children with the symptom, so it may be quite small.

When we have paired data, such as a cross-over trial (Section 2.7) or a matched case–control study (Section 3.8), the two-sample method does not work. Instead, we calculate the differences between the paired observations for each subject, then find the mean difference, its standard error, and confidence interval as in Section 8.3.

8.6 Comparison of two proportions

We can apply the method of Section 8.5 to two proportions. The standard error of a proportion p is $\sqrt{p(1-p)/n}$. For two independent proportions, p_1 and p_2, the standard error of the difference between them is

$$\sqrt{\frac{p_1(1-p_1)}{n_1} + \frac{p_2(1-p_2)}{n_2}}$$

Provided the conditions of Normal approximation are met (see Section 8.4), we can find a confidence interval for the difference in the usual way.

For example, consider Table 8.3. The researchers wanted to know to what extent children with bronchitis in infancy get more respiratory symptoms in later life than others. We can estimate the difference between the proportions reported to cough during the day or at night among children with and children without a history of bronchitis before age 5 years. We have estimates of two proportions, $p_1 = 26/273 = 0.095\,24$ and $p_2 = 44/1\,046 = 0.042\,07$. The difference between them

Table 8.3 Cough during the day or at night at age 14 and bronchitis before age 5 (data from Holland *et al.* 1978)

Cough at 14	Bronchitis at 5		
	Yes	**No**	**Total**
Yes	26	44	70
No	247	1 002	1 249
Total	273	1 046	1 319

is $p_1 - p_2 = 0.095\,24 - 0.042\,07 = 0.053\,17$. The standard error of the difference is

$$\sqrt{\frac{p_1(1-p_1)}{n_1} + \frac{p_2(1-p_2)}{n_2}}$$

$$= \sqrt{\frac{0.095\,24 \times (1 - 0.095\,24)}{273} + \frac{0.042\,07 \times (1 - 0.042\,07)}{1\,046}}$$

$$= \sqrt{0.000\,315\,639 + 0.000\,038\,528}$$

$$= \sqrt{0.000\,354\,167}$$

$$= 0.018\,8$$

The 95% confidence interval for the difference is $0.053\,17 - 1.96 \times 0.018\,8$ to $0.053\,17 + 1.96 \times 0.018\,8 = 0.016$ to 0.090. Although the difference is not very precisely estimated, the confidence interval does not include zero and gives us clear evidence that children with bronchitis reported in infancy are more likely than others to be reported to have respiratory symptoms in later life. The data on lung function in Section 8.5 gives us some reason to suppose that this is not entirely a result of response bias (Section 3.9). As in Section 8.4, the confidence interval must be estimated differently for small samples.

This difference in proportions may not be very easy to interpret. The ratio of two proportions is often more useful. Another method, the odds ratio, is described in Section 13.7. The ratio of the proportion with cough at age 14 for bronchitis before 5 to the proportion with cough at age 14 for those without bronchitis before 5 is $p_1/p_2 = 0.09524/0.04207 = 2.26$. Children with bronchitis before 5 are more than twice as likely to cough

during the day or at night at age 14 than children with no such history.

The standard error for this ratio is complex, and as it is a ratio rather than a difference it does not approximate well to a Normal distribution. If we take the logarithm of the ratio, however, we get the difference between two logarithms, because $\log(p_1/p_2) = \log(p_1) - \log(p_2)$ (Appendix 5A). We can find the standard error for the log ratio quite easily. We use the result that, for any random variable X with mean μ and variance σ^2, the approximate variance of $\log(X)$ is given by VAR $(log_e(X)) = \sigma^2/\mu^2$ (see Kendall and Stuart 1969). Hence, the variance of $\log(p)$ is

$$\mathrm{VAR}\,(\log(p)) = \frac{p(1-p)/n}{p^2} = \frac{1-p}{np}$$

For the difference between the two logarithms we get

$$\mathrm{VAR}(log_e(p_1/p_2)) = \mathrm{VAR}(log_e(p_1))$$

$$+\mathrm{VAR}(log_e(p_2))$$

$$= \frac{1-p_1}{n_1 p_1} + \frac{1-p_2}{n_2 p_2}$$

The standard error is the square root of this. (This formula is often written in terms of frequencies, but I think this version is clearer.) For the example the log ratio is $log_e(2.263\,85) = 0.817\,07$ and the standard error is

$$\sqrt{\frac{1-p_1}{n_1 p_1} + \frac{1-p_2}{n_2 p_2}}$$

$$= \sqrt{\frac{1 - 0.095\,24}{273 \times 0.095\,24} + \frac{1 - 0.042\,07}{1\,046 \times 0.042\,07}}$$

$$= \sqrt{\frac{0.904\,76}{26} + \frac{0.957\,93}{44}}$$

$$= \sqrt{0.056\,57}$$

$$= 0.237\,84$$

The 95% confidence interval for the log ratio is therefore $0.817\,07 - 1.96 \times 0.237\,84$ to $0.817\,07 + 1.96 \times 0.237\,84 = 0.350\,89$ to $1.283\,24$. The 95% confidence interval for the ratio of proportions itself is the antilog of this: $e^{0.35089}$ to $e^{1.28324} = 1.42$ to 3.61. Thus we estimate that the proportion of children reported to cough during the day or at night among those with a history of bronchitis is between 1.4 and 3.6 times the proportion among those without a history of bronchitis.

The proportion of individuals in a population who develop a disease or symptom is equal to the probability that any given individual will develop the disease, called the **risk** of an individual developing a disease. Thus in Table 8.3 the risk that a child with bronchitis before age 5 will cough at age 14 is 26/273 = 0.09524, and the risk for a child without bronchitis before age 5 is 44/1046 = 0.04207. To compare risks for people with and without a particular risk factor, we look at the ratio of the risk with the factor to the risk without the factor, the **relative risk**. The relative risk of cough at age 14 for bronchitis before 5 is thus 2.26. To estimate the relative risk directly, we need a cohort study (Section 3.7) as in Table 8.3. We estimate relative risk for a case–control study in a different way (Section 13.7).

In the unusual situation when the samples are paired, either matched or two observations on the same subject, we use a different method (Section 13.9).

8.7 Number needed to treat

When a clinical trial has a dichotomous outcome measure, such as survival or death, there are several ways in which we can express the difference between the two treatments. These include the difference between proportions of successes, ratio of proportions (risk ratio or relative risk), and the odds ratio. The **number needed to treat (NNT)** is the number of patients we would need to treat with the new treatment to achieve one more success than we would on the old treatment (Laupacis et al. 1988). It is the reciprocal of the difference between the proportion of success on the new treatment and the proportion on the old treatment. For example, in the MRC streptomycin trial (Table 2.10) the survival rates after 6 months were 93% in the streptomycin group and 73% in the control group. The difference in proportions surviving was thus 0.93 – 0.73 = 0.20 and the number needed to treat to prevent one death over 6 months was 1/0.20 = 5. The smaller the NNT, the more effective the treatment will be.

The smallest possible value for NNT is 1.0, when the proportions successful are 1.0 and 0.0. This would mean that the new treatment was always effective and the old treatment was never effective. The NNT cannot be zero.

If the treatment has no effect at all, the NNT will be infinite, because the difference in the proportion of successes will be zero. If the treatment is harmful, so that success rate is less than on the control treatment, the NNT will be negative. The number is then called the **number needed to harm (NNH)**. The NNT idea caught on very quickly and has been widely used and developed, for example as the number needed to screen (Rembold 1998).

The NNT is an estimate and should have a confidence interval. This is apparently quite straightforward. We find the confidence interval for the difference in the proportions, then the reciprocals of these limits are the confidence limits for the NNT. For the MRC streptomycin trial the 95% confidence interval for the difference is 0.0578 to 0.3352, reciprocals 17.3 and 3.0. Thus the 95% confidence interval for the NNT is 3 to 17.

This is deceptively simple. As Altman (1998) pointed out, there are problems when the difference is not significant. The confidence interval for the difference between proportions includes zero, so infinity is a possible value for NNT, and negative values are also possible, i.e. the treatment may harm. The confidence interval must allow for this.

For example, Henzi et al. (2000) calculated NNT for several studies, including that of Lopez-Olaondo et al. (1996). This study compared dexamethasone against placebo to prevent postoperative nausea and vomiting. They observed nausea in 5/25 patients on dexamethasone and 10/25 on placebo. Thus the difference in proportions without nausea (success) is 0.80 – 0.60 = 0.20, 95% confidence interval –0.0479 to 0.4479 (Section 8.6). The number needed to treat is the reciprocal of this difference, 1/0.20 = 5.0. The reciprocals of the confidence limits are 1/(–0.0479) = –20.9 and 1/0.4479 = 2.2. But the confidence interval for the NNT is not –20.9 to 2.2. Zero, which this includes, is not a possible value for the NNT. As there may be no treatment difference at all, zero difference between proportions, the NNT may be infinite. In fact, the confidence interval for NNT is not the values between –20.9 and 2.2, but the values *outside* this interval, i.e. 2.2 to infinity (number needed to achieve an extra success, NNT) and minus infinity to –20.9 (number needed to achieve an extra failure, NNH). Thus the NNT is estimated to be anything

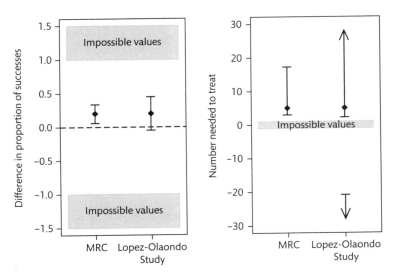

Figure 8.6 Confidence intervals for difference in proportion of successes and for number needed to treat for the data of MRC (1948) and Lopez-Olaondo et al. (1996).

greater than 2.2, and the NNH to be anything greater than 20.9. The confidence interval is in two parts, $-\infty$ to -20.9 and 2.2 to ∞. ('∞' is the symbol for infinity.) Henzi et al. (2000) quote this confidence interval as 2.2 to -21, which they say the reader should interpret as including infinity. Altman (1998) recommends 'NNTH = 21.9 to ∞ to NNTB 2.2', where NNTH means 'number needed to harm' and NNTB means 'number needed to benefit'. I prefer '$-\infty$ to -20.9, 2.2 to ∞'. Here $-\infty$ and ∞ each tell us that we do not have enough information to guide us as to which treatment should be used. The confidence intervals for the MRC and the Lopez-Olaondo trials are shown graphically in Figure 8.6.

Two-part confidence intervals are not exactly intuitive and I think that the problems of interpretation of NNT in trials which do not provide unequivocal evidence limit its value to being a supplementary description of trial results.

8.8 Standard error of a sample standard deviation

We can find a standard error and confidence interval for almost any estimate we make from a sample, but sometimes this depends on the distribution of the observations themselves. The sample standard deviation, s, is one such statistic. Provided the observations are independent and come from a Normal distribution, $(n-1)s^2/\sigma^2$ is from a Chi-squared distribution with $n-1$

degrees of freedom (Appendix 7A). The square root of this Chi-squared distribution is approximately Normal with variance 1/2 if n is large enough, so $\sqrt{(n-1)s^2/\sigma^2}$ has an approximately Normal distribution with variance 1/2. Hence s has an approximately Normal distribution with variance $\sigma^2/2(n-1)$. The standard error of s is thus $\sqrt{\sigma^2/2(n-1)}$, estimated by $s/\sqrt{2(n-1)}$. This is only true when the observations themselves are from a Normal distribution.

8.9 Confidence interval for a proportion when numbers are small

In Section 8.4 I mentioned that the standard error method for a proportion does not work when the sample is small. Instead, the confidence interval can be found using the exact probabilities of the Binomial distribution, the **Clopper Pearson method**. The method works like this. Given n, we find the value p_L for the parameter p of the Binomial distribution which gives a probability 0.025 of getting an observed number of successes, r, as big as or bigger than the value observed. We do this by calculating the probabilities from the formula in Section 6.4, iterating round different possible values of p until we get the right one. We also find the value p_U for the parameter p of the Binomial distribution which gives a probability 0.025 of getting an observed number

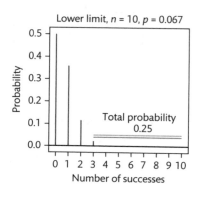

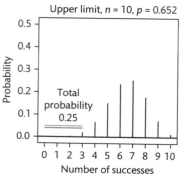

Figure 8.7 Distributions showing the calculation of the exact confidence interval for three successes out of ten trials.

of successes as small as or smaller than the value observed. The exact 95% confidence interval is p_L to p_U. For example, suppose we observe three successes out of 10 trials. The Binomial distribution with $n = 10$ which has the total probability for three or more successes equal to 0.025 has parameter $p = 0.067$. The distribution which has the total probability for three or fewer successes equal to 0.025 has $p = 0.652$. Hence the 95% confidence interval for the proportion in the population is 0.067 to 0.652. Figure 8.7 shows the two distributions. No large sample approximation is required and we can use this for any size of sample.

Unless the observed proportion is zero or one, these values are never included in the exact confidence interval. The population proportion of successes cannot be zero if we have observed a success in the sample. It cannot be one if we have observed a failure.

Although this interval is called 'exact', it can produce intervals which are too wide, in that more than 95% of possible samples give intervals which include the population proportion. Other methods have been developed, such as the Wilson interval, which give a proportion of intervals including the population proportion which is closer to 95% (see Brown *et al.* 2001, 2002).

8.10　Confidence interval for a median and other quantiles

In Section 4.5 we estimated medians and other quantiles directly from the frequency distribution. We can estimate confidence intervals for these using the Binomial distribution. This is a large sample method. The 95% confidence interval for the q quantile can be found by an application of the Binomial distribution (Section 6.4, Section 6.6) (see Conover 1980). The number of observations less than the q quantile will be an observation from a Binomial distribution with parameters n and q, and hence has mean nq and standard deviation $\sqrt{nq(1-q)}$. We calculate j and k such that:

$$j = nq - 1.96\sqrt{nq(1-q)}$$

$$k = nq + 1.96\sqrt{nq(1-q)}$$

We round j and k up to the next integer. Then the 95% confidence interval is between the jth and the kth observations in the ordered data. For the 57 FEV measurements of Table 4.4, the median was 4.1 litres (Section 4.5). For the 95% confidence interval for the median, $n = 57$ and $q = 0.5$, and

$$j = 57 \times 0.5 - 1.96\sqrt{57 \times 0.5 \times (1 - 0.5)} = 21.10$$

$$k = 57 \times 0.5 + 1.96\sqrt{57 \times 0.5 \times (1 - 0.5)} = 35.90$$

The 95% confidence interval is thus from the 22nd to the 36th observation, 3.75 to 4.30 litres from Table 4.4. Compare this to the 95% confidence interval for the mean, 3.9 to 4.2 litres, which is completely included in the interval for the median. This method of estimating percentiles is relatively imprecise. Another example is given in Section 20.7.

8.11 Bootstrap or resampling methods

Bootstrap or resampling methods (Efron and Tibshirani 1993) are an alternative way to find standard errors and confidence intervals. They takes their name, I think, from the expression 'raised up by your own bootstraps'. We use the sample itself, without any external structure of probability distributions. The idea is that the sample is a random sample of the population it represents, whatever that is, and that is the population about which we can draw conclusions. So if we draw an observation at random from our sample, it is also a random observation from the original population. All members of that population had an equal chance of being chosen. Now we record this observation, we put it back, and we draw another observation at random from our sample. It might be the same as the first one, but that doesn't matter. We record that, put it back, and draw another, and so on until we have a new sample of the same size as the first. It will contain some of the original observations, some of them repeated. That doesn't matter, the proportion of repetitions of each possible value is expected to be the same as its density in the original population. This procedure is called **resampling**.

For an example, consider Table 8.3. This comes from a sample of 1 319 children, for each of whom we have whether they had bronchitis before age 5 and cough during the day or at night reported at age 14. Using resampling, we can draw another sample of 1 319 observations. The corresponding table is shown in Table 8.4. For Table 8.3 we found the difference in the proportions with cough, the risk difference, to be 0.053 17 with

standard error 0.018 82 and 95% confidence interval calculated from these 0.016 to 0.090. For Table 8.4, the risk difference is 0.073 38 with standard error = 0.019 49 and 95% confidence interval 0.035 to 0.112.

Now instead of resampling once, we can do it many times. I chose 1 000 resamplings. Each one produced a different estimate of the risk difference. These 1 000 estimates have a distribution, shown in Figure 8.8. The mean and standard deviation of this distribution are 0.053 17 and 0.019 38. This standard deviation provides an alternative estimate of the standard error of the difference between the risks, which does not make use of any theory about the Binomial distribution. These are the bootstrap estimates. We can use them to find a confidence interval, on the assumption that the resampling distribution is Normal, which appears to be a reasonable approximation from Figure 8.8. The 95% CI will be 0.053 17 – 1.96 × 0.019 38 to 0.053 17 + 1.96 × 0.019 38 = 0.015 to 0.091. This is very similar to the 0.016 to 0.090 found using the variance formula of the Binomial distribution.

We can also use the resampling distribution directly. The 95% CI will be from the 2.5th centile to the 97.5th centile. The 2.5th centile will be between the 25th and 26th of the 1 000 observations, which are 0.015 85 and 0.016 30, and the average of these is 0.016 08. The 97.5th centile will be between observations 975 and 976, which are 0.093 23 and 0.093 78, giving us 0.093 51. Hence the bootstrap confidence interval is 0.016 to 0.094. The corresponding point estimate is the median of this distribution, 0.053.

Table 8.4 Cough during the day or at night at age 14 by bronchitis before age 5, after resampling the data of Table 8.3 (data from Holland *et al.* 1978)

Cough at 14	Bronchitis at 5		
	Yes	**No**	**Total**
Yes	34	42	76
No	263	980	1 243
Total	297	1 022	1 319

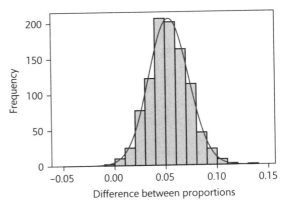

Figure 8.8 Histogram of 1 000 resampling estimates of the risk difference from Table 8.3 (data from Holland *et al.* 1978).

The two bootstrap estimates are very similar to one another and to the original and there seems little point in doing such a complicated procedure. Sometimes the bootstrap approach can be very useful, when the data do not meet the requirements of any straightforward conventional approach. We can get a bootstrap estimate for anything we can calculate from any sample. Bootstrap methods are particularly favoured by health economists, who often have cost data which have a few very extreme values, which conventional approaches might not accommodate well. This section gives the general idea of the bootstrap; there are many developments and variations. Methods which sample the possibilities in this way are (rather endearingly) called **Monte Carlo** methods.

8.12 What is the correct confidence interval?

A confidence interval only estimates errors caused by sampling. They do not allow for any bias in the sample and give us an estimate for the population of which our data can be considered a random sample. As discussed in Section 3.5, it is often not clear what this population is, and we rely far more on the estimation of differences than absolute values. This is particularly true in clinical trials. We start with patients in one locality, exclude some, allow refusals, and the patients cannot be regarded as a random sample of patients in general. However, we then randomize into two groups which are then two samples from the same population, and only the treatment differs between them. Thus the difference is the thing we want the confidence interval for, not for either group separately. Yet researchers often ignore the direct comparison in favour of estimation using each group separately.

For example, Salvesen *et al.* (1992) reported follow-up of two randomized controlled trials of routine ultrasonography screening during pregnancy. At ages 8 to 9 years, children of women who had taken part in these trials were followed up. A subgroup of children underwent specific tests for dyslexia. The test results classified 21 of the 309 screened children (7%, 95% confidence interval 3–10%) and 26 of the 294 controls (9%, 95% confidence interval 4–12%) as dyslexic. Much more useful would be a confidence interval for the difference between prevalences (−6.3 to 2.2 percentage points) or their ratio (0.44 to 1.34), because we could then compare the groups directly. See Bland and Altman (2011) for a fuller discussion.

8.13 Multiple choice questions: Confidence intervals

(Each branch is either true or false.)

8.1 The standard error of the mean of a sample:
  (a) measures the variability of the observations;
  (b) is the accuracy with which each observation is measured;
  (c) is a measure of how far a mean from a sample of this size is likely to be from the population mean;
  (d) is proportional to the number of observations;
  (e) is greater than the estimated standard deviation of the population.

8.2 95% confidence limits for the mean estimated from a set of observations:
  (a) are limits between which, in the long run, 95% of observations fall;
  (b) are a way of measuring the precision of the estimate of the mean;
  (c) are limits within which the sample mean falls with probability 0.95;
  (d) are limits calculated so as to include the population mean for 95% of possible samples;
  (e) are a way of measuring the variability of a set of observations.

8.3 If the size of a random sample were increased, we would expect:
  (a) the mean to decrease;
  (b) the standard error of the mean to decrease;
  (c) the standard deviation to decrease;
  (d) the sample variance to increase;
  (e) the degrees of freedom for the estimated variance to increase.

8.4 The prevalence of a condition in a population is 0.1. If the prevalence were estimated repeatedly from samples of size 100, these estimates would form a distribution which:

(a) is a sampling distribution;

(b) is approximately Normal;

(c) has mean = 0.1;

(d) has variance = 9;

(e) is Binomial.

8.5 It is necessary to estimate the mean FEV1 by drawing a sample from a large population. The accuracy of the estimate will depend on:

(a) the mean FEV1 in the population;

(b) the number in the population;

(c) the number in the sample;

(d) the way the sample is selected;

(e) the variance of FEV1 in the population.

8.6 In a study of 88 births to women with a history of thrombocytopenia (Samuels *et al.* 1990), the same condition was recorded in 20% of babies (95% confidence interval 13% to 30%, exact method):

(a) Another sample of the same size will show a rate of thrombocytopenia between 13% and 30%;

(b) 95% of such women have a probability of between 13% and 30% of having a baby with thrombocytopenia;

(c) It is estimated that between 13% and 30% of births to such women in the area would show thrombocytopenia;

(d) If the sample were increased to 880 births, the 95% confidence interval would be narrower;

(e) It would be impossible to get these data if the rate for all women was 10%.

8.14 Exercise: Confidence intervals in two acupuncture studies

Two short papers concerning adverse events associated with acupuncture appeared together in the *British Medical Journal*. They were very similar in the question they address and the methods used. Both papers referred to 'significant' events. The word is not used in its statistical sense.

White *et al.* (2001) recruited acupuncture practitioners through journals circulated to members of the British Medical Acupuncture Society and the Acupuncture Association of Chartered Physiotherapists. They asked acupuncturists to take part in a prospective survey, recording for each consultation adverse events, defined as 'any ill-effect, no matter how small, that is unintended and non-therapeutic, even if not un-expected'. Some events were considered to be 'significant', meaning 'unusual, novel, dangerous, significantly inconveni-ent, or requiring further information'.

White *et al.* reported that as the data were skewed, with extreme values present, confidence intervals were calculated using a bootstrapping procedure with 10 000 replications.

Data were collected from 78 acupuncturists, 31 822 (me-dian 318, range 5 to 1911) consultations were included. Altogether, 43 'significant' events were reported, giving a rate of 14 per 10 000 (95% confidence interval 8 per 10 000 to 20 per 10 000). None of these events was a serious adverse event, a category which includes death, hospital admission or prolongation of existing hospital stay, persistent or significant disability or incapacity, or otherwise life-threatening. Hence the rate of serious events was estimated as 0 per 10 000 (95% confidence interval 0 per 10 000 to 1.2 per 10 000).

MacPherson *et al.* (2001) carried out a prospective audit of treatments undertaken during a 4-week period. They invited all 1 848 professional acupuncturists who were members of the British Acupuncture Council and were practising in the UK to record details of adverse events and mild transient reactions after treatment.

A total of 574 (31%) practitioners participated, reporting on 34 407 treatments. Practitioners were asked to give details of any adverse events they considered to be 'significant', us-ing the same definition as White *et al.* (2001). There were no reports of serious adverse events, defined as described previ-ously (95% confidence interval 0 to 1.1 per 10 000 treatments). Practitioners reported 43 minor adverse events, a rate of 1.3 (0.9 to 1.7) per 1 000 treatments.

MacPherson *et al.* concluded that 'In this prospective sur-vey, no serious adverse events were reported after 34 407 acupuncture treatments. This is consistent, with 95% con-fidence, with an underlying serious adverse event rate of between 0 and 1.1 per 10 000 treatments.' They continue: 'Even given the potential bias of self reporting, this is important evidence on public health and safety as professional acupunc-turists deliver approximately two million treatments per year in the United Kingdom. Comparison of this adverse event rate for acupuncture with those of drugs routinely prescribed in primary care suggests that acupuncture is a relatively safe form of treatment'.

8.1 Are there any problems with the sampling methods used by White *et al.* and by MacPherson *et al.*? What alternative methods might have been used? Would they solve the problem?

8.2 Are there any problems with the data collection methods used in these studies? What alternatives could be used? Would they solve the problem?

8.3 White *et al.* reported the average age of their acupuncturists to be 47 (range 27 to 71) years. The median number of consultations for a practitioner was 318, range 5 to 1 911. What does this tell us about the shapes of the distributions of age and number of consultations?

8.4 Altogether, White *et al.* reported 43 'significant' events, giving a rate of 14 per 10 000 (95% confidence interval 8 per 10 000 to 20 per 10 000). What does this mean?

8.5 White *et al.* reported that none of the adverse events was serious (95% confidence interval 0 to 1.2 per 10 000 consultations). MacPherson *et al.* also reported that there were no records of serious adverse events (0 to 1.1 per 10 000 treatments). Can we conclude that there is no risk of serious events?

8.6 MacPherson *et al.* concluded that their data were consistent with an underlying serious adverse event rate of between 0 and 1.1 per 10 000 treatments. Is this a reasonable interpretation?

8.7 White *et al.* say '14 per 10 000 of these minor events were reported as significant. These event rates are per consultation, and they do not give the risk per individual patient'. Why do they not give the risk per individual patient?

8.8 MacPherson *et al.* said that further research measuring patients' experience of adverse events is merited. What would this tell us that these papers do not?

Appendix 8A: Standard error of a mean

When we calculate the mean of a sample of size n independent observations, we add n independent variables, each with variance σ^2. The variance of the sum is the sum of the variances (Section 6.6), $\sigma^2 + \sigma^2 + \cdots + \sigma^2 = n\sigma^2$. We divide this new variable by a constant, n, to get the mean. This has the effect of dividing its variance by the square of the constant, n^2. The variance on the mean is thus $n\sigma^2/n^2 = \sigma^2/n$. The standard error is the square root of this, $\sqrt{\sigma^2/n}$ or $\sigma/\sqrt{n}$.

9 Significance tests

9.1 Testing a hypothesis

In Chapter 8 I dealt with estimation and the precision of estimates. This is one form of statistical inference, the process by which we use samples to draw conclusions about the populations from which they are taken. In this chapter I shall introduce a different form of inference, the significance test or hypothesis test.

A significance test enables us to measure the strength of the evidence which the data supply concerning some proposition of interest. For example, consider the cross-over trial of pronethalol for the treatment of angina (Section 2.7). Table 9.1 shows the number of attacks over 4 weeks on each treatment. These 12 patients are a sample from the population of all patients. Would the other members of this population experience fewer attacks while using pronethalol? We can see that the number of attacks is highly variable from one patient to another, and it is quite possible that this is true from one period of time to another as well. So it could be that some patients would have fewer attacks while on pronethalol than while on placebo quite by chance. In a significance test, we ask whether the difference observed was small enough to have occurred by chance if there were really no difference in the population. If it were so, then the evidence in favour of there being a difference between the treatment periods would be weak or absent. On the other hand, if the difference were much larger than we would expect because of chance if there were no real population difference, then the evidence in favour of a real difference would be strong.

To carry out the test of significance we suppose that, in the population, there is no difference between the two treatments. The hypothesis of 'no difference' or 'no effect' in the population is called the **null hypothesis**.

Table 9.1 Trial of pronethalol for the prevention of angina pectoris (data from Pritchard *et al.* 1963)

Number of attacks while on:		Difference placebo – pronethalol	Sign of difference
placebo	pronethalol		
71	29	42	+
323	348	−25	−
8	1	7	+
14	7	7	+
23	16	7	+
34	25	9	+
79	65	14	+
60	41	19	+
2	0	2	+
3	0	3	+
17	15	2	+
7	2	5	+

If this is not true, then the **alternative hypothesis** must be true, that there is a difference between the treatments in one direction or the other. We then find the probability of getting data as different from what would be expected, if the null hypothesis were true, as are those data actually observed. If this probability is large, the data are consistent with the null hypothesis; if it is small, the data are unlikely to have arisen if the null hypothesis were true and the evidence is in favour of the alternative hypothesis.

9.2 An example: the sign test

I shall now describe a particular test of significance, the **sign test**, to test the null hypothesis that placebo and pronethalol have the same effect on angina. Consider the differences between the number of attacks on the two treatments for each patient, as in Table 9.1. If the null hypothesis were true, then differences in number of attacks would be just as likely to be positive as negative, they would be random. The probability of a change being negative would be equal to the probability of it being positive, so both probabilities would be 0.5. Then the number of negatives would be an observation from a Binomial distribution (Section 6.4) with $n = 12$ and $p = 0.5$. (If there were any subjects who had the same number of attacks on both regimes we would omit them, as they provide no information about the direction of any difference between the treatments. In this test, n is the number of subjects for whom there is a difference, one way or the other.)

If the null hypothesis were true, what would be the probability of getting an observation from this distribution as extreme or more extreme than the value we have actually observed? The expected number of negatives would be $np = 6$. What is the probability of getting a value as far from expectation as that observed? The number of negative differences is 1. The probability of getting 1 negative change would be

$$\frac{n!}{r!(n-r)!} p^r (1-p)^{n-r} = \frac{12!}{1!11!} \times 0.5^1 \times 0.5^{11}$$

$$= 12 \times 0.5^{12}$$

$$= 0.002\,93$$

if the null hypothesis were true and $p = 0.5$.

This is not a likely event in itself. However, we are interested in the probability of getting a value as far or further from the expected value, 6, as is 1, and clearly 0 is further and must be included. The probability of no negative changes is

$$\frac{12!}{0!12!} \times 0.5^0 \times 0.5^{12} = 0.000\,24$$

So the probability of one or fewer negative changes is $0.002\,93 + 0.000\,24 = 0.003\,17$. The null hypothesis is that there is no difference, so the alternative hypothesis is that there is a difference in one direction or the other.

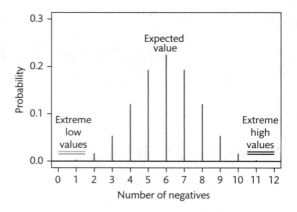

Figure 9.1 Extremes of the Binomial distribution for the sign test.

We must, therefore, consider the probability of getting a value as extreme on the other side of the mean, that is 11 or 12 negatives (Figure 9.1). The probability of 11 or 12 negatives is also 0.003 17, because the distribution is symmetrical. Hence, the probability of getting as extreme a value as that observed, in either direction, is $0.003\,17 + 0.003\,17 = 0.006\,34$. This means that if the null hypothesis were true, we would have a sample which is so extreme that the probability of it arising by chance is 0.006, less than one in a hundred.

Thus, we would have observed a very unlikely event if the null hypothesis were true. This means that the data are not consistent with null hypothesis, and we can conclude that there is strong evidence in favour of a difference between the treatments. (As this was a double blind randomized trial, it is reasonable to suppose that this was caused by the activity of the drug.)

9.3 Principles of significance tests

The sign test is an example of a test of significance. The number of negative changes is called the **test statistic**, something calculated from the data which can be used to test the null hypothesis. The general procedure for a significance test is as follows:

1 Set up the null hypothesis and its alternative.

2 Find the value of the test statistic.

3 Refer the test statistic to a known distribution which it would follow if the null hypothesis were true.

4 Find the probability of a value of the test statistic arising which is as or more extreme than that observed, if the null hypothesis were true.

5 Conclude that the data are consistent or inconsistent with the null hypothesis.

We shall deal with several different significance tests in this and subsequent chapters. We shall see that they all follow this pattern.

If the data are not consistent with the null hypothesis, the difference is said to be **statistically significant**. If the data do not support the null hypothesis, it is sometimes said that we reject the null hypothesis, and if the data are consistent with the null hypothesis, it is said that we accept it. Such an 'all or nothing' decision making approach is seldom appropriate in medical research. It is preferable to think of the significance test probability as an index of the strength of evidence against the null hypothesis. The term 'accept the null hypothesis' is also misleading because it implies that we have concluded that the null hypothesis is true, which we should not do. We cannot prove statistically that something, such as a treatment effect, does not exist. It is better to say that we have not rejected or have failed to reject the null hypothesis.

The probability of such an extreme value of the test statistic occurring if the null hypothesis were true is often called the **P value**. It is *not* the probability that the null hypothesis is true. This is a common misconception. To a frequentist statistician, the only kind to do significance tests, the null hypothesis is either true or it is not; it is not random and has no probability. I suspect that many researchers have managed to use significance tests quite effectively despite holding this incorrect view.

9.4 Significance levels and types of error

We must still consider the question of how small is small. A probability of 0.006, as in the example above, is clearly small and we have a quite unlikely event. But what about 0.06, or 0.1? Suppose we take a probability of 0.01 or

less as constituting reasonable evidence against the null hypothesis. If the null hypothesis is true, we shall make a wrong decision one in a hundred times. Deciding against a true null hypothesis is called an **error of the first kind, type I error,** or α **error**. We get an **error of the second kind, type II error,** or β **error** if we do not reject a null hypothesis which is in fact false. (α and β are the Greek letters 'alpha' and 'beta'.) Now the smaller we demand the probability should be before we decide against the null hypothesis, the larger the observed difference must be, and so the more likely we are to miss real differences. By reducing the risk of an error of the first kind, we increase the risk of an error of the second kind.

The conventional compromise is to say that differences are significant if the probability is less than 0.05. This is a reasonable guide-line, but should not be taken as some kind of absolute demarcation. There is not a great difference between probabilities of 0.06 and 0.04, and they surely indicate similar strength of evidence. It is better to regard probabilities around 0.05 as providing some evidence against the null hypothesis, which increases in strength as the probability falls. If we decide that the difference is significant, the probability is sometimes referred to as the **significance level**. We say that the significance level is high if the P value is low.

As a rough and ready guide, we can think of P values as indicating the strength of evidence like this:

Greater than 0.1:	Little or no evidence
Between 0.05 and 0.1:	Weak evidence
Between 0.01 and 0.05:	Evidence
Less than 0.01:	Strong evidence
Less than 0.001:	Very strong evidence

Because the actual value of the P value matters, it should be quoted wherever possible. Computers print out the exact P values for most test statistics. For example, using Stata 12.1 to do the sign test for the pronethalol data we get P = 0.006 3. This is the same as the 0.006 34 calculated above, but rounded to four decimal places. Before computers with powerful and easy to use statistical programs were readily available, many P values had to be found by referring the test statistic to a printed table. These often gave only a few P values, such as 0.25, 0.10, 0.05, 0.01, and the best the statistical analyst could do was to say that the P value for the data lay between two of these. Thus it was customary to quote P values as, for example, '0.05 > P > 0.01'. This was often abbreviated to 'P < 0.05', which is how our sign test might have been quoted. Old habits persist and researchers will often take the computer generated 'P = 0.006 3' and replace it in the paper by 'P < 0.05'. Even worse, 'P = 0.329 4' might be reported as 'not significant', 'ns', or 'P > 0.05'. This wastes valuable information. 'P = 0.06' and 'P = 0.6' can both get reported as 'P = NS', but 0.06 is only just above the conventional cut-off of 0.05 and indicates that there is some evidence for an effect, albeit rather weak evidence. A P value equal to 0.6, which is ten times bigger, indicates that there is very little evidence indeed. It is much better and more informative to quote the calculated P value. We do not, however, need to reproduce all the figures printed. 'P = 0.006 3' is given to four decimal places, meaning that there are four figures after the decimal point, '0', '0', '6', and '3'. It is also given to two significant figures (Section 5.2). Personally, I would quote 'P=0.006 3' to one significant figure, as P = 0.006, as figures after the first do not add much, but the first figure can be quite informative.

Sometimes the computer prints '0.000 0' or '0.000'. The programmer has set the format for the printed probability to four or three decimal places. This is done for several reasons. First, it is easier to read than printing the full accuracy to which the calculation was done. Second, if the P value is very small, it might be printed out in the standard format for very small numbers, which looks like '1.543 256E-07', meaning '0.000 000 154 325 6'. Third, almost all P values are approximations and the figures at the right hand end do not mean anything. The P value '0.000 0' may be correct, in that the probability is less than 0.000 05 and so equal to 0.000 0 to four decimal places. This is the case for '0.000 000 154 325 6'. However, the probability can rarely be exactly zero, so we usually quote this as P < 0.000 1. I have seen 'P < 0.000', which is impossible, zero is the lowest P can go. Don't do it.

9.5 One and two sided tests of significance

In the above example, the alternative hypothesis was that there was a difference in one direction or the other. This is called a **two sided** or **two tailed** test, because we

used the probabilities of extreme values in both directions (Figure 9.2). It would have been possible to have the alternative hypothesis that there was a decrease in the pronethalol direction, in which case the null hypothesis would be that the number of attacks on the placebo was less than or equal to the number on pronethalol. This would give P = 0.003 17, and of course, a higher significance level than the two sided test. This would be a **one sided** or **one tailed** test (Figure 9.3). The logic of this is that we should ignore any signs that the active drug is harmful to the patients. If what we were saying was 'if this trial does not give a significant reduction in angina using pronethalol we will not use it again', this might be reasonable, but the medical research process does not work like that. This is one of several pieces of evidence and so we should certainly use a method of inference which would enable us to detect effects in either direction.

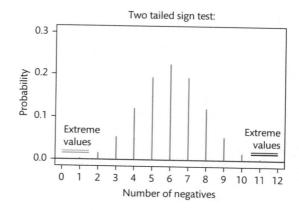

Figure 9.2 Two sided sign test.

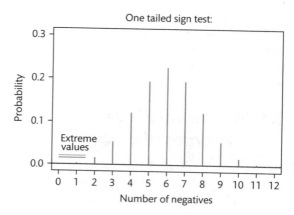

Figure 9.3 One sided sign test.

The question of whether one or two sided tests should be the norm has been the subject of considerable debate among practitioners of statistical methods. Perhaps the position taken depends on the field in which the testing is usually done. In biological science, treatments seldom have only one effect and relationships between variables are usually complex. Two sided tests are almost always preferable.

There are circumstances in which a one sided test is appropriate. In a study of the effects of an investigative procedure, laparoscopy and hydrotubation, on the fertility of sub-fertile women (Luthra *et al.* 1982), women presenting at an infertility clinic were studied. These women were observed for several months, during which some conceived, before laparoscopy was carried out on those still infertile. These were then observed for several months afterwards and some of the women conceived during this time. The conception rate in the period before laparoscopy was compared with that afterwards. Of course, women who conceived during the first period did not have a laparoscopy. It was argued that the less fertile a woman was, the longer it was likely to take her to conceive. Hence, the women who had the laparoscopy should have a lower conception rate (by an unknown amount) than the larger group who entered the study, because the more fertile women had conceived before their turn for laparoscopy came. To see whether laparoscopy increased fertility, we could test the null hypothesis that the conception rate after laparoscopy was less than or equal to that before. The alternative hypothesis was that the conception rate after laparoscopy was higher than that before. A two sided test was inappropriate because if the laparoscopy had no effect on fertility the post-laparoscopy rate was expected to be lower; chance did not come into it. In fact the post laparoscopy conception rate was very high and the difference clearly significant.

9.6 Significant, real, and important

If a difference is statistically significant, then it may well be real, but not necessarily important. For example, the UK Prospective Diabetes Study Group compared atenolol and captopril in reducing the risk of complications in type 2 diabetes. A total of 1 148 hypertensive diabetic patients were randomized. The authors reported that 'Captopril and atenolol were equally effective in reducing blood pressure to a mean of 144/83 mm Hg and 143/81 mm Hg respectively' (UKPDS 1998). The difference in diastolic pressure was statistically significant, P = 0.02. It is (statistically) significant, and real, but not (clinically) important.

On the other hand, if a difference is not statistically significant, it could still be real. We may simply have too small a sample to show that a difference exists. Furthermore, the difference may still be important. The difference in mortality in the anticoagulant trial of Carleton *et al.* (1960), described in Chapter 2, was not significant, the difference in percentage survival being 5.5 in favour of the active treatment. However, the authors also quote a confidence interval for the difference in percentage survival of 24.2 percentage points in favour of heparin to 13.3 percentage points in favour of the control treatment. A difference in survival of 24 percentage points in favour of the treatment would certainly be important if it turned out to be the case. 'Not significant' does not imply that there is no effect. It means that we have not demonstrated the existence of one. Later studies showed that anticoagulation is indeed effective.

A particular case of misinterpretation of non-significant results occurs in the interpretation of randomized clinical trials where there is a measurement before treatment and another afterwards. Rather than compare the after treatment measure between the two groups, researchers can be tempted to test separately the null hypotheses that the measure in the treatment group has not changed from baseline and that the measure in the control group has not changed from baseline. If one group shows a significant difference and the other does not, the researchers then conclude that the treatments are different.

For example, Kerrigan *et al.* (1993) assessed the effects of different levels of information on anxiety in patients due to undergo surgery. They randomized patients to receive either simple or detailed information about the procedure and its risks. Anxiety was again measured after patients had been given the information. Kerrigan *et al.* (1993) calculated significance tests for the mean change in anxiety score for each group separately. In the group given detailed information, the mean change in anxiety was not significant (P = 0.2), interpreted incorrectly as 'no change'. In the other group, the reduction in anxiety was significant (P = 0.01). They concluded that there was a difference between the two groups because the change was significant in one group but not in the other. This is incorrect. There may, for example, be a difference in one group which just fails to reach the (arbitrary) significance level and a difference in the other which just exceeds it, the differences in the two groups being similar. We should compare the two groups directly. It is these which are comparable apart from the effects of treatment, being randomized, not the before and after treatment means which could be influenced by many other factors. An alternative analysis tested the null hypothesis that, after adjustment for initial anxiety score, the mean anxiety scores are the same in patients given simple and detailed information. This showed a significantly higher mean score in the detailed information group (Bland and Altman 1993). Testing within each group separately is essentially the same error as calculating a confidence interval for each group separately (Section 8.9). See Bland and Altman (2011) for a fuller discussion.

9.7 Comparing the means of large samples

We have already seen in Section 8.5 that if we have two samples of size n_1 and n_2, with sample means $\bar{x}_1$ and $\bar{x}_2$ and with standard errors se_1 and se_2, the standard error of the difference estimate $\bar{x}_1 - \bar{x}_2$ is $\sqrt{se_1^2 + se_2^2}$. Furthermore, if n_1 and n_2 are large, $\bar{x}_1 - \bar{x}_2$ will be from a Normal distribution with mean $\mu_1 - \mu_2$, the population difference, and its standard deviation well estimated by the standard error estimate. We can use this to find a confidence interval for the difference between the means:

$$\bar{x}_1 - \bar{x}_2 - 1.96\sqrt{se_1^2 + se_2^2} \quad \text{to}$$
$$\bar{x}_1 - \bar{x}_2 + 1.96\sqrt{se_1^2 + se_2^2}$$

We can use this confidence interval to carry out a significance test of the null hypothesis that the difference

between the means is zero, i.e. the alternative hypothesis is that μ_1 and μ_2 are not equal. If the confidence interval includes zero, then the probability of getting such extreme data if the null hypothesis were true is greater than 0.05 (i.e. 1 − 0.95). If the confidence interval excludes zero, then the probability of such extreme data under the null hypothesis is less than 0.05 and the difference is significant. Another way of doing the same thing is to note that

$$z = \frac{\bar{x}_1 - \bar{x}_2 - (\mu_1 - \mu_2)}{\sqrt{se_1^2 + se_2^2}}$$

is from a Standard Normal distribution, i.e. mean 0 and variance 1. Under the null hypothesis that $\mu_1 = \mu_2$ or $\mu_1 - \mu_2 = 0$, this is

$$z = \frac{\bar{x}_1 - \bar{x}_2}{\sqrt{se_1^2 + se_2^2}}$$

This is the test statistic, and if it lies between −1.96 and +1.96 then the probability of such an extreme value is greater than 0.05 and the difference is not significant. If the test statistic is greater than 1.96 or less than −1.96, there is a less than 0.05 probability of such data arising if the null hypothesis were true, and the data are not consistent with null hypothesis; the difference is significant at the 0.05 or 5% level. This is the large sample Normal test or z test for two means.

For an example, in a study of respiratory symptoms in schoolchildren (Section 8.5), we wanted to know whether children reported by their parents to have respiratory symptoms had worse lung function than children who were not reported to have symptoms. Ninety-two children were reported to have cough during the day or at night, and their mean PEFR was 294.8 litre/min with standard deviation 57.1 litre/min. A total of 1 643 children were reported not to have the symptom, and their mean PEFR was 313.6 litre/min with standard deviation 55.2 litre/min. We thus have two large samples, and can apply the Normal test. We have

$$se_1 = \sqrt{\frac{s_1^2}{n_1}} = \sqrt{\frac{57.1^2}{92}} \qquad se_2 = \sqrt{\frac{s_2^2}{n_2}} = \sqrt{\frac{55.2^2}{1643}}$$

The difference between the two groups is $\bar{x}_1 - \bar{x}_2 = 294.8 - 313.6 = -18.8$. The standard error of the difference is

$$SE(\bar{x}_1 - \bar{x}_2) = \sqrt{\frac{s_1^2}{n_1} + \frac{s_2^2}{n_2}}$$

$$= \sqrt{\frac{57.1^2}{92} + \frac{55.2^2}{1643}}$$

$$= 6.11$$

The test statistic is

$$\frac{\bar{x}_1 - \bar{x}_2}{SE(\bar{x}_1 - \bar{x}_2)} = \frac{-18.8}{6.11} = -3.1$$

Under the null hypothesis this is an observation from a Standard Normal distribution, and so P < 0.01 (Table 7.2), or, more precisely, P = 0.002. If the null hypothesis were true, the data which we have observed would be unlikely. We can conclude that there is good evidence that children reported to have cough during the day or at night have lower PEFR than other children.

In this case, we have two ways of using the same standard error: for a confidence interval estimate or for a significance test. The confidence interval is usually superior, because we not only demonstrate the existence of a difference but also have some idea of its size. This is of particular value when the difference is not significant. For example, in the same study only 27 children were reported to have phlegm during the day or at night. These had mean PEFR of 298.0 litre/min and standard deviation 53.9 litre/min, hence a standard error for the mean of 10.4 litre/min. This is greater than the standard error for the mean for those with cough, because the sample size is smaller. The 1 708 children not reported to have this symptom had mean 312.6 litre/min and standard deviation 55.4 litre/min, giving standard error 1.3 litre/min. Hence the difference between the means was –14.6, with standard error given by $\sqrt{10.4^2 + 1.3^2} = 10.5$. The test statistic is

$$\frac{-14.6}{10.5} = -1.4$$

This has a probability of about 0.16, and so the data are consistent with the null hypothesis. However, the 95% confidence interval for the difference is $-14.6 - 1.96 \times 10.5$ to $-14.6 + 1.96 \times 10.5$ giving –35 to 6 litre/min. We see that the difference could be just as great as for cough. Because the size of the smaller sample is not so great, the test is less likely to detect a difference for the phlegm comparison than for the cough comparison.

9.8 Comparison of two proportions

Suppose we wish to compare two proportions p_1 and p_2, estimated from large independent samples sized n_1 and n_2. The null hypothesis is that the proportions in the populations from which the samples are drawn are the same, p say. As under the null hypothesis the proportions for the two groups are the same, we can get one common estimate of the proportion and use it to estimate the standard errors. We can estimate the common proportion from the data by

$$p = \frac{r_1 + r_2}{n_1 + n_2}$$

where $p_1 = r_1/n_1$, $p_2 = r_2/n_2$. We want to make inferences from the difference between sample proportions, $p_1 - p_2$, so we require the standard error of this difference.

$$SE(p_1) = \sqrt{\frac{p(1-p)}{n_1}} \qquad SE(p_2) = \sqrt{\frac{p(1-p)}{n_2}}$$

$$SE(p_1 - p_2) = \sqrt{SE(p_1)^2 + SE(p_2)^2}$$

as the samples are independent. Hence

$$SE(p_1 - p_2) = \sqrt{\frac{p(1-p)}{n_1} + \frac{p(1-p)}{n_2}}$$

$$= \sqrt{p(1-p)\left(\frac{1}{n_1} + \frac{1}{n_2}\right)}$$

As p is based on more subjects than either p_1 or p_2, if the null hypothesis were true then standard errors would be more reliable than those estimated in Section 8.6 using p_1 and p_2 separately. We then find the test statistic

$$z = \frac{p_1 - p_2}{SE(p_1 - p_2)} = \frac{p_1 - p_2}{\sqrt{p(1-p)\left(\frac{1}{n_1} + \frac{1}{n_2}\right)}}$$

Under the null hypothesis this has mean zero. Because the sample is large, we assume that p is sufficiently well estimated for

$$\sqrt{p(1-p)(1/n_1 + 1/n_2)}$$

to be a good estimate of the standard deviation of the distribution from which $p_1 - p_2$ comes, i.e. the standard error, and $p_1 - p_2$ can be assumed to come from a Normal distribution. Hence, if the null hypothesis were true, the test statistic would be from a Standard Normal distribution. This is the large sample Normal test or z test for two proportions.

In Section 8.6, we looked at the proportions of children with bronchitis in infancy and with no such history who were reported to have respiratory symptoms in later life. We had 273 children with a history of bronchitis before age 5 years, 26 of whom were reported to have day or night cough at age 14. We had 1 046 children with no bronchitis before age 5 years, 44 of whom were reported to have day or night cough at age 14. We shall test the null hypothesis that the prevalence of the symptom is the same in both populations, against the alternative that it is not.

We have $n_1 = 273, p_1 = 26/273 = 0.095\,24, n_2 = 1\,046$, and $p_2 = 44/1\,046 = 0.042\,07$. The calculation proceeds like this:

$$p = \frac{26 + 44}{273 + 1\,046} = 0.053\,07$$

$$p_1 - p_2 = 0.095\,24 - 0.042\,07 = 0.053\,17$$

$$SE(p_1 - p_2) = \sqrt{p(1-p)\left(\frac{1}{n_1} + \frac{1}{n_2}\right)}$$

$$= \sqrt{0.053\,07 \times (1 - 0.053\,07) \times \left(\frac{1}{273} + \frac{1}{1\,046}\right)}$$

$$= 0.015\,24$$

$$\frac{p_1 - p_2}{SE(p_1 - p_2)} = \frac{0.053\,17}{0.015\,24} = 3.49$$

Referring this to Table 7.2 of the Normal distribution, we find the probability of such an extreme value is less than 0.01, or, more precisely, P = 0.000 5, so we conclude that the data are not consistent with the null hypothesis. There is good evidence that children with a history of bronchitis are more likely to be reported to have day or night cough at age 14.

Note that the standard error used here is not the same as that found in Section 8.6. It is only correct if the null hypothesis is true. The formula of Section 8.6 should be used for finding the confidence interval. Thus the standard error used for testing is not identical to that used for

estimation, as was the case for the comparison of two means. It is possible for the test to be significant and for the confidence interval to include zero. This property is possessed by several related tests and confidence intervals.

This is a large sample method, and is equivalent to the chi-squared test for a 2 by 2 table (Sections 13.1–2). How small the sample can be and methods for small samples are discussed in Sections 13.3–6.

Note that we do not need a different test for the ratio of two proportions, as the null hypothesis that the ratio in the population is one is the same as the null hypothesis that the difference in the population is zero.

9.9 The power of a test

The test for comparing means in Section 9.7 is more likely to detect a large difference between two populations than a small one. The probability that a test will produce a significant difference at a given significance level is called the **power** of the test. For a given test, this will depend on the true difference between the populations compared, the sample size, and the significance level chosen. We have already noted in Section 9.4 that we are more likely to obtain a significant difference with a significance level of 0.05 than with one of 0.01. We have greater power if the P value chosen to be considered as significant is larger.

For example, we can calculate the power of the Normal comparison of two means quite easily. The sample difference $\bar{x}_1 - \bar{x}_2$ is an observation from a Normal distribution with mean $\mu_1 - \mu_2$ and standard deviation $\sqrt{\sigma_1^2/n_1 + \sigma_2^2/n_2}$, the standard error of the difference, which we shall denote by se_{diff}. The test statistic to test the null hypothesis that $\mu_1 = \mu_2$ is $(\bar{x}_1 - \bar{x}_2)/se_{diff}$. The test will be significant at the 0.05 level if the test statistic is further from zero than 1.96. If $\mu_1 > \mu_2$, it is very unlikely that we will find $\bar{x}_1$ significantly less than $\bar{x}_2$, so for a significant difference we must have $(\bar{x}_1 - \bar{x}_2)/se_{diff} > 1.96$. Subtracting $(\mu_1 - \mu_2)/se_{diff}$ from each side:

$$\frac{\bar{x}_1 - \bar{x}_2}{se_{diff}} - \frac{\mu_1 - \mu_2}{se_{diff}} > 1.96 - \frac{\mu_1 - \mu_2}{se_{diff}}$$

$$\frac{\bar{x}_1 - \bar{x}_2 - (\mu_1 - \mu_2)}{se_{diff}} > 1.96 - \frac{\mu_1 - \mu_2}{se_{diff}}$$

$(\bar{x}_1 - \bar{x}_2 - (\mu_1 - \mu_2))/se_{diff}$ is an observation from a Standard Normal distribution, because we subtract from $\bar{x}_1 - \bar{x}_2$ its expected value, $\mu_1 - \mu_2$, and divide by its standard deviation, se_{diff}. We can find the probability that this exceeds any particular value z from $1 - \Phi(z)$ in Table 7.1. So the power of the test, the probability of getting a significant result, is $1 - \Phi(z)$ where $z = 1.96 - (\mu_1 - \mu_2)/se_{diff}$.

For the comparison of PEFR in children with and without phlegm (Section 9.7), for example, suppose that the population means were in fact $\mu_1 = 310$ and $\mu_2 = 295$ litre/min, and each population had standard deviation 55 litre/min. The sample sizes were $n_1 = 1\,708$ and $n_2 = 27$, so the standard error of the difference would be

$$se_{diff} = \sqrt{\frac{55^2}{1\,708} + \frac{55^2}{27}} = 10.67 \text{ litre/min}$$

The population difference we want to be able to detect is $\mu_1 - \mu_2 = 310 - 295 = 15$, and so

$$1.96 - \frac{\mu_1 - \mu_2}{se_{diff}} = 1.96 - \frac{15}{10.67}$$
$$= 1.96 - 1.41$$
$$= 0.55$$

From Table 7.1, $\Phi(0.55)$ is between 0.691 and 0.726, about 0.71. The power of the test would be $1 - 0.71 = 0.29$. If these were the population means and standard deviation, our test would have had a poor chance of detecting the difference in means, even though it existed. The test would have low power. Figure 9.4 shows how

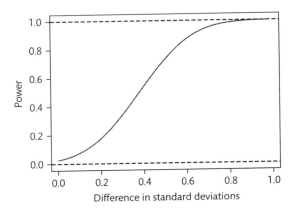

Figure 9.4 Power curve for a comparison of two means from samples of size 1 708 and 27.

the power of this test changes with the difference between population means. As the difference gets larger, the power increases, getting closer and closer to 1. The power is not zero even when the population difference is zero, because there is always the possibility of a significant difference, even when the null hypothesis is true. $1 - \text{power} = \beta$, the probability of a Type II or beta error (Section 9.4) if the population difference = 15 litre/min.

9.10 Multiple significance tests

If we test a null hypothesis which is in fact true, using 0.05 as the critical significance level, we have a probability of 0.95 of coming to a 'not significant' (i.e. correct) conclusion. If we test two independent true null hypotheses, the probability that neither test will be significant is $0.95 \times 0.95 = 0.90$ (Section 6.2). If we test 20 such hypotheses the probability that none will be significant is $0.95^{20} = 0.36$. This gives a probability of $1 - 0.36 = 0.64$ of getting at least one significant result; we are more likely to get one than not. The expected number of spurious significant results is $20 \times 0.05 = 1$.

Many medical research studies are published with large numbers of significance tests. These are not usually independent, being carried out on the same set of subjects, so the above calculations do not apply exactly. However, it is clear that if we go on testing long enough we will find something which is 'significant'. We must beware of attaching too much importance to a lone significant result among a mass of non-significant ones. It may be the one in 20 which we should get by chance alone.

This is particularly important when we find that a clinical trial or epidemiological study gives no significant difference overall, but does so in a particular subset of subjects, such as women aged over 60. For example, Lee *et al.* (1980) simulated a clinical trial of the treatment of coronary artery disease by allocating 1 073 patient records from past cases into two 'treatment' groups at random. They then analysed the outcome as if it were a genuine trial of two treatments. The analysis was quite detailed and thorough. As we would expect, it failed to show any significant difference in survival between those patients allocated to the two 'treatments'. Patients were then subdivided by two variables which affect prognosis, the number of diseased coronary vessels and whether the left ventricular contraction pattern was normal or abnormal. A significant difference in survival between the two 'treatment' groups was found in those patients with three diseased vessels (the maximum) and abnormal ventricular contraction. As this would be the subset of patients with the worst prognosis, the finding would be easy to account for by saying that the superior 'treatment' had its greatest advantage in the most severely ill patients! The moral of this story is that if there is no difference between the treatments overall, significant differences in subsets are to be treated with the utmost suspicion. This method of looking for a difference in treatment effect between subgroups of subjects is incorrect. A correct approach would be to use a multifactorial analysis, as described in Chapter 15, with treatment and group as two factors, and test for an interaction between groups and treatments (Section 15.5). The power for detecting such interactions is quite low, and we need a larger sample than would be needed simply to show a difference overall (Altman and Matthews 1996; Matthews and Altman 1996a, 1996b).

This spurious significant difference comes about because, when there is no real difference, the probability of getting no significant differences in six subgroups is $0.95^6 = 0.74$, not 0.95. We can allow for this effect by the **Bonferroni** method. In general, if we have k independent significant tests, at the α level, of null hypotheses which are all true, the probability that we will get no significant differences is $(1-\alpha)^k$. If we make α small enough, we can make the probability that none of the separate tests is significant equal to 0.95. Then if any of the k tests has a P value less than α, we will have a significant difference between the treatments at the 0.05 level. As α will be very small, it can be shown that $(1-\alpha)^k \approx 1 - k\alpha$. If we put $k\alpha = 0.05$, so $\alpha = 0.05/k$, we will have probability 0.05 that one of the k tests will have a P value less than α if the null hypotheses are true. Thus, if in a clinical trial we compare two treatments within five subsets of patients, the treatments will be significantly different at the 0.05 level if there is a P value less than 0.01 within any of the subsets. This is the Bonferroni method. Note that they are not significant at the 0.01 level, but only at the 0.05 level. The k tests together test the composite null hypothesis that there is no treatment effect on any variable.

We can do the same thing by multiplying the observed P value from the significance tests by the number of tests, k, any kP which exceeds one being ignored. Then if any kP is less than 0.05, the two treatments are significant at the 0.05 level.

For example, Williams et al. (1992) randomly allocated elderly patients discharged from hospital to two groups. The intervention group received timetabled visits by health visitor assistants, the control patients group were not visited unless there was perceived need. Soon after discharge and after 1 year, patients were assessed for physical health, disability, and mental state using questionnaire scales. There were no significant differences overall between the intervention and control groups, but among women aged 75–79 living alone, the control group showed significantly greater deterioration in physical score than did the intervention group (P = 0.04), and among men over 80 years, the control group showed significantly greater deterioration in disability score than did the intervention group (P = 0.03). The authors stated that 'Two small sub-groups of patients were possibly shown to have benefited from the intervention. ... These benefits, however, have to be treated with caution, and may be due to chance factors'. Subjects were cross-classified by age groups, whether living alone, and sex, so there were at least eight subgroups, if not more. Thus even if we consider the three scales separately, only a P value less than 0.05/8 = 0.006 would provide evidence of a treatment effect. Alternatively, the true P values are 8 × 0.04 = 0.32 and 8 × 0.03 = 0.24.

A similar problem arises if we have multiple outcome measurements. For example, Newnham et al. (1993) randomized pregnant women to receive a series of Doppler ultrasound blood flow measurements or to control. They found significantly higher proportions of birthweights below the 10th and 3rd centiles (P = 0.006 and P = 0.02) in the Doppler group. These were only two of many comparisons, however, and one would suspect that there may be some spurious significant differences among so many. At least 35 were reported in the paper, though only these two were reported in the abstract. (Birthweight was not the intended outcome variable for the trial.) These tests are not independent, because they are all on the same participants, using variables which may not be independent. The proportions of birthweights below the 10th and

3rd centiles are clearly not independent, for example. The probability that two correlated variables both give non-significant differences when the null hypothesis is true is greater than $(1 - \alpha)^2$, because if the first test is not significant, the second now has a probability greater than $1 - \alpha$ of being not significant also. (Similarly, the probability that both are significant exceeds α^2, and the probability that only one is significant is reduced.) For k tests the probability of no significant differences is greater than $(1 - \alpha)^k$ and so greater than $1 - k\alpha$. Thus if we carry out each test at the $\alpha = 0.05/k$ level, we will have a probability of no significant differences which is greater than 0.95. A P value less than α for any variable, or $kP < 0.05$, would mean that the treatments were significantly different. For the example, the P values could be adjusted by $35 \times 0.006 = 0.21$ and $35 \times 0.02 = 0.70$.

Because the probability of obtaining no significant differences if the null hypotheses are all true is greater than the 0.95 which we want it to be, the overall P value is actually smaller than the nominal 0.05, by an unknown amount which depends on the lack of independence between the tests. The power of the test, its ability to detect true differences in the population, is correspondingly diminished. In statistical terms, the test is conservative.

Other multiple testing problems arise when we have more than two groups of subjects and wish to compare each pair of groups (Section 10.9), when we have a series of observations over time, such as blood pressure every 15 minutes after administration of a drug, where there may be a temptation to test each time point separately (Section 10.7), and when we have relationships between many variables to examine, as in a survey. For all these problems, the multiple tests are highly correlated and the Bonferroni method is inappropriate, as it will be highly conservative and may miss real differences.

Because of the problem of multiple testing (and the temptation to do it), we should define a primary outcome variable for any study to investigate a specific hypothesis, such as a clinical trial. The **primary outcome variable** is the single variable which we will use to assess the strength of the evidence. We should also define a primary analysis for the main comparison of the study, including groups to be compared and any other variables used for adjustment (Section 15.3). We should do this before looking at the data, preferably we should

do it before collecting them. If the primary analysis does not produce a significant effect, we do not have sufficient evidence to conclude that an effect exists, whatever other variables and comparisons appear to show.

Some researchers want to have more than one primary outcome variable, because they think that a positive effect on any of them would be sufficient to conclude that the new treatment is more effective. This is understandable, but of course we are back to the problem of multiple testing. We can deal with this by applying the Bonferroni adjustment to the P values, but we are likely to find that these variables are related to one another and so the process becomes conservative. If we have many outcome variables and cannot pick any one of them to be the primary outcome variable, we can treat all the outcome variables as a single entity using principal component analysis (Section 20.9).

9.11 Repeated significance tests and sequential analysis

A special case of multiple testing arises in clinical trials, where participants are admitted at different times. There can be a temptation to keep looking at the data and carrying out significant tests. As described in Section 9.10, this is liable to produce spurious significant differences, detecting treatment effects where none exist. I have heard of researchers testing the difference each time a patient is added and stopping the trial as soon as the difference is significant, then submitting the paper for publication as if only one test had been carried out. I'll be charitable and put this down to ignorance.

It is quite legitimate to set up a trial where the treatment difference is tested every time a patient is added, *provided* this repeated testing is designed into the trial and the overall chance of a significant difference when the null hypothesis is true remains 0.05. Such designs are called **sequential clinical trials**. A comprehensive account is given by Whitehead (1997).

An alternative approach which is quite often used is to take a small number of looks at the data as the trial progresses, testing at a predetermined P value. For example, we could test three times, rejecting the null hypothesis of no treatment effect the first time only if P < 0.001, the second time if P < 0.01, and the third time if P < 0.04. Then if the null hypothesis is true, the probability that there will not be a significant difference is approximately 0.999 × 0.99 × 0.96 = 0.949, so the overall alpha level will be 1 − 0.949 = 0.051, i.e. approximately 0.05. (The calculation is approximate because the tests are not independent.) If the null hypothesis is rejected at any of these tests, the overall P value is 0.05, not the nominal one. This approach can be used by data monitoring committees, where if the trial shows a large difference early on the trial can be stopped yet still allow a statistical conclusion to be drawn. This is called the **alpha spending** or **P-value spending** approach.

Two particular methods which you might come across are the grouped sequential design of Pocock (1977, 1982), where each test is done at the same nominal alpha value, and the method of O'Brien and Fleming (1979), widely used by the pharmaceutical industry, where the nominal alpha values decrease sharply as the trial progresses.

9.12 Significance tests and confidence intervals

We have seen that significance tests and confidence intervals are closely related and that a confidence interval can be used to carry out a significance test. If the 95% confidence interval for a parameter does not include its null hypothesis value, then the test of that null hypothesis is significant, P < 0.05.

Why have two different ways to do what appears to be the same thing? There are several reasons, including the influence of some very argumentative statisticians in the past. Second, there can be computation problems; sometimes we cannot find a confidence interval in a straightforward way or without modern computing power, using the bootstrap, for example. Third, sometimes there is no meaningful estimate to find. We shall see in Chapters 12 and 13 some cases where it is difficult to find a suitable measure of difference or relationship, although we can still ask whether a difference or relationship exists. Fourth, sometimes we are concerned with the existence of an effect more than with how big it is. An

example was a study of the health consequences of air pollution. We looked at daily measurements of air pollution and changes in death rates and hospital admissions. Although we gave confidence intervals for the estimated effects, the important thing was to find evidence that air pollution was harmful to health at all. Fifth, we cannot always find a confidence interval; but we can almost always do a significance test.

Recommendations to authors for most major health research journals advise confidence intervals be given where possible. The advantages of confidence intervals over tests of significance are discussed by Gardner and Altman (1986). Confidence intervals are usually more informative than P values, particularly non-significant ones.

Another point worth noting about confidence intervals and significance tests is that if the 95% confidence intervals for two estimates do not overlap, those estimates are significantly different. However, this does not work the other way; confidence intervals can overlap and the difference can still be significantly different. For example, Bland and Peacock (2002) gave this example from the St George's Birthweight Study (Brooke et al. 1989). We looked at mean birthweight by social class in the subgroup of women who had missed antenatal visits. The mean birthweight for women classified as manual occupations was 3 227g (95% CI 3 140g to 3 315g). For women from non-manual occupations the mean was 3 371g (95% CI 3 274g to 3 469g). The individual confidence intervals overlap. The difference in mean birthweight, non-manual minus manual, was 144g (95% CI 14g to 274g, P = 0.03), which is, of course, statistically significant.

9.13 Multiple choice questions: Significance tests

(Each branch is either true or false.)

9.1 In a case–control study, patients with a given disease drank coffee more frequently than did controls, and the difference was highly significant. We can conclude that:

(a) drinking coffee causes the disease;

(b) there is evidence of a real relationship between the disease and coffee drinking in the sampled population;

(c) the disease is not related to coffee drinking;

(d) eliminating coffee would prevent the disease;

(e) coffee and the disease always go together.

9.2 When comparing the means of two large samples using the Normal test:

(a) the null hypothesis is that the sample means are equal;

(b) the null hypothesis is that the means are not significantly different;

(c) standard error of the difference is the sum of the standard errors of the means;

(d) the standard errors of the means must be equal;

(e) the test statistic is the ratio of the difference to its standard error.

9.3 In a comparison of two methods of measuring PEFR, six of 17 subjects had higher readings on the Wright peak flow meter, 10 had higher readings on the mini peak flow meter and one had the same on both. If the difference between the instruments is tested using a sign test:

(a) the test statistic may be the number with the higher reading on the Wright meter;

(b) the null hypothesis is that there is no tendency for one instrument to read higher than the other;

(c) a one tailed test of significance should be used;

(d) the test statistic should follow the Binomial distribution (n = 16 and p = 0.5) if the null hypothesis were true;

(e) the instruments should have been presented in random order.

9.4 In a small randomized double blind trial of a new treatment in acute myocardial infarction, the mortality in the treated group was half that in the control group, but the difference was not significant. We can conclude that:

(a) the treatment is useless;

(b) there is no point in continuing to develop the treatment;

(c) the reduction in mortality is so great that we should introduce the treatment immediately;

(d) we should keep adding cases to the trial until the Normal test for comparison of two proportions is significant;

(e) we should carry out a new trial of much greater size.

9.5 In a large sample comparison between two groups, increasing the sample size will:

(a) improve the approximation of the test statistic to the Normal distribution;

(b) decrease the chance of an error of the first kind;

(c) decrease the chance of an error of the second kind;

(d) increase the power against a given alternative;

(e) make the null hypothesis less likely to be true.

9.6 In a study of breast feeding and intelligence (Lucas *et al.* 1992), 300 children who were very small at birth were given their mother's breast milk or infant formula, at the choice of the mother. At the age of 8 years the IQ of these children was measured. The mean IQ in the formula group was 92.8, compared with a mean of 103.0 in the breast milk group. The difference was significant, $P < 0.001$:

(a) there is good evidence that formula feeding of very small babies reduces IQ at age 8;

(b) there is good evidence that choosing to express breast milk is related to higher IQ in the child at age 8;

(c) type of milk has no effect on subsequent IQ;

(d) the probability that type of milk affects subsequent IQ is less than 0.1%;

(e) if type of milk were unrelated to subsequent IQ, the probability of getting a difference in mean IQ as big as that observed is less than 0.001.

9.14 Exercise: Crohn's disease and cornflakes

The suggestion that cornflakes may cause Crohn's disease arose in the study of James (1977). Crohn's disease is an inflammatory disease, usually of the last part of the small intestine. It can cause a variety of symptoms, including vague pain, diarrhoea, acute pain, and obstruction. Treatment may be by drugs or surgery, but many patients have had the disease for many years. James' initial hypothesis was that foods taken at breakfast may be associated with Crohn's disease. James studied 16 men and 18 women with Crohn's disease, aged 19–64 years, mean time since diagnosis 4.2 years. These were compared with controls, drawn from hospital patients without major gastrointestinal symptoms. Two controls were chosen per patient, matched for age and sex. James interviewed all cases and controls himself. Cases were asked whether they ate various foods for breakfast before the onset of symptoms, and

Table 9.2 Numbers of Crohn's disease patients and controls who ate various cereals regularly (at least once per week) (data from James 1977)

		Patients	Controls	Significance test
Cornflakes	Regularly	23	17	P < 0.0001
	Rarely or never	11	51	
Wheat	Regularly	16	12	P < 0.01
	Rarely or never	18	56	
Porridge	Regularly	11	15	0.5 > P > 0.1
	Rarely or never	23	53	
Rice	Regularly	8	10	0.5 > P > 0.1
	Rarely or never	26	56	
Bran	Regularly	6	2	P = 0.02
	Rarely or never	28	66	
Muesli	Regularly	4	3	P = 0.17
	Rarely or never	30	65	

controls were asked whether they ate various foods before a corresponding time (Table 9.2). There was a significant excess of eating of cornflakes, wheat, and bran among the Crohn's patients. The consumption of different cereals was inter-related, people reporting one cereal being likely to report others. In James' opinion, the principal association of Crohn's disease was with cornflakes, based on the apparent strength of the association. Only one case had never eaten cornflakes.

Several papers soon appeared in which this study was repeated, with variations. None was identical in design to James' study and none appeared to support his findings. Mayberry et al. (1978) interviewed 100 patients with Crohn's disease, mean duration 9 years. They obtained 100 controls, matched for age and sex, from patients and their relatives attending a fracture clinic. Cases and controls were interviewed about their current breakfast habits (Table 9.3). The only significant difference was an excess of fruit juice drinking in controls. Cornflakes were eaten by 29 cases compared with 22 controls, which was not significant. In this study there was no particular tendency for cases to report more foods than controls. The authors also asked cases whether they knew of an association between food (unspecified) and Crohn's disease. The association with cornflakes was reported by 29, and 12 of these had stopped eating them, having previously eaten them regularly. In their 29 matched controls, three

Table 9.3 Number of patients and controls regularly consuming certain foods at least twice weekly (data from Mayberry et al. 1978)

Foods at breakfast	Crohn's patients (n = 100)	Controls (n = 100)	Significance Test
Bread	91	86	
Toast	59	64	
Egg	31	37	
Fruit or fruit juice	14	30	P < 0.02
Porridge	20	18	
Weetabix, Shreddies, or Shredded Wheat	21	19	
Cornflakes	29	22	
Special K	4	7	
Rice Krispies	6	6	
Sugar Puffs	3	1	
Bran or All Bran	13	12	
Muesli	3	10	
Any cereal	55	55	

were past cornflakes eaters. Of the 71 Crohn's patients who were unaware of the association, 21 had discontinued eating cornflakes compared with 10 of their 71 controls. The authors remarked 'seemingly patients with Crohn's disease had significantly reduced their consumption of cornflakes compared with controls, irrespective of whether they were aware of the possible association'.

9.1 Are the cases and controls comparable in either of these studies?

9.2 What other sources of bias could there be in these designs?

9.3 What is the main point of difference in design between the study of James and that of Mayberry *et al.*?

9.4 In the study of Mayberry *et al.*, how many Crohn's cases and how many controls had ever been regular

eaters of cornflakes? How does this compare with James' findings?

9.5 Why did James think that eating cornflakes was particularly important?

9.6 For the data of Table 9.2, calculate the percentage of cases and controls who said that they ate the various cereals. Now divide the proportion of cases who said that they had eaten the cereal by the proportion of controls who reported eating it. This tells us, roughly, how much more likely cases were to report the cereal than were controls. Do you think eating cornflakes is particularly important?

9.7 If we have an excess of all cereals when we ask what was ever eaten, and none when we ask what is eaten now, what possible factors could account for this?

10 Comparing the means of small samples

10.1 The t distribution

We have seen in Chapters 8 and 9 how the Normal distribution can be used to calculate confidence intervals and to carry out tests of significance for the means of large samples. In this chapter we shall see how similar methods may be used when we have small samples, using the t distribution, and go on to compare several means.

So far, the probability distributions we have used have arisen because of the way data were collected, either from the way samples were drawn (Binomial distribution), or from the mathematical properties of large samples (Normal distribution). The distribution did not depend on any property of the data themselves. To use the t distribution we must make an assumption about the distribution from which the observations themselves are taken, the distribution of the variable in the population. We must assume this to be a Normal distribution. As we saw in Chapter 7, many naturally occurring variables have been found to follow a Normal distribution closely. I shall discuss the effects of any deviations from the Normal later.

I have already mentioned the t distribution (Appendix 7A), as one of those derived from the Normal. I shall now look at it in more detail. Suppose we have a random sample of independent observations from a distribution with mean μ and variance σ^2. We estimate μ and σ^2 from the data by the sample mean and variance, $\bar{x}$ and s^2. The distribution of all possible sample means, i.e. of all possible $\bar{x}$s, has mean μ and standard deviation $\sqrt{\sigma^2/n}$ (Sections 8.1, 8.2), the standard error of the sample mean, estimated from the data by $\sqrt{s^2/n}$ (Section 8.2, Appendix 8A). If we had a large

sample, we would then say that the mean $\bar{x}$ comes from a Normal distribution and that $\sqrt{s^2/n}$ is a good estimate of its standard deviation. The ratio $(\bar{x} - \mu)/\sqrt{s^2/n}$ would follow a Normal distribution with mean 0 and standard deviation 1, the Standard Normal distribution. This is not true for a small sample. The estimated standard deviation, s, may vary from sample to sample. Samples with small standard deviations will give very large ratios and the distribution will have much longer tails than the Normal.

The distribution of the mean over standard error calculated from a small sample depends on the distribution from which the original observations come. As so many variables follow a Normal distribution, it is worth looking at what happens when the observations are Normal. Provided our observations are from a Normal distribution, $\bar{x}$ is too. But we cannot assume that $\sqrt{s^2/n}$ is a good estimate of its standard deviation. We must allow for the variation of s^2 from sample to sample. It can be shown that, provided the observations come from a Normal distribution, the sampling distribution of $t = (\bar{x} - \mu)/\sqrt{s^2/n}$ is Student's t distribution with $n - 1$ degrees of freedom (Appendix 10A). We can therefore replace the Normal distribution by the t distribution in confidence intervals and significance tests for small samples. In fact, when we divide anything which has a Normal distribution with mean zero, such as $\bar{x} - \mu$, by its standard error which is based on a single sum of squares of data from a Normal distribution, we get a t distribution.

Figure 10.1 shows the t distribution with 1, 4, and 20 degrees of freedom. It is symmetrical, with longer tails than the Normal distribution. For example, with 4 d.f. the probability of t being greater than 2.78 is 2.5%, whereas

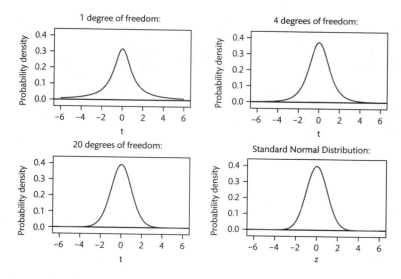

Figure 10.1 Student's t distribution with 1, 4, and 20 degrees of freedom, showing convergence to the Standard Normal distribution.

for the Standard Normal distribution the probability of being greater than 2.78 is only 0.3%. This is what we should expect, as in the expression $(\bar{x} - \mu)/\sqrt{s^2/n}$ the variation in s^2 from sample to sample will produce some samples with low values of s^2 and so large values of t. As the degrees of freedom, and hence the sample size, increase, s^2 will tend to be closer to its expected value of σ^2. The variation in s^2 will be less, and hence the variation in t will be less. This means that extreme values of t will be less likely, and so the tails of the distribution, which contain the probability associated with extreme values of t, will be smaller. We have already seen that for large samples, $(\bar{x}-\mu)/\sqrt{s^2/n}$ follows a Standard Normal distribution. The t distribution gets more and more like the Standard Normal distribution as the degrees of freedom increase.

Like the Normal distribution, the t distribution function cannot be integrated algebraically and its numerical values have been tabulated. Because the t distribution depends on the degrees of freedom, it is not usually tabulated in full like the Normal distribution in Table 7.1. Instead, probability points are given for different degrees of freedom. Table 10.1 shows two sided probability points for selected degrees of freedom. Thus, with 4 degrees of freedom, we can see that, with probability 0.05, t will be 2.78 or more from its mean, zero, as shown in Figure 10.2.

Because only certain probabilities are quoted, we cannot usually find the exact probability associated with

a particular value of t. For practical statistical analyses, a computer program calculates the required t distribution value every time, but Table 10.1 will be useful for illustration. For example, suppose we want to know the probability of t with 9 degrees of freedom being further from zero than 3.7. From Table 10.1 we see that the 0.01 point is 3.25 and the 0.001 point is 4.78. We therefore know that the required probability lies between 0.01 and 0.001. We could write this as $0.001 < P < 0.01$. Often the lower bound, 0.001, is omitted and we write $P < 0.01$.

The name 'Student's t distribution' often puzzles newcomers to the subject. It is not, as may be thought, an easy method suitable for students to use. The origin of the name is part of the folklore of statistics. The distribution was discovered by W. S. Gossett, an employee of the Guinness brewery in Dublin. At that time, the company would not allow its employees to publish the results of their work, lest it should lose some commercial advantage. Gossett therefore submitted his paper under the pseudonym 'Student' (Student 1908). In this paper he not only presented the mathematical derivation of the distribution, but also gave the results of a sampling experiment like those described in Appendix 4A and Section 8.1. He took the heights of 3000 men, obtained from a prison, wrote each onto a piece of card, then drew 750 samples of size 4 to give 750 $(\bar{x} - \mu)/\sqrt{s^2/n}$ statistics. Figure 10.3 shows the very good agreement which he obtained.

Table 10.1 Two tailed probability points of the t distribution

D.f.	Probability				D.f.	Probability			
	0.10 10%	0.05 5%	0.01 1%	0.001 0.1%		0.10 10%	0.05 5%	0.01 1%	0.001 0.1%
1	6.31	12.70	63.66	636.62	16	1.75	2.12	2.92	4.01
2	2.92	4.30	9.93	31.60	17	1.74	2.11	2.90	3.97
3	2.35	3.18	5.84	12.92	18	1.73	2.10	2.88	3.92
4	2.13	2.78	4.60	8.61	19	1.73	2.09	2.86	3.88
5	2.02	2.57	4.03	6.87	20	1.72	2.09	2.85	3.85
6	1.94	2.45	3.71	5.96	21	1.72	2.08	2.83	3.82
7	1.89	2.36	3.50	5.41	22	1.72	2.07	2.82	3.79
8	1.86	2.31	3.36	5.04	23	1.71	2.07	2.81	3.77
9	1.83	2.26	3.25	4.78	24	1.71	2.06	2.80	3.75
10	1.81	2.23	3.17	4.59	25	1.71	2.06	2.79	3.73
11	1.80	2.20	3.11	4.44	30	1.70	2.04	2.75	3.65
12	1.78	2.18	3.05	4.32	40	1.68	2.02	2.70	3.55
13	1.77	2.16	3.01	4.22	60	1.67	2.00	2.66	3.46
14	1.76	2.14	2.98	4.14	120	1.66	1.98	2.62	3.37
15	1.75	2.13	2.95	4.07	∞	1.64	1.96	2.58	3.29

D.f. = Degrees of freedom
∞ = infinity, same as the Standard Normal distribution

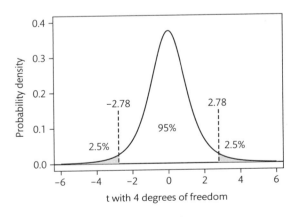

Figure 10.2 Two sided 5% probability points of the t distribution with 4 degrees of freedom.

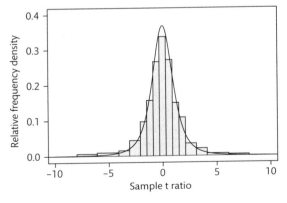

Figure 10.3 Sample t ratios derived from 750 samples of 4 human heights and the t distribution with 3 degrees of freedom (data from Student 1908).

10.2 The one sample t method

We can use the t distribution to find confidence intervals for means estimated from a small sample from a Normal distribution. We do not usually have small samples in sample surveys, but we often find them in clinical studies. For example, we can use the t distribution to find confidence intervals for the size of difference between two treatment groups, or between measurements obtained from subjects under two different conditions. I shall deal with the single sample problem first.

The population mean, μ, is unknown and we wish to estimate it using a 95% confidence interval. We can see that, for 95% of samples, the difference between $\bar{x}$ and μ is at most t standard errors, where t is the value of the t distribution such that 95% of observations will be closer to zero than t. For a large sample this will be 1.96 as for the Normal distribution. For small samples we must use Table 10.1. In this table, the probability that the t distribution is further from zero than t is given, so we must first find one minus our desired probability, 0.95. We have $1 - 0.95 = 0.05$, so we use the 0.05 column of the table to get the value of t. We then have the 95% confidence interval: $\bar{x} - t$ standard errors to $\bar{x} - t$ standard errors. The usual application of this is to differences between measurements made on the same or on matched pairs of subjects. In this application the one sample t test is also known as the **paired t test**.

Consider the data of Table 10.2. (I asked the researcher why there were so many missing data. He told me that some of the biopsies were not usable to count the capillaries, and that some of these patients were amputees and the foot itself was missing.) We shall estimate the difference in capillary density between the worse foot (in terms of ulceration, not capillaries) and the better foot for the ulcerated patients. The first step is to find the differences (worse – better). We then find the mean difference and its standard error, as described in Section 8.2. These are in the last column of Table 10.2.

To find the 95% confidence interval for the mean difference, we must suppose that the differences follow a Normal distribution and that the observations are independent. To calculate the interval, we first require the relevant point of the t distribution from Table 10.1. There are 16 non-missing differences and hence $n - 1 = 15$

degrees of freedom associated with s^2. We want a probability of 0.95 of being closer to zero than t, so we go to Table 10.1 with probability= $1 - 0.95 = 0.05$. Using the 15 d.f. row, we get $t = 2.13$. Hence the difference between a sample mean and the population mean is less than 2.13 standard errors for 95% of samples, and the 95% confidence interval is $-0.81 - 2.13 \times 1.51$ to $-0.81 + 2.13 \times 1.51$ = -4.03 to $+2.41$ capillaries/mm^2. On the basis of these data, the capillary density could be less in the worse affected foot by as much as 4.03 capillaries/mm^2, or greater by as much as 2.41 capillaries/mm^2. In the large sample case, we would use the Normal distribution instead of the t distribution, putting 1.96 instead of 2.13. We would not then need the differences themselves to follow a Normal distribution.

We can also use the t distribution to test the null hypothesis that in the population the mean difference is zero. If the null hypothesis were true, and the differences follow a Normal distribution, the test statistic mean/standard error would be from a t distribution with $n - 1$ degrees of freedom. This is because the null hypothesis is that the mean difference $\mu = 0$, hence the numerator $\bar{x} - \mu = \bar{x}$. We have the usual 'estimate over standard error' formula. For the example, we have

$$\frac{\bar{x}}{\sqrt{\frac{s^2}{n}}} = \frac{-0.81}{1.51} = -0.54$$

If we go to the 15 d.f. row of Table 10.1, we find that the probability of such an extreme value arising is greater than 0.10, the 0.10 point of the distribution being 1.75. Using a computer we would find $P = 0.6$. The data are consistent with the null hypothesis and we have not demonstrated the existence of a difference. Note that the confidence interval is more informative than the significance test.

We could also use the sign test to test the null hypothesis of no difference. This gives us 5 positives out of 12 differences (4 differences, being zero, give no useful information) which gives a two sided probability of 0.8, a little larger than that given by the t test. Provided the assumption of a Normal distribution is true, the t test is preferred because it is the most powerful test, and so most likely to detect differences should they exist.

Table 10.2 Capillary density (per mm²) in the feet of ulcerated patients and a healthy control group (data supplied by Marc Lamah)

Controls			Ulcerated patients			
Right foot	**Left foot**	**Average right and left[†]**	**Worse foot**	**Better foot**	**Average worse and better[†]**	**Difference worse – better**
19	16	17.5	9	?	9.0	?
25	30	27.5	11	?	11.0	?
25	29	27.0	15	10	12.5	5
26	33	29.5	16	21	18.5	−5
26	28	27.0	18	18	18.0	0
30	28	29.0	18	18	18.0	0
33	36	34.5	19	26	22.5	−7
33	29	31.0	20	?	20.0	?
34	37	35.5	20	20	20.0	0
34	33	33.5	20	33	26.5	−13
34	37	35.5	20	26	23.0	−6
34	?	34.0	21	15	18.0	6
35	38	36.5	22	23	22.5	−1
36	40	38.0	22	?	22.0	?
39	41	40.0	23	23	23.0	0
40	39	39.5	25	30	27.5	−5
41	39	40.0	26	31	28.5	−5
41	39	40.0	27	26	26.5	1
56	48	52.0	27	?	27.0	?
			35	23	29.0	12
			47	42	44.5	5
			?	24	24.0	?
			?	28	28.0	?
Number		19			23	16
Mean		34.08			22.59	−0.81
Sum of squares		956.13			1 176.32	550.44
Variance		53.12			53.47	36.70
Standard deviation		7.29			7.31	6.06
Standard error		1.67			1.52	1.51

† when one observation is missing the average = the other observation
? = missing data

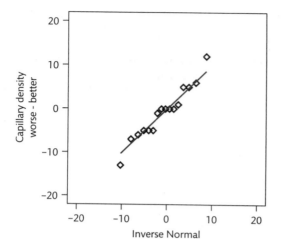

Figure 10.4 Normal plot for differences for the data of Table 10.2, ulcerated patients (data supplied by Marc Lamah).

The validity of the paired t method described above depends on the assumptions that the differences are independent and from a Normal distribution. We can check the assumption of a Normal distribution by a Normal plot (Section 7.5). Figure 10.4 shows a Normal plot for the differences. The points lie close to the expected line, suggesting that there is little deviation from the Normal.

Another plot which is a useful check here is the difference against the subject mean (Figure 10.5). If we are to estimate the mean difference, it should be constant and so unrelated to the magnitude of the observations.

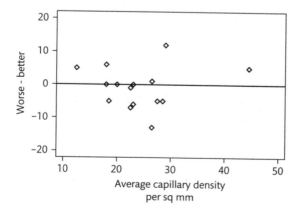

Figure 10.5 Plot of difference against average for the data of Table 10.2, ulcerated patients (data supplied by Marc Lamah).

As we use the estimate of the standard deviation, that should be constant, too. If the difference depends on magnitude, then we should be careful of drawing any conclusion about the mean difference. We may want to investigate this further, perhaps by transforming the data (Section 10.4). In this case the difference between the two feet does not appear to be related to the level of capillary density and we need not be concerned about this.

The differences may look like a fairly good fit to the Normal even when the measurements themselves do not. There are two reasons for this: the subtraction removes variability between subjects, leaving the measurement error which is more likely to be Normal, and the two measurement errors are then added by the differencing, producing the tendency of sums to the Normal seen in the Central Limit Theorem (Section 7.3). The assumption of a Normal distribution for the paired case is quite likely to be met. I discuss this further in Section 10.5.

10.3 The means of two independent samples

Suppose we have two independent samples of independent observations from populations which have a Normal distribution, with which we want to estimate the difference between the population means. If the samples were large, the 95% confidence interval for the difference would be the observed difference − 1.96 standard errors to observed difference + 1.96 standard errors. Unfortunately, we cannot simply replace 1.96 by a number from Table 10.1. This is because the standard error does not have the simple form described in Section 10.1. It is not based on a single sum of squares, but rather is the square root of the sum of two constants multiplied by two sums of squares. Hence, it does not follow the square root of the Chi-squared distribution as required for the denominator of a t distributed random variable (Appendix 7A). In order to use the t distribution, we must make a further assumption about the data. Not only must the samples be from Normal distributions, they must be from Normal distributions with the same variance. This is not as unreasonable an assumption as it may sound. A difference in mean but not in variability is a common phenomenon.

The PEFR data for children with and without symptoms analysed in Section 8.5 and Section 9.7 show the characteristic very clearly, as do the average capillary densities in Table 10.2.

We now estimate the common variance, s^2. First we find the sum of squares about the sample mean for each sample, which we can label SS_1 and SS_2. We form a combined sum of squares by $SS_1 + SS_2$. The sum of squares for the first group, SS_1, has $n_1 - 1$ degrees of freedom and the second, SS_2, has $n_2 - 1$ degrees of freedom. The total degrees of freedom is therefore $n_1 - 1 + n_2 - 1 = n_1 + n_2 - 2$. We have lost 2 degrees of freedom because we have a sum of squares about two means, each estimated from the data. The combined estimate of variance is

$$s^2 = \frac{SS_1 + SS_2}{n_1 + n_2 - 2}$$

The standard error of $\bar{x}_1 - \bar{x}_2$ is

$$\sqrt{\frac{s^2}{n_1} + \frac{s^2}{n_2}} = \sqrt{s^2\left(\frac{1}{n_1} + \frac{1}{n_2}\right)}$$

Now we have a standard error related to the square root of the Chi-squared distribution and we can get a t distributed variable by

$$\frac{\bar{x}_1 - \bar{x}_2 - (\mu_1 - \mu_2)}{\sqrt{s^2\left(\frac{1}{n_1} + \frac{1}{n_2}\right)}}$$

having $n_1 + n_2 - 2$ degrees of freedom. The 95% confidence interval for the difference between population means, $\mu_1 - \mu_2$, is

$$\bar{x}_1 - \bar{x}_2 - t\sqrt{s^2(1/n_1 + 1/n_2)}$$

to

$$\bar{x}_1 - \bar{x}_2 + t\sqrt{s^2(1/n_1 + 1/n_2)}$$

where t is the 0.05 point with $n_1 + n_2 - 2$ degrees of freedom from Table 10.1. Alternatively, we can test the null hypothesis that in the population the difference is zero, i.e. that $\mu_1 = \mu_2$, using the test statistic

$$\frac{\bar{x}_1 - \bar{x}_2}{\sqrt{s^2\left(\frac{1}{n_1} + \frac{1}{n_2}\right)}}$$

which would follow the t distribution with $n_1 + n_2 - 2$ d.f. if the null hypothesis were true.

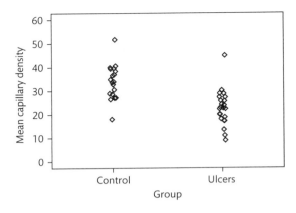

Figure 10.6 Scatter plot against group for the patient averages of Table 10.2 (data supplied by Marc Lamah).

For a practical example, Table 10.2 shows the average capillary density over both feet (if present) for control subjects as well as ulcer patients. We shall estimate the difference between the ulcerated patients and controls. We have only one observation per person, so our observations are independent. We next check the assumptions of Normal distribution and uniform variance. From Table 10.2 the variances appear remarkably similar, 53.12 and 53.47. Figure 10.6 shows that there appears to be a shift of mean only. The Normal plot (Figure 10.7) combines groups by taking the differences between each observation and its group mean, called

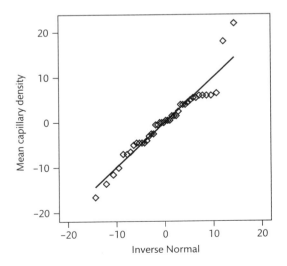

Figure 10.7 Normal plot for the patient averages of Table 10.2 (data supplied by Marc Lamah).

the **within-group residuals**. This has a slight kink at the end but no pronounced curve, suggesting that there is little deviation from the Normal. I therefore feel quite happy that the assumptions of the two sample t method are met.

First we find the common variance estimate, s^2. The sums of squares about the two sample means are 956.13 and 1 176.32. This gives the combined sum of squares about the sample means to be 956.13 + 1 176.32 = 2 132.45. The combined degrees of freedom are $n_1 + n_2 - 2 = 19 + 23 - 2 = 40$. Hence $s^2 = 2 132.45/40 = 53.31$. The standard error of the difference between means is

$$\sqrt{s^2 \left(\frac{1}{n_1} + \frac{1}{n_2} \right)} = \sqrt{53.31 \left(\frac{1}{19} + \frac{1}{23} \right)} = 2.26$$

The value of the t distribution for the 95% confidence interval is found from the 0.05 column and 40 d.f. row of Table 10.1, giving $t_{0.05} = 2.02$. The difference between means (control–ulcerated) is 34.08 – 22.59 = 11.49. Hence the 95% confidence interval is 11.49 – 2.02 × 2.26 to 11.49 + 2.02 × 2.26, giving 6.92 to 16.06 capillaries/mm^2. Hence there is clearly a difference in capillary density between controls and ulcerated patients.

To test the null hypothesis that in the population the control–ulcerated difference is zero, the test statistic is difference over standard error, 11.49/2.26 = 5.08. If the null hypothesis were true, this would be an observation from the t distribution with 40 degrees of freedom. From Table 10.1, the probability of such an extreme value is less than 0.001. Hence the data are not consistent with the null hypothesis and we can conclude that there is strong evidence of a difference in the populations which these patients represent.

What happens if we do not make the assumption of uniform variance? There is an approximate solution, the **Satterthwaite approximation**, based on the t distribution (e.g. see Davies and Goldsmith 1972; Snedecor and Cochran 1980) using the standard error formula of Section 8.5, $\sqrt{s_1^2/n_1 + s_2^2/n_2}$. Most statistical computer programs offer pooled variance and unpooled variance alternatives for the two sample t method. The difference between the variances leads to a rather complicated reduction in the degrees of freedom. For the capillary

data the variances are so similar that there is no effect. There are several other approaches based on the t test (see Armitage et al. 2002). Another approach is to abandon the use of variance altogether and use the Mann–Whitney U test (Section 12.2).

10.4 The use of transformations

We have already seen (Section 7.4) that some variables which do not follow a Normal distribution can be made to do so by a suitable transformation. The same transformation can be used to make the variance similar in different groups, called **variance stabilizing** transformations. Because mean and variance in samples from the same population are independent if and only if the distribution is Normal (Appendix 7A), stable variances and Normal distributions tend to go together.

Often standard deviation and mean are connected by a simple relationship of the form $s = a\bar{x}^b$, where a and b are constants. If this is so, it can be shown that the variance will be stabilized by raising the observations to the power $1 - b$, unless $b = 1$, when we use the log. (I shall resist the temptation to prove this, though I can. Any book on mathematical statistics will do it.) Thus, if the standard deviation is proportional to the square root of the mean (i.e. variance proportional to mean), e.g. Poisson variance (Section 6.7), $b = 0.5$, $1 - b = 0.5$, and we use a square root transformation. If the standard deviation is proportional to the mean we log. If the standard deviation is proportional to the square of the mean we have $b = 2$, $1 - b = -1$, and we use the reciprocal. Another, rarely seen transformation is used when observations are Binomial proportions. Here the standard deviation increases as the proportion goes from 0.0 to 0.5, then decreases as the proportion goes from 0.5 to 1.0. This is the arcsine square root transformation. Whether it works depends on how much other variation there is. It has now been largely superseded by logistic regression (Section 15.10).

When we have several groups we can plot log(s) against log($\bar{x}$) then draw a line through the points. The slope of the line is b (see Healy 1968). Trial and error, however, combined with scatter plots, histograms, and Normal plots, usually suffice.

Table 10.3 Biceps skinfold thickness (mm) in two groups of patients (data from Maugdal *et al.* 1985)

Crohn's disease				Coeliac disease	
1.8	2.8	4.2	6.2	1.8	3.8
2.2	3.2	4.4	6.6	2.0	4.2
2.4	3.6	4.8	7.0	2.0	5.4
2.5	3.8	5.6	10.0	2.0	7.6
2.8	4.0	6.0	10.4	3.0	

Table 10.3 shows some data from a study of anthropometry and diagnosis in patients with intestinal disease (Maugdal *et al.* 1985). The authors were interested in differences in anthropometrical measurements between patients with different diagnoses, and here we have the biceps skinfold measurements for 20 patients with Crohn's disease and nine patients with coeliac disease. The data have been put into order of magnitude and it is fairly obvious that the distribution is skewed to the right. Figure 10.8 shows this clearly. I have subtracted the group mean from each observation, giving the within-group residuals, and then found both the frequency distribution and Normal plot. The distribution is clearly skewed, and this is reflected in the Normal plot, which shows a pronounced curvature.

We need a Normalizing transformation, if one can be found. The usual best guesses are square root, log, and reciprocal, with the log being the most likely to succeed.

Figure 10.9 shows the scatter plot, histogram, and Normal plot for the residuals after transformation. (These logarithms are natural, to base *e*, rather than to base 10. It makes no difference to the final result and the calculations are the same to the computer.) The fit to the Normal distribution is not perfect, but for each transformation is much better than in Figure 10.8. The log looks the best for the equality of variance and the Normal distribution. We could use the two sample t method on these data quite happily.

Table 10.4 shows the results of the two sample t method used with the raw, untransformed data and with each transformation. The t test statistic increases and its associated probability decreases as we move closer to a Normal distribution, reflecting the increasing power of the t test as its assumptions are more closely met. Table 10.4 also shows the ratio of the variances in the two samples. We can see that as the transformed data get closer to a Normal distribution, the variances tend to become more equal also.

The transformed data clearly give a better test of significance than the raw data. The confidence intervals for the transformed data are more difficult to interpret, however, so the gain here is not so apparent. The confidence limits for the difference cannot be transformed back to the original scale. If we try it, the square root and reciprocal limits give ludicrous results. Squaring the limits for the square root transformed data always gives two positive limits, which could never include zero. Reciprocating the limits for the reciprocal transformed data gives –4.9 to 45.5, far wider than any possible difference in skinfold.

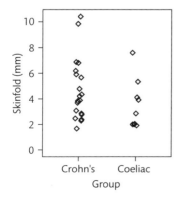
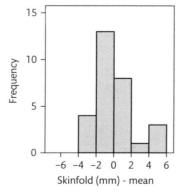
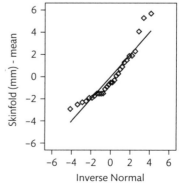

Figure 10.8 Scatter plot, histogram, and Normal plot for the biceps skinfold data (data from Maugdal *et al.* 1985).

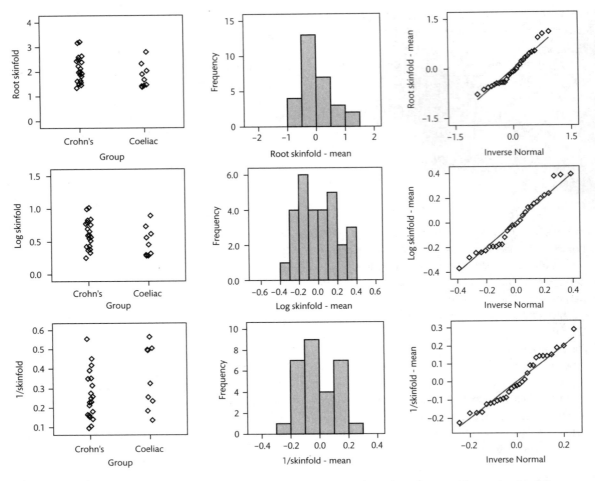

Figure 10.9 Scatter plot, histogram, and Normal plot for the biceps skinfold data, after square root, log, and reciprocal transformations (data from Maugdal *et al.* 1985).

Table 10.4 Biceps skinfold thickness (mm) compared for two groups of patients, using different transformations (data from Maugdal *et al.* 1985)

Transformation	Two sample t test, 27 d.f.		95% confidence interval for difference on transformed scale	Variance ratio, larger/smaller
	t	**P**		
None, raw data	1.28	0.21	−0.71 to 3.07	1.52
Square root	1.38	0.18	−0.140 to 0.714	1.16
Logarithm	1.48	0.15	−0.114 to 0.706	1.10
Reciprocal	−1.65	0.11	−0.203 to 0.022	1.63

If they contain zero, the narrower the reciprocal transformed limits, the wider would be the back transformed limits.

The log transformation gives interpretable results (0.89 to 2.03) but these are not limits for the difference in millimetres. How could they be, for they do not contain zero yet the difference is not significant? They are in fact the 95% confidence limits for the ratio of the Crohn's disease geometric mean to the coeliac disease geometric mean (Section 7.4). If there were no difference, of course, the expected value of this ratio would be one, not zero, and so lies within the limits. The reason is that when we take the difference between the logarithms of two numbers, we get the logarithm of their ratio, not of their difference (Appendix 5A).

Because the log transformation is the only one which gives useful confidence intervals, I would use it unless it were clearly inadequate for the data, and another transformation clearly superior. When this happens we are reduced to a significance test only, with no meaningful estimate.

10.5 Deviations from the assumptions of t methods

The methods described in this chapter depend on some strong assumptions about the distributions from which the data come. This often worries users of statistical methods, who feel that these assumptions must limit greatly the use of t distribution methods and find the attitude of many statisticians, who often use methods based on Normal assumptions almost as a matter of course, rather sanguine. We shall look at some consequences of deviations from the assumptions.

First we shall consider a non-Normal distribution. As we have seen, some variables conform very closely to the Normal distribution, others do not. Deviations occur in two main ways: grouping and skewness. **Grouping** occurs when a continuous variable, such as human height, is measured in units which are fairly large relative to the range. This happens, for example, if we measure human height to the nearest inch. The heights in Figure 10.3 were

to the nearest inch, and the fit to the t distribution is very good. This was a very coarse grouping, as the standard deviation of heights was 2.5 inches and so 95% of the 3 000 observations had values over a range of 10 inches, only 10 or 11 possible values in all. We can see from this that if the underlying distribution is Normal, rounding the measurement is not going to affect the application of the t distribution by much.

Skewness, on the other hand, can invalidate methods based on the t distribution. For small samples of highly skewed data, the t distribution does not fit the distribution of $(\bar{x} - \mu)/(\sqrt{s^2/n})$ at all well. When we have paired data this is not so important, because we have the Normalizing effect of the subtraction (Section 10.2). Skewness affects the two-sample t statistic of Section 10.3, but not so much as for one sample. In general for two equal sized samples the t method is resistant to deviations from the Normal distribution, though as the samples become less equal in size the approximation becomes less good. The most likely effect of skewness is that we lose power and may fail to detect differences which exist or have confidence intervals which are too wide. We are unlikely to get spurious significant differences. This means that we need not worry about small departures from the Normal. If there is an obvious departure from the Normal, we should try to transform the data to the Normal before we apply the t distribution.

Another assumption of the two sample t method is that the variances in the two populations are the same. If this is not correct, the t distribution will not necessarily apply. The effect is usually small if the two populations are from a Normal distribution. This situation is unusual because, for samples from the same population, mean and variance are independent if the distribution is Normal (Appendix 7A). There is an approximate t method, as we noted in Section 10.3. However, unequal variance is more often associated with skewness in the data, in which case a transformation designed to correct one fault often tends to correct the other as well.

These methods also treat the observations as independent, an assumption we often forget to mention. For comparison of ulcerated patients' feet with those of controls, I took the average of a person's feet, where possible, to give a single observation for each person.

The observations were thus independent. I could have used each foot separately. This would have given me groups of 39 observations for ulcers and 37 observations for controls, rather than 23 and 19, but it would have been wrong. The observations would not be independent and the confidence interval and significance test would not be valid.

Both the paired and two sample t methods are robust to most deviations from the distribution assumptions. Only large deviations are going to have much effect on these methods. The main problem is with skewed data in the one sample method, but for reasons given in Section 10.2, the paired test will usually provide differences with a reasonable distribution. If the data do appear to be non-Normal, then a Normalizing transformation will improve matters. If this does not work, then we must turn to methods which do not require these assumptions (Section 9.2, Section 12.2, Section 12.3).

Observations which are not independent will invalidate the method and may produce spurious results. When we have non-independent observations, for example if a sample of 30 observations is made up of three observations each from 10 people, we must take this into account in the analysis. We did this in Section 10.3 by taking the average of a person's two feet as our variable. There is another example in Section 10.13.

10.6 What is a large sample?

In this chapter we have looked at small sample versions of the large sample methods of Section 8.5 and Section 9.7. There we ignored both the distribution of the variable and the variability of s^2, on the grounds that they did not matter provided the samples were large. How small can a large sample be? This question is critical to the validity of these methods, but seldom seems to be discussed in text books.

Provided the assumptions of the t test apply, the question is easy enough to answer. Inspection of Table 10.1 will show that for 30 degrees of freedom the 5% point is 2.04, which is so close to the Normal value of 1.96 that it makes little difference which is used. So for Normal data with uniform variance, we can forget the t distribution when we have more than 30 observations.

When the data are not in this happy state, things are not so simple. If the t method is not valid, we cannot assume that a large sample method which approximates to it will be valid. I recommend the following rough guide. First, if in doubt, treat the sample as small. Second, transform to a Normal distribution if possible. In the paired case you should transform *before* subtraction. Third, the more non-Normal the data, the larger the sample needs to be before we can ignore errors in the Normal approximation.

There is no simple answer to the question: 'how large is a large sample?'. We should be reasonably safe with inferences about means if the sample is greater than 100 for a single sample, or if both samples are greater than 50 for two samples. The application of statistical methods is a matter of judgement as well as knowledge.

10.7 Serial data

Table 10.5 shows levels of zidovudine (AZT) in the blood of AIDS patients at several times after administration of the drug, for patients with normal fat absorption or fat malabsorption. A line graph of these data was shown in Figure 5.11. One common approach to such data is to carry out a two sample t test at each time separately, and researchers often ask at what time the difference becomes significant. This is a misleading question, as significance is a property of the sample rather than the population. The difference at 15 minutes may not be significant because the sample is small and the difference to be detected is small, not because there is no difference in the population. Further, if we do this for each time point, we are carrying out multiple significance tests (Section 9.10) and each test only uses a small part of the data so we are losing power (Section 9.9). It is better to ask whether there is any evidence of a difference between the responses of normal and malabsorption subjects over the whole period of observation.

The simplest approach is to reduce the data for a subject to one number. We can use the highest value attained by the subject, the time at which this peak value was reached, or the area under the curve. The first two are self-explanatory. The **area under the curve** or (**AUC**) is found by drawing a line through all the points and finding the area between it and the horizontal

Table 10.5 Blood zidovudine levels at times after administration of the drug by presence of fat malabsorption (data from Kapembwa *et al.* 1996)

Malabsorption patients:

				Time since administration of zidovudine							
0	15	30	45	60	90	120	150	180	240	300	360
0.08	13.15	5.70	3.22	2.69	1.91	1.72	1.22	1.15	0.71	0.43	0.32
0.08 .	0.08	0.14	2.10	6.37	4.89	2.11	1.40	1.42	0.72	0.39	0.28
0.08	0.08	3.29	3.47	1.42	1.61	1.41	1.09	0.49	0.20	0.17	0.11
0.08	0.08	1.33	1.71	3.30	1.81	1.16	0.69	0.63	0.36	0.22	0.12
0.08	6.69	8.27	5.02	3.98	1.90	1.24	1.01	0.78	0.52	0.41	0.42
0.08	4.28	4.92	1.22	1.17	0.88	0.34	0.24	0.37	0.09	0.08	0.08
0.08	0.13	9.29	6.03	3.65	2.32	1.25	1.02	0.70	0.43	0.21	0.18
0.08	0.64	1.19	1.65	2.37	2.07	2.54	1.34	0.93	0.64	0.30	0.20
0.08	2.39	3.53	6.28	2.61	2.29	2.23	1.97	0.73	0.41	0.15	0.08

Normal absorption patients:

				Time since administration of zidovudine							
0	15	30	45	60	90	120	150	180	240	300	360
0.08	3.72	16.02	8.17	5.21	4.84	2.12	1.50	1.18	0.72	0.41	0.29
0.08	6.72	5.48	4.84	2.30	1.95	1.46	1.49	1.34	0.77	0.50	0.28
0.08	9.98	7.28	3.46	2.42	1.69	0.70	0.76	0.47	0.18	0.08	0.08
0.08	1.12	7.27	3.77	2.97	1.78	1.27		0.83	0.57	0.38	0.25
0.08	13.37	17.61	3.90	5.53	7.17	5.16	3.84	2.51	1.31	0.70	0.37

axis. The 'curve' is usually formed by a series of straight lines found by joining all the points for the subject, and Figure 10.10 shows this for the first participant in Table 10.5. The area under the curve can be calculated by taking each straight line segment and calculating the area under this. This is the base multiplied by the average of the two vertical heights. We calculate this for each line segment, i.e. between each pair of adjacent time points, and add. Thus for the first subject we get $(15-0) \times (0.08+13.15)/2 + (30-15) \times (13.15+5.70)/2 + \cdots + (360 - 300) \times (0.43 + 0.32)/2 = 667.425$. This can be done fairly easily by most statistical computer packages. The area for each participant is shown in Table 10.6.

We can now compare the mean area by the two sample t method. As Figures 10.11 and 10.12 show,

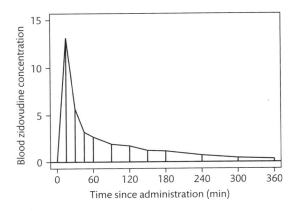

Figure 10.10 Calculation of the area under the curve for one subject (data supplied by Moses Kapembwa, personal communication).

Table 10.6 Area under the curve for data of Table 10.5 (data from Kapembwa *et al.* 1996)

Malabsorption patients		Normal patients
667.425	256.275	919.875
569.625	527.475	599.850
306.000	388.800	499.500
298.200	505.875	472.875
617.850		1 377.975

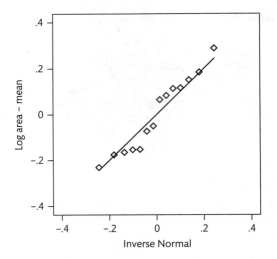

Figure 10.12 Normal plot for log area under the curve for the data of Table 10.5 (data supplied by Moses Kapembwa, personal communication).

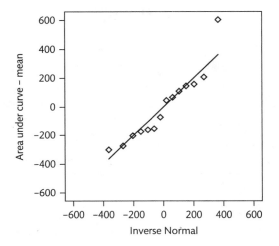

Figure 10.11 Normal plot for area under the curve for the data of Table 10.5 (data supplied by Moses Kapembwa, personal communication).

the log area gives a better fit to the Normal distribution than does the area itself. Using the log area we get $n_1 = 9$, $\bar{x}_1 = 2.639\,541$, $s_1 = 0.153\,376$ for malabsorption subjects and $n_2 = 5$, $\bar{x}_2 = 2.850\,859$, $s_2 = 0.197\,120$ for the normal subjects. The common variance is $s^2 = 0.028\,635$, standard error of the difference between the means is $\sqrt{0.028\,635 \times (1/9 + 1/5)} = 0.094\,385$, and the t statistic is $t = (2.639\,541 - 2.850\,859)/0.094\,385 = -2.24$ which has 12 degrees of freedom, $P = 0.04$. The 95% confidence interval for the difference is $2.639\,541 - 2.850\,859 \pm 2.18 \times 0.094\,385$, giving $-0.417\,078$ to $-0.005\,558$, and if we antilog this we get 0.66 to 0.99. Thus the area under the curve for malabsorption subjects is between 0.66

and 0.99 of that for normal AIDS patients, and we conclude that malabsorption inhibits uptake of the drug by this route. A fuller discussion of the analysis of serial data is given by Matthews *et al.* 1990).

10.8 Comparing two variances by the F test

We can test the null hypothesis that two population variances are equal using the F distribution. Provided the data are from a Normal distribution, the ratio of two independent estimates of the same variance will follow a F distribution (Appendix 7A), the degrees of freedom being the degrees of freedom of the two estimates. The F distribution is defined as that of the ratio of two independent Chi-squared variables divided by their degrees of freedom:

$$F_{m,n} = \frac{\chi_m^2/m}{\chi_n^2/n}$$

where m and n are the degrees of freedom (Appendix 7A). For Normal data the distribution of a sample variance s^2 from n observations is that of $\sigma^2\chi_{n-1}^2/(n-1)$, and when we divide one estimate of variance by another to give the F ratio the σ^2 cancels out. Like other distributions derived from the Normal, the F distribution cannot be integrated and so we must use a table. Because it has two degrees of freedom, the table is cumbersome, covering several pages, and I shall omit it. Most F methods are done using computer programs which calculate the probability directly. The table is usually given only as the upper percentage points.

To test the null hypothesis, we divide the larger variance by the smaller. For the capillary density data of Table 10.2, average of both feet, the variances are 53.47 for 23 people with ulcers, 22 d.f., and 53.12 for 19 controls, 18 d.f. This gives $F = 53.47/53.12 = 1.007$. The probability of this being exceeded by the F distribution with 18 and 22 degrees of freedom is 0.5, the upper 5% point of the distribution being 2.17, so there is no evidence from these data that the variance of capillary density differs between patients with foot ulcers and those without. Several variances can be compared by Bartlett's test or the Levene test (see Armitage *et al.* 2002; Snedecor and Cochran 1980).

10.9 Comparing several means using analysis of variance

Consider the data of Table 10.7. These are measures of gut permeability obtained from four groups of subjects, diagnosed with AIDS, AIDS related complex (ARC), asymptomatic HIV positive, and HIV negative controls. We want to investigate the differences between the groups.

One approach would be to use the t test to compare each pair of groups. This has disadvantages. First, there are many comparisons, $m(m-1)/2$ where m is the number of groups. The more groups we have, the more likely it is that two of them will be far enough apart to produce a 'significant' difference when the null hypothesis is true and the population means are the same (Section 9.10). Second, when groups are small, there may not be many degrees of freedom for the estimate of variance. If we can use all the data to estimate variance, we will have more degrees of freedom and hence a more powerful comparison. We can do this by **analysis of variance**, which compares the variation between the groups to the variation within the groups.

To illustrate how the analysis of variance, or **anova**, works, I shall use some artificial data, as set out in Table 10.8. In practice, equal numbers in each group are unusual in medical applications. We start by estimating the common variance within the groups, just as we do in a two sample t test (Section 10.3). We find the sum of squares about the group mean for each group and add them. We call this the **within groups sum of squares**. For Table 10.8 this gives 57.833. For each group we estimate the mean from the data, so we have estimated 4 parameters and have $24 - 4 = 20$ degrees of freedom. In general, for m groups of size n each, we have $nm - m = m(n-1)$ degrees of freedom. This gives us an estimate of variance of

$$s^2 = \frac{57.833}{20} = 2.892$$

This is the **within groups variance** or **residual variance**. There is an assumption here. For a common variance, we assume that the variances are the same in the four populations represented by the four groups.

We can also find an estimate of variance from the group means. The variance of the four group means is 5.462. If there were no difference between the means in the population from which the sample comes, this variance would be the variance of the sampling distribution of the mean of n observations, which is s^2/n, the square of the standard error (Section 8.2). Thus n times this variance should be equal to the within groups variance. For the example, this is $5.462 \times 6 = 27.375$, which is much greater than the 2.892 found within the groups. We express this by the ratio of one variance estimate to the other, between groups over within groups, which we call the variance ratio or F ratio. If the null hypothesis is true and if the observations are independent and from Normal distributions with uniform variance, this ratio follows a known distribution, the F distribution with $m-1$ and $n-m$ degrees of freedom (Section 10.8).

For the example we would have 3 and 20 degrees of freedom and

$$F_{3,20} = \frac{27.375}{2.892} = 9.47$$

If the null hypothesis were true, the expected value of this ratio would be 1.0. A large value gives us evidence of a difference between the means in the four populations. For the example we have a large value of 9.47 and

Table 10.7 Mannitol and lactulose gut permeability tests in a group of HIV patients and controls (data supplied by Moses Kapembwa, personal communication)

HIV status	Diarrhoea	%mannitol	%lactulose	HIV status	Diarrhoea	%mannitol	%lactulose
AIDS	yes	14.9	1.17	ARC	yes	10.212	0.323
AIDS	yes	7.074	1.203	ARC	no	2.474	0.292
AIDS	yes	5.693	1.008	ARC	no	0.813	0.018
AIDS	yes	16.82	0.367	HIV+	no	18.37	0.4
AIDS	yes	4.93	1.13	HIV+	no	4.703	0.082
AIDS	yes	9.974	0.545	HIV+	no	15.27	0.37
AIDS	yes	2.069	0.14	HIV+	no	8.5	0.37
AIDS	yes	10.9	0.86	HIV+	no	14.15	0.42
AIDS	yes	6.28	0.08	HIV+	no	3.18	0.12
AIDS	yes	11.23	0.398	HIV+	no	3.8	0.05
AIDS	no	13.95	0.6	HIV−	no	8.8	0.122
AIDS	no	12.455	0.4	HIV−	no	11.77	0.327
AIDS	no	10.45	0.18	HIV−	no	14.0	0.23
AIDS	no	8.36	0.189	HIV−	no	8.0	0.104
AIDS	no	7.423	0.175	HIV−	no	11.6	0.172
AIDS	no	2.657	0.039	HIV−	no	19.6	0.591
AIDS	no	19.95	1.43	HIV−	no	13.95	0.251
AIDS	no	15.17	0.2	HIV−	no	15.83	0.338
AIDS	no	12.59	0.25	HIV−	no	13.3	0.579
AIDS	no	21.8	1.15	HIV−	no	8.7	0.18
AIDS	no	11.5	0.36	HIV−	no	4.0	0.096
AIDS	no	10.5	0.33	HIV−	no	11.6	0.294
AIDS	no	15.22	0.29	HIV−	no	14.5	0.38
AIDS	no	17.71	0.47	HIV−	no	13.9	0.54
AIDS	yes	7.256	0.252	HIV−	no	6.6	0.159
AIDS	no	17.75	0.47	HIV−	no	16.5	0.31
ARC	yes	7.42	0.21	HIV−	no	9.989	0.398
ARC	yes	9.174	0.399	HIV−	no	11.184	0.186
ARC	yes	9.77	0.215	HIV−	no	2.72	0.045
ARC	no	22.03	0.651				

Table 10.8 Some artificial data to illustrate how analysis of variance works

	Group 1	Group 2	Group 3	Group 4
	6	4	7	3
	7	5	9	5
	8	6	10	6
	8	6	11	6
	9	6	11	6
	11	8	13	8
Mean	8.167	5.833	10.167	5.667

the probability of getting a value as big as this if the null hypothesis were true would be 0.000 4. Thus there is a significant difference between the four groups.

We can set these calculations out in an analysis of variance table, as shown in Table 10.9. The sum of squares in the 'between groups' row is the sum of squares of the group means times n. We call this the **between groups sum of squares**. Notice that in the 'degrees of freedom' and 'sum of squares' columns, the 'within groups' and 'between groups' rows add up to the total. The within groups sum of squares is also called the **residual sum of squares**, because it is what is left when the group effect is removed, or the **error sum of squares**, because it measures the random variation or error remaining when all systematic effects have been removed.

The sum of squares of the whole data, ignoring the groups, is called the **total sum of squares**. It is the sum of the between groups and within groups sum of squares.

Returning to the mannitol data, as so often happens the groups are of unequal size. The calculation of the between groups sum of squares becomes more complicated and we usually do it by subtracting the within groups sum of squares from the total sum of squares. Otherwise, the table is the same, as shown in Table 10.10. As these calculations are usually done by computer, the extra complexity in calculation does not matter. Here there is no significant difference between the groups.

If we have only two groups, one-way analysis of variance is another way of doing a two sample t test. For example, the analysis of variance table for the comparison of average capillary density (Section 10.3) is shown in Table 10.11. The probability is the same and the F ratio, 25.78, is the square of the t statistic, 5.08. The residual mean square is the common variance of the t test.

10.10 Assumptions of the analysis of variance

There are three assumptions for analysis of variance: that observations are independent of one another, that data come from Normal distributions within the groups, and that, in the population, the variances of these distributions are the same. The technical term for uniformity of variance is **homoscedasticity**; lack of uniformity is **heteroscedasticity**. Heteroscedasticity can affect analyses of variance greatly and we try to guard against it.

We can examine these assumptions graphically. For mannitol (Figure 10.13) the scatter plot for the groups shows that the spread of data in each group is similar, suggesting that the assumption of uniform variance is met, the histogram looks Normal and the Normal plot looks straight. This is not the case for the lactulose data, as Figure 10.14 shows. The variances are not uniform and the histogram and Normal plot suggest positive skewness. As is often the case, the group with the highest mean, AIDS, has the greatest spread. The square root

Table 10.9 One-way analysis of variance for the data of Table 10.8

Source of variation	Degrees of freedom	Sum of squares	Mean square	Variance ratio (F)	Probability
Total	23	139.958			
Between groups	3	82.125	27.375	9.47	0.0004
Within groups	20	57.833	2.892		

Table 10.10 One-way analysis of variance for the mannitol data (data supplied by Moses Kapembwa, personal communication)

Source of variation	Degrees of freedom	Sum of squares	Mean square	Variance ratio (F)	Probability
Total	58	1 559.036			
Between groups	3	49.012	16.337	0.6	0.6
Residual	55	1 510.024	27.455		

Table 10.11 One-way analysis of variance for the comparison of mean capillary density between ulcerated patients and controls, Table 10.2 (data supplied by Marc Lamah)

Source of variation	Degrees of freedom	Sum of squares	Mean square	Variance ratio (F)	Probability
Total	41	3 506.57			
Between groups	1	1 374.114	1 374.114	25.78	<0.0001
Residual	40	2 132.458	53.311		

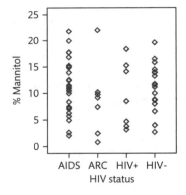 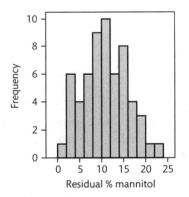 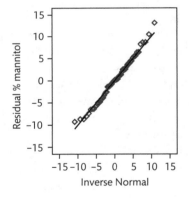

Figure 10.13 Plots of the mannitol data, showing that the assumptions of Normal distribution and homoscedasticity are reasonable (data supplied by Moses Kapembwa, personal communication).

transformation of the lactulose fits better, giving a good Normal distribution, although the variability is not uniform. The log transform over-compensates for skewness, by producing skewness in the opposite direction, though the variances appear uniform. Either the square root or the logarithmic transformation would be better than the raw data. I picked the square root because the distribution looked better. Table 10.12 shows the analysis of variance for square root transformed lactulose.

There are also significance tests which we can apply for Normal distribution and homoscedasticity. I shall omit the details.

10.11 Comparison of means after analysis of variance

Concluding from Tables 10.9 and 10.12 that there is a significant difference between the means is rather unsatisfactory. We want to know which means differ from which. There are a number of ways of doing this, called **multiple comparisons procedures**. These are mostly designed to give only one type I error (Section 9.4) per 20 analyses when the null hypothesis is true, as opposed to doing t tests for each pair of groups, which gives one error per 20 comparisons when the null hypothesis

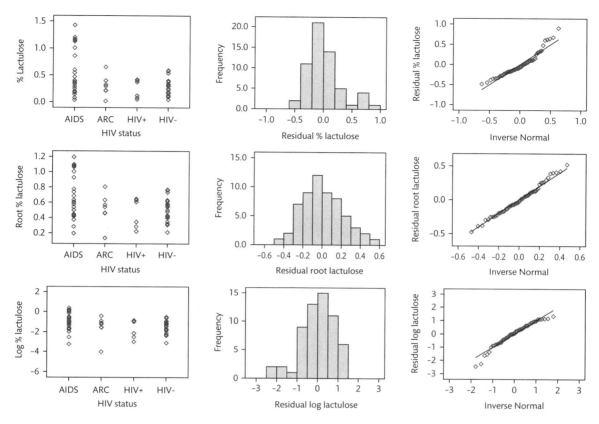

Figure 10.14 Plots of the lactulose data on the natural scale and after square root and log transformation (data supplied by Moses Kapembwa, personal communication).

Table 10.12 One-way analysis of variance for the square root transformed lactulose data of Table 10.7 (data supplied by Moses Kapembwa, personal communication)

Source of variation	Degrees of freedom	Sum of squares	Mean square	Variance ratio (F)	Probability
Total	58	3.254 41			
HIV status	3	0.428 70	0.142 90	2.78	0.049 5
Residual	55	2.825 71	0.051 38		

is true. I shall not go into details, but look at a couple of examples. There are several tests which can be used when the numbers in each group are the same, Tukey's Honestly Significant Difference, the Newman–Keuls sequential procedure (both called Studentized range tests), Duncan's multiple range test, etc. The one you use will depend on which computer program you have. The results of the Newman–Keuls sequential procedure for the data of Table 10.8 are shown in Table 10.13. Group 1 is significantly different from groups 2 and 4, and group 3 from groups 2 and 4. At the 1% level, the only significant differences are between group 3 and groups 2 and 4.

Table 10.13 The Newman–Keuls test for the data of Table 10.8

S = significant at the 0.05 level, N = not significant.				S = significant at the 0.01 level, N = not significant.			
Group	**Group**			**Group**	**Group**		
	1	2	3		1	2	3
2	S			2	N		
3	N	S		3	N	S	
4	S	N	S	4	N	N	S

Table 10.14 Gabriel's test for the root transformed lactulose data (data supplied by Moses Kapembwa, personal communication)

S = significant at the 0.05 level, N = not significant.				S = significant at the 0.01 level, N = not significant.			
Group	**Group**			**Group**	**Group**		
	AIDS	ARC	HIV+		AIDS	ARC	HIV+
ARC	N			ARC	N		
HIV+	S	N		HIV+	N	N	
HIV–	S	N	N	HIV–	N	N	N

For unequal-sized groups, the choice of multiple comparison procedures is more limited. Gabriel's test can be used with unequal sized groups. For the root transformed lactulose data, the results of Gabriel's test are shown in Table 10.14. This shows that the AIDS subjects are significantly different from the asymptomatic HIV+ patients and from the HIV– controls. For the mannitol data, most multiple comparison procedures will give no significant differences because they are designed to give only one type I error per analysis of variance. When the F test is not significant, no group comparisons will be either.

10.12 Random effects in analysis of variance

Although the technique is called analysis of variance, in Sections 10.9–10.11 we have been using it for the comparison of means. In this section we shall look at another application, where we shall indeed use anova to

look at variances. When we estimate and compare the means of groups representing different diagnoses, different treatments, etc., we call these **fixed effects**. In other applications, groups are members of a random sample from a larger population and, rather than estimate the mean of each group, we estimate the variance between them. We call these groups **random effects**.

Consider Table 10.15, which shows repeated measurements of pulse rate on a group of medical students. Each measurement was made by a different observer. Observations made repeatedly under the same circumstances are called **replicates** and here we have two replicates per subject. We can do a one-way analysis of variance on these data, with subject as the grouping factor (Table 10.16).

The test of significance in Table 10.16 is redundant, because we know each pair of measurements is from a different person, and the null hypothesis that all pairs are from the same population is clearly false. What we can use this anova for is to estimate some variances. There

Table 10.15 Paired measurements of 30 second pulse in 45 medical students

Subject	Pulse		Subject	Pulse		Subject	Pulse	
	A	B		A	B		A	B
1	46	42	16	34	36	31	43	43
2	50	42	17	30	36	32	30	29
3	39	37	18	35	45	33	31	36
4	40	54	19	32	34	34	43	43
5	41	46	20	44	46	35	38	43
6	35	35	21	39	42	36	31	37
7	31	44	22	34	37	37	45	43
8	43	35	23	36	38	38	39	43
9	47	45	24	33	34	39	48	48
10	48	36	25	34	35	40	40	40
11	32	46	26	51	48	41	46	45
12	36	34	27	31	30	42	44	42
13	37	30	28	30	31	43	36	34
14	34	36	29	42	43	44	33	28
15	38	36	30	39	35	45	39	42

Table 10.16 One-way analysis of variance for the 30 second pulse data of Table 10.15

Source of variation	Degrees of freedom	Sum of squares	Mean square	Variance ratio (F)	Probability
Total	89	3 054.99			
Between subjects	44	2 408.49	54.74	3.81	<0.0001
Within subjects	45	646.50	14.37		

are two different variances in the data. One is between measurements on the same person, the **within-subject variance** which we shall denote by σ_w^2. In this example the within-subject variance is the measurement error, and we shall assume it is the same for everyone. The other is the variance between the subjects' true or average pulse rates, about which the individual measurements for a subject are distributed. This is the average of all possible measurements for that subject, not the

average of the two measurements we actually have. This variance is the **between-subjects variance** and we shall denote it by σ_b^2. A single measurement observed from a single individual is the sum of the subject's true pulse rate and the measurement error. Such measurements therefore have variance $\sigma_b^2 + \sigma_w^2$. We can estimate both these variances from the anova table.

For the simple example of the same number of replicates m on each of n subjects, the estimation of the variances is quite simple. We estimate σ_w^2 directly from the mean square within subjects, MS_w, giving an estimate s_w^2. We can show (although I shall omit it) that the mean square between subjects, MS_b, is an estimate of $m\sigma_b^2 + \sigma_w^2$. The variance ratio, $F = MS_b/MS_w$, will be expected to be 1.0 if $\sigma_b^2 = 0$, i.e. if the null hypothesis that all subjects are the same is true. We can estimate σ_b^2 by $s_b^2 = (MS_b - MS_w)/m$.

For the example, $s_w^2 = 14.37$ and $s_b^2 = (54.74 - 14.37)/2 = 20.19$. Thus the variability between measurements by different observers on the same subject is not much less than the variability between the underlying pulse rate between different subjects. The measurement (by these untrained and inexperience observers) doesn't tell us much about the subjects. We shall see a practical application in the study of measurement error and observer variation in Section 20.2, and consider another aspect of this analysis, intraclass correlation, in Section 11.13.

If we have different numbers of replicates per subject or other factors to consider (e.g. if each observer made two repeated measurements), the analysis becomes fiendishly complicated (see Searle *et al.* 1992, if you must). These estimates of variance deserve confidence intervals like any other estimate, but these are even more fiendishly complicated, as Burdick (1992) convincingly demonstrate. I would recommend you consult a statistician experienced in these matters, if you can find one.

10.13 Units of analysis and cluster randomized trials

A cluster randomized study is one where a group of subjects, such as the patients in a hospital ward or a general practice list, are randomized to the same treatment together (Section 2.12). The treatment might be applied to participants directly, such as an offer of breast cancer screening to all eligible women in a district, or be applied to the care provider, such as treatment guidelines given to the GP. The design of the study must be taken into account in the analysis.

Table 10.17 shows an example (Oakeshott *et al.* 1994; Kerry and Bland 1998). In this study, guidelines as to appropriate referral for X-ray were given to GPs in 17

practices and another 17 practices served as controls. We could say we have 341 out of 429 appropriate referrals in the treated group and 509 out of 704 in the control group and compare these proportions as in Section 8.6 and Section 9.8. This would be wrong, because to follow a Binomial distribution, all the referrals must be independent (Section 6.4). They are not, as the individual GP may have a profound effect on the decision to refer. Even where the practitioner is not directly involved, members of a cluster may be more similar to one another then they are to members of another cluster and so not be independent. Ignoring the clustering may result in confidence intervals which are too narrow and P values which are too small, producing spurious significant differences.

The easiest way to analyse the data from such studies is to make the experimental unit, that which is randomized (Section 2.12), the unit of analysis. We can construct a summary statistic for each cluster and then analyse these summary values. The idea is similar to the analysis of repeated measurements on the same subject, where we construct a single summary statistic over the times for each individual (Section 10.7). For Table 10.17, the practice's percentage of referrals which are appropriate is the summary statistic. The mean percentages in the two groups can then be compared by the two sample t method. The observed difference is $81.6 - 73.6 = 8.0$ and the standard error of the difference is 4.3. There are 32 degrees of freedom and, from Table 10.1, the 5% point of the t distribution is 2.04. This gives a 95% confidence interval for the treatment difference of $8.0 \pm 2.037 \times 4.3$, or -1 to 17 percentage points. For the test of significance, the test statistic is $8.0/4.3 = 1.86$, $P = 0.07$.

In this example, each observation is a Binomial proportion, so we could consider an arcsine square root transformation of the proportions (Section 10.4). As Figure 10.15 shows, if anything the transformation makes the fit to the Normal distribution worse. This is reflected in a larger P value, giving $P=0.10$.

There is a widely varying number of referrals, between practices, which must reflect the list size and number of GPs in the practice. We can take this into account with an analysis which weights each observation by the numbers of referrals. Bland and Kerry (1998) give details.

Table 10.17 Number of X-ray requests conforming to the guidelines for each practice in the intervention and control groups (data from Oakeshott *et al.* 1994)

Intervention group			Control group		
Number of requests		Percentage conforming	Number of requests		Percentage conforming
Total	Conforming		Total	Conforming	
20	20	100	7	7	100
7	7	100	37	33	89
16	15	94	38	32	84
31	28	90	28	23	82
20	18	90	20	16	80
24	21	88	19	15	79
7	6	86	9	7	78
6	5	83	25	19	76
30	25	83	120	90	75
66	53	80	89	64	73
5	4	80	22	15	68
43	33	77	76	52	68
43	32	74	21	14	67
23	16	70	127	83	66
64	44	69	22	14	64
6	4	67	34	21	62
18	10	56	10	4	40
Total 429	341		704	509	
Mean		81.6			73.6
SD		11.9			13.1

10.14 Multiple choice questions: Comparisons of means

(Each branch is either true or false.)

10.1 The paired t test is:
(a) impractical for large samples;
(b) useful for the analysis of qualitative data;
(c) suitable for very small samples;
(d) used for independent samples;
(e) based on the Normal distribution.

10.2 Which of the following conditions must be met for a valid t test between the means of two samples:
(a) the numbers of observations must be the same in the two groups;
(b) the standard deviations must be approximately the same in the two groups;

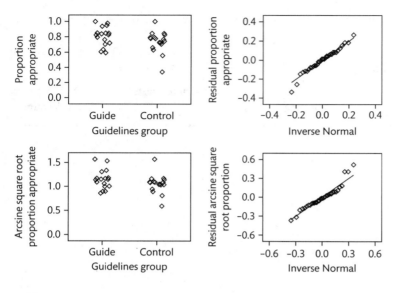

Figure 10.15 Scatter plots and Normal plots for the data of Table 10.17, showing the effect of an arcsine square root transformation. (data from Oakeshott *et al.* 1994).

(c) the means must be approximately equal in the two groups;

(d) the observations must be from approximately Normal distributions;

(e) the samples must be small.

10.3 In a two sample clinical trial, one of the outcome measures was highly skewed. To test the difference between the levels of this measure in the two groups of patients, possible approaches include:

(a) a standard t test using the observations;

(b) a Normal approximation if the sample is large;

(c) transforming the data to a Normal distribution and using a t test;

(d) a sign test;

(e) the standard error of the difference between two proportions.

10.4 In the two sample t test, deviation from the Normal distribution by the data may seriously affect the validity of the test if:

(a) the sample sizes are equal;

(b) the distribution followed by the data is highly skewed;

(c) one sample is much larger than the other;

(d) both samples are large;

(e) the data deviate from a Normal distribution because the measurement unit is large and only a few values are possible.

10.5 Table 10.18 shows a comparison of successful (i.e. fertile) and unsuccessful artificial insemination donors. The authors concluded that 'Conventional semen analysis may be too insensitive an indicator of high fertility [in AID]'.

(a) The table would be more informative if P values were given;

(b) The t test is important to the conclusion given;

(c) It is likely that semen count follows a Normal distribution;

(d) If the null hypothesis were true, the sampling distribution of the t test statistic for semen count would approximate to a t distribution;

(e) If the null hypothesis were false, the power of the t test for semen count could be increased by a log transformation.

10.6 If we take samples of size n from a Normal distribution and calculate the sample mean $\bar{x}$ and variance s^2:

(a) samples with large values of $\bar{x}$ will tend to have large s^2;

(b) the sampling distribution of $\bar{x}$ will be Normal;

(c) the sampling distribution of s^2 will be related to the chi-squared distribution with $n-1$ degrees of freedom;

(d) the ratio $\bar{x}/\sqrt{s^2/n}$ will be from a t distribution with $n-1$ degrees of freedom;

(e) the sampling distribution of s will be approximately Normal if $n > 20$.

10.7 In the one-way analysis of variance table for the comparison of three groups:

Table 10.18 Semen analyses for successful and unsuccessful sperm donors (data from Paraskevaides *et al.* 1991)

	Successful donors			Unsuccessful donors		
	n	mean	(SD)	*n*	mean	(SD)
Volume (ml)	17	3.14	(1.28)	19	2.91	(0.91)
Semen count (10^6/ml)	18	146.4	(95.7)	19	124.8	(81.8)
% motility	17	60.7	(9.7)	19	58.5	(12.8)
% abnormal morphology	13	22.8	(8.4)	16	20.3	(8.5)

All differences not significant, t test

(a) the group mean square + the error mean square = the total mean square;
(b) there are two degrees of freedom for groups;
(c) the group sum of squares + the error sum of squares = the total sum of squares;
(d) the numbers in each group must be equal;
(e) the group degrees of freedom + the error degrees of freedom = the total degrees of freedom.

10.15 Exercise: Some analyses comparing means

Liver transplant patients require drugs to suppress their immune systems and prevent rejection of the new liver. Renal dysfunction is a major complication of long-term immunosuppressive therapy with calcineurin inhibitors (CNI). Schlitt *et al.* (2001) randomly allocated 28 people, who had had renal dysfunction attributable to suspected CNI toxicity, to either replacement of CNI with mycophenolate mofetil (study patients, group A); or to remain on CNI immunosuppression (controls, group B). Renal function, blood pressure, uric acid, and blood lipids were measured before and 6 months after study entry. A figure similar to Figure 10.16 was given.

10.1 What method could be used to carry out the tests of significance shown in the figure, and why?
10.2 What can we conclude from these tests?
10.3 What test of significance would be better in this study?

The authors report: 'At the end of the study, mean (SD) serum creatinine had fallen by 44.4 (48.7) micromol/l in study

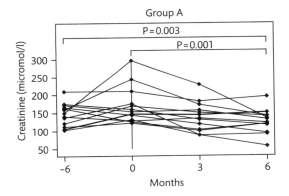

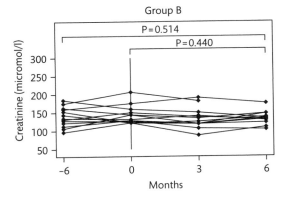

Figure 10.16 Serum creatinine concentrations in mycophenolate patients (A) and controls (B) before, at entry (0), and after study entry (reprinted from *The Lancet*, 357, 9256, Schlitt H *et al.*, "Replacement of calcineurin inhibitors with mycophenolate mofetil in liver transplant patients with renal dysfunction: a randomized controlled study", pp. 587–591, Copyright 2001, with permission from Elsevier).

patients compared with 3.1 (14.3) micromol/l in controls; a mean difference of 41.3 micromol/l (95% CI 12.4–70.2).'

10.4 What method would be used to calculate the confidence interval, and why? What condition should the data meet for this method?

10.5 The standard deviations are bigger than the means. Why should we NOT conclude that change in serum creatinine has a skew distribution?

In a different study, Paul *et al.* (1996) reported that 14 women were recruited to a cross-over trial comparing a breast pump with manual breast milk expression. Each women had three 15 minute sessions on each method: three sessions on the fourth and three on the fifth postnatal day. The order of application of the two methods was alternate. Their data were reported as shown in Table 10.19.

Table 10.19 Volume of breast milk expressed by manual and pump methods on postnatal days 4 and 5 in 15 minute sessions in 14 subjects (data from Paul *et al.* 1996)

	Pump	**Manual**
Milk expression sessions	42	42
Mean output per session (ml)	46.8	31.2
SD	26.3	15.5

Pump vs Manual t = 3.29, P<0.01

The authors do not give any further information about this t test. If we use the means and standard deviations given in the table, a two sample t test comparing two groups of 42 observations yields t = 3.31, d.f. = 82, two tailed probability P = 0.0014. This is almost the same as what they report, so this appears to be what they did, given that there would be rounding errors.

10.6 There are at least three things wrong with this test. What are they?

10.7 What effect might each of these problems have on the t test?

10.8 What better analysis could the authors have done?

Ng *et al.* (2002) evaluated the impact of early abdominopelvic computed tomography in patients with acute abdominal pain of unknown cause on length of hospital stay and accuracy of diagnosis. 120 patients admitted to hospital with acute abdominal pain for which no immediate surgical intervention or computed tomography was indicated were randomized to computed tomography within 24 hours of admission or to standard practice. They reported that early computed tomography reduced the length of hospital stay by 1.1 days (geometric mean 5.3 days (range 1 to 31) v 6.4 days (1 to 60)), but that the difference was not significant. The 95% confidence interval was 8% shorter stay to 56% longer stay, P = 0.17. They concluded that 'early abdominopelvic computed tomography for acute abdominal pain may reduce mortality and length of hospital stay'.

10.9 What can we deduce about the shape of the distribution of hospital stay?

10.10 What is a geometric mean and how was it calculated?

10.11 What does the 95% confidence interval given as '8% shorter stay to 56% longer stay' mean? What is surprising about it and why might it be wrong?

10.12 How could the 95% confidence interval given as '8% shorter stay to 56% longer stay' have been calculated?

10.13 Under Results, the authors say that 'Early computed tomography reduced the length of hospital stay by 1.1 days ... but the difference was non-significant ... '. What do you think of this statement?

10.14 The authors' first conclusion is that 'Early abdominopelvic computed tomography for acute abdominal pain may reduce mortality and length of hospital stay.' Is this a useful conclusion to be drawn from a clinical trial?

Appendix 10A: The ratio mean/standard error

We know that $\bar{x}$ has a Normal distribution with mean μ and variance σ^2/n. Hence $(\bar{x} - \mu)/\sqrt{\sigma^2/n}$ will be Normal with mean 0 and variance 1. The distribution of $(n - 1)s^2/\sigma^2$ is Chi-squared with $n - 1$ degrees of freedom (Appendix 7A). If we divide a Standard Normal variable by the square root of an independent Chi-squared variable over its degrees of freedom, we get the t distribution (Appendix 7A):

$$\frac{\dfrac{\bar{x}-\mu}{\sqrt{\sigma^2/n}}}{\sqrt{\dfrac{(n-1)s^2/\sigma^2}{n-1}}} = \frac{\dfrac{\bar{x}-\mu}{\sqrt{\sigma^2/n}}}{\sqrt{\dfrac{s^2}{\sigma^2}}}$$

$$= \frac{\bar{x}-\mu}{\sqrt{\dfrac{\sigma^2}{n}} \times \sqrt{\dfrac{s^2}{\sigma^2}}}$$

$$= \frac{\bar{x}-\mu}{\sqrt{\dfrac{\sigma^2}{n} \times \dfrac{s^2}{\sigma^2}}}$$

$$= \frac{\bar{x}-\mu}{\sqrt{\dfrac{s^2}{n}}}$$

As if by magic, we have our sample mean over its standard error. I shall not bother to go into this detail for the other similar ratios which we shall encounter. Any quantity which follows a Normal distribution with mean zero (such as $\bar{x}-\mu$), divided by its standard error, will follow a t distribution provided the standard error is based on one sum of squares and hence is related to the Chi-squared distribution.

11 Regression and correlation

11.1 Scatter diagrams

In this chapter I shall look at methods of analysing the relationship between two quantitative variables. Consider Table 11.1, which shows data collected by a group of medical students in a physiology class. Inspection of the data suggests that there may be some relationship between FEV1 and height. Before trying to quantify this relationship, we can plot the data and get an idea of its nature. The usual first plot is a scatter diagram (Section 5.6). Which variable we choose for which axis depends on our ideas as to the underlying relationship between them, as discussed below. Figure 11.1 shows the scatter diagram for FEV1 and height.

Inspection of Figure 11.1 suggests that FEV1 increases with height. The next step is to try and draw a line which best represents the relationship. The simplest line is a straight one; I shall consider more complicated relationships in Chapter 15.

The equation of a straight line relationship between variables y and x is $y = a + bx$, where a and b are constants.

Table 11.1 FEV1 and height for 20 male medical students

Height k (cm)	FEV1 (litres)	Height (cm)	FEV1 (litres)	Height (cm)	FEV1 (litres)
164.0	3.54	172.0	3.78	178.0	2.98
167.0	3.54	174.0	4.32	180.7	4.80
170.4	3.19	176.0	3.75	181.0	3.96
171.2	2.85	177.0	3.09	183.1	4.78
171.2	3.42	177.0	4.05	183.6	4.56
171.3	3.20	177.0	5.43	183.7	4.68
172.0	3.60	177.4	3.60		

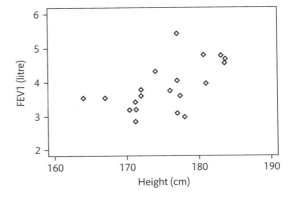

Figure 11.1 Scatter diagram showing the relationship between FEV1 and height for a group of male medical students.

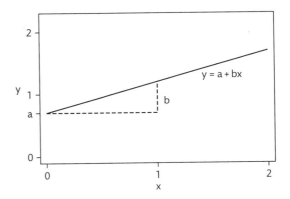

Figure 11.2 Coefficients of a straight line.

The first, a, is called the **intercept**. It is the value of y when x is 0. The second, b, is called the **slope** or **gradient** of the line. It is the increase in y corresponding to an increase of one unit in x. Their geometrical meaning is shown in Figure 11.2. We can find the values of a and b which best fit the data by regression analysis.

11.2 Regression

Regression is a method of estimating the numerical relationship between variables. For example, we would like to know what is the mean or expected FEV1 for students of a given height, and what increase in FEV1 is associated with a unit increase in height.

The name 'regression' is due to Galton (1886), who developed the technique to investigate the relationship between the heights of children and of their parents. He observed that, if we choose a group of parents of a given height, the mean height of their children will be closer to the mean height of the population than is the given height. In other words, tall parents tend to be taller than their children, short parents tend to be shorter. Galton termed this phenomenon 'regression towards mediocrity', meaning 'going back towards the average'. It is now called **regression towards the mean** (Section 11.4). The method used to investigate it was called regression analysis and the name has stuck. However, in Galton's terminology there was 'no regression' if the relationship between the variables was such that one predicted the other exactly; in modern terminology there is no regression if the variables are not related at all.

In regression problems we are interested in how well one variable can be used to predict another. In the case of FEV1 and height, for example, we are concerned with estimating the mean FEV1 for a given height rather than mean height for given FEV1. We have two kinds of variables: the **outcome** variable which we are trying to predict, in this case FEV1, and the **predictor** or **explanatory** variable, in this case height. The predictor variable is often called the **independent** variable and the outcome variable is called the **dependent** variable. However, these terms have other meanings in probability (Section 6.2), so I shall not use them. Other names for the outcome are '**left hand side variable**' and '**y variable**'. Other names for the predictor are '**right hand side variable**' and '**x variable**'. If we denote the predictor variable by X and the outcome by Y, the relationship between them may be written as

$$Y = a + bX + E$$

where a and b are constants and E is a random variable with mean 0, called the **error**, which represents that part of the variability of Y which is not explained by the relationship with X. If the mean of E were not zero, we could make it so by changing a. We assume that E is independent of X.

11.3 The method of least squares

If the points all lay along a line and there was no random variation, it would be easy to draw a line on the scatter diagram. In Figure 11.1 this is not the case. There are many possible values of a and b which could represent the data and we need a criterion for choosing the best line. Figure 11.3 shows the deviation of a point from the line, the distance from the point to the line in the Y direction. The line will fit the data well if the deviations from it are small, and will fit badly if they are large. These deviations represent the error E, that part of the variable Y not explained by X. One solution to the problem of finding the best line is to choose that which leaves the minimum amount of the variability of Y unexplained, by making the variance of E a minimum. This will be achieved by making the sum of squares of the deviations about the line a minimum. This is called the **method of least squares** and the line found is the **least squares line**.

The method of least squares is the best method if the deviations from the line follow a Normal distribution with uniform variance along the line. This is likely to be the case, as the regression tends to remove from Y the variability between subjects and leave the measurement

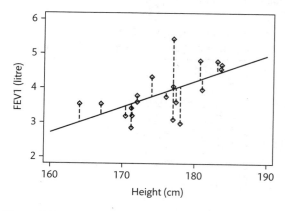

Figure 11.3 Deviations from the line in the y direction.

error, which is likely to be Normal. I shall deal with deviations from this assumption in Section 11.8.

Many users of statistics are puzzled by the minimization of variation in one direction only. Usually both variables are measured with some error and yet we seem to ignore the error in X. Why not minimize the perpendicular distances to the line rather than the vertical? There are two reasons for this. First, we are finding the best prediction of Y from the observed values of X, not from the 'true' values of X. The measurement error in both variables is one of the causes of deviations from the line, and is included in these deviations measured in the Y direction. Second, the line found in this way depends on the units in which the variables are measured. For the data of Table 11.1, the line found by this method is

FEV1 (litre) = − 9.33 + 0.075 × height (cm)

If we measure height in metres instead of centimetres, we get

FEV1 (litre) = − 34.70 + 22.0 × height (m)

Thus by this method the predicted FEV1 for a student of height 170 cm is 3.42 litres, but for a student of height 1.70 m it is 2.70 litres. This is clearly unsatisfactory and we will not consider this approach further.

Returning to Figure 11.3, the equation of the line which minimizes the sum of squared deviations from the line in the outcome variable is found quite easily (Appendix 11A). The solution is:

$$b = \frac{\sum(x_i - \bar{x})(y_i - \bar{y})}{\sum(x_i - \bar{x})^2}$$

$$= \frac{\sum x_i y_i - \frac{\left(\sum x_i\right)\left(\sum y_i\right)}{n}}{\sum x_i^2 - \frac{\left(\sum x_i\right)^2}{n}}$$

$$= \frac{\text{sum of products about the mean of } X \text{ and } Y}{\text{sum of squares about the mean of } X}$$

We then find the intercept a by

$$a = \bar{y} - b\bar{x}$$

Notice that the line has to go through the mean point, $(\bar{x}, \bar{y})$. The numerator, the **sum of products about the mean**, is similar to the sum of squares about the

mean as used in the calculation of variance. The second form, which is easier for calculator work, is found as in Appendix 4B. We shall say more about the properties of the **sum of products**, as it is usually termed, when we discuss correlation. Fitting a straight line by this method is called **simple linear regression**.

The equation Y = a+bX is called the **regression equation of Y on X**, Y being the outcome variable and X the predictor. The gradient, b, is also called the **regression coefficient**. We shall calculate this for the data of Table 11.1. We have

$$\sum x_i = 3\,507.6 \qquad \sum x_i^2 = 615\,739.24$$
$$\sum y_i = 77.12 \qquad \sum y_i^2 = 306.813\,4$$
$$n = 20 \qquad \sum x_i y_i = 13\,568.18$$
$$\bar{x} = 3\,507.6/20 = 175.38 \quad \bar{y} = 77.12/20 = 3.856$$

$$\text{sum of squares } X = \sum x_i^2 - \frac{\left(\sum x_i\right)^2}{n}$$
$$= 615\,739.24 - \frac{3\,507.6^2}{20}$$
$$= 576.352$$

$$\text{sum of squares } Y = \sum y_i^2 - \frac{\left(\sum y_i\right)^2}{n}$$
$$= 306.813\,4 - \frac{77.12^2}{20}$$
$$= 9.438\,68$$

$$\text{sum of products} = \sum x_i y_i - \frac{\left(\sum x_i\right)\left(\sum y_i\right)}{n}$$
$$= 13\,568.18 - \frac{3\,507.6 \times 77.12}{20}$$
$$= 42.874\,4$$

We do not need the sum of squares for Y yet, but we shall later.

$$b = \frac{42.874\,4}{576.352} = 0.074\,389 \text{ litre/cm}$$

$$a = \bar{y} - b\bar{x} = 3.856 - 0.074\,389 \times 175.38$$
$$= -9.19 \text{ litre}$$

Hence the regression equation of FEV1 on height is

FEV = − 9.19 + 0.074 4 × height

Figure 11.4 shows the line drawn on the scatter diagram.

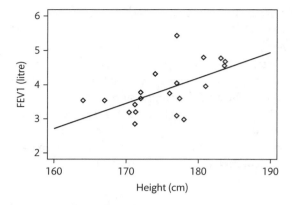

Figure 11.4 The regression of FEV1 on height.

The coefficients a and b have dimensions, depending on those of X and Y. If we change the units in which X and Y are measured we also change a and b, but we do not change the line. For example, if height is measured in metres we divide the x_i by 100 and we find that b is multiplied by 100 to give $b = 7.438\ 9$ litres/m. The line is

$$\text{FEV1 (litres)} = -9.19 + 7.44 \times \text{height (m)}$$

This is exactly the same line on the scatter diagram.

11.4 The regression of X on Y

What happens if we change our choice of outcome and predictor variables? The regression equation of height on FEV1 is

$$\text{height} = 158 + 4.54 \times \text{FEV1}$$

This is not the same line as the regression of FEV1 on height. If we rearrange this equation by dividing each side by 4.54 we get

$$\text{FEV1} = -34.8 + 0.220 \times \text{height}$$

The slope of the regression of height on FEV1 is greater than that of FEV1 on height (Figure 11.5). In general, the slope of the regression of X on Y is greater than that of Y on X, when X is the horizontal axis. Only if all the points lie exactly on a straight line are the two equations the same.

Figure 11.6 also shows the two 30 second pulse measurements of Table 10.15, with the lines representing the

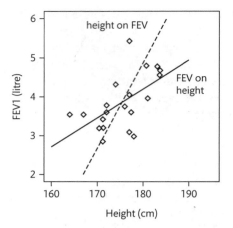

Figure 11.5 The two regression lines for the data of Table 11.1.

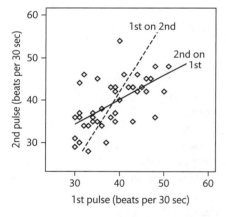

Figure 11.6 The two regression lines for the data of Table 10.15.

regression of the second measurement on the first and the first measurement on the second. The regression equations are 2nd pulse = 17.3 + 0.572 × 1st pulse and 1st pulse = 14.9 + 0.598 × 2nd pulse. Each regression coefficient is less than one. This means that for subjects with any given first pulse measurement, the predicted second pulse measurement will be closer to the mean than the first measurement, and for any given second pulse measurement, the predicted first measurement will be closer to the mean than the second measurement. This is regression towards the mean (Section 11.2). Regression towards the mean is a purely statistical phenomenon, produced by the selection of the given value of the predictor and the imperfect relationship between the variables. Regression towards the mean may manifest itself in many ways. For example, suppose we measure the blood pressure of an unselected group of people and then select subjects with high blood pressure, e.g. diastolic>95 mm Hg. If we then measure the selected group again, the mean diastolic pressure for the selected group will be less on the second occasion than on the first, without any intervention or treatment. The apparent fall is caused by the initial selection.

11.5 The standard error of the regression coefficient

In any estimation procedure, we want to know how reliable our estimates are. We do this by finding their standard errors and hence confidence intervals. We can also test hypotheses about the coefficients, for example, the null hypothesis that in the population the slope is zero and there is no linear relationship. These standard errors, confidence intervals, and t tests are only valid under the following assumptions about the data: that deviations from the line are Normal and have uniform variance and that the observations are independent of one another. The details are given in Appendix 11C. We first find the sum of squares of the deviations from the line, that is, the difference between the observed y_i and the values predicted by the regression line. This is

$$\sum (y_i - \bar{y})^2 - b^2 \sum (x_i - \bar{x})^2$$

$\sum (y_i - \bar{y})^2$ is, of course, the total sum of squares about the mean of y_i. The term $b^2 \sum (x_i - \bar{x})^2$ is called the **sum of squares due to the regression on** X. The difference between them is the **residual sum of squares** or **sum of squares about the regression**. The sum of squares due to the regression divided by the total sum of squares is called the **proportion of variability explained by the regression**.

In order to estimate the variance we need the degrees of freedom with which to divide the sum of squares. We have estimated not one parameter from the data, as for the sum of squares about the mean (Section 4.6), but

two, a and b. We lose two degrees of freedom, leaving us with $n - 2$. Hence the variance of Y about the line, called the **residual variance**, is

$$s^2 = \frac{1}{n-2} \left(\sum (y_i - \bar{y})^2 - b^2 \sum (x_i - \bar{x})^2 \right)$$

If we are to estimate the variation about the line, we must assume that it is the same all the way along the line, i.e. that the variance is uniform. This is the same as for the two sample t method (Section 10.3) and analysis of variance (Section 10.9). For the FEV1 data the sum of squares due to the regression is $0.074\,389^2 \times 576.352 = 3.189\,37$ and the sum of squares about the regression is $9.438\,68 - 3.189\,37 = 6.249\,31$. There are $20 - 2 = 18$ degrees of freedom, so the variance about the regression is $s^2 = 6.249\,3/18 = 0.347\,18$. The standard error of b is given by

$$SE(b) = \sqrt{\frac{s^2}{\sum (x_i - \bar{x})^2}}$$

$$= \sqrt{\frac{0.347\,18}{576.352}}$$

$$= 0.024\,54 \text{ litre/cm}$$

We have already assumed that the error E follows a Normal distribution, so b must do so, too. The standard error is based on a single sum of squares, so if β is the slope in the population, $(b - \beta)/SE(b)$ is an observation from the t distribution with $n - 2$ degrees of freedom (Section 10.1). We can find a 95% confidence interval for b by taking t standard errors on either side of the estimate. For the example, we have 18 degrees of freedom. From Table 10.1, the 5% point of the t distribution is 2.10, so the 95% confidence interval for b is $0.074\,389 - 2.10 \times 0.024\,54$ to $0.074\,389 + 2.10 \times 0.024\,54$ or 0.02 to 0.13 litres/cm. We can see that FEV1 and height are related, though the slope is not very well estimated.

We can also test the null hypothesis that, in the population, the slope = 0 against the alternative that the slope is not equal to 0, a relationship in either direction. The test statistic is $b/SE(b)$ and if the null hypothesis is true, this will be from a t distribution with $n - 2$ degrees of freedom. For the example,

$$t = \frac{b}{SE(b)} = \frac{0.074\,389}{0.024\,54} = 3.03$$

From Table 10.1 this has a two tailed probability of less than 0.01. The computer tells us that the probability is about 0.007. Hence the data are inconsistent with the null hypothesis and the data provide fairly good evidence that a relationship exists. If the sample were much larger, we could dispense with the t distribution and use the Standard Normal distribution in its place.

11.6 Using the regression line for prediction

We can use the regression equation to predict the mean or expected Y for any given value of X. This is called the **regression estimate** of Y. We can use this to say whether any individual has an observed Y greater or less than would be expected given X. For example, the predicted FEV1 for students with height 177 cm is $-9.19 + 0.074\,4 \times 177 = 3.98$ litres. Three subjects had height 177 cm. The first had observed FEV1 of 5.43 litres, 1.45 litres above that expected. The second had a rather low FEV1 of 3.09 litres, 0.89 litres below expectation, while the third with an FEV1 of 4.05 litres was very close to that predicted. We can use this clinically to adjust a measured lung function for height and thus get a better idea of the patient's status. We would, of course, use a much larger sample to establish a precise estimate of the regression equation. We can also use a variant of the method (Section 15.3) to adjust FEV1 for height in comparing different groups, where we can both remove variation in FEV1 due to variation in height and allow for differences in mean height between the groups. We may wish to do this to compare patients with respiratory disease on different therapies, or to compare subjects exposed to different environmental factors, such as air pollution, cigarette smoking, etc.

As with all sample estimates, the regression estimate is subject to sampling variation. We estimate its precision by standard error and confidence interval in the usual way. The standard error of the expected Y for an observed value x is

$$\text{SE(mean } Y \text{ given } X = x)$$

$$= \sqrt{s^2\left(\frac{1}{n} + \frac{(x - \bar{x})^2}{\sum(x_i - \bar{x})^2}\right)}$$

We need not go into the algebraic details of this. It is very similar to that in Appendix 11C. For $x = 177$ we have

$$\text{SE(mean } Y \text{ given } X = 177)$$

$$= \sqrt{0.347\,18^2\left(\frac{1}{20} + \frac{(177 - 175.38)^2}{576.352}\right)}$$

$$= 0.138$$

This gives a 95% confidence interval of $3.98 - 2.10 \times 0.138$ to $3.98 + 2.10 \times 0.138$, giving 3.69 litres to 4.27 litres. Here 3.98 is the estimate and 2.10 is the 5% point of the t distribution with $n - 2 = 18$ degrees of freedom.

The standard error is a minimum at $x = \bar{x}$, and increases as we move away from $\bar{x}$ in either direction. It can be useful to plot the standard error and 95% confidence interval about the line on the scatter diagram. Figure 11.7 shows this for the FEV1 data. Notice that the lines diverge considerably as we reach the extremes of the data. It is very dangerous to extrapolate beyond the data. Not only do the standard errors become very wide, but we often have no reason to suppose that the straight line relationship would persist. Figure 11.8 shows the confidence interval on a graph with a much wider scale, showing that for heights much smaller than in our own data, the predicted FEV becomes negative, clearly impossible.

The intercept a, the predicted value of Y when $X = 0$, is a special case of this. Clearly, we cannot actually have a medical student of height zero and with FEV1 of -9.19 litres. Figure 11.7 also shows the confidence interval for the regression estimate with a much smaller scale,

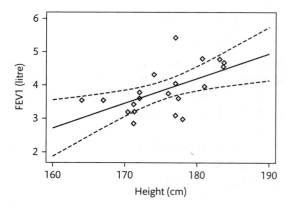

Figure 11.7 Confidence intervals for the regression estimate.

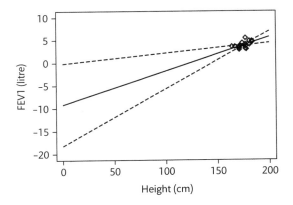

Figure 11.8 Confidence intervals for the regression estimate with an extended scale.

to show the intercept. The confidence interval is very wide at height = 0, and this does not take account of any breakdown in linearity.

We may wish to use the value of X for a subject to estimate that subject's individual value of Y, rather than the mean for all subjects with this X. The estimate is the same as the regression estimate, but the standard error is much greater:

SE(Y given $X = x$)

$$= \sqrt{s^2 \left(1 + \frac{1}{n} + \frac{(x - \bar{x})^2}{\sum(x_i - \bar{x})^2}\right)}$$

For a student with a height of 177 cm, the predicted FEV1 is 3.98 litres, with standard error 0.61 litres. Figure 11.9 shows the precision of the prediction of a further observation. As we might expect, the 95% confidence intervals

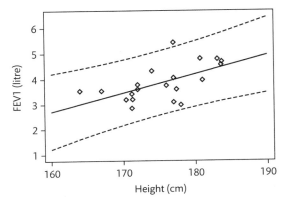

Figure 11.9 Confidence interval for a further observation.

include all but one of the 20 observations. This is only going to be a useful prediction when the residual variance s^2 is small.

We can also use the regression equation of Y on X to predict X from Y. This is much less accurate than predicting Y from X. The standard errors are

SE(mean X given $Y = y$)

$$= \sqrt{\frac{s^2}{b^2}\left(\frac{1}{n} + \frac{(y - \bar{y})^2}{b^2 \sum(x_i - \bar{x})^2}\right)}$$

SE(X given $Y = y$)

$$= \sqrt{\frac{s^2}{b^2}\left(1 + \frac{1}{n} + \frac{(y - \bar{y})^2}{b^2 \sum(x_i - \bar{x})^2}\right)}$$

For example, if we use the regression of height on FEV1 (Figure 11.5) to predict the FEV1 of an individual student with height 177 cm, we get a prediction of 4.21 litres, with standard error 1.05 litres. This is almost twice the standard error obtained from the regression of FEV1 on height, 0.61. Only if there is no possibility of deviations in X fulfilling the assumptions of Normal distribution and uniform variance, and so no way of fitting $X = a + bY$, should we consider predicting X from the regression of Y on X. This might happen if X is fixed in advance, e.g. the dose of a drug.

11.7 Analysis of residuals

It is often very useful to examine the residuals, the differences between the observed and predicted Y. This is best done graphically. We can assess the assumption of a Normal distribution by looking at the histogram or Normal plot (Section 7.5). Figure 11.10 shows these for the FEV1 data. The fit is quite good.

Figure 11.11 shows a plot of residuals against the predictor variable. This plot enables us to examine deviations from linearity. For example, if the true relationship were quadratic, so that Y increases more and more rapidly as X increases, we should see that the residuals are related to X. Large and small X would tend to have positive residuals, whereas central values would have negative residuals. Figure 11.11 shows no relationship between the residuals and height, and the linear model seems to be an adequate fit to the data.

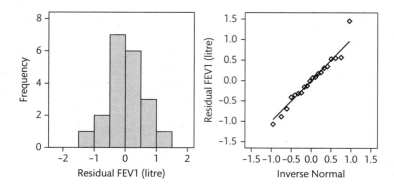

Figure 11.10 Distribution of residuals for the FEV1 data.

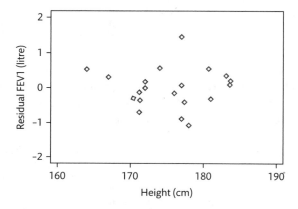

Figure 11.11 Residuals against height for the FEV1 data.

Figure 11.11 shows something else, however. One point stands out as having a rather larger residual than the others. This may be an **outlier**, a point which may well come from a different population. It is often difficult to know what to do with such data. At least we have been warned to double check this point for transcription errors. It is all too easy to transpose adjoining digits when transferring data from one medium to another. This may have been the case here, as an FEV1 of 4.53, rather than the 5.43 recorded in Table 11.1, would have been more in line with the rest of the data. If this happened at the point of recording, there is not much we can do about it. We could try to measure the subject again, or exclude him and see whether this makes any difference. I think that, on the whole, we should work with all the data unless there are very good reasons for not doing so. I have retained this case here.

11.8 Deviations from assumptions in regression

Both the appropriateness of the method of least squares and the use of the t distribution for confidence intervals and tests of significance depend on the assumption that the residuals are from a Normal distribution with uniform variance. This assumption is easily met, for the same reasons as in the paired t test (Section 10.2). The removal of the variation due to X tends to remove some of the variation between individuals, leaving the measurement error. Problems can arise, however, and it is always a good idea to plot the original scatter diagram and the residuals to check that there are no gross departures from the assumptions of the method. Not only does this help preserve the validity of the statistical method used, but it may also help us learn more about the structure of the data.

Figure 11.12 shows the relationship between gestational age and cord blood levels of AVP, the anti-diuretic hormone, in a sample of male fetuses. The variability of the outcome variable AVP depends on the actual value of the variable, being larger for large values of AVP. The assumptions of the method of least squares do not apply. However, we can use a transformation as we did for the comparison of means in Section 10.4. Figure 11.13 shows the data after AVP has been log transformed, together with the least squares line.

As in Section 10.4, the transformation is found by trial and error. The log transformation enables us to interpret the regression coefficient in a way which other transformations do not. I used logs to base 10

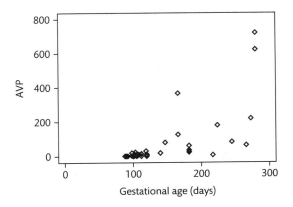

Figure 11.12 Data which do not meet the conditions of the method of least squares, before and after log transformation.

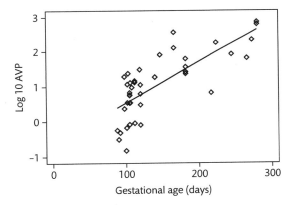

Figure 11.13 Data which do not meet the conditions of the method of least squares, after log transformation.

for this transformation and got the following regression equation:

$$\log_{10}(AVP)$$
$$= -0.651\,253 + 0.011\,771 \times \text{gestational age}$$

This means that for every 1 day increase in gestational age, $\log_{10}(AVP)$ increases by 0.011 771. Adding 0.011 771 to $\log_{10}(AVP)$ multiplies AVP by $10^{0.011\,771} = 1.027$, the antilog of 0.011 771. We can antilog the confidence limits for the slope to give the confidence interval for this factor.

It may be more convenient to report the increase per week or per month. These would be factors of $10^{0.011\,771 \times 7} = 1.209$ or $10^{0.011\,771 \times 30} = 2.255$, respectively. When the data are a random sample, it is often convenient to quote the slope calculated from logs as

the effect of a difference of one standard deviation of the predictor. For gestational age the standard deviation is 61.161 04 days, so the effect of a change of one SD is to multiply AVP by $10^{0.011\,771 \times 61.161\,04} = 5.247$, so a difference of one standard deviation is associated with a fivefold increase in AVP. Another approach is to look at the difference between two centiles, such as the 10th and the 90th. For gestational age these are 98 and 273 days, so the effect on AVP would be to multiply it by $10^{0.011\,771 \times (273-98)} = 114.796$. Thus the difference over this inter-centile range is to raise AVP 115-fold.

11.9 Correlation

The regression method tells us something about the nature of the relationship between two variables, how one changes with the other, but it does not tell us how close that relationship is. To do this we need a different coefficient, the correlation coefficient. The correlation coefficient is based on the sum of products about the mean of the two variables, so I shall start by considering the properties of the sum of products and why it is a good indicator of the closeness of the relationship.

Figure 11.14 shows the scatter diagram of Figure 11.1 with two new axes drawn through the mean point. The distances of the points from these axes represent the deviations from the mean. In the top right section of Figure 11.14, the deviations from the mean of both variables, FEV1 and height, are positive. Hence, their

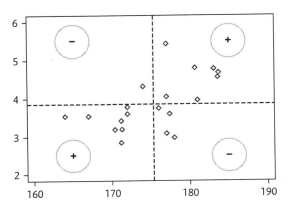

Figure 11.14 Scatter diagram with axes through the mean point.

products will be positive. In the bottom left section, the deviations from the mean of the two variables will both be negative. Again, their product will be positive. In the top left section of Figure 11.14, the deviation of FEV1 from its mean will be positive, and the deviation of height from its mean will be negative. The product of these will be negative. In the bottom right section, the product will again be negative. So in Figure 11.14 most of these products will be positive, and their sum will be positive. We say that there is a **positive correlation** between the two variables; as one increases so does the other. If one variable decreased as the other increased, we would have a scatter diagram where most of the points lay in the top left and bottom right sections. In this case the sum of the products would be negative and there would be a **negative correlation** between the variables. When the two variables are not related, we have a scatter diagram with roughly the same number of points in each of the sections. In this case, there are as many positive as negative products, and the sum is zero. There is **zero correlation** or **no correlation**. The variables are said to be **uncorrelated**.

The value of the sum of products depends on the units in which the two variables are measured. We can find a dimensionless coefficient if we divide the sum of products by the square roots of the sums of squares of X and Y. This gives us the **product moment correlation coefficient**, **Pearson's correlation coefficient**, or the **correlation coefficient** for short, usually denoted by r.

If the n pairs of observations are denoted by (x_i, y_i), then r is given by

$$r = \frac{\sum(x_i - \bar{x})(y_i - \bar{y})}{\sqrt{\left(\sum(x_i - \bar{x})^2\right)\left(\sum(y_i - \bar{y})^2\right)}}$$

$$= \frac{\sum x_i y_i - \dfrac{\left(\sum x_i\right)\left(\sum y_i\right)}{n}}{\sqrt{\left(\sum x_i^2 - \dfrac{\left(\sum x_i\right)^2}{n}\right)\left(\sum y_i^2 - \dfrac{\left(\sum y_i\right)^2}{n}\right)}}$$

$$= \frac{\text{sum of products about the mean of } X \text{ and } Y}{\sqrt{\text{sum of squares about the mean of } X \times \text{sum of squares about the mean of } Y}}$$

For the FEV1 and height we have

$$r = \frac{42.874\,4}{\sqrt{576.352 \times 9.438\,68}} = 0.58$$

The effect of dividing the sum of products by the root sum of squares of deviations of each variable is to make the correlation coefficient lie between −1.0 and +1.0. When all the points lie exactly on a straight line such that Y increases as X increases, r = 1. This can be shown by putting $a + bx_i$ in place of y_i in the equation for r; everything cancels out leaving r = 1. When all the points lie exactly on a straight line with negative slope, r = −1. When there is no relationship at all, r = 0, because the sum of products is zero. The correlation coefficient describes the closeness of the linear relationship between two variables. It does not matter which variable we take to be Y and which to be X. There is no choice of predictor and outcome variable, as there is in regression.

The correlation coefficient measures how close the points are to a straight line. Even if there is a perfect mathematical relationship between X and Y, the correlation coefficient will not be exactly 1 unless this is of the form y = a + bx. For example, Figure 11.15 shows two variables which are perfectly related but have r = 0.86. Figure 11.16 also shows two variables which are clearly related but have zero correlation, because the relationship is not linear. This shows again the importance of plotting the data and not relying on summary statistics such as the correlation coefficient only. In practice, relationships like those of Figures 11.15 and 11.16 are rare in medical data, although the possibility is always there. More often, there

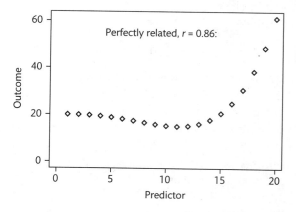

Figure 11.15 Data where the correlation coefficient may be misleading: perfect relationship.

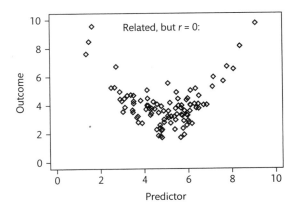

Figure 11.16 Data where the correlation coefficient may be misleading: U-shaped relationship.

is so much random variation that it is not easy to discern any relationship at all.

The correlation coefficient r is related to the regression coefficient b in a simple way. If $Y = a + bX$ is the regression of Y on X, and $X = a' + b'Y$ is the regression of X on Y, then $r^2 = bb'$. This arises from the formulae for r and b. For the FEV1 data, $b = 0.074\,389$ and $b' = 4.542\,4$, so $bb' = 0.074\,389 \times 4.542\,4 = 0.337\,90$, the square root of which is $0.581\,29$, the correlation coefficient. We also have

$$r^2 = \frac{(\text{sum of products about mean})^2}{\text{sum of squares of } X \times \text{sum of squares of } Y}$$

$$= \frac{(\text{sum of products about mean})^2}{(\text{sum of squares of } X)^2}$$
$$\times \frac{\text{sum of squares of } X}{\text{sum of squares of } Y}$$

$$= \frac{b^2 \times \text{sum of squares of } X}{\text{sum of squares of } Y}$$

This is the proportion of variability explained, described in Section 11.5.

11.10 Significance test and confidence interval for *r*

Testing the null hypothesis that $r = 0$ in the population, i.e. that there is no linear relationship, is simple. The test

is numerically equivalent to testing the null hypothesis that $b = 0$, and the test is valid provided the observations are independent of one another and at least one of the variables is from a Normal distribution. This condition is effectively the same as that for testing b, where the residuals in the Y direction must be Normal. If $b = 0$, the residuals in the Y direction are simply the deviations from the mean, and these will only follow a Normal distribution if Y does. If the condition is not met, we can use a transformation (Section 11.8), or one of the rank correlation methods (Section 12.4–5).

Because the correlation coefficient does not depend on the means or variances of the observations, the distribution of the sample correlation coefficient when the population coefficient is zero is easy to tabulate. Table 11.2 shows the correlation coefficient at the 5% and 1% level of significance. For the example we have $r = 0.58$ from 20 observations. The 1% point for 20 observations is 0.56, so we have $P < 0.01$, and the correlation is unlikely to have arisen if there were no linear relationship in the population. Note that the values of r which can arise by chance with small samples are quite high. With 10 points, r would have to be greater than 0.63 to be significant. On the other hand with 1000 points, very small values of r, as low as 0.06, will be significant.

Finding a confidence interval for the correlation coefficient is more difficult. Even when X and Y both follow Normal distributions, r does not itself approach a Normal distribution until the sample size is in the thousands. Furthermore, its distribution is rather sensitive to deviations from the Normal in X and Y. However, if both variables are from Normal distributions, Fisher's z transformation gives a variable with a Normal distribution whose mean and variance are known in terms of the population correlation coefficient which we wish to estimate. From this a confidence interval can be found. **Fisher's z transformation** is

$$z = \frac{1}{2} \log_e \left(\frac{1 + r}{1 - r} \right)$$

which follows a Normal distribution with mean

$$z_\rho = \frac{1}{2} \log_e \left(\frac{1 + \rho}{1 - \rho} \right) + \frac{\rho}{2(n - 1)}$$

and variance $1/(n-3)$ approximately, where ρ is the population correlation coefficient and n is the sample size.

Table 11.2 Two sided 5% and 1% points of the distribution of the correlation coefficient, r, under the null hypothesis

n	5%	1%	n	5%	1%	n	5%	1%
3	1.00	1.00	16	0.50	0.62	29	0.37	0.47
4	0.95	0.99	17	0.48	0.61	30	0.36	0.46
5	0.88	0.96	18	0.47	0.59	40	0.31	0.40
6	0.81	0.92	19	0.46	0.58	50	0.28	0.36
7	0.75	0.87	20	0.44	0.56	60	0.25	0.33
8	0.71	0.83	21	0.43	0.55	70	0.24	0.31
9	0.67	0.80	22	0.42	0.54	80	0.22	0.29
10	0.63	0.77	23	0.41	0.53	90	0.21	0.27
11	0.60	0.74	24	0.40	0.52	100	0.20	0.25
12	0.58	0.71	25	0.40	0.51	200	0.14	0.18
13	0.55	0.68	26	0.39	0.50	500	0.09	0.12
14	0.53	0.66	27	0.38	0.49	1000	0.06	0.08
15	0.51	0.64	28	0.37	0.48			

n = number of observations.

The 95% confidence interval for z will be approximately $z \pm 1.96\sqrt{1/(n-3)}$. For the FEV1 data, $r = 0.58$ and $n = 20$.

$$z = \frac{1}{2}\log_e\left(\frac{1+0.58}{1-0.58}\right) = 0.662\,5$$

The 95% confidence interval will be $0.662\,5 \pm 1.96\sqrt{1/17}$, giving 0.187 1 to 1.137 9. The transformation back from the z scale to the correlation coefficient scale is

$$r = \frac{\exp(2z) - 1}{\exp(2z) + 1}$$

where 'exp(x)' is the exponential or antilog, so for the lower limit we have

$$\frac{\exp(2 \times 0.187\,1) - 1}{\exp(2 \times 0.187\,1) + 1} = 0.18$$

and for the upper limit

$$\frac{\exp(2 \times 1.137\,9) - 1}{\exp(2 \times 1.137\,9) + 1} = 0.81$$

and the 95% confidence interval is 0.18 to 0.81. This is very wide, reflecting the sampling variation which the correlation coefficient has for small samples. Correlation coefficients must be treated with some caution when derived from small samples.

The ease of the significance test compared with the relative complexity of the confidence interval calculation has meant that in the past a significance test was usually given for the correlation coefficient. The increasing availability of computers with well-written statistical packages should lead to correlation coefficients appearing with confidence intervals in the future. However, I first wrote that in 1987 and I am still waiting.

11.11 Uses of the correlation coefficient

The correlation coefficient has several uses. Using Table 11.2, it provides a simple test of the null hypothesis that the variables are not linearly related, with less calculation than the regression method. It is also useful as a summary statistic for the strength of relationship between two variables. This is of great value when we are considering the inter-relationships between a large number of variables. We can set up a square array of the correlations of each pair of variables, called the **correlation matrix**. Examination of the correlation matrix can be very instructive, but we must bear in mind the possibility of non-linear relationships. There is no substitute for plotting the data. The correlation matrix also provides the starting point for a number of methods for dealing with a large number of variables simultaneously, such as principal components analysis (Section 20.9).

Of course, for the reasons discussed in Chapter 3, the fact that two variables are correlated does not mean that one causes the other. Correlation does not imply causation.

11.12 Using repeated observations

In clinical research we are often able to take several measurements on the same patient. We may want to investigate the relationship between two variables, and take pairs of readings with several pairs from each of several patients. The analysis of such data is quite complex. This is because the variability of measurements made on different subjects is usually much greater than the variability between measurements on the same subject, and we must take these two kinds of variability into account. What we must *not* do is to put all the data together, as if they were one sample. The observations would not be independent.

Consider the simulated data of Table 11.3. The data were generated from random numbers, and there is no relationship between X and Y at all. First, values of X and Y were generated for each 'subject', then a further random number was added to make the individual 'observation'. For each subject separately, there was no significant correlation between X and Y. For the subject means, the correlation coefficient was $r = 0.77$, $P = 0.23$. However, if we put all 40 observations together we get $r = 0.53$, $P = 0.0004$. Even though the coefficient is smaller than that between subject means, because it is based on 40 pairs of observations rather than 4 it becomes

Table 11.3 Simulated data showing 10 pairs of measurements of two independent variables for four subjects

	Subject 1		Subject 2		Subject 3		Subject 4	
	x	y	x	y	x	y	x	y
	47	51	49	52	51	46	63	64
	46	53	50	56	46	48	70	62
	50	57	42	46	46	47	63	66
	52	54	48	52	45	55	58	64
	46	55	60	53	52	49	59	62
	36	53	47	49	54	61	61	62
	47	54	51	52	48	53	67	58
	46	57	57	50	47	48	64	62
	36	61	49	50	47	50	59	67
	44	57	49	49	54	44	61	59
Means	45.0	55.2	50.2	50.9	49.0	50.1	62.5	62.6
	r = −0.33		r = 0.49		r = 0.06		r = −0.39	
	P = 0.35		P = 0.15		P = 0.86		P = 0.27	

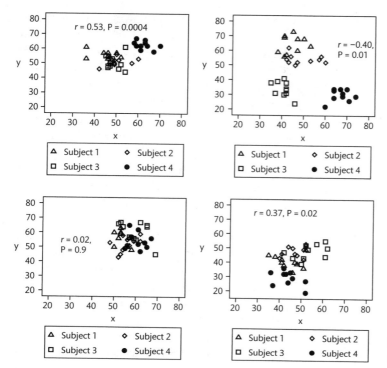

Figure 11.17 Simulations of 10 pairs of observations on four subjects.

significant. The data are plotted in Figure 11.17, with three other simulations. As the null hypothesis is always true in these simulated data, the population correlations for each 'subject' and for the means are zero. Because the numbers of observations are small, the sample correlations vary greatly. As Table 11.2 shows, large correlation coefficients can arise by chance in small samples. However, the overall correlation is 'significant' in three of the four simulations, though in different directions.

We only have four subjects and only four points. By using the repeated data, we are not increasing the number of subjects, but the statistical calculation is done as if we have, and so the number of degrees of freedom for the significance test is incorrectly increased and a spurious significant correlation produced.

There are two simple ways to approach this type of data, and which is chosen depends on the question being asked. If we want to know whether subjects with a high value of X tend to have a high value of Y also, we can use the subject means and find the correlation between them. If we have different numbers of observations for each subject, we can use a weighted analysis, weighted by the number of observations for the subject.

If we want to know whether changes in one variable in the same subject are paralleled by changes in the other, we need to use multiple regression, taking subjects out as a factor (Section 15.1, Section 15.8). In either case, we should not mix repeated observations from different subjects indiscriminately.

11.13 Intraclass correlation

Sometimes we have pairs of observations where there is no obvious choice of X and Y. The pulse data of Table 10.15 are a good example. Each subject has two measurements made by different observers, different pairs of observers being used for each subject. The choice of X and Y is arbitrary. Figure 11.18 shows the data as in Table 10.15 and with half the pairs arbitrarily reversed. The scatter plots look a little different and there is no good reason to choose one against the other. The correlation coefficients are a little different too: for the original order $r = 0.584\,8$ and for the second order $r = 0.580\,4$. These are very similar, of course, but which should we use?

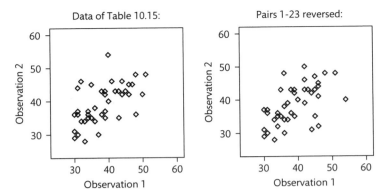

Figure 11.18 Scatter plots of the 30 second pulse data as in Table 10.15 and with half the pairs of observations reversed.

It would be nice to have an average correlation coefficient across all the 2^{45} possible orderings. This is provided by the **intraclass correlation coefficient** or **ICC**. This can be found from the estimates of within-subject variance, s_w^2, and between-subjects variance, s_b^2, found from the analysis of variance in Section 10.12. We have:

$$ICC = \frac{s_b^2}{s_b^2 + s_w^2}$$

For the example, $s_w^2 = 14.37$ and $s_b^2 = 20.19$ (Section 10.12). hence

$$ICC = \frac{20.19}{20.19 + 14.37} = 0.5842$$

The ICC was originally developed for applications such as correlation between variables measured in pairs of twins (which twin is X and which is Y?). We do not have to have pairs of measurements to use the ICC. It works just as well for triplets or for any number of observations within the groups, not necessarily all the same.

Although not used nearly as often as the product moment correlation coefficient, the ICC has some important applications. One is in the study of measurement error and observer variation (Section 20.2), where if measurements are true replicates, the order in which they were made is not important. Another is in the design of cluster randomized trials where the group is the cluster and may have hundreds of observations within it (Section 18.8).

11.14 Multiple choice questions: Regression and correlation

(Each branch is either true or false.)

11.1 In Figure 11.19:
- (a) predictor and outcome are independent;
- (b) predictor and outcome are uncorrelated;
- (c) the correlation between predictor and outcome is less than 1;
- (d) predictor and outcome are perfectly related;
- (e) the relationship is best estimated by simple linear regression.

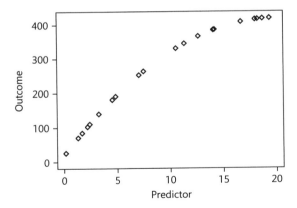

Figure 11.19 A scatter diagram.

11.2 In Figure 11.20:
- (a) predictor and outcome are independent random variables;
- (b) the correlation between predictor and outcome is close to zero;
- (c) outcome increases as predictor increases;

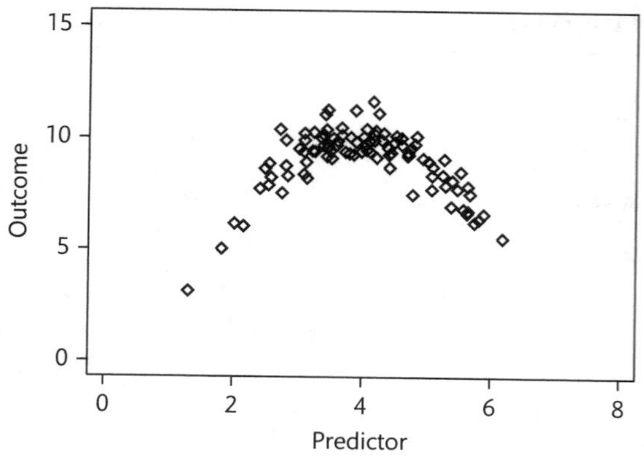

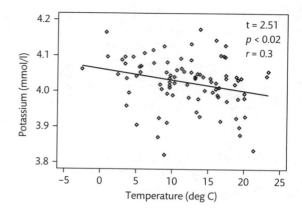

Figure 11.20 Another scatter diagram.

(d) predictor and outcome are linearly related;

(e) the relationship could be made linear by a logarithmic transformation of the outcome.

11.3 A simple linear regression equation:

(a) describes a line which goes through the origin;

(b) describes a line with zero slope;

(c) is not affected by changes of scale;

(d) describes a line which goes through the mean point;

(e) is affected by the choice of dependent variable.

11.4 If the t distribution is used to find a confidence interval for the slope of a regression line:

(a) deviations from the line in the independent variable must follow a Normal distribution;

(b) deviations from the line in the dependent variable must follow a Normal distribution;

(c) the variance about the line is assumed to be the same throughout the range of the predictor variable;

(d) the y variable must be log transformed;

(e) all the points must lie on the line.

11.5 The product moment correlation coefficient, r:

(a) must lie between −1 and +1;

(b) can only have a valid significance test carried out when at least one of the variables is from a Normal distribution;

(c) is 0.5 when there is no relationship;

(d) depends on which of the two variables is chosen as the dependent variable;

(e) measures the magnitude of the change in one variable associated with a change in the other.

Figure 11.21 Mean serum potassium and ambient temperature for hospitals and family practices (data from Ulahannan *et al.* 1998).

11.15 Exercise: Serum potassium and ambient temperature

In a study of the relationship between serum potassium concentration and ambient temperature, investigators obtained mean daily temperatures recorded in central Oxford between April 1, 1996, and Dec 31, 1997 (Ulahannan *et al.* 1998). They also obtained details of mean daily potassium concentrations from six hospital sites and family physicians in Oxfordshire for the same time. They produced a graph similar to Figure 11.21.

11.1 What kind of diagram is this?

11.2 What is the sloping straight line on the diagram?

11.3 What principle is used to calculate the line which best fits the data?

11.4 What is meant by the symbol 'r'?

11.5 Why is the value of 'r' wrong on the diagram?

11.6 What assumption is required for the tests of significance for r to be valid?

11.7 How would you describe the evidence for a relationship between ambient temperature and serum potassium based on this graph?

Appendix 11A: The least squares estimates

This section requires knowledge of calculus. We want to find a and b so that the sum of squares about the line $y = a + bx$ is a minimum. We therefore want to minimize

$\sum(y_i - a - bx_i)^2$. This will have a minimum when the partial differentials with respect to a and b are both zero.

$$\frac{\partial \sum(y_i - a - bx_i)^2}{\partial a}$$

$$= \sum 2(y_i - a - bx_i)(-1)$$

$$= -2\sum y_i + 2a\sum 1 + 2b\sum x_i$$

$$= -2\sum y_i + 2an + 2b\sum x_i$$

This must equal 0 so $\sum y_i = na + b\sum x_i$. and dividing by n we get $a = \bar{y} - b\bar{x}$.

$$\frac{\partial \sum(y_i - a - bx_i)^2}{\partial b}$$

$$= \sum 2(y_i - a - bx_i)(-x_i)$$

$$= -2\sum x_i y_i + 2a\sum x_i + 2b\sum x_i^2$$

This must equal 0 so $\sum x_i y_i = a\sum x_i + b\sum x_i^2$. We multiply the first equation by $\frac{1}{n}\sum x_i$, to make the coefficients of a equal.

$$\frac{1}{n}\sum x_i \sum y_i = a\sum x_i + \frac{b}{n}\left(\sum x_i\right)^2$$

Subtracting this from the second equation we get

$$\sum x_i y_i - \frac{1}{n}\sum x_i \sum y_i$$

$$= b\sum x_i^2 - \frac{b}{n}\left(\sum x_i\right)^2$$

$$= -b\left(\sum x_i^2 - \frac{1}{n}\left(\sum x_i\right)^2\right)$$

This gives us

$$b = \frac{\sum x_i y_i - \dfrac{\left(\sum x_i\right)\left(\sum y_i\right)}{n}}{\sum x_i^2 - \dfrac{\left(\sum x_i\right)^2}{n}}$$

Appendix 11B: Variance about the regression line

We find the formula for the variance about the regression line, s^2, as follows. The regression model is $Y = a + bX + E$, and a and b are constants. We are predicting Y for given X, so there is no random variation in X; all the random variation is in E. Hence $s^2 = \text{VAR}(Y \text{ given } X) = \text{VAR}(E)$. We

have seen in Section 11.2 that the error E is the random variable which stands for the deviations from the line in the Y direction. These deviations are $y_i - (a + bx_i)$, as $a + bx_i$ is the Y value for the line at $X = x_i$. The sum of squares of these deviations is found by a mathematical trick, replacing a by $\bar{y} - b\bar{x}$.

$$\sum(y_i - (a + bx_i))^2 = \sum(y_i - (\bar{y} - b\bar{x} + bx_i))^2$$

$$= \sum(y_i - \bar{y} - (bx_i - b\bar{x}))^2$$

$$= \sum(y_i - \bar{y} - b(x_i - \bar{x}))^2$$

$$= \sum\left((y_i - \bar{y})^2 - 2b(y_i - \bar{y})(x_i - \bar{x}) + b^2(x_i - \bar{x})^2\right)$$

$$= \sum(y_i - \bar{y})^2 - 2b\sum(y_i - \bar{y})(x_i - \bar{x}) + b^2\sum(x_i - \bar{x})^2$$

$$= \sum(y_i - \bar{y})^2 - 2b \times b\sum(x_i - \bar{x})^2 + b^2\sum(x_i - \bar{x})^2$$

$$= \sum(y_i - \bar{y})^2 - b^2\sum(x_i - \bar{x})^2$$

This is because

$$b = \left(\sum(y_i - \bar{y})(x_i - \bar{x})\right) \Big/ \left(\sum(x_i - \bar{x})^2\right)$$

so

$$\sum(y_i - \bar{y})(x_i - \bar{x}) = b\sum(x_i - \bar{x})^2$$

Appendix 11C: The standard error of b

To find the standard error of b, we must bear in mind that in our regression model all the random variation is in Y. We first rewrite the sum of products:

$$\sum(x_i - \bar{x})(y_i - \bar{y}) = \sum((x_i - \bar{x})y_i - (x_i - \bar{x})\bar{y})$$

$$= \sum(x_i - \bar{x})y_i - \sum(x_i - \bar{x})\bar{y}$$

$$= \sum(x_i - \bar{x})y_i - \bar{y}\sum(x_i - \bar{x})$$

$$= \sum(x_i - \bar{x})y_i$$

This is because $\bar{y}$ is the same for all i and so comes out of the summation, and $\sum(x_i - \bar{x}) = 0$. We now find the variance of the sampling distribution of b by

$$VAR(b) = VAR\left(\frac{\sum(x_i - \bar{x})(y_i - \bar{y})}{\sum(x_i - \bar{x})^2}\right)$$

$$= VAR\left(\frac{\sum(x_i - \bar{x})y_i}{\sum(x_i - \bar{x})^2}\right)$$

$$= \frac{1}{\left(\sum(x_i - \bar{x})^2\right)^2}VAR\sum(x_i - \bar{x})y_i$$

The variance of a constant times a random variable is the square of the constant times the variance of the random variable (Section 6.6). The x_i are constants, not random variables, so

$$VAR(b) = \frac{1}{\left(\sum(x_i - \bar{x})^2\right)^2}\sum(x_i - \bar{x})^2 VAR(y_i)$$

$VAR(y_i)$ is the same for all y_i, say $VAR(y_i) = s^2$. Hence

$$VAR(b) = \frac{s^2}{\sum(x_i - \bar{x})^2}$$

The standard error of b is the square root of this.

12 Methods based on rank order

12.1 Non-parametric methods

In Chapters 10 and 11, I described a number of methods of analysis which relied on the assumption that the data came from a Normal distribution. To be more precise, we could say the data come from one of the Normal family of distributions, the particular Normal distribution involved being defined by its mean and standard deviation, the parameters of the distribution. These methods are called **parametric** because we estimate the parameters of the underlying Normal distribution. Methods which do not assume a particular family of distributions for the data are said to be **non-parametric**. In this and the next chapter, I shall consider some non-parametric tests of significance. There are many others, but these will illustrate the general principle. We have already met one non-parametric test, the sign test (Section 9.2) and one totally non-parametric approach, bootstrapping (Section 8.11). The large sample Normal test (Section 9.7) could also be regarded as non-parametric.

It is useful to distinguish between several types of measurement scales. On an **interval scale**, the size of the difference between two values on the scale has a consistent meaning. For example, the difference in temperature between 1°C and 2°C is the same as the difference between 31°C and 32°C. Many interval scales are also **ratio scales**, which have a true zero. The °C scale has an arbitrary zero at the freezing point of water. Human height is a ratio scale and we can calculate ratios of heights: a person 2.0 metres tall is twice as tall as a person 1.0 metres tall. Water at 2.0°C is not twice as hot as water at 1.0°C. On an **ordinal scale**, observations are ordered, but differences may not have a meaning. For example, anxiety is often measured using sets of questions, the number of positive answers giving the anxiety scale. A set of 36 questions would give a scale from 0 to 36. The difference in anxiety between scores of 1 and 2 is not necessarily the same as the difference between scores 31 and 32. On a **nominal scale**, we have a qualitative or categorical variable, where individuals are grouped but not necessarily ordered. Eye colour is a good example. When categories are ordered, we can treat the scale as either ordered or nominal, as appropriate.

All the methods of Chapters 10 and 11 apply to interval data, being based on differences of observations from the mean. Most of the methods in this chapter apply to ordinal data. Any interval scale which does not meet the requirements of Chapters 10 and 11 may be treated as ordinal, as it is, of course, ordered. This is the more common application in medical work.

General texts such as Armitage *et al.* (2002), Snedecor and Cochran (1980) and Colton (1974) tend not to go into a lot of detail about rank and related methods, and more specialized books are needed (Siegel 1956; Conover 1980).

12.2 The Mann–Whitney U test

This is the non-parametric analogue of the two sample t test (Section 10.3). It works like this. Consider the following artificial data showing observations of a variable in two independent groups, A and B:

| A | 7 | 4 | 9 | 17 |
| B | 11 | 6 | 21 | 14 |

We want to know whether there is any evidence that A and B are drawn from populations with different levels of the variable. The null hypothesis is that there is no tendency for members of one population to exceed members of the other. The alternative is that there is such a tendency, in one direction or the other.

First we arrange the observations in ascending order, i.e. we rank them:

4	6	7	9	11	14	17	21
A	B	A	A	B	B	A	B

We now choose one group, say A. For each A, we count how many Bs precede it. For the first A, 4, no Bs precede. For the second A, 7, one B precedes, for the third A, 9, one B, for the fourth A, 17, three Bs. We add these numbers of preceding Bs together to give $U = 0 + 1 + 1 + 3 = 5$. Now, if U is very small, nearly all the As are less than nearly all the Bs. If U is large, nearly all As are greater than nearly all Bs. Moderate values of U mean that As and Bs are mixed. The minimum U is 0, when all Bs exceed all As, and maximum U is $n_1 \times n_2$ when all As exceed all Bs. The magnitude of U has a meaning, because $U/n_1 n_2$ is an estimate of the probability that an observation drawn at random from population A would exceed an observation drawn at random from population B.

There is another possible U, which we will call U', obtained by counting the number of As before each B, rather than the number of Bs before each A. This would be $1 + 3 + 3 + 4 = 11$. The two possible values of U and U' are related by $U + U' = n_1 n_2$. So we can subtract U' from $n_1 n_2$ to give U, $4 \times 4 - 11 = 5$.

If we know the distribution of U under the null hypothesis that the samples come from the same population, we can say with what probability these data could have arisen if there were no difference. We can carry out the test of significance. The distribution of U under the null hypothesis can be found easily. The two sets of four observations can be arranged in 70 different ways, from AAAABBBB to BBBBAAAA ($8!/4!4! = 70$, Appendix 6A). Under the null hypothesis these arrangements are all equally likely and, hence, have probability 1/70. Each has its value of U, from 0 to 16, and by counting the number of arrangements which give each value of U we can find

the probability of that value. For example, $U = 0$ only arises from the order AAAABBBB and so has probability $1/70 = 0.014$. $U = 1$ only arises from AAABABBB and so has probability $1/70 = 0.014$ also. $U = 2$ can arise in two ways: AAABBABB and AABAABBB. It has probability $2/70 = 0.029$. The full set of probabilities is shown in Table 12.1.

We apply this to the example. For groups A and B, $U = 5$ and the probability of this is 0.071. As we did for the sign test (Section 9.2) we consider the probability of more extreme values of U, $U = 5$ or less, which is $0.071 + 0.071 + 0.043 + 0.029 + 0.014 + 0.014 = 0.242$. This gives a one sided test. For a two sided test, we must consider the probabilities of a difference as extreme in the opposite direction. We can see from Table 12.1 that the distribution of U is symmetrical, so the probability of an equally extreme value in the opposite direction is also 0.242, hence the two sided probability is $0.242 + 0.242 = 0.484$. Thus the observed difference would have been quite probable if the null hypothesis were true and the two samples could have come from the same population.

In practice, there is no need to carry out the summation of probabilities described above, as these are already tabulated. Table 12.2 shows the 5% points of U for each combination of sample sizes n_1 and n_2 up to 20. For our groups A and B, $U = 5$, we find the $n_2 = 4$ column and the $n_1 = 4$ row. From this we see that the 5% point for U is 0, and so $U = 5$ is not significant. If we had calculated the larger of the two values of U, 11, we can use Table 12.2 by finding the lower value, $n_1 n_2 - U = 16 - 11 = 5$.

Table 12.1 Distribution of the Mann–Whitney U statistic, for two samples of size 4

U	probability	U	probability	U	probability
0	0.014	6	0.100	12	0.071
1	0.014	7	0.100	13	0.043
2	0.029	8	0.114	14	0.029
3	0.043	9	0.100	15	0.014
4	0.071	10	0.100	16	0.014
5	0.071	11	0.071		

Table 12.2 Two sided 5% points for the distribution of the smaller value of U in the Mann–Whitney U test

n_1	n_2 2	3	4	5	6	7	8	9	10	11	12	13	14	15	16	17	18	19	20
2	–	–	–	–	–	–	0	0	0	0	1	1	1	1	1	2	2	2	2
3	–	–	–	0	1	1	2	2	3	3	4	4	5	5	6	6	7	7	8
4	–	–	0	1	2	3	4	4	5	6	7	8	9	10	11	11	12	13	13
5	–	0	1	2	3	5	6	7	8	9	11	12	13	14	15	17	18	19	20
6	–	1	2	3	5	6	8	10	11	13	14	16	17	19	21	22	24	25	27
7	–	1	3	5	6	8	10	12	14	16	18	20	22	24	26	28	30	32	34
8	0	2	4	6	8	10	13	15	17	19	22	24	26	29	31	34	36	38	41
9	0	2	4	7	10	12	15	17	20	23	26	28	31	34	37	39	42	45	48
10	0	3	5	8	11	14	17	20	23	26	29	33	36	39	42	45	48	52	55
11	0	3	6	9	13	16	19	23	26	30	33	37	40	44	47	51	55	58	62
12	1	4	7	11	14	18	22	26	29	33	37	41	45	49	53	57	61	65	69
13	1	4	8	12	16	20	24	28	33	37	41	45	50	54	59	63	67	72	76
14	1	5	9	13	17	22	26	31	36	40	45	50	55	59	64	67	74	78	83
15	1	5	10	14	19	24	29	34	39	44	49	54	59	64	70	75	80	85	90
16	1	6	11	15	21	26	31	37	42	47	53	59	64	70	75	81	86	92	98
17	2	6	11	17	22	28	34	39	45	51	57	63	67	75	81	87	93	99	105
18	2	7	12	18	24	30	36	42	48	55	61	67	74	80	86	93	99	106	112
19	2	7	13	19	25	32	38	45	52	58	65	72	78	85	92	99	106	113	119
20	2	8	13	20	27	34	41	48	55	62	69	76	83	90	98	105	112	119	127

If U is less than or equal to the tabulated value the difference is significant.

We can now turn to the practical analysis of some real data. Consider the biceps skinfold thickness data of Table 10.3, reproduced as Table 12.3. We will analyse these using the Mann–Whitney U test. Denote the Crohn's disease group by A and the coeliac group by B. The joint order is as follows:

1.8	1.8	2.0	2.0	2.0	2.2	2.4	2.5	2.8	2.8
A	B	B	B	B	A	A	A	A	A

3.0	3.2	3.6	3.8	3.8	4.0	4.2	4.2	4.4	4.8
B	A	A	A	B	A	B	A	A	A

5.4	5.6	6.0	6.2	6.6	7.0	7.6	10.0	10.4
B	A	A	A	A	A	B	A	A

Let us count the As before each B. Immediately we have a problem. The first A and the first B have the same value. Does the first A come before the first B or after it? We resolve this dilemma by counting one half for the tied A. The ties between the second, third, and fourth Bs do not matter, as we can count the number of As before each without difficulty. We have for the U statistic:

$$U = 0.5 + 1 + 1 + 1 + 6 + 8.5 + 10.5 + 13 + 18 = 59.5$$

This is the lower value, as $n_1 n_2 = 9 \times 20 = 180$ and so the other value of U is $180 - 59.5 = 120.5$. We can therefore

Table 12.3 Biceps skinfold thickness (mm) in two groups of patients (data from Maugdal *et al.* 1985)

Crohn's disease				Coeliac disease	
1.8	2.8	4.2	6.2	1.8	3.8
2.2	3.2	4.4	6.6	2.0	4.2
2.4	3.6	4.8	7.0	2.0	5.4
2.5	3.8	5.6	10.0	2.0	7.6
2.8	4.0	6.0	10.4	3.0	

refer U to Table 12.2. The critical value at the 5% level for groups size 9 and 20 is 48, which our value exceeds. Hence the difference is not significant at the 5% level and the data are consistent with the null hypothesis that there is no tendency for members of one population to exceed members of the other. This is the same as the result of the t test of Section 10.4.

For larger values of n_1 and n_2, calculation of U can be rather tedious. A simple formula for U can be found using the ranks. The rank of the lowest observation is 1, of the next is 2, and so on. If a number of observations are tied, each having the same value and hence the same rank, we give each the average of the ranks they would have were they ordered. For example, in the skinfold data the first two observations are each 1.8. They each receive rank $(1 + 2)/2 = 1.5$. The third, fourth, and fifth are tied at 2.0, giving each of them rank $(3 + 4 + 5)/3 = 4$. The sixth, 2.2, is not tied and so has rank 6. The ranks for the skinfold data are as follows:

Skinfold	1.8	1.8	2.0	2.0	2.0	2.2	2.4	2.5
Group	A	B	B	B	B	A	A	A
Rank	1.5	1.5	4	4	4	6	7	8
		r_1	r_2	r_3	r_4			

Skinfold	2.8	2.8	3.0	3.2	3.6	3.8	3.8	4.0
Group	A	A	B	A	A	A	B	A
Rank	9.5	9.5	11	12	13	14.5	14.5	16
			r_5				r_6	

Skinfold	4.2	4.2	4.4	4.8	5.4	5.6	6.0	6.2
Group	A	B	A	A	B	A	A	A
Rank	17.5	17.5	19	20	21	22	23	24
		r_7			r_8			

Skinfold	6.6	7.0	7.6	10.0	10.4
Group	A	A	B	A	A
Rank	25	26	27	28	29
			r_9		

We denote the ranks of the B group by $r_1, r_2, \ldots, r_{n_1}$. The number of As preceding the first B must be $r_1 - 1$, as there are no Bs before it and it is the r_1th observation. The number of As preceding the second B is $r_2 - 2$, as it is the r_2th observation, and one preceding observation is a B. Similarly, the number preceding the third B is $r_3 - 3$, and the number preceding the ith B is $r_i - i$. Hence we have:

$$U = \sum_{i=1}^{n_1}(r_i - i)$$

$$= \sum_{i=1}^{n_1} r_i - \sum_{i=1}^{n_1} i$$

$$= \sum_{i=1}^{n_1} r_i - \frac{n_1(n_1 + 1)}{2}$$

That is, we add together the ranks of all the n_1 observations in Group B, subtract $n_1(n_1 + 1)/2$ and we have U. For the example, we have

$$U = 1.5 + 4 + 4 + 4 + 11 + 14.5 + 17.5 + 21$$
$$+ 27 - \frac{9 \times (9 + 1)}{2}$$
$$= 104.5 - 45$$
$$= 59.5$$

as before. This formula is sometimes written

$$U' = n_1 n_2 + \frac{n_1(n_1 + 1)}{2} - \sum_{i=1}^{n_1} r_i$$

But this is simply based on the other group, as $U + U' = n_1 n_2$. For testing we use the smaller value, as before.

As n_1 and n_2 increase, the calculation of the exact probability distribution becomes more difficult. When we cannot use Table 12.2, we use a large sample approximation instead. Because U is found by adding together a number of independent, identically distributed random variables, the central limit theorem (Section 7.2) applies. If the null hypothesis is true, the distribution of U approximates to a Normal distribution with mean $n_1 n_2 / 2$ and standard deviation is $\sqrt{n_1 n_2 (n_1 + n_2 + 1)/12}$. Hence

$$\frac{U - \dfrac{n_1 n_2}{2}}{\sqrt{\dfrac{n_1 n_2 (n_1 + n_2 + 1)}{12}}}$$

is an observation from a Standard Normal distribution. For the example, $n_1 = 9$ and $n_2 = 20$, we have

$$\frac{U - \dfrac{n_1 n_2}{2}}{\sqrt{\dfrac{n_1 n_2 (n_1 + n_2 + 1)}{12}}} = \frac{59.5 - \dfrac{9 \times 20}{2}}{\sqrt{\dfrac{9 \times 20 \times (9 + 20 + 1)}{12}}}$$
$$= -1.44$$

From Table 7.1 this gives two sided probability = 0.15, similar to that found by the two sample t test (Section 10.3).

Neither Table 12.2 nor the above formula for the standard deviation of U take ties into account; both assume the data can be fully ranked. Their use for data with ties is an approximation. For small samples we must accept this. For the Normal approximation, ties can be allowed for using the following formula for the standard deviation of U when the null hypothesis is true:

$$\sqrt{\frac{n_1 n_2}{(n_1 + n_2)(n_1 + n_2 - 1)} \times \sum_{i=1}^{n_1 + n_2} r_i^2 - \frac{n_1 n_2 (n_1 + n_2 + 1)^2}{4(n_1 + n_2 - 1)}}$$

where $\sum_{i=1}^{n_1 + n_2} r_i^2$ is the sum of the squared ranks for all observations, i.e. for both groups (see Conover 1980). The Mann–Whitney U test is not free of assumptions which may be violated. We assume that the data can be fully ordered, which in the case of ties is not so. As for the two sample t test (Section 10.3), all our observations must be independent.

The Mann–Whitney U test is a non-parametric analogue of the two sample t test. The advantage over the t test is that the only assumption about the distribution of the data is that the observations can be ranked, whereas for the t test we must assume the data are from Normal distributions with uniform variance. There are disadvantages. For data which follow a Normal distribution with uniform variance, the U test is less powerful than the t test, i.e. the t test, when valid, can detect smaller differences for given sample size. The U test is almost as powerful for moderate and large sample sizes, and this difference is important only for small samples. For very small samples, e.g. two groups of three observations, the test is useless as all possible values of U have probabilities above 0.05 (Table 12.2). The U test is primarily a test of significance. The t method also enables us to estimate the size of the difference between means and gives a confidence interval.

The null hypothesis of the Mann–Whitney test is sometimes presented as being that the populations have the same median. There is even a confidence interval for the difference between two medians based on the Mann–Whitney test (Campbell and Gardner 1989). This is surprising, as the medians are not involved in the calculation. Furthermore, we can have two groups which are significantly different using the Mann–Whitney U test yet have the same median. Table 12.4 shows an example. The majority of observations in both groups are zero, so transformation to the Normal is impossible. Although the samples are quite large, the distribution is so skew that a rank method, appropriately adjusted for ties, may be safer than the method of Section 9.7. The Mann–Whitney U test was highly significant, yet the medians are both zero. As the medians were equal, I suggested the 75th percentile as a measure of location for the distributions.

The reason for these two different views of the Mann–Whitney U test lies in the assumptions we make about the distributions in the two populations. If we make no assumptions, we can test this null hypothesis: that the probability that a member of the first population drawn at random will exceed a member of the second population drawn at random is one half. Some people choose to make an assumption about the distributions: that they have the same shape and differ only in location (mean or median). If this assumption is true, then if the distributions are different the medians must be different. The means must differ by the same amount. It is a very strong assumption. For example, if it is true then the variances

Table 12.4 Frequency distributions of number of nodes involved in breast cancers detected at screening and detected in the intervals between screens (data supplied by Mohammed Raja)

Screening cancers		Interval cancers	
Nodes	**Frequency**	**Nodes**	**Frequency**
0	291	0	66
1	43	1	22
2	16	2	7
3	20	3	7
4	13	4	2
5	3	5	4
6	1	6	4
7	4	7	3
8	3	8	3
9	1	9	2
10	1	10	2
11	2	12	2
12	1	13	1
15	1	15	1
16	1	16	1
17	2	20	1
18	2		
20	1		
27	1		
33	1		
Total	408		128
Mean	1.21		2.19
Median	0		0
75%ile	1		3

Mann–Whitney U test:

$U = 31\,555.00$, $se = 1\,281.33$

$$z = \frac{U - n_1 n_2 / 2}{se} = \frac{31\,555.00 - 408 \times 128/2}{1\,281.33} = 4.25$$

$P < 0.0001$

must be the same in the two populations. For the reasons given in Section 10.5 and Appendix 7A, it is unlikely that we could get this if the distributions were not Normal. Under this assumption the Mann–Whitney U test will rarely be valid if the two sample t test is not valid also.

There are other non-parametric tests which test the same or similar null hypotheses. Two of these, the Wilcoxon two sample test and the Kendall Tau test, are different versions of the Mann–Whitney U test which were developed around the same time and later shown to be identical. These names are sometimes used interchangeably. The test statistics and tables are not the same, and the user must be very careful that the calculation of the test statistic being used corresponds to the table to which it is referred. Another difficulty with tables is that some are drawn so that for a significant difference U must be less than or equal to the tabulated value (as in Table 12.2), for others U must be strictly less than the tabulated value.

For more than two groups, the rank analogue of one-way analysis of variance (Section 10.9) is the Kruskal–Wallis test, see Conover (1980) and Siegel (1956). Conover (1980) also describes a multiple comparison test for the pairs of groups, similar to those described in Section 10.11.

12.3 The Wilcoxon matched pairs test

This test is an analogue of the paired t test. We have a sample of independent observations measured under two conditions and the null hypothesis is that there is no tendency for the outcome on one condition to be higher or lower than the other. The alternative hypothesis is that the outcome on one condition tends to be higher or lower than the other. As the test is based on the magnitude of the differences, the data must be interval.

Consider the data of Table 12.5, previously discussed in Section 2.7 and Section 9.2, where we used the sign test for the analysis. In the sign test, we have ignored the magnitude of differences, and only considered their signs. If we can use information about the magnitude, we would hope to have a more powerful test. Clearly, we must have interval data to do this. To avoid making assumptions about the distribution of the differences,

Table 12.5 Results of a trial of pronethalol for the prevention of angina pectoris in rank order of differences (data from Pritchard *et al.* 1963)

Number of attacks while on		Difference placebo – pronethalol	Rank of difference		
placebo	pronethalol		All	Positive	Negative
2	0	2	1.5	1.5	
17	15	2	1.5	1.5	
3	0	3	3	3	
7	2	5	4	4	
8	1	7	6	6	
14	7	7	6	6	
23	16	7	6	6	
34	25	9	8	8	
79	65	14	9	9	
60	41	19	10	10	
323	348	-25	11		11
71	29	42	12	12	
Sum of ranks				67	11

we use their rank order in a similar manner to the Mann–Whitney U test.

First, we rank the differences by their absolute values, i.e. ignoring the sign. As in Section 12.2, tied observations are given the average of their ranks. We now sum the ranks of the positive differences, 67, and the ranks of the negative differences, 11 (Table 12.5). If the null hypothesis were true and there was no difference, we would expect the rank sums for positive and negative differences to be about the same, equal to 39 (their average). The test statistic is the lesser of these sums, T. The smaller T is, the lower the probability of the data arising by chance.

The distribution of T when the null hypothesis is true can be found by enumerating all the possibilities, as described for the Mann–Whitney U statistic. Table 12.6 gives the 5% and 1% points for this distribution, for sample size n up to 25. For the example, $n = 12$ and so the difference would be significant at the 5% level if T were less than or equal to 14. We have $T = 11$, so the data are

not consistent with the null hypothesis. The data support the view that there is a real tendency for patients to have fewer attacks while on the active treatment.

From Table 12.6, we can see that the probability that $T \leq 11$ lies between 0.05 and 0.01. This is greater than the probability given by the sign test, which was 0.006 (Section 9.2). Usually we would expect greater power, and hence lower probabilities when the null hypothesis is false, when we use more of the information. In this case, the greater probability reflects the fact that the one negative difference, –25, is large. Examination of the original data shows that this individual had very large numbers of attacks on both treatments, and it seems possible that he may belong to a different population from the other 11.

Like Table 12.2, Table 12.6 is based on the assumption that the differences can be fully ranked and there are no ties. Ties may occur in two ways in this test. Firstly, ties may occur in the ranking sense. In the example we had two differences of +2 and three of +7.

Table 12.6 Two sided 5% and 1% points of the distribution of T (lower value) in the Wilcoxon one sample test

Sample size	Probability that $T \leq$ the tabulated value		Sample size	Probability that $T \leq$ the tabulated value	
n	5%	1%	n	5%	1%
5	–	–	16	30	19
6	1	–	17	35	23
7	2	–	18	40	28
8	4	0	19	46	32
9	6	2	20	52	37
10	8	3	21	59	43
11	11	5	22	66	49
12	14	7	23	73	55
13	17	10	24	81	61
14	21	13	25	90	68
15	25	16			

These were ranked equally: 1.5 and 1.5, and 6, 6, and 6. When ties are present between negative and positive differences, Table 12.6 only approximates to the distribution of T.

Ties may also occur between the paired observations, where the observed difference is zero. In the same way as for the sign test, we omit zero differences (Section 9.2). Table 12.6 is used with n as the number of non-zero differences only, not the total number of differences. This seems odd, in that a lot of zero differences would appear to support the null hypothesis. For example, if in Table 12.5 we had another dozen patients with zero differences, the calculation and conclusion would be the same. However, the mean difference would be smaller and the Wilcoxon test tells us nothing about the size of the difference, only its existence. This illustrates the danger of allowing significance tests to outweigh all other ways of looking at the data.

As n increases, the distribution of T under the null hypothesis tends towards a Normal distribution, as does that of the Mann–Whitney U statistic. The sum of all the ranks, irrespective of sign, is $n(n + 1)/2$, so the expected value of T under the null hypothesis is $n(n + 1)/4$, as the

two sums should be equal. If the null hypothesis is true, the standard deviation of T is $\sqrt{\frac{1}{4}\sum r_i^2}$, where r_i is the rank of the ith difference, which is $\sqrt{n(n + 1)(2n + 1)/24}$ when there are no ties. Hence

$$\frac{T - \frac{n(n + 1)}{4}}{\sqrt{\frac{n(n + 1)(2n + 1)}{24}}}$$

is from a Standard Normal distribution if the null hypothesis is true. For the example of Table 12.5, we have:

$$\frac{T - \frac{n(n + 1)}{4}}{\sqrt{\frac{n(n + 1)(2n + 1)}{24}}} = \frac{11 - \frac{12 \times 13}{4}}{\sqrt{\frac{12 \times 13 \times 25}{24}}} = -2.197$$

From Table 7.1 this gives a two tailed probability of 0.028, similar to that obtained from Table 12.6.

We have three possible tests for paired data, the Wilcoxon, sign, and paired t methods. If the differences follow a Normal distribution, the t test is the most powerful test. The Wilcoxon test is almost as powerful, however, and in practice the difference is not great except for small samples. Like the Mann–Whitney U test, the Wilcoxon is useless for very small samples. The sign test is similar in power to the Wilcoxon for very small samples, but as the sample size increases the Wilcoxon test becomes much more powerful. This might be expected as the Wilcoxon test uses more of the information. The Wilcoxon test uses the magnitude of the differences, and hence requires interval data. This means that, as for t methods, we will get different results if we transform the data. For truly ordinal data we should use the sign test. The paired t method also gives a confidence interval for the difference. The Wilcoxon test is purely a test of significance, but a confidence interval for the median difference can be found using the Binomial method described in Section 8.9.

12.4 Spearman's rank correlation coefficient, ρ

We noted in Chapter 11 the sensitivity to assumptions of Normality of the product moment correlation coefficient, r. This led to the development of non-parametric approaches based on ranks. Spearman's approach was direct. First we rank the observations, then calculate the product moment correlation of the ranks, rather than of the observations themselves. The resulting statistic has a distribution which does not depend on the distribution of the original variables. It is usually denoted by the Greek letter ρ, pronounced 'rho', or by r_S.

Table 12.7 shows data from a study of the geographical distribution of a tumour, Kaposi's sarcoma, in mainland

Table 12.7 Incidence of Kaposi's sarcoma and access of population to health centres for each region of mainland Tanzania (data from Bland *et al.* 1977)

Region	Incidence per million per year	% population within 10 km of health centre	Rank order	
			Incidence	% Pop
Coast	1.28	4.0	1	3
Shinyanga	1.66	9.0	2	7
Mbeya	2.06	6.7	3	6
Tabora	2.37	1.8	4	1
Arusha	2.46	13.7	5	13
Dodoma	2.60	11.1	6	10
Kigoma	4.22	9.2	7	8
Mara	4.29	4.4	8	4
Tanga	4.54	23.0	9	16
Singida	6.17	10.8	10	9
Morogoro	6.33	11.7	11	11
Mtwara	6.40	14.8	12	14
Westlake	6.60	12.5	13	12
Kilimanjaro	6.65	57.3	14	17
Ruvuma	7.21	6.6	15	5
Iringa	8.46	2.6	16	2
Mwanza	8.54	20.7	17	15

Tanzania. The incidence rates were calculated from cancer registry data and there was considerable doubt that all cases were notified. The degree of reporting of cases may have been related to population density or availability of health services. In addition, incidence was closely related to age and sex (where recorded) and so could be related to the age and sex distribution in the region. To check that none of these were producing artefacts in the geographical distribution, I calculated the rank correlation of disease incidence with each of the possible explanatory variables. Table 12.7 shows the relationship of incidence to the percentage of the population living within 10 km of a health centre (Egero and Henin 1973). Figure 12.1 shows the scatter diagram of these data. The percentage within 10 km of a health centre is very highly skewed, whereas the disease incidence appears somewhat bimodal. The assumption of the product moment correlation does not appear to be met, so rank correlation was preferred.

The calculation of Spearman's ρ proceeds as follows. The ranks for the two variables are found (Table 12.7). We apply the formula for the product moment correlation (Section 11.9) to these ranks. We define:

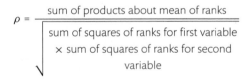

$$\rho = \frac{\text{sum of products about mean of ranks}}{\sqrt{\begin{array}{c}\text{sum of squares of ranks for first variable}\\ \times \text{ sum of squares of ranks for second}\\ \text{variable}\end{array}}}$$

The calculation is as described in Section 11.9, giving $\rho = 0.38$. We can now test the null hypothesis that the variables are independent, the alternative being that either one variable increases as the other increases, or that one decreases as the other increases. As usual with ranking statistics, the distribution of ρ for small samples can be found by listing all the possible permutations and their values of ρ. For a sample size of n there are, of course, $n!$ possibilities. Table 12.8 shows the critical value of ρ for sample sizes up to 10. Note that, although the calculation is similar to that in Sections 11.9–10, the distribution under the null hypothesis is not the same, and a different table is used. As n increases, so ρ tends to a Normal distribution when the null hypothesis is true, with expected value 0 and variance $1/(n-1)$. Thus $\rho/\sqrt{1/(n-1)} = \rho\sqrt{n-1}$ is from a Standard Normal distribution. The approximation is reasonable for $n > 10$.

For our data we have $0.38\sqrt{17-1} = 1.52$, which from Table 7.1 has a two sided probability of 0.13. Hence we have not found any evidence of a relationship between the observed incidence of Kaposi's sarcoma and access to health centres. In this study there was no significant relationship with any of the possible explanatory variables and we concluded that the observed geographical distribution did not appear to be an artefact of population distribution or diagnostic provision.

We have ignored the problem of ties in the above. We treat observations with the same value as described in

Table 12.8 Two sided 5% and 1% points of the distribution of Spearman's ρ

Sample size n	Probability that ρ is as far or further from 0 than the tabulated value	
	5%	**1%**
4	–	–
5	1.00	–
6	0.89	1.00
7	0.82	0.96
8	0.79	0.93
9	0.70	0.83
10	0.68	0.81

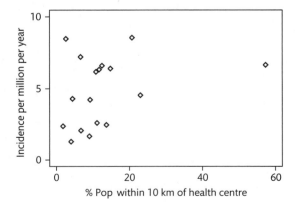

Figure 12.1 Incidence of Kaposi's sarcoma per million per year and percentage of population within 10 km of a health centre, for 17 regions of mainland Tanzania (data from Bland *et al.* 1977).

Section 12.2. We give them the average of the ranks they would have if they were separable and apply the rank correlation formula as described above. In this case the distribution of Table 12.8 is only approximate.

There are several ways of calculating this coefficient, resulting in formulae which appear quite different, though they give the same result (see Siegel 1956).

12.5 Kendall's rank correlation coefficient, τ

Spearman's rank correlation is quite satisfactory for testing the null hypothesis of no relationship, but is difficult to interpret as a measurement of the strength of the relationship. Kendall (1970) developed a different rank correlation coefficient, Kendall's τ, which has some advantages over Spearman's. (The Greek letter τ is pronounced 'tau'.) It is rather more tedious to calculate than Spearman's, but in the computer age this hardly matters. For each pair of subjects we observe whether the subjects are ordered in the same way by the two variables, a **concordant** pair, ordered in opposite ways, a **discordant** pair, or equal for one of the variables and so not ordered at all, a **tied** pair. **Kendall's** τ is the proportion of concordant pairs minus the proportion of discordant pairs. τ will be one if the rankings are identical, as all pairs will be ordered in the same way, and minus one if the rankings are exactly opposite, as all pairs will be ordered in the opposite way.

We shall denote the number of concordant pairs (ordered the same way) by n_c, the number of discordant pairs (ordered in opposite ways) by n_d, and the difference, $n_c - n_d$, by S. There are $n(n-1)/2$ pairs altogether, so

$$\tau = \frac{n_c - n_d}{\frac{1}{2}n(n-1)} = \frac{S}{\frac{1}{2}n(n-1)}$$

When there are no ties, $n_c + n_d = n(n-1)/2$.

The simplest way to calculate n_c is to order the observations by one of the variables, as in Table 12.7 which is ordered by disease incidence. Now consider the second ranking (% population within 10 km of a health centre). The first region, Coast, has 14 regions below it in Table 12.7 which have greater rank, so the pairs formed by the first region and these will be in the correct order.

There are two regions below it which have lower rank, so the pairs formed by the first region and these will be in the opposite order. The second region, Shinyanga, has 10 regions below it with greater rank and so contributes 10 further pairs in the correct order. Note that the pair 'Coast and Shinyanga' has already been counted. There are five pairs in opposite order. The third region, Mbeya, has 10 regions below it in the same order and four in opposite orders, and so on. We add these numbers to get n_c and n_d:

$$n_c = 14 + 10 + 10 + 13 + 4 + 6 + 7 + 8 + 1 + 5$$
$$+ 4 + 2 + 2 + 0 + 1 + 1 + 0$$
$$= 88$$
$$n_d = 2 + 5 + 4 + 0 + 8 + 5 + 3 + 1 + 7 + 2 + 2$$
$$+ 3 + 2 + 3 + 1 + 0 + 0$$
$$= 48$$

The number of pairs is $n(n-1)/2 = 17 \times 16/2 = 136$. Because there are no ties, we could also calculate n_d by $n_d = n(n-1)/2 - n_c = 136 - 88 = 48$. $S = n_c - n_d = 88 - 48 = 40$. Hence $\tau = S/(n(n-1)/2) = 40/136 = 0.29$.

When there are ties, τ cannot be one. However, we could have perfect correlation if the ties were between the same subjects for both variables. To allow for this, we use a different version of τ, τ_b. Consider the denominator. There are $n(n-1)/2$ possible pairs. If there are t individuals tied at a particular rank for variable X, no pairs from these t individuals contribute to S. There are $t(t-1)/2$ such pairs. If we consider all the groups of tied individuals, we have $\sum t(t-1)/2$ pairs which do not contribute to S, summing over all groups of tied ranks. Hence the total number of pairs which can contribute to S is $n(n-1)/2 - \sum t(t-1)/2$, and S cannot be greater than $n(n-1)/2 - \sum t(t-1)/2$. The size of S is also limited by ties in the second ranking. If we denote the number of individuals with the same value of Y by u, then the number of pairs which can contribute to S is $n(n-1)/2 - \sum u(u-1)/2$. We now define τ_b by

$$\tau_b = \frac{S}{\sqrt{(n(n-1)/2 - \sum t(t-1)/2) \times (n(n-1)/2 - \sum u(u-1)/2)}}$$

Note that if there are no ties, $\sum t(t-1)/2 = 0 = \sum u(u-1)/2$, so $\tau_b = \tau$. When the rankings are identical $\tau_b = 1$, no matter how many ties there are. Kendall (1970) also discusses two other ways of dealing with ties, obtaining coefficients τ_a and τ_c, but their use is restricted.

We often want to test the null hypothesis that there is no relationship between the two variables in the population from which our sample was drawn. As usual, we are concerned with the probability of S being as or more extreme (i.e. far from zero) than the observed value. Table 12.9 was calculated in the same way as Tables 12.1 and 12.2. It shows the probability of being as extreme as the observed value of S for n up to 10. For convenience, S is tabulated rather than τ. When ties are present this is only an approximation.

When the sample size is greater than 10, S has an approximately Normal distribution under the null hypothesis, with mean zero. If there are no ties, the variance is

$$VAR(S) = \frac{n(n-1)(2n+5)}{18}$$

When there are ties, the variance formula is very complicated (Kendall 1970). I shall omit it, as in practice these calculations will be done using computers anyway. If there are not many ties it will not make much difference if the simple form is used.

Table 12.9 Two sided 5% and 1% points of the distribution of S for Kendall's τ

Sample size	Probability that S is as far or further from the expected than the tabulated value	
n	**5%**	**1%**
4	–	–
5	10	–
6	13	15
7	15	19
8	18	22
9	20	26
10	23	29

For the example, $S = 40$, $n = 17$ and there are no ties, so the Standard Normal variate is

$$\frac{S}{\sqrt{Var(S)}} = \frac{S}{\sqrt{n(n-1)(2n+5)/18}}$$
$$= \frac{40}{\sqrt{17 \times 18 \times 39/18}}$$
$$= 1.55$$

From Table 7.1 of the Normal distribution we find that the two sided probability of a value as extreme as this is $0.06 \times 2 = 0.12$, which is very similar to that found using Spearman's ρ. The product moment correlation, r, gives $r = 0.30$, $P = 0.24$, but of course the non-Normal distributions of the variables make this P invalid.

Why have two different rank correlation coefficients? Spearman's ρ is older than Kendall's τ, and can be thought of as a simple analogue of the product moment correlation coefficient, Pearson's r. Kendall's τ is a part of a more general and consistent system of ranking methods, and has a direct interpretation, as the difference between the proportions of concordant and discordant pairs. In general, the numerical value of ρ is greater than that of τ. It is not possible to calculate τ from ρ or ρ from τ, they measure different sorts of correlation. ρ gives more weight to reversals of order when data are far apart in rank than when there is a reversal close together in rank, τ does not. However, in terms of tests of significance, both have the same power to reject a false null hypothesis, so for this purpose it does not matter which is used.

12.6 Continuity corrections

In this chapter, when samples were large we have used a continuous distribution, the Normal, to approximate to a discrete distribution, U, T, or S. For example, Figure 12.2 shows the distribution of the Mann–Whitney U statistic for $n_1 = 4$, $n_2 = 4$ (Table 12.1) with the corresponding Normal curve. From the exact distribution, the probability that $U < 2$ is $0.014 + 0.014 + 0.029 = 0.057$. The corresponding Standard Normal deviate is

$$\frac{U - \frac{n_1 n_2}{2}}{\sqrt{\frac{n_1 n_2 (n_1 + n_2 + 1)}{12}}} = \frac{2 - \frac{4 \times 4}{2}}{\sqrt{\frac{4 \times 4 \times 9}{12}}} = -1.732$$

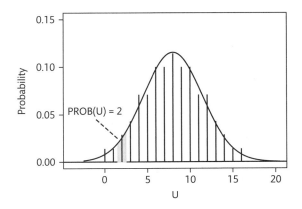

Figure 12.2 Distribution of the Mann–Whitney U statistic, $n_1 = 4$, $n_2 = 4$, when the null hypothesis is true, with the corresponding Normal distribution and area estimating PROB($U = 2$).

This has a probability of 0.048, interpolating in Table 7.1. This is smaller than the exact probability. The disparity arises because the continuous distribution gives probability to values other than the integers 0, 1, 2, etc. The estimated probability for $U = 2$ can be found by the area under the curve between $U = 1.5$ and $U = 2.5$. The corresponding Normal deviates are –1.876 and –1.588, which have probabilities from Table 7.1 of 0.030 and 0.056. This gives the estimated probability for $U = 2$ to be 0.056–0.030 = 0.026, which compares quite well with the exact figure of 0.029. Thus to estimate the probability that $U \leq 2$, we estimate the area below $U = 2.5$, not below $U = 2$. This gives us a Standard Normal deviate of –1.588, as already noted, and hence a probability of 0.056. This corresponds remarkably well with the exact probability of 0.057, especially when we consider how small n_1 and n_2 are.

We will get a better approximation from our Standard Normal deviate if we make U closer to its expected value by $\frac{1}{2}$. In general, we get a better fit if we make the observed value of the statistic closer to its expected value by half of the interval between adjacent discrete values. This is a **continuity correction**.

For S, the interval between adjacent values is 2, not 1, for $S = n_c - n_d = 2n_c - n(n - 1)/2$, and n_c is an integer. A change of one unit in n_c produces a change of two units in S. The continuity correction is therefore half of 2, which is 1. We make S closer to the expected value of

0 by 1 before applying the Normal approximation. For the Kaposi's sarcoma data, we had $S = 40$, with $n = 17$. Using the continuity correction gives

$$\frac{S - 1}{\sqrt{Var(S)}} = \frac{40 - 1}{\sqrt{17 \times 18 \times 39/18}} = \frac{39}{25.75} = 1.513$$

This gives a two sided probability of 0.066 × 2 = 0.13, slightly greater than the uncorrected value of 0.12.

Continuity corrections are important for small samples; for large samples they are negligible. We shall meet another in Section 13.5.

12.7 Parametric or non-parametric methods?

For many statistical problems there are several possible solutions, just as for many diseases there are several treatments, similar perhaps in their overall efficacy but displaying variation in their side effects, in their interactions with other diseases or treatments, and in their suitability for different types of patients. There is often no one right treatment, but rather treatment is decided on the prescriber's judgement of these effects, past experience, and plain prejudice. Many problems in statistical analysis are like this. In comparing the means of two small groups, for instance, we could use a t test, a t test with a transformation, a Mann–Whitney U test, or one of several others. Our choice of method depends on the plausibility of Normal assumptions, the importance of obtaining a confidence interval, the ease of calculation, and so on. It depends on plain prejudice, too. Some users of statistical methods are very concerned about the implications of Normal assumptions and will advocate non-parametric methods wherever possible, while others are too careless of the errors that may be introduced when assumptions are not met.

I sometimes meet people who tell me that they have used non-parametric methods throughout their analysis as if this is some kind of badge of statistical purity. It is nothing of the kind. It may mean that their significance tests have less power than they could have, and that results are left as 'not significant' when, for example, a confidence interval for a difference might be more informative.

On the other hand, such methods are very useful when the necessary assumptions of the t distribution method cannot be made, and it would be equally wrong to eschew their use. Rather, we should choose the method most suited to the problem, bearing in mind both the assumptions we are making and what we really want to know. We shall say more about what method to use when in Chapter 14.

There is a frequent misconception that when the number of observations is very small, usually said to be less than six, Normal distribution methods such as t tests and regression must not be used and that rank methods should be used instead. I have never seen any argument put forward in support of this, but inspection of Tables 12.2, 12.6, 12.8, and 12.9 will show that it is nonsense. For such small samples rank tests cannot produce any significance at the usual 5% level. Should one need statistical analysis of such small samples, Normal methods are required.

12.8 Multiple choice questions: Rank-based methods

(Each branch is either true or false.)

12.1 For comparing the responses to a new treatment of a group of patients with the responses of a control group to a standard treatment, possible approaches include:
  (a) the two sample t method;
  (b) the sign test;
  (c) the Mann–Whitney U test;
  (d) the Wilcoxon matched pairs test;
  (e) rank correlation between responses to the treatments.

12.2 Suitable methods for truly ordinal data include:
  (a) the sign test;
  (b) the Mann–Whitney U test;
  (c) the Wilcoxon matched pairs test;
  (d) the two sample t method;
  (e) Kendall's rank correlation coefficient.

12.3 Kendall's rank correlation coefficient between two variables:
  (a) depends on which variable is regarded as the predictor;
  (b) is zero when there is no relationship;

  (c) cannot have a valid significance test when there are tied observations;
  (d) must lie between –1 and +1;
  (e) is not affected by a log transformation of the variables.

12.4 Tests of significance based on ranks:
  (a) are always to be preferred to methods which assume the data to follow a Normal distribution;
  (b) are less powerful than methods based on the Normal distribution when data follow a Normal distribution;
  (c) enable confidence intervals to be estimated easily;
  (d) require no assumptions about the data;
  (e) are often to be preferred when data cannot be assumed to follow any particular distribution.

12.5 Ten men with angina were given an active drug and a placebo on alternate days in random order. Patients were tested using the time in minutes for which they could exercise until angina or fatigue stopped them. The existence of an active drug effect could be examined by:
  (a) paired t test;
  (b) Mann–Whitney U test;
  (c) sign test;
  (d) Wilcoxon matched pairs test;
  (e) Spearman's ρ.

12.9 Exercise: Some applications of rank-based methods

In a grant proposal, a researcher proposed the following statistical analysis to compare two groups with respect to length of hospital stay and number of re-admissions to hospital in 1 year: 'Outcomes will be treated as ordinal variables. Consequently the first line analysis is likely to be the Wilcoxon rank sum test'.

12.1 What kind of variables are length of hospital stay and number of re-admissions to hospital?

12.2 Might rank methods be appropriate for the analysis of these variables?

MABGEL 1 was first in a human trial of a combination of three anti-HIV1 monoclonal antibodies, called 2F5, 4E10, and 2G12, as a vaginal microbicide (Morris *et al.* 2014). Most unusually, this was first tested in women rather than men, for obvious anatomical reasons. Twenty-eight women were randomly allocated to three groups: high dose, low

Table 12.10 Concentrations of monoclonal antibody 2F5 (microgram/ml) in samples taken from the vaginal mucosa 8 hours after first dose of a gel containing three monoclonal antibodies (data from Morris *et al.* 2014)

Vehicle only *			Low dose			High dose			
<0.06	<0.06	<0.06	29.9	82.2	165	1.5	170	385	614
<0.06	<0.06	<0.06	74.6	126	195	32.3	196	481	
<0.06	<0.06	<0.06	77.4	155	424	67.1	243	503	

* sample missing for one participant

dose, and vehicle only controls. Table 12.10 shows the concentration of 2F5 for the third set of measurements, made 8 hours after the first dose of the gel. The limit of detection of the method was 0.06 and anything below this was recorded as '< 0.06'.

12.3 What feature of Table 12.10 suggests that a rank-based method will be appropriate for these data?

12.4 Which rank-based method could be used to compare the three groups?

12.5 A further question was whether 2F5 concentrations differed between the high and low doses. What rank-based method would you use to do this, omitting the vehicle only group entirely?

12.6 What other approach could we use to compare the two doses? Judging from Table 12.10, what difficulty might there be in doing this?

In a trial of metoclopramide combined with dexamethasone for the prevention of postoperative nausea and vomiting,

participants were randomized to receive 0 mg, 10 mg, 25 mg, or 50 mg metoclopramide with 8 mg dexamethasone. Hypotension was one of 20 adverse outcomes reported (Wallenborn *et al.* 2006). The results are shown in Table 12.11.

12.7 Why was Kendall's rank correlation coefficient used here?

12.8 Why was the tau b version of the Kendall's rank coefficient chosen?

12.9 This is a one sided test. Do you think this is a reasonable thing to do?

12.10 Is the null hypothesis for this test specified correctly?

12.11 One other of the 20 P values for trend in the adverse outcomes had P < 0.05. How would you interpret the test for hypotension?

12.12 The value of tau b is not given in the paper, but is easy to calculate as 0.07. How would you interpret the strength of this trend?

Table 12.11 Hypotension and dose of metoclopramide (data from Wallenborn *et al.* 2006)

	Dose of metoclopramide (mg)				Trend
	0 (*n* = 788)	10 (*n* = 783)	25 (*n* = 781)	50 (*n* = 788)	P value
Hypotension	62 (7.9%)	74 (9.5%)	88 (11.3%)	113 (14.3%)	<0.001

*One sided trend test (Kendall's tau b); null hypothesis: the event rate does not increase with the dose of metoclopramide.

13 The analysis of cross-tabulations

13.1 The chi-squared test for association

Table 13.1 shows for a sample of mothers the relationship between housing tenure and whether they had a preterm delivery. This kind of cross-tabulation of frequencies is also called a **contingency table** or **cross classification**. Each entry in the table is a frequency, the number of individuals having these characteristics (Section 4.1), each combination of row and column, e.g. private tenant having term birth, is called a **cell**. It can be quite difficult to measure the strength of the association between two qualitative variables like these, but it is easy to test the null hypothesis that there is no relationship or association between the two variables. If the sample is large, we can do this by a chi-squared test.

Table 13.1 Contingency table showing time of delivery by housing tenure (data from Brooke *et al.* 1989)

Housing tenure	Preterm	Term	Total
Owner-occupier	50	849	899
Council tenant	29	229	258
Private tenant	11	164	175
Lives with parents	6	66	72
Other	3	36	39
Total	99	1 344	1 443

The chi-squared test for association in a contingency table works like this. The null hypothesis is that there is no association between the two variables, the alternative being that there is an association of any kind. We find for each cell of the table the frequency which we would expect if the null hypothesis were true. To do this we use the row and column totals, so we are finding the expected frequencies for tables with these totals, called the **marginal** totals.

There are 1 443 women, of whom 899 were owner occupiers, a proportion 899/1 443. If there were no relationship between time of delivery and housing tenure, we would expect each column of the table to have the same proportion, 899/1 443, of its members in the first row. Thus the 99 women in the first column would be expected to have 99 × 899/1 443 = 61.7 in the first row. By 'expected' we mean the average frequency we would get in the long run in tables with these marginal totals, if there were no association. We could not actually observe 61.7 women. The 1 344 women in the second column would be expected to have 1 344 × 899/1 443 = 837.3 in the first row. The sum of these two expected frequencies is 899, the row total. Similarly, there are 258 women in the second row and so we would expect 99 × 258/1 443 = 17.7 in the second row, first column and 1 344 × 258/1 443 = 240.3 in the second row, second column. We calculate the expected frequency for each row and column combination, or cell. The 10 cells of Table 13.1 give us the expected frequencies shown in Table 13.2. Notice that the row and column totals are the

Table 13.2 Expected frequencies under the null hypothesis for Table 13.1 (data from Brooke *et al.* 1989)

Housing tenure	Preterm	Term	Total
Owner-occupier	61.7	837.3	899
Council tenant	17.7	240.3	258
Private tenant	12.0	163.0	175
Lives with parents	4.9	67.1	72
Other	2.7	36.3	39
Total	99	1 344	1 443

same as in Table 13.1. In general, the expected frequency for a cell of the contingency table is found by

$$\frac{\text{row total} \times \text{column total}}{\text{grand total}}$$

It does not matter which variable is the row and which the column.

We now compare the observed and expected frequencies. If the two variables are not associated, the observed and expected frequencies should be close together, any discrepancy being due to random variation. We need a test statistic which measures this. The differences between observed and expected frequencies are a good place to start. We cannot simply sum them, as the sum would be zero, both observed and expected frequencies having the same grand total, 1 443. We can resolve this as we resolved a similar problem with differences from the mean (Section 4.7), by squaring the differences. The size of the difference will also depend in some way on the number of patients. When the row and column totals are small, the difference between observed and expected is forced to be small. It turns out, for reasons discussed in Appendix 13A, that the best statistic is

$$\sum_{\substack{\text{all} \\ \text{cells}}} \frac{(\text{observed frequency} - \text{expected frequency})^2}{\text{expected frequency}}$$

This is often written as

$$\sum \frac{(O - E)^2}{E}$$

For Table 13.1 this is

$$\sum \frac{(O-E)^2}{E} = \frac{(50-61.7)^2}{61.7} + \frac{(849-837.3)^2}{837.3}$$
$$+ \frac{(29-17.7)^2}{17.7} + \frac{(229-240.3)^2}{240.3}$$
$$+ \frac{(11-12.0)^2}{12.0} + \frac{(164-163.0)^2}{163.0}$$
$$+ \frac{(6-4.9)^2}{4.9} + \frac{(66-67.1)^2}{67.1}$$
$$+ \frac{(3-2.7)^2}{2.7} + \frac{(36-36.3)^2}{36.3}$$
$$= 10.5$$

As will be explained in Appendix 13A, the distribution of this test statistic when the null hypothesis is true and the sample is large enough is the Chi-squared distribution (Appendix 7A) with $(r-1)(c-1)$ degrees of freedom, where r is the number of rows and c is the number of columns. I shall discuss what is meant by 'large enough' in Section 13.3. We are treating the row and column totals as fixed and only considering the distribution of tables with these totals. The test is said to be **conditional** on these totals. We can prove that we lose very little information by doing this and we get a simple test.

For Table 13.1 we have $(5-1) \times (2-1) = 4$ degrees of freedom. Table 13.3 shows some percentage points of the Chi-squared distribution for selected degrees of freedom. These are the upper percentage points, as shown in Figure 13.1. We see that for 4 degrees of freedom the 5% point is 9.49 and 1% point is 13.28, so our observed value of 10.5 has probability between 1% and 5%, or 0.01 and 0.05. If we use a computer program which prints out the actual probability, we find P = 0.03. The data are not consistent with the null hypothesis and we can conclude that there is evidence of a relationship between housing tenure and time of delivery.

The chi-squared statistic is not an index of the strength of the association. If we double the frequencies in Table 13.1, this will double chi-squared, but the strength of the association is unchanged. Note that we can only use this chi-squared test when the numbers in the cells are frequencies, not when they are percentages, proportions, or measurements.

Table 13.3 Percentage points of the Chi-squared distribution

Degrees of freedom	Probability that the tabulated value is exceeded (Figure 13.1)			
	10%	5%	1%	0.1%
1	2.71	3.84	6.63	10.83
2	4.61	5.99	9.21	13.82
3	6.25	7.81	11.34	16.27
4	7.78	9.49	13.28	18.47
5	9.24	11.07	15.09	20.52
6	10.64	12.59	16.81	22.46
7	12.02	14.07	18.48	24.32
8	13.36	15.51	20.09	26.13
9	14.68	16.92	21.67	27.88
10	15.99	18.31	23.21	29.59
11	17.28	19.68	24.73	31.26
12	18.55	21.03	26.22	32.91
13	19.81	22.36	27.69	34.53
14	21.06	23.68	29.14	36.12
15	22.31	25.00	30.58	37.70
16	23.54	26.30	32.00	39.25
17	24.77	27.59	33.41	40.79
18	25.99	28.87	34.81	42.31
19	27.20	30.14	36.19	43.82
20	28.41	31.41	37.57	45.32

13.2 Tests for 2 by 2 tables

Consider the data on cough symptom and history of bronchitis discussed in Section 9.8. We had 273 children with a history of bronchitis before age 5, of whom 26 were reported to have day or night cough at age 14, and 1 046 children without history of bronchitis, of whom 44 were reported to have day or night cough. We can set these data out as a contingency table, as in Table 13.4. We can also use the chi-squared test to test the null hypothesis of no association between cough and history.

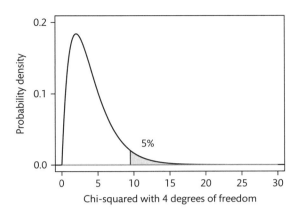

Figure 13.1 Percentage point of the Chi-squared distribution.

Table 13.4 Cough during the day or at night at age 14 for children with and without a history of bronchitis before age 5 (data from Holland *et al.* 1978)

	Bronchitis	No bronchitis	Total
Cough	26	44	70
No cough	247	1 002	1 249
Total	273	1 046	1 319

The expected frequencies are shown in Table 13.5. The test statistic is

$$\sum \frac{(O-E)^2}{E} = \frac{(26-14.49)^2}{14.49} + \frac{(44-55.51)^2}{55.51}$$
$$+ \frac{(247-258.51)^2}{258.51}$$
$$+ \frac{(1\,002-990.49)^2}{990.49}$$
$$= 12.2$$

Table 13.5 Expected frequencies for Table 13.4 (data from Holland *et al.* 1978)

	Bronchitis	No bronchitis	Total
Cough	14.49	55.51	70.00
No cough	258.51	990.49	1 249.00
Total	273.00	1 046.00	1 319.00

We have $r = 2$ rows and $c = 2$ columns, so there are $(r-1)(c-1) = (2-1) \times (2-1) = 1$ degree of freedom. We see from Table 13.3 that the 5% point is 3.84, and the 1% point is 6.63, so we have observed something very unlikely if the null hypothesis were true. Hence the data are inconsistent with the null hypothesis of no association and we can conclude that there is a relationship between present cough and history of bronchitis.

Now the null hypothesis 'no association between cough and bronchitis' is the same as the null hypothesis 'no difference between the proportions with cough in the bronchitis and no bronchitis groups'. If there were a difference, the variables would be associated. Thus we have tested the same null hypothesis in two different ways. In fact these tests are exactly equivalent. If we take the Normal deviate from Section 9.8, which was 3.49, and square it, we get 12.2, the chi-squared value. The method of Section 9.8 and Section 8.6 has the advantage that it can also give us a confidence interval for the size of the difference, which the chi-squared method does not. Note that the chi-squared test corresponds to the two sided z test, even though only the upper tail of the Chi-squared distribution is used.

13.3 The chi-squared test for small samples

When the null hypothesis is true, the test statistic $\sum (O - E)^2/E$, which we can call the **chi-squared statistic**, follows the Chi-squared distribution provided the expected values are large enough. This is a large sample test, like those of Section 9.7 and Section 9.8. The smaller the expected values become, the more dubious will be the test.

The conventional criterion for the test to be valid is usually attributed to the great statistician W. G. Cochran. The rule is this: the chi-squared test is valid if at least 80% of the expected frequencies exceed 5 and all the expected frequencies exceed 1. We can see that Table 13.2 satisfies this requirement, as only 2 out of 10 expected frequencies, 20%, are less than 5 and none is less than 1. Note that this condition applies to the expected frequencies, not the observed frequencies.

It is quite acceptable for an observed frequency to be 0, provided the expected frequencies meet the criterion.

This criterion is open to question. Simulation studies appear to suggest that the condition may be too conservative and that the chi-squared approximation works for smaller expected values, especially for larger numbers of rows and columns. As yet, no-one has succeeded in devising a better rule than Cochran's, so I would recommend keeping to it until the theoretical questions are resolved. Any chi-squared test which does not satisfy the criterion is always open to the charge that its validity is in doubt.

If the criterion is not satisfied we can usually combine or delete rows and columns to give bigger expected values. Of course, this cannot be done for 2 by 2 tables, which we consider in more detail below. For example, Table 13.6 shows data from the MRC streptomycin trial (Section 2.2), the results of radiological assessment for a subgroup of patients defined by a prognostic variable. We want to know whether there is evidence of a streptomycin effect within this subgroup, so we want to test the null hypothesis of no effect using a chi-squared test. There are 4 out of 6 expected values less than 5, so the test on this table would not be valid. We can combine the rows so as to raise the expected values. As the small expected frequencies are in the 'deterioration' and 'death' rows, it makes sense to combine these to give a 'deterioration or death' row. The expected values are then all greater than 5 and we can do the chi-squared test with 1 degree of freedom. This editing must be done with regard to the meaning of the various categories. In Table 13.6, there would be no point in combining rows 1 and 3 to give a new category of 'considerable improvement or death' to be compared with the remainder, as the comparison would be absurd. The new table is shown in Table 13.7. We have

$$\sum \frac{(O-E)^2}{E} = \frac{(13-8.4)^2}{8.4} + \frac{(5-9.6)^2}{9.6}$$
$$+ \frac{(2-6.6)^2}{6.6} + \frac{(12-7.4)^2}{7.4}$$
$$= 10.8$$

Table 13.6 Observed and expected frequencies of categories of radiological appearance at 6 months compared with appearance on admission in the MRC streptomycin trial, patients with an initial temperature of 100–100.9°F (data from MRC 1948)

Radiological assessment	Streptomycin		Control		Total
	observed	expected	observed	expected	
Improvement	13	8.4	5	9.6	18
Deterioration	2	4.2	7	4.8	9
Death	0	2.3	5	2.7	5
Total	15	15	17	17	32

Table 13.7 Reduction of Table 13.6 to a 2 by 2 table (data from MRC 1948)

Radiological assessment	Streptomycin		Control		Total
	observed	expected	observed	expected	
Improvement	13	8.4	5	9.6	18
Deterioration or death	2	6.6	12	7.4	14
Total	15	15.0	17	17.0	32

Under the null hypothesis, this is from a chi-squared distribution with one degree of freedom, and from Table 13.3 we can see that the probability of getting a value as extreme as 10.8 is less than 1%. We have data inconsistent with the null hypothesis and we can conclude that the evidence supports a treatment effect in this subgroup.

If the table does not meet the criterion even after reduction to a 2 by 2 table, we can apply either a continuity correction to improve the approximation to the Chi-squared distribution (Section 13.5), or an exact test based on a discrete distribution (Section 13.4).

13.4 Fisher's exact test

The chi-squared test described in Section 13.1 is a large sample test. When the sample is not large and expected values are less than 5, we can turn to an exact distribution, like that for the Mann–Whitney U statistic (Section 12.2). This method is called **Fisher's exact test**.

The exact probability distribution for the table can only be found when the row and column totals are given. Just as with the large sample chi-squared test, we restrict our attention to tables with these totals. This difficulty has led to much controversy about the use of this test. I shall show how the test works, then discuss its applicability.

Consider the following artificial example. In an experiment, we randomly allocate four participants to treatment A and four to treatment B, and get the outcome shown in Table 13.8. We want to know the probability of so large a difference in mortality between the two groups if the treatments have the same effect (the null hypothesis). We could have randomized the subjects into two groups in many ways, but if the null hypothesis is true the

Table 13.8 Artificial data to illustrate Fisher's exact test

	Survived	Died	Total
Treatment A	3	1	4
Treatment B	2	2	4
Total	5	3	8

Table 13.9 Possible tables for the totals of Table 13.8

i.

	S	D	T
A	4	0	4
B	1	3	4
T	5	3	8

ii.

	S	D	T
A	3	1	4
B	2	2	4
T	5	3	8

iii.

	S	D	T
A	2	2	4
B	3	1	4
T	5	3	8

iv.

	S	D	T
A	1	3	4
B	4	0	4
T	5	3	8

same three would have died. The row and column totals would therefore be the same for all these possible allocations. If we keep the row and column totals constant, there are only four possible tables, shown in Table 13.9. These tables are found by putting the values 0, 1, 2, 3 in the 'Died in group A' cell. Any other values would make the D total greater than 3.

Now, let us label our subjects a to h. The survivors we will call a to e, and the deaths f, g, h. How many ways can these patients be arranged in two groups of 4 to give tables i, ii, iii, and iv? Table i can arise in 5 ways. Patients f, g, and h would have to be in group B, to give 3 deaths, and the remaining member of B could be a, b, c, d, or e. Table ii can arise in 30 ways. The 3 survivors in group A can be abc, abd, abe, acd, ace, ade, bcd, bce, bde, cde, 10 ways. The death in A can be f, g, or h, 3 ways. Hence the group can be made up in 10 × 3 = 30 ways. Table iii is the same as table ii, with A and B reversed, so arises in 30 ways. Table iv is the same as table i with A and B reversed, so arises in 5 ways. Hence we can arrange the 8 patients into 2 groups of 4 in 5 + 30 + 30 + 5 = 70 ways. Now, the probability of any one arrangement arising by chance is 1/70, as they are all equally likely if the null hypothesis is true. Table i arises from 5 of the 70 arrangements, so has probability 5/70 = 0.071. Table ii arises from 30 out of 70 arrangements, so has probability 30/70 = 0.429. Similarly, table iii has probability 30/70 = 0.429, and table iv has probability 5/70 = 0.071.

Hence, under the null hypothesis that there is no association between treatment and survival, table ii, which we observed, has a probability of 0.429. It could easily have arisen by chance and so it is consistent with the null hypothesis. As in Section 9.2, we must also consider tables more extreme than the observed. In this case, there is one more extreme table in the direction of the observed difference, table i. In the direction of the observed difference, the probability of the observed table or a more

extreme one is 0.071 + 0.429 = 0.5. This is the P value for a one sided test (Section 9.5).

Fisher's exact test is essentially one sided. It is not clear what the corresponding deviations in the other direction would be, especially when all the marginal totals are different. This is because in that case the distribution is asymmetrical, unlike those of Sections 12.2–12.5. One solution is to double the one sided probability to get a two sided test when this is required. Another solution is to calculate probabilities for every possible table and sum all probabilities less than or equal to the probability for the observed table to give the P value. This may give a smaller P value than the doubling method.

There is no need to enumerate all the possible tables, as above. The probability can be found from a simple formula (Appendix 13B). The probability of observing a set of frequencies $f_{11}, f_{12}, f_{21}, f_{22}$, when the row and column totals are r_1, r_2, c_1, and c_2 and the grand total is n, is

$$\frac{r_1!r_2!c_1!c_2!}{n!f_{11}!f_{12}!f_{21}!f_{22}!}$$

(See Appendix 6A for the meaning of $n!$.) We can calculate this for each possible table and so find the probability for the observed table and each more extreme one. For the example:

$$\text{table i: } \frac{5!3!4!4!}{8!4!0!1!3!} = 0.071$$

$$\text{table ii: } \frac{5!3!4!4!}{8!3!1!2!2!} = 0.429$$

giving a total of 0.50 as before.

Unlike the exact distributions for the rank statistics, this distribution is fairly easy to calculate but difficult to tabulate. A good table of this distribution required a small book (Finney *et al.* 1963).

We can apply this test to Table 13.7. The 2 by 2 tables to be tested and their probabilities are:

Table:		Probability
13	5	0.001 378 2
2	12	
14	4	0.000 075 7
1	13	
15	3	0.000 001 4
0	14	

The total one sided probability is 0.001 455 3, which doubled for a two sided test gives 0.002 9. The method using all smaller probabilities gives P=0.001 6. Either is larger than the probability for the χ^2 value of 10.6, which is 0.001 1.

Fisher's exact test was originally devised for the 2 × 2 table and only used when the expected frequencies were small. This was because for larger numbers and larger tables the calculations were impractical. With computers things have changed, and Fisher's exact test can be done for any 2 × 2 table. Modern programs will also calculate Fisher's exact test for larger tables, for which we use the method of summing all probabilities as small as or smaller than the probability for the table observed. As the number of rows and columns increases, the number of possible tables for the given totals increases very rapidly and it becomes impractical to calculate and store the probability for each one. Some programs create a random sample of the possible tables and use them to estimate a distribution of probabilities whose tail area is then found. This is an example of a Monte Carlo method (Section 8.11).

13.5 Yates' continuity correction for the 2 by 2 table

The discrepancy in probabilities between the chi-squared test and Fisher's exact test arises because we are estimating the discrete distribution of the test statistic by the continuous Chi-squared distribution. A continuity correction like those of Section 12.6, called **Yates'**

correction, can be used to improve the fit. The observed frequencies change in units of one, so we make them closer to their expected values by one half. Hence the formula for the corrected chi-squared statistic for a 2 by 2 table is

$$\sum \frac{\left(|O - E| - \frac{1}{2}\right)^2}{E}$$

where $|O - E|$ means the absolute value or modulus of the difference, without sign. For Table 13.7 we have:

$$\sum \frac{\left(|O - E| - \frac{1}{2}\right)^2}{E} = \frac{\left(|13 - 8.4| - \frac{1}{2}\right)^2}{8.4}$$
$$+ \frac{\left(|5 - 9.6| - \frac{1}{2}\right)^2}{9.6}$$
$$+ \frac{\left(|2 - 6.6| - \frac{1}{2}\right)^2}{6.6}$$
$$+ \frac{\left(|12 - 7.4| - \frac{1}{2}\right)^2}{7.4}$$
$$= \frac{\left(4.6 - \frac{1}{2}\right)^2}{8.4} + \frac{\left(4.6 - \frac{1}{2}\right)^2}{9.6}$$
$$+ \frac{\left(4.6 - \frac{1}{2}\right)^2}{6.6} + \frac{\left(4.6 - \frac{1}{2}\right)^2}{7.4}$$
$$= 8.6$$

This has probability 0.003 7, which is closer to the exact probability (0.002 9 or 0.001 6, depending on how the two sided probability is calculated), though there is still a considerable discrepancy. At such extremely low values any approximate probability model such as this is liable to break down. In the critical area between 0.10 and 0.01, the continuity correction usually gives a very good fit to the exact probability. As Fisher's exact test is now so easy to do, Yates' correction may soon disappear.

13.6 The validity of Fisher's and Yates' methods

There has been much dispute among statisticians about the validity of the exact test and the continuity correction which approximates to it. Among the more argumentative of the founding fathers of statistical inference, such as Fisher and Neyman, this was quite acrimonious. The problem is still unresolved, and generating almost as much heat as light.

Note that although both are 2 by 2 tables, Tables 13.4 and 13.7 arose in different ways. In Table 13.7, the column totals were fixed by the design of the experiment and only the row totals are from a random variable. In Table 13.4 neither row nor column totals were set in advance. Both are from the Binomial distribution, depending on the incidence of bronchitis and prevalence of chronic cough in the population. There is a third possibility, that both the row and column totals are fixed. This is rare in practice, but it can be achieved by the following experimental design. We want to know whether a subject can distinguish an active treatment from a placebo. We present him with 10 tablets, 5 of each, and ask him to sort the tablets into the 5 active and 5 placebo. This would give a 2 by 2 table, subject's choice versus truth, in which all row and column totals are pre-set to 5. There are several variations on these types of table, too. It can be shown that the same chi-squared test applies to all these cases when samples are large. When samples are small, this is not necessarily so. A discussion of the problem is well beyond the scope of this book. For some of these cases, Fisher's exact test and Yates' correction may be conservative, that is, give rather larger probabilities than they should, though this is a matter of debate. My own opinion is that Yates' correction and Fisher's exact test should be used. If we must err, it seems better to err on the side of caution.

13.7 Odds and odds ratios

If the probability of an event is p, then the **odds** of that event is $o = p/(1 - p)$. The probability that a coin shows a head is 0.5, the odds is $0.5/(1 - 0.5) = 1$. Note that 'odds' is a singular word, not the plural of 'odd'. The odds has advantages for some types of analysis, as it is not constrained to lie between 0 and 1, but can take any value from zero to infinity. We often use the logarithm to the base e of the odds, the **log odds** or **logit**:

$$\log_e(o) = \log_e \left(\frac{p}{1 - p} \right)$$

This can vary from minus infinity to plus infinity and thus is very useful in fitting regression type models (Section 15.10). The logit is zero when $p = 1/2$ and the logit of $1 - p$ is minus the logit of p:

$$\log_e(o_p) = \log_e \left(\frac{p}{1 - p} \right)$$

$$= - \log_e \left(\frac{1 - p}{p} \right)$$

$$= - \log_e \left(o_{1-p} \right)$$

Consider Table 13.4. The probability of cough for children with a history of bronchitis is $26/273 = 0.095\,24$. The odds of cough for children with a history of bronchitis is $26/247 = 0.105\,26$. The probability of cough for children without a history of bronchitis is $44/1\,046 = 0.042\,07$. The odds of cough for children without a history of bronchitis is $44/1\,002 = 0.043\,91$.

One way to compare children with and without bronchitis is to find the ratio of the proportions of children with cough in the two groups (the risk ratio or relative risk, Section 8.6). Another is to find the **odds ratio**, the ratio of the odds of cough in children with bronchitis and children without bronchitis. This is $(26/247)/(44/1\,002) = 0.105\,26/0.043\,91 = 2.397\,18$. Thus the odds of cough in children with a history of bronchitis is $2.397\,18$ times the odds of cough in children without a history of bronchitis.

If we denote the frequencies in the table by a, b, c, and d, as in Table 13.10, the odds ratio is given by

$$or = \frac{a/c}{b/d} = \frac{ad}{bc}$$

This is symmetrical; we get the same thing by

$$or = \frac{a/b}{c/d} = \frac{ad}{bc}$$

Table 13.10 2 by 2 table in symbolic notation

			Total
a	b		$a + b$
c	d		$c + d$
Total	$a + c$	$b + d$	$a + b + c + d$

We can estimate the standard error and confidence interval using the log of the odds ratio (Appendix 13C). The standard error of the log odds ratio is:

$$SE\left(\log_e(or)\right) = \sqrt{\frac{1}{a} + \frac{1}{b} + \frac{1}{c} + \frac{1}{d}}$$

Hence we can find the 95% confidence interval. For Table 13.4, the log odds ratio is $\log_e(2.397\,18) = 0.874\,29$, with standard error

$$SE\left(\log_e(or)\right) = \sqrt{\frac{1}{26} + \frac{1}{44} + \frac{1}{247} + \frac{1}{1\,002}}$$

$$= \sqrt{0.066\,24}$$

$$= 0.257\,36$$

Provided the sample is large enough, we can assume that the log odds ratio comes from a Normal distribution and hence the approximate 95% confidence interval is $0.874\,29 - 1.96 \times 0.257\,36$ to $0.874\,29 + 1.96 \times 0.257\,36 = 0.369\,86$ to $1.378\,72$. To get a confidence interval for the odds ratio itself we must antilog:

$$e^{0.369\,86} \text{ to } e^{1.378\,72} = 1.45 \text{ to } 3.97$$

The odds ratio can be used to estimate the relative risk in a case–control study. The calculation of relative risk in Section 8.6 depended on the fact that we could estimate the risks. We could do this because we had a prospective study and so knew how many of the risk group developed the symptom. This cannot be done if we start with the outcome, in this case cough at age 14, and try to work back to the risk factor, bronchitis, as in a case–control study.

Table 13.11 shows data from a case–control study of smoking and lung cancer (see Section 3.8). We start with a group of cases, patients with lung cancer and a group of controls, here hospital patients without cancer. We

Table 13.11 Smokers and non-smokers among male cancer patients and controls (data from Doll and Hill 1950)

	Smokers	**Non-smokers**	**Total**
Lung cancer	647	2	649
Controls	622	27	649

Table 13.12 2 by 2 table for a case–control study in symbolic notation, multiplying frequencies in the case column by p and control column by $1 - p$

Risk factor	**Cases**	**Controls**	**Total**
Yes	ap	$b(1 - p)$	$ap + b(1 - p)$
No	cp	$d(1 - p)$	$cp + d(1 - p)$
Total	$(a + c)p$	$(b + d)(1 - p)$	$(a + c)p$ $+ (b + d)(1 - p)$

cannot calculate risks (the column totals would be meaningless and have been omitted), but we can still estimate the relative risk.

Suppose the prevalence of lung cancer is p, a small number, and the table is as Table 13.10. We can multiply the numbers in the cases column by p and the numbers in the control column by $1 - p$ to give Table 13.12. Then we can estimate the risk of being a case for those with the risk factor by $ap/(ap + b(1 - p))$ and the risk of being a case for those without the risk factor by $cp/(cp + d(1 - p))$. The relative risk of lung cancer for smokers is thus

$$\frac{ap/(ap + b(1 - p))}{cp/(cp + d(1 - p))}$$

Because p is small, much smaller than $1 - p$, $ap + b(1 - p)$ is approximately equal to $b(1 - p)$ and $cp + d(1 - p)$ is approximately equal to $d(1 - p)$. So the relative risk is approximately equal to

$$\frac{ap/(b(1 - p))}{cp/(d(1 - p))} = \frac{a/b}{c/d} = \frac{ad}{bc}$$

This is, of course, the odds ratio for the original table. Thus for case–control studies the relative risk is approximated by the odds ratio.

For Table 13.11 we have

$$\frac{ad}{bc} = \frac{647 \times 27}{2 \times 622} = 14.04$$

Thus the risk of lung cancer in smokers is about 14 times that of non-smokers. This is a surprising result from a table with so few non-smokers, but a direct estimate from the cohort study (Table 3.1) is $0.90/0.07 = 12.9$, which is very similar. The log odds ratio is $2.642\,10$ and its standard error is

$$SE\left(\log_e(or)\right) = \sqrt{\frac{1}{647} + \frac{1}{2} + \frac{1}{622} + \frac{1}{27}}$$

$$= \sqrt{0.540\,19}$$

$$= 0.734\,98$$

Hence the approximate 95% confidence interval is $2.642\,10 - 1.96 \times 0.734\,98$ to $2.642\,10 + 1.96 \times 0.734\,98 = 1.201\,54$ to $4.082\,65$. To get a confidence interval for the odds ratio itself we must antilog:

$$e^{1.201\,54} \text{ to } e^{4.082\,65} = 3.3 \text{ to } 59.3$$

The very wide confidence interval is because the numbers of non-smokers, particularly for lung cancer cases, are so small.

13.8 The chi-squared test for trend

Consider the data of Table 13.13. Using the chi-squared test described in Section 13.1, we can test the null hypothesis that there is no relationship between reported cough and smoking against the alternative that there is a relationship of some sort. The chi-squared statistic is 64.25, with 2 degrees of freedom, P < 0.001. The data are not consistent with the null hypothesis.

Now, we would have got the same value of chi-squared whatever the order of the columns. The test ignores the natural ordering of the columns, but we might expect that if there were a relationship between reported cough and smoking, the prevalence of cough would be greater for greater amounts of smoking. In other words, we look for a trend in cough prevalence from one end of the table to the other. We can test for this using the **chi-squared test for trend**.

First, we define two random variables, X and Y, whose values depend on the categories of the row and column variables. For example, we could put $X = 1$ for non-smokers, $X = 2$ for occasional smokers and $X = 3$ for regular smokers, and put $Y = 1$ for 'cough' and $Y = 2$ for 'no cough'. Then for a non-smoker who coughs, the value of X is 1 and the value of Y is 1. Both X and Y may have more than two categories, provided both are ordered. If there are n individuals, we have n pairs of observations (x_i, y_i). If there is a linear trend across the table, there will be linear regression of Y on X which has non-zero slope. We fit the usual least squares regression line, $Y = a + bX$, where

$$b = \frac{\sum(y_i - \bar{y})(x_i - \bar{x})}{\sum(x_i - \bar{x})^2} \text{ and } SE(b) = \sqrt{\frac{s^2}{(x_i - \bar{x})^2}}$$

and where s^2 is the estimated variance of Y. In simple linear regression, as described in Chapter 11, we are usually concerned with estimating b and making statements about its precision. Here we are only going to test the null hypothesis that in the population $b = 0$. Under the null hypothesis, the variance about the line is equal to the total variance of Y, as the line has zero slope. We use the estimate

$$s^2 = \frac{1}{n}\sum(y_i - \bar{y})^2$$

(We use n as the denominator, not $n-1$, because the test is conditional on the row and column totals as described in Appendix 13A. There is a good reason for it, but it is not worth going into here.) As in Section 11.5, the standard error of b is

$$SE(b) = \sqrt{\frac{s^2}{\sum(x_i - \bar{x})^2}} = \sqrt{\frac{\sum(y_i - \bar{y})^2}{n\sum(x_i - \bar{x})^2}}$$

Table 13.13 Cough during the day or at night and cigarette smoking by 12-year-old boys (data from Bland *et al.* 1978)

	Boys' smoking						Total
	Non-smoker		**Occasional**		**Regular**		
Cough	266	20.4%	395	28.8%	80	46.5%	741
No cough	1 037	79.6%	977	71.2%	92	53.5%	2 106
Total	1 303	100.0%	1 372	100.0%	172	100.0%	2 847

As in Section 11.5, b is the sum of many independent, identically distributed random variables $\sum(y_i - \bar{y})(x_i - \bar{x})$, and so follows a Normal distribution by the central limit theorem (Section 7.2). As n is large, SE(b) should be a good estimate of the standard deviation of this distribution. Hence, if the null hypothesis is true and $E(b) = 0$, b/SE(b) is an observation from a Standard Normal distribution. Hence the square of this, b^2/SE(b)^2, is from a Chi-squared distribution with one degree of freedom.

$$\frac{b^2}{SE(b)^2} = \left(\frac{\sum(y_i - \bar{y})(x_i - \bar{x})}{\sum(x_i - \bar{x})^2}\right)^2 \bigg/ \frac{\sum(y_i - \bar{y})^2}{n\sum(x_i - \bar{x})^2}$$

$$= \frac{n\left(\sum(y_i - \bar{y})(x_i - \bar{x})\right)^2}{\sum(x_i - \bar{x})^2\sum(y_i - \bar{y})^2}$$

For practical calculations we use the alternative forms of the sums of squares and products:

$$\chi_1^2 = \frac{n\left(\sum y_i x_i - \frac{(\sum y_i)(\sum x_i)}{n}\right)^2}{\left(\sum x_i^2 - \frac{(\sum x_i)^2}{n}\right)\left(\sum y_i^2 - \frac{(\sum y_i)^2}{n}\right)}$$

Note that it does not matter which variable is X and which is Y. The sums of squares and products are easy to work out. For example, for the column variable, X, we have 1 303 individuals with $X = 1$, 1 372 with $X = 2$ and 172 with $X = 3$. For our data we have

$$\sum x_i^2 = 1^2 \times 1\,303 + 2^2 \times 1\,372 + 3^2 \times 172 = 8\,339$$

$$\sum x_i = 1 \times 1\,303 + 2 \times 1\,372 + 3 \times 172 = 4\,563$$

$$\sum x_i y_i = 1 \times 1 \times 266 + 2 \times 1 \times 395$$
$$+ 3 \times 1 \times 80 + 1 \times 2 \times 1\,037$$
$$+ 2 \times 2 \times 977 + 3 \times 2 \times 92$$
$$= 7\,830$$

Similarly, $\sum y_i^2 = 9\,165$ and $\sum y_i = 4\,953$.

$$\chi_1^2 = \frac{2\,847 \times \left(7\,830 - \frac{4\,563 \times 4\,953}{2\,847}\right)^2}{\left(8\,339 - \frac{4\,563^2}{2\,847}\right)\left(9\,165 - \frac{4\,953^2}{2\,847}\right)}$$

$$= 59.47$$

If the null hypothesis were true, χ_1^2 would be an observation from the Chi-squared distribution with 1 degree of freedom. The value 59.47 is highly unlikely from this distribution and the trend is significant.

There are several points to note about this method. The choice of values for X and Y is arbitrary. By putting $X = 1, 2,$ or 3 we assumed that the difference between non-smokers and occasional smokers is the same as that between occasional smokers and smokers. This need not be so and a different choice of X would give a different chi-squared for trend statistic. The choice is not critical, however. For example, putting $X = 1, 2,$ or 4, so making regular smokers more different from occasional smokers than occasional smokers are from non-smokers, we get χ^2 for trend to be 64.22. The fit to the data is rather better, but the conclusions are unchanged.

The trend may be significant even if the overall contingency table chi-squared is not. This is because the test for trend has greater power for detecting trends than has the ordinary chi-squared test. On the other hand, if we had an association where those who were occasional smokers had far more symptoms than either non-smokers or regular smokers, the trend test would not detect it. If the hypothesis we wish to test involves the order of the categories, we should use the trend test, if it does not we should use the contingency table test of Section 13.1. Note that the trend test statistic is always less than the overall chi-squared statistic.

The distribution of the trend chi-squared statistic depends on a large sample regression model, not on the theory given in Appendix 13A. The table does not have to meet Cochran's rule (Section 13.3) for the trend test to be valid. As long as there are at least 30 observations the approximation should be valid.

Some computer programs offer a slightly different test, the Mantel–Haenzsel trend test (not to be confused with the Mantel–Haenzsel method for combining 2 by 2 tables, Section 17.9). This is almost identical to the method described here. As an alternative to the chi-squared test for trend, we could calculate Kendall's rank correlation coefficient, τ_b, between X and Y (Section 12.5). For Table 13.13 we get $\tau_b = -0.136$ with standard error 0.018. We get a χ_1^2 statistic by $(\tau_b/SE(\tau_b))^2 = 57.09$. This is very similar to the χ^2 for trend value 59.47.

13.9 Methods for matched samples

The chi-squared test described above enables us, among other things, to test the null hypothesis that binomial proportions estimated from two independent samples are the same. We can do this for the one sample or matched sample problem also. For example, Holland *et al.* (1978) obtained respiratory symptom questionnaires for 1 319 Kent schoolchildren at ages 12 and 14. One question we asked was whether the prevalence of reported symptoms was different at the two ages. At age 12, 356 (27%) children were reported to have had severe colds in the past 12 months compared with 468 (35%) at age 14. Was there evidence of a real increase? Just as in the paired t test (Section 10.2) we would hope to improve our analysis by taking into account the fact that this is the same sample. We might expect, for instance, that symptoms on the two occasions will be related.

The method which enables us to do this is **McNemar's test**, another version of the sign test (Section 9.2). We need to know that 212 children were reported to have colds on both occasions, 144 to have colds at 12 but not at 14, 256 to have colds at 14 but not at 12 and 707 to have colds at neither age. Table 13.14 shows the data in tabular form.

The null hypothesis is that the proportions saying yes on the first and second occasions are the same, the alternative being that one exceeds the other. This is a hypothesis about the row and column totals, quite different from that for the contingency table chi-squared test. If the null hypothesis were true, we would expect the frequencies for 'yes, no' and 'no, yes' to be equal. In other words, as many should go up as down. (Compare this

with the sign test, Section 9.2.) If we denote these frequencies by f_{yn} and f_{ny}, then the expected frequencies will be $(f_{yn} + f_{ny})/2$. We get the test statistic:

$$\sum \frac{(O - E)^2}{E} = \frac{\left(f_{yn} - \dfrac{f_{yn} + f_{ny}}{2}\right)^2}{\dfrac{f_{yn} + f_{ny}}{2}}$$
$$+ \frac{\left(f_{ny} - \dfrac{f_{yn} + f_{ny}}{2}\right)^2}{\dfrac{f_{yn} + f_{ny}}{2}}$$

which follows a Chi-squared distribution provided the expected values are large enough. There are two observed frequencies and one constraint, that the sum of the observed frequencies = the sum of the expected frequencies. Hence there is one degree of freedom. Like the chi-squared test (Section 13.1) and Fisher's exact test (Section 13.4), we assume a total to be fixed. In this case it is $f_{yn} + f_{ny}$, not the row and column totals, which are what we are testing. The test statistic can be simplified considerably, to:

$$\chi^2 = \frac{(f_{yn} - f_{ny})^2}{f_{yn} + f_{ny}}$$

For Table 13.14, we have

$$\chi^2 = \frac{(f_{yn} - f_{ny})^2}{f_{yn} + f_{ny}} = \frac{(144 - 256)^2}{144 + 256} = 31.4$$

This can be referred to Table 13.3 with one degree of freedom and is clearly highly significant. There was a difference in the incidence of severe colds between the two ages. As there were no changes in any of the other symptoms studied, we thought that this was possibly due to an epidemic of upper respiratory tract infection just before the second questionnaire.

There is a continuity correction, again due to Yates. If the observed frequency f_{yn} increases by 1, f_{ny} decreases by 1 and $f_{yn} - f_{ny}$ increases by 2. Thus half the difference between adjacent possible values is 1 and we make the observed difference nearer to the expected difference (zero) by 1. Thus the continuity corrected test statistic is

$$\chi^2 = \frac{(|f_{yn} - f_{ny}| - 1)^2}{f_{yn} + f_{ny}}$$

Table 13.14 Severe colds reported at two ages for Kent schoolchildren (data from Holland *et al.* 1978)

Severe colds at age 12	Severe colds at age 14		Total
	Yes	No	
Yes	212	144	356
No	256	707	963
Total	468	851	1 319

where $|f_{yn} - f_{ny}|$ is the absolute value, without sign. For Table 13.14:

$$\chi^2 = \frac{(|f_{yn} - f_{ny}| - 1)^2}{f_{yn} + f_{ny}}$$

$$= \frac{(|144 - 256| - 1)^2}{144 + 256}$$

$$= \frac{(112 - 1)^2}{400}$$

$$= 30.8$$

There is very little difference because the expected values are so large but if the expected values are small, say less than 20, the correction is advisable. For small samples, we can also take f_{ny} as an observation from the Binomial distribution with $p = \frac{1}{2}$ and $n = f_{yn} + f_{ny}$ and proceed as for the sign test (Section 9.2).

We can find a confidence interval for the difference between the proportions. The estimated difference is $p_1 - p_2 = (f_{yn} - f_{ny})/n$. We rearrange this:

$$\frac{f_{yn} - f_{ny}}{n} = \frac{f_{yn} - f_{ny}}{f_{yn} + f_{ny}} \frac{f_{yn} + f_{ny}}{n}$$

$$= \left(\frac{2f_{yn}}{f_{yn} + f_{ny}} - 1\right) \frac{f_{yn} + f_{ny}}{n}$$

We can treat the f_{yn} as an observation from a Binomial distribution with parameter $n = f_{yn} + f_{ny}$, which, of course, we are treating as fixed. (I am using n here to mean the parameter of the Binomial distribution as in Section 6.4, not to mean the total sample size.) We find a confidence interval for $f_{yn}/(f_{yn} + f_{ny})$ using either the z method of Section 8.4 or the exact method of Section 8.9. We then multiply these limits by 2, subtract 1 and multiply by $(f_{yn} + f_{ny})/n$.

For the example, the estimated difference is (144 − 256)/1 319 = −0.085. For the confidence interval, $f_{yn} + f_{ny} = 400$ and $f_{yn} = 144$. The 95% confidence interval for $f_{yn}/(f_{yn} + f_{ny})$ is 0.313 to 0.407 by the large sample method. Hence the confidence interval for $p_1 - p_2$ is $(2 \times 0.313 - 1) \times 400/1 319 = -0.113$ to $(2 \times 0.407 - 1) \times 400/1 319 = -0.056$. We estimate that the proportion of colds on the first occasion was less than that on the second by between 0.06 and 0.11.

We may wish to compare the distribution of a variable with three or more categories in matched samples.

If the categories are ordered, like smoking experience in Table 13.13, we are usually looking for a shift from one end of the distribution to the other, and we can use the sign test (Section 9.2), counting positives when smoking increased, negative when it decreased, and zero if the category was the same. When the categories are not ordered, as Table 13.1 there is a test due to Stuart (1955), described by Maxwell (1970). The test is difficult to do and the situation is very unusual, so I shall omit details.

We can also find an odds ratio for the matched table, called the **conditional odds ratio**. Like McNemar's method, it uses the frequencies in the off diagonal only. The estimate is very simple: f_{yn}/f_{ny}. Thus for Table 13.14 the odds of having severe colds at age 12 is $144/256 = 0.56$ times that at age 14. This method is particularly useful in matched case–control studies, where it provides an estimate of the relative risk. A confidence interval is provided in the same way as for the difference between proportions. We can estimate $p = f_{yn}/(f_{yn} + f_{ny})$, and then the odds ratio is given by $p/(1 - p)$. For the example, $p = 144/400 = 0.36$ and turning p back to the odds ratio $p/(1 - p) = 0.36/(1 - 0.36) = 0.56$ as before. The 95% confidence interval for p is 0.313 to 0.4071, as above. Hence the 95% confidence interval for the conditional odds ratio is $0.31/(1 - 0.31) = 0.45$ to $0.41/(1 - 0.41) = 0.69$.

13.10 The chi-squared goodness of fit test

Another use of the Chi-squared distribution is the goodness of fit test. Here we test the null hypothesis that a frequency distribution follows some theoretical distribution such as the Poisson or Normal. Table 13.15 shows a frequency distribution. We shall test the null hypothesis that it is from a Poisson distribution, i.e. that conception is a random event among fertile women.

First we estimate the parameter of the Poisson distribution, its mean, μ, in this case 0.816. We then calculate the probability for each value of the variable, using the Poisson formula of Section 6.7:

$$\frac{e^{-\mu}\mu^r}{r!}$$

Table 13.15 Parity of 125 women attending antenatal clinics at St George's Hospital, with the calculation of the chi-squared goodness of fit test (data supplied by Rebecca McNair, personal communication)

Parity	Frequency	Poisson probability	Expected frequency	$\frac{(O-E)^2}{E}$
0	59	0.442 20	55.275	0.251
1	44	0.360 83	45.104	0.027
2	14	0.147 22	18.402	1.053
3	3	0.040 04	5.005 ⎫	
4	4	0.008 17	1.021 ⎪	
5	1	0.001 33	0.167 ⎬ 6.219	1.666
> 5	0	0.000 21	0.026 ⎭	
Total	125	1.000 00	125.000	2.997

where r is the number of events. The probabilities are shown in Table 13.15. The probability that the variable exceeds 5 is found by subtracting the probabilities for 0, 1, 2, 3, 4, and 5 from 1.0. We then multiply these by the number of observations, 125, to give the frequencies we would expect from 125 observations from a Poisson distribution with mean 0.816.

We now have a set of observed and expected frequencies and can compute a chi-squared statistic in the usual way. We want all the expected frequencies to be greater than 5 if possible. We achieve this here by combining all the categories for parity greater than or equal to 3. We then add $(O-E)^2/E$ for the categories to give a χ^2 statistic. We now find the degrees of freedom. This is the number of categories minus the number of parameters fitted from the data (one in the example) minus one. Thus we have 4−1−1 = 2 degrees of freedom. From Table 13.3 the observed χ^2 value of 2.99 has P > 0.10 and the deviation from the Poisson distribution is clearly not significant.

The same test can be used for testing the fit of any distribution. For example, Wroe et al. (1992) studied diurnal variation in onset of strokes. Table 13.16 shows the frequency distribution of times of onset. If the null hypothesis that there is no diurnal variation were true, the time at which strokes occurred would follow a Uniform distribution (Section 7.2). The expected frequency in each time interval would be the same. There were 554

Table 13.16 Time of onset of 554 strokes (data from Wroe et al. 1992)

Time	Frequency	Time	Frequency
00.01–02.00	21	12.01–14.00	34
02.01–04.00	16	14.01–16.00	59
04.01–06.00	22	16.01–18.00	44
06.01–08.00	104	18.01–20.00	51
08.01–10.00	95	20.01–22.00	32
10.01–12.00	66	22.01–24.00	10

cases altogether, so the expected frequency for each time is 554/12 = 46.167. We then work out $(O - E)^2/E$ for each interval and add to give the chi-squared statistic, in this case equal to 218.8. There is only one constraint, that the frequencies total 554, as no parameters have been estimated. Hence if the null hypothesis were true we would have an observation from the Chi-squared distribution with 12 − 1 = 11 degrees of freedom. The calculated value of 218.8 is very unlikely, P < 0.001 from Table 13.3, and the data are not consistent with the null hypothesis. When we test the equality of a set of frequencies like this the test is also called the **Poisson heterogeneity test**.

13.11 Multiple choice questions: Categorical data

(Each branch is either true or false.)

13.1 The standard chi-squared test for a 2 by 2 contingency table is valid only if:
(a) all the expected frequencies are greater than 5;
(b) both variables are continuous;
(c) at least one variable is from a Normal distribution;
(d) all the observed frequencies are greater than 5;
(e) the sample is very large.

13.2 In a chi-squared test for a 5 by 3 contingency table:
(a) variables must be quantitative;
(b) observed frequencies are compared with expected frequencies;
(c) there are 15 degrees of freedom;
(d) at least 12 cells must have expected values greater than 5;
(e) all the observed values must be greater than 1.

Table 13.17 Cough first thing in the morning in a group of schoolchildren, as reported by the child and by the child's parents (data from Bland *et al.* 1979)

| | Child's report | | Total |
Parents' report	Yes	No	
Yes	29	104	133
No	172	5 097	5 269
Total	201	5 201	5 402

13.3 In Table 13.17:
(a) the association between reports by parents and children can be tested by a chi-squared test;
(b) the difference between symptom prevalence as reported by children and parents can be tested by McNemar's test;
(c) if McNemar's test is significant, the contingency chi-squared test is not valid;
(d) the contingency chi-squared test has 1 degree of freedom;
(e) it would be important to use the continuity correction in the contingency chi-squared test.

13.4 Fisher's exact test for a contingency table:
(a) applies to 2 by 2 tables;
(b) usually gives a larger probability than the ordinary chi-squared test;
(c) usually gives about the same probability as the chi-squared test with Yates' continuity correction;
(d) is suitable when expected frequencies are small;
(e) is difficult to calculate when the expected frequencies are large.

13.5 When an odds ratio is calculated from a 2 by 2 table:
(a) the odds ratio is a measure of the strength of the relationship between the row and column variables;
(b) if the order of the rows and the order of the columns is reversed, the odds ratio will be unchanged;
(c) the ratio may take any positive value;
(d) the odds ratio will be changed to its reciprocal if the order of the columns only is changed;
(e) the odds ratio is the ratio of the proportions of observations in the first row for the two columns.

Table 13.18 Bird attacks on milk bottles reported by cases of *Campylobacter jejuni* infection and controls (data from Southern *et al.* 1990)

| Number of days of week when attacks took place | Number of | | OR |
	cases	controls	
0	3	42	1
1–3	11	3	51
4–5	5	1	70
6–7	10	1	140

13.6 Table 13.18 appeared in the report of a case control study of infection with *Campylobacter jejuni* (Section 3.12):
(a) A chi-squared test for trend could be used to test the null hypothesis that risk of disease does not increase with the number of bird attacks;
(b) 'OR' means the odds ratio;
(c) A significant contingency chi-squared test for a 4 by 2 table would show that risk of disease increases with increasing numbers of bird attacks;

(d) 'OR' provides an estimate of the relative risk of *Campylobacter jejuni* infection;

(e) Kendall's rank correlation coefficient, τ_b, could be used to test the null hypothesis that risk of disease does not increase with the number of bird attacks.

13.7 McNemar's test could be used:

(a) to compare the numbers of cigarette smokers among cancer cases and age and sex matched healthy controls;

(b) to examine the change in respiratory symptom prevalence in a group of asthmatics from winter to summer;

(c) to look at the relationship between cigarette smoking and respiratory symptoms in a group of asthmatics;

(d) to examine the change in PEFR in a group of asthmatics from winter to summer;

(e) to compare the number of cigarette smokers among a group of cancer cases and a random sample of the general population.

13.12 Exercise: Some analyses of categorical data

In this exercise we shall look at some data concerning socioeconomic status and tumour stage. Brewster *et al.* (2001) investigated whether there is any relation between socioeconomic status and tumour stage at presentation in patients with

breast, colorectal, ovarian, and lung cancer. Table 13.19 shows part of the table they presented.

The authors concluded: 'We found no evidence that patients from deprived communities were likely to present with more advanced disease for breast . . . cancer'.

13.1 How could their analysis be improved?

The next questionable analysis concerns a dubious Fisher's exact test. Nuesch *et al.* (2001) studied responsiveness to treatment of hypertensive patients. Patients were classified as either responsive or non-responsive to treatment using blood pressure measurements. The authors compared the proportion of patients who were classed as responsive using clinic measurements of blood pressure with the proportion of patients who were classed as responsive using ambulatory blood pressure recording. The authors reported that: 'Measurements of clinic blood pressure at the start of the study identified 43 patients who were responsive to antihypertensive treatment and 62 who were non-responsive. With the initial ambulatory blood pressure monitoring, we reclassified 12 of the non-responsive patients as responsive (Fisher's exact test of numbers of responsive and non-responsive patients as assessed by clinic blood pressure versus ambulatory blood pressure; P = 0.127). Based on the results of ambulatory blood pressure, we classified 55 patients as responsive (control group) and 50 as non-responsive. Thus, about half of our patients taking two to four antihypertensive drugs fulfilled the criteria for treatment resistance'. We can recreate their 2 by 2 table as shown in Table 13.20.

Table 13.19 Relation between socioeconomic status and tumour size in patients with breast cancer. Values are numbers (percentages) (data from Brewster *et al.* 2001)

Tumour size (mm)	Deprivation group							
	Affluent *n* = 548		Middle *n* = 1 605		Deprived *n* = 364		Total *n* = 2 517	
0–20	271	(49.5%)	730	(45.5%)	166	(45.6%)	1 167	(46.4%)
21–50	124	(22.6%)	409	(25.5%)	109	(29.9%)	642	(25.5%)
> 50	14	(2.6%)	49	(3.1%)	13	(3.6%)	76	(3.0%)
Unknown	139	(25.4%)	417	(26.0%)	76	(20.9%)	632	(25.1%)

Significance: chi-squared = 9.89, df=6, P=0.13

Table 13.20 Response status by place of blood pressure measurement (data from Nuesch *et al.* 2001)

Status	Method of BP measurement	
	Clinic	Ambulatory
Responder	43	55
Non-responder	62	50
Total	105	105

13.2 Why is Fisher's exact test wrong here? What assumption is violated?

13.3 What effect do you think this might have on the P value?

13.4 What analysis should they do?

Hepworth *et al.* (2006) investigated the association between mobile phone use and risk of glioma in adults. They interviewed 966 people aged 18 to 69 years diagnosed with a glioma from 1 December 2000 to 29 February 2004 and 1 716 controls randomly selected from general practitioner lists. They said that the main outcome measures were 'odds ratios for risk of glioma in relation to mobile phone use'.

They reported that 'The overall odds ratio for regular phone use was 0.94 (95% confidence interval 0.78 to 1.13). There was no relation for risk of glioma and time since first use, lifetime years of use, and cumulative number of calls and hours of use. A significant excess risk for reported phone use ipsilateral to the tumour (1.24, 1.02 to 1.52) was paralleled by a significant reduction in risk (0.75, 0.61 to 0.93) for contralateral use'. They concluded that 'Use of a mobile phone, either in the short or medium term, is not associated with an increased risk of glioma'.

13.5 What kind of study design is this?

13.6 The authors say that the main outcome measures for this study are 'odds ratios for risk of glioma in relation to mobile phone use'. Is this correct?

13.7 The authors say that the overall odds ratio for regular phone use was 0.94. What is an odds ratio?

13.8 How can we interpret the odds ratio 0.94 in this study?

13.9 For the odds ratio, the authors give 95% confidence interval 0.78 to 1.13. What does this mean and how does it help us to interpret the results of this study?

13.10 What do you think of their main conclusion?

Appendix 13A: Why the chi-squared test works

We noted some of the properties of the Chi-squared distribution in Appendix 7A. In particular, it is the sum of the squares of a set of independent Standard Normal variables, and if we look at a subset of values defined by independent linear relationships between these variables we lose 1 degree of freedom for each constraint. It is on these two properties that the chi-squared test depends.

Suppose we did not have a fixed size to the birth study of Table 13.1, but observed subjects as they delivered over a fixed time. Then the number in a given cell of the table would be from a Poisson distribution and the set of Poisson variables corresponding to the cell frequency would be independent of one another. Our table is one set of samples from these Poisson distributions. However, we do not know the expected values of these distributions under the null hypothesis; we only know their expected values if the table has the row and column totals we observed. We can only consider the subset of outcomes of these variables which has the observed row and column totals. The test is said to be conditional on these row and column totals.

The mean and variance of a Poisson variable are equal (Section 6.7). If the null hypothesis is true, the means of these variables will be equal to the expected frequency calculated in Section 13.1. Thus O, the observed cell frequency, is from a Poisson distribution with mean E, the expected cell frequency, and standard deviation $\sqrt{E}$. Provided E is large enough, this Poisson distribution will be approximately Normal. Hence $(O - E)/\sqrt{E}$ is from a Normal distribution mean 0 and variance 1. Hence if we find

$$\sum \left(\frac{O-E}{\sqrt{E}}\right)^2 = \sum \frac{(O-E)^2}{E}$$

this is the sum of the squares of a set of Normally distributed random variables with mean 0 and variance 1, and so is from a Chi-squared distribution (Appendix 7A).

We will now find the degrees of freedom. Although the underlying variables are independent, we are only considering a subset defined by the row and column totals. Consider the table as in Table 13.21. Here, f_{11} to f_{22} are the observed frequencies, r_1, r_2 the row totals, c_1, c_2 the

Table 13.21 Symbolic representation of a 2 × 2 table

			Total
	f_{11}	f_{12}	r_1
	f_{21}	f_{22}	r_2
Total	c_1	c_2	n

column totals, and n the grand total. Denote the corresponding expected values by e_{11} to e_{22}. There are three linear constraints on the frequencies:

$$f_{11} + f_{12} + f_{21} + f_{22} = n$$

$$f_{11} + f_{12} = r_1$$

$$f_{11} + f_{21} = c_1$$

Any other constraint can be made up of these. For example, we must have

$$f_{21} + f_{22} = r_2$$

This can be found by subtracting the second equation from the first. Each of these linear constraints on f_{11} to f_{22} is also a linear constraint on $(f_{11} - e_{11})/\sqrt{e_{11}}$ to $(f_{22} - e_{22})/\sqrt{e_{22}}$. This is because e_{11} is fixed and so $(f_{11} - e_{11})/\sqrt{e_{11}}$ is a linear function of f_{11}. There are four observed frequencies and so four $(O - E)/\sqrt{E}$ variables, with three constraints. We lose one degree of freedom for each constraint and so have $4 - 3 = 1$ degree of freedom.

If we have r rows and c columns, then we have one constraint that the sum of the frequencies is n. Each row must add up, but when we reach the last row the constraint can be obtained by subtracting the first $r - 1$ rows from the grand total. The rows contribute only $r-1$ further constraints. Similarly the columns contribute $c - 1$ constraints. Hence, there being rc frequencies, the degrees of freedom are

$$rc - 1 - (r - 1) - (c - 1) = rc - 1 - r + 1$$
$$-c + 1$$
$$= rc - r - c + 1$$
$$= (r - 1)(c - 1)$$

So we have degrees of freedom given by the number of rows minus one times the number of columns minus one.

Appendix 13B: The formula for Fisher's exact test

The derivation of Fisher's formula is strictly for the algebraically minded. Remember that the number of ways of choosing r things out of n things (Appendix 6A) is $n!/r!(n - r)!$. Now, suppose we have a 2 by 2 table made up of n as shown in Table 13.21. First, we ask how many ways n individuals can be arranged to give marginal totals, r_1, r_2, c_1, and c_2. They can be arranged in columns in $n!/c_1!c_2!$ ways, as we are choosing c_1 objects out of n, and in rows $n!/r_1!r_2!$ ways. (Remember $n - c_1 = c_2$ and $n - r_1 = r_2$.) Hence they can be arranged in

$$\frac{n!}{c_1!c_2!} \times \frac{n!}{r_1!r_2!} = \frac{n!n!}{c_1!c_2!r_1!r_2!}$$

ways. For example, the table with totals

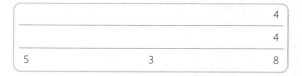

		4
		4
5	3	8

can happen in

$$\frac{8!}{5! \times 3!} \times \frac{8!}{4! \times 4!} = 56 \times 70 = 3\,920 \text{ ways.}$$

As we saw in Section 13.4, the columns can be arranged in 70 ways. Now we ask, of these ways how many make up a particular table? We are now dividing the n into four groups of sizes f_{11}, f_{12}, f_{21}, and f_{12}. We can choose the first group in $n!/f_{11}!(n - f_{11})!$ ways, as before. We are now left with $n - f_{11}$ individuals, so we can choose f_{12} in $(n - f_{11})!/f_{12}!(n - f_{11} - f_{12})!$. We are now left with $n - f_{11} - f_{12}$, and so we choose f_{21} in $(n - f_{11} - f_{12})!/f_{21}!$ ways. This leaves $n - f_{11} - f_{12} - f_{21}$, which is, of course, equal to f_{22} and so f_{22} can only be chosen in one way. Hence we have altogether:

$$\frac{n!}{f_{11}! \times (n-f_{11})!} \times \frac{(n-f_{11})!}{f_{12}! \times (n-f_{11}-f_{12})!}$$

$$\times \frac{(n-f_{11}-f_{12})!}{f_{21}! \times (n-f_{11}-f_{12}-f_{12})!}$$

$$= \frac{n!}{f_{11}! \times f_{12}! \times f_{21}! \times (n-f_{11}-f_{12}-f_{12})!}$$

$$= \frac{n!}{f_{11}! \times f_{12}! \times f_{21}! \times f_{22}!}$$

because $n - f_{11} - f_{12} - f_{12} = f_{22}$. So out of the

$$\frac{n! \times n!}{c_1! \times c_2! \times r_1! \times r_2!}$$

possible tables, the given table arises in

$$\frac{n!}{f_{11}! \times f_{12}! \times f_{21}! \times f_{22}!}$$

ways. The probability of this table arising by chance is

$$\frac{n!}{f_{11}! \times f_{12}! \times f_{21}! \times f_{22}!} \bigg/ \frac{c_1! \times c_2! \times r_1! \times r_2!}{n! \times n!}$$

$$= \frac{n! \times f_{11}! \times f_{12}! \times f_{21}! \times f_{22}!}{c_1! \times c_2! \times r_1! \times r_2!}$$

Appendix 13C: Standard error for the log odds ratio

This is for the mathematical reader. We start with a general result concerning log transformations. If X is a random variable with mean μ, the approximate variance of $\log_e(X)$ is given by

$$\mathrm{VAR}(\log_e(X)) = \frac{\mathrm{VAR}(X)}{\mu^2}$$

This is why when the standard deviation of a variable is proportional to its mean, and hence the variance is proportional to the mean squared, a log transformation makes the variance independent of the mean. For the estimate $\hat{\mu}$ of a Poisson rate μ, the approximate variance is given by

$$\mathrm{VAR}\left(\log_e(\hat{\mu})\right) = \frac{\mathrm{VAR}(\hat{\mu})}{\mu^2} = \frac{\mu}{\mu^2} = \frac{1}{\mu}$$

If an event happens a times and does not happen b times, the log odds is $\log_e(a/b) = \log_e(a) - \log_e(b)$. The frequencies a and b are from independent Poisson distributions with means estimated by a and b, respectively. Hence their variances are estimated by $1/a$ and $1/b$, respectively. The variance of the log odds is given by

$$\mathrm{VAR}\left(\log_e(o)\right) = \mathrm{VAR}\left(\log_e(a/b)\right)$$
$$= \mathrm{VAR}\left(\log_e(a) - \log_e(b)\right)$$
$$= \mathrm{VAR}\left(\log_e(a)\right) + \mathrm{VAR}\left(\log_e(b)\right)$$
$$= \frac{1}{a} + \frac{1}{b}$$

The standard error of the log odds is thus given by

$$\mathrm{SE}\left(\log_e(o)\right) = \sqrt{\frac{1}{a} + \frac{1}{b}}$$

The log odds ratio is the difference between the log odds:

$$\log_e(o_1/o_2) = \log_e(o_1) - \log_e(o_2)$$

The variance of the log odds ratio is the sum of the variances of the log odds and for Table 13.21 we have

$$\mathrm{VAR}\left(\log_e(or)\right) = \left(\frac{1}{f_{11}} + \frac{1}{f_{12}} + \frac{1}{f_{13}} + \frac{1}{f_{14}}\right)$$

The standard error is the square root of this:

$$\mathrm{SE}\left(\log_e(or)\right) = \sqrt{\frac{1}{f_{11}} + \frac{1}{f_{12}} + \frac{1}{f_{13}} + \frac{1}{f_{14}}}$$

14 Choosing the statistical method

14.1 Method oriented and problem oriented teaching

The choice of method of analysis for a problem depends on the comparison to be made and the data to be used. In Chapters 8 to 13, statistical methods have been arranged largely by type of data, large samples, Normal, ordinal, categorical, etc., rather than by type of comparison. In this chapter we look at how the appropriate method is chosen for the three most common problems in statistical inference:

- comparison of two independent groups, for example, groups of patients given different treatments;
- comparison of the response of one group under different conditions, as in a cross-over trial, or of matched pairs of subjects, as in some case–control studies;
- investigation of the relationship between two variables measured on the same sample of subjects.

This chapter acts as a map of the methods described in Chapters 8 to 13. As was discussed in Section 12.7, there are often several different approaches to even a simple statistical problem. The methods described here and recommended for particular types of question may not be the only methods, and may not always be universally agreed as the best method. Statisticians are at least as prone to disagree as clinicians. However, these would usually be considered as valid and satisfactory methods for the purposes for which they are suggested here. When there is more than one valid approach to a problem, they will usually be found to give similar answers.

14.2 Types of data

The study design is one factor which determines the method of analysis, the variable being analysed is another. We can classify variables into the following types (Section 12.1):

Ratio scales. The ratio of two quantities has a meaning, so we can say that one observation is twice another. Human height is a ratio scale. Ratio scales allow us to carry out power transformations like log or square root.

Interval scales. The interval or distance between points on the scale has precise meaning, a change of one unit at one scale point is the same as a change of one unit at another. For example, temperature in °C is an interval scale, though not a ratio scale because the zero is arbitrary. We can add and subtract on an interval scale. All ratio scales are also interval scales and I shall not suggest separate analytical methods for ratio scales. Interval scales allow us to calculate means and variances, and to find standard errors and confidence intervals for them.

Ordinal scale. The scale enables us to order the subjects, from that with the lowest value to that with the highest. Any ties which cannot be ordered are assumed to be because the measurement is not sufficiently precise. A typical example would be an anxiety score calculated from a questionnaire. A person scoring 10 is more anxious than a person scoring 8, but not necessarily higher by the same amount that a person scoring 4 is higher than a person scoring 2.

Ordered nominal scale. We can group subjects into several categories, which have an order. For example, we can ask patients if their condition is much improved, improved a little, no change, a little worse, much worse.

Nominal scale. We can group subjects into categories which need not be ordered in any way. Eye colour is measured on a nominal scale.

Dichotomous scales. Subjects are grouped into only two categories, for example: survived or died. This is a special case of the nominal scale.

Clearly these classes are not mutually exclusive, and an interval scale is also ordinal. Sometimes it is useful to apply methods appropriate to a lower level of measurement, ignoring some of the information. Sometimes we take an apparently non-interval but numerical scale, such as a questionnaire depression scale, and analyse it as if it were interval. We choose to interpret the difference between 2 and 4 as having the same meaning as the difference between 22 and 24. The difference in depression may not be the same, if such a thing could be quantified at all, but the difference in score is. The combination of the type of comparison and the scale of measurement should direct us to the appropriate method, bearing in mind the comments in Section 1.4 about the approximate nature of almost all statistical analysis.

14.3 Comparing two groups

The methods used for comparing two groups are summarized in Table 14.1.

Interval data. For large samples, say more than 50 in each group, confidence intervals for the mean can be found by the Normal approximation (Section 8.5). For smaller samples, confidence intervals for the mean can be found using the t distribution provided the data follow or can be transformed to a Normal distribution (Section 10.3, Section 10.4). If not, a significance test of the null hypothesis that the means are equal can be carried out using the Mann–Whitney U test (Section 12.2). This can be useful when the data are censored, that is, there

Table 14.1 Methods for comparing two samples

Type of data	Size of sample	Method
Interval	Large, > 50 each sample	Normal distribution for means (Section 8.5, Section 9.7)
	Small, < 50 each sample, with Normal distribution and uniform variance *	Two sample t method (Section 10.3)
	Small, < 50 each sample, non-Normal	Mann–Whitney U test (Section 12.2)
Ordinal	Any	Mann–Whitney U test (Section 12.2)
Nominal, ordered	Large, $n > 30$	Chi-squared for trend (Section 13.8), Kendall's τ_b (Section 12.5)
Nominal, not ordered	Large, most expected frequencies > 5	Chi-squared test (Section 13.1) Fisher's exact test (Section 13.4)
	Small, more than 20% expected frequencies < 5	Reduce number of categories by combining or excluding as appropriate (Section 13.3), Fisher's exact test (Section 13.4)
Dichotomous	Large, all expected frequencies > 5	Comparison of two proportions (Section 8.6, Section 9.8), chi-squared test (Section 13.1), odds ratio (Section 13.7)
	Small, at least one expected frequency < 5	Chi-squared test with Yates' correction (Section 13.5), Fisher's exact test (Section 13.4)

* Non-Normal distributions can often be transformed to make them Normal.

are values too small or too large to measure. This happens, for example, when concentrations are too small to measure and labelled 'not detectable'. Provided that data are from Normal distributions, it is possible to compare the variances of the groups using the F test (Section 10.8).

Ordinal data. The tendency for one group to exceed members of the other is tested by the Mann–Whitney U test (Section 12.2).

Ordered nominal data. First the data are set out as a two-way table, one variable being group and the other the ordered nominal data. A chi-squared test (Section 13.1) will test the null hypothesis that there is no relationship between group and variable, but takes no account of the ordering. This is done by using the chi-squared test for trend, which takes the ordering into account and provides a much more powerful test (Section 13.8).

Nominal data. Set the data out as a two-way table as described above. The chi-squared test for a two-way table is the appropriate test (Section 13.1). The condition for validity of the test, that at least 80% of the expected frequencies should be greater than 5, must be met by combining or deleting categories as appropriate (Section 13.3) or use Fisher's exact test. If the table reduces to a 2 by 2 table without the condition being met, use Fisher's exact test.

Dichotomous data. For large samples, either present the data as two proportions and use the Normal

approximation to find the confidence interval for the difference (Section 8.6), or set the data up as a 2 by 2 table and do a chi-squared test (Section 13.1). These are equivalent methods. An odds ratio can also be calculated (Section 13.7). If the sample is small, the fit to the Chi-squared distribution can be improved using Yates' correction (Section 13.5). Alternatively, use Fisher's exact test (Section 13.4).

14.4 One sample and paired samples

Methods of analysis for paired samples are summarized in Table 14.2.

Interval data. Inferences are on differences between the variable as observed on the two conditions. For large samples, say $n > 100$, the confidence interval for the mean difference is found using the Normal approximation (Section 8.3). For small samples, provided the differences are from a Normal distribution, use the paired t test (Section 10.2). This assumption is often very reasonable, as most of the variation between individuals is removed and random error is largely made up of measurement error. Furthermore, the error is the result of two added measurement errors and so tends to follow a Normal distribution anyway. If not, transformation of the original data will often make differences

Table 14.2 Methods for differences in one sample or paired samples

Type of data	Size of sample	Method
Interval	Large, > 100	Normal distribution (Section 8.3)
	Small, < 100, Normal differences *	Paired t method (Section 10.2)
	Small, < 100, non-Normal differences	Wilcoxon matched pairs test (Section 12.3), sign test (Section 9.2)
Ordinal	Any	sign test (Section 9.2)
Nominal, ordered	Any	sign test (Section 9.2)
Nominal	Any	Stuart test (Section 13.9)
Dichotomous	Any	McNemar's test (Section 13.9)

* Non-Normal distributions can often be transformed to make them Normal. Transform each variable, not the differences.

Normal (Section 10.4). If no assumption of a Normal distribution can be made, use the Wilcoxon signed-rank matched-pairs test (Section 12.3) or the sign test (Section 9.2).

It is rarely asked whether there is a difference in variability in paired data. This can be tested by finding the differences between the two conditions and their sum. Then if there is no change in variance, the correlation between difference and sum has expected value zero (Pitman's test). This is not obvious, but it is true.

Ordinal data. If the data do not form an interval scale, as noted in Section 14.2 the difference between conditions is not meaningful. However, we can say what direction the difference is in, and this can be examined by the sign test (Section 9.2).

Ordered nominal data. Use the sign test, with changes in one direction being positive, in the other negative, no change as zero (Section 9.2).

Nominal data. With more than two categories, this is difficult. Use Stuart's generalization to more than two categories of McNemar's test (Section 13.9).

Dichotomous data. Here we are comparing the proportions of individuals in a given state under the two conditions. The appropriate test is McNemar's test (Section 13.9).

14.5 Relationship between two variables

The methods for studying relationships between variables are summarized in Table 14.3. Relationships with dichotomous variables can be studied as the difference between two groups (Section 14.3), the groups being defined by the two states of the dichotomous variable. Dichotomous data have been excluded from the text of this section, but are included in Table 14.3.

Interval and interval data. Two methods are used: regression and correlation. Regression (Section 11.2, Section 11.5) is usually preferred, as it gives information about the nature of the relationship as well as about its existence. Correlation (Section 11.9) measures the strength of the relationship. For regression, residuals about the line must follow a Normal distribution with uniform variance. For estimation, the correlation coefficient requires an assumption that both variables follow a Normal distribution, but to test the null hypothesis only one variable needs to follow a Normal distribution. If neither variable can be assumed to follow a Normal distribution or be transformed to it (Section 11.8), use rank correlation (Section 12.4, Section 12.5).

Interval and ordinal data. Rank correlation coefficient (Section 12.4, Section 12.5).

Interval and ordered nominal data. This can be approached by rank correlation, using Kendall's τ_b (Section 12.5) because it copes with the large number of ties better than does Spearman's ρ, or by analysis of variance as described for interval and nominal data. The latter requires an assumption of Normal distribution and uniform variance for the interval variable. These two approaches are not equivalent.

Interval and nominal data. If the interval scale follows a Normal distribution, use one-way analysis of variance (Section 10.9). The assumption is that within categories the interval variable is from Normal distributions with uniform variance. If this assumption is not reasonable, use Kruskal–Wallis analysis of variance by ranks (Section 12.2).

Ordinal and ordinal data. Use a rank correlation coefficient, Spearman's ρ (Section 12.4) or Kendall's τ (Section 12.5). Both will give very similar answers for testing the null hypothesis of no relationship in the absence of ties. For data with many ties and for comparing the strengths of different relationships, Kendall's τ_b is preferable.

Ordinal and ordered nominal data. Use Kendall's rank correlation coefficient, τ_b (Section 12.5).

Ordinal and nominal data. Kruskal–Wallis one-way analysis of variance by ranks (Section 12.2).

Ordered nominal and ordered nominal data. Use chi-squared for trend (Section 13.8).

Ordered nominal and nominal data. Use the chi-squared test for a two-way table (Section 13.1).

Nominal and nominal data. Use the chi-squared test for a two-way table (Section 13.1), provided the expected values are large enough. Otherwise use Yates' correction (Section 13.5) or Fisher's exact test (Section 13.4).

Table 14.3 Methods for relationships between variables

	Interval, Normal	Interval, non-Normal *	Ordinal	Nominal, ordered	Nominal	Dichotomous
Interval Normal	Regression (Section 11.2), correlation (Section 11.9)	Regression (Section 11.2), rank correlation (Section 12.4, Section 12.5)	Rank correlation (Section 12.4, Section 12.5)	Kendall's rank correlation (Section 12.5)	Analysis of variance (Section 10.9)	t-test (Section 10.3), Normal test (Section 8.5, Section 9.7)
Interval, non-Normal *	Regression (Section 11.2), rank correlation (Section 12.4, Section 12.5)	Rank correlation (Section 12.4, Section 12.5)	Rank correlation Section 12.4, Section 12.5	Kendall's rank correlation (Section 12.5)	Kruskal–Wallis test (Section 12.2)	Large sample Normal test (Section 8.5, Section 9.7), Mann–Whitney U test (Section 12.2)
Ordinal	Rank correlation (Section 12.4, Section 12.5)	Rank correlation (Section 12.4, Section 12.5)	Rank correlation (Section 12.4, Section 12.5)	Kendall's rank correlation (Section 12.5)	Kruskal–Wallis test (Section 12.2)	Mann–Whitney U test (Section 12.2)
Nominal, ordered	Kendall's rank correlation (Section 12.5)	Kendall's rank correlation (Section 12.5)	Kendall's rank correlation (Section 12.5)	Chi-squared test for trend (Section 13.8), Kendall's τ_b (Section 12.5)	Chi-squared test (Section 13.1)	Chi-squared test for trend (Section 13.8)
Nominal	Analysis of variance (Section 10.9)	Kruskal–Wallis test (Section 12.2)	Kruskal–Wallis test (Section 12.2)	Chi-squared test (Section 13.1)	Chi-squared test (Section 13.1)	Chi-squared test (Section 13.1)
Dichotomous	t-test (Section 10.3), Normal test (Section 8.5, Section 9.7)	Large sample Normal test (Section 8.5, Section 9.7), Mann–Whitney U test (Section 12.2)	Mann–Whitney U test (Section 12.2)	Chi-squared test for trend (Section 13.8)	Chi-squared test (Section 13.1)	Chi-squared (Section 13.1, Section 13.5) Fisher's exact test (Section 13.4)

* Non-Normal distributions can often be transformed to make them Normal.

14.6 Multiple choice questions: Choice of statistical method

(Each branch is either true or false.)

14.1 The following variables have interval scales of measurement:
(a) height;
(b) presence or absence of asthma;
(c) Apgar score;
(d) age;
(e) Forced Expiratory Volume.

14.2 The following methods may be used to investigate a relationship between two continuous variables:
(a) paired t test;
(b) the correlation coefficient, r;
(c) simple linear regression;
(d) Kendall's τ;
(e) Spearman's ρ.

14.3 When analysing nominal data the following statistical methods may be used:
(a) simple linear regression;
(b) correlation coefficient, r;
(c) paired t test;
(d) Kendall's τ;
(e) chi-squared test.

14.4 To compare levels of a continuous variable between two groups, possible methods include:
(a) the Mann–Whitney U test;
(b) Fisher's exact test;
(c) a t test;
(d) Wilcoxon matched-pairs signed-rank test;
(e) the sign test.

14.5 Table 14.4 shows the number of rejection episodes following heart transplant in two groups of patients:
(a) The rejection rates in the two populations could be compared by a Mann–Whitney U test;
(b) The rejection rates in the two populations could be compared by a two sample t test;
(c) The rejection rates in the two populations could be compared by a chi-squared test for trend;
(d) The chi-squared test for a 4 by 2 table would not be valid;

(e) The hypothesis that the number of episodes follows a Poisson distribution could be investigated using a chi-squared test for goodness of fit.

Table 14.4 Number of rejection episodes over 16 weeks following heart transplant in two groups of patients

Episodes	Group A	Group B	Total
0	10	8	18
1	15	6	21
2	4	0	4
3	3	0	3
Total patients	**32**	**14**	**46**

14.6 Twenty arthritis patients were given either a new analgesic or aspirin on successive days in random order. The grip strength of the patients was measured. Methods which could be used to investigate the existence of a treatment effect include:
(a) Mann–Whitney U test;
(b) paired t method;
(c) sign test;
(d) Normal confidence interval for the mean difference;
(e) Wilcoxon matched-pairs signed-rank test.

14.7 In a study of boxers, computer tomography revealed brain atrophy in 3 of 6 professionals and 1 of 8 amateurs (Kaste *et al.* 1982). These groups could be compared using:
(a) Fisher's exact test;
(b) the chi-squared test;
(c) the chi-squared test with Yates' correction;
(d) McNemar's test;
(e) the two sample t test.

14.7 Exercise: Choosing a statistical method

In a cross-over trial to compare two appliances for ileostomy patients, of 14 patients who received system A first, 5 expressed a preference for A, 9 for system B, and none had no preference. Of the patients who received system B first, 7 preferred A, 5 preferred B and 4 had no preference.

14.1 How would you decide whether one treatment was preferable? How would you decide whether the order of treatment influenced the choice?

Burr *et al.* (1976) tested a procedure to remove house-dust mites from the bedding of adult asthmatics in attempt to improve subjects' lung function, which they measured by PEFR. The trial was a two period cross-over design, the control or placebo treatment being thorough dust removal from the living room. The means and standard errors for PEFR in the 32 subjects were:

active treatment:	335 litres/min, SE = 19.6 litres/min
placebo treatment:	329 litres/min, SE = 20.8 litres/min
differences within subjects: (treatment – placebo)	6.45 litres/min, SE = 5.05 litres/min

14.2 How would you decide whether the treatment improves PEFR?

Table 14.5 shows colon transit times measured in a group of elderly patients who were mobile and in a second group who were unable to move independently. Figure 14.1 shows a scatter diagram, histogram, and Normal plot of residuals for these data.

14.3 What two statistical approaches could be used here? Which would you prefer and why?

In a trial of screening and treatment for mild hypertension (Reader *et al.* 1980), 1 138 patients completed the trial on active treatment, with 9 deaths, and 1 080 completed on placebo, with 19 deaths. A further 583 patients allocated to active treatment withdrew, of whom 6 died, and 626 allocated to placebo withdrew, of whom 16 died during the trial period.

Table 14.5 Colon transit time (hours) in groups of mobile and immobile elderly patients (data supplied by Dr Michael O'Connor)

Mobile patients					Immobile patients				
8.4	21.6	45.5	62.4	68.4	15.6	38.8	54.0	63.6	69.6
14.4	25.2	48.0	66.0		24.0	42.0	54.0	64.8	
19.2	30.0	50.4	66.0		24.0	43.2	57.6	66.0	
20.4	36.0	60.0	66.0		32.4	47.0	58.8	67.2	
20.4	38.4	60.0	67.2		34.8	52.8	62.4	69.6	
$n_1 = 21$, $\bar{x}_1 = 42.57$,					$n_2 = 21$, $\bar{x}_2 = 49.63$,				
$s_1 = 20.58$					$s_2 = 16.39$				

14.4 How would you decide whether screening and treatment for mild hypertension reduces the risk of dying?

Table 14.6 shows the pH and nitrite concentrations in samples of gastric fluid from 26 patients. A scatter diagram is shown in Figure 14.2.

14.5 How would you assess the evidence of a relationship between pH and nitrite concentration?

The lung function of 79 children with a history of hospitalization for whooping cough and 178 children without a history of whooping cough, taken from the same school classes, was measured. The spirometric mean transit time for the whooping cough cases was 0.49 s (SD = 0.14 s) and for the controls 0.47 s (SD = 0.11 s) (Johnston *et al.* 1983).

14.6 How could you analyse the difference in lung function between children who had had whooping cough and those who had not? Each case had two matched controls. (Some observations were missing.) If you had all the data, how could you use this information?

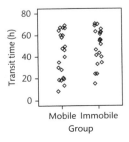 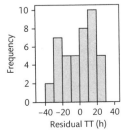 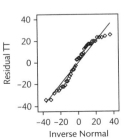

Figure 14.1 Scatter diagram, histogram, and Normal plot for the colon transit time data of Table 14.5 (data supplied by Dr Michael O'Connor).

Table 14.6 Gastric pH and urinary nitrite concentrations in 26 subjects (data supplied by Hall and Northfield, personal communication)

pH	Nitrite	pH	Nitrite	pH	Nitrite	pH	Nitrite
1.72	1.64	2.64	2.33	5.29	50.6	5.77	48.9
1.93	7.13	2.73	52.0	5.31	43.9	5.86	3.26
1.94	12.1	2.94	6.53	5.50	35.2	5.90	63.4
2.03	15.7	4.07	22.7	5.55	83.8	5.91	81.2
2.11	0.19	4.91	17.8	5.59	52.5	6.03	19.5
2.17	1.48	4.94	55.6	5.59	81.8		
2.17	9.36	5.18	0.0	5.71	21.9		

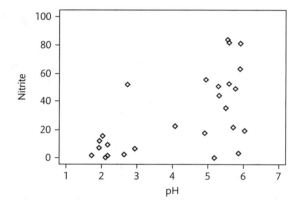

Figure 14.2 Gastric pH and urinary nitrite (data supplied by Hall and Northfield).

Table 14.7 shows some data from a pre- and post-treatment study of cataract patients. The second number in the visual acuity score represents the size of letter which can be read at a distance of 6 metres, so high numbers represent poor vision. For the contrast sensitivity test, which is a measurement, high numbers represent good vision.

14.7 What methods could be used to test the difference in visual acuity and in the contrast sensitivity test pre- and post-operation? What method could be used to investigate the relationship between visual acuity and the contrast sensitivity test post-operation?

Table 14.7 Visual acuity and results of a contrast sensitivity vision test before and after cataract surgery (data supplied by Wilkins, personal communication)

Case	Visual acuity		Contrast sensitivity test	
	before	after	before	after
1	6/9	6/9	1.35	1.50
2	6/9	6/9	0.75	1.05
3	6/9	6/9	1.05	1.35
4	6/9	6/9	0.45	0.90
5	6/12	6/6	1.05	1.35
6	6/12	6/9	0.90	1.20
7	6/12	6/9	0.90	1.05
8	6/12	6/12	1.05	1.20
9	6/12	6/12	0.60	1.05
10	6/18	6/6	0.75	1.05
11	6/18	6/12	0.90	1.05
12	6/18	6/12	0.90	1.50
13	6/24	6/18	0.45	0.75
14	6/36	6/18	0.15	0.45
15	6/36	6/36	0.45	0.60
16	6/60	6/9	0.45	1.05
17	6/60	6/12	0.30	1.05

Table 14.8 Asthma or wheeze by maternal age (data from Anderson *et al.* 1986)

Asthma or wheeze reported	Mother's age at child's birth		
	15–19	20–29	30+
Never	261	4017	2146
Onset by age 7	103	984	487
Onset from 8 to 11	27	189	95
Onset from 12 to 16	20	157	67

Table 14.8 shows the relationship between age of onset of asthma in children and maternal age at the child's birth.

14.8 How would you test whether asthma in children and maternal age were related?

14.9 The children were all born in 1 week in March, 1958. Apart from the possibility that young mothers in general tend to have children prone to asthma, what other possible explanations are there for this finding?

In a study of thyroid hormone in premature babies, we wanted to study the relationship of free T3 measured at several time points over 7 days with the number of days the babies remained oxygen dependent. Some babies died, mostly within a few days of birth, and some babies went home still oxygen dependent and were not followed any longer by the researchers.

14.10 How could you reduce the series of T3 measurements on a baby to a single variable? How could you test the relationship with time on oxygen?

15 Multifactorial methods

15.1 Multiple regression

In Chapters 10 and 11 we looked at methods of analysing the relationship between a continuous outcome variable and a predictor. The predictor could be quantitative, as in regression, or qualitative, as in one-way analysis of variance. In this chapter we shall look at the extension of these methods to more than one predictor variable, and describe related methods for use when the outcome is dichotomous or count data. These methods are very difficult to do by hand and computer programs are always used. I shall omit the formulae.

Table 15.1 shows the ages, heights, and strength as measured by the maximum voluntary contraction of the quadriceps muscle (MVC) in a group of male alcoholics. The outcome variable is MVC. Figure 15.1 shows the relationship between MVC and height. We can fit a regression line of the form MVC = $a + b \times$ height (Sections 11.2–11.3):

$$MVC = -907.6 + 7.20 \times \text{height}$$

This enables us to predict what the mean MVC would be for men of any given height. But MVC varies with other things beside height. Figure 15.2 shows the relationship between MVC and age.

We can show the strengths of the linear relationships between all three variables by their **correlation matrix**. This is a tabular display of the correlation coefficients between each pair of variables, **matrix** being used in its mathematical sense as a rectangular array of numbers. The correlation matrix for the data of Table 15.1 is shown in Table 15.2. The coefficients of the main diagonal are all 1.0, because they show the correlation of the variable with itself, and the correlation matrix is symmetrical

Table 15.1 Maximum voluntary contraction (MVC) of quadriceps muscle, age, and height, of 41 male alcoholics (data from Hickish *et al.* 1989)

Age (years)	Height (cm)	MVC (newtons)	Age (years)	Height (cm)	MVC (newtons)
24	166	466	42	178	417
27	175	304	47	162	270
28	173	343	47	171	294
28	175	404	48	177	368
31	172	147	49	177	441
31	172	294	49	178	392
32	160	392	50	167	294
32	172	147	51	176	368
32	177	412	53	159	216
32	179	270	53	172	466
34	175	402	53	173	294
34	180	368	53	175	392
35	167	491	55	155	196
37	175	196	55	170	304
38	172	343	55	178	324
39	161	387	58	160	98
39	172	319	61	162	216
39	173	441	62	159	196
40	173	441	65	168	74
41	168	343	65	168	137
41	178	540			

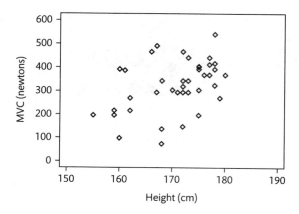

Figure 15.1 Muscle strength (MVC) against height (data from Hickish *et al.* 1989).

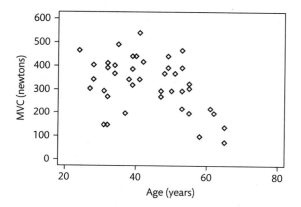

Figure 15.2 Muscle strength (MVC) against age (data from Hickish *et al.* 1989).

about this diagonal. Because of this symmetry, many computer programs print only the part of the matrix below the diagonal. Inspection of Table 15.2 shows that older men tended to be shorter and weaker than younger men, that taller men tended to be stronger than shorter men, and that the magnitudes of all three relationships were similar. Reference to Table 11.2 shows that all three correlations are significant.

We could fit a regression line of the form $MVC = a + b \times age$, from which we could predict the mean MVC for any given age:

$$MVC = 501.9 - 4.13 \times age$$

However, predicted MVC would still vary with height. To investigate the effect of both age and height, we can

Table 15.2 Correlation matrix for the data of Table 15.1 (data from Hickish *et al.* 1989)

	Age	Height	MVC
Age	1.000	−0.338	−0.417
Height	−0.338	1.000	0.419
MVC	−0.417	0.419	1.000

use multiple regression to fit a regression equation of the form

$$MVC = b_0 + b_1 \times height + b_2 \times age$$

The coefficients are calculated by a least squares procedure, exactly the same in principle as for simple regression (Section 11.3). In practice, this is always done using a computer program. For the data of Table 15.1, the multiple regression equation is

$$MVC = -466 + 5.40 \times height - 3.08 \times age$$

From this, we would estimate the mean MVC of men with any given age and height, in the population of which these are a sample. Note that the coefficients of height and age are both closer to zero than the 7.20 and −4.13 found in the simple regression. This is because height and age are themselves related. Part of the relationship of MVC with age is because older men tended to be shorter in this sample.

There are a number of assumptions implicit here. One is that the relationship between MVC and height is the same at each age, that is, that there is no interaction between height and age. Another is that the relationship between MVC and height is linear, that is of the form $MVC = a + b \times height$. Multiple regression analysis enables us to test both of these assumptions.

Multiple regression is not limited to two predictor variables. We can have any number, although the more variables we have, the more difficult it becomes to interpret the regression. We must, however, have more observations than variables, and the degrees of freedom for the residual variance are $n - 1 - q$ if q variables are fitted, and this should be large enough for satisfactory estimation of confidence intervals and tests of significance. This will become clear after the next section. A good rule of thumb is that we should have 10 observations for each predictor variable. Fewer than this and the regression may be unstable.

15.2 Significance tests and estimation in multiple regression

As we saw in Section 11.5, the significance of a simple linear regression line can be tested using the t distribution. We can carry out the same test using analysis of variance. For the FEV1 and height data of Table 11.1, the sums of squares and products were calculated in Section 11.3. The total sum of squares for FEV1 is $S_{yy} = 9.438\,68$, with $n - 1 = 19$ degrees of freedom. The sum of squares due to regression was calculated in Section 11.5 to be $3.189\,37$. The residual sum of squares, i.e. the sum of squares about the regression line, is found by subtraction as $9.438\,68 - 3.189\,37 = 6.249\,31$, and this has $n - 2 = 18$ degrees of freedom. We can now set up an analysis of variance table as described in Section 10.9, shown in Table 15.3.

The square root of the variance ratio is 3.03, the value of t found in Section 11.5. The two tests are equivalent. Note also that the regression sum of squares divided by the total sum of squares $= 3.189\,37/9.438\,68 = 0.337\,9$ is the square of the correlation coefficient, $r = 0.58$ (Section 11.5, Section 11.9). This ratio, sum of squares due to regression over total sum of squares, is the proportion of the variability accounted for by the regression. The percentage variability accounted for or explained by the regression is 100 times this, i.e. 34%.

Returning to the MVC data, we can test the significance of the regression of MVC on height and age together by analysis of variance. If we fit the regression model in Section 15.1, the regression sum of squares has two degrees of freedom, because we have fitted two regression coefficients. The analysis of variance for the MVC regression is shown in Table 15.4.

The regression is significant; it is unlikely that this association could have arisen by chance if the null hypothesis were true. The proportion of variability accounted for, denoted by R^2, is $131\,495/503\,344 = 0.26$. The square root of this is called the multiple correlation coefficient, R. R^2 must lie between 0 and 1, and as no meaning can be given to the direction of correlation in the multivariate case, R is also taken as positive. The larger R is, the

Table 15.3 Analysis of variance for the regression of FEV1 on height

Source of variation	Degrees of freedom	Sum of squares	Mean square	Variance ratio (F)	Probability
Total	19	9.438 68			
Due to regression	1	3.189 37	3.189 37	9.19	0.007
Residual (about regression)	18	6.249 31	0.347 18		

Table 15.4 Analysis of variance for the regression of MVC on height and age (data from Hickish *et al.* 1989)

Source of variation	Degrees of freedom	Sum of squares	Mean square	Variance ratio (F)	Probability
Total	40	503 344			
Regression	2	131 495	65 748	6.72	0.003
Residual	38	371 849	9 785		

more closely correlated with the outcome variable the set of predictor variables are. When $R = 1$, the variables are perfectly correlated in the sense that the outcome variable is a linear combination of the predictors. When the outcome variable is not linearly related to any of the predictor variables, R will be small, but not zero.

We may wish to know whether both or only one of our variables leads to the association. To do this, we can calculate a standard error for each regression coefficient (Table 15.5). This will be done automatically by the regression program. We can use this to test each coefficient separately by a t test. We can also find a confidence interval for each, using t standard errors on either side of the estimate. For the example, both age and height have $P = 0.04$ and we can conclude that both age and height are independently associated with MVC.

A difficulty arises when the predictor variables are correlated with one another. This increases the standard error of the estimates, and variables may have a multiple regression coefficient which is not significant despite being related to the outcome variable. We can see that this will be so most clearly by taking an extreme case. Suppose we try to fit

$$MVC = b_0 + b_1 \times height + b_2 \times height$$

For the MVC data

$$MVC = -908 + 6.20 \times height + 1.00 \times height$$

is a regression equation which minimizes the residual sum of squares. However, it is not unique, because

$$MVC = -908 + 5.20 \times height + 2.00 \times height$$

will do so too. The two equations give the same predicted MVC. There is no unique solution, and so no regression

equation can be fitted, even though there is a clear relationship between MVC and height. When the predictor variables are highly correlated the individual coefficients will be poorly estimated and have large standard errors. Correlated predictor variables may obscure the relationship of each with the outcome variable.

A different (and equivalent) way of testing the effects of two correlated predictor variables separately is to proceed as follows. We fit three models:

1 MVC on height and age, regression sum of squares = 131 495, d.f. = 2

2 MVC on height, regression sum of squares = 88 511, d.f. = 1

3 MVC on age, regression sum of squares = 87 471, d.f. = 1

Note that $88\,511 + 87\,471 = 175\,982$ is greater than 131 495. This is because age and height are correlated. We then test the effect of height if age is taken into account, referred to as the effect of height given age. The regression sum of squares for height given age is the regression sum of squares (age and height) minus regression sum of squares (age only), which is $131\,495 - 87\,471 = 44\,024$. This has degrees of freedom = $2 - 1 = 1$. Similarly, the effect of age allowing for height, i.e. age given height, is tested by regression sum of squares (age and height) minus regression sum of squares (height only) = $131\,495 - 88\,511 = 42\,984$, with degrees of freedom = $2 - 1 = 1$. We can set all this out in an analysis of variance table (Table 15.6). The third to sixth rows of the table are indented for the source of variation, degrees of freedom, and sum of squares columns, to indicate that they are different ways of looking at variation already accounted for in the second row. The indented rows are not included when the degrees of freedom and sums of

Table 15.5 Coefficients for the regression of MVC on height and age, with standard errors and confidence intervals (data from Hickish *et al.* 1989)

Predictor variable	Coefficient	Standard error	t ratio	P	95% confidence interval
Height	5.40	2.55	2.12	0.04	0.25 to 10.55
Age	−3.08	1.47	−2.10	0.04	−6.05 to −0.10
Intercept	−465.63	460.33	−1.01	0.3	−1397.52 to 466.27

Table 15.6 Analysis of variance for the regression of MVC on height and age, showing adjusted sums of squares (data from Hickish *et al.* 1989)

Source of variation	Degrees of freedom	Sum of squares	Mean square	Variance ratio (F)	Probability
Total	40	503 344			
Regression	2	131 495	65 748	6.72	0.003
age alone	1	87 471	87 471	8.94	0.005
height given age	1	44 024	44 024	4.50	0.04
height alone	1	88 511	88 511	9.05	0.005
age given height	1	42 984	42 984	4.39	0.04
Residual	38	371 849	9 785		

squares are added to give the total. After adjustment for age there is still evidence of a relationship between MVC and height, and after adjustment for height there is still evidence of a relationship between MVC and age. Note that the P values are the same as those found by a t test for the regression coefficient. This approach is essential for qualitative predictor variables with more than two categories (Section 15.8), when several t statistics may be printed for the variable.

15.3 Using multiple regression for adjustment

You will often see the words 'adjusted for' in reports of studies. This almost always means that some sort of regression analysis has been done, and if we are talking about the difference between two means this will be multiple linear regression.

In clinical trials, regression is often used to adjust for prognostic variables and baseline measurements. For example, Levy *et al.* (2000) carried out a trial of education by a specialist asthma nurse for patients who had been taken to an accident and emergency department due to acute asthma. Patients were randomized to have two 1-hour training sessions with the nurse or to usual care. The measurements were 1 week peak expiratory flow and symptom diaries made before treatment and after 3 and 6 months. We summarized the 21 PEF measurements (three daily) to give the outcome variables mean

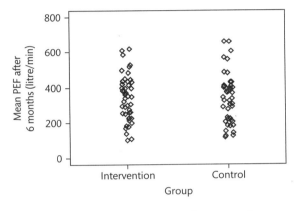

Figure 15.3 Mean of 1-week diary peak expiratory flow 6 months after training by an asthma specialist nurse or usual care (data from Levy *et al.* 2000).

and standard deviation of PEF over the week. We also analysed mean symptom score.

The primary outcome variable was mean PEF, shown in Figure 15.3. There is no obvious difference between the two groups and the mean PEF was 342 litre/min in the nurse intervention group and 338 litre/min in the control group. The 95% CI for the difference, intervention minus control, was –48 to 63 litre/min, P = 0.8, by the two-sample t method. However, although this was the primary outcome variable, it was not the primary analysis. We have the mean diary PEF measured at baseline, before the intervention, and the two mean PEFS are strongly related. We can use this to reduce the variability by carrying out multiple regression with PEF at 6 months as the outcome variable and treatment group and baseline PEF as predictors. If we control for the baseline PEF in this way, we might get a better estimate of the treatment effect because we will remove a lot of variation between people. We get:

$$PEF@6m = 18.3 + 0.99 \times PEF@base$$
95% CI   −10.5 to 47.2   0.91 to 1.06
P<0.001

$$+ 20.1 \times intervention$$
0.4 to 39.7
P = 0.046

Figure 15.4 shows the regression equation as two parallel lines, one for each treatment group. Multiple regression in which qualitative and quantitative predictor variables are both used is also known as **analysis of covariance**. The vertical distance between the lines is the coefficient for the intervention, 20.1 litre/min. By including the baseline PEF we have reduced the variability and enabled the treatment difference to become apparent.

There are clear advantages to using adjustment. In clinical trials, multiple regression including baseline measurements reduces the variability between subjects and so increases the power of the study. It makes it much easier to detect real effects and produces narrower confidence intervals. It also removes any effects of chance imbalances in the predicting variables.

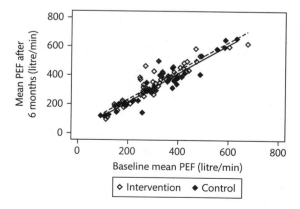

Figure 15.4 Mean PEF after 6 months against baseline PEF for intervention and control asthmatic patients, with fitted analysis of covariance lines (data from Levy *et al.* 2000).

Is adjustment cheating? If we cannot demonstrate an effect without adjustment (as in the asthma nurse trial), is it valid to show one after adjustment? Adjustment can be cheating if we keep adjusting by more and more variables until we have a significant difference. This is not the right way to proceed. We should be able to say in advance which variables we might want to adjust for because they are strong predictors of our outcome variable. Baseline measurements almost always come into this category, as should any stratification or minimization variables used in the design. If they were not related to the outcome variable, there would be no need to stratify for them. Another variable which we might expect to adjust for is centre in multi-centre trials, because there may be quite a lot of variation between centres in their patient populations and in their clinical practices. We might also want to adjust for known important predictors. If we had no baseline measurements of PEF, we would want to adjust for height and age, two known good predictors of PEF. We should state before we collect the data what we wish to adjust for and stick to it.

In the PEF analysis, we could have used the differences between the baseline and 6 month measurements rather than analysis of covariance. This is not as good because there is often measurement error in both our baseline and our outcome measurements. When we calculate the difference between them, we get two lots of error. If we do regression, we only have the error in the outcome variable. If the baseline variable has a lot of measurement error or there is only a small correlation between the baseline and outcome variables, using the difference can actually make things worse than just using the outcome variable. Using analysis of covariance, if the correlation is small the baseline variable has little effect rather than being detrimental.

15.4 Transformations in multiple regression

In the asthma nurse study, a secondary outcome measure was the standard deviation of the diary PEFs. This is because large fluctuations in PEF are a bad thing and we would like to produce less variation, both over the

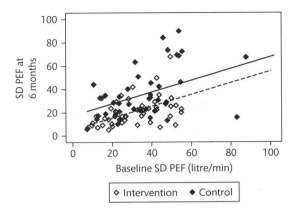

Figure 15.5 Standard deviation of diary PEF after 6 months, by baseline standard deviation and treatment group (data from Levy *et al.* 2000).

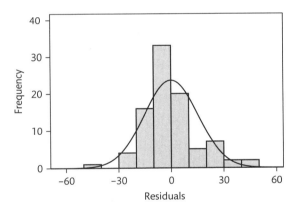

Figure 15.6 Distribution of residual standard deviation of diary PEF 6 months after regression on baseline SD and treatment group (data from Levy *et al.* 2000).

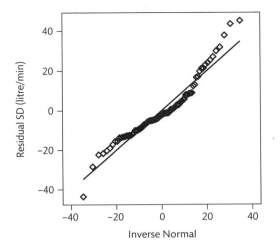

Figure 15.7 Normal plot of residual standard deviation of diary PEF 6 months after regression on baseline SD and treatment group (data from Levy *et al.* 2000).

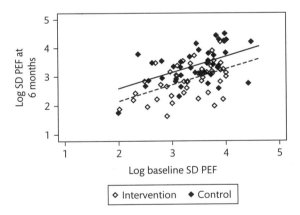

Figure 15.8 Log transformed standard deviation of diary PEF after 6 months, by baseline standard deviation and treatment group (data from Levy *et al.* 2000).

day and from day to day. Figure 15.5 shows the standard deviation at 6 months against standard deviation at baseline by treatment group. From Figure 15.5, we can see that the variability of the outcome variable increases as the baseline SD increases. Figure 15.6 shows the distribution of the residuals after regression of standard deviation at 6 months on baseline SD and treatment. Figure 15.7 shows a Normal plot. The residuals do not have a good fit to a Normal distribution.

We could try a log transformation. This gives us a much more uniform variability on the scatter diagram (Figure 15.8) and the distribution of the residuals looks a bit closer to the Normal (Figure 15.9 and Figure 15.10). The multiple regression equation is

logSD@6m	=	0.58	+ 0.56 × logSD@base	− 0.43 × intervene
95% CI		−0.16 to 1.32	0.36 to 0.77	−0.22 to −0.65
			P<0.001	P<0.001

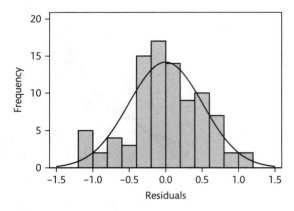

Figure 15.9 Distribution of residual log transformed standard deviation of diary PEF 6 months after regression on baseline SD and treatment group (data from Levy *et al.* 2000).

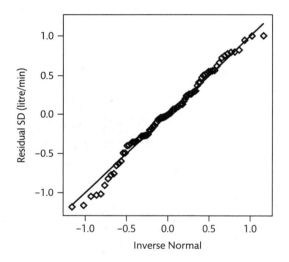

Figure 15.10 Normal plot of residual log transformed standard deviation of diary PEF 6 months after regression on baseline SD and treatment group (data from Levy *et al.* 2000).

We estimate that the mean log SD is increased by −0.43, or reduced by 0.43, by the intervention, whatever the baseline SD. Because we have used a log transformation, we can back transform just as we did for the difference between two means (Section 10.4). The antilog is exp(−0.43) = 0.65. We interpret this as that the mean standard deviation of diary PEF is reduced by a factor of 0.65 by the intervention by the specialist asthma nurse. We can antilog the confidence interval, too, giving 0.52

to 0.80 as the confidence interval for the ratio of nurse SD to control SD.

15.5 Interaction in multiple regression

An interaction between two predictor variables arises when the effect of one on the outcome depends on the value of the other. For example, tall men may be stronger than short men when they are young, but the difference may disappear as they age.

We can test for interaction as follows. We have fitted

$$MVC = b_0 + b_1 \times height + b_2 \times age$$

An interaction may take two simple forms. As height increases, the effect of age may increase so that the difference in MVC between young and old tall men is greater than the difference between young and old short men. Alternatively, as height increases, the effect of age may decrease. More complex interactions are beyond the scope of this discussion. Now, if we fit

$$MVC = b_0 + b_1 \times height + b_2 \times age + b_3 \times height \times age$$

for men of any given height the effect of age is $b_2 + b_3 \times$ height. If there is no interaction, the effect of age is the same at all heights, and b_3 will be zero. Of course, b_3 will not be exactly zero, but only within the limits of random variation. We can fit such a model just as we fitted the first one. We get

$$MVC = 4\,661 - 24.7 \times height - 112.8 \times age$$
$$+ 0.650 \times height \times age$$

The regression is still significant, as we would expect. However, the coefficients of height and age have changed; that for height has even changed sign. The coefficient of height depends on age. The regression equation can be written

$$MVC = 4\,661 + (-24.7 + 0.650 \times age) \times height$$
$$-112.8 \times age$$

The coefficient of height depends on age, the difference in strength between short and tall men being greater for older men than for younger.

Table 15.7 Analysis of variance for the interaction of height and age

Source of variation	Degrees of freedom	Sum of squares	Mean square	Variance ratio (F)	Probability
Total	40	503 344			
Regression	3	202 719	67 573	8.32	0.000 2
Height and age	2	131 495	65 748	8.09	0.001
Height × age	1	71 224	71 224	8.77	0.005
Residual	37	300 625	8 125		

The analysis of variance for this regression equation is shown in Table 15.7. The regression sum of squares is divided into two parts: that due to age and height, and that due to the interaction term after the main effects of age and height have been accounted for. The interaction row is the difference between the regression row in Table 15.7, which has 3 degrees of freedom, and the regression row in Table 15.4, which has 2. From this we see that the interaction is highly significant. The effects of height and age on MVC are not additive. Another example of the investigation of a possible interaction is given in Section 15.9.

15.6 Polynomial regression

So far, we have assumed that all the regression relationships have been linear, i.e. that we are dealing with straight lines. This is not necessarily so. We may have data where the underlying relationship is a curve rather than a straight line. Unless there is a theoretical reason for supposing that a particular form of the equation, such as logarithmic or exponential, is needed, we test for non-linearity using a polynomial. A **polynomial** is an equation or curve of the following form:

$$y = b_0 + b_1x + b_2x^2 + b_3x^3 + \ldots + b_kx^k$$

where y and x are variables and k, b_0, b_2, b_3, etc. are constants. The highest power of x, k, is called the **degree** of the polynomial. Degree = 1 gives a straight line, any higher degree gives a curve. The higher the degree is, the more complex the curve can be. Clearly, if we can fit a relationship of the form

$$MVC = b_0 + b_1 \times height + b_2 \times age$$

we can also fit one of the form

$$MVC = b_0 + b_1 \times height + b_2 \times height^2$$

to give a quadratic equation, degree 2, and continue adding powers of height to give equations which are cubic (degree = 3), quartic (degree = 4), etc.

Height and height squared are highly correlated, which can lead to problems in estimation. To reduce the correlation, we can subtract a number close to mean height from height before squaring. For the data of Table 15.1, the correlation between height and height squared is 0.999 8. Mean height is 170.7 cm, so 170 is a convenient number to subtract. The correlation between height and height minus 170 squared is –0.44, so the correlation has been reduced, though not eliminated. The regression equation is

$$MVC = -961 + 7.49 \times height + 0.092 \times (height - 170)^2$$

To test for non-linearity, we proceed as in Section 15.2. We fit two regression equations, a linear and a quadratic. The non-linearity is then tested by the difference between the sum of squares due to the quadratic equation and the sum of squares due to the linear. The analysis of variance is shown in Table 15.8. In this case the quadratic term is not significant, so there is no evidence of non-linearity. Were the quadratic term significant, we

Table 15.8 Analysis of variance for polynomial regression of MVC on height (data from Hickish *et al.* 1989)

Source of variation	Degrees of freedom	Sum of squares	Mean square	Variance ratio (F)	Probability
Total	40	503 344			
Regression	2	89 103	44 552	4.09	0.02
linear	1	88 522	88 522	7.03	0.01
quadratic	1	581	581	0.05	0.8
Residual	38	414 241	12 584		

could fit a cubic equation, degree = 3, and test the effect of the cubic term in the same way. Polynomial regression of one variable can be combined with ordinary linear regression of others to give regression equations of the form

$$MVC = b_0 + b_1 \times height + b_2 \times height^2 + b_3 \times age$$

and so on. Royston and Altman (1994) have shown that quite complex curves can be fitted with a small number of coefficients if we use $\log(x)$ and powers −1, −0.5, 0.5, 1, and 2 in the regression equation, **fractional polynomial regression**.

15.7 Assumptions of multiple regression

For the regression estimates to be optimal and the F tests, t tests, and confidence intervals valid, the residuals (the difference between observed values of the dependent variable and those predicted by the regression equation) should follow a Normal distribution and have the same variance throughout the range. The observations should be independent of one another. We also assume that the relationships which we are modelling are linear. These assumptions are the same as for simple linear regression (Section 11.7) and can be checked graphically in the same way, using histograms, Normal plots, and scatter diagrams. If the assumptions of Normal distribution and uniform variance are not met, we can use a transformation as described in Section 10.4 and Section 11.8. Non-linearity can be dealt with using polynomial regression.

The regression equation of strength on height and age is MVC = − 466 + 5.40 × height − 3.08 × age and the residuals are given by

$$residual = MVC - (-466 + 5.40 \times height$$
$$-3.08 \times age)$$

Figures 15.11 and 15.12 show a histogram and a Normal plot of the residuals for the MVC data. The distribution looks quite good. Figure 15.13 shows a plot of residuals against MVC. The variability looks uniform. We can also check the linearity by plotting residuals against the predictor variables (Figure 15.13). Figure 15.14 shows the residual against age. There is an indication that residual may be related to age. The possibility of a nonlinear relationship can be checked by polynomial regression, which, in this case, does not produce a quadratic term which approaches significance.

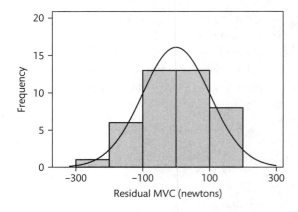

Figure 15.11 Histogram of residuals of MVC about height and age.

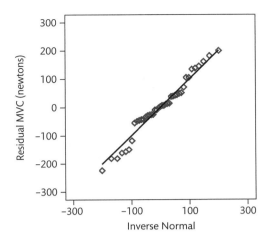

Figure 15.12 Normal plot of residuals of MVC about height and age.

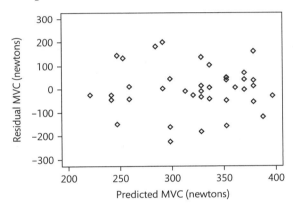

Figure 15.13 Residuals against observed MVC, to check uniformity of variance (data from Hickish *et al.* 1989).

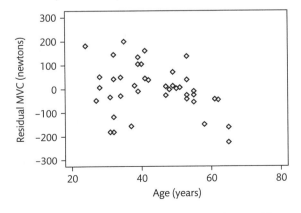

Figure 15.14 Residuals against age, to check linearity (data from Hickish *et al.* 1989).

15.8 Qualitative predictor variables

In Section 15.3 and Section 15.4 we had two predictor variables, the quantitative baseline measurement and the dichotomous treatment group. The regression coefficient of this dichotomous variable is the difference in the mean of the outcome variable between participants with the characteristic, asthma nurse, and participants without. For the mean PEF, the coefficient was positive, indicating higher mean PEF with the intervention. For the SD PEF, the coefficient was negative, indicating lower SD PEF for participants allocated to the asthma nurse. In the same way, we can use sex as a predictor variable by creating a variable which is 0 for females and 1 for males. The coefficient then represents the difference in mean between male and female. If we use only one dichotomous predictor variable in the equation, the regression is exactly equivalent to a two sample t test between the groups defined by the variable (Section 10.3).

A predictor variable with more than two categories or classes is called a **class variable** or a **factor**. We cannot simply use a class variable in the regression equation, unless we can assume that the classes are ordered in the same way as their codes, and that adjoining classes are in some sense the same distance apart. For some variables, such as the diagnosis data of Table 4.1 and the housing data of Table 13.1, this is absurd. For others, such as the AIDS categories of Table 10.7, it is a very strong assumption. What we do instead is to create a set of dichotomous variables to represent the factor. For the AIDS data of Table 10.7, we can create three variables:

hiv_1 = 1 if subject has AIDS, 0 otherwise

hiv_2 = 1 if subject has ARC, 0 otherwise

hiv_3 = 1 if subject is HIV positive but has no symptoms, 0 otherwise

If the subject is HIV negative, all three variables are zero. hiv_1, hiv_2, and hiv_3 are called **dummy variables**. Some computer programs will calculate the dummy variables automatically if the variable is declared to be a factor, for others the user must define them. We put the three

Table 15.9 Analysis of variance for the regression of mannitol excretion on HIV status (data supplied by Moses Kapembwa, personal communication)

Source of variation	Degrees of freedom	Sum of squares	Mean square	Variance ratio (F)	Probability
Total	58	1559.035			
Regression	3	49.011	16.337	0.60	0.6
Residual	55	1510.024	27.455		

dummy variables into the regression equation. This gives the equation:

$$mannitol = 11.4 - 0.066 \times hiv_1 - 2.56 \times hiv_2$$
$$-1.69 \times hiv_3$$

Each coefficient is the difference in mannitol absorption between the class represented by that variable and the class represented by all dummy variables being zero, HIV negative, called the **reference class**. The analysis of variance for this regression equation is shown in Table 15.9, and the F test shows that there is no significant relationship between mannitol absorption and HIV status. The regression program prints out standard errors and t tests for each dummy variable, but these t tests should be ignored, because we cannot interpret one dummy variable in isolation from the others.

15.9 Multi-way analysis of variance

A different approach to the analysis of multifactorial data is provided by the direct calculation of analysis of variance. Table 15.9 is identical to the one-way analysis of variance for the same data in Table 10.8. We can also produce analyses of variance for several factors at once. Table 15.10 shows the two-way analysis of variance for the mannitol data, the factors being HIV status and presence or absence of diarrhoea. This could be produced equally well by multiple regression with two categorical predictor variables. If there were the same number of patients with and without diarrhoea in each HIV group, the factors would be **balanced**. The model sum of squares would then be the sum of the sums of squares for HIV and for diarrhoea, and these could be calculated very simply from the total of the HIV groups and the diarrhoea groups. For balanced data we can assess many categorical factors and their interactions quite easily by manual calculation. See Armitage *et al.* (2002) for details. Complex multifactorial balanced experiments are rare in medical research, and they can be analysed by regression anyway to get identical results. Most computer programs in fact use the regression method to calculate analyses of variance.

For another example, consider Table 15.11, which shows the results of a study of the production of Tumour

Table 15.10 Two-way analysis of variance for mannitol excretion, with HIV status and diarrhoea as factors (data supplied by Moses Kapembwa, personal communication)

Source of variation	Degrees of freedom	Sum of squares	Mean square	Variance ratio (F)	Probability
Total	58	1559.035			
Model	4	134.880	33.720	1.28	0.3
HIV	3	58.298	19.432	0.74	0.5
Diarrhoea	1	85.869	85.869	3.26	0.08
Residual	54	1424.155	26.373		

Table 15.11 TNF measured under four different conditions using cells from 11 donors (data supplied by Dr Jan Davies)

		No MTB					MTB		
FAT	**Donor**	**TNF, 3 replicates**			**FAT**	**Donor**	**TNF, 3 replicates**		
No	1	−0.01	−0.01	−0.13	No	1	−0.05	−0.09	−0.08
No	2	16.13	−9.62	−14.88	No	2	−9.41	−6.3	5.4
No	3	missing	−0.3	−0.95	No	3	−10.13	−16.48	−14.79
No	4	3.63	47.5	55.2	No	4	8.75	134.9	203.7
No	5	−3.21	−5.64	−5.32	No	5	612.3	898.2	854.2
No	6	16.26	52.21	17.93	No	6	2 034	2 743	2 772
No	7	−12.74	−5.23	−4.06	No	7	978.5	1 137	850
No	8	−4.67	20.1	110	No	8	279.3	124.8	222.1
No	9	−5.4	20	10.3	No	9	688.1	530.9	720.2
No	10	−10.94	−5.26	−2.73	No	10	908.8	811.9	746.4
No	11	−4.19	−11.83	−6.29	No	11	439.3	960.9	593.3
Yes	1	88.16	97.58	66.27	Yes	1	709.3	874.3	630
Yes	2	196.5	114.1	134.2	Yes	2	4 541	4 106	4 223
Yes	3	6.02	1.19	3.38	Yes	3	391	194	254
Yes	4	935.4	1 011	951.2	Yes	4	2 913	3 632	3 417
Yes	5	606	592.7	608.4	Yes	5	3 801	3 112	3 681
Yes	6	1 457	1 349	1 625	Yes	6	10 150	9 410	9 243
Yes	7	139.7	399.5	91.69	Yes	7	6 736	6 323	5 117
Yes	8	196.7	270.8	160.7	Yes	8	1 454	2 250	1 092
Yes	9	135.2	221.5	268	Yes	9	857.2	1 339	1 945
Yes	10	−14.47	79.62	304.1	Yes	10	missing	739.9	4 379
Yes	11	516.3	585.9	562.6	Yes	11	6 637	6 909	6 453

Necrosis Factor (TNF) by cells *in vitro*. Two different potential stimulating factors, *Mycobacterium tuberculosis* (MTB) and Fixed Activated T-cells (FAT), have been added, singly and together. Cells from the same 11 donors have been used throughout. Thus we have three factors, MTB, FAT, and donor. Every possible combination of factors is used the same number of times in a perfect three-way factorial arrangement. There are two missing observations. These things happen, even in the best regulated laboratories. There are some negative values of TNF. This does not mean that the cells were sucking TNF in from their environment, but was an artefact of the assay method and represents measurement error.

Three measurements were made at each combination of factors; Figure 15.15 shows the means of these sets of three measurements. Figure 15.15 suggests several things: there is a strong donor effect (donor 6 is always high, donor 3 is always low, for example), MTB and FAT each

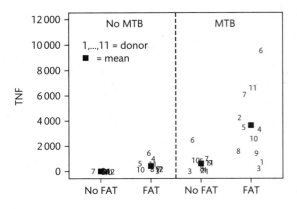

Figure 15.15 Tumour Necrosis Factor (TNF) measured in the presence and absence of Fixed Activated T-cells (FAT) and *Mycobacterium tuberculosis* (MTB) (data supplied by Dr Jan Davies).

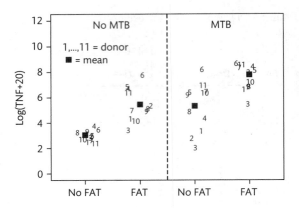

Figure 15.16 Tumour Necrosis Factor (TNF) measured in the presence and absence of Fixed Activated T-cells (FAT) and *Mycobacterium tuberculosis* (MTB), log(x + 20) transformed scale (data supplied by Dr Jan Davies).

increase TNF, both together have a greater effect than either individually, the distribution of TNF is highly skew, the variance of TNF varies greatly from group to group, and increases with the mean. As the mean for MTB and FAT combined is much greater than the sum of their individual means, the researcher thought there was synergy, i.e. that MTB and FAT worked together, the presence of one enhancing the effect of the other. She was seeking statistical support for this conclusion (Jan Davies, personal communication).

For statistical analysis, we would like Normal distributions with uniform variances between the groups. A log transformation looks like a good bet, but some observations are negative. As the log (or the square root) will

not work for negative numbers, we have to adjust the data further. The easiest approach is to add a constant to all the observations before transformation. I chose 20, which makes all the observations positive but is small compared with most of the observations. I did this by trial and error. As Figure 15.16 shows, the transformation has not been totally successful, but the transformed data look much more amenable to a Normal theory analysis than do the raw data.

The repeated measurements give us a more accurate measurement of TNF, but do not contribute anything else. I therefore analysed the mean transformed TNF. The analysis of variance is shown in Table 15.12. Donor is a factor with 11 categories, hence has 10 degrees of

Table 15.12 Analysis of variance for the effects of MTB, FAT and donor on transformed TNF (data supplied by Dr Jan Davies)

Source of variation	Degrees of freedom	Sum of squares	Mean square	Variance ratio (F)	Probability
Total	43	194.040 30			
Donor	10	38.890 00	3.889 00	3.72	0.003
MTB	1	58.493 20	58.493 20	55.88	<0.0001
FAT	1	65.244 82	65.244 82	62.33	<0.0001
MTB × FAT	1	0.008 11	0.008 11	0.01	0.9
Residual	30	31.404 18	1.046 81		

freedom. It is not of any importance to the science here, but is what we call a **nuisance variable**, one we need to allow for but are not interested in. I have included an interaction between MTB and FAT, because looking for this is one of the objectives of the experiment. The main effects of MTB and FAT are highly significant, but the interaction term is not. The estimates of the effects with their confidence intervals are shown in Table 15.13. As the analysis was on a log scale, the antilogs (exponentials) are also shown. The antilog gives us the ratio of the (geometric) mean in the presence of the factor to the mean in the absence of the factor, i.e. the amount by which TNF is multiplied by when the factor is present. Strictly speaking, of course, it is the ratio of the geometric means of TNF plus 20, but as 20 is small compared with most TNF measurements the ratio will be approximately the increase in TNF.

The estimated interaction is small and not significant. The confidence interval is wide (the sample is very small), so we cannot exclude the possibility of an interaction, but there is certainly no evidence that one exists. This was not what the researcher expected. This contradiction comes about because the statistical model used is of additive effects on the logarithmic scale, i.e. of multiplicative effects on the natural scale. This is forced on us by the nature of the data. The lack of interaction between the effects shows that the data are consistent with this model, this view of what is happening. The lack of interaction can been seen quite clearly in Figure 15.16, as the mean for MTB and FAT looks very similar to the sum of the means for MTB alone and FAT alone.

For ordinal data, there is a two-way analysis of variance using ranks, the Friedman test (see Conover 1980; Altman 1991).

15.10 Logistic regression

Logistic regression is used when the outcome variable is dichotomous, a 'yes or no', whether or not the subject has a particular characteristic such as a symptom. We want a regression equation which will predict the proportion of individuals who have the characteristic, or, equivalently, estimate the probability that an individual will have the symptom. We cannot use an ordinary linear regression equation, because this might predict proportions less than zero or greater than one, which would be meaningless. Instead we use the logit of the proportion as the outcome variable. The **logit** of a proportion p is the log odds (Section 13.7):

$$\text{logit}(p) = \log_e \left(\frac{p}{1-p} \right)$$

The logit can take any value from minus infinity, when $p = 0$, to plus infinity, when $p = 1$. We can fit regression models to the logit which are very similar to the ordinary multiple regression and analysis of variance models found for data from a Normal distribution. We assume that relationships are linear on the logistic scale:

$$\log_e \left(\frac{p}{1-p} \right) = b_0 + b_1 x_1 + b_2 x_2 + \cdots + b_m x_m$$

where $x_1, \ldots, x_m$ are the predictor variables and p is the proportion to be predicted. The method is called

Table 15.13 Estimated effects on TNF of MTB, FAT, and their interaction (data supplied by Dr Jan Davies)

	Effect (log scale)	95% confidence interval	Ratio effect (natural scale)	95% CI
With interaction term:				
MTB	2.333	(1.442 to 3.224)	10.3	(4.2 to 25.1)
FAT	2.463	(1.572 to 3.354)	11.7	(4.8 to 28.6)
MTB × FAT	0.054	(−1.206 to 1.314)	1.1	(0.3 to 3.7)
Without interaction term:				
MTB	2.306	(1.687 to 2.925)	10.0	(5.4 to 18.6)
FAT	2.435	(1.816 to 3.054)	11.4	(6.1 to 21.2)

logistic regression, and the calculation is computer intensive. The effects of the predictor variables are found as log odds ratios. We will look at the interpretation in an example.

When giving birth, women who have had a previous caesarean section usually have a trial of scar, that is, they attempt a natural labour with vaginal delivery and only have another caesarean if this is deemed necessary. Several factors may increase the risk of a caesarean, and in this study the factor of interest was obesity, as measured by the body mass index or BMI, defined as weight/height^2. The distribution of BMI is shown in Figure 15.17 (data supplied by Andreas Papadopoulos). For caesareans the mean BMI was 26.4 Kg/m^2 and for vaginal deliveries the mean was 24.9 Kg/m^2. Two other variables had a strong relationship with a subsequent caesarean. Women who had had a previous vaginal delivery (PVD) were less likely to need a caesarean, odds ratio = 0.18, 95% confidence interval 0.10 to 0.32. Women whose labour was induced had an increased

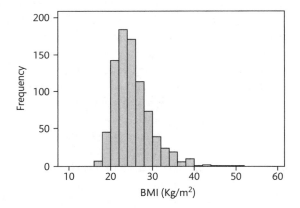

Figure 15.17 Body mass index (BMI) in women undergoing trial of scar (data supplied by Andreas Papadopoulos).

risk of a caesarean, odds ratio = 2.11, 95% confidence interval 1.44 to 3.08. All these relationships were highly significant. The question to be answered was whether the relationship between BMI and caesarean section remained when the effects of induction and previous deliveries were allowed for.

The results of the logistic regression are shown in Table 15.14. We have the coefficients for the equation predicting the log odds of a caesarean:

$$\log(o) = -3.7000 + 0.0883 \times \text{BMI} + 0.6471 \times \text{induction} - 1.7963 \times \text{PVD}$$

where induction and PVD are 1 if present, 0 if not. Thus for a woman with a BMI = 25 Kg/m^2, had not been induced and who had a previous vaginal delivery, the log odds of a caesarean is estimated to be

$$\log(o) = -3.7000 + 0.0883 \times 25 + 0.6471 \times 0$$
$$-1.7963 \times 1 = -3.2888$$

The odds is $\exp(-3.2888) = 0.03730$ and the probability is given by $p = o/(1 + o) = 0.03730/(1 + 0.03730) = 0.036$. If labour had been induced, the log odds would rise to

$$\log(o) = -3.7000 + 0.0883 \times 25 + 0.6471 \times 1$$
$$-1.7963 \times 1 = -2.6417$$

giving odds $\exp(-2.6417) = 0.07124$ and hence probability $0.07124/(1 + 0.07124) = 0.067$.

Because the logistic regression equation predicts the log odds, the coefficients represent the difference between two log odds, a log odds ratio. The antilog of the coefficients is thus an odds ratio. Some programs will print these odds ratios directly, as in Table 15.15. We can see that induction increases the odds of a caesarean by a factor of 1.910 and a previous vaginal delivery reduces

Table 15.14 Coefficients in the logistic regression for predicting caesarean section (data supplied by Andreas Papadopoulos)

	Coef.	Std. Err.	z	P	95% CI
BMI	0.0883	0.0200	4.42	<0.001	0.0492 to 0.1275
Induction	0.6471	0.2141	3.02	0.003	0.2276 to 1.0667
Prev. vag. del.	-1.7963	0.2981	-6.03	<0.001	-2.3805 to -1.2120
Intercept	-3.7000	0.5343	-6.93	<0.001	-4.7473 to -2.6528

Table 15.15 Odds ratios from the logistic regression for predicting caesarean section (data supplied by Andreas Papadopoulos)

	Odds Ratio	P	95% Confidence Interval
BMI	1.092	<0.001	1.050 to 1.136
Induction	1.910	0.003	1.256 to 2.906
Prev. vag. del.	0.166	<0.001	0.096 to 0.298

the odds by a factor of 0.166. These are often called **adjusted odds ratios**. In this example they and their confidence intervals are similar to the unadjusted odds ratios given above, because the three predictor variables happen not to be closely related to each other.

For a continuous predictor variable, such as BMI, the coefficient is the change in log odds for an increase of one unit in the predictor variable. The antilog of the coefficient, the odds ratio, is the factor by which the odds must be multiplied for a unit increase in the predictor. A two-unit increase in the predictor increases the odds by the square of the odds ratio, and so on. A difference of 5 Kg/m^2 in BMI gives an odds ratio for a caesarean of $1.092^5 = 1.55$, thus the odds of a caesarean are multiplied by 1.55. See Section 11.8 for a similar interpretation and fuller discussion when a continuous outcome variable is log transformed.

When we have a case–control study, we can analyse the data using the case or control status as the outcome variable in a logistic regression. The coefficients are then the approximate log relative risks due to the factors (Section 13.7). There is a variant called **conditional logistic regression**, which can be used when the cases and controls are in matched pairs, triples, etc.

Logistic regression is a large sample method. A rule of thumb is that there should be at least 10 'yes's and 10 'no's, and preferably 20, for each predictor variable (Peduzzi *et al.* 1996).

15.11 Stepwise regression

Stepwise regression is a technique for choosing predictor variables from a large set. The stepwise approach can be used with multiple linear, logistic, and other regression techniques (Section 15.14, Section 16.5), too.

There are two basic strategies: step-up and step-down, also called forward and backward. In **step-up** or **forward** regression, we fit all possible one-way regression equations. Having found the one which accounts for the greatest variance, all two-way regressions including this variable are fitted. The equation accounting for the most variation is chosen, and all three-way regressions including these are fitted, and so on. This continues until no significant increase in variation accounted for is found. In the **step-down** or **backward** method, we first fit the regression with all the predictor variables, and then the variable is removed which reduces the amount of variation accounted for by the least amount, and so on. There are also more complex methods, in which variables can both enter and leave the regression equation.

These methods must be treated with care. Different stepwise techniques may produce different sets of predictor variables in the regression equation. This is especially likely when the predictor variables are correlated with one another. The technique is very useful for selecting a small set of predictor variables for purposes of standardization and prediction. For trying to get an understanding of the underlying system, stepwise methods can be very misleading. When predictor variables are highly correlated, once one has entered the equation in a step-up analysis, the other will not enter, even though it is related to the outcome. Thus it will not appear in the final equation.

15.12 Seasonal effects

Sometimes we look at data over time, for example daily admissions to hospital, where there might be seasonal or day of the week effects, which produce cycles in the data. We shall see an example in Section 15.13. If we are doing regression over time, we may need to model these. We can model such effects mathematically using a sine or cosine function, like the one shown in Figure 15.18.

This has three parameters. The **amplitude**, a, is how much the curve varies, so measures how big the cyclic effect is. The **lag**, b, is where the curve crosses zero, so tells us the positions of peaks and troughs. The **period**, p, is the distance between peaks. For weekly or seasonal

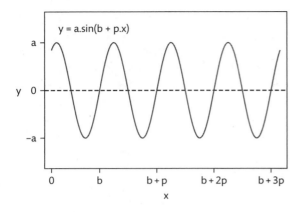

Figure 15.18 A sine curve, $y = a \times \sin(b + p \times x)$.

effects, we know what this period should be and can fit it in advance. For example, for seasonal effects and using time measured in years and decimal fractions of a year, the period is 1 year. Statistical computer programs have their sine and cosine functions in radians rather than degrees, with one complete cycle being 2π radians, so $p = 2\pi$. We would want to include in our regression equation a term $a \times \sin(b + 2\pi \times x)$. To make this into a simple linear function we use a bit of school mathematics, which I expect most readers will have long forgotten. (If not, good for you!) This is that if A and B are two angles, $\sin(A + B) = \sin(A)\cos(B) + \cos(A)\sin(B)$. We apply this to $a \times \sin(b + 2\pi \times x)$ and get $a \times (\sin(b)\cos(2\pi \times x) + \cos(b)\sin(2\pi \times x))$. This is equal to $a\sin(b)\cos(2\pi \times x) + a\cos(b)\sin(2\pi \times x)$. So if we create two variables, one equal to $\cos(2\pi \times x)$ and the other equal to $\sin(2\pi \times x)$ and put them both into our regression equation, we can fit the cyclic effect. The coefficients of these two variables can be used to estimate the amplitude and the lag, if we wish to do this. We shall fit a seasonal model in Section 15.13.

15.13 Dealing with counts: Poisson regression and negative binomial regression

If the outcome variable is a count of independent events, such as hospital admissions in a day or deaths related to

a specific cause per week or month, we can use **Poisson regression**. This is particularly useful when we have many time intervals but the numbers of events per interval is small, so that the assumptions of multiple regression (Section 15.7) do not apply.

For an example, Figure 15.19 shows deaths attributed to volatile substance abuse (VSA) in England, Wales, and Scotland between 1983 and 1991, as recorded in a register of such deaths maintained at St George's University of London (Butland et al. 2012). (The number of deaths is a 3-month moving average, so the number for each month is an average of the count for that month and the months before and after it. This is done to remove some random variation produced by the small numbers to make the pattern easier to see.) VSA is the deliberate inhalation of any of a variety of substances, including solvents from glues, office materials, cleaning products, aerosol propellants, and fuels such as butane or petrol, to produce intoxication. Deaths were from several causes, including acute physiological effects such as sudden cardiac arrest, suffocation from plastic bags over the face, and accidental trauma or drowning while intoxicated. Two important public health issues are apparent: the numbers of deaths were increasing and the majority of these deaths were among children. This led the UK Department of Health to carry out a media-based health education campaign, beginning in February 1992, directed at parents and informing them about the dangers of VSA and

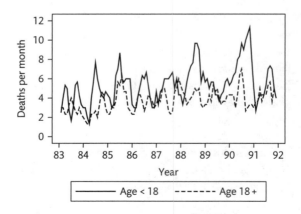

Figure 15.19 Monthly deaths (3-month moving average) attributed to volatile substance abuse, England, Wales, and Scotland, 1983–1991, by age group (data from St George's register of deaths associated with VSA).

warning signs to watch for among their children. We used the register to evaluate this campaign (Field-Smith *et al.* 2002). The data for childhood deaths up to 2000 are shown in Table 15.16.

The deaths in Table 15.16 can be assumed to be happening independently of one another, so the number of deaths should be an observation from a Poisson distribution (Section 6.7), the mean of which depends on the time. We can carry out a Poisson regression, to estimate the effects of time on the rate at which deaths occur. Inspection of Figure 15.19 suggests that the increase is not a straight line but a curve, so we will include a time squared term, and that there may be a seasonal effect, so we will include a sine and a cosine variable as described in Section 15.12. We will also include a dichotomous variable, equal to zero before the campaign and one from February 1992 onwards.

We have one more complication for this analysis. The counts are per month, and months are not of equal length. We can allow for this by including an exposure variable equal to the number of days in the month.

We can now do the Poisson regression, which predicts the rate at which events, in this case deaths, happen. The results are shown in Table 15.17.

Table 15.17 is estimated using an iterative, maximum likelihood procedure, like logistic regression (Section 15.10). The equation formed by these coefficients predicts the log rate at which events happen. Here time is calendar time since January 1st 1900 in years as a decimal, so April 1999 is 99.333, and time squared is time minus 91 all squared. The variable seasonal1 is $\cos(2\pi \times \text{time})$ and seasonal2 is $\sin(2\pi \times \text{time})$ (Section 15.12). The effect of the health education campaign is represented by campaign = 0 before February 1992 and = 1 from then onwards. The natural logarithm of the rate at which events happen is estimated by the sum of each of these variables multiplied by its coefficient, including the log of the number of days in the month. If we omit the last term, we get the log of the daily rate.

The antilog of the coefficient gives the amount by which this variable multiplies the rate at which events happen. For example, for the campaign, $exp(-0.855) = 0.425$. This is called the **incident rate ratio**. Thus the rate at which events happen after the campaign is estimated to be 0.425 times the rate before it, a reduction of 0.575 or 57.5%. This type of study, where the outcome variable is measured over time and we have an intervention, then look at the same time relationship before and after with a sharp change included in the model, is called an **interrupted time series**.

The Poisson regression produces other statistics, including a chi-squared statistic which tests the null hypothesis that the entire set of variables in the equation does not predict the outcome. For Table 15.17 this is 195.27 with 5 degrees of freedom, one for each variable in the model. This is highly significant, P<0.0001. It can be useful if we want to add some more variables which we want to test together. For example, the model for Table 15.17 assumes that the relationship with calendar time is the same before and after the campaign. We can test this by adding two interaction variables (Section 15.5), created by multiplying the time and the time squared variables each by the campaign variable. This model can then have different relationships with time before and after the campaign. If we do this we get chi-squared = 196.48 with 7 degrees of freedom, because we have added two more variables. The increase in the chi-squared statistic is 196.48 – 195.27 = 1.21 and the increase in the degrees of freedom is 7 – 5 = 2. The probability that a Chi-squared variable with 2 d.f. will exceed 1.21 is P = 0.5, so there is no evidence that adding these two interaction variables improves the prediction of death rates and we can drop them.

This is an observational study, not a randomized trial, but it seems to me wildly unlikely that some other factor arose at exactly the same time to have this effect. So I think that the campaign saved many children's lives and, as our register was very influential in raising the alarm, so did we. The numbers of events over the whole period, with the numbers predicted by the Poisson regression model, are shown in Figure 15.20. The fit of the model looks pretty good. When the same model was used for deaths among adults, the campaign effect was not significant, P = 0.08, and the only significant predictor was linear time. Figure 15.21 shows the data and fitted model. As the campaign was aimed specifically at parents with the objective of reducing VSA among children, this provided further evidence of its efficacy.

Table 15.16 Death at ages less than 18 years attributed to volatile substance abuse, England, Wales, and Scotland, by month and year of death (data from Field-Smith *et al.* 2002)

Month	1983	1984	1985	1986	1987	1988	1989	1990	1991
Jan	2	3	4	3	7	3	3	4	2
Feb	3	2	3	3	1	5	5	7	4
Mar	7	1	2	3	6	5	7	8	5
Apr	6	1	5	7	8	7	5	5	4
May	2	10	12	6	4	8	5	11	4
Jun	0	6	4	6	6	7	3	9	5
Jul	3	7	10	6	8	8	5	9	7
Aug	6	5	4	8	5	14	3	9	9
Sep	7	3	3	2	7	7	5	12	6
Oct	4	5	11	2	3	6	6	11	6
Nov	2	4	4	5	8	4	6	11	3
Dec	4	5	3	2	2	10	6	2	3

Month	1992	1993	1994	1995	1996	1997	1998	1999	2000
Jan	2	0	1	1	0	4	1	0	1
Feb	3	3	0	2	2	0	2	3	2
Mar	1	2	0	5	2	2	3	2	0
Apr	3	4	4	4	2	1	1	2	1
May	3	1	2	3	2	4	0	1	1
Jun	3	2	3	0	7	0	1	2	1
Jul	6	4	3	2	4	1	5	3	0
Aug	5	2	4	7	4	5	2	2	1
Sep	4	3	0	2	3	0	3	4	0
Oct	3	1	1	3	6	4	4	2	2
Nov	0	4	0	0	2	2	1	1	2
Dec	2	1	2	0	0	3	2	0	3

Table 15.17 Poisson regression estimates for deaths below age 18 years (data from Field-Smith *et al.* 2002)

	Coef.	Std. Err.	z	P value	95% Conf. Interval
Time	0.009	0.014	0.63	0.5	−0.019 to 0.037
Time squared	−0.0067	0.0017	−3.95	<0.001	−0.0100 to −0.0034
Seasonal1	−0.226	0.050	−4.50	<0.001	−0.325 to −0.128
Seasonal2	−0.168	0.050	−3.35	0.001	−0.267 to −0.070
Campaign	−0.855	0.148	−5.80	<0.001	−1.144 to −0.566
Constant	−2.43	1.25	−1.94	0.05	−4.88 to 0.02
ln(number days)	1 (exposure)				

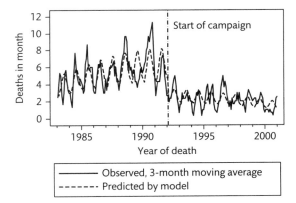

Figure 15.20 Monthly deaths aged less than 18 years (3-month moving average) attributed to volatile substance abuse, England, Wales, and Scotland, 1983–2000, with estimated model (data from Field-Smith *et al.* 2002).

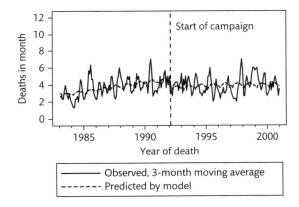

Figure 15.21 Monthly deaths aged 18 years or more (3-month moving average) attributed to volatile substance abuse, England, Wales, and Scotland, 1983–2000, with estimated model (data from Field-Smith *et al.* 2002).

The key assumption of Poisson regression is that the counts are of events which are independent of one another. This is not always the case. For example, a Ph.D. student randomized elderly people who had experienced a fall to one of three groups: occupational therapist-led environmental assessment, trained assessor-led environmental assessment, and usual care control (Pighills *et al.* 2011). Among the outcome variables was the number of falls experienced over the 12 months following randomization. Some participants had several falls, some had none, and there was clearly variation between people in the risk of falling. Some people are more fall-prone than others. Because of this

lack of independence, we could not do a Poisson regression. A method which allows for this dependence in count data is **negative binomial regression**. The **Negative Binomial distribution** is related to the Binomial distribution, as you might expect. The Binomial distribution is the distribution of the number of successes in a fixed number of trials, the Negative Binomial distribution is the number of trials required to achieve a fixed number of successes. We can completely ignore the mathematics and say that negative binomial regression is just a name for a method suitable for this type of data. The method gives us an incidence rate ratio, as does Poisson regression, and Pighills *et al.* (2011) reported that the falls rate in the occupational therapy group was approximately half that of the controls (IRR = 0.54, 95% CI 0.36 to 0.83, P = 0.005). For the trained assessor group compared with the control group, IRR = 0.78 (95% CI 0.51 to 1.21, P = 0.3).

15.14 Other regression methods

The choice of regression method (multiple, logistic, Poisson, negative binomial) is determined by the nature of the outcome variable: continuous, dichotomous, or count. There are other types of outcome variable and corresponding multifactorial techniques. We shall deal with the one most often seen, time to event or survival data, in Chapter 16. I shall not go into any details of other techniques, but this list may help should you come across any of them. I would recommend you consult a statistician should you actually need to use one of these methods. The techniques for dealing with predictor variables described in Sections 15.2–15.6 and Section 15.8 apply to all of them.

There is another variant of regression for counts, where we have a lot of zero counts and the non-zero counts can be assumed to be like a Poisson distribution, called **zero-inflated Poisson regression**.

If the outcome variable is categorical with more than two categories, e.g. several diagnostic groups, we use a procedure called **multinomial logistic regression**. This estimates for a subject with given values of the predictor variable, the probability that the subject will be in each category. If the categories are ordered, e.g. tumour stage, we can take the ordering into account using **ordered logistic regression**. Both these techniques are closely related to logistic regression (Section 15.10).

A slightly different problem arises with multi-way contingency tables where there is no obvious outcome variable. We can use a technique called **log linear modelling**. This enables us to test the relationship between any two of the variables in the table holding the others constant. You will very rarely see this.

There are also non-parametric regression methods and more are being developed to solve more complicated and specialized problems all the time. I couldn't possibly cover them all, but the general principles in this chapter will usually apply.

15.15 Data where observations are not independent

All the analyses of Section 15.1 to Section 15.14 require observations to be independent. When they are not, as in Section 10.13 and Section 11.12, we must adapt our analysis to take the structure of the data into account. There are several ways to do this, of which the most comprehensive is multi-level modelling (Goldstein 1995). This was developed to analyse data of the type 'children within classes within schools', where we might want to investigate variables reported at each of these levels. The main limitation is that we need a fairly large number of observations, such as >40, at the highest level (e.g. school) for this to be reliable. Another approach is general estimating equations, GEE models. General estimating equation models were originally designed for analysing panel data, when we have a group of participants whom we follow over time. This method copes only with two levels and also needs a fairly large number of observations at the top level.

A simpler approximation is provided by robust standard errors. This method, also known as the Huber White sandwich estimator, produces the same estimates as we would get if we assume the observations are independent, but adjusts the standard errors to allow for the data structure. It gets its second name from the appearance of a matrix equation. It can deal with only two levels, but can accommodate slightly smaller samples, >30 at the top level rather than >40. In a cluster randomized trial, the standard errors are increased compared with those ignoring the clustering, as we would expect.

These methods can all be used with smaller samples, but the smaller the sample is, the less reliable the estimates and their standard errors become. Bland (2010) compares analyses of a cluster randomized trial by all these methods and by summary statistics.

There are many other methods used for complex datasets which you will come across from time to time.

15.16 Multiple choice questions: Multifactorial methods

(Each answer is true or false.)

15.1 In a trial of the treatment of warts and verrucae, carried out for the television series *Health Freaks*, 11 people were allocated by minimization to duct tape applied over the wart for a month and 11 to surgical tape as a control group (Bland 2014). After a month, 10 duct tape and 7 control participants were available to be measured. The difference in mean diameter of the wart (duct tape minus control) was –1.9mm (P = 0.2, 95% CI – 4.9 to +1.0mm, two sample t method). The results of a regression analysis including treatment and the size of the wart at baseline are shown in Table 15.18.

(a) There is evidence that initial size is related to final size;

(b) There are insufficient data for us to be sure the analysis is valid;

(c) The results of the multiple regression are not consistent with the results of the t test;

(d) There is no evidence that duct tape reduces the size of warts;

(e) This analysis is according to intention to treat.

15.2 In multiple regression, R^2:

(a) is the square of the multiple correlation coefficient;

(b) would be unchanged if we exchanged the outcome (dependent) variable and one of the predictor (independent) variables;

(c) is called the proportion of variability explained by the regression;

(d) is the ratio of the error sum of squares to the total sum of squares;

(e) would increase if more predictor variables were added to the model.

15.3 The analysis of variance table for a study of the distance between the pupils of the eyes is shown in Table 15.19:

(a) There were 34 observations;

(b) There is good evidence of an ethnic group difference in the population;

(c) We can conclude that there is no difference in inter-pupil distance between men and women;

(d) There were two age groups;

(e) The difference between ethnic groups is likely to be due to a relationship between ethnicity and age in the sample.

Table 15.18 Regression analysis of duct tape data

Final size	Coef.	Std. Err.	t	P	95% Conf. Interval
Initial size	0.832	0.056	14.80	<0.001	0.711 to 0.953
Duct tape	–2.097	0.353	5.95	<0.001	–2.853 to –1.340
Constant	–3.280	0.624	–5.26	<0.001	–4.618 to –1.943

Table 15.19 Analysis of variance for the effects of age, sex, and ethnic group (Afro-Caribbean vs White) on inter-pupil distance (data supplied by Imafedon, personal communication)

Source of variation	Degrees of freedom	Sum of squares	Mean square	Variance ratio (F)	Probability
Total	37	603.586			
Age group	2	124.587	62.293	6.81	0.003
Sex	1	1.072	1.072	0.12	0.7
Ethnic group	1	134.783	134.783	14.74	0.000 5
Residual	33	301.782	9.145		

Table 15.20 Logistic regression of vein graft failure after 6 months (data from Thomas *et al.* 1993)

Variable	Coef.	Std. Err.	coef/se	P	95% CI
White cell count	1.238	0.273	4.539	<0.001	0.695 to 1.781
Graft type 1	0.175	0.876	0.200	0.842	–1.570 to 1.920
Graft type 2	0.973	1.030	0.944	0.348	–1.080 to 3.025
Graft type 3	0.038	1.518	0.025	0.980	–2.986 to 3.061
Female	–0.289	0.767	–0.377	0.708	–1.816 to 1.239
Age	0.022	0.035	0.633	0.528	–0.048 to 0.092
Smoker	0.998	0.754	1.323	0.190	–0.504 to 2.501
Diabetic	1.023	0.709	1.443	0.153	–0.389 to 2.435
Constant	–13.726	3.836	–3.578	0.001	–21.369 to –6.083

Number of observations = 84, chi squared = 38.05, d.f. = 8, P < 0.0001

15.4 Table 15.20 shows the logistic regression of vein graft failure on some potential explanatory variables. From this analysis:

(a) patients with high white cell counts were more likely to have graft failure;

(b) the log odds of graft failure for a diabetic patient is estimated to be between 0.389 less and 2.435 greater than that for a non-diabetic;

(c) grafts were more likely to fail in female patients in this sample, though this is not significant;

(d) there were four types of graft;

(e) any relationship between white cell count and graft failure may be due to smokers having higher white cell counts.

15.5 For the data in Figure 15.22:

(a) the relationship could be investigated by linear regression;

(b) an 'oral squared' term could be used to test whether there is any evidence that the relationship is not a straight line;

(c) if an 'oral squared' term were included there would be 2 degrees of freedom for the model;

(d) the coefficients of an 'oral' and an 'oral squared' term would be uncorrelated;

(e) the estimation of the coefficients would be improved by subtracting the mean from the oral temperature before squaring.

15.17 Exercise: A multiple regression analysis

Trisomy-16 mice can be used as an animal model for Down's syndrome. This analysis looks at the volume of a region of the heart, the atrioventricular cushion, of a mouse embryo, compared between trisomic and normal embryos. The embryos were at varying stages of development, indicated by the number of pairs of somites (precursors of vertebrae).

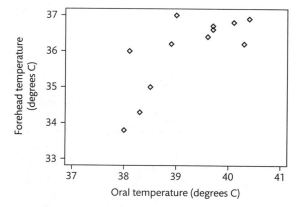

Figure 15.22 Oral and forehead temperature measurements made in a group of pyrexic patients.

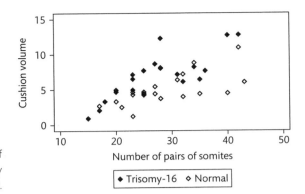

Figure 15.23 Cushion volume against number of pairs of somites for two groups of mouse embryos (data supplied by Webb and Brown, personal communication).

Table 15.21 Number of somites and cushion volume in mouse embryos (data supplied by Webb and Brown, personal communication)

Normal				Trisomy-16			
somites	volume	somites	volume	somites	volume	somites	volume
17	2.674	28	3.704	15	0.919	28	8.033
20	3.299	31	6.358	17	2.047	28	12.265
21	2.486	32	3.966	18	3.302	28	8.097
23	1.202	32	7.184	20	4.667	31	7.145
23	4.263	34	8.803	20	4.930	32	6.104
23	4.620	35	4.373	23	4.942	34	8.211
25	4.644	40	4.465	23	6.500	35	6.429
25	4.403	42	10.940	23	7.122	36	7.661
27	5.417	43	6.035	25	7.688	40	12.706
27	4.395			25	4.230	42	12.767
				27	8.647		

Figure 15.23 and Table 15.21 show the data. The group was coded 1 = normal, 2 = trisomy-16.

Table 15.22 shows the results of a regression analysis and Figures 15.24 and 15.25 shows residual plots.

15.1 Is there any evidence of a difference in volume between groups for given stage of development?

15.2 Are there any features of the data which might make the analysis invalid?

15.3 It appears from Figure 15.23 that the relationship between volume and number of pairs of somites may not be the same in the two groups. Table 15.23 shows the results of a regression analysis including an interaction term. Is there any evidence that there is an interaction?

Table 15.22 Regression of cushion volume on number of pairs of somites and group in mouse embryos (data supplied by Webb and Brown, personal communication)

Source of variation	Degrees of freedom	Sum of squares	Mean square	Variance ratio (F)	Probability
Total	39	328.976			
Due to regression	2	197.708	98.854	27.86	P < 0.0001
Residual (about regression)	37	131.268	3.548		

Variable	Coef.	Std. Err.	t	P	95% Conf. Int.
Group	2.44	0.60	4.06	<0.001	1.29 to 3.65
Somites	0.274	0.041	6.69	<0.001	0.191 to 0.357
Constant	−5.43	1.57	−3.45	0.001	−8.62 to −2.24

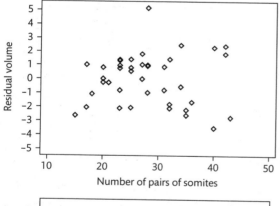

Figure 15.24 Residual against number of pairs of somites for the analysis of Table 15.22 (data supplied by Webb and Brown, personal communication).

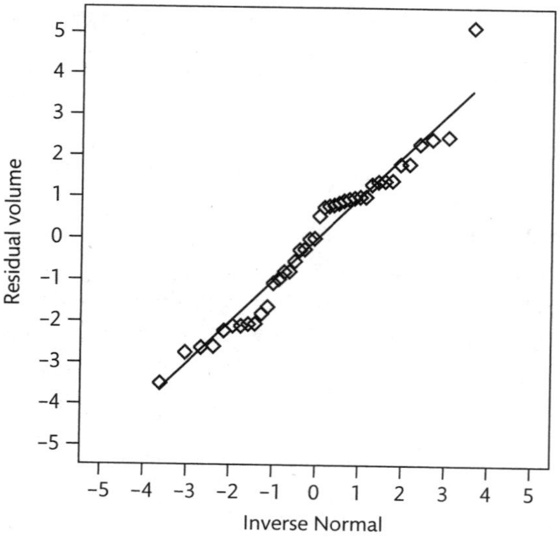

Figure 15.25 Normal plot of residuals for the analysis of Table 15.22 (data supplied by Webb and Brown, personal communication).

Table 15.23 Regression of cushion volume on number of pairs of somites, group, and number of pairs of somites × group interaction in mouse embryos (data supplied by Webb and Brown, personal communication)

Source of variation	Degrees of freedom	Sum of squares	Mean square	Variance ratio (F)	Probability
Total	39	328.976			
Due to regression	3	207.139	69.046	20.40	P < 0.0001
Residual (about regression)	36	121.837	3.384		

Variable	Coef.	Std. Err.	t	P	95% Conf. Int.
Group	−1.31	2.32	−0.57	0.6	−6.02 to 3.39
Somites	0.204	0.058	3.52	0.001	0.086 to 0.322
Interaction	0.134	0.080	1.67	0.1	−0.029 to 0.296
Constant	0.336	3.782	0.090	0.9	−7.335 to 8.007

It appears from Figure 15.24 that there may be a non-linear relationship of cushion volume with somite number. A term in somite number squared was added to the regression. The mean somite number was 27.95. The term added to the regression was $(somites-28)^2$.

15.4 Why was 28 subtracted from the somite number before squaring?

15.5 The results of the regression are shown in Table 15.24. Is there any need to include the somites squared term?

Table 15.24 Regression of cushion volume on number of pairs of somites, group, and somites squared in mouse embryos (data supplied by Webb and Brown, personal communication)

Source of variation	Degrees of freedom	Sum of squares	Mean square	Variance ratio (F)	Probability
Total	39	328.976			
Due to regression	3	203.302	67.767	19.41	P < 0.0001
Residual (about regression)	36	125.674	3.491		

Variable	Coef.	Std. Err.	t	P	95% Conf. Int.
Group	2.46	0.60	4.13	<0.001	1.26 to 3.67
Somites	0.291	0.043	6.80	<0.001	0.204 to 0.378
$(Somites -28)^2$	−0.0063	0.0050	−1.27	0.2	−0.0166 to 0.0038
Constant	−5.61	1.57	−3.58	0.001	−8.80 to −2.43

16 Time to event data

16.1 Time to event data

We often have data which represent the time until some event takes place. Early studies looked at the time to death, for example in a randomized trial or to estimate the 5-year survival rate in cancer. The methods of analysis developed were called **survival analysis** for this reason, but we can use the same methods for time to many other kinds of event. In cancer studies we can use survival analysis for the time to metastasis or to local recurrence of a tumour, in a study of medical care we can use it to analyse the time to readmission to hospital, in a study of breast-feeding we could look at the age at which breast-feeding ceased or at which bottle feeding was first introduced, in a study of the treatment of infertility we can treat the time from treatment to conception as survival data, in a study of chronic wounds we can use the time until the wound has healed. We usually refer to the terminal event, death, conception, etc., as the **endpoint**.

Problems arise in the analysis of time to event data because often we do not know the exact survival times of all subjects. This is because some will still be surviving when we want to analyse the data. When cases have entered the study at different times, some of the recent entrants may be surviving event-free, but have been observed for a short time only. Their observed survival time may be less than those cases admitted early in the study and who have since had an event. The method of calculating survival curves described below takes this into account. Observations which are known only to be greater than some value are **right censored**, often shortened to **censored**. (We get **left censored** data when the measurement method cannot detect anything below some cut-off value, and observations are recorded as 'none detectable'. The rank methods in Chapter 12 are useful for such data.)

16.2 Kaplan–Meier survival curves

Table 16.1 shows some survival data for patients with parathyroid cancer. The survival times are recorded in completed years. A patient who survived for 6 years and then died can be taken as having lived for 6 years and then died in the seventh. In the first year from diagnosis, one patient died, two patients were observed for only part of this year, and 17 survived into the next year. The subjects who have only been observed for part of the year are censored, also called **lost to follow-up** or **withdrawn from follow-up**. (These are rather misleading names, often wrongly interpreted as meaning that these subjects have dropped out of the study. This may be the case, but most of these subjects are simply still alive and their further survival is unknown.) There is no information about the survival of these subjects after the first year, because it has not happened yet. These patients are only at risk of dying for part of the year and we cannot say that 1 out of 20 died as they may yet contribute another death in the first year. We can say that such patients will contribute half a year of risk, on average, so the number of patient years at risk in the first year is 18 (17 who survived and 1 who died) plus 2 halves for those withdrawn from follow-up, giving 19 altogether. We get an estimate of the probability of dying in the first year of 1/19, and an estimated probability of surviving of $1 - \frac{1}{19}$.

Table 16.1 Survival time in years of 20 patients after diagnosis of parathyroid cancer

Still alive	<1	<1	1	1	4	5	6	8	10	10	17
Deaths		<1	2	6	6	7	9	9	11	14	

We can do this for each year until the limits of the data are reached. We thus trace the survival of these patients, estimating the probability of death or survival at each year and the cumulative probability of survival to each year. This set of probabilities is called a **life table**.

To carry out the calculation, we first set out for each year, x, the number alive at the start, n_x, the number withdrawn during the year, w_x, the number at risk, r_x, and the number dying, d_x (Table 16.2). Thus in year 1 the number at the start is 20, the number withdrawn is 2, the number at risk $r_1 = n_1 - \frac{1}{2}w_1 = 20 - \frac{1}{2} \times 2 = 19$ and the number of deaths is 1. As there were 2 withdrawals and 1 death, the number at the start of year 2 is 17. For each year we calculate the probability of dying in that year for patients who have reached the beginning of it, $q_x = d_x/r_x$, and hence the probability of surviving to the next year, $p_x = 1 - q_x$. Finally we calculate the cumulative survival probability. For the first year, this is the probability of surviving that year, $P_1 = p_1$. For the second year, it is the probability of surviving up to the start of the second year, P_1, times the probability of surviving that year, p_2, to give $P_2 = p_2 P_1$. The probability of surviving for 3 years is similarly $P_3 = p_3 P_2$, and so on. From this life table we can estimate the **5-year survival rate**, a useful measure of prognosis in cancer. For the parathyroid cancer, the 5-year survival rate is 0.884 2, or 88%. We can see that

Table 16.2 Life table calculation for parathyroid cancer survival

Year	Number at start	Withdrawn during year	At risk	Deaths	Prob of death	Prob of surviving year x	Cumulative prob of surviving x years
x	n_x	w_x	r_x	d_x	q_x	p_x	P_x
1	20	2	19	1	0.052 6	0.947 4	0.947 4
2	17	2	16	0	0	1	0.947 4
3	15	0	15	1	0.066 7	0.933 3	0.884 2
4	14	0	14	0	0	1	0.884 2
5	14	1	13.5	0	0	1	0.884 2
6	13	1	12.5	0	0	1	0.884 2
7	12	1	11.5	2	0.173 9	0.826 1	0.730 4
8	9	0	9	1	0.111 1	0.888 9	0.649 3
9	8	1	7.5	0	0	1	0.649 3
10	7	0	7	2	0.285 7	0.714 3	0.463 8
11	5	2	4	0	0	1	0.463 8
12	3	0	3	1	0.333 3	0.666 7	0.309 2
13	2	0	2	0	0	1	0.309 2
14	2	0	2	0	0	1	0.309 2
15	2	0	2	1	0.500 0	0.500 0	0.154 6
16	1	0	1	0	0	1	0.154 6
17	1	0	1	0	0	1	0.154 6
18	1	1	0.5	0	0	1	0.154 6

$r_x = n_x - \frac{1}{2}w_x, \quad q_x = d_x/r_x, \quad p_x = 1 - q_x, \quad P_x = p_x P_{x-1}$

the prognosis for this cancer was quite good. If we know the exact time of death or withdrawal for each subject, then instead of using fixed time intervals we use x as the exact time, with a row of the table for each time when either an endpoint or a withdrawal occurs. Then $r_x = n_x$ and we can omit the $r_x = n_x - \frac{1}{2}w_x$ step.

We can draw a graph of the cumulative survival probability, the **survival curve**. This is usually drawn in steps, with abrupt changes in probability (Figure 16.1). This convention emphasizes the relatively poor estimation at the long survival end of the curve, where the small numbers at risk produced large steps. When the exact times of death and censoring are known, this is called a **Kaplan–Meier survival curve**.

There is an important assumption made in this method. It is that observations which are censored represent a population who would experience the same risk of an event following the moment at which data were censored as would those whom we can observe beyond that time.

Sometimes we want to show the proportion who have experienced the event, rather than the proportion who have yet to experience it. This is one minus the survival function and is called the **failure function**. Despite the name, this is useful when the event is a positive one. For example, Figure 16.2 shows the proportion of people with sloughy leg ulcers whose wounds have debrided, i.e. had all the dead tissue removed, following treatment with larval therapy or hydrogel (Dumville *et al.* 2009). The larval therapy was the application of the maggots of the greenbottle fly, which eat only dead tissue, here either placed loose upon the wound or in a mesh bag like a teabag. As the graph shows, debridement is clearly faster with larval therapy of either type than with hydrogel. Unfortunately, this was not translated into faster wound healing.

The times at which observations are censored may be marked by small vertical lines above the survival curve (Figure 16.2) and the number remaining at risk may be written at suitable intervals below the time axis (Figure 16.2). These pieces of additional information are sometimes given, sometimes not.

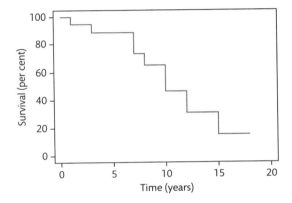

Figure 16.1 Survival curve for parathyroid cancer patients.

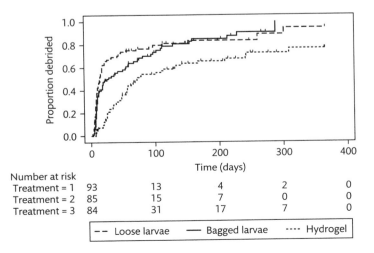

Number at risk				
Treatment = 1	93	13	4	2	0
Treatment = 2	85	15	7	0	0
Treatment = 3	84	31	17	7	0

Figure 16.2 Time to debridement of sloughy venous leg ulcers following treatment with two methods of larval therapy (maggots) or hydrogel (data from Dumville *et al.* 2009).

Table 16.3 Time to recurrence of gall stones following dissolution, whether previous gall stones were multiple, maximum diameter of previous gall stones, and months previous gall stones took to dissolve (data from Petroni *et al.* 2000)

Time	Rec.	Mult.	Diam.	Dis.	Time	Rec.	Mult.	Diam.	Dis.	Time	Rec.	Mult.	Diam.	Dis.	Time	Rec.	Mult.	Diam.	Dis.
3	No	Yes	4	10	13	No	No	11	6	11	No	Yes	13	18	25	No	No	4	11
3	No	No	18	3	13	No	No	22	33	11	Yes	No	7	8	26	No	No	17	5
3	No	Yes	5	27	13	No	No	13	9	12	Yes	Yes	5	7	26	No	Yes	6	12
4	No	Yes	4	4	13	Yes	Yes	8	12	12	Yes	Yes	8	12	26	Yes	No	16	8
5	No	No	19	20	14	No	Yes	6	6	12	No	Yes	4	6	28	No	No	20	3
6	No	Yes	3	10	14	No	No	23	15	12	No	Yes	4	8	28	Yes	No	30	4
6	No	Yes	4	6	14	No	No	15	10	12	Yes	Yes	7	19	29	No	No	16	3
6	No	Yes	4	20	16	Yes	Yes	5	6	12	Yes	No	7	3	29	Yes	No	12	15
6	Yes	Yes	5	8	16	Yes	Yes	6	8	12	No	Yes	5	22	29	Yes	Yes	10	7
6	Yes	Yes	3	18	16	No	No	18	4	12	Yes	No	8	1	29	No	Yes	7	6
6	Yes	Yes	7	9	17	No	No	7	10	12	No	No	6	6	30	No	Yes	4	4
6	No	No	25	9	17	No	Yes	4	3	12	No	No	26	4	30	No	No	9	12
6	No	Yes	4	6	17	No	Yes	7	6	13	No	Yes	5	6	30	Yes	Yes	22	10
6	Yes	Yes	10	38	17	Yes	No	8	8	13	No	No	13	6	30	Yes	Yes	6	3
6	Yes	Yes	8	15	18	Yes	No	5	6	31	No	Yes	5	6	38	No	No	10	18
6	No	Yes	4	13	18	Yes	Yes	10	9	31	No	No	26	3	38	Yes	Yes	5	10
7	Yes	Yes	4	15	18	No	Yes	8	38	31	No	No	7	24	38	No	No	7	4
7	No	Yes	3	7	19	No	No	26	6	32	Yes	Yes	10	12	40	No	No	23	1
7	Yes	Yes	10	48						32	No	Yes	5	6	41	No	No	16	2

8	Yes	Yes	14	29	19	No	Yes	11	16	32	No	No	4	6	41	No	No	4	14
8	Yes	No	18	14	19	Yes	Yes	5	7	32	No	No	18	10	42	No	No	15	43
8	Yes	Yes	6	6	20	No	No	11	2	33	No	No	13	9	42	No	Yes	16	6
8	No	No	15	1	20	No	No	13	9	34	No	No	15	8	42	No	Yes	9	11
8	No	Yes	1	12	20	No	No	6	7	34	No	No	20	30	42	No	Yes	14	9
8	No	No	5	6	21	No	Yes	11	1	34	No	Yes	15	8	43	Yes	No	4	17
9	No	Yes	2	15	21	No	Yes	13	24	34	No	No	27	8	44	No	Yes	7	6
9	Yes	Yes	7	6	21	No	Yes	4	11	35	No	No	6	12	44	No	Yes	10	8
9	No	No	19	8	22	No	No	10	4	36	No	No	18	5	45	No	Yes	12	17
10	Yes	Yes	14	8	22	No	No	20	20	36	No	Yes	6	16	47	No	No	4	3
11	No	No	8	12	23	No	No	16	6	36	No	Yes	5	6	48	No	No	21	11
11	No	No	15	15	24	No	No	15	4	36	No	Yes	8	17	48	No	No	9	10
11	Yes	No	5	8	24	No	Yes	3	6	36	No	No	5	4	53	No	Yes	6	9
11	No	Yes	3	6	24	Yes	No	15	2	37	No	Yes	5	7	60	Yes	No	15	15
11	Yes	Yes	5	12	24	Yes	Yes	7	6	37	No	No	19	4	61	No	No	10	11
11	No	Yes	4	6	25	No	No	13	10	37	No	Yes	4	4	65	No	Yes	5	3
11	No	Yes	4	3	25	Yes	Yes	6	3	37	No	Yes	4	12	70	No	Yes	7	12

16.3 The logrank test

Standard errors and confidence intervals for the survival probabilities can be found (see Armitage *et al.* 2002). These are useful for estimates such as 5-year survival rate. They do not provide a good method for comparing survival curves, as they do not include all the data, only using those up to the chosen time. Survival curves start off together at 100% survival, possibly diverge, but, for many endpoints eventually come together at zero survival, if we follow for long enough. Thus the comparison would depend on the time chosen. Survival curves can be compared by several significance tests, of which the best known is the **logrank** test (Peto and Peto 1972). This is a non-parametric test which makes use of the full survival data without making any assumption about the shape of the survival curve.

Table 16.3 shows the time to recurrence of gall stones following dissolution by bile acid treatment or lithotripsy. Here we shall compare the two groups defined by having single or multiple gall stones, using the logrank test. We shall look at the quantitative variables diameter of gall stone and months to dissolve in Section 16.5. Figure 16.3 shows the time to recurrence for subjects with single primary gall stones and multiple primary gall stones. The null hypothesis is that there is no difference in recurrence-free survival time, the alternative that there is such a difference. The calculation of the logrank test is set out in Table 16.4. For each time at which a recurrence or a censoring occurred, we have the numbers under observation in each group, n_1 and n_2, the number of recurrences, d_1 and d_2 (d for death), and the number of censorings, w_1 and w_2 (w for withdrawal). For each time, we calculate the probability of recurrence, $p_d = (d_1 + d_2)/(n_1 + n_2)$, which each subject would have if the null hypothesis were true. For each group, we calculate the expected number of recurrences, $e_1 = p_d \times n_1$ and $e_2 = p_d \times n_2$. We then calculate the numbers at risk at the next time, $n_1 - d_1 - w_1$ and $n_2 - d_2 - w_2$. We do this for each time. We then add the d_1 and d_2 columns to get the observed numbers of recurrences, and the e_1 and e_2 columns to get the numbers of recurrences expected if the null hypothesis were true.

We have observed frequencies of recurrence d_1 and d_2, and expected frequencies e_1, and e_2. Of course,

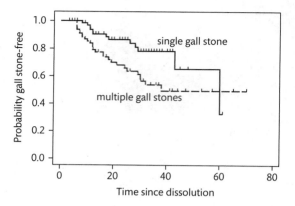

Figure 16.3 Gall stone-free survival after the dissolution of single and multiple gall stones.

$d_1 + d_2 = e_1 + e_2$, so we only need to calculate e_1 as in Table 16.4, and hence e_2 by subtraction. This only works for two groups, however, and the method of Table 16.4 works for any number of groups.

We can test the null hypothesis that the risk of recurrence in any month is equal for the two populations by a chi-squared test:

$$\sum \frac{(d_i - e_i)^2}{e_i} = \frac{(12 - 20.032)^2}{20.032}$$
$$+ \frac{(27 - 18.968)^2}{18.968}$$
$$= 6.62$$

There is one constraint, that the two frequencies add to the sum of the expected (i.e. the total number of recurrences), so we lose 1 degree of freedom, giving $2 - 1 = 1$ degree of freedom. From Table 13.3, this has a probability of 0.01.

Some texts describe this test differently, saying that under the null hypothesis d_1 is from a Normal distribution with mean e_1 and variance $e_1 e_2/(e_1 + e_2)$. This is algebraically identical to the chi-squared method, but only works for two groups.

The logrank test is non-parametric, because we make no assumptions about either the distribution of survival time or any difference in recurrence rates. It requires the survival or censoring times to be exact. A similar method for grouped data, as in Table 16.2, is given by Mantel (1966). We make the same assumption about censoring as for the Kaplan–Meier survival curve, that

Table 16.4 Calculation for the logrank test

Time	n_1	d_1	w_1	n_2	d_2	w_2	p_d	e_1	e_2
3	65	0	1	79	0	2	0.000	0.000	0.000
4	64	0	0	77	0	1	0.000	0.000	0.000
5	64	0	1	76	0	0	0.000	0.000	0.000
6	63	0	1	76	5	5	0.036	2.266	2.734
7	62	0	0	66	2	1	0.016	0.969	1.031
8	62	1	1	63	2	2	0.024	1.488	1.512
9	60	0	1	59	1	1	0.008	0.504	0.496
10	59	0	0	57	1	0	0.009	0.509	0.491
11	59	2	1	56	1	5	0.026	1.539	1.461
12	56	2	2	50	3	3	0.047	2.642	2.358
13	52	0	4	44	1	1	0.010	0.542	0.458
14	48	0	2	42	0	1	0.000	0.000	0.000
16	46	0	1	41	2	0	0.023	1.057	0.943
17	45	1	1	39	0	3	0.012	0.536	0.464
18	43	1	0	36	1	1	0.025	1.089	0.911
19	42	0	1	34	1	1	0.013	0.553	0.447
20	41	0	3	32	0	0	0.000	0.000	0.000
21	38	0	0	32	0	3	0.000	0.000	0.000
22	38	0	2	29	0	0	0.000	0.000	0.000
23	36	0	1	29	0	0	0.000	0.000	0.000
24	35	0	2	29	1	1	0.016	0.547	0.453
25	33	0	2	27	1	0	0.017	0.550	0.450
26	31	1	1	26	0	1	0.018	0.544	0.456
28	29	1	1	25	0	0	0.019	0.537	0.463
29	27	1	1	25	1	1	0.038	1.038	0.962
30	25	0	1	23	2	1	0.042	1.042	0.958
31	24	0	2	20	0	1	0.000	0.000	0.000
32	22	0	2	19	1	1	0.024	0.537	0.463
33	20	0	1	17	0	0	0.000	0.000	0.000
34	19	0	3	17	0	1	0.000	0.000	0.000

continued

Table 16.4 (continued)

Time	n_1	d_1	w_1	n_2	d_2	w_2	p_d	e_1	e_2
35	16	0	1	16	0	0	0.000	0.000	0.000
36	15	0	2	16	0	3	0.000	0.000	0.000
37	13	0	1	13	0	3	0.000	0.000	0.000
38	12	0	2	10	1	0	0.045	0.545	0.455
40	10	0	1	9	0	0	0.000	0.000	0.000
41	9	0	2	9	0	0	0.000	0.000	0.000
42	7	0	1	9	0	3	0.000	0.000	0.000
43	6	1	0	6	0	0	0.083	0.500	0.500
44	5	0	0	4	0	2	0.000	0.000	0.000
45	5	0	1	4	0	0	0.000	0.000	0.000
47	4	0	0	4	0	1	0.000	0.000	0.000
48	4	0	2	3	0	0	0.000	0.000	0.000
53	2	0	0	3	0	1	0.000	0.000	0.000
60	2	1	0	2	0	0	0.250	0.500	0.500
61	1	0	1	2	0	0	0.000	0.000	0.000
65	0	0	0	2	0	1	0.000	0.000	0.000
70	0	0	0	1	0	1	0.000	0.000	0.000
Total		12			27			20.032	18.968

$p_d = (d_1 + d_2)/(n_1 + n_2)$, $e_1 = p_d n_1$, $e_2 = p_d n_2$

censored subjects have the same chance of an event at subsequent times as do observed subjects. It is sometimes said that the curves must not cross, but it is because the test is not good at detecting complex differences in time to event such as those where this happens rather than that it finds differences which are not there.

16.4 The hazard ratio

The logrank test is a test of significance and, of course, an estimate of the difference is preferable if we can get one. The logrank test calculation can be used to give us one: the **hazard ratio**. This is the ratio of the risk of death in group 1 to the risk of death in group 2. For this to make sense, we have to assume that this ratio is the

same at all times, otherwise there could not be a single estimate. (Compare the paired t method, Section 10.2.) This is called the assumption of **proportional hazards**. The risk of death is the number of deaths divided by the population at risk, but the population keeps changing due to censoring. However, the populations at risk in the two groups are proportional to the numbers of expected deaths, e_1 and e_2. We can thus calculate the hazard ratio by

$$h = \frac{d_1/e_1}{d_2/e_2}$$

For Table 16.4, we have

$$h = \frac{12/20.032}{27/18.968} = 0.42$$

Thus we estimate the risk of recurrence with single stones to be 0.42 times the risk for multiple stones. The direct calculation of a confidence interval for the hazard ratio is tedious and I shall omit it. Altman (1991) gives details. It can also be done by Cox regression (Section 17.9).

16.5 Cox regression

One problem of survival data, the censoring of individuals who have not died at the time of analysis, has been discussed in Section 16.1 and Section 16.2. There is another which is important for multifactorial analysis. We often have no suitable mathematical model of the way survival is related to time, i.e. the survival curve. The solution now widely adopted to this problem was proposed by Cox (1972), and is known as **Cox regression** or the **proportional hazards model**. In this approach, we say that for subjects who have lived to time t, the probability of an endpoint (e.g. dying) instantaneously at time t is $h(t)$, which is an unknown function of time. We call the probability of an endpoint the **hazard**, and $h(t)$ is the **hazard function**. We then assume that anything which affects the hazard does so by the same ratio at all times, the proportional hazards assumption. Thus, something which doubles the risk of an endpoint on day one will also double the risk of an endpoint on day two, day three, and so on. Thus, if $h_0(t)$ is the hazard function for subjects with all the predictor variables equal to zero, and $h(t)$ is the hazard function for a subject with some other values for the predictor variables, $h(t)/h_0(t)$ depends only on the predictor variables, not on time t. We call $h(t)/h_0(t)$ the **hazard ratio**, as in Section 16.4. It is the relative risk of an endpoint occurring at any given time.

In statistics, it is convenient to work with differences rather than ratios, so we take the logarithm of the ratio (see Appendix 5A) and have a regression-like equation:

$$\log_e \left(\frac{h(t)}{h_0(t)} \right) = b_1 x_1 + b_2 x_2 + \cdots + b_p x_p$$

where $x_1, \ldots, x_p$ are the predictor variables and $b_1, \ldots, b_p$ are the coefficients which we estimate from the data. This is Cox's proportional hazards model. Cox regression enables us to estimate the values of $b_1, \ldots, b_p$ which best predict the observed survival. There is no constant term b_0, its place being taken by the **baseline hazard** function $h_0(t)$.

Table 16.3 shows the time to recurrence of gall stones, or the time for which patients are known to have been gall stone-free, following dissolution by bile acid treatment or lithotripsy, with the number of previous gall stones, their maximum diameter, and the time required for their dissolution. The difference between patients with a single and with multiple previous gallstones was tested using the logrank test (Section 16.3). Cox regression enables us to look at continuous predictor variables, such as diameter of gall stone, and to examine several predictor variables at once. Table 16.5 shows the result of the Cox regression. We can carry out an approximate test of significance dividing the coefficient by its standard error, and if the null hypothesis that the coefficient would be zero in the population is true, this should follow a Standard Normal distribution. The chi-squared statistic tests the relationship between the time to recurrence and the three variables together. The maximum diameter has no significant relationship to time to recurrence, so we can try a model without it (Table 16.6). As the change in

Table 16.5 Cox regression of time to recurrence of gall stones on presence of multiple stones, maximum diameter of stone, and months to dissolution (data from Petroni *et al.* 2000)

Variable	Coef.	Std. Err.	z	P	95% Conf. Interval
Mult. gall st.	0.838	0.401	2.09	0.038	0.046 to 1.631
Max. diam.	−0.023	0.036	−0.63	0.532	−0.094 to 0.049
Months to dissol.	0.044	0.017	2.64	0.009	0.011 to 0.078

$\chi^2 = 12.57$, 3 d.f., P = 0.006

Table 16.6 Cox regression of time to recurrence of gall stones on presence of multiple stones and months to dissolution (data from Petroni *et al.* 2000)

Variable	Coef.	Std. Err.	z	P	95% Conf. Interval
Mult. gall st.	0.963	0.353	2.73	0.007	0.266 to 1.661
Months to dissol.	0.043	0.017	2.59	0.011	0.010 to 0.076

$\chi^2 = 12.16$, 2 d.f., P = 0.002

overall chi-squared shows, removing diameter has had very little effect.

The coefficients in Table 16.6 are the log hazard ratios. The coefficient for multiple gall stones is 0.963. If we antilog this, we get exp(0.963) = 2.62. As multiple gall stones is a 0 or 1 variable, the coefficient measures the difference between those with single and multiple stones. A patient with multiple gall stones is 2.62 times as likely to have a recurrence at any time than a patient with a single stone. The 95% confidence interval for this estimate is found from the antilogs of the confidence interval in Table 16.6, 1.30 to 5.26. Note that a positive coefficient means an increased risk of the event, in this case recurrence. The coefficient for months to dissolution is 0.043, which has antilog = 1.04. This is a quantitative variable, and for each month to dissolve the hazard ratio increases by a factor of 1.04. Thus a patient whose stone took 2 months to dissolve has a risk of recurrence 1.04 times that for a patient whose stone took 1 month, a patient whose stone took 3 months has a risk 1.04^2 times that for a 1-month patient, and so on.

If we have only the dichotomous variable multiple gall stones in the Cox model, we get for the overall test statistic $\chi^2 = 6.11$, 1 d.f. In Section 15.6 we analysed these data by comparison of two groups using the logrank test which gave $\chi^2 = 6.62$, 1 d.f. The two methods give similar, but not identical results. The logrank test is non-parametric, making no assumption about the distribution of survival time. The Cox method is said to be **semi-parametric**, because although it makes no assumption about the shape of the distribution of survival time, it does require assumptions about the hazard ratio.

Like logistic regression (Section 15.10), Cox regression is a large sample method. A rule of thumb is that there should be at least 10, and preferably 20, events (deaths) for each predictor variable. Fuller accounts of Cox regression are given by Altman (1991); Matthews and Farewell (1988); Parmar and Machin (1995); and Hosmer and Lemeshow (1999).

Proportional hazards regression differs from least squares regression in an important way. Adjustment for other variables, even in a randomized trial, can produce significant differences by changing the estimate rather than the standard error. For example, in an individual participant data meta-analysis (see Section 17.11), O'Meara *et al.* (2009) compared the treatment of venous leg ulcers using four-layer elastic bandages with treatment using short-stretch elastic bandages. Unadjusted analysis indicated no significant difference in time to healing between bandage types: hazard ratio = 1.15, 95% confidence interval 0.97 to 1.37; P=0.11. After adjustment for ulcer duration before and ulcer area at randomization, the hazard ratio for bandage type was 1.31 (95% CI 1.09 to 1.58; P=0.005). It is not unusual to find that in randomized trials adjustment for prognostic variables produces a significant treatment difference where there was none in the unadjusted analysis. What surprised readers here was that the treatment estimate changed but the precision of the estimate did not, rather than the estimate becoming more precise. The confidence interval was calculated on the log scale, of course, and if we log the confidence limits, the width of the confidence interval was log(1.37) – log(0.97) = 0.345 for the unadjusted estimate and log(1.58) – log(1.09) = 0.371 for the adjusted, actually slightly wider. The explanation for this lies in the non-linear nature of the model and the fitting. Ford and Norrie (2002) give a fairly mathematical explanation of this phenomenon, which I have known to confuse some very competent statisticians (and myself).

For Cox regression we must make the assumption about event rates after censoring being the same as for uncensored observations. We must also make the assumption of proportional hazards. We can test this in several ways, both analytical and graphical. These include Kaplan–Meier plots, described above, log minus log survival plots, and Schoenfeld residuals. I shall omit the last two here. If we find problems of non-proportionality, there are more advanced methods of analysis which can be used, such as the use of time-dependent covariates. There are also several parametric models of survival time which can be used. At the time of writing, however, the Cox proportional hazards model is, by far, the one most often seen in the medical research literature.

According to Ryan and Woodall (2005), Kaplan and Meier (1958) and Cox (1972) are the two most highly cited statistical papers ever.

16.6 Multiple choice questions: Time to event data

(Each answer is true or false.)

16.1 When a survival curve is calculated from censored survival times:
(a) the estimated proportion surviving becomes less reliable as survival time increases;
(b) individuals withdrawn during the first time interval are excluded from the analysis;
(c) survival estimates depend on the assumption that survival rates for any given time of follow-up remain constant over the study period;
(d) it may be that the survival curve will not reach zero survival;
(e) the 5-year survival rate can be calculated even if some of the subjects were identified less than 5 years ago.

16.2 Figure 16.4 shows data from a study of conception by women attending a subfertility clinic (Luthra *et al.* 1982). Conceptions are compared for women observed before laparoscopy was carried out and for women who had had laparoscopy.

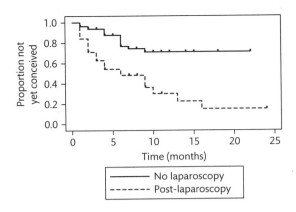

Figure 16.4 Conception without and following a laparoscopy in a women attending a subfertility clinic (data from Luthra *et al.* 1982).

(a) Survival curves are useful when subjects are followed up for different lengths of time;
(b) The effect of the woman's age on the difference in conception rates could be examined by Cox regression;
(c) The logrank test could be used to test the null hypothesis that the conception rates are the same;
(d) The method requires the assumption that women observed for a short time have the same conception pattern as women observed for a long time;
(e) The small vertical lines on the graph represent censored observations.

16.3 Patients with metastatic renal cell carcinoma were randomly assigned in a two to one ratio to receive everolimus 10 mg once daily (n = 272) or placebo (n = 138). The trial was halted after 191 progression events had been observed, 101 (37%) events in the everolimus group and 90 (65%) in the placebo group. The median duration of treatment was 95 days (range 12 to 315 days) in the everolimus group and 57 days (range 21 to 327) in the control group. The hazard ratio was 0.30, 95% CI 0.22 to 0.40, P< 0.0001, and median progression-free survival was 4.0 months (95% CI 3.7 to 5.5) months in the everolimus group vs. 1.9 (1.8 to 1.9) months in the control group (Motzer *et al.* 2008).
(a) The analysis assumes that the chance of progression in the everolimus group is the same throughout follow-up;

(b) If we followed all patients treated with everolimus, we estimate that, by a time between 3.7 and 5.5 months, half of them would have progressed;

(c) Everolimus patients in the trial were more likely to be observed to progress than were controls;

(d) The analysis assumes that the chance of progression in the everolimus group is a constant proportion of the chance of progression in the placebo group;

(e) We estimate that the rate at which events happened in the everolimus group was 0.30 times the rate in the placebo group.

16.4 Table 16.7 shows the results of an observational study following up asthmatic children discharged from hospital. From this table:

(a) the analysis could only have been done if all children had been readmitted to hospital;

(b) the proportional hazards model would have been better than Cox regression;

(c) boys have a shorter average time before readmission than do girls;

(d) the use of theophyline prevents readmission to hospital;

(e) children with several previous admissions have an increased risk of readmission.

16.5 Figure 16.5 shows time to diagnosis of breast cancer in women from families with a high risk of carrying the BRCA1 or BRCA2 genes, classified by the exon in which a mutation occurred:

(a) This graph shows the failure function;

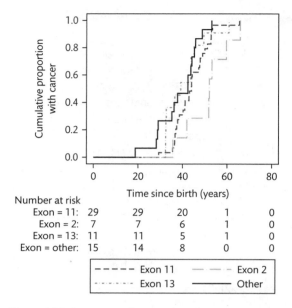

Number at risk				
Exon = 11:	29	29	20	1	0
Exon = 2:	7	7	6	1	0
Exon = 13:	11	11	5	1	0
Exon = other:	15	14	8	0	0

Figure 16.5 Proportion of women from families with a high risk of carrying the BRCA1 or BRCA2 genes diagnosed with breast cancer, by age, classified by the exon bearing a mutation (data from Al-Mulla *et al.* 2009).

(b) Exon 11 mutations are the largest group;

(c) As there are four groups, we could not do a logrank test;

(d) We could estimate differences between these groups using three hazard ratios;

(e) Only three women were observed at age 60 because all the others had developed breast cancer before that age.

Table 16.7 Cox regression of time to readmission for asthmatic children following discharge from hospital (data from Mitchell *et al.* 1994)

Variable	Coef.	Std. Err.	coef/se	P
Boy	−0.197	0.088	−2.234	0.026
Age	−0.126	0.017	−7.229	<0.001
Previous admissions (square root)	0.395	0.034	11.695	<0.001
Inpatient i.v. therapy	0.267	0.093	2.876	0.004
Inpatient theophyline	−0.728	0.295	−2.467	0.014

Number of observations = 1 024, χ^2 = 167.15, 5 d.f., P < 0.0001

16.7 Exercise: Survival after retirement

Tsai *et al.* (2005) studied the age at retirement and long-term survival of an industrial population, using a prospective cohort study. They wanted to know whether early retirement was associated with better survival. They noted that 'Some researchers had concluded that early retirement harms health, attributing this to illness before retirement or the change of life events associated with retirement. On the other hand, there is a widespread perception that early retirement is associated with longer life expectancy and that retiring later leads to early death. The possible health benefits of retirement, such as reduced role demand and a more relaxed lifestyle, have been postulated to improve longevity among people who retire early'.

The sample were past employees of Shell Oil who retired at ages 55, 60, and 65 between 1 January 1973 and 31 December 2003. They looked only at those who reached the age of 65 and they compared survival beyond that point. Figure 16.6 shows the survival after age 65 of subjects who retired early at age 55 compared with those who retired age at 65. The authors say that there was a consistently lower probability of survival for employees who retired at 55 (173 deaths) than for those who retired at 65 (462 deaths). This difference was not, however, statistically significant (P = 0.09, logrank test).

Women accounted for about 11% (10% among early retirees and 12% among those retiring at 65) of the study population during follow-up. More than half of early retirees who reached 65 (57% who retired at 55 and 53% who retired at 60) were in the high socioeconomic group, whereas less than half (44%) of those who retired at 65 were in this group. The authors used the Cox proportional hazards model to estimate the hazard ratios of death between the early and normal retirement groups, with adjustment for sex, calendar year of entry into the study, and socioeconomic group. After adjustment, employees who retired at 55 and were still alive at 65 had significantly higher mortality than those who retired at 65 (hazard ratio 1.37, 95% CI 1.09 to 1.73).

The authors concluded that retiring early at 55 or 60 was not associated with better survival than retiring at 65 in a cohort of past employees of the petrochemical industry. Mortality was higher in employees who retired at 55 than in those who continued working.

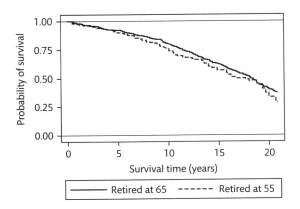

Figure 16.6 Survival beyond age 65 for Shell Oil employees who retired early at age 55 compared with those who retired age at 65 (reproduced from Tsai *et al.*, *The BMJ*, 'Age at retirement and long term survival of an industrial population: prospective cohort study', 331, 995, copyright 2005, with permission from BMJ Publishing Group Ltd).

16.1 What kind of graph is this? What assumptions are required about the data? Do you think they are plausible?

16.2 Why do you think the curves become steadily steeper as survival increases?

16.3 What is a logrank test and what can we conclude from this one?

16.4 What is the Cox proportional hazards model, what are its assumptions, and why was it used here?

16.5 Why do they say that employees who retired at 55 and were still alive at 65 had significantly higher mortality than those who retired at 65, when no P value is given?

16.6 Why did they adjust for socioeconomic group? What would we expect the effects of this adjustment to be?

16.7 Why did they adjust for sex, which is very similar in the early and late retirement groups? What would we expect the effect of this to be?

16.8 Why did they adjust for calendar year at entry, i.e. the year at which subjects became 65 years old?

16.9 The authors concluded that retiring early at 55 or 60 was not associated with better survival than retiring at 65 in a cohort of past employees of the petrochemical industry. Why do think they put the conclusion in this way, rather than concluding that early retirement was associated with worse survival?

17 Meta-analysis

17.1 What is a meta-analysis?

Meta-analysis is a statistical technique, or set of statistical techniques, for summarizing the results of several studies into a single estimate. Meta-analysis takes data from several different studies and produces a single estimate of the effect, usually of a treatment or risk factor. We improve the precision of an estimate by making use of all available data. Meta-analysis is often linked to systematic review and many systematic reviews include a meta-analysis, but not all. Some meta-analyses are not part of a systematic review, either, being planned to summarize several linked studies.

The Greek root 'meta' means 'with', 'along' 'after', or 'later', so here we have an analysis after the original analysis has been done. Boring pedants think that 'metanalysis' would have been a better word, and more euphonious, but we boring pedants can't have everything.

For us to do a meta-analysis, we must have more than one study which has estimated something, usually the effect of an intervention or of a risk factor. The participants, interventions, or risk factors, and settings in which the studies were carried out need to be sufficiently similar for us to say that there is something in common for us to investigate. We might not want do a meta-analysis of two studies, one of which was in adults and the other in children, for example. We must make a judgement that the studies do not differ in ways which are likely to affect the outcome substantially. We need outcome variables in the different studies which we can somehow get into a common format, so that they can be combined. Finally, the necessary data must be available. If we have only published papers, we need to get estimates of both the effect and its standard error from what is published in them, for example.

Meta-analysis can be done whenever we have more than one study addressing the same issue. The sort of subjects addressed in meta-analysis include:

- interventions: usually randomized trials to give treatment effect,

- epidemiological: usually case–control and cohort studies to give relative risk,

- diagnostic: combined estimates of sensitivity, specificity, positive predictive value,

- population estimates, such as prevalence.

In this chapter I shall concentrate on studies which compare two groups, but the principles are the same for other types of estimate.

Systematic review and accompanying meta-analysis has been a great advance in the study of medical evidence. At the time of writing, meta-analysis is a rapidly advancing field. There are many books on the subject; in preparing this chapter I relied heavily on Borenstein *et al.* (2009). The methods are implemented in readily available software. This changes too fast to make recommendations, but I used Stata and Comprehensive Meta Analysis 2. I hope that this chapter will enable readers to understand the meta-analyses they see and even to try their own. But meta-analysis can be complex and difficult; do not be afraid to seek help.

17.2 The forest plot

Figure 17.1 shows an example of a **forest plot**, a graphical representation of the results of a meta-analysis, in this case of the association between migraine and ischaemic stroke. A forest plot shows the estimate and associated confidence interval for each of the studies. In Figure 17.1,

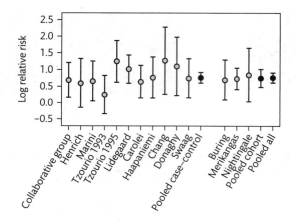

Figure 17.1 Meta-analysis of the association between migraine and ischaemic stroke (data from Etminan *et al.* 2005). (Log relative risks for case–control studies are in fact log odds ratios, Section 13.7.)

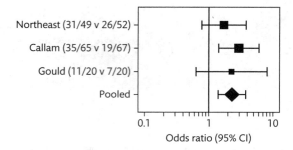

Figure 17.2 Meta-analysis of the effect of elastic multilayer high compression bandaging versus inelastic multilayer compression for venous leg ulcers (complete healing, after varying lengths of treatment) (data from Fletcher *et al.* 1997).

the grey circles represent the logarithms of the relative risks for the individual studies and the vertical lines their confidence intervals. It is called a forest plot because the vertical lines are thought to resemble trees in a forest. There are three pooled or meta-analysis estimates: one for all the studies combined, at the extreme right of the picture, and one each for the case–control and the cohort studies, shown as black circles. The pooled estimates have much narrower confidence intervals than any of the individual studies and are therefore much more precise estimates than any one study can give. In this case the study difference is shown as the log of the relative risk. The value for no difference in stroke incidence between migraine sufferers and non-sufferers is therefore zero, which is well outside the confidence interval for the pooled estimates, showing good evidence that migraine is a risk factor for stroke.

Figure 17.1 is a rather old-fashioned forest plot. The studies are arranged horizontally, with the outcome variable on the vertical axis in the conventional way for statistical graphs. This makes it difficult to put in the study labels, which are too big to go in the usual way and have been slanted to make them legible. The imprecise studies with wide confidence intervals are much more visible than those with narrow intervals and look the most important, which is quite wrong. The three meta-analysis estimates look quite unimportant by comparison. These

are distinguished by colour in the original, shaded in my version, but otherwise look like the other studies.

Figure 17.2 shows the results of a meta-analysis of elastic multilayer high compression bandaging versus inelastic multilayer compression for venous leg ulcers (Fletcher *et al.* 1997). The outcome variable is complete healing, after lengths of treatment which varied between the three trials. This is based on a graph which was actually published several years before the study shown in Figure 17.1, but is a more developed version of the forest plot. This forest plot has been rotated so that the outcome variable is shown along the horizontal axis and the studies are arranged vertically. The squares represent the odds ratios for the three individual studies and the horizontal lines their confidence intervals. This orientation makes it much easier to label the studies and also to include other information, here the numbers healed and treated in each group. The size of the squares can represent the amount of information which the study contributes. If they are not all the same size, their area should be proportional to the weight given to them, their contribution to the overall estimate. This depends at least partly on the standard error of the estimates and hence on the study sample sizes. This means that larger studies appear more important than smaller studies, as they are. A different point symbol is shown for the pooled estimate, a diamond rather than a square, making it easy to distinguish.

The horizontal scale in Figure 17.2 is logarithmic, labelling the scale with the numerical odds ratio rather than showing the logarithm itself. A vertical line is shown

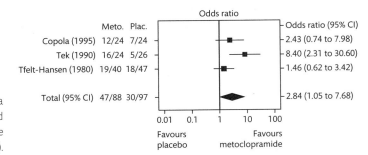

Figure 17.3 Graphical representation of a meta-analysis of metoclopramide compared with placebo in reducing pain from acute migraine (data from Colman *et al.* 2004).

at 1.0, the odds ratio for no effect, making it easy to see whether this is included in any of the confidence intervals.

Figure 17.3 shows a more evolved forest plot, showing the meta-analysis of three studies of metoclopramide for the treatment of migraine. On the right-hand side of Figure 17.3 are the individual trial estimates and the combined meta-analysis estimate in numerical form. On the left-hand side are the raw data from the three studies. The pooled estimate is now represented by a diamond or lozenge shape, making it much easier to distinguish from the individual study estimates than in Figure 17.1. The deepest point marks the position of the point estimate and the width of the diamond is the confidence interval. The choice of the diamond is now widely accepted, but other point symbols may yet be used for the individual study estimates. The vertical caps at the ends of the confidence interval lines have been dropped. I think this was a good idea; graphs like Figure 17.2 remind me of the view in Luke Skywalker's rear-view mirror.

17.3 Getting a pooled estimate

Most meta-analyses are done using the summary statistics representing the effect and its standard error in each study. We use the estimates of treatment effect for each trial and obtain the common estimate of the effect by averaging the individual study effects. We do not use a simple average of the effect estimates, because this would treat all the studies as if they were of equal value. Some studies have more information than others, e.g. are larger. We weight the trials before we average them. In this section we shall look at the simple case where we assume that each trial provides an estimate of the same

population value, what we call a **fixed effect model**. 'Effect' is singular, because there is assumed to be only one effect, which is estimated by each study. If we assume that the studies vary in what they estimate and that we want a mean value, we use a random effects model (Section 17.7). Here 'effects' is plural, because each study estimates a slightly different effect.

To get a weighted average, we must define weights which reflect the importance of the trial. The usual weights are the inverse variance weights:

$$\text{weight} = 1/\text{variance of trial estimate}$$
$$= 1/\text{standard error squared.}$$

We multiply each trial difference by its weight and add, then divide by sum of weights. If a study estimate has high variance, this means that the study estimate contains a low amount of information and the study receives low weight in the calculation of the common estimate. If a study estimate has low variance, the study estimate contains a high amount of information and the study has high weight in the common estimate. If we give the trials equal weight, setting all the weights equal to one, we get the ordinary average.

There are several different ways to produce the pooled estimate, some of which are discussed in Section 17.9. These are slightly different solutions to the same problem. The pooled estimates in Figure 17.1 were done using inverse variance weighting with the assumption that they all estimated the same effect. Those in Figure 17.3 were done by a different method, using a random effects model (Section 17.7). Having found the pooled estimate, it is straightforward to calculate a standard error and confidence interval for it and to test the null hypothesis that the pooled effect is zero.

17.4 Heterogeneity

Studies can differ in several ways, including participants, interventions, outcome definitions, and study design. These differences can produce **clinical heterogeneity**, meaning that the clinical question addressed by these studies is not the same for all of them. We have to consider whether we should be trying to combine them, or whether they differ too much for this to be a sensible thing to do. We detect clinical heterogeneity from the descriptions of the trial populations, treatments, and outcome measurements.

We may also have variation between studies in the true treatment effects or risk ratios, either in magnitude or direction. If this is greater than the variation between individual subjects would lead us to expect, we call this **statistical heterogeneity**. We detect statistical heterogeneity on purely statistical grounds, using the study data. Statistical heterogeneity may be caused by clinical differences between studies, i.e. by clinical heterogeneity, by methodological differences, or by unknown characteristics of the studies or study populations. Even if studies are clinically homogeneous there may be statistical heterogeneity.

To identify statistical heterogeneity, we can test the null hypothesis that the studies all have the same treatment (or other) effect in the population. The test looks at the differences between observed treatment effects for the trials and the pooled treatment effect estimate. We square these differences, divide each by the variance of the study effect, and then sum them. This statistic, usually denoted by Q, gives a chi-squared test with degrees of freedom = number of studies – 1. For the observational studies of migraine as a risk factor for stroke (Figure 17.1) we have 14 studies, $Q = 9.48$, d.f. = 13, P = 0.7. There is no evidence of heterogeneity. Inspection of Figure 17.1 also suggests that the studies are all estimating the same thing. All the study confidence intervals overlap and the common estimate falls within all them. There is nothing to suggest that the studies do not agree.

In the metoclopramide trials in Figure 17.3, the test for heterogeneity gives $Q = 4.91$, d.f. = 2, P = 0.086. This is not conventionally significant. Of course, a non-significant test does not imply that there is no heterogeneity, only that we have not demonstrated that there is heterogeneity. The test for heterogeneity has low power, particularly when the number of studies is small, as in this example. To compensate for the low power of the test, some researchers accept a larger P value as being significant, often using P < 0.1 rather than P < 0.05. This is what Colman *et al.* (2004) elected to do and they used a random effects model (Section 17.7).

If there is significant heterogeneity, then we have evidence that there are differences between the studies. It may therefore be invalid to pool the results and generate a single summary result. There are a number of possibilities:

- First, we could decide not to pool the study estimates at all. Instead, we would carry out a narrative review. We do not get any numerical estimate.

- Second, we could ignore the heterogeneity and analyse the data as described in Section 17.3, using a fixed effect model and assuming that the underlying effects are the same for all studies. As we shall see, this can result in a confidence interval which is too narrow and a pooled estimate which is difficult to interpret.

- Third, we could explore the heterogeneity and try to explain it and remove it. We may be able to find a variable or variables which explain this heterogeneity and so give our meta-analysis estimate depending on this variable.

- Fourth, we could allow for the heterogeneity in our analysis and produce a much wider confidence interval, using what is called a random effects model (Section 17.7).

17.5 Measuring heterogeneity

We can ask: how much heterogeneity is there? The chi-squared test provides a test of significance for heterogeneity, but it does not measure it. An index of heterogeneity can be defined as I^2 (Higgins *et al.* 2002), where

$$I^2 = 100\% \times \frac{Q - df}{Q}$$

and Q is the chi-squared heterogeneity statistic with df degrees of freedom. If I^2 is negative we set it to zero. The value which we expect chi-squared to have if there is no heterogeneity is equal to its degrees of freedom

(Appendix 7A). Hence I^2 is the percentage of the chi-squared statistic which is not explained by the variation within the studies. It represents the percentage of the total variation which is due to variation between studies. It is similar to the intraclass correlation coefficient (Section 11.13). For the migraine and stroke data,

$$I^2 = 100\% \times \frac{9.48 - 13}{9.48} = -37.1\%$$

This is negative, so we set I^2 to zero. For the metoclopramide data, we have

$$I^2 = 100\% \times \frac{4.91 - 2}{4.91} = 59.3\%$$

For interpreting I^2, Deeks *et al.* in chapter 9 of the Cochrane Handbook (Cochrane Collaboration 2013) suggest as a rough guide:

- 0% to 40%: might not be important;
- 30% to 60%: may represent moderate heterogeneity;
- 50% to 90%: may represent substantial heterogeneity;
- 75% to 100%: considerable heterogeneity.

I^2 can never actually reach 100% and values above 90% are very rare. Deeks *et al.* note that the importance of the observed value of I^2 depends on (i) magnitude and direction of effects and (ii) strength of evidence for heterogeneity (e.g. P value from the chi-squared test, or a confidence interval for I^2). Judgement is therefore involved here. We would interpret the $I^2 = 59.3\%$ for the metoclopramide analysis as moderate heterogeneity.

Table 17.1 shows a set of data with fairly obvious heterogeneity. These were collected in a systematic review

Table 17.1 Packed red cell transfusion after cardiac surgery with tranexamic acid compared with no treatment (data from Ngaage and Bland 2010)

Study	Tranexamic acid		Control		Odds ratio	95% CI
	No.	Transfusion	No.	Transfusion		
Penta de Peppo (1995)	15	1	15	3	0.29	0.03 to 3.12
Speekenbrink (1995)	15	14	15	11	5.09	0.50 to 52.29
Katsaros (1996)	104	11	106	27	0.35	0.16 to 0.74
Brown (1997)	30	8	30	20	0.18	0.08 to 0.55
Hardy (1998)	43	28	45	27	1.24	0.52 to 2.96
Mongan (1998)	75	19	30	20	0.17	0.07 to 0.43
De Bonis (2000)	20	3	20	4	0.71	0.14 to 3.66
Nuttal (2000)	45	16	43	21	0.58	0.25 to 1.36
Armellin (2001)	143	35	140	63	0.40	0.24 to 0.66
Zabeeda (2002)	25	9	25	25	0.01	0.00 to 0.21
Pleym (2003)	40	7	39	8	0.82	0.27 to 2.54
Andreasen (2004)	21	6	23	5	1.44	0.37 to 5.67
Diprose (2005)	60	20	60	27	0.61	0.29 to 1.28
Karski (2005)	147	24	165	41	0.59	0.34 to 1.04
Vanek (2005)	29	3	30	6	0.46	0.10 to 2.05
Santos (2006)	29	7	31	12	0.50	0.17 to 1.54
Baric (2007)	97	51	96	51	0.98	0.56 to 1.72

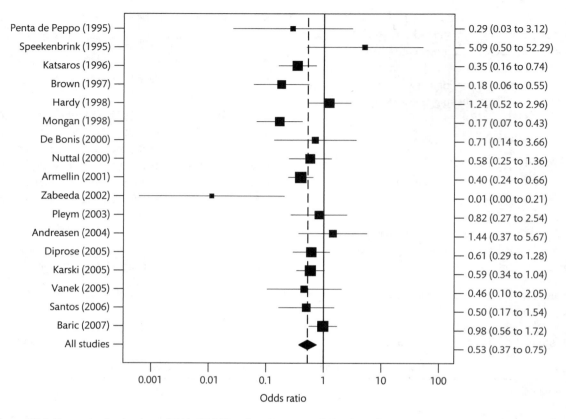

Figure 17.4 Forest plot for the data of Table 17.1 (data from Ngaage and Bland 2010).

of the effect of tranexamic acid during surgery. Table 17.1 shows the outcome variable 'need for blood transfusion'. There is a lot of variability in the number receiving transfusions in these trials and we might expect from this that there might be heterogeneity of effects. The forest plot reflects this (Figure 17.4). Some confidence intervals do not overlap at all, showing that they are unlikely to be estimating the same population value. The heterogeneity test gives $Q = 33.86$, d.f. $= 16$, $P = 0.006$, $I^2 = 52.7\%$, which would be interpreted as an estimate of moderate heterogeneity, with strong evidence that heterogeneity exists.

17.6 Investigating sources of heterogeneity

Heterogeneity comes about because the effects in the populations which the studies represent are not the same. We can look for possible explanations of this in variations in study characteristics. For example, there may be subsets of studies within which there is little heterogeneity. These may be defined by different categories of participants, such as hospital-based and community-based patients, or variations in treatments, such as different antibiotics being compared with none, or different study designs, cohort or case–control studies, or crossover or parallel groups trials. These subsets should be pre-specified, if possible, so as to avoid bias. For example, Sattar *et al.* (2010) reported a meta-analysis of 13 large trials of statins against placebo or no treatment (Table 17.2). They considered only the 91 140 participants who were non-diabetic at the start of the trial and looked at the increased risk of developing diabetes. The average follow-up was 4 years and 4 278 participants developed diabetes, 4.7%. Some of the data are shown in Table 17.2.

Table 17.2 Characteristics of and results from 13 trials of statins (data from Sattar et al. 2010)

Trial	Statin used and dose	Control treatment	Participant population	Number of non-diabetics	Odds ratio	95% confidence interval	Mean age at start	Mean BMI at start	Mean % reduction in LDL cholesterol achieved
ASCOT-LLA	Atorvastatin 10 mg	Placebo	Hypertension, CVD risk factors, no CHD	7773	1.14	0.89 to 1.46	63.0	28.6	34.8
AFCAPS/TexCAPS	Lovastatin 20–40 mg	Placebo	No CVD	6211	0.98	0.70 to 1.38	58.0	27.0	26.7
WOSCOPS	Pravastatin 40 mg	Placebo	No MI, raised cholesterol	5974	0.79	0.58 to 1.10	55.0	25.9	23.7
LIPID	Pravastatin 40 mg	Placebo	MI unstable angina in previous 3 years	6997	0.91	0.71 to 1.17	62.0	.	25
PROSPER	Pravastatin 40 mg	Placebo	Elderly people with CVD or at high risk	5023	1.32	1.03 to 1.69	76.0	26.5	30.7
MEGA	Pravastatin 10–20 mg	No treatment	No CVD, raised cholesterol, Japanese	6086	1.07	0.86 to 1.35	58.3	23.8	17.1
ALLHAT-LLT	Pravastatin 40 mg	No treatment	CHD or CHD risk factors	6087	1.15	0.95 to 1.41	66.4	29.0	18.1
GISSI PREV	Pravastatin 20 mg	No treatment	MI within past 6 months	3460	0.89	0.67 to 1.20	59.3	26.3	11.5
JUPITER	Rosuvastatin 20 mg	Placebo	No CVD	17802	1.26	1.04 to 1.51	66.0	28.4	50
CORONA	Rosuvastatin 20 mg	Placebo	Systolic heart failure (NYHA II–IV)	3534	1.14	0.84 to 1.55	73.0	27.0	45.1
GISSI HF	Rosuvastatin 10 mg	Placebo	Chronic heart failure (NYHA II–IV)	3378	1.10	0.89 to 1.35	67.0	26.7	34.9
HPS	Simvastatin 40 mg	Placebo	History of CVD	14573	1.15	0.98 to 1.35	65.0	27.2	29.4
4S	Simvastatin 20–40 mg	Placebo	Previous MI or angina	4242	1.03	0.84 to 1.28	58.6	25.9	36.7

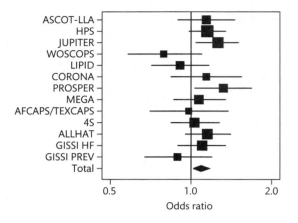

Figure 17.5 Forest plot for the meta-analysis of the data of Table 17.2 (data from Sattar *et al.* 2010).

Their meta-analysis is shown in Figure 17.5. The chi-squared test for heterogeneity gave $Q = 14.6$ with 12 degrees of freedom, $P = 0.3$, $I^2 = 11.2\%$. There is very little statistical heterogeneity. However, as Table 17.2 shows, there is considerable clinical heterogeneity. Sattar *et al.* investigated possible sources of heterogeneity, including drug used, age, body mass index, and reduction in LDL cholesterol achieved. Inspection of Table 17.2, which is arranged by statin used, shows that the effect is seen within each of the statins except lovastatin, represented by only one trial.

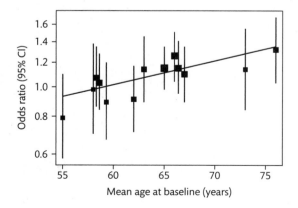

Figure 17.6 Odds ratio for developing diabetes after statin use against mean age at the start of the trial, with meta-regression line (data from Sattar *et al.* 2010).

Figure 17.6 shows a plot of odds ratio against mean age at the start of the trial. The regression line in Figure 17.6 was fitted by a method called **meta-regression**, which allows for variation within studies and between studies separately. We use a special form of regression because ordinary least squares regression would not allow for the uncertainty in the individual trial estimates. In this example, it would give a very similar regression equation but with narrower confidence intervals and smaller P values. (The term 'meta-regression' upsets boring pedants even more than does 'meta-analysis'. It is not a regression of regressions, but a regression applied to meta-analysis. 'Meta-analytic regression' would be better, but it is too late!) The regression in Figure 17.6 is statistically significant ($P = 0.02$) and after allowing for it the recalculated $I^2 = 0\%$, suggesting that age differences can explain all the statistical heterogeneity present. Similar analyses of the effects of body mass index (BMI) and LDL-cholesterol reduction achieved show increases in the odds ratio which are not statistically significant. Age, BMI, and cholesterol reduction achieved are all positively, but weakly, correlated between these trials.

17.7 Random effects models

We cannot always explain heterogeneity. We have already noted the clear heterogeneity in the tranexamic acid data of Table 17.1. This cannot be explained by the great variation in transfusion rate between the trials, as Figure 17.7 shows. The meta-regression is not significant ($P = 0.5$) and leaves $I^2 = 52.2\%$ after the adjustment. To estimate the average effect of tranexamic acid, we therefore have to use a method of estimation which allows for the variation between studies. This is the **random effects model**. In a random effects model, we regard each study as estimating a different effect and we then estimate the average effect over all studies. The study effects for all the studies which could be done form a population, of which the studies actually carried out are a sample. The mean of this population will be our best measure of the overall effect. We estimate both the variability between participants within the studies and the

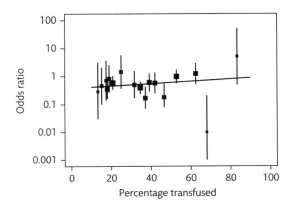

Figure 17.7 Odds ratio for transfusion with tranexamic acid against percentage of trial participants transfused, with meta-regression line (data from Ngaage and Bland 2010).

Table 17.3 Inverse variance weights for the data of Table 17.1 under the fixed effect and random effects models (data from Ngaage and Bland 2010)

Study	Fixed effect model	Random effects model
Penta de Peppo (1995)	0.67	0.58
Speekenbrink (1995)	0.71	0.61
Katsaros (1996)	6.61	2.58
Brown (1997)	3.12	1.79
Hardy (1998)	5.13	2.32
Mongan (1998)	4.54	2.19
De Bonis (2000)	1.42	1.06
Nuttal (2000)	5.26	2.34
Armellin (2001)	14.99	3.29
Zabeeda (2002)	0.45	0.41
Pleym (2003)	3.03	1.76
Andreasen (2004)	2.05	1.38
Diprose (2005)	7.03	2.64
Karski (2005)	12.16	3.13
Vanek (2005)	1.72	1.22
Santos (2006)	3.08	1.78
Baric (2007)	12.02	3.12

variation between studies. By contrast, the fixed effect model assumes that all the studies are estimating the same effect and only random variation between research participants leads the observed study effects to vary. In the random effects model, we estimate variance between studies, which is usually denoted by τ^2 (tau squared). There are several ways to estimate τ^2, the most popular of which is due to DerSimonian and Laird (1986). The variance of the estimated effect for a study is no longer given by the standard error squared, but by the standard error squared plus the inter-study variance. Using inverse variance weights, the weight of a study is no longer $1/SE^2$, but $1/(SE^2 + \tau^2)$. The effect of this is to make the weights less variable. Table 17.3 shows the inverse variance weights for the tranexamic acid data under the two models. Two things are apparent: the random effects weights are all smaller and the weights are much more similar. Random effects models give relatively less weight to large studies and more weight to small studies than do fixed effect models.

For the data of Table 17.1, the random effects estimated odds ratio = 0.53 (95% CI 0.38 to 0.75, P < 0.001), compared with the fixed effect estimated odds ratio = 0.54 (95% CI 0.47 to 0.67, P < 0.001). The main difference is that the random effects model gives a wider and, I think, more realistic confidence interval. The differences between models can be much greater, however.

The change in relative weight can even have the effect of changing the direction of estimated effects. Using a fixed effect model when it is not valid can have misleading results. On the other hand, if a fixed effect model is valid, a random effects model may result in a confidence interval which is unnecessarily wide and a P value which is unnecessarily large. Random effects models can be inefficient when a fixed effect model is valid. How do we decide between these two methods of meta-analysis? There is no universally accepted method for choosing. I think that the following approach is reasonable:

1 Irrespective of the numerical data, decide whether the assumption of a fixed effect model is plausible. Could the studies all be estimating the same effect? If not, consider a random effects model.

2 If fixed effect assumption is plausible, are the data compatible with it? We can do this using graphical methods, such as a forest plot, and analytical methods such as the chi-squared heterogeneity test and the I^2 statistic. If the fixed effect assumption looks compatible with the data, use a fixed effect model, otherwise consider random effects.

3 If we consider a random effects model, do the studies represent a population where the average effect is interesting? Do we want to pool them? If yes, then use a random effects model. If no, then do a narrative review and do not try to get a numerical estimate.

It is worth noting that random effects models in use at the time of writing do not take into account the uncertainty in the estimate of τ^2. As DerSimonian and Kacker (2007) note, it is difficult to determine an expression for the standard error of a pooled estimate involving the uncertainty that arises from the use of estimates of the within-study and between-study variances. This is why, when τ^2 is estimated to be zero, the confidence interval is the same as for a fixed effect model. It should really be wider to allow for the uncertainty in that zero estimate.

17.8 Continuous outcome variables

All the meta-analyses we have seen so far have had dichotomous outcome measures. Table 17.4 and Figure 17.8 shows a continuous outcome variable, blood loss measured in ml, from the systematic review of tranexamic acid in surgery (Ngaage and Bland 2010).

Table 17.4 Mean and standard deviation of blood loss (ml) during surgery reported in 12 trials comparing tranexamic acid with no treatment, where the standard deviation was available (data from Ngaage and Bland 2010)

Study name	Tranexamic acid			Control		
	Number	**Mean**	**SD**	**Number**	**Mean**	**SD**
Karski (1995)	99	610	125	48	980	220
Penta de Peppo (1995)	15	534	288	15	724	280
Speekenbrink (1995)	15	700	375	15	1 000	680
Katsaros (1996)*	104	474	244.75	106	906	525.08
De Bonis (2000)	20	573	164	20	739	228
Nuttal (2000)	45	600	300	43	800	450
Armellin (2001)	143	447	262	140	720	357
Zabeeda (2002)	25	194	135	25	488	238
Pleym (2003)	40	475	274	39	713	243
Karski (2005)	147	550	200	165	800	400
Abul-Azm (2006)	50	733	93	50	1 208	121
Baric (2007)	97	633	343	96	903	733

* Standard deviations calculated from standard error and sample size.

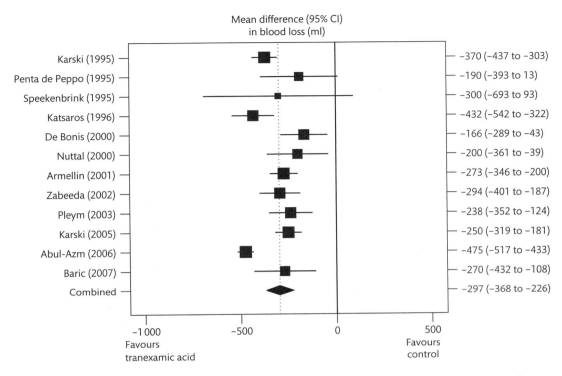

Figure 17.8 Mean reduction in blood loss due to tranexamic acid (adapted from Ngaage D and Bland M, 'Lessons from aprotinin: is the routine use and inconsistent dosing of tranexamic acide prudent? Meta-analysis of randomised and large matched observational studies', *European Journal of Cardiothoracic Surgery*, 2010, 37, 6, pp. 1375–1383, by permission of Oxford University Press and European Association for Cardio-Thoracic Surgery (EACTS)).

Figure 17.8 includes a vertical line through the treatment estimate, quite often added to forest plots. Here it is dotted, to distinguish it from the solid zero effect line. There are two main measures of effect in use for a continuous outcome variable: **mean difference**, and **standardized mean difference**. Mean difference is also referred as **weighted mean difference** or as the somewhat sinister '**WMD**', but the 'weighted' is redundant. All meta-analysis estimates are weighted. The mean difference takes the difference in effect, measured in the units of the original variable, and weights it by the inverse of the variance of the estimate. It is in the same units as the observations, which makes it easy to interpret. It is useful when the outcome is always the same measurement. These are usually physical measurements.

For the data of Table 17.4, there is clear heterogeneity, with confidence intervals for several pairs of individual studies not overlapping at all. Testing, we get $Q = 68.3$,

d.f. $= 11$, $P < 0.001$, $I^2 = 84\%$. We therefore used a random effects model and obtained an estimated mean reduction in mean blood loss $= -279$ ml, 95% CI $= -368$ to -226 ml. We can do this because blood loss is always measured as a volume of blood. In the same way, if we are evaluating treatments to lower high blood pressure, we are always going to be looking at blood pressure in mm Hg. We do not always have all the trials measuring the outcome in the same units. For example, Table 17.5 shows data for a meta-analysis of grip strength in studies comparing internal and external fixation for fractures of the wrist. The outcome variable was measured as Kg force. Grip strength varies greatly between people, and surgeons often dealt with this by making the measurement in both hands and then reporting the grip strength in the hand which had been injured as a percentage of the uninjured hand. Only Belloti reported strength in Kgf.

Table 17.5 Data for a meta-analysis of grip strength in wrist fracture (data supplied by Chinyelu Menekaya)

Study name	How reported	Internal fixation			External fixation		
		Number	Mean	SD	Number	Mean	SD
Harley 2004	% uninjured	90	19	15	79	25	15
Grewal 2005	% uninjured	86	16	24	97	16	29
Egol 2008	% uninjured	85	27.5	36	100	57	36
Abramo 2009	% uninjured	78	17	22	90	17	24
Wei 2009	% uninjured	66	19.7	19	69	34	17
Xu 2009	% uninjured	80.76	17.5	13	79.4	16.4	12
Belloti 2010	Kgf	5.6	8.2	48	5.8	8.9	48
Wilcke 2011	% uninjured	94	23.0	33?	85	16.4	30?

To combine these measurements, we need to convert them to a common unit and the one we use is the standard deviation of the measurement. We divide the effect estimate for the study by the standard deviation of the measurement, to give the standardized difference between the treatment means. This standardized difference is also called the effect size. We also divide the standard error of the difference by this standard deviation. We then find the weighted average as above. The forest plot and common estimate of the standardized difference is shown in Figure 17.9. This is useful when the outcome is not always the same measurement. It is often used for psychological scales. The common estimate is usually referred to as the **standardized mean difference** or **SMD**, though it is in fact, a mean of standardized differences.

There are several possibilities for the standard deviation we use as the unit. We could use the common standard deviation within groups for the study, as found in a two sample t test (Section 10.3), or the standard deviation in the control group, or if we have a baseline measurement before any treatment we can use the standard deviation of that. These are not interchangeable. For example, in the CADET study of collaborative care for depression in primary care (Richards *et al.* 2013), the standard deviation of the PHQ9 depression score at baseline was 5.13. After treatment the SD was 6.83 for

the treatment as usual group and for the collaborative care intervention group it was 7.32. This was because depression scores were all high at baseline and so were crowded at the top of the scale. They fell after treatment in both groups, spreading across the available range and so increasing the variability, and also some patients responded to treatment more than others. The intervention group had a lower mean score than the treatment as usual group, so these effects were greater for them. Which of these standard deviations we chose to use for standardization would affect the standardized mean difference. We should be consistent about this choice and try to use the same standard deviation for all studies in the meta-analysis.

The usual standard deviation used for standardization is the pooled within-groups standard deviation, as for a two sample t test. Dividing the observed difference by the pooled standard deviation gives **Cohen's d**. The problem is now that there are two sources of uncertainty: the estimates of the means and the estimate of the standard deviation. We can estimate the standard error of d as

$$\sqrt{\frac{n_1 + n_2}{n_1 n_2} + \frac{d^2}{2(n_1 + n_2)}}$$

and use this to produce the inverse variance weights either for a fixed effect model as in Section 17.3 or a

Standardized difference (95% CI)

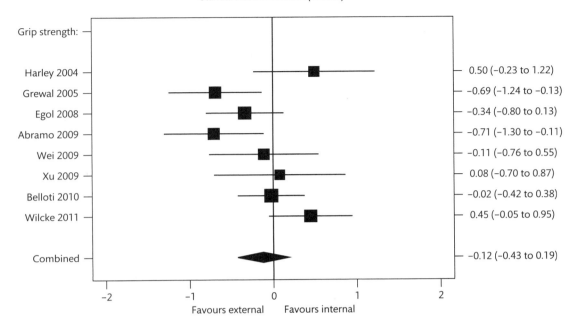

Figure 17.9 Meta-analysis of grip strength in eight trials of external vs. internal fixation of wrist fractures (data supplied by Chinyelu Menekaya).

random effects model as in Section 17.7. Figure 17.9 shows a random effects meta-analysis for the grip strength data, using Cohen's d. There is a small bias in d as an estimate of the standardized difference in the whole population. This can be corrected by **Hedges' g**. We use a factor J defined by

$$J = 1 - \frac{3}{4df - 1}$$

where df is the degrees of freedom for the within-groups variance, usually $n_1 + n_2 - 2$. Then $g = J \times d$ and $SE(g) = J \times SE(d)$. All these calculations are built into software. J increases as the sample size increases, reaching 0.98 for two groups of size 20, so the difference in the estimate will be small unless the studies themselves are small. For the blood loss data of Table 17.4, the random effects estimate of the pooled treatment effect using Cohen's d is −1.21 (95% CI = −1.62 to −0.79) standard deviations, using Hedges' g it is −1.20 (95% CI = −1.61 to −0.78). For this example there is not much difference, as we would expect given the sample sizes.

Another method found in meta-analysis software is **Glass's delta**. This standardizes by the control group standard deviation rather than the pooled standard deviation from the control group and the intervention group. For the tranexamic acid blood loss data, the pooled standardized difference estimated by Glass's method is −0.98 (95% CI = −1.30 to −0.66). Inspection of Table 17.4 shows that the standard deviations in the control groups tend to be larger than those in the tranexamic acid group, so dividing only by the control SDs results in a smaller standardized estimate. Neither the pooled SD nor the control SD approach are incorrect, they are just different, but the contrast illustrates that it is important to know what you want to standardize for and to stick to it.

What effect size in standard deviations are we looking for? Cohen (1992) suggested that 0.8 should be considered a large effect, 0.5 a moderate effect, and 0.2 a small effect. Jacob Cohen was a psychologist, a field where it is difficult to measure anything directly and many important quantities have no true units. These recommended interpretations of effect size values are now widely accepted in many fields, including medicine. Cohen said that he thought 0.5, half a standard deviation, represented 'an effect likely to be visible to the naked eye of a careful observer', and that 0.2 was 'noticeably smaller than medium but not so small as to be trivial'. The large effect size was the same distance above the medium as small was below it. Figure 17.10 shows pairs of Normal curves 0.2, 0.5, and 0.8 standard deviations apart. Effect size = 0.5 does not look very big. To help see what this might mean, imagine that the variable is a measurement where high values are detrimental, such as blood pressure or cholesterol. The higher the value, the worse it is. As Figure 17.10 shows, an effect size of 0.5 would mean that, for a Normal distribution, 31% of observations would be expected to fall above the control median, rather than 50%. So even a small shift in mean may result in a marked reduction in the proportion in the most dangerous part of the range.

The data required for meta-analysis of a continuous outcome variable are, for each study, the difference between means and its standard error or the mean, standard deviation, and sample size for each group. Unfortunately, the required data are not always available for all published studies. Studies sometimes report different measure of variation. In the systematic review of tranexamic acid and blood loss (Ngaage and Bland 2010), we identified 11 studies which gave means and standard deviations and one where we had the standard errors for the means. It is easy to calculate the standard deviation from the standard error of the mean; we just multiply by the square root of the sample size. These studies are included in Table 17.4. We found a further eight studies where blood loss was reported but standard deviations were not given. Instead, authors reported statistics such as the median, range, and interquartile range. We estimated the means and standard deviations as best we could from these data. We presented pooled estimates for the first 12 trials, as above, and for all 20 trials including the estimated ones.

We need to extract the information required, means and standard deviations, from what is available in the paper. These might be:

- standard errors – this is straightforward, as we know the formula for the standard error and so provided we have the sample sizes we can calculate standard deviation.

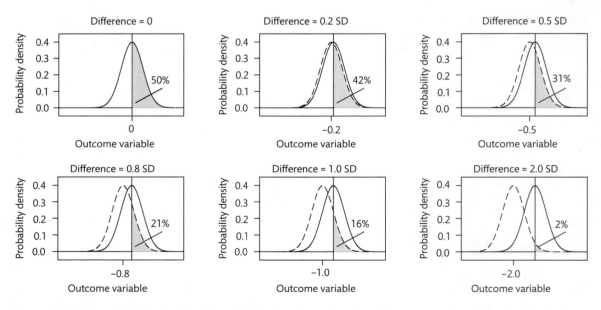

Figure 17.10 The meaning of effect size: Normal distribution curves at varying distances apart measured in standard deviations, with area above the median of the first curve indicated for the second.

- confidence intervals – this is also straightforward, as we can work back to the standard error, the width of the confidence interval = four standard errors approximately.

- 95% reference ranges (Section 20.7) – again straightforward, as the reference range is four standard deviations wide.

- medians – we can use the difference between two medians as an estimate of the difference between two means, but it is not a very good one. The median is less well estimated than the mean and if the distribution is skew they will not be the same. The bias should be in the same direction in the two groups, but will not necessarily be the same size.

- interquartile ranges – here we need an assumption about distribution; provided this is Normal we know how many standard deviations wide the IQR should be, but of course this is often not the case.

- range – this is very difficult, as not only do we need to make an assumption about the distribution, but the estimates are unstable and affected by outliers.

- significance test – sometimes we can work back from a t value to the standard error, but not from some other tests, such as the Mann–Whitney U test.

- P value – if we have a t test we can work back to a t value hence to the standard error, but not for other tests, and we need the exact P value. The authors may be particularly annoying and give a non-significant P value, so you can estimate the test statistic and hence the absolute magnitude of the difference in standard deviations, but not the direction of the difference.

- 'Not significant' or 'P < 0.05' – this is hopeless.

Research, like politics, is an art of the possible and sometimes we have to use a bit of ingenuity, make the best of what we have, and present the results with appropriate caution. One strategy which is sometimes used is to borrow the standard deviation from studies where this was published. This would have been a dubious method in the tranexamic acid review, because the standard deviations varied greatly.

17.9 Dichotomous outcome variables

For a dichotomous outcome measure we can present the comparison of two proportions as a relative risk or risk ratio (RR), odds ratio (OR), or absolute risk difference (ARD) and its reciprocal, the number needed to treat (NNT) (Sections 8.6, 8.7, 13.7). Most of the examples of meta-analyses given so far reported dichotomous outcomes. The stroke and migraine study reported relative risk, the others all reported odds ratios.

Both odds ratios and relative risks are presented logarithmically. In Figure 17.1 the log relative risks are shown, though in fact the log relative risks for case–control studies are log odds ratios. They have used the odds ratio as an approximation to the relative risk, as described in Section 13.7. In Figures 17.2 to 17.5 the odds ratios are shown on logarithmic scales (Section 5.10). There are two reasons for this. First, ratios equal to 2 and to $\frac{1}{2}$ are shown as equal and opposite on a logarithmic scale. Hence similar differences in opposite directions are shown similarly. Second, as we saw in Sections 8.6 and 13.7, the confidence intervals for both odds ratios and relative risks are symmetrical on the log scale. On the natural scale, the graph can look very cramped on the left, as Figure 17.11 shows. Even if we cut off most of the confidence interval for the Speekenbrink study and use an arrow to indicate that it goes on to the right, things are not much better (Figure 17.12). (The common practice of indicating in forest plots that the confidence intervals go on beyond the scale of the graph with a right or left arrow irritates me, as it means that to see the data I have to re-draw the graph mentally. Graphs are intended to convey information quickly.)

Odds ratios are symmetrical in another way, too. If we reverse the characteristic being analysed, and estimate the effect of tranexamic acid on not being transfused, the combined odds ratio for not being transfused is 1.89. The reciprocal of this is 1/1.89 = 0.53, the odds ratio for being transfused. We get the same answer. This is not the case for relative risk. The combined estimate of relative risk for transfusion is 0.67. The combined estimate of relative risk for no transfusion is 1.18 and 1/1.18 = 0.85. We get a different answer. As we saw in Section 13.7, the odds ratio has several mathematical advantages over the

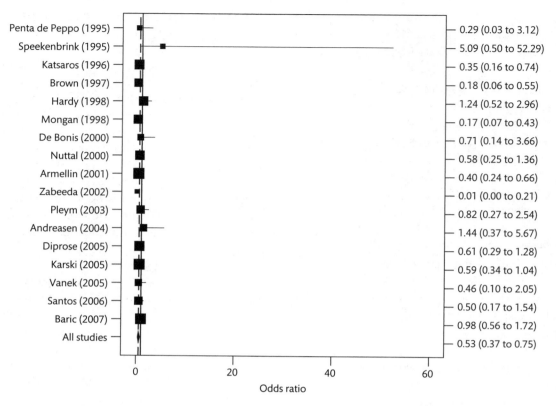

Figure 17.11 Figure 17.4 redrawn with a natural scale for odds ratio (data from Ngaage and Bland 2010).

risk ratio. Another disadvantage of risk ratios is that if the lower of the two risks is large, the risk ratio must be close to 1.0. In Table 17.1, some studies have much higher transfusion rates than others. This leads to increased heterogeneity. For the odds ratio, $I^2 = 53\%$, for the risk ratio $I^2 = 68\%$. As we saw in Section 15.10, if we want to adjust the effect of interest for other variables, it is easiest to use the odds ratio and logistic regression. If some of our studies have done an adjustment and we want to use the adjusted estimate in the meta-analysis, we must use odds ratios. On the other hand, the risk ratio has more intuitive interpretation and may be preferred for this reason.

We can also analyse risk differences. These can be even more heterogeneous, because if the risks are small or large the differences are going to be smaller than differences for risks in the middle of the scale. For the meta-analysis of the risk differences for the transfusion data, $I^2 = 73\%$, greater than for either odds ratios or risk

ratios. Risk differences appear to be the approach used least frequently in the medical research literature, odds ratios being the most frequent.

For odds ratios, three methods of pooling are routinely used: the inverse variance method for log odds ratios described above, the Mantel–Haenszel method, and the Peto method. The inverse variance method is straightforward, using the study standard error described in Section 17.3 as a basis for the weights. The analyses in Figures 17.2 and 17.3 were done in this way. Everything is done using the log odds ratios and the results are antilogged at the end. One problem with the log odds ratio is when a frequency is zero. Neither the log odds ratio nor the standard error will be defined, because zero has no logarithm or reciprocal. The usual correction is to add 0.5 to all four frequencies for that study. The study will then have a very large standard error which will reflect the uncertainty. The software will do this automatically. For the tranexamic transfusion data, this happens for the

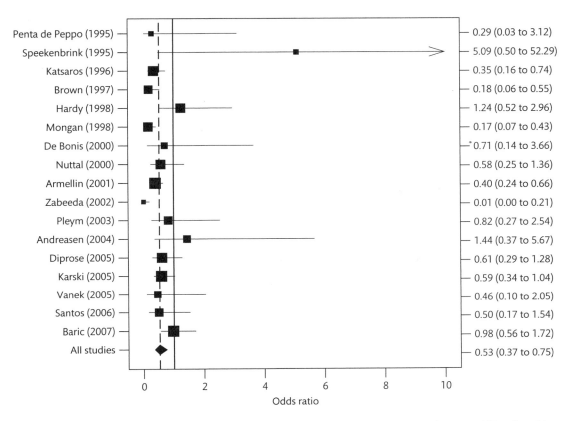

Figure 17.12 Figure 17.4 redrawn with a natural scale for odds ratio and one confidence interval truncated (data from Ngaage and Bland 2010).

study of Zabeeda. By the inverse variance method, the pooled odds ratio was 0.53 (95% CI 0.37 to 0.75).

The Mantel–Haenszel method was developed for epidemiologists to combine the odds ratios calculated for more than one 2 by 2 table. It is a weighted combination of odds ratios, rather than log odds ratios. It is a fixed effect analysis. For the tranexamic acid transfusion data, the Mantel–Haenszel pooled odds ratio estimate is 0.53 (95% CI 0.37 to 0.75).

The Peto method is a weighted log odds ratio, which uses a slightly different estimate of the odds ratio and of its standard error to that used in the usual method. It, too, is at heart a fixed effect method, but a random effects version has been adapted. For the tranexamic acid data, we have the estimated odds ratio = 0.51 (95% CI 0.35 to 0.73). It agrees fairly closely with the other two methods. The Peto method does not have any problems with zero frequencies and might be preferred if this is a problem.

For relative risk, there are two main methods: inverse variance and a development of the Mantel–Haenszel method. For the tranexamic acid transfusion data, the inverse variance method gives RR = 0.68 (95% CI 0.54 to 0.85) and the Mantel–Haenszel method gives RR = 0.67 (0.53 to 0.85), so there is little to choose between them.

It is unusual to use risk difference in a meta-analysis, because of the problem that the potential difference is so dependent on the risk in the control group. For a treatment that lowers risk, such as tranexamic acid, the maximum possible magnitude of the difference is equal to the control risk, so small risks enforce small differences. If researchers do feel the need to do use risk difference in a meta-analysis, the inverse variance method can be used. For the tranexamic acid data, the estimated risk difference, TA minus control, is –0.14 (95% CI –0.22 to –0.06). Because a constant odds ratio is much more plausible than a constant risk difference, some researchers advocate carrying out the meta-analysis using the odds ratio, then using the pooled estimate of the odds ratio to estimate the risk difference for a few possible values of the control risk. If the treatment and control proportions are p_t and p_c, the odds ratio is given by

$$o = \frac{p_t/(1-p_t)}{p_c/(1-p_c)} = \frac{p_t(1-p_c)}{p_c(1-p_t)}$$

Hence we can calculate the risk difference, $p_t - p_c$, from p_c and o by

$$op_c - op_c p_t = p_t - p_t p_c$$

$$op_c = p_t(1 - p_c + op_c)$$

$$p_t = \frac{op_c}{1 - p_c + op_c}$$

$$p_t - p_c = \frac{op_c}{1 - p_c + op_c} - p_c$$

For some specimen values of the control proportion, we can estimate the treatment difference and its confidence interval by putting the estimated pooled odds ratio and its confidence interval into this formula. For the tranexamic acid transfusion data, OR = 0.53 (95% CI 0.37 to 0.75), and the risk difference for specimen control proportions would be:

Control proportion	p_t	Difference	95% CI
0.80	0.68	−0.12	(−0.20 to −0.05)
0.50	0.35	−0.15	(−0.22 to −0.07)
0.20	0.12	−0.08	(−0.11 to −0.04)

These calculations can also be done starting with the risk ratio, which would work well if the risks themselves were fairly small. If the risk ratio is r, the risk difference = $p_c(1 - r)$.

The number needed to treat has an attractive intuitive interpretation, but also has some awkward mathematical properties (Section 8.7). For this reason, it is not used directly in a meta-analysis. It is calculated from $1/(p_c - p_t)$

and, as above, the risk difference is best calculated indirectly from the odds ratio or risk ratio (Smeeth et al. 1999). For the number needed to be treated with tranexamic acid to prevent one blood transfusion, we would have:

Control proportion	p_t	NNT	95% CI
0.80	0.68	8.3	(5.1 to 20.0)
0.50	0.35	6.5	(4.5 to 8.3)
0.20	0.12	12.0	(8.8 to 23.8)

17.10 Time to event outcome variables

Time to event data (Chapter 16) are straightforward to deal with in meta-analysis, provided we have the estimated hazard ratio (Section 16.4) and a measure of its precision (the standard error of the log hazard ratio or some derivative of it, such as a confidence interval) for all studies. We can then analyse the log hazard ratio using the inverse variance method to get a pooled estimate and antilog to get the pooled hazard ratio. For example, Maier et al. (2005) analysed the time to visual field loss or deterioration of the optic disc, or both, in patients with ocular hypertension (Figure 17.13). The patients were randomized to pressure lowering treatment or to no treatment. A hazard ratio which is equal to 1.0 represents no difference between the groups. The hazard ratio is active treatment divided by no treatment, so if the hazard ratio is less than one, this means that the risk of visual field loss is less for patients given pressure lowering treatment. As for risk ratios and odds ratios, hazard ratios are analysed by taking the log and the results are shown on a logarithmic scale on the forest plot.

The problems arise when the hazard ratio is not available. We may have Kaplan–Meier survival curves (Section 16.2) or logrank tests (Section 16.3). Parmar et al. (1998); Tudur et al. (2001); Williamson et al. (2002); and Tierney et al. (2007) describe methods for estimating log hazard ratios and their standard errors from such statistics. This is not a trivial job, be warned.

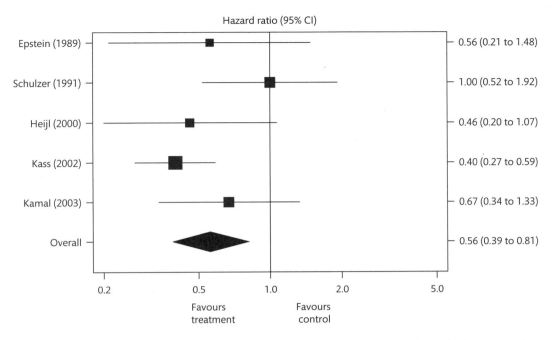

Figure 17.13 Example of time to event data: time to visual field loss or deterioration of optic disc, or both, among patients randomized to pressure lowering treatment vs. no treatment in ocular hypertension (data from Maier *et al.* 2005).

17.11 Individual participant data meta-analysis

In view of the problems in extracting the desired information from published studies, some researchers try to get the raw data from each study. We may then combine them into a single dataset and analyse them like a single, multi-centre study. Alternatively, we may use the individual data to extract the corresponding summary statistics from each study then proceed as we would using summary statistics from published reports. Either way, we call this an **individual participant data meta-analysis**, **individual patient data meta-analysis**, or **IPD data meta-analysis**. Stewart and Tierney (2002) give a good account of how this is organized.

There are several advantages:

- data can be checked and cleaned in a consistent way,
- we can perform statistical analyses in the same way in each study,
- we can adjust for covariates much more easily.

The disadvantage is that it involves many more people than a literature-based meta-analysis and, as a result, takes longer and costs more.

For an example, we can look at the review comparing four layer bandage with short stretch bandage for the treatment of venous leg ulcers (O'Meara *et al.* 2009). Some published trials had reported the proportion healed at some fixed follow-up time, different in different studies, and we wanted to use the full available follow-up in a time to event analysis. This had already been done for a fairly large trial in the department (Nelson *et al.* 2004; Iglesias *et al.* 2004). A search was done to identify trials and authors were contacted. We asked triallists to provide anonymized baseline and outcome data for each randomized patient, including those excluded from their own analyses, to maintain randomized groups and to provide as complete a dataset as possible for the meta-analysis. All data were systematically checked for completeness, duplication, consistency, feasibility, and integrity of randomization. Queries were resolved by discussion with the relevant triallist. Six published trials were

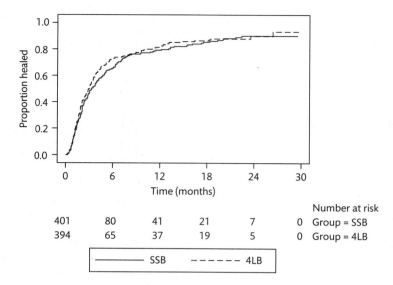

Figure 17.14 Results of an individual participant data meta-analysis comparing time to healing of venous leg ulcers between compression supplied by short stretch bandages (SSB) and four layer bandages (4LB) (data from O'Meara *et al.* 2009).

identified. For one all data had been destroyed, as they had for the one unpublished trial found. We obtained data from the other five trials, 797 out of 887 patients ever randomized (89.9%). We analysed the data as a single dataset, allowing for trial as a fixed effect by a five level factor (Section 15.8). Figure 17.14 shows the Kaplan–Meier curves (Section 16.2) for the whole dataset. After adjustment for ulcer duration and ulcer area, the hazard ratio for bandage type was 1.31 (95% CI 1.09 to 1.58, P = 0.005), providing clear evidence that the four layer bandage resulted in faster healing.

17.12 Publication bias

One of the great problems with systematic review is that not all studies carried out are published. Those which are published may be different from those which are not. Research with statistically significant results may be more likely to be submitted and published than work with null or non-significant results. Any experienced researcher will tell you that they have not published all their results and that they have not published some because they were negative and did not appear interesting. I have certainly done this, in my salad days, when I was green in judgement. Any medical statistician will tell you that they have done a stack of analyses for clinical researchers

which never saw the press. People change jobs, have other things to do, it is inevitable. This is known as the **file drawer problem**, the dull stuff is left in the filing cabinet rather than being published. Furthermore, research with statistically significant results is likely to be published more prominently than work with null or non-significant results, for example in English, in higher impact journals. To make things worse, well designed and conducted research is less likely to produce statistically significant results than badly designed and conducted research. Combining only published studies may lead to an over-optimistic conclusion.

As many meta-analyses are done as part of a systematic review, the detection of publication bias is closely linked to meta-analysis and specialized meta-analysis software is where the methods for this are found. There are graphical and analytical methods to detect publication bias, as for many other deviations from assumptions. I think that graphical methods are more useful, as analytical methods are not powerful for small numbers of primary studies. Graphical methods can still warn us of the possibility of bias, even though we cannot be sure that it is present.

The main graphical method for identifying publication bias is the use of funnel plots. A **funnel plot** is a plot of effect size against sample size or some other indicator of the precision of the estimate. Figure 17.15 shows some

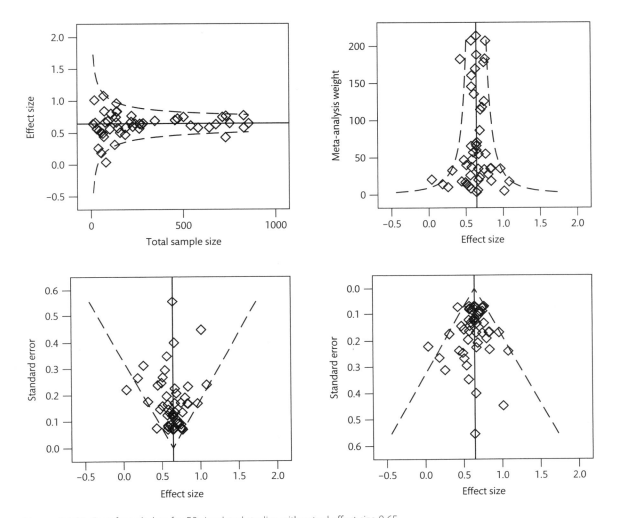

Figure 17.15 Four funnel plots for 50 simulated studies with actual effect size 0.65.

styles of funnel plot for 50 simulated studies. The first panel shows the original funnel plot, with effect size on the vertical axis and sample size in each group on the horizontal axis. There is a horizontal line through the pooled effect and dashed lines at 1.96 standard errors on either side of this. We expect most of the effect estimates to be between the outer lines and to be distributed symmetrically about the central line. The second panel shows the effect size plotted against the meta-analysis weight rather than the sample size. The effect size has been plotted on the horizontal axis, as in a forest plot (Section 17.2). Both styles may be seen in the literature. The third panel shows effect size plotted against standard error. This gives the outer limits as straight lines and is the most popular method at the time of writing. The fourth panel shows the standard error scale reversed, so that the values increase down the scale. This version is implemented in some popular meta-analysis software. Figure 17.16 shows the same 50 simulated studies where the non-significant effects have been highlighted in the first panel and omitted in the second panel, showing publication bias. The graph appears asymmetrical when the non-significant studies do not get published.

Figure 17.17 shows a funnel plot for the tranexamic acid transfusion data. This appears to be fairly symmetrical, with nothing to suggest that there was any

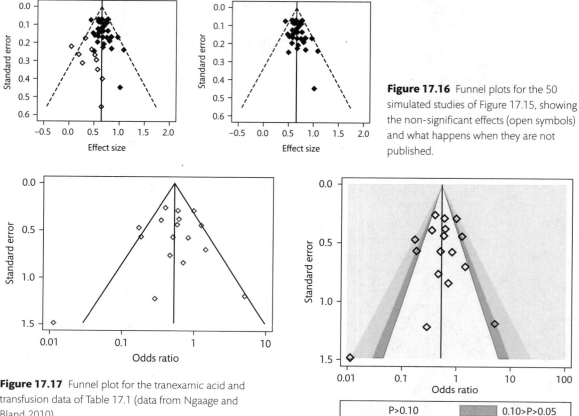

Figure 17.16 Funnel plots for the 50 simulated studies of Figure 17.15, showing the non-significant effects (open symbols) and what happens when they are not published.

Figure 17.17 Funnel plot for the tranexamic acid and transfusion data of Table 17.1 (data from Ngaage and Bland 2010).

Figure 17.18 Contour enhanced funnel plot for the tranexamic acid and transfusion data of Table 17.1 (data from Ngaage and Bland 2010).

publication bias in that review. Figure 17.18 shows a variant on this plot (Peters *et al.* 2008), with shaded contours marking areas where observations would be likely or unlikely to be if there were no asymmetry and a fixed effect model were valid. Although there are several points in the low-probability zones, they appear to be symmetrically so.

Figure 17.19 shows a funnel plot from data by a review by Torgerson and Bell-Syer (2001). This shows some studies which had published the results for fractures and others which had not, but were obtained for the review. This certainly suggests that among the studies which carried low weight in the meta-analysis, those which were published were reporting a bigger reduction in the risk of fracture than were the studies which were not published.

Publication bias is only one of the possible explanations for asymmetry in a funnel plot (Sterne *et al.* 2011).

We may have bias due to selective reporting in published studies, either of outcome variables which show the biggest difference or of analyses which produce the lowest P values, though both of these could be argued to be just other aspects of publication bias. Poor methodology may lead to inflated estimates of effects in small studies. There may be a genuine relationship, where small studies tend to include participants who are particularly suited to the treatment or be done by clinicians particularly committed to it. There may be some relationship between the estimate and its standard error, for example if we have greatly varying odds ratios.

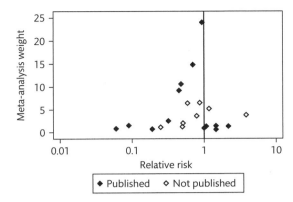

Figure 17.19 Funnel plot showing the relative risk of fracture non-vertebral fractures for women on hormone replacement therapy, published and unpublished data (data from Torgerson and Bell-Syer 2001).

There are several significance tests which have been developed to identify funnel plot asymmetry: Begg's and Mazumdar's test (Begg and Mazumdar 1994), Egger's test (Egger *et al.* 1997) and a variant due to Tang and Liu (2000) can be used for any kind of outcome variable, several others have been developed for dichotomous outcome variables only. All ask: 'Is the study estimate related to the size of the study or standard error?'. The Egger test appears to have greater power than the Begg test. For example, in their meta-analysis of the effect of breast feeding in infancy on blood pressure in later life, Owen *et al.* (2003) published a funnel plot (Figure 17.20) and

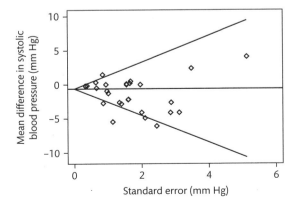

Figure 17.20 Funnel plot for 27 differences in mean blood pressure, systolic pressure for people who were breastfed minus those who were not (data from Owen *et al.* 2003).

reported that 'The Egger test was significant (P = 0.033) for publication bias but not the Begg test (P = 0.186)'. The Begg and Mazumdar test is non-parametric, which reduces its power, but even so the discrepancy is large. The funnel plot appears to show some departure from symmetry and Owen *et al.* (2003) concluded: 'Selective publication of small studies with positive findings may have exaggerated claims that breast feeding in infancy reduces systolic blood pressure in later life. The results of larger studies suggest that feeding in infancy has at most a modest effect on blood pressure ...'.

Sterne *et al.* (2011) recommend the Egger test. I shall omit the details, but will note that you need quite a lot of studies, certainly more than 10, to make these tests worthwhile at all. For example, Begg and Mazumdar (1994) say that their test is 'fairly powerful with 75 studies, moderate power with 25 studies'. Even 25 studies is a pretty large meta-analysis. Two other methods you may come across are Rosenthal's and Orwin's fail-safe N methods. These predict the number of studies with a null effect that would need to be added to make the significant result of the meta-analysis non-significant.

Table 17.6 shows another set of observational data, the estimated reduction in birthweight associated with passive smoking by the mother. Figure 17.21 shows a funnel plot. This plot shows the pooled estimate, too. There appears to be some asymmetry in the graph. The Begg and Mazumdar test produced P = 0.3 and the Egger test produced P = 0.04, so again we have different conclusions from the tests. I think there is evidence of publication bias. Here publication bias might be expected. There have been many studies of birthweight and many have collected data on smoking by the parents. Some of these may not have analysed for passive smoking, others may have analysed for it but either not published it at all or published it with little prominence, as many potential risk factors would be considered. In these studies, low prominence is more likely if the difference is small, negative, or not significant. The funnel plot shows a lack of studies in the small sample, negative results region, where they might be expected if the review had obtained all the studies which had been carried out. Hence we may be missing studies which would lower the overall effect.

Can we correct for the effects of publication bias using the data we have? One possible approach is the **trim**

Table 17.6 Estimated differences between the mean birthweights for non-smoking mothers not exposed to the cigarette smoke of others, and the mean birthweights for mothers who were passive smokers (data from Peacock et al. 1998)

Study	Number	Estimated reduction in birth-weight (g)	(95% CI) (g)	Standard error (g)
Rubin et al. (1986)	500	60*		47.4**
Martin et al. (1986)	2 473	24	(−13 to 60)	21.3
Haddow et al. (1988)	1 231	108		30.2**
Lazzaroni et al. (1990)	647	38	(−31 to 107)	41.7
Ogawa et al. (1991)	5 336	11	(−11 to 32)	14.5
Mathai et al. (1992)	994	63	(12 to 114)	33.6
Zhang et al. (1993)	1 785	30*	(−7 to 66)	25.1
Martinez et al. (1994)	907	34	(5 to 63)	35.2
Mainous et al. (1994)	1 173	84	(15 to 153)	31.0
Eskenazi et al. (1995)	2 243	45	(−36 to 125)	22.4
Peacock et al. (1998)	818	6.7	(−84 to 97)	31.4

* Estimated from a rate per pack per day, as the difference for half a pack.
** Estimated by taking the SD of birthweight as 500 g.

and fill method of Duval and Tweedie (2000). To quote them: 'Simply put, we trim off the asymmetric outlying part of the funnel after estimating how many studies are in the asymmetric part. We then use the symmetric remainder to estimate the true centre of the funnel and then replace the trimmed studies and their missing counterparts around the centre. The final estimate of the true mean, and also its variance, are then based on the filled funnel plot'.

Figure 17.22 shows the birthweight data after trim and fill. The method estimates how many extra studies might be needed to make the funnel plot symmetrical

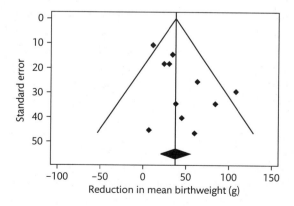

Figure 17.21 Funnel plot for the reduction in mean birthweight associated with passive smoking (data from Peacock et al. 1998).

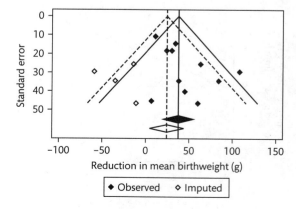

Figure 17.22 Funnel plot for the reduction in mean birthweight associated with passive smoking showing the effect of trim and fill (data from Peacock et al. 1998).

about the common estimate. We then drop that num-·
ber of studies to make the plot more symmetrical. We
recalculate the common estimate and repeat. Once we
have a symmetrical plot about its own common estimate, we put the deleted observations back and impute
some more observations, reflections of these about the
last common estimate. Finally we calculate the common
estimate and its confidence interval again. The original
estimated mean reduction in birthweight was 38 g (95%
CI 21 to 55 g), and after the trim and fill procedure the
estimated mean was 24 g (95% CI 5 to 44 g). Mean
birthweight is about 3 400 g in Caucasian populations,
so either estimate would tell us that the effect was quite
small. The estimated bias is in the direction predicted.

Other methods proposed to estimate the effect of
publication bias are selection models and the use of
meta-regression. In a selection model, we try to model
the selection process that determines which results are
published. With only the published papers to go on, this
is going to be pretty difficult. The regression approach
uses study characteristics, e.g. quality score, sample size,
etc., to predict outcome. We then estimate the outcome
we would get from the best studies.

A note of caution should be sounded. These methods
require large numbers of studies. They are not powerful
in most meta-analyses. Furthermore, a relationship between trial outcome and sample size may not result from
publication bias. As noted above, small trials may differ
in nature, e.g. have more intensive treatment or treatment by more committed clinicians (i.e. more committed
to the technique, not to their patients!). Furthermore,
publication bias may not result from significance or sample size. Researchers or sponsors may simply not like
the result. Many healthcare researchers are healthcare
professionals but amateur researchers, with other de-
mands on their attention (e.g. their patients). It is easy
for them not to publish their work. It is better to think of
these methods as a way of exploring possibilities than to
produce definitive answers.

17.13 Network meta-analysis

Network meta-analysis (Lumley 2002) is used when
we have trials of more than two treatments, where

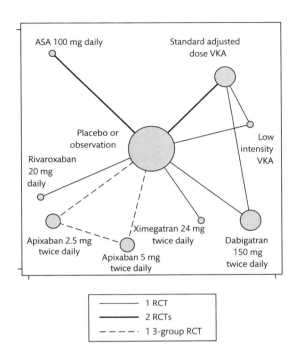

Figure 17.23 Evidence network for recurrence of venous
thromboembolism (data from Castellucci *et al.* 2013). (ASA =
aspirin, VKA = Vitamin K antagonists.)

the treatment comparisons vary between trials. For example, Figure 17.23 shows the network of trials of oral
anticoagulants and antiplatelet drugs given to prevent
the recurrence of venous thromboembolism (Castellucci
et al. 2013). There are 11 trials which involve eight active treatment regimens and placebo or no treatment.
We can use these to get an estimate of the difference between any pair of treatments, even though there might
be no trial comparing them directly. For example, we
have the difference ASA 100 mg daily minus placebo
and the difference standard adjusted dose VKA minus
placebo. The difference between these is ASA 100 mg
daily minus standard adjusted dose VKA, because (ASA
– placebo) – (VKA – placebo) = ASA – placebo – VKA
+ placebo = ASA – VKA. If this were all we had, we
could estimate the differences for the each pair of trials by standard meta-analysis and then the standard
error for the difference between them by the square
root of the sum of the standard errors squared. The network meta-analysis also enables the information from

the trials comparing standard adjusted dose VKA with low intensity VKA and comparing low intensity VKA with placebo, and the trials comparing standard adjusted dose VKA with dabigatran and comparing dabigatran with placebo, to provide information to improve this estimate. The other trials can provide information about variability to further improve the estimate of the confidence interval.

There is almost certain to be clinical heterogeneity and so random effects models are used. The approach is often Bayesian (Chapter 22), but there is more than one possibility and results may not be consistent. Details are beyond this introduction, but Mills *et al.* (2013) point out some of the pitfalls. For another example of a network meta-analysis see Exercise 22.11.

17.14 Multiple choice questions: Meta-analysis

(Each answer is true or false.)

17.1 Figure 17.24 shows a graph similar to one published in a systematic review of a bundled intervention of decolonization and prophylaxis to decrease Gram positive surgical site infections after cardiac or orthopaedic surgery. In Figure 17.24:
(a) the figure shows the results of a meta-analysis;
(b) the risk ratios are shown on a logarithmic scale;
(c) the horizontal lines represent confidence intervals;
(d) the study by Jog shows a significant advantage for the intervention;
(e) this is a forest plot.

17.2 In Figure 17.24:
(a) the squares represent the observed treatment ratios for the trials;
(b) the areas of the squares depend on the weight given to each study;
(c) studies with long horizontal lines should be given most weight in the meta-analysis;
(d) there is clear evidence of a relationship between the intervention and surgical site infection;
(e) none of the individual trials was big enough to detect the difference which might exist between these two treatments.

17.3 Figure 17.24 comes with the following information: 'Test for heterogeneity: $\tau^2 = 0.00$, $\chi^2 = 4.50$, d.f. = 6, P = 0.61, $I^2 = 0\%$.' The Methods section tells us 'Pooled

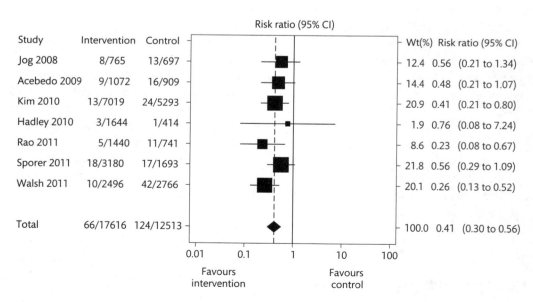

Figure 17.24 Bundle intervention to prevent surgical site infections caused by Gram positive bacteria. All studies were observational (data from Schweizer *et al.* 2013).

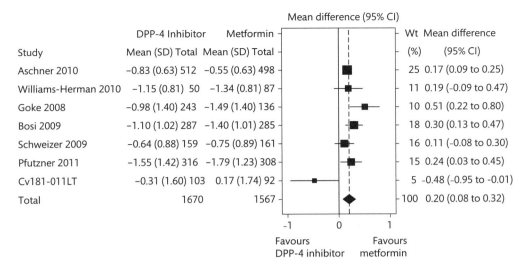

Figure 17.25 Weighted mean difference in change in HbA1c (%) from baseline comparing DPP-4 inhibitors and metformin in type 2 diabetes (data from Karagiannis *et al.* 2012).

relative risk estimates from random effect models are presented'. This tells us that:

(a) there is strong evidence for heterogeneity;

(b) a fixed effects analysis would give the same estimates;

(c) τ^2 and I^2 are inconsistent;

(d) the plot suggests considerable heterogeneity;

(e) the chi-squared statistic is less than its expected value if there were no heterogeneity.

17.4 Karagiannis *et al.* (2012) reported a systematic review and meta-analysis of a group of drugs called dipeptidyl peptidase-4 inhibitors for the treatment of type 2 diabetes. Figure 17.25 shows the result of a comparison with the standard drug, metformin. The test for heterogeneity gave

$\tau^2 = 0.01$, $\chi^2 = 9.14$, d.f. = 6, P = 0.17, $I^2 = 34\%$. The test for overall effect was $z = 3.40$, P < 0.001:

(a) the differences are measured in standard deviations;

(b) there is heterogeneity apparent in Figure 17.25;

(c) a random effects model would be appropriate here;

(d) there is good evidence that metformin is superior to the average effect of DPP-4 inhibitors;

(e) the horizontal scale is logarithmic.

17.5 Figure 17.26 shows data from a systematic review of the effects of beta blockers on mortality in patients with heart failure and reduced ejection fraction (Chatterjee *et al.* 2013). In Figure 17.26:

(a) Figure 17.26(a) shows a funnel plot;

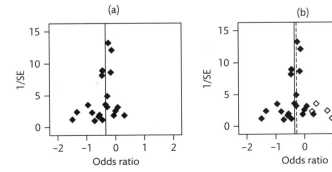

Figure 17.26 Effects of beta blockers on mortality in patients with heart failure and reduced ejection fraction (data from Chatterjee *et al.* 2013).

(b) there is nothing in Figure 17.26(a) to suggest there might be publication bias;

(c) Figure 17.26(b) shows the results of a trim and fill analysis;

(d) the smallest studies are at the top of the plot;

(e) possible publication bias appears to have little effect on the estimate of treatment effect.

17.15 Exercise: Dietary sugars and body weight

Te Morenga, Mallard, and Mann (2012) carried out a systematic review and meta-analyses of randomized controlled trials and cohort studies of the impact of dietary sugars and body weight. The question is whether reducing or increasing intake of dietary sugars influences measures of body fatness in adults, and whether the existing evidence provides support for the recommendation to reduce intake of free sugars. In this exercise we will look at some of the analyses for the randomized trials in adults. In these trials, participants in the intervention arm were advised to decrease or increase their intake of sugars, or foods and drinks containing sugars, usually with the recommendation to increase or decrease other forms of carbohydrate.

17.1 Figure 17.27 shows the effect of decreasing free sugars on body fatness in adults. What is the outcome measure of this meta-analysis and what type of outcome variable is this? What is the effect measure?

17.2 What kind of a graph is Figure 17.27 and what do the squares, horizontal lines, and diamond each represent? Why are the squares of different sizes?

17.3 In Figure 17.27, the line for 'Smith 1996' has an arrowhead on the right end. What is the purpose of this? Do you think it was a sensible thing to do?

17.4 Te Morenga et al. (2012) give the following information for Figure 17.27: 'Test for heterogeneity: $\tau^2 = 0.04$, $\chi^2 = 4.85$, d.f. = 4, P = 0.30, $I^2 = 17\%$'. What is heterogeneity in this context and what is each part of this statement telling us?

17.5 Te Morenga et al. (2012) used an inverse variance model with random effects to estimate the analysis weights and the combined estimate of difference in mean body weight. What does this mean and what reasons might there be for using a random effects model?

17.6 Figure 17.28 shows the effect of increasing dietary sugars on body weight in adults. Trials are divided into those with shorter and longer duration, with combined estimates for each group as well as for all trials. What feature of the plot suggests that there is much greater heterogeneity for the short trials in Figure 17.28 than there is in Figure 17.27?

17.7 For Figure 17.28, Te Morenga et al. (2012) give three tests for heterogeneity. For trials < 8 weeks: $\tau^2 = 0.20$, $\chi^2 = 30.39$, d.f. = 7, P < 0.0001, $I^2 = 77\%$. For trials > 8 weeks: $\tau^2 = 0.00$, $\chi^2 = 0.56$, d.f. = 1, P = 0.46, $I^2 = 0\%$.

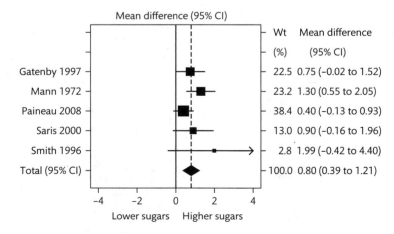

Figure 17.27 Differences in mean body weight (Kg) in trials where the intervention group were asked to decrease their intake of sugars (data from Te Morenga et al. 2012).

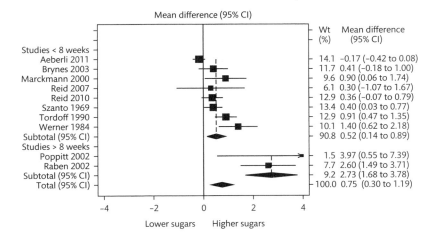

Figure 17.28 Differences in mean body weight (Kg) in trials where the intervention group were asked to increase their intake of sugars (data from Te Morenga *et al.* 2012).

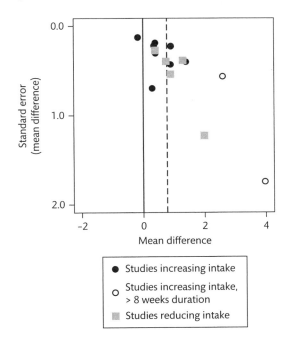

Figure 17.29 Plot of standard error (order reversed) against difference in mean body weight for 15 trials of sugar increase or decrease. The dashed line indicates the pooled estimate for all trials (data from Te Morenga *et al.* 2012).

For all trials: $\tau^2 = 0.35$, $\chi^2 = 50.93$, d.f. = 9, P < 0.0001, $I^2 = 82\%$. What do these tell us about heterogeneity and the effect of trial duration upon it?

17.8 What do you think of the use of the arrowhead in Figure 17.28?

17.9 What kind of plot is Figure 17.29 and what is its purpose?

17.10 Te Morenga *et al.* (2012) reported that 'the Egger's test for bias was significant (P = 0.001)'. What does this add to Figure 17.29?

17.11 Te Morenga *et al.* (2012) report that there was 'significant heterogeneity between the relatively short term crossover trials with small variances and the longer term parallel trials with larger variances'. How might this influence the interpretation of Figure 17.29?

17.12 The combined estimate of the difference in mean body weight for all 15 trials was 0.78 kg (95% CI 0.43 to 1.12), more sugar producing more weight. After adjustment using the trim and fill method, the estimated difference was reduced to 0.50 kg (95% CI 0.18 to 0.81, correcting an apparent typographical error in the original). What is 'trim and fill' and how should we interpret this?

18 Determination of sample size

18.1 Estimation of a population mean

One of the questions most frequently asked of a medical statistician is 'How large a sample should I take?'. In this chapter we shall see how statistical methods for deciding sample sizes can be used in practice as an aid in designing investigations. To illustrate the principles, the methods we shall use are large sample methods, that is, they assume that large sample methods will be used in the analysis and so take no account of degrees of freedom. It is possible to do this, however, and some of the many software packages available for sample size calculation do allow for small sample methods of analysis. Also, as well as the formulae-led approach described here, there is increasing interest in simulation methods to estimate sample sizes.

We can use the concepts of standard error and confidence interval to help decide how many subjects should be included in a sample. If we want to estimate some population quantity, such as the mean, and we know how the standard error is related to the sample size, then we can calculate the sample size required to give a confidence interval with the desired width. The difficulty is that the standard error may also depend either on the quantity we wish to estimate, or on some other property of the population, such as the standard deviation. We must estimate these quantities from data already available, or carry out a pilot study to obtain a rough estimate. The calculation of sample size can only be approximate anyway, so the estimates used to do it need not be precise.

If we want to estimate the mean of a population, we can use the formula for the standard error of a mean,

$s/\sqrt{n}$, to estimate the sample size required. For example, suppose we wish to estimate the mean FEV1 in a population of young men. We know that in another study FEV1 had standard deviation $s = 0.67$ litre (Section 4.8). We therefore expect the standard error of the mean to be $0.67/\sqrt{n}$. We can set the size of standard error we want and choose the sample size to achieve this. We might decide that a standard error of 0.1 litre is what we want, so that we would estimate the mean to within $1.96 \times 0.1 = 0.2$ litre. Then: SE $= 0.67/\sqrt{n}$, $n = 0.67^2/SE^2 = 0.67^2/0.1^2 = 45$. We can also see what the standard error and width of the 95% confidence interval would be for different values of n:

n	standard error	95% confidence interval
10	0.212	±0.42
20	0.150	±0.29
50	0.095	±0.19
100	0.067	±0.13
200	0.047	±0.09
500	0.030	±0.06

So that if we had a sample size of 200, we would expect the 95% confidence interval to be 0.09 litre on either side of the sample mean (1.96 standard errors), whereas with a sample of 50 the 95% confidence interval would be 0.19 litre on either side of the mean.

To do these calculations there are now many good software packages available. As these things change rapidly, I will not give recommendations, but if you search the World Wide Web you will find several good programs available free and some very comprehensive commercial packages.

18.2 Estimation of a population proportion

When we wish to estimate a proportion we have a further problem. The standard error depends on the very quantity which we wish to estimate. We must guess the proportion first. For example, suppose we wish to estimate the prevalence of a disease, which we suspect to be about 2%, to within 5%, i.e. to the nearest 1 per 1 000. The unknown proportion, p, is guessed to be 0.02 and we want the 95% confidence interval to be 0.001 on either side, so the standard error must be half this, 0.000 5.

$$0.000\,5 = \sqrt{\frac{p(1-p)}{n}} = \sqrt{\frac{0.02(1-0.02)}{n}}$$

$$n = \frac{0.02(1-0.02)}{0.000\,5^2} = 78\,400$$

The accurate estimation of very small proportions requires very large samples. This is a rather extreme example and we do not usually need to estimate proportions with such accuracy. A wider confidence interval, obtainable with a smaller sample is usually acceptable. We can also ask 'If we can only afford a sample size of 1 000, what will be the standard error?'

$$\sqrt{\frac{0.02(1-0.02)}{1\,000}} = 0.004\,4$$

The 95% confidence limits would be, roughly, $p \pm 0.009$. For example, if the estimate were 0.02, the 95% confidence limits would be 0.011 to 0.029. If this accuracy were sufficient, we could proceed.

These estimates of sample size are based on the assumption that the sample is large enough to use the Normal distribution. If a very small sample is indicated it will be inadequate and other methods must be used which are beyond the scope of this book.

18.3 Sample size for significance tests

We often want to demonstrate the existence of a difference or relationship as well as wanting to estimate its magnitude, as in a clinical trial, for example. We base these sample size calculations on significance tests, using the power of a test (Section 9.9) to help choose the sample size required to detect a difference if it exists. The power of a test is related to the postulated difference in the population, the standard error of the sample difference (which in turn depends on the sample size), and the significance level, which we usually take to be $\alpha = 0.05$. These quantities are linked by an equation which enables us to determine any one of them given the others. We can then say what sample size would be required to detect any given difference. We then need to decide what difference we need to be able to detect. This might be a difference which would have clinical importance, or a difference which we think the treatment may produce.

Suppose we have a sample which gives an estimate d of the population difference μ_d. We assume d comes from a Normal distribution with mean μ_d and has standard error SE(d). Here d might be the difference between two means, two proportions, or anything else we can calculate from data. We are interested in testing the null hypothesis that there is no difference in the population, i.e. $\mu_d = 0$. We are going to use a significance test at the α level, and want the power, the probability of detecting a significant difference, to be P.

I shall define u_α to be the value such that the Standard Normal distribution (mean 0 and variance 1) is less than $-u_\alpha$ or greater than u_α with probability α. For example, $u_{0.05} = 1.96$. The probability of lying between $-u_\alpha$ and u_α is $1 - \alpha$. Thus u_α is the two sided α probability point of the Standard Normal distribution, as shown in Table 7.2.

If the null hypothesis were true, the test statistic $d/\mathrm{SE}(d)$ would be from a Standard Normal distribution. We reject the null hypothesis at the α level if the test statistic is greater than u_α or less than $-u_\alpha$, 1.96 for the usual 5% significance level. For significance we must have:

$$\frac{d}{\mathrm{SE}(d)} < -u_\alpha \text{ or } \frac{d}{\mathrm{SE}(d)} > u_\alpha$$

Let us assume that we are trying to detect a difference such that d will be greater than 0. The first alternative is then extremely unlikely and can be ignored. Thus we must have, for a significant difference: $d/\mathrm{SE}(d) > u_\alpha$ so $d > u_\alpha \mathrm{SE}(d)$. The critical value which d must exceed is $u_\alpha \mathrm{SE}(d)$.

Now, d is a random variable, and for some samples it will be greater than its mean, μ_d, for some it will be less than its mean. The sample difference d is an observation from a Normal distribution with mean μ_d and variance $SE(d)^2$. We want d to exceed the critical value with probability P, the chosen power of the test. The value of the Standard Normal distribution which is exceeded with probability P is $-u_{2(1-P)}$ (see Figure 18.1). $(1 - P)$ is often represented as β (beta). This is the probability of failing to obtain a significant difference when the null hypothesis is false and the population difference is μ_d. It is the probability of a Type II error (Section 9.4). The value which d exceeds with probability P is the mean minus $-u_{2(1-P)}$ standard deviations: $\mu_d - u_{2(1-P)}SE(d)$. Hence for significance this must exceed the critical value, $u_\alpha SE(d)$. This gives

$$\mu_d - u_{2(1-P)}SE(d) = u_\alpha SE(d)$$

Putting the correct standard error formula for d into this equation will yield the required sample size. We can rearrange it as

$$\mu_d^2 = \left(u_\alpha + u_{2(1-P)}\right)^2 SE(d)^2$$

This is the condition which must be met if we are to have a probability P of detecting a significant difference at the α level. We shall use the expression $(u_\alpha + u_{2(1-P)})^2$ a lot, so for convenience I shall denote it by $f(\alpha, P)$. Table 18.1 shows the values of the factor $f(\alpha, P)$ for different values of α and P. The usual value used for α is 0.05, and P is usually 0.80, 0.90, or 0.95.

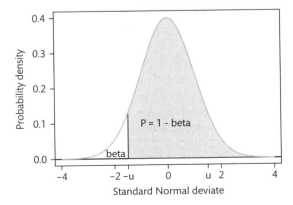

Figure 18.1 Relationship between P, β (beta), and $u = u_{2(1-P)}$.

Table 18.1 Values of $f(\alpha, P) = (u_\alpha + u_{2(1-P)})^2$ for different P and α, for large sample tests

Power, P	Significance level, α	
	0.05	**0.01**
0.50	3.8	6.6
0.70	6.2	9.6
0.80	7.9	11.7
0.90	10.5	14.9
0.95	13.0	17.8
0.99	18.4	24.0

Sometimes we do not expect the new treatment to be better than the standard treatment, but hope that it will be as good. We want to test treatments which may be as good as the existing treatment because the new treatment may be cheaper, have fewer side effects, be less invasive, or under our patent. We cannot use the power method based on the difference we want to be able to detect, because we are not looking for a difference. What we do is specify how different the treatments might be in the population and still be regarded as equivalent, and design our study to detect such a difference. This can get rather complicated and specialized, so I shall leave the details to Machin et al. (1998).

I have mentioned the superiority of confidence intervals to significance tests (Section 9.12). Most major medical journals have in their instructions to authors that the results of randomized clinical trials should be reported in the form of confidence intervals for differences rather than significance tests. However, despite telling triallists not to rely on significance tests, we continue to estimate the sample size based on a significance test, which we then tell them not to do. Why we do this is a mystery to me and I repeatedly argue against it (Bland 2009), but if you want a research grant you will need to do this.

18.4 Comparison of two means

When we are comparing the means of two samples, sample sizes n_1 and n_2, from populations with means

μ_1 and μ_2, with the variance of the measurements being σ^2, we have $\mu_d = \mu_1 - \mu_2$ and

$$SE(d) = \sqrt{\frac{\sigma^2}{n_1} + \frac{\sigma^2}{n_2}}$$

so the equation becomes:

$$(\mu_1 - \mu_2)^2 = f(\alpha, P)\sigma^2 \left(\frac{1}{n_1} + \frac{1}{n_2}\right)$$

For example, suppose we want to compare biceps skinfold in patients with Crohn's disease and coeliac disease, following up the inconclusive comparison of biceps skinfold in Table 10.4 with a larger study. We shall need an estimate of the variability of biceps skinfold in the population we are considering. We can usually get this from the medical literature or, as here, from our own data. If not we must do a pilot study, a small preliminary investigation to collect some data and calculate the standard deviation. For the data of Table 10.4, the within-groups standard deviation is 2.3 mm. We must decide what difference we want to detect. In practice this may be difficult. In my small study the mean skinfold thickness in the Crohn's patients was 1 mm greater than in my coeliac patients. I will design my larger study to detect a difference of 0.5 mm. I shall take the usual significance level of 0.05. I want a fairly high power, so that there is a high probability of detecting a difference of the chosen size should it exist. I shall take 0.90, which gives $f(\alpha, P) = 10.5$ from Table 18.1. The equation becomes:

$$0.5^2 = 10.5 \times 2.3^2 \times \left(\frac{1}{n_1} + \frac{1}{n_2}\right)$$

We have one equation with two unknowns, so we must decide on the relationship between n_1 and n_2. I shall try to recruit equal numbers in the two groups:

$$0.5^2 = 10.5 \times 2.3^2 \times \left(\frac{1}{n} + \frac{1}{n}\right)$$

$$n = \frac{10.5 \times 2.3^2 \times 2}{0.5^2} = 444.36$$

and I need 444 subjects in each group.

It may be that we do not know exactly what size of difference we are interested in. A possible approach is to look at the size of the difference we could detect using different sample sizes, as in Table 18.2. This done by putting different values of n in the sample size equation. However, if we are planning a clinical trial which we want to give us a clear answer to help decide whether to introduce a new treatment, the difference we are looking for should be the smallest difference which would convince clinicians to adopt the new treatment. What we should not do is to decide the sample size that we think we can get, work out the difference we would be powered to detect, then claim that this is the difference we actually wanted to detect in the first place. Grant committees can spot that sort of thing and are not impressed.

If we measure the difference in terms of standard deviations, we can make a general table. Table 18.3 gives the sample size required to detect differences between two equally sized groups. Altman (1991) gives a neat graphical method of calculation.

We do not need to have $n_1 = n_2 = n$. We can calculate $\mu_1 - \mu_2$ for different combinations of n_1 and n_2. The size of difference which would be detected, in terms of standard deviations, is given in Table 18.4. We can see

Table 18.2 Difference in mean biceps skinfold thickness (mm) detected at the 5% significance level with power 90% for different sample sizes, equal groups (data from Maugdal *et al.* 1985)

Size of each group, *n*	Difference detected with probability 0.90	Size of each group, *n*	Difference detected with probability 0.90
10	3.33	200	0.75
20	2.36	500	0.47
50	1.49	1 000	0.33
100	1.05		

Table 18.3 Sample size required in each group to detect a difference between two means at the 5% significance level with power 90%, using equally sized samples

Difference in standard deviations	n	Difference in standard deviations	n	Difference in standard deviations	n
0.01	210 000	0.1	2 100	0.6	58
0.02	52 500	0.2	525	0.7	43
0.03	23 333	0.3	233	0.8	33
0.04	13 125	0.4	131	0.9	26
0.05	8 400	0.5	84	1.0	21

Table 18.4 Difference (in standard deviations) detectable at the 5% significance level with power 90% for different sample sizes, unequal groups

n_2	n_1						
	10	**20**	**50**	**100**	**200**	**500**	**1 000**
10	1.45	1.25	1.13	1.08	1.05	1.03	1.03
20	1.25	1.03	0.85	0.80	0.75	0.75	0.73
50	1.13	0.85	0.65	0.55	0.50	0.48	0.48
100	1.08	0.80	0.55	0.45	0.40	0.35	0.35
200	1.05	0.75	0.50	0.40	0.33	0.28	0.25
500	1.03	0.75	0.48	0.35	0.28	0.20	0.18
1 000	1.03	0.73	0.48	0.35	0.25	0.18	0.15

from this that what matters is the size of the smaller sample. For example, if we have 10 in group 1 and 20 in group 2, we do not gain very much by increasing the size of group 2; increasing group 2 from 20 to 100 produces less advantage than increasing group 1 from 10 to 20. In this case the optimum is clearly to have samples of equal size.

The previous text enables us to compare independent samples. When we have paired observations, as in a cross-over trial, we need to take into account the pairing. If we have data on the distribution of differences, and hence their variance, s_d^2, the standard error of the mean difference is $SE(d) = \sqrt{s_d^2/n}$. If we do not, but have an estimate of the correlation, r, between repeated measurements of the quantity over a time similar to that

proposed, then $SE(d) = \sqrt{2s^2(1-r)/n}$, where s is the usual standard deviation between subjects. If we have neither of these, which happens often, we need a pilot study. As we need about 20 subjects for such a study, and many cross-over trials are of this order (Section 2.7), we could carry out a small trial. The difference will either be so large that we have the answer, or, if not, we will have sufficient data with which to design a much larger study.

18.5 Comparison of two proportions

Using the same approach, we can also calculate the sample sizes for comparing two proportions. If we have two samples with sizes n_1 and n_2 from Binomial populations with proportions p_1 and p_2, the difference is $\mu_d = p_1 - p_2$, the standard error of the difference between the sample proportions (Section 8.6) is:

$$SE(d) = \sqrt{\frac{p_1(1-p_1)}{n_1} + \frac{p_2(1-p_2)}{n_2}}$$

If we put these into the previous formula we have:

$$(p_1 - p_2)^2 = f(\alpha, P) \left(\frac{p_1(1-p_1)}{n_1} + \frac{p_2(1-p_2)}{n_2} \right)$$

The size of the proportions, p_1 and p_2, is important, as well as their difference. (The significance test implied here is similar to the chi-squared test for a 2 by 2 table). When the sample sizes are equal, i.e. $n_1 = n_2 = n$, we have

$$n = \frac{f(\alpha, P)(p_1(1-p_1) + p_2(1-p_2))}{(p_1 - p_2)^2}$$

There are several slight variations on this formula. Different computer programs may therefore give slightly different sample size estimates.

Suppose we wish to compare the survival proportion with a new treatment with that with an old treatment, where it is about 60%. What values of n_1 and n_2 will have 90% chance of giving significant difference at the 5% level for different values of p_2? For $P = 0.90$ and $\alpha = 0.05$, $f(\alpha, P) = 10.5$. Suppose we wish to detect an increase in the survival proportion on the new treatment to 80%, so $p_2 = 0.80$, and $p_1 = 0.60$, using equally sized samples.

$$n = \frac{10.5 \times (0.8(1-0.8) + 0.6(1-0.6))}{(0.8 - 0.6)^2}$$
$$= \frac{10.5 \times (0.16 + 0.24)}{0.2^2}$$
$$= 105$$

We would require 105 in each group to have a 90% chance of showing a significant difference if the population proportions were 0.6 and 0.8.

When we don't have a clear idea of the value of p_2 in which we are interested, we can calculate the sample size required for several proportions, as in Table 18.5. It is immediately apparent that to detect small differences between proportions we need very large samples.

Table 18.5 Sample size in each group required to detect different proportions p_2 when $p_1 = 0.6$ at the 5% significance level with power 90%, equal groups

p_2	n
0.90	39
0.80	105
0.70	473
0.65	1 964

The case where samples are of equal size is usual in experimental studies, but not in observational studies. Suppose we wish to compare the prevalence of a certain condition in two populations. We expect that in one population it will be 5% and that it may be more common in the second. We can rearrange the equation:

$$n_2 = \frac{f(\alpha, P)p_2(1-p_2)}{(p_1 - p_2)^2 - f(\alpha, P)\frac{p_1(1-p_1)}{n_1}}$$

Table 18.6 shows n_2 for different n_1 and p_2. For some values of n_1 we get a negative value of n_2. This means that no value of n_2 is large enough. When the proportions themselves are small, the detection of small differences requires very large samples indeed.

18.6 Detecting a correlation

Investigations are often set up to look for a relationship between two continuous variables. It is convenient to treat this as an estimation of, or test of, a correlation coefficient. The correlation coefficient has an awkward distribution, which tends only very slowly to the Normal, even when both variables themselves follow a Normal distribution. We can use Fisher's z transformation:

$$z = \frac{1}{2} \log_e \left(\frac{1+r}{1-r} \right)$$

which follows a Normal distribution with mean

$$z_\rho = \frac{1}{2} \log_e \left(\frac{1+\rho}{1-\rho} \right) + \frac{\rho}{2(n-1)}$$

and variance $1/(n-3)$ approximately, where ρ is the population correlation coefficient and n is the sample

Table 18.6 n_2 for different n_1 and p_2 when $p_1 = 0.05$ at the 5% significance level with power 90%

p_2	n_1								
	50	100	200	500	1 000	2 000	5 000	10 000	100 000
0.06	·	·	·	·	·	·	237 000	11 800	7 900
0.07	·	·	·	·	·	4 500	2 300	2 000	1 800
0.08	·	·	·	·	1 900	1 200	970	900	880
0.10	·	·	1 500	630	472	420	390	390	380
0.15	5 400	270	180	150	140	140	140	140	130
0.20	134	96	84	78	76	76	75	75	75

size (Section 11.10). For sample size calculations we can approximate z_ρ by

$$z_\rho = \frac{1}{2} \log_e \left(\frac{1 + \rho}{1 - \rho} \right)$$

The 95% confidence interval for z will be $z_\rho \pm 1.96\sqrt{1/(n - 3)}$, approximately. Given a rough idea of ρ we can estimate n required for any accuracy. For example, suppose we want to estimate a correlation coefficient, which we guess to about 0.5, and we want it to within 0.1 either way, i.e. we want a confidence interval like 0.4 to 0.6. The z transformations of these values of r are $z_{0.4} = 0.423\,65$, $z_{0.5} = 0.549\,31$, $z_{0.6} = 0.693\,15$, the differences are $z_{0.5} - z_{0.4} = 0.125\,66$ and $z_{0.6} - z_{0.5} = 0.143\,84$, and so to get the sample size we want, we need to set 1.96 standard errors to the smaller of these differences. We get $1.96\sqrt{1/(n - 3)} = 0.125\,66$, giving $n = 246$.

We more often want to see whether there is any evidence of a relationship. When $r = 0$, $z_r = 0$, so to test the null hypothesis that $\rho = 0$ we can test the null hypothesis that $z_\rho = 0$. The difference we wish to test is $\mu_d = z_\rho$, which has $SE(d) = \sqrt{1/(n - 3)}$. Putting this into the formula of Section 18.3 we get

$$z_\rho^2 = f(\alpha, P)\frac{1}{n - 3}$$

Thus we have

$$\left(\frac{1}{2} \log_e \left(\frac{1 + \rho}{1 - \rho} \right) \right)^2 = f(\alpha, P)\frac{1}{n - 3}$$

Table 18.7 Approximate sample size required to detect a correlation at the 5% significance level with power 90%

ρ	n	ρ	n	ρ	n
0.01	100 000	0.1	1 000	0.6	25
0.02	26 000	0.2	260	0.7	17
0.03	12 000	0.3	110	0.8	12
0.04	6 600	0.4	62	0.9	8
0.05	4 200	0.5	38		

and we can estimate n, ρ, or P given the other two. Table 18.7 shows the sample size required to detect a correlation coefficient with a power of $P = 0.9$ and a significance level $\alpha = 0.05$.

18.7 Accuracy of the estimated sample size

In this chapter I have assumed that samples are sufficiently large for sampling distributions to be approximately Normal and for estimates of variance to be good estimates. With very small samples this may not be the case. Various more accurate methods exist, but any sample size calculation is approximate and except for very small samples, say less than 10, the methods described above should be adequate. When the sample is small, we might need to replace the significance test component of $f(\alpha, P)$ by the corresponding number from the t distribution.

These methods depend on assumptions about the size of difference sought and the variability of the observations. It may be that the population to be studied does not have exactly the same characteristics as those from which the standard deviation or proportions were estimated. The likely effects of changes in these can be examined by putting different values of them in the formula. However, there is always an element of venturing into the unknown when embarking on a study and we can never be sure that the sample and population will be as we expect. The determination of sample size as described above is thus only a guide, and it is as well always to err on the side of a larger sample when coming to a final decision.

The choice of power is arbitrary, in that there is no optimum choice of power for a study. I usually recommend 90%, but 80% is often quoted. This gives smaller estimated sample sizes, but, of course, a greater chance of failing to detect effects.

For a fuller treatment of sample size estimation and fuller tables see Machin *et al.* (1998) and Lemeshow *et al.* (1990).

18.8 Trials randomized in clusters

When we randomize by cluster rather than individual (Sections 2.12, 2.14) we lose power compared with an individually randomized trial of the same size. Hence to get the power we want, we must increase the sample size from that required for an individually randomized trial. The ratio of the number of patients required for a cluster trial to that for a simply randomized trial is called the **design effect** of the study. It depends on the number of subjects per cluster. For the purpose of sample size calculations, we usually assume this is constant.

If the outcome measurement is continuous, e.g. serum cholesterol, a simple method of analysis is based on the mean of the observations for all subjects in the cluster, and compares these means between the treatment

groups (Section 10.13). We will denote the variance of observations within one cluster by s_w^2 and assume that this variance is the same for all clusters. If there are m subjects in each cluster then the variance of a single sample mean is s_w^2/m. The true cluster mean (unknown) will vary from cluster to cluster, with variance s_c^2 (see Section 10.12). The observed variance of the cluster means will be the sum of the variance between clusters and the variance within clusters, i.e. variance of outcome = $s_c^2 + s_w^2/m$. Hence the standard error for the difference between means is given by

$$SE(d) = \sqrt{\left(s_c^2 + \frac{s_w^2}{m}\right)\left(\frac{1}{n_1} + \frac{1}{n_2}\right)}$$

where n_1 and n_2 are the numbers of clusters in the two groups. For most trials $n_1 = n_2 = n$. so

$$SE(d) = \sqrt{\left(s_c^2 + \frac{s_w^2}{m}\right) \times \frac{2}{n}}$$

Hence, using the general method of Section 18.3, we can calculate the required number of clusters by

$$\mu_d^2 = f(\alpha, P)\left(s_c^2 + \frac{s_w^2}{m}\right) \times \frac{2}{n}$$

When the outcome is a dichotomous, 'yes or no' variable, we replace s_w^2 by $p(1 - p)$, where p is the probability of a 'yes'.

For example, in a proposed study of a behavioural intervention to lower cholesterol in general practice, practices were to be randomized into two groups, one to offer intensive dietary intervention by specially trained practice nurses using a behavioural approach and the other to usual general practice care. The outcome measure would be mean cholesterol levels in patients attending each practice 1 year later. Estimates of between-practice variance and within-practice variance were obtained from the MRC thrombosis prevention trial (Meade *et al.* 1992) and were $s_c^2 = 0.004\,6$ and $s_w^2 = 1.28$, respectively. The minimum difference considered to be clinically relevant was 0.1 mmol/l. If we recruit 50 patients per practice, we would have $s^2 = s_c^2 + s_w^2/m = 0.004\,6 + 1.28/50 = 0.030\,2$. If we choose power $P = 0.90$ and significance level $\alpha = 0.05$, from Table 18.1 $f(P, \alpha) = 10.5$.

The number of practices required to detect a difference of 0.1 mmol/l is given by $n = 10.5 \times 0.0302 \times 2/0.1^2 = 63$ in each group. This would give us $63 \times 50 = 3150$ patients in each group. A completely randomized trial without clusters would have $s^2 = 0.0046 + 1.28 = 1.2846$ and we would need $n = 10.5 \times 1.2846 \times 2/0.1^2 = 2698$ patients per group. Thus the design effect of having clusters of 50 patients is $3150/2698 = 1.17$.

The equation for the design effect is

$$DEFF = \frac{s_c^2 + s_w^2/m}{s_c^2 + s_w^2}$$

If we calculate an intraclass correlation coefficient (ICC) for these clusters (Section 11.13), we have

$$ICC = \frac{s_c^2}{s_c^2 + s_w^2}$$

In this context, the ICC is called the **intracluster correlation coefficient**. By a bit of algebra we get

$$DEFF = 1 + (m - 1) \times ICC$$

If there is only one observation per cluster, $m = 1$ and the design effect is 1.0, and the two designs are the same. Otherwise, the larger the ICC, i.e. the more important the variation between clusters is, the bigger the design effect and the more subjects we will need to get the same power as a simply randomized study. Even a small ICC will have an impact if the cluster size is large. The X-ray guidelines study (Section 10.13) had ICC = 0.019. A study with the same ICC and $m = 50$ referrals per practice would have design effect $D = 1 + (50 - 1) \times 0.019 = 1.93$. Thus it would require almost twice as many subjects as a trial where patients were randomized to treatment individually.

The main difficulty in calculating sample size for cluster randomized studies is obtaining an estimate of the between-cluster variation or ICC. Estimates of variation between individuals can often be obtained from the literature but even studies that use the cluster as the unit of analysis may not publish their results in such a way that the between-practice variation can be estimated. Donner *et al.* (1990), recognizing this problem, recommended that authors publish the cluster-specific event rates observed in their trial. This would enable other workers to use this information to plan further studies.

In some trials, where the intervention is directed at the individual subjects and the number of subjects per cluster is small, we may judge that the design effect can be ignored. On the other hand, where the number of subjects per cluster is large, an estimate of the variability between clusters will be very important. When the number of clusters is very small, we may have to use small sample adjustments mentioned in Section 18.7.

18.9 Multiple choice questions: Sample size

(Each answer is true or false.)

18.1 The power of a two sample t test:
(a) increases if the sample sizes are increased;
(b) depends on the difference between the population means which we wish to detect;
(c) depends on the difference between the sample means;
(d) is the probability that the test will detect a given population difference;
(e) cannot be zero.

18.2 The sample size required for a study to compare two proportions:
(a) depends on the magnitude of the effect we wish to detect;
(b) depends on the significance level we wish to employ;
(c) depends on the power we wish to have;
(d) depends on the anticipated values of the proportions themselves;
(e) should be decided by adding subjects until the difference is significant.

18.3 The sample size required for a study to estimate a mean:
(a) depends on the width of the confidence interval which we want;
(b) depends on the variability of the quantity being studied;
(c) depends on the power we wish to have;
(d) depends on the anticipated value of the mean;
(e) depends on the anticipated value of the standard deviation.

18.4 Blackberry *et al.* (2013) reported a cluster randomized trial of telephone coaching by practice nurses in improving glycaemic control in patients with type 2 diabetes. The unit of randomization was the general practice. The trial was designed to detect a specified difference in change in HbA1c over 18 months. Information required to estimate the sample size included:

(a) the difference in mean fall in HbA1c which the study was aimed to detect;

(b) the intracluster correlation coefficient between practices for change in HbA1c;

(c) the average fall in HbA1c expected for the 'treatment as usual' practices;

(d) the anticipated number of patients to be recruited in a practice;

(e) the desired power of the trial.

18.10 Exercise: Estimation of sample sizes

18.1 An opinion pollster wanted to estimate voter preferences to within two percentage points. How could the sample size to do this be decided?

The paper 'Defibrotide for prophylaxis of hepatic veno-occlusive disease in paediatric haemopoietic stem-cell transplantation: an open-label, phase 3, randomized controlled trial' (Corbacioglu *et al.* 2012) contains the following statement:

'We estimated the sample size on the basis of the primary endpoint, assuming rates of veno-occlusive disease to be 30% [four references] in the control group and 15% in the defibrotide group. Assuming a two-sided level of significance at 0.05, power of 80%, and a 10% dropout rate, 135 patients per group were needed (270 patients in total)'.

18.2 What is meant by 'two-sided level of significance at 0.05' and why did they need to specify this?

18.3 What are 30% and 15% in this statement and from where do they come?

18.4 What is meant by 'power of 80%'?

The authors go on to report that:

'The data and safety monitoring board inspected the planned adaptive interim analysis on the primary endpoint, and recommended that the sample size be increased to 180 patients per group to achieve a conditional power for significance of 80%'.

The results were that:

'22 (12%) of 180 participants in the defibrotide group had veno-occlusive disease by 30 days after HSCT compared with 35 (20%) of 176 controls (risk difference −7.7%, 95% CI −15.3 to −0.1; Z test . . . p = 0.048 8 . . .)'.

The 95% confidence intervals for the proportions with veno-occlusive disease were 7% to 17% for the defibrotide group and 14% to 26% for the control group.

18.5 How do the results of the study compare with the sample size calculations?

In a proposed trial of a health promotion programme, the programme was to be implemented across a whole county. The plan was to use four counties, two counties to be allocated to receive the programme and two counties to act as controls. The programme would be evaluated by a survey of samples of about 750 subjects drawn from the at-risk populations in each county. A conventional sample size calculation, which ignored the clustering, had indicated that 1 500 subjects in each treatment group would be required to give power 80% to detect the required difference. The applicants were aware of the problem of cluster randomization and the need to take it into account in the analysis, e.g. by analysis at the level of the cluster (county). They had an estimate of the intracluster correlation = 0.005, based on a previous study. They argued that this was so small that they could ignore the clustering.

18.6 Were they correct?

19 Missing data

19.1 The problem of missing data

Missing data are an almost inevitable part of research on people, whether it is medical, educational, or social. People who participate in these studies are usually free agents and can decide to withhold information at any time or may omit information by accident, or information might be misrecorded or lost.

For an example, we shall look at what happened in CADET (Richards *et al.* 2009, 2013), a randomized controlled trial of treatments for people presenting with depression in primary care. In this cluster randomized trial, 582 patients were allocated to collaborative care provided by a mental health worker or to treatment as usual by the primary care doctor. The trial was done at three geographical sites (Manchester, Bristol, and London). Fifty-one primary care practices were allocated using minimization within each site (Section 2.14), balanced for the index of multiple deprivation (IMD), number of primary care doctors, and the list size (the number of patients registered). Two practices recruited no patients, leaving us with 49. (The data presented here come from a preliminary analysis of CADET, we later filled in some of the missing data.)

The data which were collected included

- primary care practice size (number of patients and number of doctors) and the index of multiple deprivation for catchment area,
- participant age, sex, employment, marital status, etc.,
- participant depression (using the nine-item PHQ9 scale), anxiety (using the seven-item GAD7 scale), and quality of life (using the widely used SF36 scale) at recruitment to the trial, i.e. at baseline, all from multi-item questionnaire scales,

- participant depression (PHQ9), anxiety (GAD7), quality of life (SF36), and a multi-item client satisfaction with care questionnaire scale (using the CSQ scale) after 4 months.

Data were missing in several ways:

- for four participants the sex was not recorded, which must be a data entry error by researchers,
- for some of the completed scales, one or more items were omitted while other items had been completed,
- for some participants, all items were omitted in a scale, so the scale had not been completed at all.

The planned primary analysis for CADET was to use the PHQ9 depression score at 4 months as the primary outcome variable and to adjust the estimated effect of collaborative care for three cluster level variables (geographical site, IMD, and list size) and two individual level variables (age and PHQ9 at baseline). Because there were three sites, two dummy variables (Section 15.8) were needed for these and with treatment, IMD, and list size that made five predictor variables at the practice level. With 49 practices, we thought that five was all that we should include for a valid multiple regression giving us almost 10 observations per variable (Section 15.1). Number of doctors was highly correlated with list size, so we did not think that omitting it would be a problem. As this was a cluster randomized trial, we needed to take the clustering into account in the analysis. For CADET, we used the robust standard errors method (Section 15.15).

One possible approach to the analysis is to leave out all the incomplete cases and use only those for which all variables are available. If we do this **available data** or **complete case** data analysis, we have 499 complete cases for the required variables. We get the adjusted estimate, collaborative care minus treatment as usual, = −1.42 PHQ9 scale points, SE = 0.50, 95% confidence interval = −2.44 to −0.41, P = 0.007. So this would suggest that collaborative care results in lower mean depression scores than does treatment as usual.

The variable with most missing values in this analysis is PHQ9 at 4 months, where 13.6% were missing altogether, 17.3% of the collaborative care group and 10.2% of the treatment as usual group. This difference in missingness is significant, P = 0.01 by a chi-squared test. It would be easy to criticise the trial on the grounds that the difference in proportion of missing depression scores may explain the treatment difference. We need to find a way of taking the missing data into account.

Available data analysis is also inefficient. Some of the cases were omitted because the baseline PHQ9 was missing (all because some, but not all, items in the nine-item scale were omitted) but had PHQ9 after 4 months.

19.2 Types of missing data

It is usual to define three kinds of missing data:

- missing completely at random (MCAR);
- missing at random (MAR);
- missing not at random (MNAR).

These terms are widely used, but are a bit misleading. When we say data are **missing completely at random**, we mean that the missingness is nothing to do with the person being studied. For example, a questionnaire might be lost in the post, or a blood sample might be damaged in the lab. In CADET, sex might be MCAR. Of course, this is not truly random, but means that whether something is missing is not related to the subject of the missing data.

When we say data are **missing at random**, we mean that the missingness is to do with the person but can be predicted from other information about the person. It is not specifically related to the missing information. For example, if a child does not attend an educational assessment because the child is (genuinely) ill, this might be predictable from other data we have about the child's health, but it would not be related to what we

would have measured had the child not been ill. Are the depression data MAR? We cannot tell this from the data. We know that the PHQ9 scores are not MCAR, because the proportions missing in the two treatment groups are different. We know that at least one observation is not MAR, because, tragically, the participant had committed suicide. This is always a danger in depression research.

When data are **missing not at random**, the missingness is specifically related to what is missing, e.g. a person does not attend a drug test because the person took drugs the night before. The suicide victim has the PHQ9 at 4 months MNAR. The problem is to decide which of these situations we have and in the same dataset we may have some data missing for each reason.

We had some missing data in the foot ulcer data in Table 10.2. Some of the capillary densities were missing because the skin biopsy was not usable to count the capillaries. We could regard these as MCAR. Some were missing because the foot had been amputated. As a frequent reason for foot amputation is gangrene from severe foot ulcers, I think we would have to classify these as MNAR.

There are several strategies which can be applied:

- try to obtain the missing data;
- leave out incomplete cases and use only those for which all variables are available;
- replace missing data by a conservative estimate, e.g. the sample mean;
- try to estimate the missing data from the other data on the person.

Trying to obtain missing data is obviously a good idea if we can do it. For the missing recording of sex, we were able to fill in two observations from the participants' forenames. Often, this is not possible.

One participant committed suicide. The PHQ9 for this person cannot be regarded as missing at random. The 4-month PHQ9 was set to the maximum 27. We checked whether this had a large effect on the estimates by running the analysis with and without this participant.

Leaving out incomplete cases and using only the available data may cause bias, as we have seen, and is inefficient. If all our missing data are MCAR there should be no bias, at least, but this is unusual in health applications.

19.3 Using the sample mean

We can replace missing data by a conservative estimate, such as the sample mean. If we have data which are MCAR there should be no bias. However, it might lead to some silly values. If we score sex as 1 = male and 2 = female, we could score those with missing sex 1.5, or, given that there are 72% women in the study, 1.72. It might also lead to some outliers in the analysis and have a bad effect on the variance. We would not use the mean for the intervention group, this would definitely cause problems, e.g. the variance would be too small.

If we replace the missing depression scores by the mean for the whole sample, we have 582 observations. We can run the regression and our adjusted estimate of the treatment effect becomes –1.02, SE = 0.44, 95% CI = –1.91 to –0.13, P = 0.026. The standard error is too small, however, because we do not really have 582 observations, but 503. The standard error is proportional to one over the sample size, so we can estimate the true standard error by multiplying the standard error given by $\sqrt{582/503}$. This gives 0.48. The t statistic becomes 1.02/0.48 = 2.13, P = 0.034 and the 95% confidence interval –1.02 – 1.96 × 0.48 to –1.02 + 1.96 × 0.48 = –1.96 to –0.08. Compare this with the available data estimate, –1.42 PHQ9 scale points, SE = 0.50, 95% CI = –2.44 to

–0.41, P = 0.007. The estimate when we replace missing data by the mean is closer to zero and has a larger P value. Estimates by each adjustment method are shown in Table 19.1.

This estimate is conservative. If we are going to have a bias, it is better for it to be in the direction of missing effects which are there rather than of finding effects which are not there. However, it does not deal with the problem of data which are not missing completely at random. If participants who did not complete the depression inventory are systematically different to those who did, using the overall mean will not necessarily compensate. We know that in CADET this is true, because there are more missing data in the collaborative care group than in treatment as usual.

I have used this method in the past for data such as the zidovudine data (Section 10.7) where I wanted to calculate an area under the curve. Using the overall mean for that time-point in place of missing observations before calculating the area can be a useful expedient. I think that I would now be inclined to use simple imputation (Section 19.5).

19.4 Last observation carried forward

Rather than use the sample mean, we could try to estimate the missing data from the other data on the person. This would be useful for both MCAR and MAR, though not for MNAR. However, even for MNAR, it may

Table 19.1 Summary of estimates adjusted for missing data in preliminary analyses of the CADET trial (data from Richards *et al.* 2009, 2013)

Missingness adjustment method	Estimated difference in mean PHQ9	Standard error	95% CI	P
Complete cases	–1.42	0.50	–2.44 to –0.41	0.007
Using sample mean	–1.02	0.48	–1.96 to –0.08	0.034
Last observation carried forward	–0.96	0.45	–1.86 to –0.07	0.036
Simple imputation	–1.35	0.50	–2.36 to –0.34	0.010
Multiple imputation	–1.30	0.52	–2.34 to –0.26	0.016

still be better than making no attempt to adjust. How do we do this?

If we have more than one observation over time, we can use the last one made before the missing one as an estimate, called the method of **last observation carried forward** or **LOCF**. This method has been used often, but it is usually not a good idea. For example, suppose the measure is a reading ability score in children. We expect reading ability to increase over time, so the last observation carried forward would underestimate the missing measurement. We can try this in CADET. We can replace the missing PHQ9 scores at 4 months by the baseline PHQ9. The missing baseline scores we will have to omit, because there was no prior observation. The estimated treatment effect is −0.96, SE = 0.45, 95% CI = −1.86 to −0.07, P = 0.036.

The result here is a smaller treatment effect, because the missing data are replaced by the higher baseline PHQ9. The mean PHQ9 score fell from 17.8 at baseline to 11.9 after 4 months. More observations are missing in the collaborative care group and so the upward bias is greater than in the treatment as usual group. Compare the zidovudine data (Section 10.7), which rise and then fall over time. Replacement of a missing observation by the last observation carried forward would cause a downward bias for early dropouts, as zidovudine concentrations would be rising, and an upward bias for later ones. The use of the last observation carried forward can cause bias in both directions and is not recommended.

19.5 Simple imputation

Imputation means using the data on non-missing cases to predict the missing variable from other variables for which we do have data. We then use this estimate in place of the missing data. We may need to adjust the standard error for the true sample size, and to adjust degrees of freedom in small samples. Using the data on non-missing cases, we make a regression equation to predict the missing variable from other variables. We use the values predicted by the regression equation to estimate the missing data. Imputation is the modern way, enabled by modern computer power.

There are two broad approaches to imputation of missing data, simple and multiple. I shall describe **simple imputation** first, in which the estimate of a single value for a missing item is made from the data which have actually been observed. In CADET, individual items were missing from the depression and anxiety scales. For PHQ9 and GAD7, we could find no recommended method for handling missing items. We therefore imputed values for these missing observations from the other, observed items in the scale. We did this unless half or more of the items were missing, when the whole scale would be regarded as missing.

For example, for the baseline PHQ9 scale, six individual item answers were missing. For the 4-month PHQ9 scale, only one individual item answer was missing. These missing item answers were imputed using simple imputation from the completed items. For each scale item variable which had a missing observation, we carried out regression of the item on the other eight items in the scale. We used this regression equation to predict the missing observation. As the scale items were all recorded as 0, 1, 2, or 3, these imputed item scores were rounded to the nearest integer. Total PHQ9 scores were then calculated. The total scores were then used in the analysis, with no further adjustment being made. Because the total scores had been calculated using only partly imputed information, no adjustment was made to standard errors or to degrees of freedom.

No special imputation software is needed to do this, any multiple regression program will do, though some statistical programs have imputation commands to guide users in the right direction. If the missing observation is not numerical but dichotomous, we use logistic regression, and other regression methods for other variable types.

The same simple imputation approach was used for the GAD7 anxiety score. It was not used for the SF36 quality of life measure. SF36 is a long and complex instrument. It produces two main scales: Physical Health and Mental Health. It produces eight subscales: Physical Functioning, Physical Role Functioning, Bodily Pain, and General Health, which together make the composite Physical Health Component scale; and Social Functioning, Emotional Role Functioning, Mental Health, and Vitality, which together make the composite Mental

Health Component scale. Coding the SF36 is complex. Some items are recoded in a non-linear way and the scales are standardized to a reference population. Missing data in SF36 are dealt with by averaging the items which have been completed for a scale if fewer than half are missing and by making the whole scale missing if more than half are missing. This is the standard method so we used it. This means that SF36 scores are comparable across the many studies where SF36 is used. It, too, is a form of simple imputation, where the missing items are replaced by the average of available items in the subscale.

When I had completed the simple imputation, I ran the analysis again. I now had 504 observations and the treatment estimate was −1.35, SE = 0.50, 95% CI = −2.36 to −0.34, P = 0.010. I didn't think I should omit participants because they had missed one or two items on a scale, so I reported this as the available data analysis.

19.6 Multiple imputation

This method applies to data which are missing completely at random or missing at random. It is the currently accepted statistical approach to missing data. At the time of writing, it is a hot research topic for statisticians and rapidly changing. I think that this really does require purpose-written software.

Multiple imputation means that we impute not just once but several times, and not just one missing observation at a time but all of them. There are three steps:

1 generate multiple imputed datasets,
2 analyse each of the multiple datasets,
3 combine these analyses into a single analysis.

There are several ways to generate multiple imputed datasets. I am going to describe the **chained equations** method, also known as the **fully conditional specification** method and the **sequential regression multivariate imputation method**, following White et al. (2011).

First we replace each missing observation by an observation of the same variable randomly chosen from the dataset. This is called the **hot deck** method, a name that

dates back to the days of punch cards. Then for the first variable with missing data, we impute the missing observations by regression, just as for simple imputation. We then replace the missing observation by the predicted value from the regression plus a random error found from the residual error about that regression. We repeat this for the second variable with missing data, and so on. We use an appropriate regression method, least squares for continuous variables, logistic for dichotomous data, and so on. When we have done this for all the variables with missing values we have completed one cycle. This procedure is repeated for several cycles to produce a single imputed dataset. We then repeat this whole process several times to give a set of imputed datasets. Of course, this complex procedure can be accomplished by a single computer command, we do not do the whole thing in detail.

In the CADET study, we had a considerable amount of missing data at the 4-month follow-up and a few missing baseline observations. To investigate the potential effect of these missing data we used the method of chained regression equations as implemented by Patrick Royston in the 'ice' and 'micombine' commands in Stata. Here 'ice' is the imputation by chained equations command. We have to tell the program several things.

First, we need the list of variables to be used in the imputation. This includes both the variables we want to impute, such as the depression and anxiety scores at 4 months, and the variables which we want to use to predict them. These included all the variables which we wanted to use in the subsequent analyses and others, such as sex and number of primary care doctors, which I thought might be helpful as predictors in the imputation. We had to specify the number of imputed datasets which we wanted to generate. We chose 100 imputed datasets for this analysis, which I shall explain later. For each of the variables to be imputed, the program works out what kind of variable it is and from this what is the appropriate regression method to use: logistic for a variable with two possible values, multinomial for a variable with three, four, or five possible values, and ordinary least squares regression otherwise. If you would like something else, you can tell the program. For the CADET data, the program automatically chose logistic regression for sex, which had only two possible values, and chose ordinary least squares for the other variables with missing observations, all of which had more than five different values. Finally, a file was specified to save the 100 imputed datasets.

We next analyse each of the multiple datasets. This is easy for the computer, because for each of the 100 datasets we carry out the required regression analysis using the usual computer routine. We then combine these multiple data analyses into a single analysis. In the program I used, this was all accomplished using a single command, putting 'micombine' (combine multiple imputations) in front of the usual regression command. The standard errors for the coefficients are a combination of the variation in the individual regression estimate and the variation between samples produced by the simulation, a method due to Rubin (1987).

For the multiply imputed data, the treatment estimate was −1.30, SE = 0.52, 95% CI = −2.34 to −0.26, P = 0.016. The results are very similar to the estimate found after simple imputation (Section 19.5), which was −1.35, SE = 0.50, 95% CI = −2.36 to −0.34, P = 0.010. This suggested that, if the missing at random assumption is correct, missing data have very little effect on this estimate. All the estimates adjusted for missingness are summarized in Table 19.1. The standard error for the imputation is almost the same as for the available data. We might expect the standard error to be less than for the dataset after simple imputation, as there are more observations, but this is counteracted by the extra imprecision added by the simulation.

Multiple imputation is a simulation method and so it produces slightly different results each time the analysis is run. I ran the program again and the estimated regression coefficient was −1.27, SE = 0.53, 95% CI = −2.33 to −0.20, P = 0.021. This is similar to, but not identical to, the first run. As we might expect, the more imputations we do, the more consistent the estimates will be if we repeat the process. Some authors recommend that only a small number of imputations need be used, three, four, or five, for example. The default for the program I used is one. White *et al.* (2011) point out that such small numbers can lead to inconsistent estimates, which might be particularly important for coefficients close to the critical value for statistical significance. They suggest a guideline that the number of imputations should be should be at least equal to the percentage of incomplete cases, which

in the case of CADET is 18%, leading to 20 imputations being reasonable for this example. They go on to say that this rule is not always appropriate and that sometimes we may need more. I used 100 because I ran the analysis a few times with a small number of imputations and did not get consistent treatment estimates. I boosted the number to 100 and found that gave highly consistent estimates, so I stuck with that. Given that this only required waiting for an extra minute compared to the 20 imputations to which the guideline would lead, I felt quite happy with that.

Multiple imputation is another example of a Monte Carlo method (Section 8.11).

19.7 Why we should not ignore missing data

The analysis in Section 19.1 using 499 available data cases for the required variables gave the adjusted estimate, collaborative care minus treatment as usual, = −1.42 PHQ9 scale points, SE = 0.50, 95% confidence interval = −2.44 to −0.41, P = 0.007. For the multiply imputed data, the treatment estimate was −1.30, SE = 0.52, 95% CI = −2.34 to −0.26, P = 0.016. In this study, the available data analysis gave an estimate further from zero and with a smaller P value than the multiple imputation estimate. The estimates are sufficiently similar for us not to be concerned about the validity of the trial and we would draw the same conclusions from both. What would we do if they were different? As the missing data are clearly not missing completely random, the available data analysis is likely to be biased and the imputation estimate would be more reliable. I think we should choose that.

Nüesch *et al.* (2009) reviewed 167 trials of therapeutic interventions compared with no active treatment in patients with osteoarthritis of the hip or knee, identified in 14 meta-analyses. They analysed the effect size in standard deviations for patient reported pain (Section 17.8). They reported that 39 trials had included all patients in the analysis, mostly using last observation carried forward or multiple imputation to allow for missing data. In 128 trials some patients were excluded from the analysis. Effect sizes from trials with exclusions tended to favour the intervention by more than those from trials without exclusions. The difference was −0.13 standard deviations,

95% CI −0.29 to 0.04. So the difference was not significant, but in the direction a cynic would predict. Nüesch *et al.* (2009) concluded that 'Trialists should always report results of intention to treat analyses, including all randomized patients in the analysis in the group to which they were originally allocated. If data imputations are necessary to carry out an intention to treat analysis, multiple imputation should be used to replace missing data'. Nine of the 167 trials reported that they had full data on all participants, which strikes me as quite a lot, so for most of them imputation was the way to get as close as possible to the analysis according to intention to treat, which was advocated in Chapter 2 (Section 2.6).

Multiple imputation is only valid if data are missing at random. What should we do when data are missing not at random, so that we do not have a reliable way to estimate the missing? So far as I know, at the time of writing we do not yet have a generally accepted way to proceed. People are working on it, of course. But for now, multiple imputation is the way to go and if data truly are missing not at random, then multiple imputation will give a much more reliable estimate than available data.

Several other approaches are also being used to allow for missing data. I do not have the space (or the knowledge) to discuss them all here, but I think that, in general, any attempt to allow for and to investigate the effects of missing data is a good thing. I might sometimes make an exception for last observation carried forward.

Soon after the previous edition of this book was published, I was at a statistical meeting on multiple imputation. It occurred to me that in the future, we would be as familiar with multiple imputation as we now are with randomization and that we would regard it as the natural and automatic thing to do. I think that future is here.

For more information than you will ever need about missing data, see <http://www.missingdata.org.uk/>.

19.8 Multiple choice questions: Missing data

(Each answer is true or false.)

19.1 If, in a randomized trial, data are missing completely at random:
  (a) omitting the cases with missing data will introduce bias;
  (b) omitting the cases with missing data will still be analysis by intention to treat;
  (c) using last observation carried forward will remove bias;
  (d) there should be no systematic difference between participants with and without full data;
  (e) missingness is unrelated to characteristics of the participants.

19.2 If data in a randomized trial are 'missing at random':
  (a) whether data are missing is unrelated to characteristics of the participants;
  (b) there should be no systematic difference between participants with and without missing data;
  (c) multiple imputation is a possible approach to the analysis;
  (d) an available data analysis may introduce bias;
  (e) the fact that a variable is missing is related primarily to the unobserved value of the missing variable.

19.3 Using the overall sample mean to fill in for missing observations in a randomized trial:
  (a) gives the same value for all missing observations of the same variable;
  (b) uses the observations on other variables to estimate the missing one;
  (c) is less likely to introduce bias than using the randomized group mean;
  (d) uses the available data in the most informative way;
  (e) is an approach which may produce bias toward a smaller treatment effect.

19.4 Multiple imputation:
  (a) is unsuitable for data which are missing at random;
  (b) may give different results if repeated for the same dataset;
  (c) is a random simulation method;
  (d) corrects reliably for data missing not at random;
  (e) can make use of several regression methods.

19.5 Simple imputation:
  (a) is unsuitable for data which are missing at random;
  (b) may give different results if repeated for the same dataset;
  (c) is a random simulation method;
  (d) corrects reliably for data missing not at random;
  (e) can make use of several regression methods.

19.9 Exercise: Last observation carried forward

Antonioli and Reveley (2005) randomly allocated 30 people with mild to moderate depression either to an intervention where they swam with dolphins or to an outdoor nature programme. Of the 15 participants allocated to the dolphins, 13 completed the programme, the other two dropping out after a week. Of the 15 allocated to the nature programme without dolphins, 12 completed, the other three refused when they found they had not been allocated to the dolphins.

Using the data for completers only, for both the Hamilton rating scale for depression and for the Beck depression inventory there was a significantly greater reduction in depression score in the dolphin group, P = 0.002 and P = 0.006. For their main analysis, Antonioli and Reveley used the last observation carried forward method to replace the depression scores for the five participants who were missing at 2 weeks. Table 19.2 shows the mean and standard deviation of the changes in depression scores from baseline to final scores 2 weeks later, both using the available complete data and the last observation carried forward.

19.1 What are the main differences between the complete data analysis and the LOCF analyses? Why do you think this is?

19.2 Why might missing data be a problem in this study?

19.3 What problems are there using LOCF in this study?

19.4 Antonioli and Reveley described their LOCF analysis as a 'modified analysis by intention to treat and last observation carried forward'. In what sense is this analysis by intention to treat? Do you think this was a reasonable thing to do?

Antonioli and Reveley also reported the depression scores before and after the intervention, using LOCF. Table 19.3 shows the means and standard deviations for the post-intervention scores.

19.5 What effect will the LOCF have had on the means and standard deviations in Table 19.3?

19.6 This is slightly off-topic, but what is noticeable about the standard deviations in Table 19.3 compared with those in for LOCF in Table 19.2? What explanation would you give for this?

Table 19.2 Reductions in depression scores following exposure to dolphins or an outdoor nature programme (data from Antonioli and Reveley 2005)

Scale	Method	Dolphins			Nature			95% CI for difference	P value
		n	mean	SD	*n*	mean	SD		
Hamilton	Complete	13	8.4	2.0	12	4.5	3.2	1.7 to 6.1	0.002
	LOCF	15	7.3	3.5	15	3.6	3.4	1.1 to 6.2	0.007
Beck	Complete	13	15.5	5.7	12	7.6	7.4	2.4 to 13.3	0.006
	LOCF	15	13.4	7.6	15	6.1	7.3	1.8 to 12.9	0.01

Table 19.3 Depression scores following exposure to dolphins or an outdoor nature programme, after addition of LOCF estimates for missing observations (data from Antonioli and Reveley 2005)

	Dolphins			Nature			95% CI for difference	P value
Scale	*n*	mean	SD	*n*	mean	SD		
Hamilton	15	7.3	2.5	15	10.9	3.4	−5.8 to −1.4	0.003
Beck	15	6.9	5.6	15	12.7	7.6	−10.9 to −0.8	0.02

20 Clinical measurement

20.1 Making measurements

In this chapter we shall look at a number of problems associated with clinical measurement. These include how precisely we can measure, how different methods of measurement can be compared, how measurements can be used in diagnosis, and how composite scale measurements are constructed.

When we make a measurement, particularly a biological measurement, the number we obtain is the result of several things: the true value of the quantity we want to measure, biological variation, the measurement instrument itself, the position of the subject, the skill,

experience, and expectations of the observer, and even the relationship between observer and subject. Some of these factors, such as the variation within the subject, are outside the control of the observer. Others, such as position, are not, and it is important to standardize these. One which is most under our control is the precision with which we read scales and record the result. When blood pressure is measured, for example, some observers record to the nearest 5 mm Hg, others to the nearest 10 mm Hg. Table 20.1 shows 210 systolic blood pressures recorded at baseline in a trial of coronary artery bypass surgery (Motallebzadeh *et al.* 2007). If observers did not record zero and five in preference

Table 20.1 210 measurements of systolic blood pressure (mm Hg) from CABG patients (data from Motallebzadeh *et al.* 2007)

16	105	110	116	120	123	126	130	130	135	140	144	150	160
88	105	110	116	120	123	126	130	131	135	140	145	152	160
95	106	111	117	120	123	126	130	131	135	140	145	153	160
98	106	112	117	120	123	127	130	131	135	140	145	153	160
99	107	112	117	120	123	127	130	132	135	140	145	154	160
99	107	112	117	120	124	127	130	132	136	140	145	154	164
99	107	112	118	120	125	127	130	132	138	140	145	154	165
100	108	112	118	120	125	128	130	132	138	140	146	155	165
100	108	112	118	120	125	128	130	132	139	140	147	155	166
100	109	113	119	121	125	128	130	132	139	140	147	156	170
100	109	113	119	122	125	128	130	132	139	141	148	158	170
102	109	115	120	122	125	128	130	132	140	141	148	158	175
102	110	115	120	122	126	128	130	133	140	142	150	159	176
103	110	115	120	123	126	128	130	134	140	143	150	159	189
104	110	116	120	123	126	129	130	135	140	143	150	160	198

to other digits we would expect one in ten observations, 10%, to end in zero and 10% to end in five. In the 210 blood pressure measurements of Table 20.1, there are 62 which end in zero, 30%, and 29 which end in five, 14%. This tendency to record some terminal digits rather than others is called **digit preference**. Observer training and awareness of the problem help to minimize digit preference, but, if possible, readings should be taken to sufficient significant figures for the last digit to be unimportant. Digit preference is particularly important when differences in the last digit are of importance to the outcome, as it might be in Table 20.2, where we are dealing with the difference between two similar numbers. Because of this it is a mistake to have one measurer take readings under one set of conditions and a second under another, as their degree of digit preference may differ.

Some observers may record diastolic pressure at Korotkov sound four, others at five. Observers may think that as blood pressure is such a variable quantity, errors in recording of this magnitude are unimportant. In the monitoring of the individual patient, such lack of uniformity may make apparent changes difficult to interpret. In research, imprecise measurement can lead to problems in the analysis and to loss of power.

How precisely should we record data? While this must depend to some extent on the purpose for which the data are to be recorded, any data which are to be subjected to statistical analysis should be recorded as precisely as possible. A study can only be as good as the data, and data are often very costly and time-consuming to collect. The precision to which data are to be recorded and all other procedures to be used in measurement should be decided in advance and stated in the protocol, the written statement of how the study is to be carried out. We should bear in mind that the precision of recording depends on the number of significant figures (Section 5.2) recorded, not the number of decimal places. The observations 0.15 and 1.66 from the serum triglyceride measurements in Table 4.8, for example, are both recorded to two decimal places, but 0.15 has two significant figures and 1.66 has three. The second observation is recorded more precisely. This becomes very important when we come to analyse the data, for the data of Table 4.8 have a skew distribution which we wish to log transform (Section 10.4). The greater imprecision of recording at the lower end of the scale is magnified by the transformation. It is important to agree the precision to which data are to be recorded and to ensure that instruments have sufficiently fine scales for the job in hand.

Table 20.2 Pairs of readings made with a Wright Peak Flow Meter on 17 healthy volunteers

Subject	PEFR (litres/min)		Subject	PEFR (litres/min)	
	First	Second		First	Second
1	494	490	10	433	429
2	395	397	11	417	420
3	516	512	12	656	633
4	434	401	13	267	275
5	476	470	14	478	492
6	557	611	15	178	165
7	413	415	16	423	372
8	442	431	17	427	421
9	650	638			

20.2 Repeatability and measurement error

I have already discussed some factors which may produce bias in measurements (Sections 2.9, 2.10, 3.9). I have not yet considered the natural biological variability, in subject and in measurement method, which may lead to measurement error. 'Error' comes from a Latin root meaning 'to wander', and its use in statistics in closely related to this, as in Section 11.2, for example. By 'error', we do not mean 'mistake'. A mistake might occur, for example, if we write the measurement incorrectly. In Table 20.1 the first entry, 16, must be a mistake. I suspect that it should be 160 mm Hg. Thus error in measurement may include the natural continual variation of a biological quantity, when a single observation will be used to characterize the individual. For example, in the measurement of blood pressure we are dealing with a quantity that varies continuously, not only from heart-beat to heart-beat but from day to day, season to season, and even with the sex of the measurer. The measurer, too, will show variation in the perception of the Korotkov sound and reading of the manometer. Because of this, most clinical measurements cannot be taken at face value without some consideration being given to their error.

The quantification of measurement error is not difficult in principle. To do it we need a set of replicate readings, obtained by measuring each member of a sample of subjects more than once. We can then estimate the standard deviation of repeated measurements on the same subject. Table 20.2 shows some replicated measurements of peak expiratory flow rate, made by the same observer (myself) with a Wright Peak Flow Meter. For each subject, the measured PEFR varies from observation to observation. This variation is the measurement error. We can quantify measurement error in two ways: using the standard deviation for repeated measurements on the same subject and by correlation.

We can find the standard deviation within the subject by one-way analysis of variance (Section 10.9), the subjects being the 'groups' (Table 20.3). As we are only going to use the residual variance estimate, it does not matter whether we think of the subjects as fixed or random (Section 10.12). The **variance within subjects** is the residual mean square in the analysis of variance table, and the **standard deviation within subjects**, s_w, is the square root of this. From Table 20.3, this is $s_w = \sqrt{234.3} = 15.3$ litres/min.

There are a number of ways in which the measurement error may be presented to the user of the measurement. It may be as the standard deviation calculated above. This within-subject standard deviation is also called the **standard error of measurement (SEM)**, because it is the standard error of the sample observation as an estimate of the subject's true value. The difference between the observed value, with measurement error, and the subject's true value will be at most two standard deviations with probability 0.95. By 'true value' here, I mean the average value which would be obtained over many measurements. The precision may be quoted as being within two standard deviations, $2 \times 15.3 = 30$ litres/min. We can follow the British Standards Institution (1979) and quote the **repeatability**, the value below which the difference between two measurements will lie with probability 0.95. Provided the measurement errors are from a Normal distribution, this is estimated by $1.96 \times \sqrt{2s_w^2} = 2.77s_w$. BSI (1979) recommend $2 \times \sqrt{2s_w^2} = 2.83s_w$. Clearly, 2.77 is more exact, but it

Table 20.3 Analysis of variance by subject for the PEFR data of Table 20.2

Source of variation	Degrees of freedom	Sum of squares	Mean square	Variance ratio (F)	Probability
Total	33	445 581.5			
Between subjects	16	441 598.5	27 599.9	117.8	P < 0.000 1
Residual (within subjects)	17	3 983.0	234.3		

makes no practical difference. Throughout this chapter I have used two standard deviations on either side of the mean rather than 1.96, for simplicity. The repeatability is also called the **smallest real difference**, **minimal detectable change**, and **minimum clinical difference**, because it is the smallest difference that can be interpreted as evidence for a real change in the subject's true value.

Measurement error may also be reported as the **within-subjects coefficient of variation**, which is the standard deviation divided by the mean, often multiplied by 100 to give a percentage. For our data the mean PEFR is 447.9 litres/min, so the coefficient of variation is 15.3/447.9 = 0.034 or 3.4%. The trouble with quoting the error as a percentage in this example is that 7% of the smallest observation, 165 litres, is only 12 litres/min, compared with 7% of the largest, 656, which is 46 litres/min. This is not a good method if the top of the range of possible values is great compared with the bottom and the error does not depend on the value of the measurement. This is a good method if the standard deviation is proportional to the mean. In that case a logarithmic transformation (Section 10.4) can be used. Although there is no compelling reason to apply the log transformation to the data of Table 20.2, I shall do it for illustration. Table 20.4 gives the within-subjects standard deviation on the $\log_e$ scale as $s_w = \sqrt{0.001\,227} = 0.035\,0$. This standard deviation does not have the same units as the original data, but is a pure number (Section 7.4). If we back-transform by taking the antilog to give $\exp(0.035\,0) = 1.036$, we do not get a standard deviation on the PEFR scale. This is because to get s_w we subtracted the log of one number from the log of another, the mean on the log scale from

the observations on the log scale (Appendix 5A). Now, the difference between the logs of two numbers is the log of their ratio. By subtracting on the log scale we divide one PEFR by the other to get a dimensionless ratio. Thus the antilog of s_w is what we multiply by on the natural scale to get the effect of adding s_w on the log scale. If we multiply the mean by this factor we get the equivalent of the mean plus one standard deviation on the log scale. If we subtract one from this ratio, we get the ratio of the standard deviation to the mean, which is the coefficient of variation. For the example this is 1.036 − 1 = 0.036, or 3.6%, actually very similar to the 3.4% by the crude method above. When the standard deviation is proportional to the mean we therefore can have a valid use and method of estimation of the coefficient of variation. From it, we can estimate the standard deviation of repeated measurements at any point within the interval of measurement. If we calculate a standard deviation on the log scale, it is the same whatever units we have used for the measurement. The standard deviation of log(weight in Kg) is the same as the standard deviation of log(weight in lb).

We should check to see whether the error does depend on the value of the measurement, usually being larger for larger values. We can do this by plotting a scatter diagram of the absolute value of the difference (i.e. ignoring the sign) and the mean of the two observations (Figure 20.1). For the PEFR data, there is no obvious relationship. We can check this by calculating a correlation (Section 11.9) or rank correlation coefficient (Sections 12.4, 12.5). For Figure 20.1 we have $\tau = 0.17$, $P = 0.3$, so there is little to suggest that the measurement error is related to the size of the PEFR. Hence the coefficient of variation is not as appropriate as the within-subjects

Table 20.4 Analysis of variance by subject for the log (base e) transformed PEFR data of Table 20.2

Source of variation	Degrees of freedom	Sum of squares	Mean square	Variance ratio (F)	Probability
Total	33	3.160 104			
Subjects	16	3.139 249	0.196 203	159.9	P < 0.000 1
Residual (within subjects)	17	0.020 855	0.001 227		

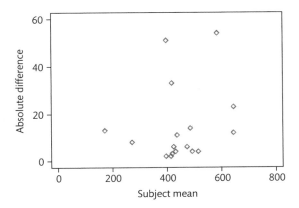

Figure 20.1 Absolute difference versus sum for 17 pairs of Wright Peak Flow Meter measurements.

standard deviation as a representation of the measurement error. For most medical measurements, the standard deviation is either independent of or proportional to the magnitude of the quantity being measured and so one of these two approaches can be used.

Measurement error may also be presented as the correlation coefficient between pairs of readings. This is sometimes called the **reliability** of the measurement, and is often used for psychological measurements using questionnaire scales. However, the correlation depends on the amount of variation between subjects. If we deliberately choose subjects to have a wide spread of possible values, the correlation will be bigger than if we take a random sample of subjects. Thus this method should only be used if we have a representative sample of the subjects in whom we are interested. The intraclass correlation coefficient (Section 11.13), which does not take into account the order in which observations were taken and which can be used with more than two observations per subject, is preferred for this application. Applying the method of Section 11.13 to Table 20.2 we get ICC = 0.98. ICC and s_w are closely related, because ICC $= 1 - s_w^2/(s_b^2 + s_w^2) = s_b^2/(s_b^2 + s_w^2)$. ICC therefore depends also on the variation between subjects, and thus relates to the population, of which the subjects can be considered a random sample. It is the proportion of the variance of measurements which is due to the variation between true values of the quantity being measured, rather than to measurement error. Streiner and Norman (2008) provide an interesting discussion.

20.3 Assessing agreement using Cohen's kappa

Table 20.5 shows answers to the question 'Have you ever smoked a cigarette?' obtained from a sample of children on two occasions, using a self-administered questionnaire and an interview (Bland *et al.* 1975). We would like to know how closely the children's answers agree.

One possible method of summarizing the agreement between the pairs of observations is to calculate the percentage of agreement, the percentage of subjects observed to be the same on the two occasions. For Table 20.5, the percentage agreement is $100 \times (61 + 25)/94 = 91.5\%$. However, this method can be misleading because it does not take into account the agreement which we would expect even if the two observations were unrelated.

Consider Table 20.6, which shows some artificial data relating observations by one observer, A, to those by three others, B, C, and D. For Observers A and B, the percentage agreement is 80%, as it is for Observers A and C. This would suggest that Observers B and C are equivalent in their agreement with A. However, Observer C always chooses 'No'. Because Observer A chooses 'No' often, A and C appear to agree, but in fact they are using different and unrelated strategies for forming their opinions. Observers A and D give ratings which are independent of one another, the frequencies in Table 20.6 being equal to the expected frequencies under the null hypothesis of independence (chi-squared = 0.0), calculated by the method described in Section 13.1. The percentage agreement is 68%, which may not sound very much worse than 80% for A and B. However, there is no more agreement

Table 20.5 Answers to the question: 'Have you ever smoked a cigarette?', by Derbyshire schoolchildren (data from Bland *et al.* 1975)

Self-administered questionnaire	Interview		Total
	Yes	**No**	
Yes	61	2	63
No	6	25	31
Total	67	27	94

Table 20.6 Artificial tabulation of observations by four observers

Observer A	Observer B			Observer C			Observer D		
	Yes	**No**	**Total**	**Yes**	**No**	**Total**	**Yes**	**No**	**Total**
Yes	10	10	20	0	20	20	4	16	20
No	10	70	80	0	80	80	16	64	80
Total	20	80	100	0	100	100	20	80	100

than we would expect by chance. The proportion of subjects for which there is agreement tells us nothing at all. To look at the extent to which there is agreement other than that expected by chance, we need a different method of analysis: Cohen's kappa.

Cohen's kappa (Cohen 1960) was introduced as a measure of agreement which avoids the previously described problems by adjusting the observed proportional agreement to take account of the amount of agreement which would be expected by chance.

First, we calculate the proportion of units where there is agreement, p, and the proportion of units which would be expected to agree by chance, p_e. The expected numbers agreeing are found as in chi-squared tests, by row total times column total divided by grand total (Section 13.1).

For Table 20.5, for example, we get $p = (61 + 25)/94 = 0.915$ and

$$p_e = \frac{63 \times 67/94 + 31 \times 27/94}{94} = 0.572$$

Cohen's kappa (κ) is then defined by

$$\kappa = \frac{p - p_e}{1 - p_e}$$

For Table 20.5 we get:

$$\kappa = \frac{0.915 - 0.572}{1 - 0.572} = 0.801$$

Cohen's kappa is thus the agreement adjusted for that expected by chance. It is the amount by which the observed agreement exceeds that expected by chance alone, divided by the maximum which this difference could be. Kappa distinguishes between the agreement shown between pairs of observers A and B, A and C, and A and D in Table 20.6 very well. For Observers A and B,

$\kappa = 0.37$, whereas for Observers A and C $\kappa = 0.00$, as it does for Observers A and D.

We will have perfect agreement when all agree, so $p = 1$. For perfect agreement $\kappa = 1$. We may have no agreement in the sense of no relationship, when $p = p_e$ and so $\kappa = 0$. We may also have no agreement when there is an inverse relationship. In Table 20.5, this would be if children who said 'no' the first time said 'yes' the second and vice versa. We would have $p < p_e$ and so $\kappa < 0$. The lowest possible value for κ is $-p_e/(1 - p_e)$, so depending on p_e, κ may take any negative value. Thus κ is not like a correlation coefficient, lying between -1 and $+1$. Only values between 0 and 1 have any useful meaning.

Note that kappa is always less than the proportion agreeing, p, unless agreement is perfect. You could just trust me, or we can see this mathematically because:

$$p - \kappa = p - \frac{p - p_e}{1 - p_e}$$

$$= \frac{p \times (1 - p_e) - p_e}{1 - p_e}$$

$$= \frac{p - p \times p_e - p + p_e}{1 - p_e}$$

$$= \frac{p_e - p \times p_e}{1 - p_e}$$

$$= \frac{p_e \times (1 - p)}{1 - p_e}$$

and this must be greater than 0 because p_e, $1 - p$, and $1 - p_e$ are all greater than 0 unless $p = 1$, when $p - \kappa$ is equal to 0. Hence p must be greater than kappa.

How large should kappa be to indicate good agreement? This is a difficult question, as what constitutes good agreement will depend on the use to which the assessment will be put. Kappa is not easy to interpret in

Table 20.7 Interpretation of kappa (data from Landis and Koch 1977 and Altman 1991)

Value of kappa	Strength of agreement	
	Landis and Koch	Altman
<0.00	Poor	—
0.00–0.20	Slight	Poor
0.21–0.40	Fair	Fair
0.41–0.60	Moderate	Moderate
0.61–0.80	Substantial	Good
0.81–1.00	Almost perfect	Very good

terms of the precision of a single observation. The problem is the same as arises with correlation coefficients for measurement error in continuous data. Table 20.7 gives two guidelines for its interpretation, one by Landis and Koch (1977), the other, slightly adapted from Landis and Koch, by Altman (1991). I prefer the Altman version, because kappa less than zero to me suggests positive disagreement rather than poor agreement and 'almost perfect' seems too good to be true. Table 20.7 is only a guide, and does not help much when we are interested in the clinical meaning of an assessment.

There are problems in the interpretation of kappa. Kappa depends on the proportions of subjects who have true values in each category. For a simple example, suppose we have two categories, the proportion in the first category is p_1, and the probability that an observer is correct is q. For simplicity, we shall assume that the probability of a correct assessment is unrelated to the subject's true status. This gives us for kappa:

$$\kappa = \frac{p_1(1 - p_1)}{\dfrac{q(1 - q)}{(2q - 1)^2} + p_1(1 - p_1)}$$

Trust me. Inspection of this equation shows that unless $q = 1$ or 0.5, i.e. all observations always correct, $\kappa = 1$, or random assessments, $\kappa = 0$, kappa depends on p_1, having a maximum when $p_1 = 0.5$. Thus kappa will be specific for a given population. This is like the intraclass correlation coefficient, to which kappa is related, and has the same implications for sampling. If we choose a group of subjects to have a larger number in rare categories than does the population we are studying, kappa will be larger in the observer agreement sample than it would be in the population as a whole.

Figure 20.2 shows the predicted two-category kappa against the proportion who are 'yes' for different probabilities that the observer's assessment will be correct under this simple model. Kappa is maximum when the probability of a true 'yes' is 0.5. As this probability gets closer to zero or to one, the expected kappa gets smaller, quite dramatically so at the extremes when agreement is very good. Unless the agreement is perfect, if one of two

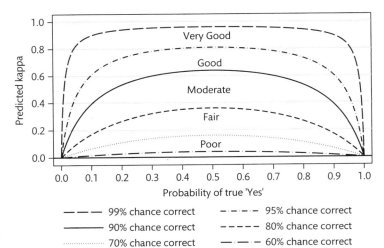

Figure 20.2 Predicted kappa for two categories, 'yes' and 'no', by probability of a 'yes' and probability observer will be correct. The verbal categories of Altman's classification are shown.

categories is small compared with the other, kappa will almost always be small, no matter how good the agreement is. This causes grief for a lot of users. We can see that the lines in Figure 20.2 correspond quite closely to the categories shown in Table 20.7.

A large-sample approximation standard error and confidence interval can be found for kappa. The standard error of κ is given by

$$SE(\kappa) = \sqrt{\frac{p \times (1 - p)}{n \times (1 - p_e)^2}}$$

where n is the number of subjects. The 95% confidence interval for κ is $\kappa - 1.96 \times SE(\kappa)$ to $\kappa + 1.96 \times SE(\kappa)$ as κ is approximately Normally Distributed, provided np and $n(1 - p)$ are large enough, say greater than five.

For the data of Table 20.5:

$$SE(\kappa) = \sqrt{\frac{p \times (1 - p)}{n \times (1 - p_e)^2}}$$

$$= \sqrt{\frac{0.915 \times (1 - 0.915)}{94 \times (1 - 0.572)^2}}$$

$$= 0.067$$

For the 95% confidence interval we have: $0.801 - 1.96 \times 0.067$ to $0.801 + 1.96 \times 0.067 = 0.67$ to 0.93.

We can also carry out a significance test of the null hypothesis of no agreement. The null hypothesis is that in the population $\kappa = 0$, or $p = p_e$. This affects the standard error of kappa because the standard error depends on p, in the same way that it does for proportions (Section 8.4). Under the null hypothesis, p can be replaced by p_e in the standard error formula:

$$SE(\kappa) = \sqrt{\frac{p \times (1 - p)}{n \times (1 - p_e)^2}}$$

$$= \sqrt{\frac{p_e \times (1 - p_e)}{n \times (1 - p_e)^2}}$$

$$= \sqrt{\frac{p_e}{n \times (1 - p_e)}}$$

If the null hypothesis were true, $\kappa/SE(\kappa)$ would be from a Standard Normal Distribution. For the example, $\kappa/SE(\kappa) = 6.71$, $P < 0.000\,1$. This test is one tailed (Section 9.5), as zero and all negative values of κ mean no

agreement. Because the confidence interval and the significance test use different standard errors, it is possible to get a significant difference when the confidence interval contains zero. In that case, there would be evidence of some agreement, but kappa would be poorly estimated.

Cohen (1960) dealt with only two observers. In many observer variation studies, we have observations on a group of subjects by many observers. For an example, Table 20.8 shows the results of a study of observer variation in transactional analysis (Falkowski et al. 1980). Observers watched video recordings of discussions between people with anorexia and their families. Observers classified 40 statements as being made in the role of 'adult', 'parent' or 'child', as a way of understanding the psychological relationships between the family members. For some statements, such as statement 1, there was perfect agreement, all observers giving the same classification. Others statements, e.g. statement 15, produced no agreement between the observers. These data were collected as a validation exercise, to see whether there was any agreement at all between observers.

Fleiss (1971) extended Cohen's kappa to the study of agreement between many observers. To estimate kappa by Fleiss's method, we ignore any relationship between observers for different subjects. This method does not take any weighting of disagreements into account, and so is suitable for the data of Table 20.8. We shall omit the details. For Table 20.8, $\kappa = 0.43$.

Fleiss only gives the standard error of kappa for testing the null hypothesis of no agreement. For Table 20.8 it is $SE(\kappa) = 0.02198$. If the null hypothesis were true, the ratio $\kappa/SE(\kappa)$ would be from a Standard Normal Distribution; $\kappa/SE(\kappa) = 0.43156/0.02198 = 19.6$, $P < 0.001$. The agreement is highly significant and we can conclude that transactional analysts' assessments are not random. We can extend Fleiss's method to the case when the number of observers is not the same for each subject but varies, and for weighted kappa (Section 20.4).

Kappa statistics have several applications. They are used to assess agreement between classifications made on the same participants on different occasions, between classifications made by different observers, between classifications made by different methods, and by different reviewers identifying relevant studies or extracting data from studies in systematic reviews.

Table 20.8 Ratings of 40 statements as 'adult', 'parent' or 'child' by 10 transactional analysts (data from Falkowski *et al.* 1980)

Statement	Observer									
	A	**B**	**C**	**D**	**E**	**F**	**G**	**H**	**I**	**J**
1	C	C	C	C	C	C	C	C	C	C
2	P	C	C	C	C	P	C	C	C	C
3	A	C	C	C	C	P	P	C	C	C
4	P	A	A	A	P	A	C	C	C	C
5	A	A	A	A	P	A	A	A	A	P
6	C	C	C	C	C	C	C	C	C	C
7	A	A	A	A	P	A	A	A	A	A
8	C	C	C	C	A	C	P	A	C	C
9	P	P	P	P	P	P	P	A	P	P
10	P	P	P	P	P	P	P	P	P	P
11	P	C	C	C	C	P	C	C	C	C
12	P	P	P	P	P	P	A	C	C	P
13	P	A	P	P	P	A	P	P	A	A
14	C	P	P	P	P	P	P	C	A	P
15	A	A	P	P	P	C	P	A	A	C
16	P	A	C	P	P	A	C	C	C	C
17	P	P	C	C	C	C	P	A	C	C
18	C	C	C	C	C	A	P	C	C	C
19	C	A	C	C	C	A	C	A	C	C
20	A	C	P	C	P	P	P	A	C	P
21	C	C	C	P	C	C	C	C	C	C
22	A	A	C	A	P	A	C	A	A	A
23	P	P	P	P	P	A	P	P	P	P
24	P	C	P	C	C	P	P	C	P	P
25	C	C	C	C	C	C	C	C	C	C
26	C	C	C	C	C	C	C	C	C	C
27	A	P	P	A	P	A	C	C	A	A
28	C	C	C	C	C	C	C	C	C	C
29	A	A	C	C	A	A	A	A	A	A

continued

Table 20.8 (continued)

Statement	Observer									
	A	**B**	**C**	**D**	**E**	**F**	**G**	**H**	**I**	**J**
30	A	A	C	A	P	P	A	P	A	A
31	C	C	C	C	C	C	C	C	C	C
32	P	C	P	P	P	P	C	P	P	P
33	P	P	P	P	P	P	P	P	P	P
34	P	P	P	P	A	C	C	A	C	C
35	P	P	P	P	P	A	P	P	A	P
36	P	P	P	P	P	P	P	C	C	P
37	A	C	P	P	P	P	P	P	C	A
38	C	C	C	C	C	C	C	C	C	P
39	A	C	C	C	C	C	C	C	C	C
40	A	P	C	A	A	A	A	A	A	A

20.4 Weighted kappa

Table 20.9 shows the agreement between two ratings of physical health, obtained from a sample of mainly elderly stoma patients. For the data of Table 20.9, kappa is low, 0.13. However, this may be misleading. Here the categories are ordered. The disagreement between 'good' and 'excellent' is not as great as between 'poor' and 'excellent'. We may think that a difference of one category is reasonable whereas others are not. We can take this into account if we allocate weights to the importance of disagreements, as shown in Table 20.10.

We suppose that the disagreement between 'Poor' and 'Excellent' is three times that between 'Poor' and 'Fair'. As the weight is for the degree of disagreement, a weight of zero means that observations in this cell agree.

Now for another little mathematical diversion, which you could skip. Denote the weight for cell in row i and

Table 20.9 Physical health of 366 subjects as judged by a health visitor and the subject's general practitioners (data supplied by Lea MacDonald)

General practitioner	Health visitor				Total
	Poor	**Fair**	**Good**	**Excellent**	
Poor	2	12	8	0	22
Fair	9	35	43	7	94
Good	4	36	103	40	83
Excellent	1	8	36	22	67
Total	16	91	190	69	366

$p = 0.443$, $p_e = 0.361$, $\kappa = 0.13$

Table 20.10 Weights for disagreement between ratings of physical health as judged by health visitor and general practitioner (data supplied by Lea MacDonald)

General practitioner	Health visitor			
	Poor	Fair	Good	Excellent
Poor	0	1	2	3
Fair	1	0	1	2
Good	2	1	0	1
Excellent	3	2	1	0

Table 20.11 Alternative weights for disagreement between ratings of physical health as judged by health visitor and general practitioner (data supplied by Lea MacDonald)

General practitioner	Health visitor			
	Poor	Fair	Good	Excellent
Poor	0	1	4	9
Fair	1	0	1	4
Good	4	1	0	1
Excellent	9	4	1	0

column j (cell i, j) by $w_{i,j}$, the proportion in cell i, j by $p_{i,j}$, and the expected proportion in cell i, j by $p_{e,i,j}$. The weighted disagreement will be found by multiplying the proportion in each cell by its weight and adding, $\Sigma w_{i,j} p_{i,j}$. We can turn this into a weighted proportion disagreeing by dividing by the maximum weight, w_{max}. This is the largest value which $\Sigma w_{i,j} p_{ij}$ can take, attained when all observations are in the cell with the largest weight. The weighted proportion agreeing would be one minus this. Thus the weighted proportion agreeing is $p = 1 - \Sigma w_{i,j} p_{i,j} / w_{max}$. Similarly, the weighted expected proportion agreeing is $p_e = 1 - \Sigma w_{i,j} p_{e,i,j} / w_{max}$. We then define weighted kappa as for standard kappa, using these values for p and p_e. If all the $w_{i,j} = 1$ except on the main diagonal, where $w_{i,j} = 0$, we get the usual unweighted kappa.

For Table 20.9, using the weights of Table 20.10, we get $\kappa_w = 0.23$, larger than the unweighted value of 0.13.

The standard error of weighted kappa is given by the approximate formula:

$$\sqrt{\frac{\Sigma w_{i,j}^2 p_{i,j} - (\Sigma w_{i,j} p_{i,j})^2}{m(\Sigma w_{i,j} p_{e,i,j})^2}}$$

For the significance test this reduces to

$$\sqrt{\frac{\Sigma w_{i,j}^2 p_{e,i,j} - (\Sigma w_{i,j} p_{e,i,j})^2}{m(\Sigma w_{i,j} p_{e,i,j})^2}}$$

by replacing the observed p_{ij} by their expected values under the null hypothesis. We use these as we did for unweighted kappa.

The choice of weights is important. If we define a new set, the squares of the old, as shown in Table 20.11, we get $\kappa_w = 0.35$.

In the example, the agreement is better if we attach a bigger relative penalty to disagreements between 'poor' and 'excellent'. Clearly, we should define these weights in advance rather than derive them from the data. The weights in Table 20.10 are called linear weights. **Linear weights** are proportional to number of categories apart. The weights in Table 20.11 are called quadratic weights. **Quadratic weights** are proportional to the square of the number of categories apart. Cohen (1968) recommended that a committee of experts decide the weights, but in practice it seems unlikely that this happens very often. In any case, when using weighted kappa we should state the weights used. I suspect that in practice people use the default weights of the program.

Tables 20.10 and 20.11 show weights for disagreement, as originally defined by Cohen (1968). It is also possible to describe the weights as weights for the agreement rather than the disagreement. Agreement weights would give the weight for perfect agreement along the main diagonal (i.e. 'poor'; and 'poor', 'fair' and 'fair', etc.) as 1.0. We then give smaller weights for the other cells, the smallest weight being for the biggest disagreement (i.e. 'poor' and 'excellent'). Table 20.12 shows linear weights for agreement rather than for disagreement, standardized so that 1.0 is perfect agreement. Like Table 20.10, in Table 20.12 the weights are equally spaced, going down to zero. To get the weights for agreement from those for disagreement, we subtract the disagreement

Table 20.12 Linear weights for agreement between ratings of physical health as judged by health visitor and general practitioner (data supplied by Lea MacDonald)

General practitioner	Health visitor			
	Poor	**Fair**	**Good**	**Excellent**
Poor	1.00	0.67	0.33	0.00
Fair	0.67	1.00	0.67	0.33
Good	0.33	0.67	1.00	0.67
Excellent	0.00	0.33	0.67	1.00

Table 20.13 Quadratic weights for agreement between ratings of physical health as judged by health visitor and general practitioner (data supplied by Lea MacDonald)

General practitioner	Health visitor			
	Poor	**Fair**	**Good**	**Excellent**
Poor	1.00	0.89	0.56	0.00
Fair	0.89	1.00	0.89	0.56
Good	0.56	0.89	1.00	0.89
Excellent	0.00	0.56	0.89	1.00

weights from their maximum value and divide by that maximum value. For the quadratic weights of Table 20.11, we get the quadratic weights for agreement shown in Table 20.13. Both versions of linear weights give the same kappa statistic, as do both versions of quadratic weights.

20.5 Comparing two methods of measurement

In clinical measurement, most of the things we want to measure, hearts, lungs, livers and so on, are deep within living bodies and out of reach. This means that many of the methods we use to measure them are indirect and we cannot be sure how closely they are related to what we really want to know. When a new method of measurement is developed, rather than compare its outcome with a set of known values we must often compare it with

Table 20.14 Comparison of two methods of measuring PEFR

Subject number	PEFR (litres/min)		Difference Wright–mini
	Wright meter	**Mini meter**	
1	494	512	-18
2	395	430	-35
3	516	520	-4
4	434	428	6
5	476	500	-24
6	557	600	-43
7	413	364	49
8	442	380	62
9	650	658	-8
10	433	445	-12
11	417	432	-15
12	656	626	30
13	267	260	7
14	478	477	1
15	178	259	-81
16	423	350	73
17	427	451	-24
Total			-36
Mean	·		2.1
S.d.			38.8

another method just as indirect. This is a common type of study, and one which is often badly done (Altman and Bland 1983; Bland and Altman 1986).

Table 20.14 shows measurements of PEFR by two different methods, the Wright meter data coming from Table 20.2. For simplicity, I shall use only one measurement by each method here. We could make use of the duplicate data by using the average of each pair first, but this introduces an extra stage in the calculation. Bland and Altman (1986, 1999, 2007) give details.

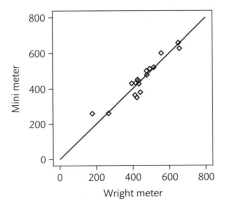

Figure 20.3 PEFR measured by two different instruments, mini meter vs Wright meter.

The first step in the analysis is to plot the data as a scatter diagram (Figure 20.3). If we draw the line of equality, along which the two measurements would be exactly equal, this gives us an idea of the extent to which the two methods agree. This is not the best way of looking at data of this type, because much of the graph is empty space and the interesting information is clustered along the line. A better approach is to plot the difference between the methods against the sum or average. The sign of the difference is important, as there is a possibility that one method may give higher values than the other, and this may be related to the true value we are trying to measure. This plot is shown in Figure 20.4. The line of equality is now a horizontal line through zero.

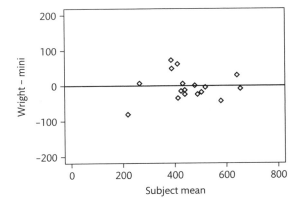

Figure 20.4 PEFR measured by two different instruments, difference versus mean of mini and Wright meters.

Two methods of measurement agree if the difference between observations on the same subject using both methods is small enough for us to use the methods interchangeably. How small this difference has to be depends on the measurement and the use to which it is to be put. It is a clinical, not a statistical, decision. We quantify the differences by estimating the bias, which is the mean difference, and the limits within which most differences will lie. We estimate these limits from the mean and standard deviation of the differences. If we are to estimate these quantities, we want them to be the same for high values and for low values of the measurement. We can check this from the plot of difference against average. There is no clear evidence of a relationship between difference and mean in Figure 20.4, and we can check this by a test of significance using the correlation coefficient. We get $r = 0.19$, $P = 0.5$.

The mean difference is close to zero, so there is little evidence of overall bias. We can find a confidence interval for the mean difference as described in Section 10.2. The differences have a mean $\bar{d} = -2.1$ litres/min, and a standard deviation of 38.8. The standard error of the mean is thus $s/\sqrt{n} = 38.8/\sqrt{17} = 9.41$ litres/min and the corresponding value of t with 16 degrees of freedom is 2.12 (Table 10.1). The 95% confidence interval for the bias is thus $-2.1 \pm 2.12 \times 9.41 = -22$ to $+18$ litres/min. Thus on the basis of these data we could have a bias of as much as 22 litres/min, which could be clinically important. The original comparison of these instruments used a much larger sample and found that any bias was very small (Oldham *et al.* 1979).

The standard deviation of the differences between measurements made by the two methods provides a good index of the comparability of the methods. If we can estimate the mean and standard deviation reliably, with small standard errors, we can then say that the difference between methods will be at most two standard deviations on either side of the mean for 95% of observations. These $\bar{d} \pm 2s$, or, more precisely, $\bar{d} \pm 1.96s$, limits for the difference are called the **95% limits of agreement**. For the PEFR data, the standard deviation of the differences is estimated to be 38.8 litres/min and the mean is -2 litres/min. Two standard deviations is therefore 78 litres/min. The reading with the mini meter is

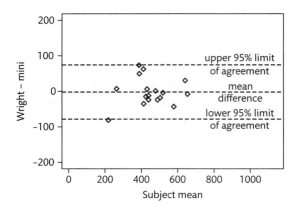

Figure 20.5 PEFR measured by two different instruments, difference versus mean of mini and Wright meters.

expected to be 80 litres below to 76 litres above for most subjects. These limits are shown as horizontal lines in Figure 20.5. The limits depend on the assumption that the distribution of the differences is approximately Normal, which can be checked by histogram and Normal plot (Section 7.5) (Figure 20.6).

On the basis of these data we would not conclude that the two methods are comparable or that the mini meter could reliably replace the Wright peak flow meter. As remarked in Section 10.2, this meter had received considerable wear.

When there is a relationship between the difference and the mean, we can try to remove it by a transformation. This is usually accomplished by the logarithm, and leads to an interpretation of the limits similar to that described in Section 20.2. Bland and Altman (1986, 1999) give details. Figure 20.5 is called a **Bland Altman plot**.

20.6 Sensitivity and specificity

One of the main reasons for making clinical measurements is to aid in diagnosis. This may be to identify one of several possible diagnoses in a patient, or to find people with a particular disease in an apparently healthy population. The latter is known as **screening**. In either case the measurement provides a test which enables us to classify subjects into two groups, one group whom we think are likely to have the disease in which we are interested, and another group unlikely to have the disease. When developing such a test, we need to compare the test result with a true diagnosis. The test may be based on a continuous variable and the disease indicated if it is above or below a given level, or it may be a qualitative observation such as carcinoma *in situ* cells on a cervical smear. In either case I shall call the test positive if it indicates the disease and negative if not, and the disease positive if the disease is later confirmed, negative if not.

How do we measure the effectiveness of the test? Table 20.15 shows three artificial sets of test and disease data. We could take as an index of test effectiveness the proportion giving the correct diagnosis from the test. For Test 1 in the example it is 94%. Now consider Test 2, which always gives a negative result. Test 2 will never detect any cases of the disease. We are now right for 95% of the subjects! However, the first test is useful, in that it detects some cases of the disease, and the second is not, so this is clearly a poor index.

There is no one simple index which enables us to compare different tests in all the ways we would like. This is because there are two things we need to measure: how good the test is at finding disease positives, i.e. those

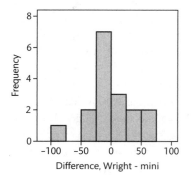

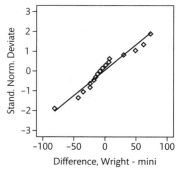

Figure 20.6 Distribution of differences between PEFR measured by two methods.

Table 20.15 Some artificial test and diagnosis data

Disease	Test 1		Test 2		Test 3		Total
	+ve	–ve	+ve	–ve	+ve	–ve	
Yes	4	1	0	5	2	3	5
No	5	90	0	95	0	95	95
Total	9	91	0	100	2	98	100

with the condition, and how good the test is at excluding disease negatives, i.e. those who do not have the condition. The indices conventionally employed to do this are:

sensitivity = Number of people who are both disease positive and test positive divided by the number who are disease positive,

specificity = Number who are both disease negative and test negative divided by the number who are disease negative.

In other words, the sensitivity is a proportion of disease positives who are test positive, and the specificity is the proportion of disease negatives who are test negatives. For our three tests these are:

	Test 1	Test 2	Test 3
Sensitivity	0.80	0.00	0.40
Specificity	0.95	1.00	1.00

Test 2, of course, misses all the disease positives and finds all the disease negatives, by saying all are negative. The difference between Tests 1 and 3 is brought out by the greater sensitivity of 1 and the greater specificity of 3. We are comparing tests in two dimensions. We can see that Test 3 is better than Test 2, because its sensitivity is higher and specificity the same. However, it is more difficult to see whether Test 3 is better than Test 1. We must come to a judgement based on the relative importance of sensitivity and specificity in the particular case.

Sensitivity and specificity are often multiplied by 100 to give percentages. They are both binomial proportions, so their standard errors and confidence intervals are found as described in Sections 8.4 and 8.9. Because the proportions are often near to 1.0, the large sample approach (Section 8.4) may not be valid. The exact method using the Binomial probabilities (Section 8.9) is preferable. Harper and Reeves (1999) point out that confidence intervals are almost always omitted in studies of diagnostic tests reported outside the major general medical journals, and recommend that they should always be given. As the reader might expect, I agree with them! The sample size required for the reliable estimation of sensitivity and specificity can be calculated as described in Section 18.2.

Sometimes a test is based on a continuous variable. For example, Table 20.16 shows measurements of creatine kinase (CK) in patients with unstable angina and acute myocardial infarction (AMI), two conditions which can be hard to tell apart clinically. Figure 20.7 shows a scatter plot. We wish to detect patients with AMI among patients who may have either condition and this measurement is a potential test, AMI patients tending to have high values. How do we choose the cut-off point? The lowest CK in AMI patients is 90, so a cut-off below this will detect all AMI patients. Using 80, for example, we would detect all AMI patients, sensitivity = 1.00, but would also only have 42% of angina patients below 80, so the sensitivity = 0.42. We can alter the sensitivity and specificity by changing the cut-off point. Raising the cut-off point will mean fewer cases will be detected and so the sensitivity will be decreased. However, there will be fewer false positives, positives on test but who do not in fact have

Table 20.16 Creatine kinase in patients with unstable angina and acute myocardial infarction (AMI) (data supplied by Frances Boa)

Unstable angina							AMI	
23	48	62	83	104	130	307	90	648
33	49	63	84	105	139	351	196	894
36	52	63	85	105	150	360	302	962
37	52	65	86	107	155		311	1 015
37	52	65	88	108	157		325	1 143
41	53	66	88	109	162		335	1 458
41	54	67	88	111	176		347	1 955
41	57	71	89	114	180		349	2 139
42	57	72	91	116	188		363	2 200
42	58	72	94	118	198		377	3 044
43	58	73	94	121	226		390	7 590
45	58	73	95	121	232		398	11 138
47	60	75	97	122	257		545	
48	60	80	100	126	257		577	
48	60	80	103	130	297		629	

the disease, and the specificity will be increased. For example, if CK $\geq$ 100 were the criterion for AMI, sensitivity would be 0.96 and specificity 0.62. There is a trade-off between sensitivity and specificity. It can be helpful to plot sensitivity against specificity to examine this trade-off. This is called a **receiver operating characteristic** or **ROC** curve. (The name comes from telecommunications.) We often plot sensitivity against one minus specificity, as in Figure 20.8. We can see from Figure 20.8 that we can get both high sensitivity and high specificity if we choose the right cut-off. With 1-specificity less than 0.1, i.e. specificity greater than 0.9, we can get sensitivity greater than 0.9 also. In fact, a cut-off of 200 would give sensitivity = 0.93 and specificity = 0.91 in this sample. These estimates will be biased, because we are estimating the cut-off and testing it in the same sample. We should check the sensitivity and specificity of this cut-off in a different sample to be sure.

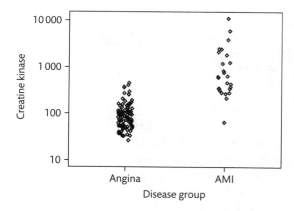

Figure 20.7 Scatter diagram for the data of Table 20.16 (data supplied by Frances Boa).

The area under the ROC curve is often quoted (here it is 0.975 3). It estimates the probability that a member of one population chosen at random will exceed a

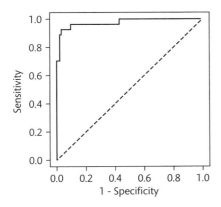

Figure 20.8 ROC curve for the data of Table 20.16 (data supplied by Frances Boa).

member of the other population, in the same way as does U/n_1n_2 in the Mann–Whitney U test (Section 12.2). It can be useful in comparing different tests. In this study another blood test gave us an area under the ROC curve = 0.9825, suggesting that the test may be slightly better than CK.

We can also estimate the **positive predictive value** or **PPV**, the probability that a subject who is test positive will be a **true positive** (i.e. has the disease and is correctly classified), and the **negative predictive value** or **NPV**, the probability that a subject who is test negative will be a **true negative** (i.e. does not have the disease and is correctly classified). These depend on the prevalence of the condition, p_{prev}, as well as the sensitivity, p_{sens}, and the specificity, p_{spec}. If the sample is a single group of people, not selected by diagnosis, we know the prevalence and can estimate PPV and NPV for this population directly as simple proportions. If we started with a sample of cases with a true positive diagnosis and a sample of controls with a true negative diagnosis, we could not calculate the prevalence from the sample. We can still use the sensitivity and specificity to estimate PPV and NPV for a population with any given prevalence. As described in Section 6.8, p_{sens} is the conditional probability of a positive test given the disease, so the probability of being both test positive and disease positive is $p_{sens} \times p_{prev}$. Similarly, the probability of being both test positive and disease negative is $(1 - p_{spec}) \times (1 - p_{prev})$. The probability of being test positive is the sum of these (Section 6.2):

$p_{sens} \times p_{prev} + (1 - p_{spec}) \times (1 - p_{prev})$ and the positive predictive value is

$$PPV = \frac{p_{sens} p_{prev}}{p_{sens} p_{prev} + (1 - p_{spec})(1 - p_{prev})}$$

Similarly, the negative predictive value is

$$NPV = \frac{p_{spec}(1 - p_{prev})}{p_{spec}(1 - p_{prev}) + (1 - p_{sens})p_{prev}}$$

In screening situations the prevalence is almost always small and the PPV is low. Suppose we have a fairly sensitive and specific test, $p_{sens} = 0.95$ and $p_{spec} = 0.90$, and the disease has prevalence $p_{prev} = 0.01$ (1%). Then

$$PPV = \frac{0.95 \times 0.01}{0.95 \times 0.01 + (1 - 0.90) \times (1 - 0.01)}$$
$$= 0.088$$
$$NPV = \frac{0.90 \times (1 - 0.01)}{0.90 \times (1 - 0.01) + (1 - 0.95) \times 0.01}$$
$$= 0.999$$

so only 8.8% of test positives would be true positives, but almost all test negatives would be true negatives. Most screening tests are dealing with much smaller prevalences than this, so most screening test positives are false positives.

20.7 **Normal range or reference interval**

In Section 20.6 we were concerned with the diagnosis of particular diseases. In this section we look at it the other way round and ask what values measurements on normal, healthy people are likely to have. There are difficulties in doing this. Who is 'normal' anyway? In the UK population almost everyone has hard fatty deposits in their coronary arteries, which result in death for many of them. Very few rural Africans have this; they die from other causes. So it is normal in the UK to have an abnormality. We usually say that normal people are the apparently healthy members of the local population. We can draw a sample of these as described in Chapter 3 and make the measurement on them.

The next problem is to estimate the set of values. If we use the range of the observations, the difference between the two most extreme values, we can be fairly confident that if we carry on sampling we will eventually find observations outside it, and the range will get bigger and bigger (Section 4.7). To avoid this we use a range between two quantiles (Section 4.7), usually the 2.5 centile and the 97.5 centile, which is called the **normal range**, **95% reference range**, or **95% reference interval**. This leaves 5% of normals outside the 'normal range', which is the set of values within which 95% of measurements from apparently healthy individuals will lie.

A third difficulty comes from confusion between 'normal' as used in medicine and 'Normal distribution' as used in statistics. This has led some people to develop approaches which say that all data which do not fit under a Normal curve are abnormal! Such methods are simply absurd, there is no reason to suppose that all variables follow a Normal distribution (Sections 7.4, 7.5). The term 'reference interval' has the advantage of avoiding this confusion. However, the most frequently used method of estimation rests on the assumption that the variable follows a Normal distribution.

We have already seen that in general most observations fall within two standard deviations of the mean, and that for a Normal distribution 95% are within these limits, with 2.5% below and 2.5% above. If we estimate the mean and standard deviation of data from a Normal population we can estimate the reference interval as $\bar{x}-2s$ to $\bar{x}+2s$.

Consider the FEV1 data of Table 4.5. We will estimate the reference interval for FEV1 in male medical students. We have 57 observations, mean 4.06 and standard deviation 0.67 litres. The reference interval is thus $4.06 - 2 \times 0.67 = 2.7$ to $4.06 + 2 \times 0.67 = 5.4$ litres. From Table 4.4 we see that in fact only one student (2%) is outside these limits, although the sample is rather small.

As the observations are assumed to be from a Normal distribution, standard errors and confidence intervals for these limits are easy to find. The estimates $\bar{x}$ and s are independent (Appendix 7A) with standard errors $\sqrt{s^2/n}$ and $\sqrt{s^2/2(n-1)}$ (Sections 8.2, 8.8). $\bar{x}$ follows a Normal distribution and s a distribution which is approximately

Normal. Hence $\bar{x} - 2s$ is from a Normal distribution with variance:

$$VAR(\bar{x} - 2s) = VAR(\bar{x}) + VAR(2s)$$
$$= VAR(\bar{x}) + 4VAR(s)$$
$$= \frac{s^2}{n} + 4 \times \frac{s^2}{2(n-1)}$$
$$= s^2 \left(\frac{1}{n} + \frac{2}{n-1} \right)$$

Hence, provided Normal assumptions hold, the standard error of the limit of the reference interval is

$$\sqrt{s^2 \left(\frac{1}{n} + \frac{2}{n-1} \right)}$$

If n is large, this is approximately $\sqrt{3s^2/n}$. For the FEV1 data, the standard error is $\sqrt{3 \times 0.67^2/57} = 0.15$. Hence the 95% confidence intervals for these limits are $2.7 \pm 1.96 \times 0.15$ and $5.4 \pm 1.96 \times 0.15$, i.e. from 2.4 to 3.0 and 5.1 to 5.7 litres.

Compare the serum triglyceride measurements of Table 4.8. As already noted (Sections 4.4, 7.4), the data are highly skewed, and we cannot use the Normal method directly. If we did, the lower limit would be 0.07, well below any of the observations, and the upper limit would be 0.94, greater than which are 5% of the observations. It is possible for such data to give a negative lower limit.

Figure 7.15 shows the $\log_{10}$ transformed data, which give a breathtakingly symmetrical distribution ($\bar{x} = -0.331$, $s = 0.171$). The lower limit in the transformed data is −0.67, corresponding to a triglyceride level of 0.21, below which are 2.1% of observations. The upper limit is 0.01, corresponding to 1.02, above which are 2.5% of observations. The fit to the log transformed data is excellent. For the standard error of the reference limit we have $\sqrt{3 \times 0.171^2/282} = 0.0176$. The 95% confidence intervals are thus $-0.673 \pm 1.96 \times 0.0176$ and $0.011 \pm 1.96 \times 0.0176$, i.e. −0.707 to −0.639 and −0.023 to 0.045. Transforming back to the linear scale, we get 0.196 to 0.230 and 0.948 to 1.109, found by taking the antilogs. These confidence limits can be transformed back to the original scale, unlike those in Section 10.4, because no subtraction of means has taken place.

Because of the obviously unsatisfactory nature of the Normal method for some data, some authors have advocated the estimation of the percentiles directly (Section 4.5), without any distributional assumptions. This is an attractive idea. We want to know the point below which 2.5% of values will fall. Let us simply rank the observations and find the point below which 2.5% of the observations fall. For the 282 triglycerides, the 2.5 and 97.5 centiles are found as follows. For the 2.5 centile, we find $i = q(n + 1) = 0.025 \times (282 + 1) = 7.08$. The required quantile will be between the 7th and 8th observation. The 7th is 0.21, the 8th is 0.22 so the 2.5 centile would be estimated by $0.21 + (0.22 - 0.21) \times (7.08 - 7) = 0.211$. Similarly the 97.5 centile is 1.039.

This approach gives an unbiased estimate whatever the distribution. The log transformed triglyceride would give exactly the same results. Note that the Normal theory limits from the log transformed data are very similar. We now look at the confidence interval. The 95% confidence interval for the q quantile, here q being 0.025 or 0.975, estimated directly from the data is found by the Binomial distribution method (Section 8.10). For the triglyceride data, $n = 282$ and so for the lower limit, $q = 0.025$, we have

$$j = 282 \times 0.025 - 1.96\sqrt{282 \times 0.025 \times 0.975}$$

$$k = 282 \times 0.025 + 1.96\sqrt{282 \times 0.025 \times 0.975}$$

This gives $j = 1.9$ and $k = 12.2$, which we round up to $j = 2$ and $k = 13$. In the triglyceride data the second observation, corresponding to $j = 2$, is 0.16 and the 13th is 0.26. Thus the 95% confidence interval for the lower reference limit is 0.16 to 0.26. The corresponding calculation for $q = 0.975$ gives $j = 270$ and $k = 281$. The 270th observation is 0.96 and the 281st is 1.64, giving a 95% confidence interval for the upper reference limit of 0.96 to 1.64. These are wider confidence intervals than those found by the Normal method, those for the long tail particularly so. This method of estimating percentiles in long tails is relatively imprecise.

20.8 Centile charts

Centile charts show the reference range for different values of some other variable, usually age. For example,

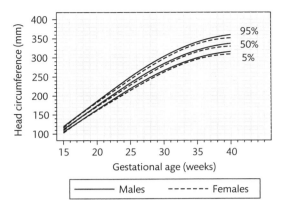

Figure 20.9 Centile chart of fetal head circumference by gestational age (data from Schwarzler *et al.* 2004).

Figure 20.9 shows a 90% reference range for fetal head circumference at different times of gestation.

This enables us to see at a glance the range for fetuses of any gestational age. Like any reference range, the centile chart is estimated from data on an apparently normal set of subjects. The data used to produce the chart for males in Figure 20.9 are shown in Figure 20.10. In this case, it was important to exclude any extra measurements on fetuses made because there was concern about the development of the pregnancy, as these would produce a bias in the estimate.

Several different methods have been used to generate centile charts, but I think that the best is due to Altman (1993). First we carry out regression with head

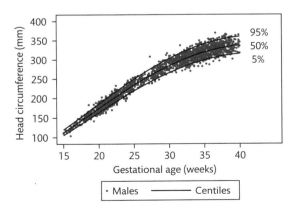

Figure 20.10 Fetal head circumference by gestational age for males, with fitted centile curves (data from Schwarzler *et al.* 2004).

circumference as the outcome (or dependent) variable
and gestational age as the predictor (explanatory or independent) variable. We use a regression method which
enables us to fit curves rather than straight lines (Section 15.6). This enables us to estimate the mean head
circumference for any gestational age. The problem is
that the standard deviation can vary with gestational age,
too. It clearly does so in Figure 20.10. We can estimate
the standard deviation from the residuals, the differences
between the observed values and those predicted by the
regression equation. Altman (1993) showed that, provided the residuals for any given gestational age followed
a Normal distribution, the absolute value of the residual,
without the plus or minus sign, can be used to estimate
the standard deviation. We do regression with the absolute residual as the outcome variable and gestational age
as the predictor. The standard deviation is given by the
predicted absolute residual multiplied by $\sqrt{\pi/2}$. We now
have equations to predict the mean and the standard deviation from the gestational age and we can use these to
calculate the centiles as we did for a simple reference
range.

20.9 Combining variables using principal components analysis

Sometimes we have several outcome variables and we
are interested in the effect of treatment on all of them.
For example, Motallebzadeh et al. (2007) compared the
neurocognitive function of 212 coronary artery bypass
surgery patients who were randomized to have the procedure on-pump, i.e. an artificial pump took over the
function of the heart, or off-pump, where the heart continued to function. An observational study had suggested
that using the pump resulted in long-term damage to
neurocognitive function. We had doubts about this and
carried out a randomized clinical trial. The participants
did a battery of neuropsychological tests which produced 21 different outcome variables. If we compared
each of these between the treatment groups, each individual variable would include only a small part of
the information, so power would be reduced. Also, the

possibility of a Type I error, where we have a significant
difference in the sample but no real difference in the
population, would be increased. We could deal with the
type I error by the Bonferroni correction (Section 9.10),
multiplying each P value by 21, but this would reduce the
power further.

The approach used by Motallebzadeh et al. (2007)
was to find a combination of the 21 variables which
contained as much of the available information as possible. This was done using a method called **principal
component analysis** or **PCA**. This finds a new set of
variables, each of which is a linear combination of the
original variables. A linear combination is found by multiplying each variable by a constant coefficient and adding,
as in a multiple regression equation. In PCA, we standardize the variables (subtracting the mean and dividing
by the standard deviation) and make the sum of the
coefficients squared equal to one. This is an arbitrary
method of enabling us to assign numerical values to
the components. First, we find the linear combination
which has the greatest possible variance. We call this the
first principal component. We then consider all the
possible linear combinations which are not correlated
with the first component and find the one with the largest variance. This combination is the **second principal
component**. We then consider all the possible linear
combinations which are not correlated with either the
first or the second principal component and find the one
with the largest variance. This combination is the **third
principal component**. We can go on like this until we
have as many principal components as there are variables. The advantage that the principal components have
over the original variables is that they are all uncorrelated
and that they are ordered by how much variance they
have, which tells us how much information they contain.
These calculations are all done by computer programs
and the mathematics is all done using matrix algebra. We
will omit this and go straight to the computer output (in
this case from Stata). Table 20.17 shows the eigenvalues
of the principal components.

Eigenvalues are a mathematical construct much used
in matrix algebra and in the study of linear transformation. As far as we are concerned it is just a name for
something which tells us how variable the principal components are. The column of eigenvalues adds to 21,

Table 20.17 Eigenvalues for the principal components of 21 neurocognitive test variables (data from Motallebzadeh *et al.* 2007)

Component	Eigenvalue	Percentage of variability explained	Cumulative percentage of variability
1	8.35	39.8	39.8
2	2.39	11.4	51.2
3	1.82	8.7	59.8
4	1.17	5.6	65.4
5	1.05	5.0	70.4
6	0.88	4.2	74.6
7	0.76	3.6	78.2
8	0.70	3.3	81.6
9	0.67	3.2	84.8
10	0.47	2.2	87.0
11	0.42	2.0	89.0
12	0.39	1.9	90.9
13	0.34	1.6	92.5
14	0.31	1.5	93.9
15	0.26	1.2	95.2
16	0.25	1.2	96.3
17	0.21	1.0	97.4
18	0.20	1.0	98.3
19	0.18	0.8	99.2
20	0.14	0.7	99.8
21	0.03	0.2	100.0
Total	21.00	100.0	100.0

the number of variables. The variances of the principal components are equal to the eigenvalues. Hence the eigenvalue divided by the sum of all the eigenvalues is the proportion of the total amount of variance which that component represents. In Table 20.17, this is shown in the column headed 'Percentage of variability explained'. We can see that our first principle component has eigenvalue 8.351 96 and 8.351 96/21 = 0.397 7. Hence our first principal component includes a proportion 0.397 7,

or 39.8%, of the total variation of all the 21 variables. The second principle component contains a further 0.1140, or 11.4% of the total variance, and so on. For this study, we just used the first principal component as our outcome variable.

Table 20.18 shows the coefficients for the first principal component. If we square these coefficients and add them, we get 1.00. Table 20.18 enables us to calculate the first principal component for each subject.

Table 20.18 Coefficients of the first principal component for 21 neurocognitive variables (data from Motallebzadeh *et al.* 2007)

Variable	Component 1
cft	0.033 47
cft1	0.245 94
cft2	0.248 18
gpt	-0.191 08
gpt1	-0.166 09
ravlt1	0.222 61
ravlt2	0.234 34
ravlt3	0.271 29
ravlt4	0.271 77
ravlt5	0.254 37
ravltb	0.157 45
ravlt6	0.254 08
ravlt30min	0.255 88
lct	-0.168 18
lct1	-0.146 15
tmt	-0.199 57
tmt1	-0.254 76
sdrt	-0.252 51
vft	0.200 14
vft1	0.192 92
vft2	0.214 12

We standardize each variable (i.e. subtract the mean and divide by the standard deviation), multiply each by the coefficient, and add. The program would do this for us directly, but having the coefficients meant that we could calculate it for the same variables measured after surgery and at the 3- and 6-months follow-up. (The result was that there was indeed a reduction in test score after surgery for on-pump patients, but this was entirely recovered after 6 months, Motallebzadeh *et al.* 2007.)

The reason a single linear combination of the 21 variables can include 39.8% of the variation is that many of these neurocognitive test outcomes are correlated with one another. Compare Table 20.19, which shows the result of a simulation, where PCA was done using 21 randomly generated Normal variables for 200 subjects. Here the first principal component explains only 7.8% of the variation. With 21 principal components, the average percentage of variability explained by a component is $1/21 = 0.48$ or 4.8%. The average eigenvalue will be 1.00, as the 21 eigenvalues add up to 21. In Table 20.17, the first component explains a lot more variability than we would expect if the variables were uncorrelated, 39.8% compared with 7.8% in Table 20.19.

Principal component analysis is described as a method for reducing the dimensions of a set of data. With 21 separate measurements we have 21 dimensions to our outcome variables. But if we describe them instead by the first few principal components, we reduce the dimensions considerably. For example, in Table 20.17 the first five components explain 70.5% of the variability. We could just analyse these five components and discard the remaining 16. We would still have most of the information. The remaining components will consist mainly of measurement error anyway and will have little real information in them.

There are two frequently used methods used to decide how many dimensions our variables really have. One is the **Kaiser criterion**. This states that we take all those components with eigenvalues greater than the average, which is 1.00. So in Table 20.17, we would have five dimensions to our data. In Table 20.19, we would have 10. This cut-off should be about halfway down the table if the variables are not correlated. An alternative method is the **Cattell scree plot**. This is a plot of the eigenvalue against the principal component number. Figure 20.11 shows the scree plot for Table 20.17. It is called a scree plot because it resembles the scree formed by fallen rocks at the bottom of an escarpment. There are two fairly distinct parts to it forming two straight lines, the large eigenvalues and the small eigenvalues, as indicated in Figure 20.11. The point where the divide occurs is decided by subjective judgement and different observers may not agree what the dimension of the data is. For the neurocognitive test data in Figure 20.11,

Table 20.19 Eigenvalues for PCA using 21 randomly generated Normal variables for 200 subjects

Component	Eigenvalue	Percentage of variability explained	Cumulative percentage of variability
1	1.64	7.8	7.8
2	1.52	7.2	15.0
3	1.42	6.8	21.8
4	1.32	6.3	28.1
5	1.29	6.1	34.3
6	1.28	6.1	40.4
7	1.21	5.8	46.1
8	1.14	5.4	51.5
9	1.09	5.2	56.7
10	1.00	4.8	61.5
11	0.95	4.5	66.0
12	0.92	4.4	70.4
13	0.88	4.2	74.6
14	0.83	4.0	78.5
15	0.79	3.8	82.3
16	0.78	3.7	86.0
17	0.73	3.5	89.5
18	0.63	3.0	92.5
19	0.59	2.8	95.3
20	0.51	2.4	97.7
21	0.48	2.3	100.0
Total	21.00	100.0	100.0

I think there are three dimensions and would not use more than the first three principal components. These would include 59.8% of the variability in the 21 variables. Although the scree plot is subjective, I think it produces a more useful answer than the objective Kaiser criterion. Compare the scree plot for the random numbers of Table 20.19, shown in Figure 20.12. The eigenvalues all lie roughly along a single line, with no scree. We cannot reduce the dimensions of the problem. We should regard all 21 eigenvalues as large eigenvalues.

20.10 Composite scales and subscales

In health research we often want to measure ill-defined and abstract things, like disability, depression, anxiety, and health. The obvious way to decide how depressed someone is to ask them. We could just ask 'how depressed are you on a scale of 1 to 10?', or use a visual analogue scale, but our subjects may not use that label for their problem. Instead we form a composite scale. We

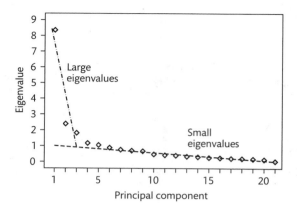

Figure 20.11 Scree plot for Table 20.17, showing the presence of structure in the real data (data from Motallebzadeh *et al.* 2007).

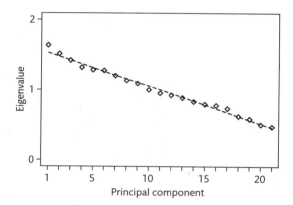

Figure 20.12 Scree plots for Table 20.19, showing the absence of structure in the simulated data.

ask a series of questions relating to different aspects of depression and then combine them to give a depression score.

To form questions into a scale, we first devise a set of questions which are expected to be related to the concepts of interest, based on experience. These questions usually have a few possible answers, which are ordered categories. The questions are answered by test subjects. We usually remove questions for which the lowest category is the answer for most respondents (called the **floor effect**) or the highest category is the most frequent (the **ceiling effect**) or are highly correlated with other answers and so do not carry much or new information.

We then need to know whether the questions form a coherent scale and whether they measure one or more than one underlying construct.

For example, Table 20.20 shows a questionnaire, the Hull Reflux Cough Questionnaire, devised by Dr Alyn Morice (Morice *et al.* 2011). This questionnaire was devised using experience and evidence about the nature of respiratory symptoms. It gives a single score, but does it really measure one thing? To answer this we can do principal component analysis. The data were obtained from 83 attendees at a chronic cough clinic. The eigenvalues for the PCA are shown in Table 20.21. The scree plot is shown in Figure 20.13.

By the Kaiser criterion for Table 20.21, we would have four dimensions. From the scree plot in Figure 20.13, two or three dimensions looks better. We could try either two or three dimensions, to help decide which is better, but for reasons of space we will just try two dimensions here. Having decided the dimensions of the data, we now need to find a good description of them. To do this we use a statistical method developed by psychologists: factor analysis. This was originally introduced to answer questions like 'Is there more than one kind of intelligence?'. By carrying out principal component analysis on a set of variables, we can decide whether there is more than one dimension. There are other methods to do this as well, but we shall stick to PCA for this chapter. The statistical program Stata, for example, offers methods called principal factor (the default), iterated principal factor, and maximum likelihood, in addition to principal component analysis. SPSS offers seven methods and has principal component analysis as the default.

The factor analysis model is that each of our variables can be represented as a linear combination of other variables, called **factors**, which we cannot actually see. The factors are all set to have mean zero and variance one. Each standardized observed variable is the sum of each factor multiplied by a coefficient plus some unique factor of its own. The coefficients are called **factor loadings**. Table 20.22 shows the factor loadings for two factors, which are the first two principal components. The uniqueness is the coefficient by which we would multiply a standard Normal variable to give the extra error not explained by the factors. Hence we predict

Table 20.20 Hull Reflux Cough Questionnaire (reproduced from *Lung*, 189, 1, 2011, pp. 73–79, 'Cough hypersensitivity syndrome: a distinct clinical entity', Morice A *et al.*, with permission from Springer Science and Business Media)

Please circle the most appropriate response for each question						
Within the last MONTH, how did the following problems affect you?	**0 = no problem and** **5 = severe or frequent problem**					
1. Hoarseness or a problem with your voice	0	1	2	3	4	5
2. Clearing your throat	0	1	2	3	4	5
3. The feeling of something dripping down the back of your nose or throat	0	1	2	3	4	5
4. Retching or vomiting when you cough	0	1	2	3	4	5
5. Cough on first lying down or bending over	0	1	2	3	4	5
6. Chest tightness or wheeze when coughing	0	1	2	3	4	5
7. Heartburn, indigestion, stomach acid coming up (or do you take medications for this, if yes score 5)	0	1	2	3	4	5
8. A tickle in your throat, or a lump in your throat	0	1	2	3	4	5
9. Cough with eating (during or soon after meals)	0	1	2	3	4	5
10. Cough with certain foods	0	1	2	3	4	5
11. Cough when you get out of bed in the morning	0	1	2	3	4	5
12. Cough brought on by singing or speaking (for example, on the telephone)	0	1	2	3	4	5
13. Coughing more when awake rather than asleep	0	1	2	3	4	5
14. A strange taste in your mouth	0	1	2	3	4	5
TOTAL SCORE =						/70

that the standardized value of the first variable, hoarse, is given by

$$\text{hoarse} = 0.64 \times \text{factor 1} - 0.11 \times \text{factor 2} + 0.57 \times \text{error}$$

where error is a Standard Normal random variable.

Such factors are called **latent variables**. A dictionary definition of 'latent' is that it is concealed, not visible or apparent, dormant, undeveloped, but capable of development. In statistics, we mean something which is not measured directly and the existence of which is inferred in some way. We can estimate the numerical values of the factors from sets of coefficients like those of Table 20.18. These are not the same as the factor loadings. The factor

loadings are for calculating the variables from the factors, the factor coefficients are for calculating the factors from the variables.

In Table 20.22, most of the loadings for Factor 1 are positive numbers and mostly of similar size. The loadings for Factor 2 tend to be smaller and half of them are negative. If we can predict our variables from two factors, we could also predict them from two other factors, each of which is a linear combination of the first two. This is called a **factor rotation**.

For example,

$$\text{hoarse} = 0.64 \times \text{factor}_1 - 0.11 \times \text{factor}_2$$
$$+ 0.57 \times \text{error}$$

Table 20.21 Eigenvalues for the principal components of 14 respiratory questions (data from Morice *et al.* 2011)

Component	Eigenvalue	Percentage of variability explained	Cumulative percentage of variability
1	5.02	35.9	35.9
2	1.64	11.7	47.6
3	1.30	9.3	56.8
4	1.07	7.6	64.5
5	0.92	6.6	71.1
6	0.74	5.3	76.4
7	0.68	4.9	81.2
8	0.59	4.2	85.4
9	0.44	3.1	88.6
10	0.39	2.8	91.4
11	0.36	2.6	93.9
12	0.34	2.4	96.3
13	0.26	1.9	98.2
14	0.25	1.8	100.0
Total	14.00		100.0

Define two new variables, new_1 and new_2, so that

$$new_1 = factor_1 + factor_2$$
$$new_2 = factor_1 - factor_2$$

Then

$$factor_1 = (new_1 + new_2)/2$$
$$factor_2 = (new_1 - new_2)/2$$

If we replace the old factors by the new:

$$hoarse = 0.64 \times (new_1 + new_2)/2$$
$$-0.11 \times (new_1 - new_2)/2$$
$$+ 0.57 \times error$$
$$= 0.27 \times new_1 + 0.38 \times new_2$$
$$+ 0.57 \times error$$

There are many possible new pairs of factors which we could use. We will only use rotations which keep the

standard deviations of the factors equal to one,' which this simple example does not. Note that the uniqueness remains the same.

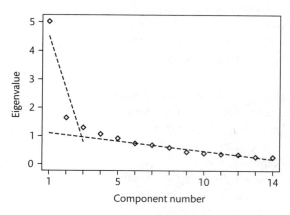

Figure 20.13 Scree plot for The Hull Reflux Cough Questionnaire, Table 20.21 (data from Morice *et al.* 2011).

Table 20.22 Factor loadings for the first two factors from Table 20.21 (data from Morice *et al.* 2011)

Variable	Factor Loadings		
	Factor 1	**Factor 2**	**Uniqueness**
hoarse	0.64	−0.11	0.57
throat	0.58	−0.58	0.33
mucus	0.60	−0.33	0.53
retching	0.62	0.21	0.57
lyingdwn	0.66	0.24	0.51
wheeze	0.67	0.12	0.53
heartbrn	0.41	0.45	0.64
tickle	0.64	−0.18	0.56
eating	0.75	0.15	0.42
foods	0.65	0.48	0.35
outofbed	0.58	−0.22	0.61
speaking	0.62	−0.38	0.47
day	0.39	−0.33	0.74
taste	0.46	0.53	0.51

Table 20.23 Factor loadings after varimax rotation for two factors from Table 20.21 (data from Morice *et al.* 2011)

Variable	Factor Loadings		
	Factor 1	**Factor 2**	**Uniqueness**
Hoarse	0.53	0.38	0.57
Throat	0.82	0.01	0.33
Mucus	0.65	0.19	0.53
Retching	0.28	0.59	0.57
Lying down	0.29	0.64	0.51
Wheeze	0.39	0.57	0.53
Heartburn	−0.03	0.60	0.64
Tickle	0.58	0.33	0.56
Eating	0.42	0.64	0.42
Foods	0.11	0.80	0.35
Out of bed	0.57	0.26	0.61
Speaking	0.71	0.17	0.47
Day	0.51	0.05	0.74
Taste	−0.06	0.70	0.51

We find a rotation to produce two new factors which have as many factor loadings as close to zero as possible. This means that as many variables as possible will be predicted mainly by only one factor. This in turn helps us to interpret the factors. Table 20.23 shows the factor loadings after a rotation.

There are several methods of rotation; Table 20.23 is the result of a varimax rotation, which keeps the factors uncorrelated. It is also possible to have correlated factors. Rotations methods which produce them are called **oblique**. Methods for rotation have names like quartimax, promax, quartimin, oblimax, and oblimin.

In Table 20.23, Factor 1 mainly loads on hoarseness, clearing the throat, feeling of mucus, tickle in the throat, cough on getting out of bed, cough on singing or speaking, and cough more when awake. Factor 2 mainly loads on retching when coughing, cough on lying down, tightness or wheeze, heartburn, cough with eating, cough with foods, and taste in the mouth. These are chosen because the factor loading is greater than 0.5. We then have the task of deciding from this what each factor represents. We might, for example, label them as 'respiratory tract cough' and 'alimentary tract cough'.

The factor loadings are the contribution of the factors to the items. We estimate the values of the factors for each person from a set of **factor coefficients**, which predict the factor from the items. Table 20.24 shows these for the loadings in Table 20.23. We standardize each individual item by subtracting its mean and dividing by its standard deviation, multiply by the coefficient, then add. We rarely do this for composite scales, however. Having decided that a group of variables make up our scale, we usually then simplify by making the coefficients for them

Table 20.24 Scoring coefficients for the three factor solution of Table 20.23 (data from Morice *et al.* 2011)

Variable	Scoring coefficients	
	Factor 1	Factor 2
Hoarse	0.139 99	0.042 26
Throat	0.331 77	−0.164 84
Mucus	0.226 52	−0.056 66
Retching	−0.005 79	0.178 55
Lying down	−0.011 42	0.195 89
Wheeze	0.041 12	0.148 08
Heartburn	−0.136 59	0.248 41
Tickle	0.168 87	0.012 48
Eating	0.040 19	0.169 25
Foods	−0.116 60	0.296 32
Out of bed	0.177 27	−0.011 49
Speaking	0.251 83	−0.075 18
Day	0.196 83	−0.085 10
Taste	−0.166 36	0.293 09

all equal to one and adding. Thus the 'throat cough scale' becomes the sum of the scores for hoarseness, clearing the throat, feeling of mucus, tickle in the throat, cough on getting out of bed, cough on singing or speaking, and cough more when awake.

Factor analysis is often treated sceptically by statisticians. For example, Feinstein (2001, page 623) quoted Donald Mainland: 'If you don't know what you're doing, factor analysis is a great way to do it'. There is actually a book called *Factor Analysis as a Statistical Method* (Lawley and Maxwell 1971), which would imply that readers might not think of factor analysis as a statistical method at all!

There are several practical problems with factor analysis:

- Factor analysis may be unstable over the items we use. We may not get the same factors if we change some of the items, or add other items. This is particularly true if we have a small number of subjects relative to the number of variables. Random numbers can form factors.

- Factor analysis may be unstable over the population of subjects. If we use a different group of subjects, we might get different factors.

- The choice of number of factors is subjective. Even if we use the objective Kaiser criterion, we may conclude that a factor is meaningless or uninterpretable and drop it.

- The factor analysis model, with each observed variable being a linear combination of factors, means that the observed variables should be able to take any value in a range, i.e. should be continuous. In our Hull Reflux Cough Questionnaire example (Table 20.20), the variables are all integers between 0 and 5, and certainly not continuous. This is typical of the sort of data often used in factor analysis. If anything, we have more possible values than is usual. This means that the prediction of our observed variables from the factors is very approximate.

- The choice of label for the factor is subjective. Different observers may interpret the same factor differently. This leads to what is called the **reification problem**, that having labelled our factors, we then treat them as real things.

- There are many variations on the factor analysis method and these may produce different structures.

For all these reasons, we need to test our scales, by repeating them among other groups of subjects, by estimating their repeatability, and by comparing them with other observations.

Despite all these caveats, factor analysis remains the main method for establishing composite scales. Apart from simply going on expert opinion, there is not much else to do. It is also a complicated process, full of choices and pitfalls, and not to be undertaken lightly! Don't try this at home. If you are going to do factor analysis 'for real' you should consult an expert. For more on factor analysis, see Streiner and Norman (2008).

20.11 Internal consistency of scales and Cronbach's alpha

If a series of items are to form a scale, they should be correlated with one another. A useful coefficient for assessing internal consistency is Cronbach's alpha (Cronbach 1951). Alpha is a measure of how closely the items that make up the scale are correlated. If the items are all perfectly correlated, which usually means identical, then alpha will be one, its maximum possible value. If the items are all independent, having no relationship at all, then alpha will be zero. In this case, of course, there is no coherent scale formed by summing them.

Mathematically, the coefficient alpha is given by:

$$\alpha = \frac{k}{k-1}\left(1 - \frac{\sum \sigma_i^2}{\sigma_T^2}\right)$$

where k is the number of items, σ_i^2 is the variance of the i'th item and σ_T^2 is the variance of the total scale formed by summing all the items. So the essential part of alpha is the sum of the variances of the items divided by the variance of the sum of all the items. If the items are all independent, then the variance of the sum will be the sum of the individual variances, $\sigma_T^2 = \sum \sigma_i^2$. The ratio will be one and $\alpha = 0$. If the items are all identical and so perfectly correlated, all the σ_i^2 will be equal and $\sigma_T^2 = k^2\sigma_i^2$. Because all the item variances are the same, $\sum \sigma_i^2 = k\sigma_i^2$, so $= \sum \sigma_i^2/\sigma_T^2 = 1/k$ and $\alpha = 1$.

Alpha is based on the idea that our items are a sample from a large population of possible items which could be used to measure the construct which the scale represents. If alpha is low, then the items will not be coherent and the scale will not necessarily be a good estimate of the construct. Alpha can be thought of as an estimate of the correlation between the scale and another similar scale made from a different set of the possible items.

For use in research, alpha values of 0.7 or greater are considered acceptable. A very high value, like 0.95, might indicate some redundancy in the scale, because if our items are very highly correlated we may not need them all. For use in making clinical decisions about individual patients, it is considered that alpha should be higher, say 0.9 or greater. For the Hull Reflux Cough Questionnaire,

the alpha coefficient is 0.86 and for the two subscales it is 0.79 and 0.81

Alpha is often called a coefficient of reliability, or alpha reliability. It is not the same as the correlation between repeated administrations of the scale (Section 20.2) but if the model is correct it should be similar. We can increase alpha by adding in more items, though the gain gets smaller as the number of items in the scale increases. We can also increase alpha by dropping items which are not highly correlated with others in the scale.

20.12 Presenting composite scales

Composite scales that measure artificial constructs, whether assembled from questionnaires like a depression score or by summing the results of disparate measures as for IQ tests, have the disadvantage that they do not have natural units. Blood concentrations are naturally measured in physical units, such as milligrams per decilitre or millimoles per litre. Even when more than one unit system is in use it is easy to convert from one to another. We do not need to state the particular measurement instrument being employed to understand the result. There are hundreds of depression scales, each with its own unit of measurement. To understand a depression score, we must be told which of these many scales is being used. To get round this problem of the arbitrary nature of composite scales and to establish a common unit for them, we sometimes employ a statistical approach which relates the measurement to its distribution in the general population.

If we know the mean and standard deviation of a score in the population as a whole, we can use an individual's measurement to locate that individual in the distribution. The simplest way to do this is to subtract the population mean from the measurement and divide by the population standard deviation. This tells us how many standard deviations the measured individual is from the population mean. This is called a **standardized score** or **z score**.

The disadvantage of standardized scores is that half of them are negative and they include decimal points. A depression score recorded as −1.2, meaning 1.2 standard deviations below the population mean, is not very user friendly. The minus sign problem is sometimes solved by transforming the standardized data to have a mean greater than zero. The decimal point problem is solved by using a standard deviation greater than one. One method often used is the **T-score**. For this we use an arbitrary mean = 50 and standard deviation = 10. A standardized score = −1.2 would become a T-score = −1.2 × 10 + 50 = −12 + 50 = 38. Most T-scores will lie between 30 and 70 and it would be very unusual to get one which was greater than 100 or negative.

IQ uses a different mean, 100, and standard deviation 15. Hence an IQ score which was 1.2 standard deviations less than the population mean would be presented as 100 − 1.2 × 15 = 100 − 18 = 82 on the IQ scale. Some other similar scales also use this system.

There are many types of scale in regular use. This is one of several possible formats. Scales are difficult to design and validate, and so whenever possible we use one which has been developed previously. This also makes it easier to plan and to interpret the results of studies, as the properties of the scale are already known. There is a wide range of scales which have been used in many studies, and are readily available to the researcher. A review of the literature in the field in which you propose to research will reveal what scales are available and which are used most often. It should then be possible to find information about the performance of the scales, such as measurement error, to help in choosing one for you.

McDowell and Newell (1996) review a large number of scales useful in medical research, including full lists of questions. Bowling (1997) gives a review of quality of life scales.

20.13 Multiple choice questions: Measurement

(Each answer is true or false.)

20.1 The repeatability or precision of measurements may be measured by:

(a) the coefficient of variation of repeated measurements;

(b) the standard deviation of measurements between subjects;

(c) the standard deviation of the difference between pairs of measurements;

(d) the standard deviation of repeated measurements within subjects;

(e) the difference between the means of two sets of measurements on the same set of subjects.

Table 20.25 Reliability of COOP/WONCA charts (data from Ettema *et al.* 2007)

COOP/WONCA chart	Inter-observer reliability		Test-retest reliability	
	n	κ_w	*n*	κ_w
Physical function	28	0.94	34	0.67
Feelings	28	0.98	34	0.56
Daily activities	27	0.94	33	0.23
Social activities	27	0.90	29	0.27
QOL	28	0.97	34	0.30
Pain	28	0.97	34	0.46

κ_w: Linear weighted Cohen's Kappa.

20.2 The Dartmouth Cooperative Functional Assessment Charts/World Organization of General Practitioners/ Family Physicians (COOP/WONCA) charts are a measure of quality of life in people with dementia. Each chart consists of one statement that is printed on a separate sheet, followed by five response options, which are illustrated with drawings, such as a smiling or sad looking face. Higher scores indicate worse functional status. Ettema *et al.* (2007) administered COOP/WONCA charts to a group of people with dementia, both using two observers simultaneously and one of these observers 1 week later. Table 20.25 shows some of their results.

(a) Inter-observer agreement would be regarded as very good or almost perfect;

(b) Kappa statistics must lie between −1 and +1;

(c) Test-retest reliability for Feelings is moderate;

(d) Test-retest reliability for Daily activities is poor;

(e) Disagreements between categories which adjoin are treated like disagreements between categories at opposite ends of the scale.

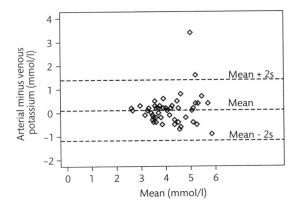

Figure 20.14 Plot of difference between potassium measurements against average (data from Johnston and Murphy 2005).

20.3 Johnston and Murphy (2005) studied the agreement between an arterial blood gas analyser and a venous blood analyser in the measurement of potassium in patients in cardiac arrest. Their paper, which handily includes a table of the data, included a graph like Figure 20.14.
(a) the two outer horizontal lines are the 95% limits of agreement;
(b) agreement is poor because not all the observations in Figure 20.14 are between the limits of agreement;
(c) the data meet the assumptions of the limits of agreement method well;
(d) a logarithmic transformation would be worth trying here;
(e) the distribution of the differences would make the limits invalid.

20.4 The specificity of a test for a disease:
(a) has a standard error derived from the Binomial distribution;
(b) measures how well the test detects cases of the disease;
(c) measures how well the test excludes subjects without the disease;
(d) measures how often a correct diagnosis is obtained from the test;
(e) is all we need to tell us how good the test is.

20.5 The level of an enzyme measured in blood is used as a diagnostic test for a disease, the test being positive if the enzyme concentration is above a critical value. The sensitivity of the diagnostic test:
(a) is one minus the specificity;
(b) is a measure of how well the test detects cases of the disease;
(c) is the proportion of people with the disease who are positive on the test;
(d) increases if the critical value is lowered;
(e) measures how well people without the disease are excluded.

20.6 A 95% reference interval, 95% reference range, or normal range:
(a) may be calculated as two standard deviations on either side of the mean;
(b) may be calculated directly from the frequency distribution;
(c) can only be calculated if the observations follow a Normal distribution;
(d) gets wider as the sample size increases;
(e) may be calculated from the mean and its standard error.

20.7 If the 95% reference interval for haematocrit in men is 43.2 to 49.2:
(a) any man with haematocrit outside these limits is abnormal;
(b) haematocrits outside these limits are proof of disease;
(c) a man with a haematocrit of 46 must be very healthy;
(d) a woman with a haematocrit of 48 has a haematocrit within normal limits;
(e) a man with a haematocrit of 42 may be ill.

20.8 Lock *et al.* (2012) evaluated the Eating and Meal Preparation Skills Assessment (EMPSA) as an outcome measure in a study of a cookery group-based occupational therapy intervention for adult inpatients and day patients with severe eating disorders. Twenty-seven participants completed EMPSAs at their first, 10th and final sessions, plus 1 year later. EMPSA has two subscales: Ability and Motivation. Cronbach's alpha was 0.71 for the Ability subscale and 0.95 for the Motivation subscale.
(a) Cronbach's alpha measures the internal consistency of a scale;
(b) The Ability subscale would be suitable for clinical use with individual patients;

(c) The Motivation subscale would be suitable only for use at a group level;

(d) Cronbach's alpha can take any value between −1 and +1;

(e) The Ability subscale would be suitable for use as a research instrument.

20.9 If we have a large number of outcome measurements in a randomized trial, suitable approaches to the analysis include:

(a) publish only those which show significant differences;

(b) apply a Bonferroni correction to all the P values;

(c) combine the variables using principle component analysis;

(d) before looking at the data, choose a variable to be the primary outcome variable and rely on that for the main significance test;

(e) choose the variable which has the smallest P value as the primary outcome variable.

20.14 Exercise: Two measurement studies

In the first study we shall look at the distribution of plasma magnesium and estimate a reference interval. Mather *et al.* (1979) measured plasma magnesium in 140 apparently healthy people, to compare with a sample of diabetics. The normal sample was chosen from blood donors and people attending day centres for the elderly in the area of St George's Hospital, to give 10 male and 10 female subjects in each age decade from 15–24 to 75 years and over. Questionnaires were used to exclude any subject with persistent diarrhoea, excessive alcohol intake, or who was on regular drug therapy other than hypnotics and mild analgesics in the elderly. The distribution of plasma magnesium is shown in Figure 20.15 and a Normal quantile plot in Figure 20.16. The mean was 0.810 mmol/litre and the standard deviation 0.057 mmol/litre.

20.1 What do you think of the sampling method? Why use blood donors and elderly people attending day centres?

20.2 Why were some potential subjects excluded? Was this a good idea? Why were certain drugs allowed for the elderly?

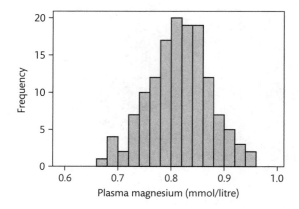

Figure 20.15 Distribution of plasma magnesium in 140 apparently healthy people (data from Mather *et al.* 1979).

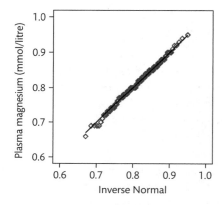

Figure 20.16 Normal plot of plasma magnesium in 140 apparently healthy people (data from Mather *et al.* 1979).

20.3 Does plasma magnesium appear to follow a Normal distribution?

20.4 How could we estimate a reference interval for plasma magnesium?

20.5 How could we find confidence intervals for the reference limits?

20.6 Would it matter if mean plasma magnesium in normal people increased with age? What method might be used to improve the estimate of the reference interval in this case?

The second study is of the development of a composite scale. Minaya *et al.* (2012) set out to develop and validate a specific quality of life (QoL) questionnaire for caregivers of cancer patients, the CareGiver Oncology Quality of Life questionnaire (CarGOQoL), based on the point of view of the caregivers. A 75-item questionnaire generated from content analysis of interviews with caregivers was self-completed by 837 caregivers of cancer patients. To reduce the number of items, each of the 75 items was reviewed for adverse characteristics regarding item distribution, missing data per item, and inter-item correlations. Items considered for deletion included those with more than 15% missing data, ceiling or floor effects over 70%, a distribution which was highly skewed, or with correlation coefficients with other items over 0.80. At the end of this step, 16 items were removed.

They selected a final set of 29 items which assessed 10 dimensions: psychological well-being, burden, relationship with health care, administration and finances, coping, physical wellbeing, self-esteem, leisure time, social support, and private life. These were identified after a principal component analysis which explained 73% of the total variance. The missing data and the floor effects were low. Some ceiling effects were found, the highest was for burden (34%). Cronbach's alpha coefficients ranged from 0.72 to 0.89, except private life (0.55).

The questionnaire is in the French language, but the authors give a rough translation into English. Each item has five options:

1 Never/Not at all
2 Rarely/A little
3 Sometimes/Somewhat
4 Often/A lot
5 Always/Very much

Some questions had negative worded item scores that were reversed so that higher scores indicated a higher QoL, indicated by '∗'. The start of the questions is 'Concerning the person you help, have you . . .'. The 'burden' subscale had four items:

- felt lack of freedom?∗
- bothered because you are confined?∗
- bothered because your life is devoted to the care-receiver?∗
- felt being alone for caregiving?∗

The 'private life' subscale had two questions:

- had difficulties with your private life?∗
- had a satisfied sentimental/sexual life?

The wording looks better in French.

20.7 Why did they drop questions with more than 15% missing data?

20.8 What are floor and ceiling effects for a question and why did they drop questions with ceiling or floor effects over 70%?

20.9 Why did they drop questions with highly skewed distributions?

20.10 Why did they drop questions which had correlation coefficients with other items over 0.80?

20.11 Having selected a final set of 29 items, they carried out a principal components analysis. What does this mean?

20.12 The principal components analysis explained 73% of the variance with 10 components. What does this mean and where is the other 27% of the variance?

20.13 They reported that some ceiling effects were found for the dimension 'burden' (34%). What might a ceiling effect mean for a subscale? Is it a problem and what could be done about it if it is?

20.14 Cronbach's alpha coefficients ranged from 0.72 to 0.89, except 'private life' (0.55). How would we interpret these figures?

20.15 How might we try to increase the internal consistency for 'private life'?

21 Mortality statistics and population structure

21.1 Mortality rates

Mortality statistics are one of our principal sources of information about the changing pattern of disease within a country and the differences in disease between countries. In most developed countries, any death must be certified by a doctor, who records the cause, date, and place of death, and some data about the deceased. In Britain, these include the date of birth, area of residence, and last known occupation. These death certificates form the raw material from which mortality statistics are compiled by a national bureau of censuses, in Britain the Office for National Statistics. The numbers of deaths can be tabulated by cause, sex, age, types of occupation, area of residence, and marital status. Table 5.1 shows one such tabulation, of deaths by cause and sex.

For purposes of comparison we must relate the number of deaths to the number in the population in which they occur. We have this information fairly reliably at 10-year intervals from the decennial census of the country. We can estimate the size and age and sex structure of the population between censuses using registration of births and deaths. Each birth or death is notified to an official registrar, and so we can keep some track of changes in the population. There are other, less well-documented changes taking place, such as immigration and emigration, which mean that population size estimates between the census years are only approximations. Some estimates, such as the numbers in different occupations, are so unreliable that mortality data are only tabulated by them for census years. In the UK, this system is changing, however.

If we take the number of deaths over a given period of time and divide it by the number in the population

and the time period, we get a mortality rate, the number of deaths per unit time per person. We usually take the number of deaths over 1 calendar year, although when the number of deaths is small we may take deaths over several years, to increase the precision of the numerator. The number in the population is changing continually, and we take as the denominator the estimated population at the mid-point of the time period. Mortality rates are often very small numbers, so we usually multiply them by a constant, such as 1 000 or 100 000, to avoid strings of zeros after the decimal point.

When we are dealing with deaths in the whole population, irrespective of age, the rate we obtain is called the **crude mortality rate** or **crude death rate**. The terms 'death rate' and 'mortality rate' are used interchangeably. We calculate the crude mortality rate for a population as:

$$\frac{\text{deaths occurring over given period}}{\begin{array}{c}\text{number in population at mid-point}\\\text{of period} \times \text{length of period}\end{array}} \times 1\,000$$

If the period is in years, this gives the crude mortality rate as deaths per 1 000 population per year.

The crude mortality rate is so called because no allowance is made for the age distribution of the population, and comparisons may be influenced by populations having different age structures. For example, in 1901 the crude mortality rate among adult males (aged over 15 years) in England and Wales was 15.7 per 1 000 per year, and in 1981 it was 14.8 per 1 000 per year. It seems strange that with all the improvements in medicine, housing, and nutrition between these times there had been so little improvement in the crude mortality rate. To see why we must look at the **age specific**

mortality rates, the mortality rates within narrow age groups. Age specific mortality rates are usually calculated for 1-, 5-, or 10-year age groups. In 1901 the age specific mortality rate for men aged 15 to 19 was 3.5 deaths per 1 000 per year, whereas in 1981 it was only 0.8. As Table 21.1 shows, the age specific mortality rate in 1901 was greater than that in 1981 for every age group. However, in 1901 there was a much greater proportion of the population in the younger age groups, where mortality was low, than there was in 1981. Correspondingly, there was a smaller proportion of the 1901 population than the 1981 population in the higher mortality older age groups. Although mortality was lower at any given age in 1981, the greater proportion of older people meant that there were almost as many deaths as in 1901.

To eliminate the effects of different age structures in the populations which we want to compare, we can look at the age specific death rates. But if we are comparing several populations, this is a rather cumbersome procedure, and it is often more convenient to calculate a single summary figure from the age specific rates. There are many ways of doing this, of which three are frequently used: the direct and indirect methods of age standardization and the life table.

21.2 Age standardization using the direct method

I shall describe the **direct method** first. We use a standard population structure, i.e. a standard age distribution or set of proportions of people in each age group. We then calculate the overall mortality rate which a population with the standard age structure would have if it experienced the age specific mortality rates of the observed population, the population whose mortality rate is to be adjusted. We shall take the 1901 population as the standard and calculate the mortality rate the 1981 population would have experienced if the age distribution were the same as in 1901. We do this by multiplying each 1981 age specific mortality rate by the proportion in that age group in the standard 1901 population, and adding. This then gives us an average mortality rate for the whole population, the **age standardized mortality rate**. For example, the 1981 mortality rate in age group 15–19 was 0.8 per 1 000 per year and the proportion in the standard population in this age group is 15.36% or 0.153 6. The contribution of this age group is 0.8 × 0.153 6 = 0.122 9. The calculation is set out in Table 21.2.

Table 21.1 Age specific mortality rates and age distribution in adult males, England and Wales, 1901 and 1981

Age group (years)	Age specific death rate per 1 000 per year		% adult population in age group	
	1901	1981	1901	1981
15–19	3.5	0.8	15.36	11.09
20–24	4.7	0.8	14.07	9.75
25–34	6.2	0.9	23.76	18.81
35–44	10.6	1.8	18.46	15.99
45–54	18.0	6.1	13.34	14.75
55–64	33.5	17.7	8.68	14.04
65–74	67.8	45.6	4.57	10.65
75–84	139.8	105.2	1.58	4.28
85+	276.5	226.2	0.17	0.64

Table 21.2 Calculation of the age standardized mortality rate by the direct method

Age group (years)	Standard proportion in age group (a)	Observed mortality rate per 1 000 (b)	$a \times b$
15–19	0.153 6	0.8	0.122 9
20–24	0.140 7	0.8	0.112 6
25–34	0.237 6	0.9	0.213 8
35–44	0.184 6	1.8	0.332 3
45–54	0.133 4	6.1	0.813 7
55–64	0.086 8	17.7	1.536 4
65–74	0.045 7	45.6	2.083 9
75–84	0.015 8	105.2	1.662 2
85+	0.001 7	226.2	0.384 5
Sum			7.262 3

If we used the population's own proportions in each age group in this calculation we would get the crude mortality rate. As 1901 has been chosen as the standard population, its crude mortality rate of 15.7 is also the age standardized mortality rate. The age standardized mortality rate for 1981 was 7.3 per 1 000 men per year. We can see that there was a much higher age standardized mortality in 1901 than 1981, reflecting the difference in age specific mortality rates. This is despite the crude mortality rates, 15.7 and 14.8 per 1 000 per year, being very similar.

21.3 Age standardization by the indirect method

The direct method relies on age specific mortality rates for the observed population. If we have very few deaths, these age specific rates will be very poorly estimated. This will be particularly so in the younger age groups, where we may even have no deaths at all. Such situations arise when considering mortality caused by particular conditions or in relatively small groups, such as those defined by occupation. The **indirect method** of standardization is used for such data. We calculate the number of deaths we would expect in the observed population if it experienced the age specific mortality rates of a standard population. We then compare the expected number of deaths with that actually observed.

I shall take as an example the deaths because of cirrhosis of the liver among male qualified medical practitioners in England and Wales, recorded around the 1971 census. There were 14 deaths among 43 570 doctors aged below 65, a crude mortality rate of 14/43 570 = 321 per million, compared with 1 423 out of 15 247 980 adult males (aged 15–64), or 93 per million. The mortality among doctors appears high, but the medical population may be older than the population of men as a whole, as it will contain relatively few below the age of 25. Also the actual number of deaths among doctors is small and any difference not explained by the age effect may be a result of chance. The indirect method enables us to test this. Table 21.3 shows the age specific mortality rates for cirrhosis of the liver among all men aged 15–65, and the number of men estimated in each 10-year age group, for

Table 21.3 Age specific mortality rates because of cirrhosis of the liver and age distributions of all men and medical practitioners, England and Wales, 1971

Age group (years)	Mortality per million men per year	Number of men	Number of doctors
15–24	5.859	3 584 320	1 080
25–34	13.050	3 065 100	12 860
35–44	46.937	2 876 170	11 510
45–54	161.503	2 965 880	10 330
55–64	271.358	2 756 510	7 790

all men and for doctors. We can see that the two age distributions do appear to be different.

The calculation of the expected number of deaths is similar to the direct method, but different populations and rates are used. For each age group, we take the number in the observed population, and multiply it by the standard age specific mortality rate, which would be the probability of dying if mortality in the observed population were the same as that in the standard population. This gives us the number we would expect to die in this age group in the observed population. We add these over the age groups and obtain the expected number of deaths. The calculation is set out in Table 21.4.

The expected number of deaths is 4.496 5, which is considerably less than the 14 observed. We usually express the result of the calculation as the ratio of observed to expected deaths, called the **standardized mortality ratio** or **SMR**. Thus the SMR for cirrhosis among doctors is

$$SMR = \frac{14}{4.496\,5} = 3.11$$

We usually multiply the SMR by 100 to get rid of the decimal point, and report the SMR as 311. If we do not adjust for age at all, the ratio of the crude death rates is 3.44, compared with the age adjusted figure of 3.11, so the adjustment has made some, but not much, difference in this case.

We can calculate a confidence interval for the SMR quite easily. Denote the observed deaths by O and

Table 21.4 Calculation of the expected number of deaths because of cirrhosis of the liver among medical practitioners, using the indirect method

Age group (years)	Standard mortality rate	Observed population: number of doctors	a × b
	(a)	(b)	
15–24	0.000 005 859	1 080	0.006 3
25–34	0.000 013 050	12 860	0.167 8
35–44	0.000 046 937	11 510	0.540 2
45–54	0.000 161 503	10 330	1.668 3
55–64	0.000 271 358	7 790	2.113 9
Total			4.496 5

expected by E. It is reasonable to suppose that the deaths are independent of one another and happening randomly in time, so the observed number of deaths is from a Poisson distribution (Section 6.7). The standard deviation of this Poisson distribution is the square root of its mean and so can be estimated by the square root of the observed deaths, $\sqrt{O}$. The expected number is calculated from a very much larger sample and is so well estimated it can be treated as a constant, so the standard deviation of $100 \times O/E$, which is the standard error of the SMR, is estimated by $100 \times \sqrt{O}/E$. Provided the number of deaths is large enough, say more than 10, an approximate 95% confidence interval is given by

$$100 \times \frac{O}{E} - 1.96 \times 100 \times \frac{\sqrt{O}}{E}$$

$$\text{to } 100 \times \frac{O}{E} + 1.96 \times 100 \times \frac{\sqrt{O}}{E}$$

For the cirrhosis data the formula gives

$$100 \times \frac{14}{4.4965} - 1.96 \times 100 \times \frac{\sqrt{14}}{4.4965}$$

$$\text{to } 100 \times \frac{14}{4.496\,5} + 1.96 \times 100 \times \frac{\sqrt{14}}{4.496\,5}$$

$$= 311 - 163 \text{ to } 311 + 163$$

$$= 148 \text{ to } 474$$

The confidence interval clearly excludes 100 and the high mortality cannot be ascribed to chance.

For small observed frequencies, tables based on the exact probabilities of the Poisson distribution are available (Pearson and Hartley 1970). The calculations are easily done by computer. There is also an exact method for comparing two SMRs. For the cirrhosis data the exact 95% confidence interval is 170 to 522. This is not quite the same as the large sample approximation. Better approximations and exact methods of calculating confidence intervals are described by Morris and Gardner (1989) and Breslow and Day (1987).

We can also test the null hypothesis that in the population the SMR = 100. If the null hypothesis is true, O is from a Poisson distribution with mean E and hence standard deviation $\sqrt{E}$, provided the sample is large enough, say $E > 10$. Then $(O - E)/\sqrt{E}$ would be an observation from the Standard Normal distribution if the null hypothesis were true. The sample of doctors is too small for this test to be reliable, but if it were, we would have $(O - E)/\sqrt{E} = (14 - 4.496\,5)/\sqrt{4.496\,5} = 4.48$, $P = 0.000\,1$. Again, there is an exact method. This gives $P = 0.000\,5$. As so often happens, large sample methods become too liberal and give P values which are too small when used with samples which are too small for the test to be valid.

The highly significant difference suggests that doctors are at increased risk of death from cirrhosis of the liver, compared with employed men as a whole. The news is not all bad for medical practitioners, however. The corresponding SMR for cancer of the trachea, bronchus, and lung was only 32. Doctors may drink, but they don't smoke!

21.4 Demographic life tables

We have already discussed a use of the life table technique for the analysis of clinical survival data (Section 16.2). The life table was found by following the survival of a group of subjects from some starting point to death. In **demography**, which means the study of human populations, this longitudinal method of analysis is impractical, because we could only study people born more than 100 years ago. Demographic life tables are generated in a different way, using a cross-sectional approach. Rather than charting the progress of a group from birth to death, we start with the present age specific mortality rates. We then calculate what would happen to a cohort of people from birth if these age specific mortality rates applied unchanged throughout their lives. We denote the probability of dying between ages x and $x + 1$ years (the age specific mortality rate at age x) by q_x. As in Table 16.2, the probability of surviving from age x to $x + 1$ is $p_x = 1 - q_x$. We now suppose that we have a cohort of size l_0 at age 0, i.e. at birth. l_0 is usually 100 000 or 10 000. The number who would still be alive after x years is l_x. We can see that the number alive after $x + 1$ years is $l_{x+1} = p_x \times l_x$, so given all the p_x from $x = 0$ onwards we can calculate the l_x. The cumulative survival probability to age x is then $P_x = l_x/l_0$.

Table 21.5 shows an extract from Life Table Number 11, 1950–52, for England and Wales. With the exception of 1941, a life table like this has been produced every 10 years since 1871, based on the decennial census year. The life table is based on the census year because only then do we have a good measure of the number of

people at each age, the denominator in the calculation of q_x. A 3-year period is used to increase the number of deaths for a year of age and so improve the estimation of q_x. Separate tables are produced for males and females because the mortality of the two sexes is very different. Age specific death rates are higher in males than females at every age. Between census years, life tables are still produced but are only published in an abridged form, giving l_x at 5-year intervals only after age 5 (Table 21.6).

Table 21.5 Extract from English Life Table Number 11, 1950–52, Males

Age in years	Expected number alive at age x	Probability an individual dies between ages x and $x + 1$	Expected life at age x years
x	l_x	q_x	e_x
0	100 000	0.032 66	66.42
1	96 734	0.002 41	67.66
2	96 501	0.001 41	66.82
3	96 395	0.001 02	65.91
4	96 267	0.000 84	64.98
⋮	⋮	⋮	⋮
100	23	0.440 45	1.67
101	13	0.450 72	1.62
102	7	0.460 11	1.58
103	4	0.468 64	1.53
104	2	0.476 36	1.50

Table 21.6 Abridged Life Table 1988–90, England and Wales

Age	Males		Females	
x	l_x	e_x	l_x	e_x
0	10 000	73.0	10 000	78.5
1	9 904	72.7	9 928	78.0
2	9 898	71.7	9 922	77.1
3	9 893	70.8	9 919	76.1
4	9 890	69.8	9 916	75.1
5	9 888	68.8	9 914	74.2
10	9 877	63.9	9 907	69.2
15	9 866	58.9	9 899	64.3
20	9 832	54.1	9 885	59.4
25	9 790	49.3	9 870	54.4
30	9 749	44.5	9 852	49.5
35	9 702	39.7	9 826	44.6
40	9 638	35.0	9 784	39.8
45	9 542	30.3	9 718	35.1
50	9 375	25.8	9 607	30.5
55	9 097	21.5	9 431	26.0
60	8 624	17.5	9 135	21.7
65	7 836	14.0	8 645	17.8
70	6 689	11.0	7 918	14.2
75	5 177	8.4	6 869	11.0
80	3 451	6.4	5 446	8.2
85	1 852	4.9	3 659	5.9

The final columns in Tables 21.5 and 21.6 are the **expected life**, **expectation of life**, or **life expectancy**, e_x. This is the average life still to be lived by those reaching age x. We can do the calculation in a number of ways. For example, if we add l_{x+1}, l_{x+2}, l_{x+3}, etc., we will get the total number of years to be lived, because the l_{x+1} who survive to $x+1$ will have added l_{x+1} years to the total, the l_{x+2} of these who survive from $x + 1$ to $x + 2$ will add a further l_{x+2} years, and so on. If we divide this sum by l_x we get the average number of whole years to be lived. If we then remember that people do not die on their birthdays, but scattered throughout the year, we can add half to allow for the average of half year lived in the year of death. We thus get

$$e_x = \frac{1}{2} + \frac{1}{l_x} \sum_{i=x+1}^{\infty} l_i$$

i.e. summing the l_i from age $x + 1$ to the end of the life table.

If many people die in early life, with high age specific death rates for children, this has a great effect on expectation of life at birth. Table 21.7 shows expectation of life at selected ages from five English Life Tables (Office for National Statistics). In 1991, for example, expectation of life at birth for males was 74 years, compared with only 40 years in 1841, an improvement of 34 years. However, expectation of life at age 45 in 1991 was 31 years

compared with 23 years in 1841, an improvement of only 8 years. At age 65, male expectation of life was 11 years in 1841 and 14 years in 1991, an even smaller change. Hence the change in life expectancy at birth was a result of changes in mortality in early life, not late life.

One notable thing about Table 21.7 is that although between 1841 and 1951 life expectancy at birth increased by 26 years for males and by 30 years for females, at age 65 it increased by only 1 and 2 years respectively. Far more people were surviving childhood, but in later life the survival was almost unchanged. Life expectancy for both men and women at age 65 then increased between 1951 and 2011, by 6 and 7 years. I think that this must be mainly the result of improved medicine, the result in turn of improved medical research into both the causes and the treatment of disease. There was a greater increase in life expectancy for men at age 65 in the 20 years after 1991 than in the 150 years before it. We can also note that in 1841 life expectancy for men and women was similar at every age. During the 20th century, women's life expectancy increased faster than men's, but in the 21st century men are catching up. Women having considerably longer lives than men was a 20th-century phenomenon, it is not an immutable law of nature.

There is a common misconception that a life expectancy at birth of 40 years, as in 1841, meant that most people died about age 40. For example (Rowe 1992):

'Mothers have always provoked rage and resentment in their adult daughters, while the adult daughters have always provoked anguish and guilt in their mothers. In past centuries, however, such matched misery did not last for long. Daughters could bury their rage and resentment under a concern for duty while they cared for their mothers who, turning 40, rapidly aged, grew frail and died. Now mothers turning 40 are strong and healthy, and only half way through their lives'.

This is absurd. As Table 21.7 shows, since life expectancy was first estimated, women turning 40 have had

Table 21.7 Life expectancy in 1841, 1901, 1951, 1991, and 2011, England and Wales

Age	Sex	Expectation of life in years				
		1841	1901	1951	1991	2011
Birth	Males	40	49	66	74	79
	Females	42	52	72	79	83
15 years	Males	43	47	54	59	64
	Females	44	50	59	65	68
45 years	Males	23	23	27	31	36
	Females	24	26	31	36	39
65 years	Males	11	11	12	14	18
	Females	12	12	14	18	21

average remaining lives of more than 20 years. They did not rapidly age, grow frail, and die.

Life expectancy is the average duration of life, not its maximum. Here 'expectation' is used in its statistical sense of the average of a distribution (Section 6.5). It does not mean that each person can know when they will die. From the most recent life table for England and Wales, for 2010–2012, a man aged 67 (myself, for example) has a life expectancy of 16.8 years. This is the average life time which all men aged 67 years would have if the present age specific mortality rates do not change. (These should go down over time, putting life-spans up.) About half of these men will have shorter lives and half longer. If we could calculate life expectancies for men with different combinations of risk factors, we might find that my life expectancy would be decreased because I am short (so unfair I think) and increased because I don't smoke (like almost all medical statisticians) and am of professional social class. However my expectation of life was adjusted, it would remain an average, not a guaranteed figure for me.

Life tables have a number of uses, both medical and non-medical. Expectation of life provides a useful summary of mortality without the need for a standard population. The table enables us to predict the future size of and age structure of a population given its present state, called a **population projection**. This can be very useful in predicting such things as the future requirement for geriatric beds in a health district. Life tables are also invaluable in non-medical applications, such as the calculation of insurance premiums, pensions, and annuities.

The main difficulty with prediction from a life table is finding a table which applies to the populations under consideration. For the general population of, say, a health district, the national life table will usually be adequate, but for special populations this may not be the case. If we want to predict the future need for care of an institutionalized population, such as in a long stay psychiatric hospital or old peoples' home, the mortality may be considerably greater than that in the general population. Predictions based on the national life table can only be taken as a very rough guide. If possible, life tables calculated for that type of population should be used.

21.5 Vital statistics

We have seen a number of occasions where ordinary words have been given quite different meanings in statistics from those they have in common speech; 'Normal' and 'significant' are good examples. 'Vital statistics' is the opposite, a technical term which has acquired a completely unrelated popular meaning. As far as the medical statistician is concerned, vital statistics have nothing to do with the dimensions of female bodies. That usage began as a joke. They are the statistics relating to life and death: birth rates, fertility rates, marriage rates, and death rates. I have already mentioned crude mortality rate, age specific mortality rates, age standardized mortality rate, standardized mortality ratio, and expectation of life. In this section I shall define a number of other statistics which are often quoted in the medical literature. Many of these are called rates but they are not, in fact, per unit time (Section 5.1).

The **infant mortality rate** is the number of deaths under 1 year of age divided by the number of live births, usually expressed as deaths per 1 000 live births. The **neonatal mortality rate** is the same thing for deaths in the first 4 weeks of life. The **stillbirth rate** is the number of stillbirths divided by the total number of births, live and still. A stillbirth is a child born dead after 28 weeks' gestation. The **perinatal mortality rate** is the number of stillbirths and deaths in the first week of life divided by the total births, again usually presented per 1 000 births. Infant and perinatal mortality rates are regarded as particularly sensitive indicators of the health status of the population. The **maternal mortality rate** is the number of deaths of mothers ascribed to problems of pregnancy and birth, divided by the total number of births. The **birth rate** is the number of live births per year divided by the total population. The **fertility rate** is the number of live births per year divided by the number of women of childbearing age, taken as 15–44 years.

The **attack rate** for a disease is the proportion of people exposed to infection who develop the disease. The **case fatality rate** is the proportion of people with the disease who die from it. The **prevalence** of a disease is the proportion of people who have it at one point in time. The **incidence rate** is the number of new cases in 1 year divided by the number at risk. Incidence really is a rate.

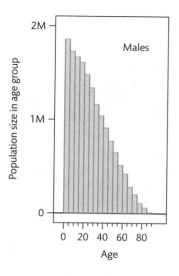

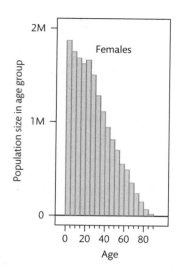

Figure 21.1 Age distributions for the population of England and Wales, by sex, 1901.

21.6 The population pyramid

The age distribution of a population can be presented as histogram, using the methods of Section 4.3. However, because the mortality of males and females is so different, the age distributions for males and females are also different. It is usual to present the age distributions for the two sexes separately. Figure 21.1 shows the age distributions for the male and female populations of England and Wales in 1901. Now, these histograms have the same horizontal scale. The conventional way to display them is with the age scale vertically and the frequency scale horizontally as in Figure 21.2. The frequency scale has zero in the middle and increases to the right for females and to the left for males. This is called a **population pyramid**, because of its shape.

Figure 21.3 shows the population pyramid for England and Wales in 2011. The shape is quite different. Instead of a triangle we have an irregular figure with almost vertical sides which begin to bend very sharply inwards at about age 65. The post-war and 1960s baby booms can be seen as bulges at ages 60–65 and 40–50. A major change in population structure has taken place, with a vast increase in the proportion of elderly. This has major implications for medicine, as the care of the elderly has become a large proportion of the work of doctors, nurses, and their colleagues. It is interesting to see how this has come about.

It is popularly supposed that people are now living much longer as a result of modern medicine, which

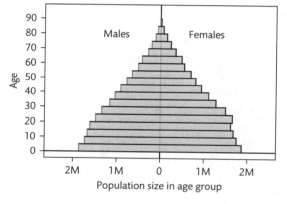

Figure 21.2 Population pyramid for England and Wales, 1901.

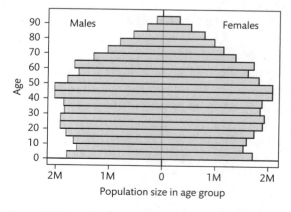

Figure 21.3 Population pyramid for England and Wales, 2011.

prevents deaths in middle life. This is only partly true. As Table 21.7 shows, life expectancy at birth increased dramatically between 1901 and 2001, but the increase in later life is much less. The change is not an extension of every life by 25 years, which would be seen at every age, but mainly a reduction in mortality in childhood and early adulthood. Mortality in later life has changed relatively little. Now, a big reduction in mortality in childhood would result in an increase in the base part of the pyramid, as more children survived, unless there was a corresponding fall in the number of babies being born. In the 19th century, women were having many children and despite the high mortality in childhood the number who survived into adulthood to have children of their own exceeded that of their own parents. The population expanded and this history is embodied in the 1901 population pyramid. In the 20th century, infant mortality fell and people responded to this by having fewer children. In 1841–5, the infant mortality rates were 148 per 1 000 live births, 138 in 1901–5, 10 in 1981–5 (OPCS 1992), and only 5.9 in 1997 (ONS 1999). The birth rate was 32.2 per 1 000 population per year in 1841–5, in 1901–5 it was 28.2, and in 1987–97 it was 13.5 (Office for National Statistics). The base of the pyramid ceased to expand. As those who were in the base of the 1901 pyramid grew older, the population in the top half of the pyramid increased. Had the birth rate not fallen, the population would have continued to expand and we would have as great or greater a proportion of young people in 1991 as we did in 1901, and a vastly larger population. Thus the increase in the proportion of the elderly is not primarily because adult lives have been extended, although this has a small effect, but because fertility has declined. Life expectancy for the elderly has changed relatively little. Most developed countries have stable population pyramids like Figure 21.3 and those of most developing countries have expanding pyramids like Figure 21.2.

21.7 Multiple choice questions: Population and mortality

(Each branch is either true or false.)

21.1 Age specific mortality rate:
  (a) is a ratio of observed to expected deaths;
  (b) can be used to compare mortality between different age groups;
  (c) is an age adjusted mortality rate;
  (d) measures the number of deaths in a year;
  (e) measures the age structure of the population.

21.2 Expectation of life:
  (a) is the number of years most people live;
  (b) is a way of summarizing age specific death rates;
  (c) is the expected value of a particular probability distribution;
  (d) varies with age;
  (e) is derived from life tables.

21.3 In a study of post-natal suicide (Appleby 1991), the SMR for suicide among women who had just had a baby was 17 with a 95% confidence interval 14 to 21 (all women = 100). For women who had had a stillbirth, the SMR was 105 (95% confidence interval 31 to 277). We can conclude that:
  (a) women who had just had a baby were less likely to commit suicide than other women of the same age;
  (b) women who had just had a stillbirth were less likely to commit suicide than other women of the same age;
  (c) women who had just had a live baby were less likely to commit suicide than women of the same age who had had a stillbirth;
  (d) it is possible that having a stillbirth increases the risk of suicide;
  (e) suicidal women should have babies.

21.4 In 1971, the SMR in England and Wales for cirrhosis of the liver for men was 773 for publicans and innkeepers and 25 for window cleaners, both being significantly different from 100 (Donnan and Haskey 1977). We can conclude that:
  (a) between 1970 and 1972, publicans were more than seven times as likely as the average person of similar age to die from cirrhosis of the liver;
  (b) the high SMR for publicans may be because they tend to be found in the older age groups;
  (c) being a publican causes cirrhosis of the liver;

(d) window cleaning protects men from cirrhosis of the liver;

(e) window cleaners are at high risk of cirrhosis of the liver.

21.5 The age and sex structure of a population may be described by:

(a) a life table;

(b) a correlation coefficient;

(c) a standardized mortality ratio;

(d) a population pyramid;

(e) a bar chart.

21.6 The following statistics are adjusted to allow for the age distribution of the population:

(a) age standardized mortality rate;

(b) fertility rate;

(c) perinatal mortality rate;

(d) crude mortality rate;

(e) expectation of life at birth.

21.8 Exercise: Mortality and type 1 diabetes

Harjutsalo *et al.* (2011) compared mortality in patients with type 1 diabetes between those with early onset, before age 15 years, and later onset, age 15–30 years, in a nationwide population-based cohort study using data from Finland, the country with the world's highest incidence of type 1 diabetes. They studied 17 306 people diagnosed as having type 1 diabetes below 30 years of age between 1970 and 1999. They obtained information on date and cause of deaths from the Finnish cause of death register. They calculated both crude and standardized mortality ratios for the entire follow-up period, as well as at 20 years' duration of diabetes, separately for the early onset and late onset cohorts. The standardized mortality ratio (SMR) for all causes was 3.6 (95% confidence interval 3.3 to 3.9) in the early onset cohort and 2.8 (2.6 to 3.0) in the late onset cohort.

21.1 What do the authors mean by 'standardized mortality ratio' and how should we interpret 3.6 here?

21.2 Why was it important to standardize the death rates to compare people with earlier and later onset diabetes?

21.3 Why can deaths before the actual age of onset not be included?

21.4 What information other than information about the study cohort would be needed to calculate the SMRs?

21.5 Was the difference between early onset and late onset diabetes statistically significant?

22 The Bayesian approach

22.1 Bayesians and Frequentists

Statistical inference, the process of drawing conclusions from data, can be done in several different ways. The two main contending schools are the Bayesian school, who base their methods on the work of Thomas Bayes and the approach to probability as a measure of knowledge or belief, and the Frequentist or sampling school, whose approach is based on the frequency theory of probability and idea of sampling distributions. The argument between these groups can be as bitter as that between Swift's Big-endians and Little-endians, who fought a war over the way to open a boiled egg. At the moment almost all the analysis in the medical literature is of the frequency type (confidence intervals, significance tests, etc.). Bayesian methods of meta-analysis (Section 17.13) are an exception to this and are becoming quite frequent at the time of writing. Bayesian methods have had a resurgence of interest among statisticians and this will lead to an increase in their use in medicine.

Many statisticians, like me, have been taught by the majority party, the Frequentists, and do not actually know very much about the Bayesian approach. What follows is a very crude account of the Bayesian viewpoint and the choice between these alternative approaches.

22.2 Bayes' theorem

Bayes' theorem states that the probability of a proposition given data is proportional to the probability of the data given the proposition multiplied by the probability that the proposition is true.

Suppose there are a set of possible events or propositions (things which can be true or false) $Q_1, Q_2, \ldots, Q_n$. These are mutually exclusive and exhaustive. This means

that one and only one can be true (Sections 6.2, 6.3). For example, a coin can come down head or tail, not both, and nothing else. Then the probability of Q_i given some data D is $\text{PROB}(Q_i|D)$ and

$$\text{PROB}(Q_i|D) = \frac{\text{PROB}(D|Q_i)\text{PROB}(Q_i)}{\sum_j \text{PROB}(D|Q_j)\text{PROB}(Q_j)}$$

This may also be written as:

$$\text{PROB}(Q_i|D) \propto \text{PROB}(D|Q_i)\text{PROB}(Q_i)$$

where the symbol '$\propto$' means 'is proportional to'. The application of Bayes' theorem is at the heart of the Bayesian approach to statistical analysis.

22.3 An example: the Bayesian approach to computer-aided diagnosis

Bayes' theorem may be stated in terms of the probability of Diagnosis A having observed Data B, as:

$$\text{PROB}(\text{Diagnosis A} \mid \text{Data B})$$
$$\propto \text{PROB}(\text{Data B} \mid \text{Diagnosis A})$$
$$\times \text{PROB}(\text{Diagnosis A})$$

If we have a large dataset of known diagnoses and their associated symptoms and signs, we can estimate PROB(Diagnosis A) easily. It is simply the proportion of times A has been diagnosed. For a patient, the data B are the particular combination of signs and symptoms with which the patient presents. The problem of finding the probability of a particular combination of symptoms and signs for each diagnosis is more difficult. We can say that the probability of a given symptom for a given diagnosis is the proportion of times the symptom occurs in patients with that diagnosis. If the symptoms are all independent, the probability of any combination of symptoms can be then found by multiplying their individual probabilities together (Section 6.2). In practice the assumption that signs and symptoms are independent is most unlikely to be met and a more complicated analysis would be required to deal with this. However, some systems of computer-aided diagnosis have been found to work quite well with the simple approach.

We thus have the probability of each diagnosis and the probability of each combination of symptoms and signs for each diagnosis. When a new patient presents, we obtain the data and compute

$$PROB(Data|Diagnosis) \times PROB(Diagnosis)$$

for each diagnosis and sum these. We then divide the product by this sum for each diagnosis and this gives us the probability for each diagnosis given the signs and symptoms.

PROB(Diagnosis A) is called the **prior probability** of Diagnosis A, because it is the probability of Diagnosis A before the data are observed. PROB(Diagnosis A|Data B) is called the **posterior probability** of Diagnosis A given Data B, the probability of the diagnosis for someone with the observed signs and symptoms denoted by B. PROB(Data B|Diagnosis A) is called the **likelihood** of Diagnosis A for Data B, the probability of the observed signs and symptoms for someone with the diagnosis.

22.4 The Bayesian and frequency views of probability

In the diagnosis example, we could give prior probabilities for the diagnoses easily. They were given by the proportions of people with the diagnoses in the population of patients. But suppose we want to use the Bayesian approach to estimate a population mean. We must attach a prior probability to each possible value of the mean, that is, we must find a prior probability distribution.

From the frequency definition of probability, that it is the proportion of times the event would happen in

the long run, this is meaningless. The population mean is seen as a constant, not a random variable, and so it cannot have probability attached to it.

Bayesians solve this problem by saying that the population mean is a random variable with a probability distribution and that the probability expresses our degree of knowledge about or belief held with respect to it. The frequency definition then is included as the method of calculating this degree of knowledge or belief when appropriate. From the Bayesian viewpoint it quite reasonable to talk about the probability that Liverpool will be league champions next year, but this probability will vary depending on the allegiance of the believer; it is subjective. Thus we can talk about the probability that a population mean will be, say, between 900 and 910. The probability expresses the strength of our knowledge or belief that this will be so. We can also estimate, as a result of a randomized clinical trial, the probability that one treatment is better than the other, something which would be meaningless from the Frequentist viewpoint. Thus the Bayesian view of probability, much more general than the Frequentist, is much closer to the usual popular view, where 'I will probably go to the pub tonight' is a meaningful statement.

22.5 An example of Bayesian estimation

An artificial example will illustrate the Bayesian approach to estimation. Two researchers, A and B, wish to estimate the prevalence of a condition X in a population. Researcher A is more familiar with condition X than is B. A can make a reasonable guess as to the unknown prevalence μ, which A reckons to be around 0.15, and at least 0.10 and not more than 0.20. We can represent A's prior opinion about μ by a distribution with mean = 0.15 and standard deviation = 0.025. B guesses that μ could be anywhere between 0 and 0.5. We can represent B's prior opinion about μ by a distribution with mean = 0.25 and standard deviation = 0.125. The shape of the distribution is more than either A or B could be expected to specify. In traditional Bayesian analysis, we choose one that makes the mathematics easy. For estimating a Binomial proportion, the appropriate family of distributions is

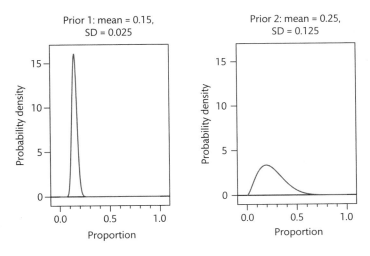

Figure 22.1 Prior distributions for estimating a binomial proportion.

one called the Beta distribution. Like a proportion, this is constrained to have values between 0 and 1. The prior probability distributions for Researchers A and B, which have the required means and standard deviations, are shown in Figure 22.1.

We can now start collecting data. We observe the number of people with X in a sample. This count will be an observation from a Binomial distribution (Section 6.4), with parameters equal to the unknown proportion with condition X, μ, and the sample size, n, which we choose. We will start by collecting a few subjects, say 20, of whom four have condition X. The posterior probability distribution of μ is the product of the prior probability and the likelihood, standardized to have a total probability of one. This is another Beta distribution, which is why this form for the prior distribution is chosen.

For Researcher A, the posterior distribution has mean = 0.154, SD = 0.024. For B the posterior distribution has mean = 0.218, SD = 0.073. Researcher B's estimate is influenced more by the data than is A's, because B's prior knowledge was weaker. Figure 22.2 shows these posterior distributions.

Now, suppose we increase the size of the sample to 100, and observe a sample number with condition X of 21. The posterior distribution for Researcher A now has mean = 0.170, SD = 0.022 and for Researcher B the posterior distribution now has mean = 0.214, SD = 0.039 (Figure 22.3). The two posterior distributions are closer together, as more data have been used.

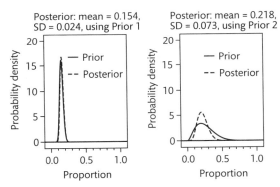

Figure 22.2 Posterior distributions for estimating a binomial proportion after observing 20 subjects.

Finally, we might have a much larger sample of 1 000 subjects, 192 of whom have condition X. The posterior distribution for Researcher A now has mean = 0.185, SD = 0.011 and for Researcher B the posterior distribution now has mean = 0.193, SD = 0.012 (Figure 22.4). These are fairly similar as the data have almost outweighed the prior differences.

Each posterior distribution gives us an estimate, the mean of the posterior, and we can calculate a region of substantial probability in which the μ is believed to lie, such as two standard deviations of the posterior distribution on either side of the estimate. Bayesians often calculate a **credible interval**, an interval in which the estimate has a high probability, often 95%. There are several ways of doing this, including a **higher posterior**

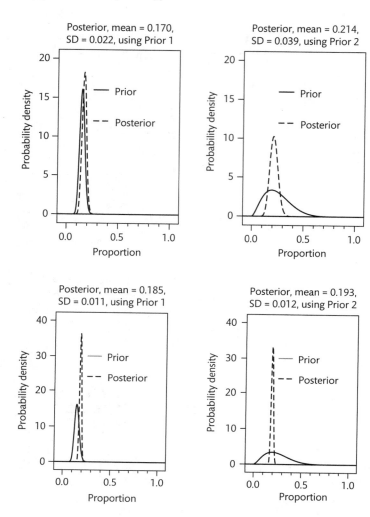

Figure 22.3 Posterior distributions for estimating a binomial proportion after observing 100 subjects.

Figure 22.4 Posterior distributions for estimating a binomial proportion after observing 1 000 subjects.

density interval (H.P.D. interval), where the interval is chosen so that values within it have greater probability density than any of those outside it, and a **central credibility interval**, where the total probability at either end is the same, usually 0.025 or 2.5%. As the posterior distribution here is a member of the Beta distribution family, this can be found by numerical integration of the incomplete Beta function, a long way beyond the scope of this book. However, provided the mean and one minus the mean are much greater than the standard deviation, the distribution will be approximately Normal and we can use the mean ± 1.96 standard deviations in the usual way. For Researcher A this gives 0.163 to 0.207. For Researcher B this gives 0.169 to 0.217.

Compare this with the frequency approach. Here we estimate the population proportion from the sample, giving 192/1 000 = 0.192 with standard error $\sqrt{0.192 \times (1 - 0.192)/1\,000}$ = 0.012 and a 95% confidence interval of 0.192 – 1.96 × 0.012 = 0.168 to 0.192 + 1.96 × 0.012 = 0.216. We get very similar numerical results here by both approaches. The interpretation is different, however. We noted in Section 8.3 that we should not interpret the 95% confidence interval as meaning that there is a probability of 0.95 that the unknown proportion lies between 0.168 and 0.216. That is the Frequentist view, that we can say only that for 95% of confidence intervals the population value lies within the interval. This is a real problem for the Frequentist approach: it does not give users what they want and think they have got.

Note that the frequency answer is closer to that of Researcher B. This is because B's prior knowledge was weaker than A's and so had less influence.

22.6 Prior distributions

One difficulty with Bayesian methods lies in the choice of the prior distribution. Unless we have strong prior knowledge or belief about the thing we wish to estimate, we usually want the prior to have little influence on the estimate. Prior distributions can be chosen so that they are relatively uninformative compared with the data. This happens if the distribution has a large variance and the prior probability curve is fairly flat or uniform in the region of the estimate. There are several possible approaches to this question of the form of the prior distribution.

Bayes suggested that in the absence of grounds for choosing a particular form for the prior, one should be chosen which gives equal probability to all the possibilities. This is known as **Bayes' Postulate**, but as Bayes' work was published posthumously by a friend, it is unclear to what extent Bayes himself was willing to apply this.

A prior distribution which gives the same probability to all possibilities is called an **uninformative prior**. For the estimation of a proportion, the uninformative prior would be one which gives all proportions from 0 to 1 equal probability, the Uniform distribution. This is a special case of the Beta distribution, with mean 0.5 and standard deviation 0.290.

If we were to use an uninformative prior in the example of estimation of a proportion in Section 22.5, the first sample, 20 people with four positives, gives a posterior mean = 0.227, which is higher than for either of the informative priors. This is not surprising, because the prior mean is 0.5, higher than for either. The posterior standard deviation is 0.087, also higher than for either prior, again to be expected because the uninformative prior has a much higher standard deviation. For the sample of 100 people with 21 positives, the posterior distribution has mean 0.216 and SD 0.041. This is very similar to Researcher B, 0.214 and 0.039, whose prior

knowledge was weak, but not to Researcher A, 0.170 and 0.022, whose prior knowledge and belief was strong. For the large sample with 1 000 people and 192 positives, we get mean = 0.193, SD = 0.012, almost identical to Researcher B, also 0.193 and 0.012 to three decimal places, and not very different from Researcher A, 0.185 and 0.011. The frequentist estimate is also very similar, 0.192 with standard error 0.012. With the larger sample, only the strong belief of Researcher A has much effect.

We can also have a **vague prior**, which, while not being totally uninformative, has a very big standard deviation and so gives a small prior probability to a very wide range of possible values. This is used when the prior distribution has a form which does not have fixed upper and lower limits, such as the Normal, for a parameter which does not have fixed upper and lower limits, such as the difference between two means. We choose a prior distribution with a very large variance, which therefore contains very little information about the parameter rather than none at all, and which will be very quickly overwhelmed by the data.

22.7 Maximum likelihood

Followers of the frequency school of probability have adopted a different approach to estimation, that of **maximum likelihood**. This states that the best estimate is the one that maximizes the likelihood of the estimate, the probability of the data given the estimate. We choose the estimate which would give the greatest probability to the observed data. For variables which follow a Normal distribution, the usual least squares estimates (as in linear regression, etc.) are the maximum likelihood estimates. Most of the methods in this book are frequency methods and have maximum likelihood properties.

If we adopt Bayes' Postulate, and have equal prior probability for all possibilities, the posterior probability will be proportional to the likelihood and the estimate with maximum posterior probability will also be the maximum likelihood estimate. Thus the two approaches are often going to lead to the same conclusions. Bayesian methods with priors of this type lead to results very similar to the two sample t method, etc.

22.8 Markov Chain Monte Carlo methods

Careful choice of the family of distributions used for the prior distribution can make calculation of the posterior distribution feasible. One of the great problems with analytical Bayesian methods is that such a choice of prior distribution may not be available. In that case, calculation of the posterior distribution may be very difficult.

The modern Bayesian approach gets around this by using numerical methods called Markov Chain Monte Carlo (MCMC) to make calculation of posterior distributions possible even when an exact mathematical solution is not available. A **Markov chain** is a process in which the future state is random and depends only on the present state, rather than the past. A **Monte Carlo** method is one which relies on chance. The bootstrap method (Section 8.11) and the multiple imputation method (Section 19.6) are both Monte Carlo methods.

Any method which relies on generating thousands of random steps will be much easier using a computer and MCMC Bayesian methods are very much a product of the computer age. Early practitioners would set their computer running to carry out an analysis before leaving the office and go home, hoping that by the morning the process would have finished. The great increases in computer speed have rendered this unnecessary and Bayesian methods using MCMC can now be carried out quickly and conveniently. This has enabled Bayesian statisticians to solve some difficult problems and statisticians now talk about analysing data 'in a Bayesian framework' or 'in a Frequentist framework' and most are willing (and some are able) to switch between the two approaches. A few are still fighting the war, however.

To see how this works, I shall describe the MCMC Bayesian estimation of a simple proportion, which I did analytically in Section 22.5. I used a program called WinBUGS, which is the Windows version of BUGS (Bayesian inference Using Gibbs Sampling), developed in Cambridge by the Medical Research Council Biostatistics Unit (Lunn *et al.* 2000). At the time of writing, this program is freely available from http://www.mrc-bsu.cam.ac.uk/bugs/.

As an example I shall use Researcher B's estimate of the proportion after observing 21 positives out of a sample of size 100. First I told the program what the problem was, including for the prior distribution the Beta distribution I worked out for Observer B, and gave it the data. I told it that a good starting guess for the proportion would be Observer B's expected proportion, 0.25, then I accepted the default number of iterations or **updates**, 1 000, and let it run. One of the outputs of the MCMC procedure is a series of random draws from the posterior distribution. These can be collected to give an estimate of the posterior distribution and its parameters Figure 22.5 shows a record of the history of the 1 000 estimates, as produced by WinBUGS.

This was a very simple analysis and the graph looks the same all the way along. More complex analyses may take a lot of updates before this is achieved and a run-in or 'burn-in' period is needed before we have satisfactory convergence and the distribution is not changing.

Another output of WinBUGS is a table of the statistics produced by the estimation process (Table 22.1). The mean and standard deviation of the posterior distribution are very similar to the 0.214 and 0.039 found by the analytic approach (Section 22.5). We also have some centiles of the posterior distribution. The interval from the 2.5%ile to the 97.5%ile, 0.1439 to 0.295 or 14.4% to 29.5%, gives a 95% central credible interval (Section 22.5). (The different numbers of decimal places for the two centiles reflects the irritating way computer programs

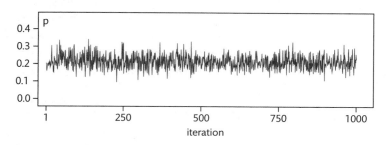

Figure 22.5 History of the WinBUGS estimation of a proportion for Observer B. (The vertical axis shows the estimated proportion, p.)

Table 22.1 Statistics produced by WinBUGS estimation of a proportion for Researcher B, using the Beta distribution prior

Node	Mean	SD	MC error	2.5%	Median	97.5%	Start	Sample
p	0.2138	0.039 09	0.001 305	0.143 9	0.210 5	0.295	1	1 000

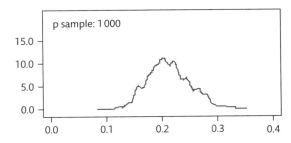

Figure 22.6 Posterior density plot from the WinBUGS estimation of a proportion for Observer B. (The vertical axis shows the probability density.).

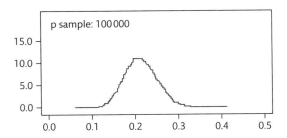

Figure 22.7 Posterior density plot from the WinBUGS estimation of a proportion for Observer B with 100 000 updates. (The vertical axis shows the probability density.).

drop trailing zeros.) The estimate used all the iterations, from 1 to 1 000. We can also get a picture of the empirical posterior distribution (Figure 22.6). It looks quite like the posterior distribution in Figure 22.3, though the scale is different, making it appear to be stretched horizontally, and it is bumpy, a result of the simulation process.

Table 22.2 shows the same analysis with 100 000 iterations or updates rather than 1 000, for which I had to wait 63 seconds. The estimated mean, standard deviation, and centiles are very similar, but not quite the same, and the Monte Carlo error, 1.294E-4 or 0.000 129 4 is much smaller, reflecting the improved estimation produced by the greater number of updates. The graph of the posterior density is also considerably smoother, too (Figure 22.7).

The great advantage of the MCMC approach, however, is that it can solve problems which are very difficult using an analytic approach. We do not need to choose a form for the prior distribution which makes the mathematics work. So I tried saying that the prior distribution was

Normal with mean 0.25 and standard deviation 0.125, as for Researcher B, but omitting the step of finding the Beta distribution with these properties. Now this is not a particularly good choice, because it attaches non-trivial probability (0.025) to proportions which are less than zero, impossible values. WinBUGS refused to cooperate, giving no estimates with the default 1 000 iterations that worked for the Beta prior distribution. I increased the number of iterations to 10 000 and Table 22.3 resulted. The result is very similar to Table 22.1, except for the start point and the sample count. The algorithm usedthe first 4 000 iterations to prepare for the estimation process and used only the last 6 000 actually to estimate the posterior distribution. The standard deviation and the Monte Carlo error are both greater than in Table 22.1, despite the greater number of updates, which I think is a result of the less appropriate, though simpler, prior distribution.

I am not an experienced user of Bayesian MCMC methods and this was a learning experience for me, too. I included it to illustrate the basic idea, which was

Table 22.2 Statistics produced by WinBUGS estimation of a proportion for Observer B, using the Beta distribution prior and 100 000 updates

Node	Mean	SD	MC error	2.5%	Median	97.5%	Start	Sample
p	0.213 7	0.038 74	1.294E-4	0.143 1	0.212	0.294 4	1	100 000

Table 22.3 Statistics produced by WinBUGS estimation of a proportion for Observer B, using the Normal distribution prior

Node	Mean	SD	MC error	2.5%	Median	97.5%	Start	Sample
p	0.2143	0.04243	0.001355	0.139	0.2097	0.3039	4001	6000

used, for example, in the network meta-analysis in Section 17.13. There are now many Bayesian meta-analyses in the literature. I expect readers of medical research to come across its use with increasing frequency in the future. If your own research should require a Bayesian analysis, for a network meta-analysis (Section 17.13), for example, then I would strongly recommend finding an experienced collaborator to do it, rather than trying to climb the steep learning curve alone.

22.9 Bayesian or Frequentist?

There are arguments against the Bayesian view:

(a) philosophical – can we ascribe probability to the mean of a population or is it really a constant?

(b) practical – Bayesian methods can be computationally much more difficult than the familiar frequency ones and suitable software, easy to use for the non-statistician, is not readily available.

Against the frequency approach it can be argued that:

(a) philosophical – sampling theory, based on the idea of an infinite number of samples, only one of which exists, is erecting a huge hypothetical structure to arrive at its simple conclusions. Confidence intervals and significance tests are not what researchers actually want, which is why they continually misinterpret them. Also, should we really ignore all other knowledge in our formal analysis of our data?

(b) practical – some problems are very difficult to solve from the frequency viewpoint but can be solved using Bayesian methods, such as network meta-analysis (Section 17.13).

The philosophical arguments against Bayes' approach seem rather weak, and if we want to see why Bayesian methods are not more widely used we have to look elsewhere. Although modern computers can deal with

the problems of calculation, they can only do this if there is readily available, easy to use software. There is, as yet, no Bayesian equivalent of SPSS. But the main reason, I think, is inertia. Many statisticians, trained in the frequency school, are not well informed about the practicalities of Bayesian methods, and are sometimes quite prejudiced against them. (I include myself among the ignorant, though, I hope, less prejudiced than I used to be.) The opposite, however, is also true.

To learn more about Bayesian methods, you could start with Sivia and Skilling (2006) or Kruschke (2010).

Finally, we should ask whether it matters. As we have seen, many Bayesian and frequency approaches arrive at the same conclusion. Perhaps the best approach is to ignore the philosophical problems and use whichever analysis seems best suited to the problem in hand. Open the egg at whichever end you like.

22.10 Multiple choice questions: Bayesian methods

(Each branch is either true or false.)

22.1 In a Bayesian analysis, a prior distribution:
   (a) expresses our knowledge of the quantity of interest before data are observed;
   (b) is based on the data to be analysed;
   (c) will influence the final estimate;
   (d) can be different for different researchers;
   (e) must be from a particular family to match the data.

22.2 When we have no knowledge about the likely value of a parameter, the prior distribution:
   (a) does not require any decision to be made about it;
   (b) can be a vague prior;
   (c) should have as little influence on the estimate as possible;
   (d) will have no influence on the final estimate;
   (e) can be an uninformative prior.

22.3 In a Bayesian analysis, a posterior distribution:
  (a) expresses our knowledge of the quantity of interest after new data are observed;
  (b) is based on the data to be analysed;
  (c) should be uninformative;
  (d) will be influenced by the prior distribution;
  (e) expresses uncertainty about the final estimate.

22.4 Markov Chain Monte Carlo methods:
  (a) enable a wide range of problems to be solved;
  (b) can give slightly different answers if repeated;
  (c) always use all updates to estimate the posterior distribution;
  (d) are often used in network meta-analysis;
  (e) are much more flexible than analytical Bayesian methods.

22.5 A credible interval
  (a) can be chosen so that values within it have greater probability than any of those outside it;
  (b) can be derived from the centiles of the prior distribution;
  (c) can be chosen so that the probabilities above the upper limit and below the lower limit are the same;
  (d) expresses our knowledge of a parameter after data have been analysed;
  (e) is the Bayesian analogue of a confidence interval.

22.11 Exercise: A Bayesian network meta-analysis

Patients who are in intensive therapy units and on ventilation are at risk of potentially fatal infections associated with the ventilator. Three types of preventive treatments are in use: topical oropharyngeal antiseptic agents (mostly chlorhexidine), selective digestive decontamination (SDD), and selective oropharyngeal decontamination (SOD). Price *et al.* (2014) carried out a systematic review of trials to compare these approaches. They found only one trial comparing any two of these three approaches, but found 28 trials comparing one of these with control/usual care treatments. A summary of the results of meta-analyses using only direct comparisons between pairs of treatments is shown in Table 22.4. One trial, by de Smet *et al.* (2009), is so large that it dwarfs the other, but as it was a cluster randomized trial it is not quite as dominant as it appears. It contributes 31% of the weight for the SDD vs. control estimate, but 88% for the SOD vs. control estimate.

22.1 What conclusions might we draw from Table 22.4?

Price *et al.* (2014) carried out a network meta-analysis using the log odds ratios and their standard errors for each trial. They report that 'All model parameters were estimated within a Bayesian framework with WinBUGS software'. There were several parameters to be estimated, including the log

Table 22.4 Results of three Frequentist meta-analyses of the relationship of death to interventions to reduce the risk of oropharyngeal infection in ITU (data from Price *et al.* 2014)

Comparison	No. of trials	Numbers of participants	I^2	OR (95% confidence interval)	P
SDD vs. SOD *	1	3 904	N.A.	0.97 (0.79 to 1.18)	0.8
SDD vs. control **	15	5 891	13%	0.73 (0.64 to 0.84)	<0.001
SOD vs. control **	4	4 266	0%	0.85 (0.74 to 0.97)	0.02
Chlorhexidine vs. control	11	2 618	0%	1.25 (1.05 to 1.50)	0.01

* From a single trial (de Smet *et al.* 2009), P value estimate from confidence interval.
** Includes the comparison with Control from de Smet *et al.* (2009).

odds ratios of each of the interventions versus control and the standard deviation between studies. They used vague prior distributions for these. A run-in period of 50 000 iterations was adequate to achieve convergence, and a further 100 000 samples were taken.

Table 22.5 Results of a network meta-analysis of interventions to prevent death in intensive care (data from Price *et al.* 2014)

Comparison	OR (95% Credible interval)
SDD vs. SOD	0.91 (0.70 to 1.19)
SDD vs. chlorhexidine	0.61 (0.47 to 0.78)
SOD vs. chlorhexidine	0.67 (0.48 to 0.91)
SDD vs. control	0.74 (0.63 to 0.86)
SOD vs. control	0.82 (0.62 to 1.02)
Chlorhexidine vs. control	1.23 (0.99 to 1.49)

22.2 Why did they use vague prior distributions rather than uninformative priors?

Table 22.5 shows the odds ratios of death estimated in the network meta-analysis, giving an odds ratio for the comparison of each pair of interventions.

22.3 What can we conclude from Table 22.5 and what does it add to Table 22.4?

Table 22.6 shows the estimated probabilities of death for patients receiving each treatment. These are quite high, because these are ITU patients, many of whom are very sick. It also shows the posterior probability that each of the interventions is the best of the four.

22.4 Could the estimated probabilities of death be interpreted from a Frequentist perspective? Would this be different from a Bayesian perspective?

22.5 Could the estimated probabilities of the intervention being best be interpreted from a Frequentist perspective? How would they be interpreted from a Bayesian perspective?

Table 22.6 Estimated probability of death and probability of the intervention being the best of the four, ranked by this probability (data from Price *et al.* 2014)

Intervention	Rank order of intervention	Estimated probability of death	Probability of intervention being best
SDD	1	0.213	0.740
SOD	2	0.228	0.260
Control	3	0.266	<0.001
Chlorhexidine	4	0.305	<0.001

Appendix 1
Suggested answers to multiple choice questions and exercises

These are suggested answers to the exercises. Some of them are matters of opinion and I am sometimes wrong. You may disagree with me.

Some of the multiple choice questions are quite hard. If you score +1 for a correct answer, –1 for an incorrect answer, and 0 for a part which you omitted, I would regard 40% as the pass level, 50% as good, 60% as very good, and 70% as excellent. These questions are hard to set and some may be ambiguous, so you will not score 100%. If you appear to fail, remember Samuel Beckett: 'No matter. Try again. Fail again. Fail better'. And it's not you, it's me.

Chapter 2

Answers to 2.15 Multiple Choice Questions: Clinical trials

2.1. FFFFF. Controls should be treated in the same place at the same time, under the same conditions other than the treatment under test (Section 2.1). All must be willing and eligible to receive either treatment (Section 2.13).

2.2. FTFTF. Random allocation is done to achieve comparable groups, allocation being unrelated to the subjects' characteristics (Section 2.2). The use of random numbers helps to prevent bias in allocation (Section 2.4).

2.3. TFFFT. Patients do not know their treatment, but they usually do know that they are in a trial (Section 2.9). Not the same as a cross-over trial (Section 2.7).

2.4. FFFFF. Vaccinated and refusing children are self-selected (Section 2.5). We analyse by intention to treat (Section 2.6). We can compare effect of a vaccination programme by comparing the whole vaccination group, vaccinated and refusers to the controls.

2.5. TFTTT. Section 2.7. The order is randomized.

2.6. FFTTT. Sections 2.9, 2.10. The purpose of placebos is make dissimilar treatments appear similar. Only in randomized trials

can we rely on comparability, and then only within the limits of random variation (Section 2.2).

Answers to 2.16 Exercise: The 'Know Your Midwife' trial

2.1. It was hoped that women in the KYM group would be more satisfied with their care. The knowledge that they would receive continuity of care was an important part of the treatment, and so the lack of blindness is essential. More difficult is that KYM women were given a choice and so may have felt more committed to whichever scheme, KYM or standard, they had chosen, than did the control group. We must accept this element of patient control as part of the treatment.

2.2. The study should be (and was) analysed by intention to treat (Section 2.6). As often happens, the refusers did worse than did the acceptors of KYM, and worse than the control group. When we compare all those allocated to KYM with those allocated to control, there is very little difference (Table A.1).

2.3. Women had booked for hospital antenatal care expecting the standard service. Those allocated to this therefore received what they had requested. Those allocated to the KYM scheme were offered a treatment which they could refuse

Table A.1 Method of delivery in the KYM study (data from Flint and Poulengeris 1986)

Method of delivery	Allocated to KYM		Allocated to control	
	%	*n*	%	*n*
Normal	79.7	382	74.8	354
Instrumental	12.5	60	17.8	84
Caesarean	7.7	37	7.4	35

if they wished, refusers getting the care for which they had originally booked. No extra examinations were carried out for research purposes, the only special data being the questionnaires, which could be refused. There was therefore no need to get the women's permission for the randomization. I thought this was a convincing argument.

Chapter 3

Answers to 3.11 Multiple choice questions: Observational studies

3.1. FTTTT. A population can be any group we wish to study (Section 3.3).

3.2. TFFFT. A census tells us who is there on that day, and only applies to current in-patients. The hospital could be quite unusual. Some diagnoses are less likely than others to lead to admission or to long stay (Section 3.2).

3.3. TFFTF. All members and all samples have equal chances of being chosen (Section 3.4). We must stick to the sample the random process produces. Errors can be estimated using confidence intervals and significance tests. Choice does not depend on the subject's characteristics at all, except for its being in the population.

3.4. FTTFT. Some populations are unidentifiable and some cannot be listed easily (Section 3.4).

3.5. FFFTF. In a case-control study we start with a group with the disease (here eczema), the cases, and a group without the disease, the controls (Section 3.8).

3.6. FTFTT. We must have a cohort or case-control study to get enough cases (Sections 3.7, 3.8).

3.7. TTTTF. This is a random cluster sample (Section 3.4). Each patient had the same chance of their hospital being chosen and then the same chance of being chosen within the hospital. This would not be so if we chose a fixed number from each hospital rather than a fixed proportion, as those in small hospitals would be more likely to be chosen than those in large hospitals. In part (e), what about a sample with patients in every hospital?

Answers to 3.12 Exercise *Campylobacter jejuni* infection

3.1. Many cases of infection may be unreported, but there is not much that could be done about that. Many organisms produce similar symptoms, hence the need for laboratory confirmation. There are many sources of infection, including direct transmission, hence the exclusion of cases exposed to other water supplies and to infected people.

3.2. Controls can be matched for age and sex as these may be related to their exposure to risk factors such as handling raw meat. If not, we would need to adjust for these in the analysis. Inclusion of controls who may have had the disease would have weakened any relationships with the cause, and the same exclusion criteria were applied as for the cases, to keep them comparable.

3.3. Data are obtained by recall. Cases may remember events in relation to the disease more easily than controls in relation to the same time. Cases may have been thinking about possible causes of the disease and so be more likely to recall milk attacks. The lack of positive association with any other risk factor suggests that this is not important here.

3.4. I was convinced. The relationship is very strong and these scavenging birds are known to carry the organism. There was no relationship with any other risk factor. The only problem is that there was little evidence that these birds had actually attacked the milk. Others have suggested that cats may also remove the tops of milk bottles to drink the milk and may be the real culprits (Balfour 1991).

3.5. Further studies include testing of attacked milk bottles for campylobacter (we would have to wait for the next year). Possibly a cohort study, asking people about history of bird attacks and drinking attacked milk, then follow for future campylobacter (and other) infections. Possibly an intervention study. Advise people to protect their milk and observe the subsequent pattern of infection.

Chapter 4

Answers to 4.9 Multiple choice questions: Summarizing data

4.1. TFFTF. Section 4.1. Parity is quantitative and discrete, height and blood pressure are continuous.

4.2. TTFTF. Section 4.1. Age last birthday is discrete, exact age includes years and fraction of a year.

4.3. FFTFT. Sections 4.4, 4.6. It could have more than one mode, we cannot say. Standard deviation is less than variance if the variance is greater than one (Sections 4.7-8). This is not related to the shape of the distribution.

4.4. TTTFT. Sections 4.2-4. Mean and variance only tell us the location and spread of the distribution (Sections 4.6-7).

4.5. TFTFF. Sections 4.5–7. Median = 2 , the observations must be ordered before the central one is found, mode = 2, range = 7 – 1 = 6. The standard deviation = 2.35; it could not possibly be so large as 6, the range.

4.6. FFFFT. Sections 4.6–8. There would be more observations below the mean than above, because the median would be less than the mean. Most observations will be within one standard deviation of the mean whatever the shape. The standard deviation measures how widely the blood pressure is spread between people, not for a single person, which would be needed to estimate accuracy. See also Section 20.2.

Answers to 4.10 Exercise: Student measurements and a graph of study numbers

4.1. Arm circumference is quantitative, because it has a numerical value. Arm circumference is also continuous, because any arm circumference within the range could have been recorded, limited only by the accuracy to which the scale could be read (Section 4.1).

4.2. This is a histogram, a graphical representation of a frequency distribution (Section 4.2).

4.3. The mode is the value of the variable at the highest part of the graph, the region of highest frequency (Figure A.1). This is where arm circumference is between 240 and 260 mm. The lower tail is the part of the distribution where there are relatively few observations and these are small. This is where the arm circumference is below 240 mm. The upper tail is the part of the distribution where there are relatively few observations and these are large. This is where the arm circumference is above 300 mm (Section 4.4).

4.4. The distribution appears to be skewed to the right or positively skewed. The lower tail is much shorter than the upper tail.

4.5. The median is the value which divides the distribution into two equal parts. The middle of the distribution looks to be just above 260 mm. The first quartile, which cuts off the bottom quarter of the observations, would be somewhere near the lower end of the tallest bar, in the 240 to 260 mm interval, perhaps around 245 mm. The third quartile, which cuts off the top quarter of the observations, appears to be in the 280 to 300 mm interval, perhaps around 290 mm. In fact, the median is 265 mm, the first quartile is 245.5 mm and the third quartile 281 mm. Of course, it is difficult to judge accurately from the histogram and any answers within 10 mm of the correct one are good. Figure A.1 shows how they look on

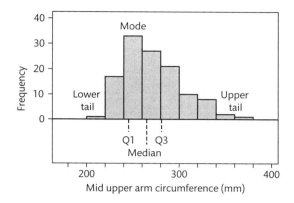

Figure A.1 Quartiles of arm circumference in a group of female students.

the histogram. My estimate of the third quartile was high because in the interval 280 to 300⁻, 11 of the 25 observations were 280 mm.

4.6. The mean will be higher than the median, because the distribution is positively skew. We would expect it to be greater than the 260 estimated for the median, perhaps about 270 mm. To estimate the standard deviation, we know that about 95% of observations will be within two standard deviations of the mean and that the 5% outside this will be mostly, if not all, at the higher end of the distribution. There are 120 students, so only six would be expected to be outside the limits. There look to be three above 340 mm and more than this between 320 and 340, so we might estimate four standard deviations as being from the lowest arm circumference to 330, that is from 200 to 330 or 130 mm. A quarter of this is 32.5, so we could estimate the standard deviation to be about 33 mm. In fact the mean is 268.8 mm and the standard deviation is 31.6 mm, so my estimates were good. If you got within 10 mm for the mean and 5 mm for the standard deviation, that was good. Figure A.2 shows how they appear on the histogram.

4.7. Eye colour is a qualitative variable, also called a categorical variable. The categories are not ordered. Such a variable is also called nominal. Sex is also a qualitative variable. Because there are only two categories, it is also called dichotomous or binary.

4.8. This is highly skew to the right. If you said symmetrical, you were misled by a very confusing display. Read on!

4.9. The intervals are of very different sizes. The first interval has width 20, the second, third, and fourth have width 10, the fifth has width 50, the sixth has width 100, and so on.

4.10. The horizontal scale should show the number of cases, positive plus negative. The scale would start at zero. The top of the scale would be uncertain, because we know that the

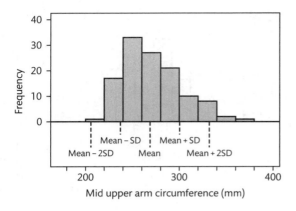

Figure A.2 Mean and standard deviation of arm circumference in a group of female students.

highest group is greater than or equal to 1 001, but not what the upper limit is. I have arbitrarily chosen 2 000 as the upper limit.

4.11. On a histogram, the vertical scale shows the frequencies in some form. As the intervals for the frequency distribution are unequal, we must use frequency density rather than frequency. Hence we get number of studies per case. The histogram should look like Figure A.3. It is difficult for us to see clearly the rightmost bar of the histogram, which covers the interval 1 000 to 2 000 and has height = 0.004 studies per case.

4.12. The tail is on the right is much longer than the tail on the left, so this is highly skew to the right.

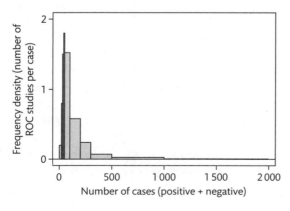

Figure A.3 Histogram for the distribution of sample size in 233 diagnostic studies.

Chapter 5

Answers to 5.11 Multiple choice questions: Data presentation

5.1. FTTTT. Sections 5.1, 5.2. Without a control group we have no idea how many would get better anyway (Section 2.1). 66.67% is 2/3. We may only have three patients.

5.2. TFFTT. Section 5.2. To three significant figures, it should be 1 730. We round up because of the 9 in the fourth place. To six decimal places it is 1 729.543 710.

5.3. FTTFT. This is a bar chart showing the relationship between two variables (Section 5.5). See Figure A.4. Calendar time has no true zero to show.

5.4. TTFFT. Section 5.10, Appendix 5A. There is no logarithm of zero.

5.5. FFTTT. Sections 5.5–7. A histogram (Section 4.3) and a pie chart (Section 5.4) each show the distribution of a single variable.

Answers to 5.12 Exercise: Creating presentation graphs

5.1. This is the frequency distribution of a qualitative variable, so a pie chart can be used to display it. The calculations are set out in Table A.2. Notice that we have lost one degree through rounding errors. We could work to fractions of a degree, but the eye is unlikely to spot the difference. In practice we would use a computer to do these calculations and draw

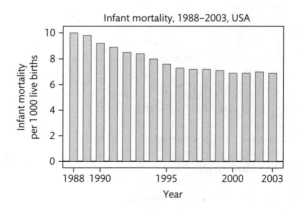

Figure A.4 A dubious graph revised.

Table A.2 Calculations for a pie chart for the Tooting Bec data (data from Bewley *et al.* 1975)

Category	Frequency	Relative frequency	Angle
Schizophrenia	474	0.323 11	116
Affective illness	277	0.188 82	68
Organic brain syndrome	405	0.276 07	99
Subnormality	58	0.039 54	14
Alcoholism	57	0.038 85	14
Other	196	0.133 61	48
Total	1 467	1.000 00	359

the graph. The pie chart is shown in Figure A.5. We could also show these data as a bar chart (Figure A.6). I have used a horizontal bar chart to make it easy to read the names of diagnoses. Personally, I find the table better than either, but numbers speak to me.

5.2. See Figure A.7.

5.3. There are several possibilities. In the original paper, Doll and Hill used a separate bar chart for each disease, similar to Figure A.8. We could also combine them into a single bar chart as shown in Figure A.9.

Chapter 6

Answers to 6.9 Multiple choice questions: Probability

6.1. TTFFF. Section 6.2. If they are mutually exclusive they cannot both happen. There is no reason why they should

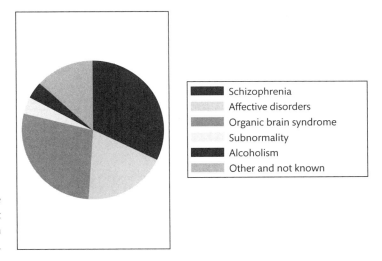

Figure A.5 Pie chart showing the distribution of patients in Tooting Bec Hospital by diagnostic group (data from Bewley *et al.* 1975).

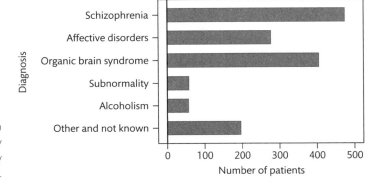

Figure A.6 Bar chart showing the distribution of patients in Tooting Bec Hospital by diagnostic group (data from Bewley *et al.* 1975).

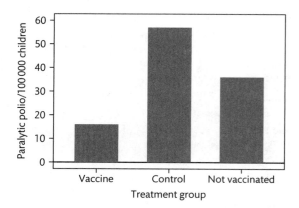

Figure A.7 Bar chart showing the results of the Salk vaccine trial (data from Meier 1977).

be equiprobable or exhaustive, the only events which can happen (Section 6.3).

6.2. TFTFT. For both, the probabilities are multiplied, $0.2 \times 0.05 = 0.01$ (Section 6.2). Clearly the probability of both must be less than that for each one separately. The probability of both is 0.01, so the probability of X alone is $0.20 - 0.01 = 0.19$ and the probability of Y alone is

$0.05 - 0.01 = 0.04$. The probability of having X or Y is the probability of X alone + probability of Y alone + probability of X and Y together, because these are three mutually exclusive events. Having X and having Y are not mutually exclusive as she can have both. Having X tells us nothing about whether she has Y. If she has X, the probability of having Y is still 0.05, because X and Y are independent.

6.3. TFTFF. Section 6.4. Weight is continuous. Patients respond with equal probability, being selected at random from a population where the probability of responding varies. The number of red cells might follow a Poisson distribution (Section 6.7); there is no set of independent trials. The *number* of hypertensives follows a Binomial distribution, not the proportion.

6.4. TTTTF. The probability of clinical disease is $0.5 \times 0.5 = 0.25$. The probability of carrier status = probability that father passes the gene and mother does not + probability that mother passes the gene and father does not = $0.5 \times 0.5 + 0.5 \times 0.5 = 0.5$. Probability of not inheriting the gene = $0.5 \times 0.5 = 0.25$. Probability of not having clinical disease = $1 - 0.25 = 0.75$. Successive children are independent, so the probabilities for the second child are unaffected by the first (Section 6.2).

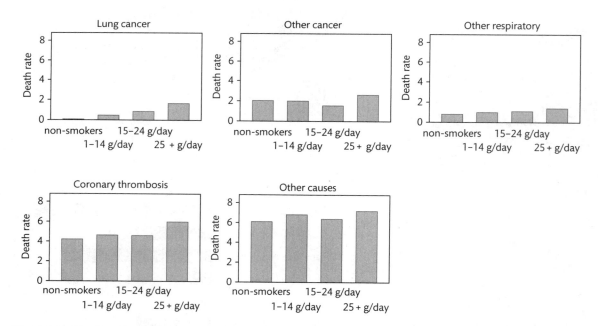

Figure A.8 Mortality in British doctors by smoking habits (data from Doll and Hill 1956).

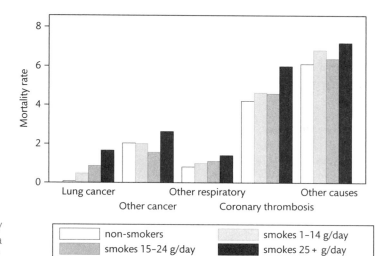

Figure A.9 Mortality in British doctors by smoking habits, alternative version (data from Doll and Hill 1956).

6.5. FTTFT. Section 6.3–4. The expected number is one (Section 6.6). The spins are independent (Section 6.2). At least one tail means one tail (PROB = 0.5) or two tails (PROB = 0.25). These are mutually exclusive, so the probability of at least one tail is 0.5 + 0.25 = 0.75.

6.6. FTTFT. Section 6.6. $E(X + 2) = \mu + 2$, $VAR(2X) = 4\sigma^2$.

6.7. TTTFF. Section 6.6. The variance of a difference is the sum of the variances. Variances cannot be negative. $VAR(X - Y) = VAR(X) + VAR(Y)$, $VAR(-X) = (-1)^2 \times VAR(X) = VAR(X)$.

Answers to 6.10 Exercise: Probability in court

6.1. This is the multiplicative rule, that the probability that two independent events would both happen is found by multiplying their individual probabilities.

6.2. The assumption is that the two deaths are independent, that the fact of the first child dying does not influence the probability that the second child will die. This seems to me inherently implausible. Unexplained death is not the same as random. There may be several factors which increase the risk of cot death. Prone sleeping position and amount of thermal insulation around the baby spring to mind, there may be undiscovered genetic factors and other environmental factors which would also make the events not independent. Watkins (2000) mentions studies which do appear to show that, indeed, one cot death does increase the chance of another.

6.3. Rather than

$$PROB(cot\ death) \times PROB(cot\ death)$$

we would need

$$PROB(second\ cot\ death\ |\ first\ cot\ death) \times PROB(cot\ death)$$

and as we think that Prob(second cot death | first cot death) is less than Prob(cot death), the probability of two cot deaths would be less than if the deaths were independent.

6.4. It would tell us that two cot deaths would be very unlikely in a family of two children chosen at random. But we knew that already.

6.5. The probability that there are two cot deaths given that we have two unexplained deaths would be useful, or the probability that the mother is or is not a murderer given that there are two unexplained deaths. Of course, we do not know either of these.

6.6. This was an example of the prosecutor's fallacy, where the calculated probability of the evidence (unexplained deaths of two children) given that the accused is not guilty (mother is not a murderer) is presented as the probability that the accused is not guilty (mother is not a murderer) given the evidence (unexplained deaths of two children), which is quite different.

Chapter 7

Answers to 7.6 Multiple choice questions: The Normal distribution

7.1. TTTFT. Sections 7.2–4.

7.2. FFFTT. Symmetrical, $\mu = 0, \sigma = 1$ (Section 7.3, Section 4.6).

7.3. TTFFF. Section 7.2. Median = mean. The Normal distribution has nothing to do with normal physiology. 2.5% will be less than 260, 2.5% will be greater than 340 litres/min.

7.4. FTTFF. Sections 4.6, 7.3. The sample size should not affect the mean. The relative sizes of mean, median, and standard deviation depend on the shape of the frequency distribution.

7.5. TFTTF. Sections 7.2, 7.3. Adding, subtracting, or multiplying by a constant, or adding or subtracting an independent Normal variable gives a Normal distribution. X^2 follows a very skew Chi-squared distribution with one degree of freedom and X/Y follows a t distribution with one degree of freedom (Appendix 7A).

7.6. TTTTT. A gentle slope indicates that observations are far apart, a steep slope that there are many observations close together. Hence gentle-steep-gentle ('S' shaped) indicates long tails (Section 7.5).

Answers to 7.7 Exercise: Distribution of some measurements obtained by students

7.1. This is a Normal quantile plot, often simply called a Normal plot (Section 7.5).

7.2. The points lie close to the straight line on which they would be expected to lie for a Normal distribution, except for the first and the last. The distribution would appear to be close to a Normal distribution except for two extreme points, which make the tails rather long. For comparison, Figure A.10 shows a histogram with a superimposed Normal curve, which supports this interpretation. As we shall see in Chapter 10, differences from the Normal like this do not usually matter for comparisons of means, but in Chapter 20 we shall see that they do matter for estimating reference intervals.

7.3. This is a standardized Normal probability plot or p-p plot. The points lie fairly close to the line, indicating a good fit to the Normal distribution, but the two extreme values are not apparent.

7.4. The histogram appears to have two peaks, around the intervals 165 to 170 cm and 180 to 185 cm. The Normal plot

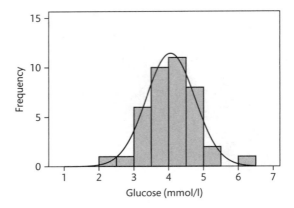

Figure A.10 Histogram of the blood glucose data with the corresponding Normal distribution curve.

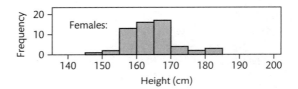

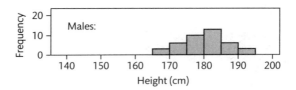

Figure A.11 Histograms showing heights of 99 postgraduate students and their friends and family, divided by sex.

appears to have several curves, first becoming less steep, then becoming more steep, and then becoming less steep again. Both these things indicate a bimodal distribution (Section 4.4).

7.5. This suggests that there might be two different populations here, for such a sample males and females are plausible, as we know men tend to be taller than women. Figures A.11 and A.12 show the distribution separately for females and for males, suggesting that within the sexes, height follows a distribution closer to Normal, though not so closely for females, where there appear to be some departures.

7.6. This appears to curve upwards and become steeper as BMI gets bigger, suggesting a distribution which is positively skewed. The effect is quite marked, suggesting considerable skewness. The histogram shown in Figure A.13 confirms that this is the case.

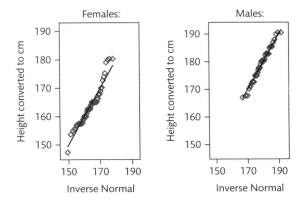

Figure A.12 Normal plots showing heights of 99 postgraduate students and their friends and family, divided by sex.

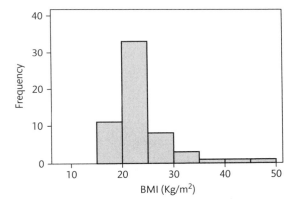

Figure A.13 Histogram showing body mass index (BMI) of 58 female postgraduate students and friends and family.

Chapter 8

Answers to 8.13 Multiple choice questions: Confidence intervals

8.1. FFTFF. Section 8.2. Variability of observations is measured by the standard deviation, s. Standard error of the mean = $\sqrt{s^2/n}$.

8.2. FTFTF. Section 8.3. The sample mean is always in the middle of the limits.

8.3. FTFFT. $SE(\bar{x}) = s/\sqrt{n}$, d.f. = $n - 1$.

8.4. TTTFF. Sections 8.1–2, Section 6.4) Variance is $p(1 - p)/n = 0.1 \times 0.9/100 = 0.0009$. The *number* in the sample with the condition follows a Binomial distribution, not the proportion.

8.5. FFTTT. It depends on the variability of FEV1 and the number in the sample (Section 8.2). The sample should be random (Sections 3.3–4).

8.6. FFTTF. Sections 8.3–4. It is unlikely that we would get these data if the population rate were 10%, but not impossible.

Answers to 8.14 Exercise: Confidence intervals in two acupuncture studies

8.1. White *et al.* (2001) asked people to volunteer. There may be a problem in that the sample of practitioners will not be representative. They may, for example, be more likely to think that their adverse events are low than are practitioners who do not volunteer. An alternative would be to take a representative sample of practitioners, if there were a suitable list of practitioners from which to sample. This would solve the problem if all those sampled agreed to take part. The intended sample of MacPherson *et al.* (2001) was all professional acupuncturists who were members of the British Acupuncture Council and were practising in the UK. This would be a very good sample if they could get information from them all. However, fewer than one in three agreed to take part, giving the same problem as the sample of White *et al.* There may be a problem in that the sample of acupuncturists will not be representative. Acupuncturists who refuse, for example, may be more likely to think that their adverse events are high than those acupuncturists who agree to take part.

8.2. The adverse events in both studies were recorded by the practitioners. This may lead to bias, because practitioners may tend to minimize adverse events. Also they will vary in their interpretation of what constitutes an event worth reporting. The alternative would be to ask the patients. This would make the study much more cumbersome, but might remove some potential bias in the reporting. It would not prevent variability in what people regard as worth reporting, but we could argue that the patient's perception is the more important thing anyway.

8.3. For age, the mean is close to the middle of the range (49 years) so the distribution should be roughly symmetrical, possibly very slightly skewed to the right. For the number of consultations, the median is much closer to the lower limit than to the higher. This distribution will be pronounced skewed to the right. Some practitioners are reporting very few consultations. Either they do very little or are not reporting those that they do.

8.4. In this sample, for every 10 000 consultations we have an average of 14 adverse events. This will not necessarily be true for all consultations. In the population which these consultations represent, we estimate that there are between 8 and 20 events per 10 000 consultations.

8.5. No, we cannot conclude that there is no risk and the authors of these papers do not do so. Just because we have seen no serious events does not mean that there will never be one. The confidence intervals tell us that the data are consistent with there being as many as 1.2 or 1.1 serious events per 10 000 consultations. In fact, there are several reports in the literature of hepatitis transmission being linked with acupuncture, though these are very rare.

8.6. Yes, I think that this is a reasonable interpretation of the confidence interval means.

8.7. This is because a patient might have many consultations. Thus the risk for a patient will be higher than these estimates of a risk for a consultation.

8.8. These papers tell us about the acupuncturists' view of events. Patients might regard more incidents as important than do the acupuncturists, or they might regard fewer incidents as important.

Chapter 9

Answers to 9.13 Multiple choice questions: Significance tests

9.1. FTFFF. There is evidence for a relationship (Section 9.6), which is not necessarily causal. There may be other differences related to coffee drinking, such as smoking (Section 3.8).

9.2. FFFFT. The null hypothesis is that the *population* means are equal (Section 9.7). Significance is a property of the sample, not the population. $SE(\bar{x}_1 - \bar{x}_2) = \sqrt{SE(\bar{x}_1)^2 - SE(\bar{x}_2)^2}$ (Section 8.5).

9.3. TTFTT. Section 9.2. It is quite possible for either to be higher and deviations in either direction are important (Section 9.5). $n = 16$ because the subject giving the same reading on both gives no information about the difference and is excluded from the test. The order should be random, as in a cross-over trial (Section 2.7).

9.4. FFFFT. The trial is small and the difference may be the result of chance, but there may also be a large treatment effect. We must do a bigger trial to increase the power (Section 9.9). Adding cases would completely invalidate the test. If the null hypothesis were true, the test would give a 'significant' result one in 20 independent tests. If we keep adding cases and doing many tests, we have a very high chance of getting a 'significant' result on one of them, even though there is no treatment effect (Section 9.10).

9.5. TFTTF. Large sample methods depend on estimates of variance obtained from the data. This estimate gets closer to the population value as the sample size increases (Section 9.7, Section 9.8). The chance of an error of the first kind is the significance level set in advance, say 5%. The larger the sample, the more likely we are to detect a difference should one exist (Section 9.9). The null hypothesis depends on the phenomena we are investigating, not on the sample size.

9.6. FTFFT. We cannot conclude causation in an observational study (Sections 3.6–8), but we can conclude that there is evidence of a difference (Section 9.6). 0.001 is the probability of getting so large a difference if the null hypothesis were true (Section 9.3).

Answers to 9.14 Exercise: Crohn's disease and cornflakes

9.1. Both control groups are drawn from populations which were easy to get to, one being hospital patients without gastrointestinal symptoms, the other being fracture patients and their relatives. Both are matched for age and sex; Mayberry *et al.* also matched for social class and marital status. Apart from the matching factors, we have no way of knowing whether cases and controls are comparable, or any way of knowing whether controls are representative of the general population. This is usual in case–control studies and is a major problem with this design.

9.2. There are two obvious sources of bias: interviews were not blind and information is being recalled by the subject. The latter is particularly a problem for data about the past. In James' study subjects were asked what they used to eat several years in the past. For the cases this was before a definite event, onset of Crohn's disease, for the controls it was not, the time being time of onset of the disease in the matched case.

9.3. The question in James' study was 'what did you to eat in the past?', that in Mayberry *et al.* was 'what do you eat now?'.

9.4. Of the 100 patients with Crohn's disease, 29 were current eaters of cornflakes. Of 29 cases who knew of the cornflakes association, 12 were ex-eaters of cornflakes, and among the other 71 cases 21 were ex-eaters of cornflakes, giving a total of 33 past but not present eaters of cornflakes. Combining these with the 29 current consumers, we get 62 cases who had at some time been regular eaters of cornflakes. If we carry out the same calculation for the controls, we obtain 3 + 10 = 13 past eaters, and with 22 current eaters this gives 35 sometime regular cornflakes eaters. Cases were more likely than controls to have eaten cornflakes regularly at some time, the proportion of cases reporting having eaten cornflakes being almost twice as great as for controls. Compare this with James' data, where 17/68 = 25% of controls and 23/34 = 68% of cases, 2.7 times as many, had eaten cornflakes regularly. The results are similar.

9.5. The relationship between Crohn's disease and reported consumption of cornflakes had a much smaller probability for the significance test and hence stronger evidence that a relationship existed. Also, only one case had never eaten cornflakes (it was also the most popular cereal among controls).

9.6. Of the Crohn's cases, 67.6% (i.e. 23/34) reported having eaten cornflakes regularly compared with 25.0% of controls. Thus cases were 67.6/25.0 = 2.7 times as likely as controls to report having eaten cornflakes. The corresponding ratios for the other cereals are: wheat, 2.7; porridge, 1.5; rice, 1.6; bran, 6.1; muesli, 2.7. Cornflakes do not stand out when we look at the data in this way. The small probability simply arises because it is the most popular cereal. The P value is a property of the sample, not of the population.

9.7. We can conclude that there is no evidence that eating cornflakes is more closely related to Crohn's disease than is consumption of other cereals. The tendency for Crohn's cases to report excessive eating of breakfast foods before onset of the disease may be a result of greater variation in diet than in controls, as they try different foods in response to their symptoms. They may also be more likely to recall what they used to eat, being more aware of the effects of diet because of their disease.

Chapter 10

Answers to 10.14 Multiple choice questions: Comparisons of means

10.1. FFTFT. Section 10.2. For large samples, it is equivalent to the Normal distribution method (Section 8.3).

10.2. FTFTF. Section 10.3. Whether the (population) means are equal is what we are trying to find out. The large sample case is like the Normal test of Section 9.7, except for the common variance estimate. It is valid for any sample size.

10.3. FTTFF. The assumption of Normality would not be met for a small sample t test (Section 10.3) without transformation (Section 10.4), but for a large sample the distribution followed by the data would not matter (Section 9.7). The sign test is for paired data. We have measurements, not qualitative data.

10.4. FTTFF. Section 10.5. The more different the sample sizes are, the worse is the approximation to the t distribution. When

both samples are large, this becomes a large sample Normal distribution test (Section 9.7). Grouping of data is not a serious problem.

10.5. TFFTT. A P value conveys more information than a statement that the difference is significant or not significant. A confidence interval would be even better. What is important is how well the diagnostic test discriminates, i.e. by how much the distributions overlap, not any difference in mean. Semen count cannot follow a Normal distribution because two standard deviations exceeds the mean and some observations would be negative (Section 7.4). Approximately equal numbers make the t test very robust but skewness reduces the power (Section 10.5).

10.6. FTTFT. Appendix 7A, Section 8.8. For a Normal distribution $\bar{x}$ and s^2 are independent. s^2 will follow this distribution multiplied by $\sigma^2/(n-1)$, where σ^2 is the population variance. $\bar{x}/\sqrt{s^2/n}$ follows a t distribution only if the mean of the population distribution is zero (Section 10.1).

10.7. FTTFT. Section 10.9. Sums of squares and degrees of freedom add up, mean squares do not. Three groups gives two degrees of freedom. We can have any sizes of groups.

Answers to 10.15 Exercise: Some analyses comparing means

10.1. Paired t test, because we have the same subject measured on two occasions.

10.2. We can conclude that there is good evidence that in group A creatinine fell between the start of treatment and the 6th month of follow-up, and between 6 months before treatment and the 6th month of follow-up. There is no evidence for any fall in creatinine in group B. We cannot conclude that creatinine did not fall in group B, or that groups A and B differ.

10.3. We should compare the two groups directly, using two sample t test for the creatinine at 6-month follow-up. Even better would be to use the 3-month data as well, perhaps by averaging the two or using an area under the curve method (Section 10.7). We should also control for the pre-treatment levels. We could compare the mean difference between pre- and post-treatment creatinine between the two groups. An even better way to do this, which we will look at later in the book (Section 15.3), would be to use analysis of covariance of the post-treatment creatinine using the pre-treatment creatinine as a covariate.

10.4. This is a comparison of two samples, so we would use an unpaired or two sample t method (Section 10.3). The data should be from Normal distributions with the same variance for the standard two sample t method. However, in this study the standard deviations in the two samples are very different, 48.7 micromol/l in study patients compared with 14.3 micromol/l in controls. We should therefore use the two sample t method for unequal variances, the Satterthwaite correction to the degrees of freedom.

10.5. The changes could be positive or negative, so it is quite possible to have observations two standard deviations below the mean, even though two standard deviations is bigger than the mean and mean minus two standard deviations would be negative.

10.6. There are actually four things you might have noted. First, they have treated 42 observations on 14 subjects as independent. They are not, because repeated observations on the same woman will be more like one another than they are like observations on a different woman. Second, they have ignored that the same women use both pump and manual methods and treated them as though they are independent. They have carried out a two sample t test on paired data. Third, in the sample, the standard deviations are different between pump and manual. We cannot assume they are the same in the population from which the sample comes. Also, the condition with the bigger standard deviation also has the bigger mean. When the standard deviation increases with the mean, we usually have skewness. Fourth, the standard deviations are large compared with the means. For the pump measurements the SD is greater than half the mean, for the manual measurements it is almost half the mean. When the standard deviation is large compared with the mean, we usually have skewness.

10.7. Treating repeated observations on the same subject as independent gives us a false idea of the amount of information. This makes P values smaller than they should be. Carrying out a two sample t test on paired data means that all the variation between women goes into the random variation. This tends to make the P value too large. Carrying out a test when variances are unequal and distributions skew may make the P value too large.

10.8. They should take the women as the unit of analysis (Section 10.13) and for each woman find the mean volume for all the sessions using the same method. This would give 14 pairs of means. Then they could apply the paired t method. If the 14 differences between these woman means display skewness and unequal variance, they could try a suitable transformation of the means, or of the individual observations, which would be preferable. Finally, they could present the results as a confidence interval for the mean difference in volume expressed per session, in addition to a P value.

10.9. The geometric mean was 5.3 days (range 1 to 31) in the intervention group and 6.4 days (range 1 to 60) in the control group. The geometric mean is very close to the left hand or lower end of the range, so we can deduce that the distribution must be positively skew or skew to the right. This is typical of lengths of stay.

10.10. The geometric mean is found by multiplying all the n observations together and then taking the nth root. In practice, we calculate the geometric mean using a logarithmic transformation of the data. If we find the mean on the log scale, taking the antilog of this mean gives us the geometric mean.

10.11. This comes from a 95% confidence interval for the ratio of the geometric means of the length of stay. The geometric mean length of stay in one group is estimated to be between 8% less than the geometric mean length of stay in the other group and 56% greater. What is surprising is that the full sentence reads: 'Early computed tomography reduced the length of hospital stay by 1.1 days (geometric mean 5.3 days (range 1 to 31) v 6.4 days (1 to 60)), but the difference was non-significant (95% confidence interval, 8% shorter stay to 56% longer stay, P = 0.17)'. If early computed tomography shortened stay, the confidence interval should show the estimated shortening at the lower end to be much greater than the estimated lengthening at the upper end. In the results section of the paper we read: 'Hospital stay was 1.1 days shorter in the computed tomography arm than in the standard practice arm (geometric mean 5.3 (range 1 to 31) days v 6.4 (1 to 60) days, respectively), but the difference was non-significant (95% confidence interval −0.034 to 0.194; P = 0.17). This corresponded to patients in the standard practice arm staying 20% longer than those in the early computed tomography arm (95% confidence interval 8% shorter stay to 56% longer stay)'. When editing this sentence to put it into the abstract, they have cut out 'This corresponded to patients in the standard practice arm staying 20% longer than those in the early computed tomography arm . . .'.

10.12. This comes from a 95% confidence interval for the ratio of the geometric means of the length of stay. The antilog or back transformation of the difference in mean log length of stay is the ratio of the two geometric means. A 95% confidence interval for the difference in mean log length of stay was also calculated and the antilog of the confidence limits gives the 95% confidence interval for the ratio of geometric means. Here they will have a 95% confidence interval for the ratio equal to 0.92 to 1.56, which has been presented as 8% reduction (1 − 0.92 = 0.08) to 56% increase. I know that readers will want to know where those numbers come from. The 95% confidence interval −0.034 to 0.194 is on the log scale and these are logs to base 10 rather than being natural logs. The antilog of −0.034 is 0.924 698, or 0.92 to two decimal places. The antilog of 0.194 is 1.563 148 or 1.56 to two decimal places. These correspond to 92% to 156%, or a fall from 100% of 8 percentage points to an increase of 56 percentage points.

10.13. They cannot state this as a result of the study. They have no way of knowing whether the difference they observed was because of the difference in treatment. It could easily have arisen by chance, even if the treatment difference had no effect on length of stay. They quote P = 0.17 for the comparison of lengths of stay between the treatment groups. We usually take a P value greater than 0.1, as this is, as indicating little or no evidence against the null hypothesis.

10.14. They knew this before they did the trial. If they did not think that the intervention *may* be beneficial, they would not have thought of doing the trial in the first place. It is as if they have learned nothing from their trial at all. What they could conclude is that early abdominopelvic computed tomography for acute abdominal pain may not reduce length of hospital stay or may reduce it by as much as 56%.

Chapter 11

Answers to 11.14 Multiple choice questions: Regression and correlation

11.1. FFTTF. Outcome and predictor variables are perfectly related but do not lie on a straight line, so $r < 1$ (Section 11.9).

11.2. FTFFF. Knowledge of the predictor tells us something about the outcome variable (Section 6.2). This is not a straight line relationship. For part of the scale the outcome variable increases as the predictor increases, then the outcome variable decreases again. The correlation coefficient will be close to zero (Section 11.9). A logarithmic transformation would work if the outcome increased more and more rapidly as the predictor increased, but not here (Section 5.9).

11.3. FFFTT. A regression line usually has non-zero intercept and slope, which have dimensions (Section 11.3). Exchanging X and Y changes the line (Section 11.4)

11.4. FTTFF. The predictor variable has no error in the regression model (Section 11.3). Transformations are only used if needed to meet the assumptions (Section 11.8). There is a scatter about the line (Section 11.3).

11.5. TTFFF. Sections 11.9–10. There is no distinction between dependent and independent variables, or outcome and predictor variables. r should not be confused with the regression coefficient (Section 11.3).

Answers to 11.15 Exercise: Serum potassium and ambient temperature

11.1. This is a scatter diagram.

11.2. This is a simple linear regression line.

11.3. The line was fitted using the principle of least squares. We find the line which makes the sum of the squares of the differences between the observed potassium and that predicted by the regression line a minimum. On the graph, these would be the vertical distances from the point to the line.

11.4. The symbol 'r' represents the correlation coefficient, also called Pearson's correlation coefficient or the product moment correlation coefficient.

11.5. Mean serum potassium tends to be smaller when the temperature is higher, so r should be negative. Judging from the strength of the relationship on the scatter diagram, $r = -0.3$ looks quite plausible.

11.6. At least one of the variables should follow a Normal distribution. This looks quite plausible from the scatter diagram.

11.7. The P value is less than 0.02, so the correlation coefficient is significantly different from zero. There is evidence that mean serum potassium and temperature are related.

Chapter 12

Answers to 12.8 Multiple choice questions: Rank-based methods

12.1. TFTFF. Section 10.3, Section 12.2. The sign and Wilcoxon tests are for paired data (Section 9.2, Section 12.3). Rank correlation looks for the existence of relationships between two ordinal variables, not a comparison between two groups (Section 12.4, Section 12.5).

12.2. TTFFT. Section 9.2, Section 12.2, Section 10.3, Section 12.5. The Wilcoxon test is for interval data (Section 12.3).

12.3. FTFTT. Section 12.5. There is no predictor variable in correlation. Log transformation would not affect the rank order of the observations.

12.4. FTFFT. If Normal assumptions are met, the methods using them are better (Section 12.7). Estimation of confidence intervals using rank methods is difficult. Rank methods require the assumption that the scale is ordinal, i.e. that the data can be ranked.

12.5. TFTTF. We need a paired test: t, sign, or Wilcoxon (Sections 10.2, 9.2, 12.3).

Answers to 12.9 Exercise: Some applications of rank-based methods

12.1. Length of hospital stay and number of re-admissions to hospital in 1 year are both numerical, ratio scale variables. They have a true zero and we can, for example, say that a subject re-admitted twice and staying in hospital for a total of 30 days has twice as many re-admissions and three times the length of stay as a subject re-admitted once for 10 days.

12.2. Rank methods may still be appropriate, but not for the reason given. Although ratio level data, the distributions are likely to be positively skewed, discrete, and have a large number of zeros, because of people who are not re-admitted at all. This could make t methods invalid and transformation to a Normal distribution difficult or impossible.

12.3. Nine observations are recorded as '<0.06'. We have no numerical value for these. We could set them all to the same low value, e.g. zero, but the distribution would then be highly positively skewed and we would not be able to transform to Normal. A rank method would enable us to have them all tied at the lowest rank.

12.4. To compare three groups we can use the Kruskal–Wallis one-way analysis of variance by ranks (Section 12.2). This gives a chi-squared statistic: $\chi^2 = 17.49$ with 2 degrees of freedom, P = 0.0002.

12.5. We now have two groups, so we can use the Mann–Whitney U test, or some other version of the two sample rank sum test (Section 12.2). This gives $U = 30$, P = 0.2.

12.6. As we have all the values, we could consider a two sample t test. This gives t = 1.51, d.f. = 17, P = 0.15, very similar to the U test. However, from Table 12.10, the distributions look to be positively skewed and the variability in the high dose group looks to be considerably greater than in the low dose group. Figure A.14 shows a scatter plot and a Normal plot of the residuals. The difference in variability is clear, but the Normal plot does not have a clear curve. A logarithmic transformation (Figure A.15) does not appear to help as we now have an outlier in the high dose group, making the residual distribution negatively skewed. A square root transformation (Figure A.16) looks better, possibly having slightly more uniform variation and a reasonably straight line in the Normal plot. This gives P = 0.29. The Mann–Whitney U test looks to be a good option here and this was used in the analysis of the trial (Morris et al. 2014).

12.7. The dose of metoclopramide is ordered, but it could be regarded as a ratio scale, because it clearly has a numerical value and a zero. However, there are only a few possible values. The presence or absence of hypotension is dichotomous,

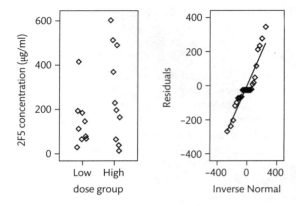

Figure A.14 Scatter plot and Normal plot for 2F5 concentrations in low dose and high dose groups in the MABGEL 1 trial (data from Morris et al. 2014).

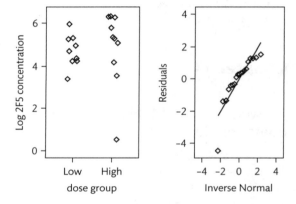

Figure A.15 Scatter plot and Normal plot for log to base e transformed 2F5 concentrations in low dose and high dose groups in the MABGEL 1 trial (data from Morris et al. 2014).

but we could also regard this as an ordinal, in that the presence of hypertension is consistently 'more hypotension' than the absence of hypotension. Thus we could take this as two ordered variables. We could also use several other methods, such as a Mann–Whitney U test comparing the dose of metoclopramide in those who experienced hypotension with those who did not. We could also use the chi-squared test for trend described in Section 13.8

12.8. Because there will be many ties between participants on the same dose of metaclopramide and between those with hypotension or between those without hypotension, we need the version of Kendall's tau modified for ties, tau b.

12.9. Hypotension is specified to be an adverse event, so if the metoclopramide decreased the risk of hypertension,

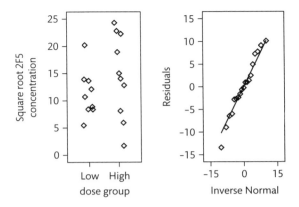

Figure A.16 Scatter plot and Normal plot for square root transformed 2F5 concentrations in low dose and high dose groups in the MABGEL 1 trial (data from Morris *et al.* 2014).

this would not be adverse. We would be quite happy with that. Even so, I would have wanted to know about this and would have wanted my statistical analysis to detect it. I would have done a two sided test (which would still have given P < 0.001).

12.10. I think it is specified correctly, because it is specified as 'the event rate does not increase with the dose of metoclopramide'. rather than 'the event rate is not related to the dose of metoclopramide'.

12.11. I would apply the Bonferroni correction (Section 9.10) and multiply the P values by 20, the number of tests, and if any of the tests then still had P < 0.05, I would have said that there was a significant trend in adverse events. In fact, 20 × 0.001 = 0.02, so the trend remains significant.

12.12. Kendall's tau b is zero for no relationship and −1 or +1 for a perfect relationship, so 0.07 is a weak positive relationship.

Chapter 13

Answers to 13.11 Multiple choice questions: Categorical data

13.1. TFFFF. Section 13.3. 80% of 4 is greater than 3, so all four expected frequencies must exceed 5. The sample size can be as small as 20, if all row and column totals are 10.

13.2. FTFTF. Sections 13.1, 13.3. (5 − 1) × (3 − 1) = 8 d.f., 80% × 15 = 12 cells must have expected frequencies > 5. It is acceptable for an *observed* frequency to be zero.

13.3. TTFTF. Sections 13.1, 13.9. The two tests are independent. There are (2 − 1) × (2 − 1) = 1 d.f. With such large numbers Yates' correction does not make much difference. Without it we get $\chi^2 = 124.5$, with it we get $\chi^2 = 119.4$ (Section 13.5.).

13.4. TTTTT. Sections 13.4–5. The factorials of large numbers can be difficult to calculate and the number of possible tables with the same row and column totals can be astronomical.

13.5. TTTTF. Section 13.7.

13.6. TTFTT. Chi-squared for trend and τ_b will both test the null hypothesis of no trend in the table, but an ordinary chi-squared test will not (Section 13.8). The odds ratio (OR) is an estimate of the relative risk for a case–control study (Section 13.7).

13.7. TTFFF. The test compares proportions in matched samples (Section 13.9). For a relationship, we use the chi-squared test (Section 13.1). PEFR is a continuous variable, we use the paired t method (Section 10.2). For two independent samples, we use the contingency table chi-squared test (Section 13.1).

Answers to 13.12 Exercise: Some analyses of categorical data

13.1. The analysis does not take into account the ordering of the categories. The deprivation group is clearly ordered and so is the tumour size. Thus the data could have been analysed with a method which takes these orderings into account, such as the chi-squared test for trend. To do this we must omit the 'unknown' row, of course. When we do, the chi-squared test for trend yields the following P values:

trend chi-squared = 5.16, d.f. = 1, P = 0.02
about trend chi-squared = 0.49, d.f. = 3, P = 0.9
total chi-squared = 5.65, d.f. = 4, P = 0.2

Hence we have a significant trend and inspection of the table shows that more deprived subjects tend to have bigger tumours. We can see this if we omit the unknowns from the table, as shown in Table A.3. The authors disagree with me, and you can judge for yourself from the *BMJ* on:

http://www.bmj.com/content/322/7290/830.1?tab =responses.

13.2. The subjects in the table are not independent. The authors have completely ignored the fact that the 105 subjects classified by clinic measurements are the same as the 105

Table A.3 Deprivation and tumour size data, omitting tumour size not known (data from Brewster *et al.* 2001)

Tumour size (mm)	Affluent n = 409		Middle n = 1 188		Deprived n = 288		Total n = 2 185	
				Deprivation group				
0–20	271	(66.3)	730	(61.4)	166	(57.6)	1 167	(61.9)
21–50	124	(30.3)	409	(34.4)	109	(37.8)	642	(34.1)
>50	14	(3.4)	49	(4.1)	13	(4.5)	76	(4.0)
Total	409	(100.0)	1 188	(100.0)	288	(100.0)	1 885	(100.0)

classified by ambulatory measurements. They count every subject twice and ignore the fact that they are the same subjects. Fisher's exact test requires the observations to be independent.

13.3. They have ignored the pairing of the data, so they have ignored some important information. If they were to take the pairing into account, using all the information, they might have a more powerful study. This could decrease the P value. On the other hand, they have inflated the sample size, doubling it. Reducing the sample size to the true 105 might increase the P value.

13.4. The correct analysis for comparing two proportions in paired samples is McNemar's test. To do McNemar's test we usually redraw the table in a paired structure, as in Table A.4. There were 12 changes from non-response to response and none from response to non-response. This gives P = 0.0015. Fisher's exact test requires the observations to be independent. By using a test the assumptions of which are not met by the data, these authors missed a highly significant effect.

13.5. This is a retrospective case–control study.

Table A.4 Place of blood pressure measurement by responder status

Ambulatory	Clinic		
	Responder	Non-responder	Total
Responder	43	12	55
Non-responder	0	50	50
Total	43	62	105

13.6. The outcome measure in a research study is not the results of the analysis but the variable which we are trying to predict. We could take two views of this in a case–control study: it is either the possible causal variable, mobile phone use, or the possible consequence of this variable, glioma.

13.7. The odds of a subject having a characteristic is the ratio of the number of such subjects with the characteristic to the number without the characteristic. The odds of being a mobile phone user is the number of mobile phone users divided by the number who do not use a mobile phone. The odds ratio is the odds of phone use for cases divided by the odds of phone use for controls. Cases were slightly less likely to be mobile phone users than were controls.

13.8. This is case–control study and glioma is a rare condition, so we can interpret the odds ratio as an estimate of the relative risk. We estimate that the risk of glioma for mobile phone users is 0.94 times the risk among non-mobile-phone-users. This is because the odds ratio is unaffected by the ratio of cases to controls and so the odds ratio from the case–control study is an estimate of the odds ratio for the entire population. Provided the proportion of cases in the whole population is small, the odds ratio and the relative risk will be very similar.

13.9. We are using the subjects in this study as a sample to estimate the odds ratio in the whole population from which they come. Some samples will give us estimates above the population odds ratio, others will give estimates below it. We estimate a range of values which we think should include the population value. This is called an interval estimate. A 95% confidence interval is chosen so that 95% of intervals from such samples will include the population odds ratio. In this study, we estimate that the odds ratio in the population, and hence the relative risk, is between 0.78 and 1.13. We estimate that the risk of glioma is increased by at most a factor 1.13, or 13%.

13.10. The main conclusion is 'use of a mobile phone, either in the short or medium term, is not associated with an increased risk of glioma'. It is always rash to conclude that there is no association. We could conclude that we estimate that the risk of glioma is increased by not more than 13%.

Chapter 14

Answers to 14.6 Multiple choice questions: Choice of statistical method

14.1. TFFTT. Section 12.1.

14.2. FTTTT. Section 14.5.

14.3. FFFFT. Regression, correlation, and paired t methods need continuous data (Sections 11.3, 11.9, 10.2). Kendall's τ can be used for *ordered* categories.

14.4. TFTFF. Section 14.2.

14.5. TFTTT. A t test could not be used because the data do not follow a Normal distribution (Section 10.3). The expected frequencies will be too small for a chi-squared test (Section 13.3), which we can tell from the very small row totals, but a trend test would be acceptable (Section 13.8). A goodness of fit test could be used (Section 13.10).

14.6. FTTFT. A small-sample, paired method is needed (Table 14.4).

14.7. TFTFF. For a 2 by 2 table with small expected frequencies, we can use Fisher's exact test or Yates' correction (Sections 13.4–5). McNemar's test is inappropriate because the groups are not matched (Section 13.9).

Answers to 14.7 Exercise: Choosing a statistical method

14.1. For overall preference, we have one sample of patients so we use Table 14.2. Of these 30 people, 12 preferred A, 14 preferred B and four did not express a preference. We can use a Binomial or sign test (Section 9.2), only considering those who expressed a preference. Those for A are positives, those for B are negatives. We get two sided P = 0.85, not significant. For preference and order, we have the relationship between two variables (Table 14.3), preference and order, both nominal. We set up a two way table and do a chi-squared test. For the 3 by 2 table (Table A.5), we have two expected frequencies less than five, so we must edit the table. There are no obvious combinations, but we can delete those who expressed no preference, leaving a 2 by 2 table, χ^2 = 1.3, 1 d.f.,

Table A.5 Results of a cross-over trial to compare two appliances for ileostomy patients

Preference	A first	B first	Total
A	5	7	12
Neither	0	4	4
B	9	5	14
Total	14	16	30

P > 0.05. We can do Fisher's exact test instead, which would give P = 0.095.

14.2. The data are paired (Table 14.2) so we use a paired t test (Section 10.2). The assumption of a Normal distribution for the differences should be met as PEFR itself follows a Normal distribution fairly well. We get t = 6.45/5.05 = 1.3, d.f. = 31, which is not significant. Using t = 2.04 (Table 10.1) we get a 95% confidence interval of –3.85 to 16.75 litres/min.

14.3. This is a comparison of two independent samples, so we use Table 14.1. The variable is interval and the samples are small. We could either use the two sample t method (Section 10.3) or the Mann–Whitney U test (Section 12.2). The groups have similar variances, but the distribution shows a slight negative skewness and is possibly bimodal. As the two sample t method is fairly robust to deviations from the Normal distribution and as I wanted a confidence interval for the difference, I chose this option. I did not think that the slight skewness was sufficient to cause any problems. By the two sample t method we get the difference between the means, immobile – mobile, to be 7.06, standard error = 5.74, t = 1.23, P = 0.23, 95% CI to –4.54 to 18.66 hours. By the Mann–Whitney, we get U = 178.5, z = – 1.06, P = 0.29. The two methods give very similar results and lead to similar conclusions, as we expect them to do when both methods are valid.

14.4. We have two independent samples (Table 14.1). We must use the total number of patients we randomized to treatments, in an intention to treat analysis (Section 2.6). Thus we have 1 721 patients allocated to active treatment, including 15 deaths, and 1 706 patients allocated to placebo, with 35 deaths. A chi-squared test gives us χ^2 = 8.3, d.f. = 1, P < 0.01. A comparison of two proportions gives a difference of –0.012 with 95% confidence interval –0.020 to –0.004 (Section 8.6) and test of significance using the Standard Normal distribution gives a value of z = 2.88, P < 0.01, (Section 9.8).

14.5. We are looking at the relationship between two variables (Table 14.3). Both variables have very non-Normal distributions. Nitrite is highly skew and pH is bimodal. It might be possible to transform the nitrites to a Normal distribution but the transformation would not be a simple one. The zero prevents a simple logarithmic transformation, for example. Because of this, regression and correlation are not appropriate and rank correlation can be used. Spearman's $\rho = 0.58$ and Kendall's $\tau = 0.40$, both giving a probability of 0.004.

14.6. We have two independent samples (Table 14.1). We have two large samples and can do the Normal comparison of two means (Sections 8.5, 9.7). The standard error of the difference is 0.0178 s and the observed difference is 0.02 s, giving a 95% confidence interval of −0.015 to 0.055 for the excess mean transit time in the controls. If we had all the data, for each case we could calculate the mean MTT for the two controls matched to each case, find the difference between case MTT and control mean MTT, and use the one sample method of Section 8.3.

14.7. These are paired data, so we refer to Table 14.2. The unequal steps in the visual acuity scale suggest that it is best treated as an ordinal scale, so the sign test is appropriate. Pre minus post, there are 10 positive differences, no negative differences and 7 zeros. Thus we refer 0 to the Binomial distribution with $p = 0.5$ and $n = 10$. The probability is given by

$$\frac{10!}{10! \times 0!} \times 0.5^0 \times 0.5^{10} = 0.00098$$

For a two sided test we can double this to give P = 0.002. The contrast sensitivity test is a measurement, and hence an interval scale. We could carry out the paired t test or the Wilcoxon signed-rank test on the differences. The distribution of the differences is grouped, as the scale is clearly discrete with intervals of 0.5, but not skewed, so either would be valid. For the paired t test, the mean difference (pre–post) is −0.335, standard deviation = 0.180, standard error of mean = $0.180/\sqrt{17} = 0.044$, and the t statistic for testing the null hypothesis that the population mean is zero is t = 0.335/0.044 = 7.61, with 16 degrees of freedom, P < 0.001. For the Wilcoxon signed-rank test, all the differences are negative, so T = 0, which is also highly significant. For the relationship between visual acuity and the contrast sensitivity test, visual acuity is ordinal so we must use rank correlation. Spearman's $\rho = -0.49$, P = 0.05, Kendall's $\tau = -0.40$, P = 0.06.

14.8. We want to test for the relationship between two variables, which are both presented as categorical (Table 14.3). We use a chi-squared test for a contingency table, $\chi^2 = 38.1$, d.f. = 6, P < 0.001.

14.9. One possibility is that some other variable, such as the mother's smoking or poverty, is related to both maternal age and asthma. Another is that there is a cohort effect. All the age 14–19 mothers were born during the Second World War, and some common historical experience may have produced the asthma in their children.

14.10. The serial measurements of thyroid hormone could be summarized using the area under the curve (Section 10.7). The oxygen dependence is tricky. The babies who died had the worst outcome, but if we took their survival time as the time they were oxygen dependent, we would be treating them as if they had a good outcome. We must also allow for the babies who went home on oxygen having a long but unknown oxygen dependence. My solution was to assign an arbitrary large number of days, larger than any for the babies sent home without oxygen, to the babies sent home on oxygen. I assigned an even larger number of days to the babies who died. I then used Kendall's tau b (Section 12.5) to assess the relationship with thyroid hormone AUC. Kendall's rank correlation was chosen in preference to Spearman's because of the large number of ties which the arbitrary assignment of large numbers produced.

Chapter 15

Answers to 15.16 Multiple choice questions: Multifactorial methods

15.1. TTFFF. Sections 15.1–3. Both baseline size and duct tape are highly significant predictors of final wart size (P < 0.001). The negative coefficient of duct tape shows that the mean wart size is reduced. The confidence interval for the regression estimate of the treatment effect is entirely within the interval by the two sample t method, so they are consistent, the adjusted regression estimate is just a lot more precise. We are missing data from one participant in the duct tape group and four in the control group, so we do not really have analysis by intention to treat. We do not have 10 observations per variable, though we are close, so, by the usual guideline, we should not have full confidence in the validity of the analysis

15.2. TFTFT. Section 15.2. It is the ratio of the regression sum of squares to the total sum of squares.

15.3. FTFFF. Section 15.2. There were 37 + 1 = 38 observations. There is a highly significant ethnic group effect. The non-significant sex effect does *not* mean that there is no difference (Section 9.6). There are three age groups, so two degrees of freedom. If the effect of ethnicity were entirely because of age, it would have largely disappeared when age was included in the model.

15.4. TTTTF. Section 15.10. A four-level factor has three dummy variables (Section 15.8). If the effect of white cell count were entirely because of smoking, it would have largely disappeared when smoking was included in the model.

15.5. TTTFT. Section 15.6

Answers to 15.17 Exercise: A multiple regression analysis

15.1. The difference is highly significant (P < 0.001) and is estimated to be between 1.3 and 3.7, i.e. volumes are higher in group 2, the trisomy-16 group.

15.2. From both the Normal plot and the plot against number of pairs of somites, there appears to be one point which may be rather separate from the rest of the data, an outlier. Inspection of the data showed no reason to suppose that the point was an error, so it was retained. Otherwise, the fit to the Normal distribution seems quite good. The plot against number of pairs of somites shows that there may be a relationship between mean and variability, but this is small and will not affect the analysis too much. There is also a possible non-linear relationship.

15.3. The interaction term has P = 0.1, not significant. I would remove the interaction term from the model.

15.4. If we were to include somites and somites squared in our model, they would be highly correlated. In fact, r = 0.99. This would make the coefficients very difficult to interpret. By subtracting a number close to the mean of somites, we remove most of this correlation, making the coefficients straightforward to interpret. The effect of subtracting 28 before squaring is to reduce the correlation with somites to 0.31.

15.5. The somites squared term has P = 0.2, not significant. I would remove the somites squared term from the model and use the regression in Table 15.20, which is what I recommended to the researchers.

Chapter 16

Answers to 16.6 Multiple choice questions: Time to event data

16.1. TFTTT. Section 16.2. As time increases, rates are based on fewer potential survivors. Withdrawals during the first interval contribute half an interval at risk. If survival rates change, those

subjects starting later in calendar time, and so more likely to be withdrawn, will have a different survival to those starting earlier. The first part of the curve will represent a different population to the second. The longest survivor may still be alive and so become a withdrawal.

16.2. TTTTT. These are survival curves, although the outcome is conception, not death. They were calculated by the Kaplan–Meier method, which allows for some women being observed for longer periods than others. When a woman has been followed for a length of time and has not yet conceived, we say she is censored at the time point. These are marked on the graph by short vertical lines. We could test the null hypothesis that the conception rates in the two populations are the same at each time, though they may vary over time, using the logrank test. To have another predicting variable, we use Cox proportional hazards regression. We assume that women who are censored have the same probability of conceiving as do women who continue to be observed. Hence women who enter early, and so can be followed for longer, should have the same probability of conception as do women who enter late and cannot be followed for as long. Otherwise the survival probabilities at long times are biased.

16.3. FTFTT. This trial has been analysed using Cox regression, which gives a hazard ratio and confidence interval. The hazard ratio is the hazard in the everolimus divided by the hazard in the placebo group, the hazard being the instantaneous rate at which events happen. We assume this ratio to be a constant, though the hazard itself can change over the time of follow-up. The median time to progression is estimated by the Kaplan–Meier survival curve and does not require all subjects to be observed for the full duration. They can be censored, that is observed for a time and still not have progressed at the end of the trial. This censoring time might be quite short for some patients in this trial, which was stopped earlier. Some patients will have been recruited very recently when the trial was stopped. In fact, only 47 of the 272 everolimus patients were observed to be symptom-free at 4 months, many having been censored before that duration of follow-up. The confidence interval, 3.7 to 5.5 months, tells us that in the whole population of everolimus treated patients, the median survival would be between 3.7 and 5.5, so half would have progressed sometime between these limits. More everolimus patients progressed than controls, but there were twice as many of them. The proportion who progressed was less.

16.4. FFFFT. Section 16.5. Boys have a lower risk of readmission than girls, shown by the negative coefficient, and hence a longer time before being readmitted. Theophylline is related to a lower risk of readmission but we cannot conclude causation. Treatment may depend on the type and severity of asthma. Cox regression and the proportional hazards model are the same thing.

16.5. TTFTF. Sections 16.2–16.4. The proportion who have experienced the event, here diagnosis of breast cancer, is called the failure function. The numbers below the time axis show the numbers observed at that age. The numbers go down because some people are diagnosed but also because some have yet to reach that age but have not yet been diagnosed, so are censored. The logrank test can be used for any numbers of groups. Four groups require three variables to represent them, one group being the reference group.

Answers to 16.7 Exercise: Survival after retirement

16.1. This graph shows two Kaplan–Meier survival curves, for those who retired at age 65 and those who retired at age 55. The curves are calculated as follows. At each time when there is an event, we calculate the proportion of those followed to this time who do not experience an event. We multiply these together for all the times up to the index time to give the proportion who have not experienced the event up to and including this time. The assumptions required are that observations are independent and that those who are censored are not different from those followed up to death, so that those who are recruited at the end of the study should not differ in their survival probabilities from those at the beginning. The latter is unlikely to be true. People were recruited over a 30-year period, when mortality rates at all ages were falling, so the mortality rates experienced by the earliest recruits may be greater than those experienced by the latest recruits at corresponding ages.

16.2. These survival curves cover ages 65 to 85, an age range when mortality rates get bigger as age increases. So the hazard is getting bigger all the time and the proportion dying in each year is getting bigger all the time. Hence the curves get steeper.

16.3. A logrank test is used to compare two or more survival curves. It uses data from all subjects, including those who are still surviving. It tests the null hypothesis that the risk of death in the groups is the same at any given time of follow-up. The P value is 0.09. This is larger than the conventional cut-off point of 0.05, so we would regard this as not providing good evidence for a difference. However, we can think of P values between 0.05 and 0.1 as providing rather weak evidence for a difference, not enough on its own to draw any firm conclusion.

16.4. The Cox proportional hazards model provides a regression method for survival data. It uses data from all subjects,

including those who are still surviving. The assumptions required include independence, that those who are censored are not different from those followed up to death, and that the ratio of the risks of events for different values of the predicting variables is not related to time of follow-up, even though the risks themselves may change (the proportional hazards assumption). It was used here because there are several variables which may be related to survival. These may be related to the predictor variable of interest (age at retirement), in which case Cox regression will remove at least part of any spurious relationship between age at retirement and survival which might be produced by the factor, or may be related only to survival, in which case they will improve the fit of the regression model.

16.5. The difference is significant at the 0.05 level because the 95% confidence interval for the hazard ratio, which is 1.09 to 1.73, does not include 1.00. This is the value the hazard ratio for the population would have if the null hypothesis were true

16.6. Socioeconomic group is well known to be a predictor of mortality. People in higher socioeconomic groups have lower average mortality at any given age and longer average survival than those in lower economic groups. Also, age at retirement is related to socioeconomic group. The early retirers tended to be from higher socioeconomic groups than the later retirers. This could produce a difference in survival between early and late retirers which was a result of differences in socioeconomic group rather than age at retirement itself. The effect would be to remove at least some of the spurious effect on survival of the differences in socioeconomic groups. We expect it to change the estimated hazard ratio for age at retirement.

16.7. Sex is a strong predictor of the risk of death, males having a greater risk of death than females at all ages. As sex is not related to age at retirement, we might expect intuitively that adjusting for it should not alter the estimated hazard ratio. In multiple regression, it would improve the prediction and make the unexplained variance smaller. The standard errors would then be smaller and the estimate would be better. This would in turn narrow the confidence interval for the estimated coefficient of retirement age. In Cox regression, improving the prediction may alter the hazard ratio rather than narrow the confidence interval. Because sex is a strong predictor of the risk of death after age 65, adjusting for it should improve the prediction and make the estimate of the hazard ratio more accurate. It may do this by removing some bias rather than by making the estimate more precise.

16.8. Calendar year may be a predictor of risk of dying at any given age, because death rates tend to decline over time. We do not know whether it is associated with age at retirement, but we do know that it makes it plausible that the assumption that risk of death is unrelated to when the subject entered the study is violated. Adjusting for calendar year should make the data fit the assumptions of Cox regression better. We cannot say what the effects would be, because we do not know whether age at retirement was related to calendar year, i.e. whether the rate of early retirement had changed over the period of the study.

16.9. We might have a healthy worker effect, where people in ill health retired early for that reason. Hence there is good reason to expect that early retirement would be associated with increased mortality which is not actually the result of retirement itself. Indeed, there was much greater mortality before age 65 in early retirers than later retirers, suggesting that this happened. The authors were interested in whether early retirement increased later survival. They could have done a legitimate one tailed test here.

Chapter 17

Answers to 17.14 Multiple choice questions: Meta-analysis

17.1. TTTFT. Section 17.2. This is a forest plot showing the results of a meta-analysis. The horizontal scale is logarithmic, because the equal intervals marked on the scale each represent a multiple by 10 of the preceding level. The horizontal lines represent the widths of the confidence intervals for the individual study estimates. For the study by Jog, the confidence interval includes 1.0, the null hypothesis value for a ratio, so the difference between treatments is not statistically significant.

17.2. TTFTF. Section 17.2. The squares do indeed represent the individual trial estimates. The area of the square is proportional to the meta-analysis weight given to the trial. Studies with the smallest standard errors and hence the narrowest confidence intervals and shortest lines on the forest plot should be given the most weight. The pooled estimate has a confidence interval 0.30 to 0.56, a fairly narrow interval which does not include the null value 1.0 and so provides strong evidence for a treatment effect. Three of the individual trials, Kim, Rao, and Walsh, have confidence intervals which do not include the null value and so provided individual significant effects. They were therefore sufficient alone to provide evidence of a treatment effect in their populations.

17.3. FTFFT. Sections 17.4, 17.5, 17.7. The estimated proportion of the variation caused by heterogeneity, I^2, is zero as is the estimated variance between studies, τ^2, which are therefore consistent and estimate no heterogeneity. The expected

value of the chi-squared statistic is its degrees of freedom, 6, so χ^2 is less than the expected value. In the forest plot, all the confidence intervals overlap and all include the pooled estimate, also consistent with no heterogeneity. In the absence of any statistical heterogeneity at all, fixed and random effects estimates are identical.

17.4. FTTTF. Sections 17.4, 17.5, 17.7. The differences are measured in the units of HbA1c, which is reported here as a percentage. There appears to be some heterogeneity, because not all confidence intervals overlap and not all include the overall estimate. Even though the heterogeneity is neither large nor significant, this suggests that a random effects model would be prudent. Also, 'a group of drugs' suggests that all the trials do not use the same drug, implying clinical heterogeneity. The trial Cv181-011LT appears to be an outlier from the rest. The difference in favour of metformin has 95% confidence interval 0.08 to 0.32 percentage points of HbA1c, which does not include zero, the null value, and so provides clear evidence in favour of metformin, the standard treatment. The intervals on the scale represent equal linear quantities, each representing 1.0, so this is not logarithmic.

17.5. TFTFT. Section 17.2. Figure 17.26(a) shows a funnel plot, with one over the standard error on the vertical axis, so the studies at the top have the smallest standard errors and hence are the largest. The graph does not appear to be symmetrical about the central vertical line representing the pooled estimate, with more studies at the bottom left than at the bottom right. As publication bias is one possible cause of funnel plot asymmetry, this might be the case here. Some studies have been added to Figure 17.26(b), the result of a trim and fill analysis. The vertical lines representing the new estimate and the old estimate appear very similar, suggesting very little effect of the asymmetry on the estimate.

Answers to 17.15 Exercise: Dietary sugars and body weight

17.1. The outcome measure is body weight measured in kilograms. This is a quantitative, continuous variable. All measurements are in kilograms, and so the authors have presented the effect as the mean difference in kilograms, rather than as a standardized mean difference measured in standard deviations.

17.2. This is a forest plot (Section 17.2), with the outcome variable on the horizontal scale and the individual studies on the vertical scale. The squares represent the point estimates of the differences in mean weight found in the individual trials, with their 95% confidence intervals being represented by the width of the horizontal lines. The diamond shows the combined estimate over the trials, the deepest point of the diamond being the point estimate and the width of the diamond showing the 95% confidence interval. The squares have different sizes because the studies contribute different amounts of information and so carry different weights in the analysis. The area of the square should be proportional to the analysis weight.

17.3. The confidence interval, –0.42 to 4.40, has its upper limit beyond the highest point of the horizontal scale. The arrow head indicates to the reader that this confidence interval is wider than the graph suggests. Personally, I find this graphical approach counter-productive. The purpose of a graph is to convey information quickly and intuitively and this does not happen when the reader has to redraw the graph mentally to get a true representation of the data. In this case, the end of the confidence interval is so close to the scale limit that it would be very easy to extend the scale, as in Figure A.17. (The *BMJ* redraws all graphs, so we do not know whether the decision to use the arrowhead was made by the authors or was editorial.)

17.4. 'Heterogeneity' here means the extent to which the trials are estimating different treatment effects. 'τ^2' is the estimated variance between studies. This is the variability which is not simply caused by the variability between individual study participants. 'τ^2 = 0.04' tells us that to estimate the variance between all the people in these studies we would add 0.04 to the variance between participants in the same trial. 'χ^2 = 4.85, d.f. = 4, P = 0.30' is the result of a test of the null hypothesis that all the trials are estimating the same intervention effect. 'χ^2' is the chi-squared test statistics, often called Cochran's Q. Its expected value is the degrees of freedom, 'd.f.', equal to the number of studies minus one. 'P = 0.30' is the proportion of possible meta-analyses which would give this amount of heterogeneity or more if there were really no heterogeneity in the population. We have little or no evidence

of heterogeneity here. 'I^2' is a measure of the amount of heterogeneity present, the difference between χ^2 and d.f. as a percentage of the observed χ^2. 17% would usually be interpreted as little heterogeneity.

17.5. The effect estimates from individual studies are not simply averaged, the studies with more information are given more weight. One way to do this is to weight them by multiplying each study difference by one over the variance of the estimate before adding. The variance of an estimate is the square of its standard error. In a random effects model we can include the variability between studies by adding τ^2, the variance between studies, to the within-study variance. We use a random effects model because we think there is heterogeneity between the studies. This might be because the statistical analysis suggests it, which it does not do here, or because there is clinical heterogeneity, differences between the studies in intervention, participant population, or methodology which lead us to think that it would not be valid to assume that they all estimate exactly the same treatment effect. These studies varied quite a lot in age and sex of participants, duration of intervention, and amount of sugar reduction.

17.6. In Figure 17.27, all the confidence intervals overlap. For each pair of studies, the point estimate of one is within the confidence interval of the other. They could all plausibly be estimating the same thing. In Figure 17.28, the confidence intervals do not all overlap. For example, Aeberli does not overlap with either Tordoff or Werner. The confidence intervals for Aeberli and for Werner do not include the common estimate. They could not all plausibly be estimating the same thing.

17.7. For all trials and for short trials there was highly significant, high heterogeneity. For long trials there was no evidence of heterogeneity, although as there were only two trials we

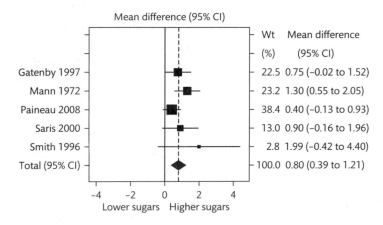

Figure A.17 Forest plot of differences in mean body weight (Kg) in trials where the intervention group were asked to decrease their intake of sugars, redrawn without the need for an arrowhead (data from Te Morenga *et al.* 2012).

could not conclude much from this. The heterogeneity overall was greater than for either of the subgroups, which suggests that trial duration was one of the factors contributing to the heterogeneity.

17.8. Personally, I thought it was poor. The point estimate, 3.97, is almost on the scale limit, 4.0, and the arrowhead covers it. Figure A.18 shows a version without an arrowhead. I prefer it; you can judge for yourself.

17.9. This is a funnel plot. It is used to detect evidence of possible publication bias. If publication bias were caused by trials with large P values being unpublished, we would expect lack of lateral symmetry about the common effect (dashed) line in Figure 17.29. This seems to be the case here, though some of it is explained by the longer duration trials of increased sugar, which had the largest effects, also having larger standard errors.

17.10. This test is a bit dodgy, in my opinion, but here it very highly significant and reinforces the visual impression that there is very definitely asymmetry in the funnel plot.

17.11. I think this suggests that there might be other explanations for the asymmetry beyond publication bias.

17.12. Trim and fill is a method for making an asymmetrical funnel plot more symmetrical. Essentially, we add in dummy

studies with large standard errors and differences in the opposite direction from the real ones. The estimate is reduced by this, but remains clearly greater than zero. We could conclude that if the asymmetry really were a result of publication bias and there were other trials, unpublished because of small and non-significant effects, there would still be evidence for a weight increase with sugar consumption.

Chapter 18

Answers to 18.9 Multiple choice questions: Sample size

18.1. TTFTT. Section 9.9. Power is a property of the test, not the sample. It cannot be zero, as even when there is no population difference at all, the test may be significant.

18.2. TTTTF. Section 18.5. If we keep on adding observations and testing, we are carrying out multiple testing and so invalidate the test (Section 9.10).

18.3. TTFFT. Section 18.1. Power is not involved in estimation.

18.4. TTFTT. Section 18.8. As this trial is aimed to detect a specified effect size, we are doing a power calculation, for which

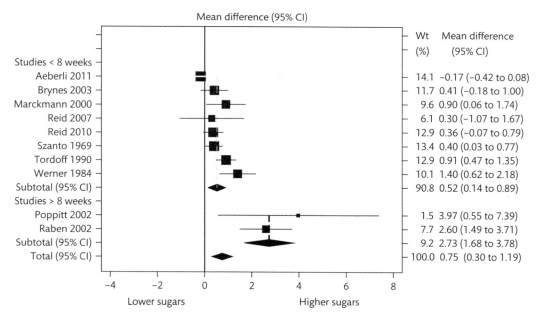

Figure A.18 Differences in mean body weight (Kg) in trials where the intervention group were asked to increase their intake of sugars, without the arrowhead (data from Te Morenga et al. 2012). (Note that for Aeberli the confidence interval is shown in white so that the box will not obliterate it.)

we need to specify the size of difference we want the trial to detect, the power with which we want to detect it, the standard deviation of change in HbA1c, and the planned ratio of group sizes. This trial aimed for equal-sized groups to detect a difference of 0.5 in HbA1c in percentage units with power 80% (alpha 0.05), and used an expected standard deviation 1.44 percentage units. This would require 131 patients per group in an individually randomized trial. In a cluster randomized trial we also need the number of participants in a cluster and the intracluster correlation coefficient to enable us to allow for the extra uncertainty which cluster randomization introduces. In this trial, they planned for eight patients per cluster and used ICC = 0.05 and multiplied the sample size by the estimated design effect, 1.3, then increased it by a further 20% to allow for loss of follow-up. We do not need the change from baseline, as this will happen in both groups, it is the difference between treatments we need.

Answers to 18.10 Exercise: Estimation of sample sizes

18.1. The accuracy is to two standard errors, and for a proportion this is $2\sqrt{p(1-p)/n}$. The maximum value of the standard error is when $p = 0.5$. Two percentage points is 0.02, so from Section 18.2:

$$0.02 = 2\sqrt{\frac{0.5 \times (1 - 0.5)}{n}}$$

$$0.02^2 = 2^2 \times \frac{0.5 \times 0.5}{n}$$

$$n = \frac{4 \times 0.25}{0.0004}$$

$$= 2\,500$$

A sample of size 2 500 would give a confidence interval of at most two percentage points on each side of the estimate for any sample proportion.

18.2. This means that a difference would be regarded as statistically significant, and so would provide evidence of a treatment effect, if the difference observed were such that the proportion of samples which would produce a difference as large as or larger than that observed, in either direction, was 0.05 or less. They set this as the level of evidence which would enable them to conclude that defibrotide is different from the control treatment.

18.3. 30% is the proportion of patients undergoing paediatric haemopoietic stem-cell transplantation who will develop veno-occlusive disease. This is derived from several studies, to which references are given. 15% is the proportion after

treatment which this trial is designed to be able to detect. It is not clear from the statement how this was chosen, nor could I find any other comment on it in the paper. It could be the difference that would lead to a change in treatment policy, or it could be what they hoped the drug would achieve. It could be what the sample size they could achieve would be able to detect, but I doubt this. As we shall see, they increased the sample size.

18.4. Some possible samples would produce differences larger than that in the whole population of patients, some would produce differences which were smaller. The larger the observed difference is, the smaller will be the P value for the significance test comparing the proportions with veno-occlusive disease between the treatment groups. The proportion of studies that will produce a difference big enough to be significant, if in the population the difference is that postulated, is called the power (Section 9.9). This is also the probability that a study will produce a significance difference. Here it has been set to 80%, so that 80% of possible studies would produce a significant difference if defibrotide reduces the risk of hepatic veno-occlusive disease from 30% to 15%. This means, of course, that 20% of possible studies would not be significant.

18.5. The percentage developing disease in the control group is considerably less than the postulated 30%. This is why they increased the planned sample size to maintain the power. The proportion in the treated group is similar to what the study was designed to detect. The confidence interval for the difference just includes the 15 percentage point difference which the study was designed to have 80% power to detect and just excludes zero. Either the population difference is smaller than they planned for or they were unlucky and their sample was one with a difference considerably smaller than they planned for. They were lucky, of course, in that the difference was just statistically significant and they got into the *Lancet*.

18.6. When the number of clusters is very small and the number of individuals within a cluster is large, as in this study, clustering can have a major effect. The design effect, by which the estimated sample size should be multiplied, is DEFF = $1 + (m - 1) \times$ ICC = $1 + (750 - 1) \times 0.005 = 4.745$. Thus the estimated sample size for any given comparison should be multiplied by 4.745. Looking at it another way, the effective sample size is the actual sample size, 3 000, divided by 4.745, about 632. Further, sample size calculations should take into account degrees of freedom. In large sample approximation sample size calculations, power 80% and alpha 5% are embodied in the multiplier $f(\alpha, P) = f(0.05, 0.80) = (1.96+0.85)^2 = 7.90$ (Table 18.1). For a small sample calculation using the t test, 1.96 must be replaced by the corresponding 5% point of the t distribution with the appropriate degrees of freedom, here 2 degrees of freedom giving t = 4.30 (Table 10.1). Hence the multiplier is $(4.30 + 0.85)^2$ = 26.52, 3.36 times that for the large sample. The effect of the small number of clusters would reduce the effective sample size even more, down to 630/3.36 = 188. Thus the 3 000 men in two groups of two clusters would give the same power to detect the same difference as 188 men randomized individually. The applicants resubmitted a proposal with many more clusters.

Chapter 19

Answers to 19.8 Multiple choice questions: Missing data

19.1. FFFTT. 'Missing completely at random' (Section 19.2) means that the missingness is entirely unrelated to the participant, for example when forms are lost in the post or samples are destroyed in laboratory accidents. Hence there is no systematic difference between participants who have missing data and those with full data. If we omit these participants there should, therefore, be no bias. If we omit anyone, we are not analysing all participants and so, I think, not analysing strictly according to intention to treat, though we should still be guided by this principle (Section 2.6). Use of the last observation carried forward will introduce bias when the variable which is missing is changing over time. If it is not changing over time, why record it more than once?

19.2. FFTTF. 'Missing at random' (Section 19.2) means that whether the data are missing may be related to the other characteristics of the participants, but not to the actual unobserved value in a such way that it cannot be estimated from the observed data. Thus there are likely to be systematic differences between participants for whom all data are observed and participants for whom some data are missing. Multiple imputation, which predicts the missing observations from the data we have, is a possible method of analysis. Because missingness may be related to participant characteristics, omitting such participants may lead to complete cases being unrepresentative and so using only them may lead to bias.

19.3. TFTFT. Section 19.3. Using the mean for all other observations of the variable produces only one number, so all missing values are replaced by the same. No other variables are used. The substitution of the overall mean should make the groups appear more similar, a bias which we do not mind very much. The substitution of the randomized group mean should make the groups appear more different, a bias which we should always try to avoid. Other methods, such as

multiple imputation, can use the available data much more informatively.

19.4. FTTFT. Section 19.6. Multiple imputation is for data which are MAR, MNAR data may give incorrect estimates because the missing observations cannot be predicted from existing data.

19.5. FFFFT. Section 19.5. Simple imputation, like multiple imputation, is for data which are MAR, MNAR data may give incorrect estimates because the missing observations cannot be predicted from existing data. It does not use random estimation but instead uses the regression estimate (Section 11.6) to replace the missing observation.

Answers to 19.9 Exercise: Last observation carried forward

19.1. The mean reductions are greater for the complete data than for the LOCF, whereas the standard deviations are greater for the LOCF. These are differences from baseline, and the cases for which the last observation was carried forward must give zero differences. This will reduce the mean. Most of the observed differences must be considerably greater than zero, judging from the means and standard deviations. Adding in some zero observations, a long way from the mean, will therefore tend to increase the variability and hence the standard deviation.

19.2. The numbers in this study are small, but there is differential dropout between the two groups. The nature of the missingness is also different. In the dolphin group it was after the two who have missing data had tried and quit the programme. In the outdoor nature group it was after the three who have missing data had learned that they were not going to get the dolphins. There is no way to tell how these groups may have differed, or whether had they stayed the results might have been different, but this may have made the groups non-comparable. The authors quite rightly attempted to allow for the missingness.

19.3. There was differential dropout between the two groups. The effects of the LOCF in reducing the mean reduction and inflating the variance may thus be greater in the study with greater dropout, the outdoor nature programme. This may have inflated the difference in mean reduction slightly.

19.4. All the participants were included and analysed as they were allocated. This is what makes an analysis according to the intention to treat principle (Section 2.6). However, it is modified in the sense that we do not have outcome observations for five of the participants who were allocated. By carrying forward the baseline measurements, we are in effect assigning a zero value to the reduction in depression score to these five people. So in effect, they are asking what we could conclude if the five who dropped out experienced no change at all. This seems like a reasonable sensitivity analysis to me.

19.5. Because in this study the depression scores fell considerably in both groups, the baseline depression scores are likely to be higher than most of the scores at 2 weeks. Thus LOCF will have raised both the means and the standard deviations of the outcome scores.

19.6. The standard deviations in Table 19.3 are noticeably smaller than those in the LOCF rows in Table 19.2. These are the rows which cover the same participants. When we take change scores, we include two measurement errors, one from each of the scores, but we remove systematic variation between the participants. Sometimes removing between-participants variation is sufficient to make the total variability less, but often it is not and by using change scores we can actually increase the variance. In fact, if the variance of the measurements is given by $\sigma_b^2 + \sigma_w^2$, the variance of the differences is $2\sigma_w^2$. So we increase the variance by using change scores instead of final scores if $\sigma_w^2 > \sigma_b^2$. This will be the case if the correlation between baseline and outcome measurements is less than 0.5. Analysis of covariance (Section 15.3) is always better.

Chapter 20

Answers to 20.13 Multiple choice questions: Measurement

20.1. TFTTF. Section 20.2. Unless the measurement process changes the subject, we would expect the difference in mean to be zero.

20.2. TFTFF. Section 20.3. Cohen's kappa is measure of agreement between two observations of a categorical variable (Section 20.3). The maximum value of kappa is +1, zero indicates no agreement, there is no lower limit. Values of kappa between 0.0 and 0.2 are interpreted as slight or poor agreement, 0.2–0.4 as fair, 0.4–0.6 as moderate, 0.6–0.8 as substantial or good, and 0.8–1.0 as very good or almost perfect. Weighting enables disagreement where the chosen categories are similar to have less effect than those when the categories are very different (Section 20.4).

20.3. TFFTF. Section 20.5. This plot of difference against average shows the 95% limits of agreement, estimates of the limits within which 95% of differences should lie. We expect 5% of difference to be outside these limits; here 4% are outside.

This should be true whatever the distribution and, for an approximately symmetrical distribution, as here, 2.5% would be below the lower limit and 2.5% above the upper limit. However, the assumptions are not met, the variability of the difference clearly increases greatly with increasing magnitude. A log transformation may help and, as Figure A.19 shows, does so, though it does not remove all the relationship.

20.4. TFTFF. Section 20.6. We need the sensitivity as well as specificity. There are other things, dependent on the population studied, which may be important too, like the positive predictive value.

20.5. FTTTF. Section 20.6. Specificity, not sensitivity, measures how well people without the disease are eliminated.

20.6. TTFFF. Section 20.7. The 95% reference interval should not depend on the sample size.

20.7. FFFFT. Section 20.7. We expect 5% of 'normal' men to be outside these limits. The patient may have a disease which does not produce an abnormal haematocrit. This reference interval is for men, not women who may have a different distribution of haematocrit. It is dangerous to extrapolate the reference interval to a different population. In fact, for women the reference interval is 35.8 to 45.4, putting a woman with a haematocrit of 48 outside the reference interval. A haematocrit outside the 95% reference interval suggests that the man may be ill, although it does not prove it.

20.8. TFFFT. Section 20.11. Cronbach's alpha is a measure of internal consistency which lies between 0 and 1. Alpha $\geqslant 0.7$ is usually interpreted as being good enough for use as a research instrument to compare groups, alpha $\geqslant 0.9$ is usually interpreted as being good enough for use as a clinical instrument to inform decisions about an individual patient.

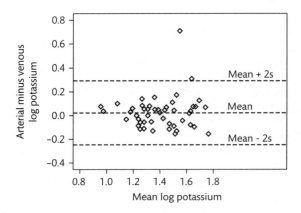

Figure A.19 Plot of difference against average for $\log_e$ transformed potassium (data from Johnston and Murphy 2005).

20.9. FTTTF. There is great danger of multiple testing, which may be highly misleading (Section 9.10). We can avoid this by use of the Bonferroni correction, but, as our variables are unlikely to be independent, this procedure may be very conservative and have low power. It would be better to choose a primary outcome variable, which we should be able to choose before we do the trial and certainly before we look at the data and which we should not change during the analysis, as this would risk greatly biasing the P value. A method of using all the variables in a single analysis might be preferable if there is no single variable more important than the others, which principal components analysis provides (Section 20.9).

Answers to 20.14 Exercise: Two measurement studies

20.1. The blood donors were used because it was easy to get the blood. This would produce a sample deficient in older people, so it was supplemented by people attending day centres. This would ensure that these were reasonably active, healthy people for their age. Given the problem of getting blood and the limited resources available, this seems a fairly satisfactory sample for the purpose. The alternative would be to take a random sample from the local population and try to persuade them to give the blood. There might have been so many refusals that volunteer bias would make the sample unrepresentative anyway. The sample is also biased geographically, being drawn from one part of London. In the context of the study, where we wanted to compare people with diabetes with people without diabetes, this did not matter so much, as both groups came from the same place. For a reference interval which would apply nationally, if there were a geographical factor the interval would be biased in other places. To look at this we would have to repeat the study in several places, compare the resulting reference intervals and pool as appropriate.

20.2. We want normal, healthy people for the sample, so we want to exclude people with obvious pathology and especially those with disease known to affect the quantity being measured. However, if we excluded all elderly people currently receiving drug therapy we would find it very difficult to a sufficiently large sample. It was indeed 'normal' for the elderly to be taking analgesics and hypnotics, so these were permitted.

20.3. From the shape of the histogram and the Normal plot, the distribution of plasma magnesium does indeed appear to be a very good fit to the Normal distribution.

20.4. As the data appear a good fit to the Normal distribution, we could do this using the Normal distribution method. The reference interval, outside which about 5% of normal values are expected to lie, is $\bar{x} - 2s$ to $\bar{x} + 2s$, or $0.810 - 2 \times 0.057$ to $0.810 + 2 \times 0.057$, which is 0.696 to 0.924, or 0.70 to 0.92 mmol/litre.

20.5. As the sample is large and the data from an approximately Normal distribution, the standard error of the limits (Section 20.7) is approximately

$$\sqrt{\frac{3s^2}{n}} = \sqrt{\frac{3 \times 0.057^2}{140}} = 0.008\,343\,9$$

For the 95% confidence interval we take 1.96 standard errors on either side of the limit, $1.96 \times 0.008\,343\,9 = 0.016$. The 95% confidence interval for the lower reference limit is $0.696 - 0.016$ to $0.696 + 0.016 = 0.680$ to 0.712 or 0.68 to 0.71 mmol/litre. The confidence interval for the upper limit is $0.924 - 0.016$ to $0.696 + 0.016 = 0.908$ to 0.940 or 0.91 to 0.94 mmol/litre. The reference interval is well estimated as far as sampling errors are concerned.

20.6. Plasma magnesium did indeed increase with age. The variability did not. This would mean that for older people the lower limit would be too low and the upper limit too high, as the few above the upper limit would all be elderly. We could simply estimate the reference interval separately at different ages. We could do this using separate means but a common estimate of variance, obtained by one-way analysis of variance (Section 10.9). Or we could use the regression of magnesium on age to get a formula which would predict the reference interval for any age. We could then construct a centile chart (Section 20.8). The method chosen would depend on the nature of the relationship.

20.7. If a question has a lot of missing data, i.e. has not been answered by many respondents, this suggests that it is difficult to answer or does not apply to a substantial proportion of people. Missing data in turn means that either the full score cannot be calculated, or we have to impute the missing value in some way, often by the average of items which are not missing. This in turn will mean that the questionnaire and the scale score will be slightly different for those who complete the item and those who do not. For these reasons it is better to drop such items at an early stage.

20.8. Floor effects arise when most people answering a question give the same answer, which is the lowest possible in the ordering. Ceiling effects arise when most people answering a question give the same answer, which is the highest possible in the ordering. If more than 70% of respondents give the same extreme answer, the question does not distinguish well between people and does not convey much information. It is likely to have only weak relationships with other variables and so to reduce the internal consistency of the score.

20.9. Like questions with floor and ceiling effects, questions with highly skewed distributions do not distinguish well between people and do not convey a lot of information. They are likely to have weak relationships with other variables and so to reduce the internal consistency of the score.

20.10. If an item is closely related to another item, it does not carry much information that the second item does not. If the second item is present in the questionnaire, the first need not be. We might wish to drop such an item from the scale to shorten the questionnaire without losing much information. Such questions may be described as redundant.

20.11. Principal components analysis (Section 20.9) is a way of reducing the dimensions of a dataset by finding combinations of the variables which have most of the variability and hence most of the information. These combinations estimate variables which can be used to predict those observed and, if this can be done with fewer composite variables than the total number of variables with which we started, they can be used to reduce the dimensions of the data. The composite variables are formed as linear combinations of the existing variable, i.e. by multiplying each variable by a coefficient and adding. We use the standardized form of the variables, i.e. subtract the mean and divide by the standard deviation to give mean zero and standard deviation one. The coefficients are constrained so that their squares sum to 1.0. The first principal component is the combination which has the maximum variance, the second component is the combination which is not correlated with the first and which has the maximum variance, the third is the combination which is not correlated with the first or the second and which has the maximum variance, and so on until we have as many combinations as there are variables.

20.12. The variances of the principal components are estimated by mathematical quantities called eigenvalues (Section 20.9). The sum of the eigenvalues is equal to the number of variables. The percentage of variance which the component contains is thus given by the eigenvalue divided by the number of variables, here 29. The first 10 components altogether have 73% of the total variance. The remaining 19 components have 27% of the variance and so each explains much less than we would expect if the components were all similar. This shows that there is structure in the data and that the 29 variables can be predicted by only 10 components. The remaining 19 components represent variability which cannot be so explained and is interpreted as random information, not part of the constructs in which we are interested.

20.13. A ceiling effect is when a large number of the observed values are the highest possible. In this case 34% of the answers are the maximum. (Note that the scoring of all four questions was reversed; a high score means a low burden and thus higher quality of life.) It suggests that the scale is not estimating the underlying construct well, and information about respondents who score high for the 'burden' construct is being lost. They could have tried adding a couple of questions specifically on this topic to try to overcome this. As these 34% of respondents have answered 'never / not at all' to all four questions which form this subscale, it may also be that about one-third of caregivers do not feel any burden whatsoever from their caregiving and we would just have to accept this ceiling effect. It would make statistical analysis much easier if we could remove the ceiling, however.

20.14. Cronbach's alpha measures the internal consistency of a scale or subscale. Values of alpha greater than 0.7 are usually regarded as being sufficiently consistent for use in research, where we want to estimate the average value of a construct to compare groups, but we want alpha to be 0.9 or greater if we wish to use the scale to inform us about individuals. Hence most of the subscales here would be good enough for use in research projects. For the 'private life' subscale, alpha = 0.55 suggests that this scale would be poor even as a research instrument.

20.15. We could increase alpha by adding more items to the scale. We have only two items in this scale, so there is plenty of scope for this. We cannot drop items which are not highly correlated with others in the scale, because there are only two items.

Chapter 21

Answers to 21.7 Multiple choice questions: Population and mortality

21.1. FTFFF. Section 21.1. It is for a specific age group, not age adjusted. It measures the number of deaths per person at risk, not the total number. It tells us nothing about age structure.

21.2. FTTTT. Section 21.4. The life table is calculated from age specific death rates. Expectation of life is the expected value of the distribution of age at death if these mortality rates apply. It usually decreases with age in resource-rich populations, though in resource-poor populations it may increase in the years of infancy, when mortality rates are particularly high. For example, see England in 1841 (Table 21.7).

21.3. TFTTF. The SMR (Section 21.3) for women who had just had a baby is lower than 100 (all women) and 105 (stillbirth women). The confidence intervals do not overlap so there is good evidence for a difference. Women who had had a stillbirth may be less or more likely than all women to commit suicide, we cannot tell. We cannot conclude that giving birth prevents suicide—it may be that optimists conceive, for example.

21.4. TFFFF. Section 21.3. Age effects have been adjusted for. It may also be that heavy drinkers become publicans. It is difficult to infer causation from observational data. Men at high risk of cirrhosis of the liver, i.e. heavy drinkers, may not become window cleaners, or window cleaners who drink may change their occupation, which requires good balance. Window cleaners have low risk. The 'average' ratio is 100, not 1.0.

21.5. FFFTF. Section 21.6. A life table tells us about mortality, not population structure. A bar chart shows the relationship between two variables, not their frequency distribution (Section 5.5).

21.6. TFFFT. Sections 21.1, 21.2, 21.5. Expectation of life does not depend on age distribution (Section 21.4).

Answers to 21.8 Exercise: Mortality and type 1 diabetes

21.1. A standardized mortality ratio (Section 21.3) is the number of deaths observed in the index group, here people with type 1 diabetes diagnosed before age 15, divided by the number of deaths we would expect to see in the same number of people from the standard or reference population if they had the same age and sex distribution as the index group (Section 21.3). We have seen 3.6 times the number of deaths in people with early onset type 1 diabetes as would be expected in a similar group from the Finnish population as a whole.

21.2. The people in the later onset group will tend to be older than the earlier onset group, because nobody under age 15 is in the later onset group and there must always be new people aged under 15 coming into the earlier onset group.

21.3. Because these deaths take place before diagnosis, such unfortunate people will never be included in either diabetes group.

21.4. They would need age and sex specific death rates for a standard population, in this case the population of Finland.

21.5. Yes, it has to be, because the confidence intervals, 3.3 to 3.9 and 2.6 to 3.0, do not overlap (Section 9.12).

Chapter 22

Answers to 22.10 Multiple choice questions: Bayesian methods

22.1. TFTTF. A prior distribution is not based on the data to be analysed, but should express our prior knowledge or belief. We may have no prior knowledge, in which case we can choose a vague or an uninformative prior. The final estimate, the posterior distribution, will depend on our choice of prior, less so if we have a lot of data than if we have little. For an analytical solution, we need to choose a prior from a family of distributions with suitable properties, but this is less important when using Markov Chain Monte Carlo methods.

22.2. FTTFT. We have to choose a prior distribution which reflects the state of our knowledge, so we will have to choose one which reflects our ignorance and will have little effect on the estimate. This can be uninformative and give equal probability to all possibilities when the parameter has a finite range, such as a proportion or a correlation coefficient. When the range is not bounded at the low end, the high end, or both, we cannot do this, as all possibilities would have zero probability. Instead we choose a vague prior, which has a very high variance so any plausible value has a similar, very low but non-zero probability. An uninformative or a vague prior will still have an influence on the estimate, because this will be different from the estimate using an informative prior.

22.3. TTFTT. The posterior distribution combines the knowledge which had before we collected our data, as expressed by the prior distribution, with the data themselves. It must therefore tell us something. It tells us what our final estimate is and how certain we can be about it.

22.4. TTFTT. MCMC methods are very flexible and enable us to solve a very wide range of analytical problems. Because they make use of chance, the answers vary, depending on things like the number of updates and the seed used to start the random number generation used in the simulation. There is usually a burn-in period when the updates are not included in the final estimate of the posterior distribution. Network meta-analysis is one of the areas in medical research where MCMC has been widely used.

22.5. TFTTT. A Bayesian credible interval does a similar job to a Frequentist confidence interval, telling us how good our estimate of the parameter might be after we have analysed data. It can be derived from the posterior distribution in more than one way. We can take the region where the probability density is highest so as to give a total probability equal to that desired, typically 95%, giving a higher posterior density or

H.P.D. interval. We can also do this by cutting off equal probabilities at either end, usually 2.5%, to give a central credibility interval.

Answers to 22.11 Exercise: A Bayesian network meta-analysis

22.1. We have enough evidence to conclude that chlorhexidine increases the odds of death compared with control, by a factor between 1.05 and 1.50. We have enough to conclude that both SDD and SOC reduce the odds of death compared with control, but not enough to say which is preferable.

22.2. Log odds ratios can take any numerical value between minus and plus infinity, standard deviations can take any value between zero and plus infinity. Thus a distribution which gives equal probability to all possibilities will have to give zero probability everywhere and it just will not work. Instead we choose a vague prior with a very large variance.

22.3. The evidence suggests that SDD and SOD are each superior to control and also superior to chlorhexidine. We can also conclude that chlorhexidine may be inferior to control and at best has very little advantage. We have added the estimates of the effects of SDD and SOD relative to chlorhexidine. All the estimates are based on more data; for example the SDD vs. SOD comparison includes all the studies comparing SDD and SOD to control. However, because the effect of the very large de Smet et al. (2009) study is so great, the estimates are quite similar in the two tables.

22.4. The estimated probabilities of death can be given the straightforward Frequentist interpretation that the proportion of intubated patients who would die if given SDD is 0.213. From the Bayesian perspective we would say the same, as the rational degree of belief that such a patient, chosen at random, would die, must be the proportion of such patients who die.

22.5. The estimated probability that the SDD intervention is the best of the four is meaningless from a frequency point of view. There is no long run of repetitions which we could imagine. From a Bayesian perspective it is straightforward. For SDD, the probability 0.740 represents our degree of belief, arising from the observed data, that SDD is the best of the four treatments.

References

Abul-Azm, A. and Abdullah, K.M. (2006). Effect of topical tranexamic acid in open heart surgery. *European Journal of Anaesthesiology*, **23**, 380–4.

Abramo, A., Kopylov, P., Geijer, M., and Tägil, M. (2009). Open reduction and internal fixation compared to closed reduction and external fixation in distal radial fractures: a randomized study of 50 patients. *Acta Orthopaedica*, **80**, 478–85.

Al-Mulla, F., Bland, J.M., Serratt, D., Miller, J., Chu, C., and Taylor, G.T. (2009). Age-dependent penetrance of different germline mutations in the BRCA1 gene. *Journal of Clinical Pathology*, **62**, 350–6.

Altman, D.G. (1982). Statistics and ethics in medical research. In *Statistics in Practice* (ed. S.M. Gore and D.G. Altman). British Medical Association, London.

Altman, D.G. (1991). *Practical Statistics for Medical Research*. Chapman and Hall, London.

Altman, D.G. (1993). Construction of age-related reference centiles using absolute residuals. *Statistics in Medicine*, **12**, 917–24.

Altman, D.G. (1998). Confidence intervals for the number needed to treat. *British Medical Journal*, **317**, 1309–12.

Altman, D.G. and Bland, J.M. (1983). Measurement in medicine: the analysis of method comparison studies. *The Statistician*, **32**, 307–17.

Altman, D.G. and Matthews, J.N.S. (1996). Statistics Notes: Interaction 1: heterogeneity of effects. *British Medical Journal*, **313**, 486.

Anderson, H.R., Bland, J.M., Patel, S., and Peckham, C. (1986). The natural history of asthma in childhood. *Journal of Epidemiology and Community Health*, **40**, 121–9.

Andreasen, J.J. and Nielsen, C. (2004). Prophylactic tranexamic acid in elective, primary coronary artery bypass surgery using cardiopulmonary bypass. *European Journal of Cardiothoracic Surgery*, **26**, 311–17.

Anon (1997). All trials must have informed consent. *British Medical Journal*, **314**, 1134–5.

Antonioli, C. and Reveley, M.A. (2005). Randomised controlled trial of animal facilitated therapy with dolphins in the treatment of depression. *British Medical Journal*, **331**, 1231.

Appleby, L. (1991). Suicide during pregnancy and in the first postnatal year. *British Medical Journal*, **302**, 137–40.

Armitage, P., Berry, G., and Matthews, J.N.S. (2002). *Statistical Methods in Medical Research*. Blackwell, Oxford.

Armellin, G., Vinciguerra, A., Bonato, R., Pittarello, D., and Giron, G.P. (2001). Tranexamic acid in primary CABG surgery: high vs. low dose. *Minerva Anestesiologica*, **70**, 97–107.

Balfour, R.P. (1991). Birds, milk and campylobacter. *Lancet*, **337**, 176.

Banks, M.H., Bewley, B.R., Bland, J.M., Dean, J.R., and Pollard, V.M. (1978). A long term study of smoking by secondary schoolchildren. *Archives of Disease in Childhood*, **53**, 12–19.

Baric, D., Biocina, B., Unic, D., Sutlic, Z., Rudez, I., Vrca, V.B., Brkic, K., and Ivkovic, M. (2007). Topical use of antifibrinolytic agents reduces postoperative bleeding: a double-blind, prospective, randomized study. *European Journal of Cardiothoracic Surgery*, **31**, 366–71.

Begg, C.B. and Mazumdar, M. (1994). Operating characteristics of a rank correlation test for publication bias. *Biometrics*, **50**, 1088–1101.

Belloti, J.C., Tamaoki, M.J.S., Atallah, A.N., Albertoni, W.M., dos Santos, J.B.G., and Faloppa, F. (2010). Treatment of reducible unstable fractures of the distal radius in adults: a randomised controlled trial of De Palma percutaneous pinning versus bridging external fixation. *BMC Musculoskeletal Disorders*, **11**, 137.

Bewley, B.R. and Bland, J.M. (1976). Academic performance and social factors related to cigarette smoking by schoolchildren. *British Journal of Preventive and Social Medicine*, **31**, 18–24.

Bewley, B.R., Bland, J.M., and Harris, R. (1974). Factors associated with the starting of cigarette smoking by primary school children. *British Journal of Preventive and Social Medicine*, **28**, 37–44.

Bewley, T.H., Bland, J.M., Ilo, M., Walch, E., and Willington, G. (1975). Census of mental hospital patients and life expectancy of those unlikely to be discharged. *British Medical Journal*, **4**, 671–5.

Bewley, T.H., Bland, J.M., Mechen, D., and Walch, E. (1981). 'New chronic' patients. *British Medical Journal*, **283**, 1161–4.

Blackberry, I.D., Furler, J.S., Best, J.D., Chondros, P., Vale, M., Walker, C., Dunning, T., Segal, L., Dunbar, J., Audehm, R., Liew, D., and Young, D. (2013). Effectiveness of general practice based, practice nurse led telephone coaching on glycaemic control of type 2 diabetes: the Patient Engagement And Coaching for Health (PEACH) pragmatic cluster randomised controlled trial. *British Medical Journal*, **347**, f5272.

Bland, J.M. (2004). Cluster randomised trials in the medical literature: two bibliometric surveys. *BMC Medical Research Methodology*, **4**, 21.

Bland, J.M. (2009). The tyranny of power: is there a better way to calculate sample size? *British Medical Journal*, **339**, b3985.

Bland, J.M. (2010). The analysis of cluster-randomised trials in education. *Effective Education*, **2**, 165–80.

Bland, J.M. and Altman, D.G. (1986). Statistical methods for assessing agreement between two methods of clinical measurement. *Lancet*, **i**, 307–10.

Bland, J.M. and Altman, D.G. (1993). Informed consent. *British Medical Journal*, **306**, 928.

Bland, J.M. and Altman, D.G. (1999). Measuring agreement in method comparison studies. *Statistical Methods in Medical Research*, **8**, 135–60.

Bland, J.M. and Altman, D.G. (2007). Agreement between methods of measurement with multiple observations per individual. *Journal of Biopharmaceutical Statistics*, **17**, 571–82.

Bland, J.M. and Altman, D.G. (2011). Comparisons against baseline within randomised groups are often used and can be highly misleading. *Trials*, **12**, 264.

Bland, J.M., Bewley, B.R., Banks, M.H., and Pollard, V.M. (1975). Schoolchildren's beliefs about smoking and disease. *Health Education Journal*, **34**, 71–8.

Bland, J.M., Bewley, B.R., Pollard, V., and Banks, M.H. (1978). Effect of children's and parents' smoking on respiratory symptoms. *Archives of Disease in Childhood*, **53**, 100–5.

Bland, J.M., Bewley, B.R., and Banks, M.H. (1979). Cigarette smoking and children's respiratory symptoms: validity of questionnaire method. *Revue d'Epidemiologie et Santé Publique*, **27**, 69–76.

Bland, J.M., Holland, W.W., and Elliott, A. (1974). The development of respiratory symptoms in a cohort of Kent schoolchildren. *Bulletin Physio-Pathologie Respiratoire*, **10**, 699–716.

Bland, J.M. and Kerry, S.M. (1998). Statistics Notes: Weighted comparison of means. *British Medical Journal*, **316**, 129.

Bland, J.M., Mutoka, C., and Hutt, M.S.R. (1977). Kaposi's sarcoma in Tanzania. *East African Journal of Medical Research*, **4**, 47–53.

Bland, J.M. and Peacock, J.L. (2000). *Statistical Questions in Evidence-based Medicine*. Oxford University Press, Oxford.

Bland, M. (1997). Informed consent in medical research: Let readers judge for themselves. *British Medical Journal*, **314**, 1477–8.

Bland, M. (2014). Health freaks on trial: duct tape, bull semen and the call of television. *Significance*, **11(2)**, 32–35.

Bland, M. and Peacock, J. (2002). Interpreting statistics with confidence. *The Obstetrician and Gynaecologist*, **4**, 176–80.

BMJ (1996a). The Declaration of Helsinki. *British Medical Journal*, **313**, 1448.

BMJ (1996b). The Nuremberg code (1947). *British Medical Journal*, **313**, 1448.

Borenstein, M., Hedges, L.V., Higgins, J.P.T., and Rothstein, H. (2009). *Introduction to Meta-Analysis*. Wiley, Chichester.

Bowling, A. (1997). *Measuring Health: A Review Of Quality Of Life Measurement Scales, 2nd Ed*. Open University Press, Milton Keynes.

Brawley, O.W. (1998). The study of untreated syphilis in the negro male. *International Journal of Radiation Oncology, Biology, Physics*, **40**, 5–8.

Breslow, N.E. and Day, N.E. (1987). *Statistical methods in cancer research. Volume II—the design and analysis of cohort studies*. IARC, Lyon.

Brewster, D.H., Thomson, C.S., Hole, D.J., Black, R.J., Stroner, P.L., and Gillis, C.R. (2001). Relation between socioeconomic status and tumour stage in patients with breast, colorectal, ovarian, and lung cancer: results from four national, population based studies. *British Medical Journal*, **322**, 830–1.

British Standards Institution (1979). *Precision of test methods. 1: Guide for the determination and reproducibility of a standard test method (BS5497, part 1)*. BSI, London.

Brooke, O.G., Anderson, H.R., Bland, J.M., Peacock, J., and Stewart, M. (1989). Effects on birth weight of smoking, alcohol, caffeine, socio-economic factors, and psychosocial stress. *British Medical Journal*, **298**, 795–801.

Brown, L.D., Cai, T., and DasGupta, A. (2001). Interval estimation for a binomial proportion. *Statistical Science*, **16**, 101–33.

Brown, L.D., Cai, T.T., and DasGupta, A. (2002). Confidence intervals for a binomial proportion and asymptotic expansions. *Annals of Statistics*, **30**, 160–201.

Brown, R.S., Thwaites, B.K., and Mongan, P.D. (1997). Tranexamic acid is effective in decreasing postoperative bleeding and transfusions in primary coronary artery bypass operations: a double-blind, randomized, placebo-controlled trial. *Anesthesia and Analgesia*, **85**, 963–70.

Bryson, M.C. (1976). The *Literary Digest* poll: making of a statistical myth. *The American Statistician*, **30**, 184–5.

Bulletin of Medical Ethics (1998). News: Lively debate on research ethics in the US. November, 3–4.

Burdick, R.K. and Graybill, F.A. (1992). *Confidence intervals on variance components*. Dekker, New York.

Burr, M.L., St Leger, A.S., and Neale, E. (1976). Anti-mite measures in mite-sensitive adult asthma: a controlled trial. *Lancet*, **i**, 333–5.

Butland, B.K., Field-Smith, M.E., Ramsey, J.D., and Anderson, H.R. (2012). Twenty-five years of volatile substance abuse mortality: a national mortality surveillance programme. *Addiction*, **108**, 385–93.

Campbell, M.J. and Gardner, M.J. (1989). Calculating confidence intervals for some non-parametric analyses. In *Statistics with Confidence* (ed. M.J. Gardner and D.G. Altman). British Medical Journal, London.

Carleton, R.A., Sanders, C.A., and Burack, W.R. (1960). Heparin administration after acute myocardial infarction. *New England Journal of Medicine*, **263**, 1002–4.

Casey, A.T.H., Crockard, H.A., Bland, J.M., Stevens, J., Moskovich, R., and Ransford, A. (1996). Predictors of outcome in the quadriparetic nonambulatory myelopathic patient with rheumatoid-arthritis – a prospective study of 55 surgically treated Ranawat class IIIB patients. *Journal of Neurosurgery*, **85**, 574–81.

Castellucci, L.A., Cameron, C., Le Gal, G., Rodger, M.A., Coyle, D., Wells, P.S., Clifford, T., Gandara, E., Wells, G., and Carrier, M. (2013). Efficacy and safety outcomes of oral anticoagulants and antiplatelet drugs in the secondary prevention of venous thromboembolism: systematic review and network meta-analysis. *British Medical Journal*, **347**, f5133.

Chatterjee, S., Biondi-Zoccai, G., Abbate, A., D'Ascenzo, F., Castagno, D., Van Tassell, B., Mukherjee, D., and Lichstein, E. (2013). Benefits of beta blockers in patients with heart failure and reduced ejection fraction: network meta-analysis. *British Medical Journal*, **346**, f55.

Cheyne, H., Hundley, V., Dowding, D., Bland, J.M., McNamee, P., Greer, I., Styles, M., Barnett, C.A., Scotland, G., and Niven, C. (2008). Effects of algorithm for diagnosis of active labour: cluster randomised trial. *BMJ*, **337**, a2396.

Christie, D. (1979). Before-and-after comparisons: a cautionary tale. *British Medical Journal*, **2**, 1629–30.

Cochran, W.G. (1977). *Sampling Techniques*. Wiley, New York.

Cochrane Collaboration (2013). <http://www.mrc-bsu.cam.ac.uk/cochrane/handbook/>.

Cohen, J. (1960). A coefficient of agreement for nominal scales. *Educational and Psychological Measurement*, **20**, 37–47.

Cohen, J. (1968). Weighted kappa: nominal scale agreement with provision for scaled disagreement or partial credit. *Psychological Bulletin*, **70**, 213–20.

Cohen, J. (1992). A power primer. *Psychological Bulletin*, **112**, 155–9.

Colman, I., Brown, M.D., Innes, G.D., Grafstein, E., Roberts, T.E., and Rowe, B.H. (2004). Parenteral metoclopramide for acute migraine: meta-analysis of randomised controlled trials. *British Medical Journal*, **329**, 1369.

Colton, T. (1974). *Statistics in Medicine*. Little Brown, Boston.

Conover, W.J. (1980). *Practical Nonparametric Statistics*. John Wiley and Sons, New York.

Corbacioglu, S., Cesaro, S., Faraci, M., Valteau-Couanet, D., Gruhn, B., Rovelli, A., Boelens, J.J., Hewitt, A., Schrum, J., Schulz, A.S., Müller, I., Stein, J., Wynn, R., Greil, J., Sykora, K-W., Matthes-Martin, S., Führer, M., O'Meara, A., Toporski, J., Sedlacek, P., Schlegel, P.G., Ehlert, K., Fasth, A., Winiarski, J., Arvidson, J., Mauz-Körholz, C., Ozsahin, H., Schrauder, A., Bader, P., Massaro, J., D'Agostino, R., Hoyle, H., Iacobelli, M., Debatin, K-M., Peters, C., and Dini, G. (2012). Defibrotide for prophylaxis of hepatic veno-occlusive disease in paediatric haemopoietic stem-cell transplantation: an open-label, phase 3, randomised controlled trial. *Lancet*, **379**, 1301–9.

Cox, D.R. (1972). Regression models and life tables. *Journal of the Royal Statistical Society Series B*, **34**, 187–220.

Cronbach, L.J. (1951). Coefficient alpha and the internal structure of tests. *Psychometrika*, **16**, 297–334.

Davies, O.L. and Goldsmith, P.L. (1972). *Statistical Methods in Research and Production*. Oliver and Boyd, Edinburgh.

De Bonis, M., Cavaliere, F., Alessandrini, F., Lapenna, E., Santarelli, F., Moscato, U., Schiavello, R., and Possati, G.F. (2000). Topical use of tranexamic acid in coronary artery bypass operations: a double-blind, prospective, randomized, placebo-controlled study. *Journal of Thoracic and Cardiovascular Surgery*, **119**, 575–80.

Dennis, M. (1997). Commentary: Why we didn't ask patients for their consent. *British Medical Journal*, **314**, 1077.

Dennis, M., O'Rourke, S., Slattery, J., Staniforth, T., and Warlow, C. (1997). Evaluation of a stroke family care worker: results of a randomised controlled trial. *British Medical Journal*, **314**, 1071–6.

DerSimonian, R. and Laird, N. (1986). Meta-analysis in clinical trials. *Controlled Clinical Trials*, **7**, 177–87.

DerSimonian, R. and Kacker, R. (2007). Random-effects model for meta-analysis of clinical trials: an update. *Contemporary Clinical Trials*, **28**, 105–14.

DHSS (1976). *Prevention and Health: Everybody's Business*. HMSO, London.

Diprose, P., Herbertson, M.J., O'Shaughnessy, D., Deakin, C.D., and Gill, R.S. (2005). Reducing allogeneic transfusion in cardiac surgery: a randomized double-blind placebo-controlled trial of antifibrinolytic therapies used in addition to intra-operative cell salvage. *British Journal of Anaesthesia*, **94**, 271–8.

Doll, R. and Hill, A.B. (1950). Smoking and carcinoma of the lung. *British Medical Journal*, **ii**, 739–48.

Doll, R. and Hill, A.B. (1956). Lung cancer and other causes of death in relation to smoking: a second report on the mortality of British doctors. *British Medical Journal*, **ii**, 1071–81.

Doll, R., Peto, R., Boreham, J., and Sutherland, I. (2004). Mortality in relation to smoking: 50 years' observations on male British doctors. *British Medical Journal*, **328**, 1519–28.

Donnan, S.P.B. and Haskey, J. (1977). Alcoholism and cirrhosis of the liver. *Population Trends*, **7**, 18–24.

Donner, A., Brown. K.S., and Brasher, P. (1990). A methodological review of non-therapeutic intervention trials employing cluster randomisation 1979–1989. *International Journal of Epidemiology*, **19**, 795–800.

Donner, A. and Klar, N. (2000). *Design and Analysis of Cluster Randomization Trials in Health Research*. Arnold, London.

Doyal, L. (1997). Informed consent in medical research: Journals should not publish research to which patients have not given fully informed consent—with three exceptions. *British Medical Journal*, **314**, 1107–11.

Dumville, J.C., Worthy, G., Bland, J.M., Cullum, N., Dowson, C., Iglesias, C., Mitchell, J.L., Nelson, E.A., Soares, M.O., and Torgerson, D.J. (2009). Larval therapy for leg ulcers (VenUS II): randomised controlled trial. *British Medical Journal*, **338**, b773.

Duval, S. and Tweedie, R. (2000). Trim and fill: a simple funnel-plot-based method of testing and adjusting for publication bias in meta-analysis. *Biometrics*, **56**, 455–63.

Efron, B. and Tibshirani, R.J. (1993). *An Introduction to the Bootstrap*. Chapman and Hall, New York.

Egero, B. and Henin, R.A. (1973). *The Population of Tanzania*. Bureau of Statistics, Dar es Salaam.

Egger, M., Smith, G.D., Schneider, M., and Minder, C. (1997). Bias in meta-analysis detected by a simple, graphical test. *British Medical Journal*, **315**, 629–34.

Egol, K., Walsh, M., Tejwani, N., McLaurin, T., Wynn, C., and Paksima, N. (2008). Bridging external fixation and supplementary Kirschner-wire fixation versus volar locked plating for unstable fractures of the distal radius: a randomised, prospective trial. *Journal of Bone and Joint Surgery (British Volume)*, **90-B**, 1214–21.

Eldridge, S. and Kerry, S. (2012). *A Practical Guide to Cluster Randomised Trials in Health Services Research*. Wiley, Chichester.

Eskenazi, B., Prehn, A.W., and Christianson, R.E. (1995). Passive and active maternal smoking as measured by serum cotinine: the effect on birthweight. *American Journal of Public Health*, **85**, 395–8.

Esmail, A., Warburton, B., Bland, J.M., Anderson, H.R., and Ramsey, J. (1997). Regional variations in deaths from volatile solvent abuse in Great Britain. *Addiction*, **92**(12), 1765–71.

Etminan, M., Takkouche, B., Isorna, F.C., and Samii, A. (2005). Risk of ischaemic stroke in people with migraine: systematic review and meta-analysis of observational studies. *British Medical Journal*, **330**, 63.

Ettema, T.P., Hensen, E., De Lange, J., Dröes, R.M., Mellenbergh, G.J., and Ribbe, M.W. (2007). Self report on quality of life in dementia with modified COOP/WONCA charts. *Aging & Mental Health*, **11**, 734–42.

Falkowski, W., Ben-Tovim, D.I., and Bland, J.M. (1980). The assessment of the ego states. *British Journal of Psychiatry*, **137**, 572–3.

Feinstein, A.R. (2001). *Principles of Medical Statistics*. Chapman and Hall/CRC, Boca Raton, Florida.

Field-Smith, M.E., Bland, J.M., Taylor, J.C., Ramsey, J.D., and Anderson, H.R. (2002). *Trends in deaths associated with abuse of volatile substances 1971–2000. Report no 15*. St George's Hospital Medical School, London.

Finney, D.J., Latscha, R., Bennett, B.M., and Hsa, P. (1963). *Tables for Testing Significance in a 2 × 2 Contingency Table*. Cambridge University Press, London.

Fleiss, J.L. (1971). Measuring nominal scale agreement among many raters. *Psychological Bulletin*, **76**, 378–82.

Fletcher, A., Cullum, N., and Sheldon, T.A. (1997). A systematic review of compression treatment for venous leg ulcers. *British Medical Journal*, **315**, 576–80.

Flint, C. and Poulengeris, P. (1986). *The 'Know Your Midwife' Report*. Caroline Flint, London.

Ford, I. and Norrie, J. (2002). The role of covariates in estimating treatment effects and risk in long-term clinical trials. *Statistics in Medicine*, **21**, 2899–908.

Friedland, J.S., Porter, J.C., Daryanani, S., Bland, J.M., Screaton, N.J., Vesely, M.J.J., Griffin, G.E., Bennett, E.D., and Remick, D.G. (1996). Plasma proinflammatory cytokine concentrations, Acute Physiology and Chronic Health Evaluation (APACHE) III scores and survival in patients in an intensive care unit. *Critical Care Medicine*, **24**, 1775–81.

Galton, F. (1886). Regression towards mediocrity in hereditary stature. *Journal of the Anthropological Institute*, **15**, 246–63.

Gardner, M.J. and Altman, D.G. (1986). Confidence intervals rather than P values: estimation rather than hypothesis testing. *British Medical Journal*, **292**, 746–50.

Goldacre, B. (2014). Take with a pinch of salt. *The Guardian*, London, 10 April, pp.6–9 (G2).

Goldstein, H. (1995). *Multilevel Statistical Models, 2nd Ed.* Arnold, London.

Grewal, R., Perey, B., Wilmink, M., and Stothers, K. (2005). A randomized prospective study on the treatment of intra-articular distal radius fractures: open reduction and internal fixation with dorsal plating versus mini open reduction, percutaneous fixation, and external fixation. *The Journal of Hand Surgery (American Volume)*, **30A**, 764–72.

Haddow, J.E., Knight, G.J., Palomaki, G.E., Kloza, E.M., and Wald, N.J. (1988). Cigarette consumption and serum cotinine in relation to birthweight. *British Journal of Obstetrics and Gynaecology*, **94**, 678–81.

Hardy, J.F., Belisle, S., Dupont, C., Harel, F., Robitaille, D., Roy, M., and Gagnon, L. (1998). Prophylactic tranexamic acid and epsilon-aminocaproic acid for primary myocardial revascularization. *Annals of Thoracic Surgery*, **65**, 371–6.

Harjutsalo, V., Forsblom, C., and Groop, P-H. (2011). Time trends in mortality in patients with type 1 diabetes: nationwide population based cohort study. *British Medical Journal*, **343**, d5364.

Harley, B.J., Scharfenberger, A., Beaupre, L.A., Jomha, N., and Weber, D.W. (2004). Augmented external fixation versus percutaneous pinning and casting for unstable fractures of the distal radius – a prospective randomized trial. *Journal of Hand Surgery (American Volume)*, **29A**, 815–24.

Harper, R. and Reeves, B. (1999). Reporting of precision of estimates for diagnostic accuracy: a review. *British Medical Journal*, **318**, 1322–3.

Hart, P.D. and Sutherland, I. (1977). BCG and vole bacillus in the prevention of tuberculosis in adolescence and early adult life. *British Medical Journal*, **2**, 293–5.

Healy, M.J.R. (1968). Disciplining medical data. *British Medical Bulletin*, **24**, 210–14.

Hedges, B.M. (1978). Question wording effects: presenting one or both sides of a case. *The Statistician*, **28**, 83–99.

Henzi, I., Walder, B., and Tramèr, M.R. (2000). Dexamethasone for the prevention of postoperative nausea and vomiting: a quantitative systematic review. *Anesthesia-Analgesia*, **90**, 186–94.

Hepworth, S.J., Schoemaker, M.J., Muir, K.R., Swerdlow, A.J., Tongeren, M.J.A., and McKinney, P.A. (2006). Mobile phone use and risk of glioma in adults: case-control study. *British Medical Journal*, **332**, 883–7.

Hickish, T., Colston, K., Bland, J.M., and Maxwell, J.D. (1989). Vitamin D deficiency and muscle strength in male alcoholics. *Clinical Science*, **77**, 171–6.

Higgins, J.P.T. and Thompson, S.G. (2002). Quantifying heterogeneity in a meta-analysis. *Statistics in Medicine*, **21**, 1539–58.

Hill, A.B. (1962). *Statistical Methods in Clinical and Preventive Medicine*. Churchill Livingstone, Edinburgh.

Hill, A.B. (1977). *A Short Textbook of Medical Statistics*. Hodder and Stoughton, London.

Holland, W.W., Bailey, P., and Bland, J.M. (1978). Long-term consequences of respiratory disease in infancy. *Journal of Epidemiology and Community Health*, **32**, 256–9.

Holten, C. (1951). Anticoagulants in the treatment of coronary thrombosis. *Acta Medica Scandinavica*, **140**, 340–8.

Horizon (2014). *The Power of the Placebo*, BBC 2 Television, London.

Hosmer, D.W. and Lemeshow, S. (1999). *Applied Survival Analysis*. John Wiley and Sons, New York.

Huff, D. (1954). *How to Lie with Statistics*. Gollancz, London.

Hundley, V., Cheyne, H., Bland, J.M., Styles, M., and Barnett, C.A. (2010). So you want to conduct a cluster randomized controlled trial? Lessons from a national cluster trial of early labour. *Journal of Evaluation in Clinical Practice*, **16**, 632–8.

Huskisson, E.C. (1974). Simple analgesics for arthritis. *British Medical Journal*, **4**, 196–200.

Iglesias, C., Nelson, E.A., Cullum, N.A., and Torgerson, D.J. (2004). VenUS I: a randomised controlled trial of two types of bandage for treating venous leg ulcers. *Health Technology Assessment*, **8**, 29.

James, A.H. (1977). Breakfast and Crohn's disease. *British Medical Journal*, **1**, 943–7.

Jefferson, T., Jones, M., Doshi, P., Spencer, E.A., Onakpoya, I., and Heneghan, C.J. (2014). Oseltamivir for influenza in adults and children: systematic review of clinical study reports and summary of regulatory comments. *British Medical Journal*, **348**, g2545.

Johnson, F.N. and Johnson, S. (eds) (1977). *Clinical Trials*. Blackwell, Oxford.

Johnston, H.L.M. and Murphy, R. (2005). Agreement between an arterial blood gas analyser and a venous blood analyser in the measurement of potassium in patients in cardiac arrest. *Emergency Medicine Journal*, **22**, 269–71.

Johnston, I.D.A., Anderson, H.R., Lambert, H.P., and Patel, S. (1983). Respiratory morbidity and lung function after whooping cough. *Lancet*, **ii**, 1104–8.

Jones, B. and Kenward, M.G. (1989). *Design and Analysis of Cross-Over Trials*. Chapman and Hall, London.

Kapembwa, M.S., Fleming, S.C., Orr, M., Wells, C., Bland, M., Back, D., and Griffin, G.E. (1996). Impaired absorption of zidovudine in patients with AIDS-related small intestinal disease. *AIDS*, **10**, 1509–14.

Kaplan, E.L. and Meier, P. (1958). Nonparametric estimation from incomplete observations. *Journal of the American Statistical Association*, **53**, 457–81.

Kaptchuk, T.J. , Friedlander, E., Kelley, J.M., Sanchez, M.N., Kokkotou, E., Singer, J.P., Kowalczykowski, M., Miller, F.G., Kirsch, I., and Lembo, A.J. (2010). Placebos without deception: a randomized controlled trial in irritable bowel syndrome. *PLoS ONE*, **5**, e15591.

Karagiannis, T., Paschos, P., Paletas, K., Matthews, D.R., and Tsapas, A. (2012). Dipeptidyl peptidase-4 inhibitors for treatment of type 2 diabetes mellitus in the clinical setting: systematic review and meta-analysis. *British Medical Journal*, **344**, e1369.

Karski, J., Djaiani, G., Carroll, J., Iwanochko, M., Seneviratne, P., Liu, P., Kucharczyk, W., Fedorko, L., David, T., and Cheng, D. (2005). Tranexamic acid and early saphenous vein graft patency in conventional coronary artery bypass graft surgery: a prospective randomized controlled clinical trial. *Journal of Thoracic and Cardiovascular Surgery*, **130**, 309–14.

Karski, J.M., Teasdale, S.J., Norman, P., Carroll, J., VanKessel, K., Wong, P., and Glynn, M.F. (1995). Prevention of bleeding after cardiopulmonary bypass with high-dose tranexamic acid. Double-blind, randomized clinical trial. *Journal of Thoracic and Cardiovascular Surgery*, **110**, 835–42.

Kaste, M., Kuurne, T., Vilkki, J., Katevuo, K., Sainio, K., and Meurala, H. (1982). Is chronic brain damage in boxing a hazard of the past? *Lancet*, **ii**, 1186–8.

Katsaros, D., Petricevic, M., Snow, N.J., Woodhall, D.D., and Van Bergen, R. (1996). Tranexamic acid reduces post-bypass blood use: a double-blinded, prospective, randomized study of 210 patients. *Annals of Thoracic Surgery*, **61**, 1131–5.

Kendall, M.G. (1970). *Rank Correlation Methods*. Charles Griffin, London.

Kendall, M.G. and Babington Smith, B. (1971). *Tables of Random Sampling Numbers*. Cambridge University Press, Cambridge.

Kendall, M.G. and Stuart, A. (1969). *The Advanced Theory of Statistics, 3rd Ed., vol. 1*. Charles Griffin, London.

Kerrigan, D.D., Thevasagayam, R.S., Woods, T.O., McWelch, I., Thomas, W.E., Shorthouse, A.J., and Dennison, A.R. (1993). Who's afraid of informed consent? *British Medical Journal*, **306**, 298–300.

Kerry, S.M. and Bland, J.M. (1998). Statistics Notes: Analysis of a trial randomized in clusters. *British Medical Journal*, **316**, 54.

Kiely, P.D.W., Bland, J.M., Joseph, A.E.A., Mortimer, P.S., and Bourke, B.E. (1995). Upper limb lymphatic function in inflamatory arthritis. *Journal of Rheumatology*, **22**, 214–17.

Kish, L. (1994). *Survey Sampling*. Wiley Classic Library, New York.

Kramer, A.D.I., Guillory, J.E., and Hancock, J.T. (2014). Experimental evidence of massive-scale emotional contagion through social networks. *Proceedings of the National Academy of Sciences of the United States of America*, **111**, 8788–90.

Kruschke, J.K. (2010). *Data Analysis: A Bayesian Tutorial*. Academic Press, Waltham, Mass.

Lancet (1980). BCG: bad news from India. *Lancet*, **i**, 73–4.

Landis, J.R. and Koch, G.G. (1977). The measurement of observer agreement for categorical data. *Biometrics*, **33**, 159–74.

Laupacis, A., Sackett, D.L., and Roberts, R.S. (1988). An assessment of clinically useful measures of the consequences of treatment. *New England Journal of Medicine*, **318**, 1728–33.

Lawley, D.N. and Maxwell, A.E. (1971). *Factor Analysis as a Statistical Method, 2nd Ed*. Butterworth, London.

Lazzaroni, F., Bonassi, S., Manniello, E., Morcaldi, L., Repetto, E., Ruocco, A., Calvi, A., and Cotellessa, G. (1990). Effect of passive smoking during pregnancy on selected perinatal parameters. *International Journal of Epidemiology*, **19**, 960–5.

Leaning, J. (1996). War crimes and medical science. *British Medical Journal*, **313**, 1413–15.

Lee, K.L., McNeer, J.F., Starmer, F.C., Harris, P.J., and Rosati, R.A. (1980). Clinical judgements and statistics: lessons from a simulated randomized trial in coronary artery disease. *Circulation*, **61**, 508–15.

Lemeshow, S., Hosmer, D.W., Klar, J., and Lwanga, S.K. (1990). *Adequacy of Sample Size in Health Studies*. John Wiley and Sons, Chichester.

Levine, M.I. and Sackett, M.F. (1946). Results of BCG immunization in New York City. *American Review of Tuberculosis*, **53**, 517–32.

Levy, M.L., Robb, M., Allen, J., Doherty, C., Bland, J.M., and Winter, R.J.D. (2000). A randomized controlled evaluation of specialist nurse education following accident and emergency department attendance for acute asthma. *Respiratory Medicine*, **94**, 900–8.

Lindley, M.I. and Miller, J.C.P. (1955). *Cambridge Elementary Statistical Tables*. Cambridge University Press, Cambridge.

Lock, L., Williams, H., Bamford, B., and Lacey, J.H. (2012). The St George's eating disorders service meal preparation group for inpatients and day patients pursuing full recovery: a pilot study. *European Eating Disorders Review*, **20**, 218–24.

Lopez-Olaondo, L., Carrascosa, F., Pueyo, F.J., Monedero, P., Busto, N., and Saez, A. (1996). Combination of ondansetron and dexamethasone in the prophylaxis of postoperative nausea and vomiting. *British Journal of Anaesthesia*, **76**, 835–40.

Lucas, A., Morley, R., Cole, T.J., Lister, G., and Leeson-Payne, C. (1992). Breast milk and subsequent intelligence quotient in children born preterm. *Lancet*, **339**, 510–5.

Lumley, T. (2002). Network meta-analysis for indirect treatment comparisons. *Statistics in Medicine*, **21**, 2313–24.

Lunn, D.J., Thomas, A., Best, N., and Spiegelhalter, D. (2000). WinBUGS – a Bayesian modelling framework: concepts, structure, and extensibility. *Statistics and Computing*, **10**, 325–37.

Luthra, P., Bland, J.M., and Stanton, S.L. (1982). Incidence of pregnancy after laparoscopy and hydrotubation. *British Medical Journal*, **284**, 1013.

Machin, D., Campbell, M.J., Fayers, P., and Pinol, A. (1998). *Statistical Tables for the Design of Clinical Studies, Second Ed.* Blackwell, Oxford.

MacPherson, H., Thomas, K., Walters, S., and Fitter, M. (2001). The York acupuncture safety study: prospective survey of 34 000 treatments by traditional acupuncturists. *British Medical Journal*, **323**, 486–7.

Maier, P.C., Funk, J., Schwarzer, G., Antes, G., and Falck-Ytter, Y.T. (2005). Treatment of ocular hypertension and open angle glaucoma: meta-analysis of randomised controlled trials. *British Medical Journal*, **331**, 134.

Mainous, A.G. and Hueston, W.J. (1994). Passive smoking and low birth weight. Evidence of a threshold effect. *Archives of Family Medicine*, **3**, 875–8.

Mantel, N. (1966). Evaluation of survival data and two new rank order statistics arising in its consideration. *Cancer Chemotherapy Reports*, **50**, 163–70.

Martinez, F.D., Wright, A.L., and Taussig, L.M. (1994). The effect of paternal smoking on the birthweight of newborns whose mothers did not smoke. *Public Health Briefs*, **84**, 1489–91.

Martin, T.R. and Bracken, M.B. (1986). Association of low birth weight with passive smoke exposure in pregnancy. *American Journal of Epidemiology*, **124**, 633–42.

Mathai, M., Vijayasn, R., Babu, S., and Jeyaseelan, L. (1992). Passive maternal smoking and birthweight in a South Indian population. *British Journal of Obstetrics and Gynaecology*, **99**, 342–3.

Mather, H.M., Nisbet, J.A., Burton, G.H., Poston, G.J., Bland, J.M., Bailey, P.A., and Pilkington, T.R.E. (1979). Hypomagnesaemia in diabetes. *Clinica Chemica Acta*, **95**, 235–42.

Matthews, D.E. and Farewell, V. (1988). *Using and Understanding Medical Statistics, 2nd Ed.* Karger, Basel.

Matthews, J.N.S. and Altman, D.G. (1996a). Statistics Notes: Interaction 2: compare effect sizes not P values. *British Medical Journal*, **313**, 808.

Matthews, J.N.S. and Altman, D.G. (1996b). Statistics Notes: Interaction 3: how to examine heterogeneity. *British Medical Journal*, **313**, 862.

Matthews, J.N.S., Altman, D.G., Campbell, M.J., and Royston, P. (1990). Analysis of serial measurements in medical research. *British Medical Journal*, **300**, 230–5.

Maugdal, D.P., Ang, L., Patel, S., Bland, J.M., and Maxwell, J.D. (1985). Nutritional assessment in patients with chronic gastro-intestinal symptoms: comparison of functional and organic disorders. *Human Nutrition: Clinical Nutrition*, **39**, 203–12.

Maxwell, A.E. (1970). Comparing the classification of subjects by two independent judges. *British Journal of Psychiatry*, **116**, 651–5.

Mayberry, J.F., Rhodes, J., and Newcombe, R.G. (1978). Breakfast and dietary aspects of Crohn's disease. *British Medical Journal*, **2**, 1401.

McDowell, I. and Newell, C. (1996). *Measuring Health: A Guide To Rating Scales and Questionnaires, 2nd Ed.* Oxford University Press, Oxford.

McKie, D. (1992). Pollsters turn to secret ballot. *The Guardian*, London, 24 August, p.20.

McLean, S. (1997). Commentary: No consent means not treating the patient with respect. *British Medical Journal*, **314**, 1076.

Meade, T.W., Roderick, P.J., Brennan, P.J., Wilkes, H.C., and Kelleher, C.C. (1992). Extra-cranial bleeding and other symptoms due to low dose aspirin and low intensity oral anticoagulation. *Thrombosis and Haematosis,* **68**, 1–6.

Meier, P. (1977). The biggest health experiment ever: the 1954 field trial of the Salk poliomyelitis vaccine. In *Statistics: A Guide to the Biological and Health Sciences* (ed. J.M. Tanur, *et al.*). Holden-Day, San Francisco.

Mills, E.J., Thorlund, K., and Ioannidis, J.P.A. (2013). Demystifying trial networks and network meta-analysis. *British Medical Journal,* **346**, f2914.

Minaya, P., Baumstarck, K., Berbis, J., Goncalves, A., Barlesi, F., Michel, G., Salas, S., Chinot, O., Grob, J.J., Seitz, J.F., Bladou, F., Clement, A., Mancini, J., Simeoni, M.C., and Auquier, P. (2012). The CareGiver Oncology Quality of Life questionnaire (CarGOQoL): development and validation of an instrument to measure the quality of life of the caregivers of patients with cancer. *European Journal of Cancer,* **48**, 904–11.

Mitchell, E.A., Bland, J.M., and Thompson, J.M.D. (1994). Risk factors for readmission to hospital for asthma. *Thorax,* **49**, 33–6.

Mongan, P.D., Brown, R.S., and Thwaites, B.K. (1998). Tranexamic acid and aprotinin reduce postoperative bleeding and transfusions during primary coronary revascularization. *Anesthesia and Analgesia,* **87**, 258–65.

Morice, A.H., Faruqi, S., Wright, C.E., Thompson, R., and Bland, J.M. (2011). Cough hypersensitivity syndrome: a distinct clinical entity. *Lung,* **189**, 73–9.

Morris, G.C., Wiggins, R.C., Woodhall, S.C., Bland, J.M., Taylor, C.R., Jespers, V., Vcelar, B.A., and Lacey, C.J. (2014). MABGEL 1: First phase 1 trial of the anti-HIV1 monoclonal antibodies 2F5, 4E10 and 2G12 as a vaginal microbicide. *PLoS ONE,* Submitted for publication.

Morris, J.A. and Gardner, M.J. (1989). Calculating confidence intervals for relative risks, odds ratios and standardized ratios and rates. In *Statistics with Confidence* (ed. M.J. Gardner and D.G. Altman). British Medical Journal, London.

Moseley, J.B., O'Malley, K., Petersen, N.J., Menke, T.J., Brody, B.A., Kuykendall, D.H., Hollingsworth, J.C., Ashton, C.M., and Wray, N.P. (2002). A controlled trial of arthroscopic surgery for osteoarthritis of the knee. *New England Journal of Medicine,* **347**, 81–8.

Motallebzadeh, R., Bland, J.M., Markus, H.S., Kaski, J.C., and Jahangiri, M. (2007). Neurocognitive function and cerebral emboli: randomised study of on-pump versus off-pump coronary artery bypass surgery. *Annals of Thoracic Surgery,* **83**, 475–82.

Motzer, R.J., Escudier, B., Oudard, S., Hutson, T.E., Porta, C., Bracarda, S., Grunwald, V., Thompson, J.A., Figlin, R.A., Hollaender, N., Urbanowitz, G., Berg, W.J., Kay, A., Lebwohl, D., and Ravaud, A. (2008). Efficacy of everolimus in advanced renal cell carcinoma: a double-blind, randomised, placebo-controlled phase III trial. *Lancet,* **372**, 449–56.

MRC (1948). Streptomycin treatment of pulmonary tuberculosis. *British Medical Journal,* **2**, 769–82.

Mudur, G. (1997). Indian study of women with cervical lesions called unethical. *British Medical Journal,* **314**, 1065.

Nelson, E.A., Iglesias, C.P., Cullum, N., and Torgerson, D.J. (2004). Randomized clinical trial of four-layer and short-stretch compression bandages for venous leg ulcers (VenUS I). *British Journal of Surgery,* **91**, 1292–9.

Newcombe, R.G. (1992). Confidence intervals: enlightening or mystifying. *British Medical Journal,* **304**, 381–2.

Newnham, J.P., Evans, S.F., Con, A.M., Stanley, F.J., and Landau, L.I. (1993). Effects of frequent ultrasound during pregnancy: a randomized controlled trial. *Lancet,* **342**, 887–91.

Ng, C.S., Watson, C.J.E., Palmer, C.R., See, T.C., Beharry, N.A., Housden, B.A., Bradley, J.A., and Dixon, A.K. (2002). Evaluation of early abdominopelvic computed tomography in patients with acute abdominal pain of unknown cause: prospective randomised study. *British Medical Journal,* **325**, 1387.

Ngaage, D.L. and Bland, J.M. (2010). Lessons from aprotinin: is the routine use and inconsistent dosing of tranexamic acid prudent? Meta-analysis of randomised and large matched observational studies. *European Journal of Cardio-Thoracic Surgery,* **37**, 1375–83.

Nüesch, E., Trelle, S., Reichenbach, S., Rutjes, A.W.S., Bürgi, E., Scherer, M., Altman, D.G., and Jüni, P. (2009). The effects of excluding patients from the analysis in randomised controlled trials: meta-epidemiological study. *British Medical Journal,* **339**, b3244.

Nuesch, R., Schroeder, K., Dieterle, T., Martina, B., and Battegay, E. (2001). Relation between insufficient response to antihypertensive treatment and poor compliance with treatment: a prospective case-control study. *British Medical Journal,* **323**, 142–6.

Nuttall, G.A., Oliver, W.C., Ereth, M.H., Santrach, P.J., Bryant, S.C., Orszulak, T.A., and Schaff, H.V. (2000). Comparison of blood-conservation strategies in cardiac surgery patients at high risk for bleeding. *Anesthesiology,* **92**, 674–82.

Oakeshott, P., Kerry, S.M., and Williams, J.E. (1994). Randomised controlled trial of the effect of the Royal College of Radiologists' guidelines on general practitioners' referral for radiographic examination. *British Journal of General Practice,* **44**, 197–200.

O'Brien, P.C. and Fleming, T.R. (1979). A multiple testing procedure for clinical trials. *Biometrics*, **35**, 549–56.

Office for National Statistics. (1999). *Mortality Statistics, Childhood, Infant and Perinatal, Series DH3, No 30.* HMSO, London.

Ogawa, H., Tominaga, S., Hori, K., Noguchi, K., Kanou, I., and Matsubara, M. (1991). Passive smoking by pregnant women and fetal growth. *Journal of Epidemiology and Community Health*, **45**, 164–8.

Oldham, H.G., Bevan, M.M., and McDermott, M. (1979). Comparison of the new miniature Wright peak flow meter with the standard Wright peak flow meter. *Thorax*, **34**, 807–8.

O'Meara, S., Tierney, J., Cullum, N., Bland, J.M., Franks, P.J., Mole, T., and Scriven, M. (2009). Four layer bandage compared with short stretch bandage for venous leg ulcers: systematic review and meta-analysis of randomised controlled trials with data from individual patients. *British Medical Journal*, **338**, b1344.

OPCS (1992). *Mortality statistics, Series DH1, No 24.* HMSO, London.

Osborn, J.F. (1979). *Statistical Exercises in Medical Research.* Blackwell, Oxford.

Owen, C., Whincup, P.H., Gilg, J.A., and Cook, D.G. (2003). Effect of breast feeding in infancy on blood pressure in later life: systematic review and meta-analysis. *British Medical Journal*, **327**, 1189–95.

Paraskevaides, E.C., Pennington, G.W., Naik, S., and Gibbs, A.A. (1991). Pre-freeze/post-freeze semen motility ratio. *Lancet*, **337**, 366–7.

Parmar, M. and Machin, D. (1995). *Survival Analysis.* John Wiley and Sons, Chichester.

Parmar, M.K., Torri, V., and Stewart, L. (1998). Extracting summary statistics to perform meta-analyses of the published literature for survival endpoints. *Statistics in Medicine*, **17**, 2815–34.

Paul, V.K., Singh, M., Deorari, A.K., Pacheco, J., and Taneja, U. (1996). Manual and pump methods of expression of breast milk. *Indian Journal of Pediatrics*, **63**, 87–92.

Peacock, J.L., Cook, D.G., Carey, I.M., Jarvis, M.J., Bryant, A.E., Anderson, H.R., and Bland, J.M. (1998). Maternal cotinine level during pregnancy and birthweight for gestational age. *International Journal of Epidemiology*, **27**, 647–56.

Pearson, E.S. and Hartley, H.O. (1970). *Biometrika Tables for Statisticians, volume 1.* Cambridge University Press, Cambridge.

Peduzzi, P., Concato, J., Kemper, E., Holford, T.R., and Feinstein, A.R. (1996). A simulation study of the number of events per variable in logistic regression analysis. *Journal of Clinical Epidemiology*, **49**, 1373–9.

Penta de Peppo, A., Pierri, M.D., Scafuri, A., De Paulis, R., Colantuono, G., Caprara, E., Tomai, F., and Chiariello, L. (1995). Intraoperative antifibrinolysis and blood-saving techniques in cardiac surgery: prospective trial of 3 antifibrinolytic drugs. *Texas Heart Institute Journal*, **22**, 231–6.

Peters, J.L., Sutton, A.J., Jones, D.R., Abrams, K.R., and Rushton, L. (2008). Contour-enhanced meta-analysis funnel plots help distinguish publication bias from other causes of asymmetry. *Journal of Clinical Epidemiology*, **61**, 991–6.

Peto, R. and Peto, J. (1972). Asymptotically efficient rank invariant test procedures. *Journal of the Royal Statistical Society Series A*, **135**, 185–207.

Petroni, M.L., Jazrawi, R.P., Pazzi, P., Zoin, M., Lanzini, A., Fracchia, M., Facchinetti, D., Alrisi, V., Ferraris, R., Bland, J.M., Heaton, K.W., Podda, M., and Northfield, T.C. (2000). Risk factors for the development of gallstone recurrence following medical dissolution. *European Journal of Gastroenterology & Hepatology*, **12**, 695–700.

Pighills, A.C., Torgerson, D.J., Sheldon, T.A., Drummond, A.E., and Bland, J.M. (2011). Environmental assessment and modification to prevent falls in older people. *Journal of the American Geriatrics Society*, **59**, 26–33.

Pleym, H., Stenseth, R., Wahba, A., Bjella, L., Karevold, A., and Dale, O. (2003). Single-dose tranexamic acid reduces postoperative bleeding after coronary surgery in patients treated with aspirin until surgery. *Anesthesia and Analgesia*, **96**, 923–8.

Pocock, S.J. (1977). Group sequential methods in the design and analysis of clinical trials. *Biometrika*, **64**, 191–9.

Pocock, S.J. (1982). Interim analyses for randomised clinical trials: the group sequential approach. *Biometrika*, **38**, 153–62.

Pocock, S.J. (1983). *Clinical Trials: A Practical Approach.* John Wiley and Sons, Chichester.

Price, R., MacLennan, G., and Glen, J. (2014). Selective digestive or oropharyngeal decontamination and topical oropharyngeal chlorhexidine for prevention of death in general intensive care: systematic review and network meta-analysis. *British Medical Journal*, **348**, g2197.

Pritchard, B.N.C., Dickinson, C.J., Alleyne, G.A.O., Hurst, P., Hill, I.D., Rosenheim, M.L., and Laurence, D.R. (1963). Report of a clinical trial from Medical Unit and MRC Statistical Unit, University College Hospital Medical School, London. *British Medical Journal*, **2**, 1226–7.

Radical Statistics Health Group (1976). *Whose Priorities?* Radical Statistics, London.

Ramsay, S. (1998). Miss Evers' Boys (review). *Lancet*, **352**, 1075.

Reader, R., *et al.* (1980). The Australian trial in mild hypertension: report by the management committee. *Lancet*, **i**, 1261–7.

Rembold, C. (1998). Number needed to screen: development of a statistic for disease screening. *British Medical Journal*, **317**, 307–12.

Richards, D.A., Hill, J.J., Gask, L., Lovell, K., Chew-Graham, C., Bower, P., Cape, J., Pilling, S., Araya, R., Kessler, D., Bland, J.M., Green, C., Gilbody, S., Lewis, G., Manning, C., Hughes-Morley, A., and Barkham, M. (2013). Clinical effectiveness of collaborative care for depression in UK primary care (CADET): cluster randomised controlled trial. *British Medical Journal*, **347**, f4913.

Richards, D.A., Hughes-Morley, A., Hayes, R.A., Araya, R., Barkham, M., Bland, J.M., Bower, P., Cape, J., Chew-Graham, C.A., Gask, L., Gilbody, S., Green, C., Kessler, D., Lewis, G., Lovell, K., Manning, C., and Pilling, S. (2009). Collaborative Depression Trial (CADET): multicentre randomised controlled trial of collaborative care for depression – study protocol. *BMC Health Services Research*, **9**, 188.

Richards, D.A., Lovell K., Gilbody, S., Gask, L., Torgerson, D., Barkham, M., Bland, M., Bower, P., Lankshear, A.J., Simpson, A., Fletcher, J., Escott, D., Hennessy, S., and Richardson, R. (2008). Collaborative care for depression in UK primary care: a randomized controlled trial. *Psychological Medicine*, **38**, 279–87.

Rodin, D.A., Bano, G., Bland, J.M., Taylor, K., and Nussey, S.S. (1998). Polycystic ovaries and associated metabolic abnormalities in Indian subcontinent Asian women. *Clinical Endocrinology*, **49**, 91–9.

Rose, G.A., Holland, W.W., and Crowley, E.A. (1964). A sphygmomanometer for epidemiologists. *Lancet*, **i**, 296–300.

Rowe, D. (1992). Mother and daughter aren't doing well. *The Guardian*, London, 14 July, p.33.

Royston, P. and Altman, D.G. (1994). Regression using fractional polynomials of continuous covariates: parsimonious parametric modelling. *Applied Statistics*, **43**, 429–67.

Rubin, D.B. (1987). *Multiple Imputation for Nonresponse in Surveys*. Wiley, New York.

Rubin, D.H., Krasilnikoff, P.A., Leventhal, J.M., Welle, P.A., and Berget, A. (1986). Effect of passive smoking on birthweight. *Lancet*, **11**, 415–17.

Ryan, T.P. and Woodall, W.H. (2005). The most-cited statistical papers. *Journal of Applied Statistics*, **32**, 461–74.

Salvesen, K.A., Bakketeig, L.S., Eik-nes, S.H., Undheim, J.O., and Okland, O. (1992). Routine ultrasonography in utero and school performance at age 8–9 years. *Lancet*, **339**, 85–9.

Samuels, P., Bussel, J.B., Braitman, L.E., Tomaski, A., Druzin, M.L., Mennuti, M.T., and Cines, D.B. (1990). Estimation of the risk of thrombocytopenia in the offspring of pregnant women with presumed immune thrombocytopenia purpura. *New England Journal of Medicine*, **323**, 229–35.

Santos, A.T., Kalil, R.A., Bauemann, C., Pereira, J.B., and Nesralla, I.A. (2006). A randomized, double-blind, and placebo-controlled study with tranexamic acid of bleeding and fibrinolytic activity after primary coronary artery bypass grafting. *Brazilian Journal of Medical and Biological Research*, **39**, 63–9.

Sattar, N., Preiss, D., Murray, H.M., Welsh, P., Buckley, B.M., de Craen, A.J.M., Seshasai, S.R.K., McMurray, J.J., Freeman, D.J., Jukema, J.W., Macfarlane, P.W., Packard, C.J., Stott, D.J., Westendorp, R.G., Shepherd, J., Davis, B.R., Pressel, S.L., Marchioli, R., Marfisi, R.M., Maggioni, A.P., Tavazzi, L., Tognoni, G., Kjekshus, J., Pedersen, T.R., Cook, T.J., Gotto, A.M., Clearfield, M.B., Downs, J.R., Nakamura, H., Ohashi, Y., Mizuno, K., Ray, K.K., and Ford, I. (2010). Statins and risk of incident diabetes: a collaborative meta-analysis of randomised statin trials. *Lancet*, **375**, 735–42.

Schapira, K., McClelland, H.A., Griffiths, N.R., and Newell, D.J. (1970). Study on the effects of tablet colour in the treatment of anxiety states. *British Medical Journal*, **2**, 446–9.

Schlitt, H.J., Barkmann, A., Boker, K.H.W., Schmidt, H.H.J., Emmanouilidis, N., Rosenau, J., Bahr, M.J., Tusch, G., Manns, M.P., Nashan, B., and Klempnauer, J. (2001). Replacement of calcineurin inhibitors with mycophenolate mofetil in liver-transplant patients with renal dysfunction: a randomised controlled study. *Lancet*, **357**, 587–91.

Schmid, H. (1973). Kaposi's sarcoma in Tanzania: a statistical study of 220 cases. *Tropical Geographical Medicine*, **25**, 266–76.

Schulz, K.F., Chalmers, I., Hayes, R.J., and Altman, D.G. (1995). Bias due to non-concealment of randomization and non-double-blinding. *Journal of the American Medical Association*, **273**, 408–12.

Schwarzler, P., Bland, J.M., Holden, D., Campbell, S., and Ville, Y. (2004). Sex-specific antenatal reference growth charts for uncomplicated singleton pregnancies at 15–40 weeks of gestation. *Ultrasound in Obstetrics & Gynaecology*, **23**, 23–9.

Schweizer, M., Perencevich, E., McDanel, J., Carson, J., Formanek, M., Hafner, J., Braun, B., and Herwaldt,

L. (2013). Effectiveness of a bundled intervention of decolonization and prophylaxis to decrease Gram positive surgical site infections after cardiac or orthopedic surgery: systematic review and meta-analysis. *British Medical Journal*, **346**, f2743.

Searle, S.R., Cassela, G., and McCulloch, C.E. (1992). *Variance Components*. Wiley, New York.

Senn, S. (2002). *Cross-Over Trials in Clinical Research, 2nd Ed.* Wiley, Chichester.

Shaker, J.L., Brickner, R.C., Findling, J.W., Kelly, T.M., Rapp, R., Rizk, G., Haddad, J.G., Schalch, D.S., and Shenker, Y. (1997). Hypocalcemia and skeletal disease as presenting features of celiac disease. *Archives of Internal Medicine*, **157**, 1013-16.

Shiraishi, J., Pesce, L.L., Metz, C.E., and Doi, K. (2009). Experimental design and data analysis in receiver operating characteristic studies: lessons learned from reports in *Radiology* from 1997 to 2006. *Radiology*, **253**, 822-30.

Sibbald, B., Addington Hall, J., Brenneman, D., and Freeling, P. (1994). Telephone versus postal surveys of general practitioners. *British Journal of General Practice*, **44**, 297-300.

Siegel, S. (1956). *Non-parametric Statistics for the Behavioural Sciences*. McGraw-Hill Kagakusha, Tokyo.

Sivia, D. and Skilling, J. (2006). *Data Analysis: A Bayesian Tutorial*. Oxford University Press, Oxford.

Smeeth, L., Haines, A., and Ebrahim, S. (1999). Numbers needed to treat derived from meta-analyses – sometimes informative, usually misleading. *British Medical Journal*, **318**, 1548-51.

de Smet, A.M.G.A., Kluytmans, J.A.J.W., Cooper, B.S., Mascini, E.M., Benus, R.F.J., van der Werf, T.S., van der Hoeven, J.G., Pickkers, P., Bogaers-Hofman, D., van der Meer, N.J.M., Bernards, A.T., Kuijper, E.J., Joore, J.C.A., Leverstein-van Hall, M.A., Bindels, A.J.G.H., Jansz, A.R., Wesselink, R.M.J., de Jongh, B.M., Dennesen, P.J.W., van Asselt, G.J., te Velde, L.F., Frenay, I.H.M.E., Kaasjager, K., Bosch, F.H., van Iterson, M., Thijsen, S.F.T., Kluge, G.H., Pauw, W., de Vries, J.W., Kaan, J.A., Arends, J.P., Aarts, L.P.H.J., Sturm, P.D.J., Harinck, H.I.J., Voss, A., Uijtendaal, E.V., Blok, H.E.M., Thieme Groen, E.S., Pouw, M.E., Kalkman, C.J., and Bonten, M.J.M. (2009). Decontamination of the digestive tract and oropharynx in ICU patients. *New England Journal of Medicine*, **360**, 20-31.

Smith, J.B., Niven, B.E., and Mann, J.I. (1996). The effect of reduced extrinsic sucrose intake on plasma triglyceride levels. *European Journal of Clinical Nutrition*, 1996, **50**, 498-504.

Snedecor, G.W. and Cochran, W.G. (1980). *Statistical Methods, 7th Ed.* Iowa State University Press, Ames, Iowa.

Snowdon, C., Garcia, J., and Elbourne, D.R. (1997). Making sense of randomisation: Responses of parents of critically ill babies to random allocation of treatment in a clinical trial. *Social Science and Medicine*, **15**, 1337-55.

South-east London Screening Study Group (1977). A controlled trial of multiphasic screening in middle-age: results of the South-east London Screening Study. *International Journal of Epidemiology*, **6**, 357-63.

Southern, J.P., Smith, R.M.M., and Palmer, S.R. (1990). Bird attack on milk bottles: possible mode of transmission of *Campylobacter jejuni* to man. *Lancet*, **336**, 1425-7.

Speekenbrink, R.G., Vonk, A.B., Wildevuur, C.R., and Eijsman, L. (1995). Hemostatic efficacy of dipyridamole, tranexamic acid, and aprotinin in coronary bypass grafting. *Annals of Thoracic Surgery*, **59**, 438-42.

Sterne, J.A.C., Sutton, A.J., Ioannidis, J.P.A., Terrin, N., Jones, D.R., Lau, J., Carpenter, J., Rücker, G., Harbord, R.M., Schmid, C.H., Tetzlaff, J., Deeks, J.J., Peters, J., Macaskill, P., Schwarzer, G., Duval, S., Altman, D.G., Moher, D., and Higgins, J.P.T. (2011). Recommendations for examining and interpreting funnel plot asymmetry in meta-analyses of randomised controlled trials. *British Medical Journal*, **342**, d4002.

Stewart, L.A. and Tierney, J.F. (2002). To IPD or not to IPD? Advantages and disadvantages of systematic reviews using individual patient data. *Evaluation & the Health Professions*, **25**, 76-97.

Streiner, D.L. and Norman, G.R. (2008). *Health Measurement Scales: A Practical Guide to their Development and Use, 4th Ed.* Oxford University Press, Oxford.

Stuart, A. (1955). A test for homogeneity of the marginal distributions in a two-way classification. *Biometrika*, **42**, 412.

'Student' (1908). The probable error of a mean. *Biometrika*, **6**, 1-24.

'Student' (1931). The Lanarkshire Milk Experiment. *Biometrika*, **23**, 398-406.

Tang, J-L. and Liu, J.L. (2000). Misleading funnel plot for the detection of bias in meta-analysis. *Journal of Clinical Epidemiology*, **53**, 477-84.

Taves, D.R. (1974). Minimization – new method of assigning patients to treatment and control groups. *Clinical Pharmacology & Therapeutics*, **15**, 443-53.

Te Morenga, L.T., Mallard, S., and Mann, J. (2012). Dietary sugars and body weight: systematic review and meta-analyses of randomised controlled trials and cohort studies. *British Medical Journal*, **345**, e7492.

Thomas, P.R.S., Queraishy, M.S., Bowyer, R., Scott, R.A.P., Bland, J.M., and Dormandy, J.A. (1993). Leucocyte count: a predictor of early femoropopliteal graft failure. *Cardiovascular Surgery*, **1**, 369–72.

Tierney, J.F., Stewart, L.A., Ghersi, D., Burdett, S., and Sydes, M.R. (2007). Practical methods for incorporating summary time-to-event data into meta-analysis. *Trials*, **8**, 16.

Torgerson, D.J. and Bell-Syer, S.E.M. (2001). Hormone replacement therapy and prevention of nonvertebral fractures. A meta-analysis of randomized trials. *JAMA*, **285**, 2891–7.

Torgerson, D.J. and Torgerson, C. (2008). *Designing Randomized Trials in Health, Education, and the Social Sciences: An Introduction*. Palgrave Macmillan, Basingstoke.

Todd, G.F. (1972). *Statistics of Smoking in the United Kingdom, 6th Ed.* Tobacco Research Council, London.

Tsai, S.P., Wendt, J.K., Donnelly, R.P., de Jong, G., and Ahmed, F.S. (2005). Age at retirement and long term survival of an industrial population: prospective cohort study. *British Medical Journal*, **331**, 995.

Tudur, C., Williamson, P.R., Khan, S., and Best, L.Y. (2001). The value of the aggregate data approach in meta-analysis with time-to-event outcomes. *Journal of the Royal Statistical Society Series A – Statistics in Society*, **164**, 357–70.

Tukey, J.W. (1977). *Exploratory Data Analysis*. Addison-Wesley, New York.

Turnbull, P.J., Stimson, G.V., and Dolan, K.A. (1992). Prevalence of HIV infection among ex-prisoners. *British Medical Journal*, **304**, 90–1.

UKPDS Group (1998). Efficacy of atenolol and captopril in reducing risk of macrovascular and microvascular complications in type 2 diabetes. *British Medical Journal*, **317**, 713–20.

Ulahannan, T.J., McVittie, J., and Keenan, J. (1998). Ambient temperatures and potassium concentrations. *Lancet*, **352**, 1680–1.

Vanek, T., Jares, M., Fajt, R., Straka, Z., Jirasek, K., Kolesar, M., Brucek, P., and Maly, M. (2005). Fibrinolytic inhibitors in off-pump coronary surgery: a prospective, randomized, double-blind TAP study (tranexamic acid, aprotinin, placebo). *European Journal of Cardiothoracic Surgery*, **28**, 563–8.

Velzeboer, S.C.J.M., Frenkel, J., and de Wolff, F.A. (1997). A hypertensive toddler. *Lancet*, **349**, 1810.

Victora, C.G. (1982). Statistical malpractice in drug promotion: a case-study from Brazil. *Social Science and Medicine*, **16**, 707–9.

Wallenborn, J., Gelbrich, G., Bulst, D., Behrends, K., Wallenborn, H., Rohrbach, A., Krause, U., Kühnast, T., Wiegel, M., and Olthoff, D. (2006). Prevention of postoperative nausea and vomiting by metoclopramide combined with dexamethasone: randomised double blind multicentre trial. *British Medical Journal*, **333**, 324.

Watkins, S.J. (2000). Conviction by mathematical error? *British Medical Journal*, **320**, 2–3.

Wei, D.H., Raizman, N.M., Bottino, C.J., Jobin, C.M., Strauch, R.J., and Rosenwasser, M.P. (2009). Unstable distal radial fractures treated with external fixation, a radial column plate, or a volar plate: a prospective randomized trial. *Journal of Bone and Joint Surgery (American Volume)*, **91A**, 1568–77.

White, A., Hayhoe, S., Hart, A., and Ernst, E. (2001). Adverse events following acupuncture: prospective survey of 32 000 consultations with doctors and physiotherapists. *British Medical Journal*, **323**, 485–6.

White, I.R., Royston, P., and Wood, A.M. (2011). Multiple imputation using chained equations: issues and guidance for practice. *Statistics in Medicine*, **30**, 377–99.

White, P.T., Pharoah, C.A., Anderson, H.R., and Freeling, P. (1989). Improving the outcome of chronic asthma in general practice: a randomized controlled trial of small group education. *Journal of the Royal College of General Practitioners*, **39**, 182–6.

Whitehead, J. (1997). *The Design and Analysis of Sequential Clinical Trials, revised 2nd Ed.* Wiley, Chichester.

Whittington, C. (1977). Safety begins at home. *New Scientist*, **76**, 340–2.

Wilcke, M.K.T., Abbaszadegan, H., and Adolphson, P.Y. (2011). Wrist function recovers more rapidly after volar locked plating than after external fixation but the outcomes are similar after 1 year. *Acta Orthopaedica*, **82**, 76–81.

Williams, E.I., Greenwell, J., and Groom, L.M. (1992). The care of people over 75 years old after discharge from hospital: an evaluation of timetabled visiting by Health Visitor Assistants. *Journal of Public Health Medicine*, **14**, 138–44.

Williamson, P.R., Smith, C.T., Hutton, J.L., and Marson, A.G. (2002). Aggregate data meta-analysis with time-to-event outcomes. *Statistics in Medicine*, **21**, 3337–51.

Wroe, S.J., Sandercock, P., Bamford, J., Dennis, M., Slattery, J., and Warlow, C. (1992). Diurnal variation in incidence of stroke: Oxfordshire community stroke project. *British Medical Journal*, **304**, 155-7.

Xu, G.G.Q., Chan, S.P., Puhaindran, M.E., and Chew, W.Y.C. (2009). Prospective randomised study of intra-articular fractures of the distal radius: comparison between external fixation and plate fixation. *Annals, Academy of Medicine, Singapore*, **38**, 600-5.

Zabeeda, D., Medalion, B., Sverdlov, M., Ezra, S., Schachner, A., Ezri, T., and Cohen, A.J. (2002). Tranexamic acid reduces bleeding and the need for blood transfusion in primary myocardial revascularization. *Annals of Thoracic Surgery*, **74**, 733-8.

Zelen, M. (1979). A new design for clinical trials. *New England Journal of Medicine*, **300**, 1242-5.

Zelen, M. (1992). Randomized consent designs for clinical trials: an update. *Statistics in Medicine*, **11**, 131-2.

Zhang, J. and Radcliffe, J.M. (1993). Paternal smoking and birthweight in Shanghai. *American Journal of Public Health*, **83**, 207-10.

Index